THE MACROECONOMY OF IRELAND

Second Edition

Anthony J. Leddin
University of Limerick

Brendan M. Walsh
University College, Dublin

Gill and Macmillan

Published in Ireland by
Gill and Macmillan Ltd
Goldenbridge
Dublin 8
with associated companies in
Auckland, Budapest, Delhi, Gaborone, Harare,
Hong Kong, Kampala, Kuala Lumpur, Lagos, London,
Madras, Manzini, Melbourne, Mexico City, Nairobi,
New York, Singapore, Sydney, Tokyo, Windhoek
© Anthony J. Leddin and Brendan M. Walsh, 1990, 1992
0 7171 1951 3
Index compiled by Helen Litton
Printed by
The Bath Press, Avon

A catalogue record is available for
this book from the British Library.

Technical note
The text of this book was composed by the authors using Microsoft Word. The
graphs and drawings were generated on Gem and Designer software respectively.
The final document was brought to camera ready copy, to the publishers' design
specifications, on Ventura Desk Top Publisher using the facilities of the
Department of Information Technology at the University of Limerick.

To

Celeste, Sofia and Alana
A.J.L.

Patricia, Colm, Nessa and Ben
B.M.W.

PREFACE

A macroeconomic text that combines theory with empirical analysis needs constant revision. The process of revising this text in fact began as soon as the first edition appeared and continued for two years. It led to a much more radical revision than was originally planned. In addition to updating statistical material, the text was completely rewritten, introductory material added and the discussion of open economy macroeconomic theory and developments in Europe extended. Our aim has been to provide a comprehensive and up-to-date survey of modern macroeconomic theory and policy with particular reference to developments in the Irish economy.

In the preparation of the second edition we benefited from reactions to the first edition. Very helpful comments were received from colleagues, in particular, Donal Byard of the University of Limerick, Joseph Durkan, J. Peter Neary, Cormac O Gráda of University College, Dublin and Finola Kennedy of the Institute of Public Administration. We are also most grateful to Michael Kennedy and Margaret Kilmartin of the University of Limerick for reading earlier drafts of various chapters and making valuable comments and suggestions. We are indebted to Martin Leonard and John Fitzgerald of the University of Limerick, Department of Information Technology, for putting their technical expertise at our disposal.

Finally, we wish to again acknowledge successive generations of students in our courses in University College, Dublin and the University of Limerick who, perhaps unwittingly, helped us improve the presentation of the concepts in this book.

Plassey, Limerick   AJL
Belfield, Dublin   BMW
April, 1992

Contents

Chapter 7   Interest Rates and Money in a Closed Economy

Chapter 8   Unemployment and Inflation

Chapter 9   **The Labour Market and the Problem of Unemployment in Ireland**

Chapter 1

Introduction to Macroeconomics

1.1   Introduction

Macroeconomics is concerned with the study of whole economies. It deals with topics such as the growth of national output and income, the level of unemployment, the rate of inflation, interest rates and exchange rates. One of the main reasons for studying macroeconomics is the hope that by obtaining a better understanding of how the economy works we shall be able to suggest policies that will improve the economy's performance and raise the living standards of the population. Microeconomics, on the other hand, is concerned with the behaviour of individual firms and households, and with relative prices (as distinct from the aggregate price level). The two branches of economics are not rigidly segregated, however. In many areas, macroeconomists draw on the analytical techniques developed by microeconomists.

Although we usually deal with national economic aggregates, many macroeconomic topics can be studied at regional as well as at national level. Many small economies are smaller than the major regions of the economic giants, such as the United States. The economy of Ireland is smaller than that of the German states. Furthermore, with the evolution of closer economic integration in Europe, countries like Ireland have sacrificed some economic sovereignty, and the scope for independent macroeconomic policies has diminished. However, we are still a long way from the situation in which it would be possible to study the Irish economy as if it were merely a region of Europe, as New England is of the United States or Brittany of France. An independent nation, however small, can use certain *policy instruments* that are not available to a region of a larger political entity to try to influence the level of income, the rate of inflation, the level of unemployment and other *targets*. None the less, when we discuss macroeconomic policy in Ireland we have to take account of the fact that we are dealing with a very small, open economy, constrained in many areas by obligations as a member of the European Community (EC) and of the European Monetary System (EMS).

An economy is a complex and ever changing system whose behaviour reflects the choices of the population in millions of everyday transactions. Such a system is not subject to precise laws like those that apply in astronomy. None the less, in order to understand how an economy works economists find it helpful to try to summarise it in a minimum of abstract statements about the relationships between key variables.

This is called *model-building* and it is a distinguishing feature of all economic theorising. If we stick too closely to the facts and ignore theory we shall not gain a profound understanding of what causes an economy to behave as it does. On the other hand, theory divorced from the detailed study of a real economy tends to become too remote from the complexities of economic life to make much of a contribution to policy formulation. In this book we have therefore linked our discussion of macroeconomic theory closely to a description of the Irish economy. The aim of this chapter is to introduce the student to some of the basic concepts of macroeconomics, and to touch briefly on the main topics that will occupy us throughout the rest of the book.

1.2   National Income and Product

In order to track the performance of an economy over time and to compare it with other economies, we have to measure the flow of goods and services being produced and the incomes being earned by the population in an easily understood index. The branch of macroeconomics that deals with this subject is called *national income accounting*. Chapter 3 contains a technical account of the main indices of economic activity that have been developed. In this brief introduction we sketch the principal concepts without going into technical details.

Imagine that you have a bird's eye view of Ireland. Think of the hundreds of thousands of different goods and services produced in the country, and the innumerable ways in which people earn money. A list of the transactions taking place in a single day in even the smallest economy would be extremely long, and would include millions of goods and services. If we add together the value of all the goods and services produced in the country over the course of a year, we obtain the value of the *total output* of the economy. One such index is *Gross National Product* (GNP). The Central Statistics Office (CSO) estimate that GNP in Ireland in 1990 was IR£22,911 million, or IR£6,569 per person.

Closely related to GNP is the concept of *national income*. This is the total amount of income received by residents in the country. The nation's output is closely linked to the nation's income. If a person works harder at his job and produces more, then he would expect his income to rise accordingly. The same is true at national level: the more the nation produces, the more income is generated. We stated that a principal objective of macroeconomics is to find ways of increasing GNP and national income. If this objective is achieved, then the *standard of living* of the population is raised. There is more income for the country as a whole to use, and in principle this means that everyone could be made better off. In fact, as economic growth occurs there are *losers* as well as *gainers*. This issue relates to the *distribution* of national income, which falls between microeconomics and macroeconomics, and tends to be neglected by textbooks on both subjects.

Finally, note that income and product are *flow* concepts, that is they measure a stream of activity over a *period of time*, as distinct from *national wealth*, which measures the value of a stock of assets at a *point of time*.

1.3 Measuring Economic Activity

In a later chapter we explain in more detail how the CSO estimates the nation's output and income. In this section we summarise some of the broad issues that arise in national income accounting.

Double counting When we measure the value of output in the economy, we must avoid *double counting*. In the time-honoured example of a simple economy, in which the only product being produced is bread, we should count only the value of the *final* goods (bread), and not the *intermediate* goods (wheat, flour) as well. Bread is a final good because it is consumed and not used to produce any other good. Wheat and flour, on the other hand, are intermediate goods as they are inputs in the production of bread. However, the distinction between intermediate and final output is not always as clear-cut as in this example. A feature of complex economies is the growing proportion of effort that has to be devoted to commuting, crime prevention and health care. Longer traffic jams and higher bills for policing are *inputs* to the process of producing and enjoying all the other things we really want: they should not be counted as part of national output. But in fact national income, as conventionally measured, treats the value of policing and commuting as if they were final goods and services. There is therefore a serious element of double counting in national income. Moreover, since the importance of expenditure on these items tends to increase as a country grows richer, this problem distorts the comparison of national income between rich and poor countries.

Non-market activities National income is primarily concerned with magnitudes that can be brought under the measuring rod of money. Non-market activities are in general excluded. This can give rise to some unsatisfactory results. An old-fashioned, somewhat sexist, example is that if a man marries his housekeeper, the value of national income falls, because her work moves out of the market economy and becomes an intra-familial activity. It is possible, in principle, to *impute* the value of non-market work in the national income accounts, but in practice this is done only for a limited range of items. (In Ireland an imputed value of the produce consumed on farms is included in national income.) Another problem with the conventional national income accounts is that no account is taken of the country's climate, the amount of leisure its population enjoys or the pleasure derived from family life. This distorts comparisons between countries. In general the poorer the country, the greater the importance of non-market activities as a component of the welfare of the people. In some poor countries most of the population lives a leisurely

3

life under relatively pleasant conditions, which goes some way towards compensating them for the lower material standard of living they enjoy, compared with the harried citizens of rich countries.

Spillover effects   A particularly important ramification of the failure to include a value for items that are not bought and sold is the treatment of pollution, or what economists more generally call *external costs* or *spillover effects*. These *social costs* are not reflected in the *private costs* of firms producing national product. As a result, the cost of activities that cause pollution are understated, and this results in their over-production.   Waste of limited resources such as clean air and water is encouraged.   The national accounts should include a negative item reflecting the damage inflicted on the environment by the production of GNP.

1.4   The Business Cycle

So far we have been concerned with the output or the GNP of the nation in a particular year. However, we are also interested in changes in GNP from year to year. In this context, it is important to distinguish between changes in *nominal* and *real* GNP. Note that *value* equals *quantity* multiplied by *price*. For example, the value of a fleet of cars is equal to the number of cars multiplied by the price of one car. Similarly, nominal GNP is equal to real GNP multiplied by the price level. In analysing changes in nominal GNP over time, it makes a great deal of difference whether the change is due to a change in the price level or a change in the volume of GNP.

Consider the hypothetical data in Table 1.1. In case 1, nominal GNP increases from £100 to £200 due to a doubling of the price level. Real GNP remains constant. In case 2, nominal GNP again increases from £100 to £200, but this time real GNP doubles while the price level remains constant. Improvements in a country's standard of living only come about through changes in *real* GNP. If increases in nominal GNP are due to price increases only, as in case 1, people are not becoming any better off.

The *real growth rate* measures the percentage change in real GNP from one year to the next. A high and stable rate of economic growth is one of the principal goals of macroeconomic policy. Ideally, an economy should expand steadily at the rate which realises its full growth potential. This rate depends on factors such as the rate of growth of the labour force and the rate of improvement in its skills, the rate of technical progress and the growth of the country's productive capital.

Table 1.1
Nominal and Real GNP

	Nominal GNP (Value)	=	Real GNP (Quantity)	×	Price level (Price)
Case 1					
Year 1	£100	=	50	×	£2
Year 2	£200	=	50	×	£4
Case 2					
Year 1	£100	=	50	×	£2
Year 2	£200	=	100	×	£2

The variability of the rate of growth of GNP over time, and the way in which it falls below and rises above its trend growth path, is referred to as the *business cycle*. It can be seen from Figure 1.1 that the Irish growth rate has fluctuated widely from year to year.[1] In the 1960s and early 1970s high growth rates in real GNP were recorded, but real GNP declined in the early 1980s.

The growth rate of GNP is a barometer of business activity. During periods of rapid growth, firms find that sales rise and order books fill up. In periods of slow growth or decline, sales fall and unsold stocks accumulate. Because of their importance for business, firms are willing to pay a lot for economic forecasts. If slow growth is predicted, they will cut back production and reduce the size of their labour force. If, on the other hand, a high growth rate is expected, they will increase production, hire additional workers and contemplate new investment projects.

The following terms are useful when describing the business cycle. A *peak* describes the upper turning point, and a *trough* is the lower turning point. A downturn in the business cycle is referred to as a *contraction* in output, and an increase in the growth rate is referred to as an *expansion*. In the US, if a contraction lasts for two or more consecutive calendar quarters, the economy is said to be in a *recession*. If a recession is prolonged and deep, it may be called a *depression*. The distinction between recession and depression is not always clear-cut. President Harry S. Truman remarked that a recession was when your neighbour was out of work and a depression was when you were out of work!

One of the main goals of macroeconomics is to increase real GNP and raise the standard of living in the country. The objective is to smooth out the boom and the bust of the business cycle, and maintain a stable level of economic activity. If the *actual* growth rate exceeds the *potential*, upward pressure is put on the price level, and inflation results. On the other hand, if the actual growth rate falls below the potential, unemployment will tend to rise. Good macroeconomic management

5

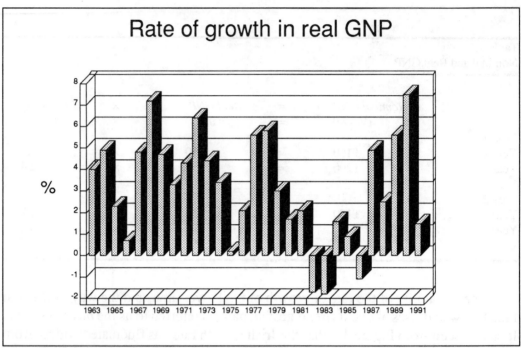

Rate of growth in real GNP

Figure 1.1 The Irish business cycle, 1963-91

---

avoids inflation on the one hand and excessive unemployment on the other, by keeping the actual growth rate close to the economy's potential. Unfortunately, on this score the Irish economy has not performed well: as may be seen from Figure 1.1, the business cycle has been extremely pronounced in Ireland. In fact the Irish economy has gone through much wider swings from boom to bust than most others during the post war years.

Note:
Potential GNP is that level of output that could be produced given the state of technology and the size of the labour force and without increasing inflation. It is frequently referred to as "full employment" GNP.

International comparisons

Figure 1.2 shows the level of real income per person in 1990 for a few countries which are of interest to Irish students.[2] The low level of income in Ireland relative to the United States, Germany, France and the United Kingdom is evident. In fact, out of the 24 member states of the Organisation for Economic Cooperation and Development (OECD), only Turkey, Portugal and Greece are poorer than Ireland. However, even if we are still relatively poor, we are much richer than we used to be. Such is the power of compound interest that if real GNP were to grow at a steady 3 per cent per annum, real output would double every twenty-five years, that is, each

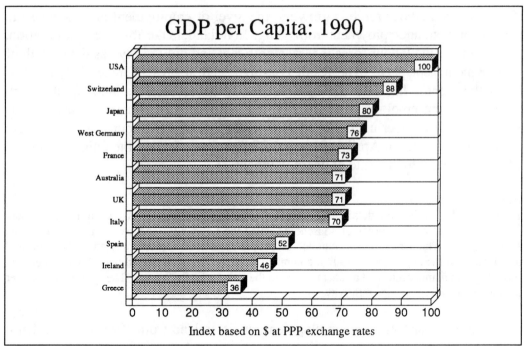

Figure 1.2 International comparisions

generation would be twice as well-off as the preceding one. In fact real income per person in Ireland is now about double what it was at the beginning of the 1960s.

1.5 Unemployment

Economic growth is not an end in itself, but a means towards improving the well-being of the population. This link is made very clear by the close relationship between the business cycle and the level of unemployment. During periods of rapid growth, more jobs are created and this leads to a fall in unemployment. Conversely, during periods when output is falling, employment falls and unemployment rises.

The definition and measurement of unemployment are fraught with difficulties. A person is regarded as being unemployed if he or she is currently out of work, but willing to accept a job at the going rate for the type of work that he or she is qualified to do. If someone is only casually looking for a job or holding out until a suitable position with a high wage becomes available, then he or she is not regarded as being unemployed.

The *labour force* is defined as the sum of the numbers employed and unemployed.

(1)   Labour force = employed + unemployed

When the labour force is growing, the level of employment must increase in order to prevent unemployment from rising. In Ireland, in the absence of emigration, the growth of the labour force is very significant and only rarely has the growth of employment kept pace. The result is a high, and at present increasing, level of unemployment. In 1991 the Irish labour force totalled 1,330,000, of whom 1,120,000 were employed and 210,000 unemployed. The *unemployment rate* is defined as the number unemployed as a percentage of the labour force. The Irish unemployment rate in April 1991 was 15.8 per cent. Among the OECD countries only Spain has a higher rate of unemployment.

Note:
As we shall discuss in more detail in Chapter 9, there are two principal measures of unemployment in Ireland. The first is a survey of households called the *Labour Force Survey*. The second is the *Live Register*, which records the number of people registered for unemployment benefits and assistance. At the beginning of 1992 the number registered as unemployed was about 15 per cent more than the number returned as unemployed in the Labour Force Survey. The data in this chapter are based on the Labour Force Survey.

Figure 1.3 shows the unemployment rate in Ireland from 1961 to 1991. Until the mid-1970s, the rate remained in a range between 4 and 6 per cent. However, it rose to 9 per cent in 1976 and in 1987 it reached a peak of 17.6 per cent, a level which would have been unimaginable in the 1960s. Although the rate declined slightly during the late 1980s, when emigration fell, as the economy slowed in 1991 it began to increase again. By the beginning of 1992 *registered* unemployment was approaching 300,000, the highest ever recorded in the history of the state.

Types of unemployment   We have stated that one of the principal objectives of macroeconomic policy is to minimise the rate of unemployment. In a dynamic economy, the pattern of demand is ever changing, new technologies are constantly being introduced, and the relative costs of factors of production vary. As a consequence some firms have to close down, while others open up. There are always people losing their jobs, switching between one job and another, and entering and leaving the labour force. But in addition to this type of *frictional* unemployment, which is present in any dynamic economy, most economies are now suffering from deep-seated *structural* unemployment. Whole regions and sectors have declined and many of those who lost their jobs may never work again. In addition, during the contractionary phase of the business cycle, firms lay off workers and unemployment rises. This *cyclical* unemployment can turn into structural unemployment if the recession is prolonged or the recovery weak.

Unemployment and the business cycle   A comparison of Figures 1.1 and 1.3 suggests that there has been a reasonably close relationship between cyclical swings in the level of output and the level of unemployment in Ireland. This is to be expected

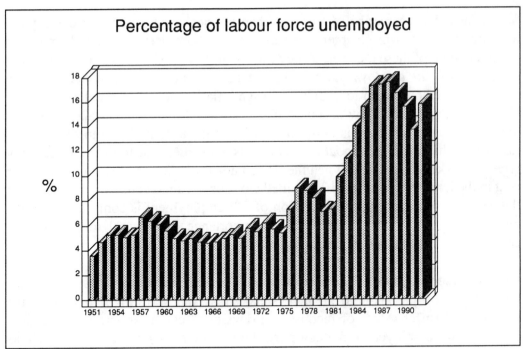

Figure 1.3 Unemployment rate in Ireland, 1961-91

because as firms increase output they hire more workers. If the labour force were constant, an increase in employment would be associated with a fall in unemployment. With a growing labour force, employment must increase to prevent unemployment from rising. In the 1960s the high growth rate in real output was associated with falling unemployment. Conversely, when the economy goes into recession and firms reduce output, workers are made redundant and unemployment rises. Recession and slow growth during the 1970s and 1980s were associated with large increases in unemployment. The resumed growth recorded at the end of the 1980s was associated with a decline in unemployment, but it was not sustained for very long and its effects on unemployment were quickly swamped by the fall in the level of emigration.

Note:
It is estimated that between 1980 and 1990 about 360,000 people emigrated from Ireland.[3] If the option of emigration had not been available, undoubtedly the level of unemployment would have risen much more over this period.

While accelerated economic growth may not automatically reduce unemployment and poverty as rapidly as we would wish, and additional targeted policies are undoubtedly needed to help disadvantaged groups, the importance of maintaining a high rate of economic growth as a means of reducing poverty can hardly be exaggerated.

In later chapters we shall explore the theories that have been proposed to explain unemployment, and in Chapter 9 we examine the problem of unemployment in Ireland in light of these theories. A key issue in this context is to arrive at a working definition of *full employment*, that is, the rate of unemployment below which shortages of labour begin to be felt and wage inflation begins to accelerate. In the US, for example, it is now accepted that when 5 per cent of the labour force is unemployed, the economy is close to full employment. If the unemployment rate falls below this level, the labour market begins to overheat due to shortages of many types of workers. Similarly, when the British unemployment rate fell to under 6 per cent in the late 1980s, shortages of skilled workers began to constrain the growth of the economy. In Ireland, the definition of full employment is complicated by the openness of the labour market and the importance of external migration as a component of the change in the supply of labour.

Costs of unemployment The costs of unemployment are very serious. First, most unemployed people undergo great personal stress and suffering.[4] Secondly, the unemployed suffer a loss of income. In developed countries this loss is shared between the employed and unemployed through *transfer payments* such as unemployment benefits, which are paid for by taxes levied on the working population. However, these transfers do not make up all of the income lost through unemployment, and as a result there is a close, relationship between the rate of unemployment and the incidence of poverty in a country.[5] Thirdly, the budgetary implications of high unemployment are very serious. The 1992 Budget included a figure of £680 million for unemployment assistance. In addition, high unemployment results in a loss of tax revenue. A country with a high rate of unemployment, therefore, faces the unpalatable prospect of having to impose a heavy tax burden on the employed population. As we shall see, a heavy burden of taxation makes it harder to alleviate the unemployment problem. Finally, the national economy loses the output and income that would be produced if the unemployed could find work. The extra output that could be produced by those looking for work in Ireland today would increase GNP by over a billion pounds.

1.6   Inflation

Microeconomics is concerned with the prices of individual goods and services relative to each other. Macroeconomics, on the other hand, is concerned with the *aggregate* price level. This is measured using a *price index*, which is a weighted average of the individual prices included in it. The most widely used price index in Ireland is the *Consumer Price Index* (CPI). To construct the CPI, the CSO collects the prices of 700 different goods and services every three months and averages them on the basis of their relative importance in the typical household's budget. (These expenditure shares are known as the *weights* of the price index.) The value of the

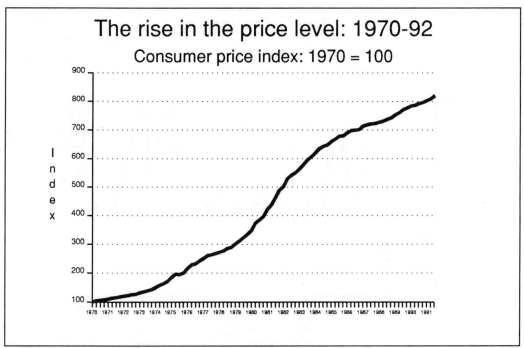

Figure 1.4 Consumer price index, 1970-91

---

index in the *base year* is set equal to 100. Changes in the index are then monitored relative to the base year. Figure 1.4 shows the CPI for Ireland for the period 1970 to 1991. It rose from 100 to 775, or by 675 per cent, over this 21-year period.

The annual *inflation rate* is defined as being equal to the percentage change in the price index over a year:

(2)   Inflation rate = $[(P_t - P_{t-1})/P_{t-1}] \times 100$

where P_t and P_{t-1} are the price indices in year t and year t-1 respectively. Figure 1.5 displays the annual rate of inflation (measured by the CPI) since the formation of the state. There were periods of *deflation* or falling prices in the 1920s and 1930s, but since 1951 there was only one year (1959) when there was no inflation. High rates of inflation were recorded in the late 1930s, and there was a massive rise in prices between the early 1960s and the mid-1980s. After 1986, however, inflation subsided and it has remained very low in recent years. Between 1970 and 1985 the annual average rate of inflation was over 13 per cent. However, since 1986 it has been just over 3 per cent.

Costs of inflation Why do economists worry about inflation? Should we be willing to undergo the adjustment required to squeeze inflation out of the economy if this

11

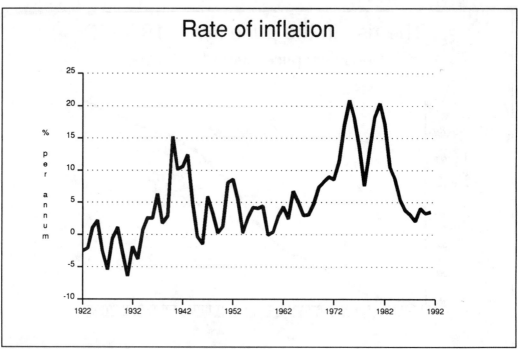

Figure 1.5 Inflation rate in Ireland, 1922-91

---

entails high unemployment and slow growth? To answer these questions we need to consider the costs of inflation.

Inflation raises the cost of living, or, equivalently, lowers the value of money. We have come to think of an inflation rate of 3 per cent as acceptably low, but we should bear in mind that if prices go on rising at this rate they will double in less than 24 years. At this rate of inflation over a century the price index would rise from 100 to 1,922 (that is, more than 19-fold). Thus, even a modest rate of inflation implies a major long-term rise in the price level.

The long-run decline in the purchasing power of money as a result of inflation is illustrated by the fact that one of today's pounds is only worth the equivalent of about three pence in 1922 money. A wage of £3 a week in 1922 was the equivalent of £100 a week in today's money.

Note:
James Joyce's *Ulysses* takes place in Dublin on 16 June 1904. There are numerous references to the cost of living in the course of the book. A pint of milk and a pint of stout both cost 2d. The morning newspaper cost 1d. A domestic servant was paid £12 a year. (Remember that d was the symbol for a penny and there were 240 pence in the pound in pre-decimal currency.)

Because inflation erodes the value of money, people dependent on savings and those living on fixed incomes are taxed by inflation. In fact, inflation threatens any long-term contract which specifies amounts in money terms. Unless people have the foresight or luck to anticipate future inflation and build it into their contracts, this can have very unfair effects. Consider, for example, a person who saved and invested her money in long-term government securities back in the 1960s, before the major inflation of the 1970s. For every £1 placed in these securities the government is obliged to repay £1 when they mature. But £1 in today's money is worth less than 10 pence in the money of 1960. Moreover, the rate of interest offered on long-term securities back in the 1960s was only about 5.5 per cent, and this did not compensate the saver for the inflation that occurred in subsequent years, which was largely unanticipated.

On the other hand, consider a person who borrowed in 1960 to buy a house. He incurred a debt that was specified in money terms (a mortgage), but acquired a real asset (a house). During the 1960s and 1970s the value of the house would have soared, but the amount owed on the mortgage remained unchanged. Consequently, the borrower benefited enormously from the *leverage* obtained by having his debt expressed in nominal values. Furthermore, the rate of interest did not rise as rapidly as the rate of inflation: the money was borrowed at an interest rate that remained low relative to the rate of inflation. This gain, however, was at the expense of savers who left their money in building societies or banks, earning a rate of interest that did not compensate them for inflation. In fact there was no convenient way the typical saver could have earned a positive real return on savings at the time.

In general, inflation takes purchasing power from savers and gives it to borrowers. The biggest borrower in most countries is the government, so inflation acts as an arbitrary tax on the population. However, a situation in which borrowers are in effect confiscating savers' money cannot last indefinitely. In the 1980s interest rates eventually rose to compensate savers for the higher inflation that had become the norm. Inflation is much lower now, and interest rates are relatively high, so savers can easily earn a positive real return. Borrowers have to pay a more realistic rate of interest on their debt, and the rate of inflation in the price of real assets, such as houses, is low.

In addition to its impact on borrowers and lenders, inflation can also have very serious implications for an economy's *competitiveness*, that is, the ability of domestic producers to compete with their international rivals. A loss of competitiveness threatens the attainment of a high and stable rate of growth of GNP. To see how inflation affects competitiveness, consider the case of a country whose inflation in running at 10 per cent a year. If inflation among its trading partners is running at only 5 per cent, the country's products will be progressively priced out of both the domestic and export markets by those of other countries. Local firms will be forced out of business, employment will fall and unemployment will rise. As we shall see in later chapters, these effects could be avoided by *devaluing* the currency, but this gives another twist to the inflationary spiral. It is therefore desirable that a country keep its rate of inflation lower than that of its main trading partners in order to maintain international competitiveness without recourse to repeated devaluations.

The gravest problem is not a high rate of inflation, but an *rising* rate of inflation. Once inflation becomes entrenched, the risk is that it will increase. This can lead to *hyperinflation.* In many Latin American countries inflation has been as high as 50,000 per cent a year. When this happens the currency's value in terms of hard currencies falls daily. Faced with this situation people will try to spend their money as fast as they can before rising prices further reduce its value. They will also seek to be paid in a stable currency, usually US dollars. The local currency will only be used to pay taxes. This response to inflation is known as "dollarisation". Hyperinflation undermines the whole economy and renders economic growth virtually impossible. There are no examples of countries that have recorded sustained economic growth combined with high rates of inflation. In general there is a tendency for high inflation to lead to low growth and high unemployment. For example, in Ireland between 1971 and 1991 the annual average rate of inflation was 11 per cent and the average rate of unemployment was also 11 per cent. Over the same period, countries such as Switzerland, Germany and Japan had an average rate of inflation of about 5 per cent and an average rate of unemployment of less than 6 per cent.[6]

Thus, in addition to acting as an unfair tax on savers, inflation lowers the rate of real economic growth. It is therefore essential that inflation be controlled if a country is to achieve a high growth rate and a low rate of unemployment.

1.7   Constraints

From the outset we should be conscious of two very important constraints that policy-makers face when pursuing the goals of high growth and low unemployment. The first is the country's *fiscal deficit,* the second is its *balance of payments.* These can act as major constraints on the authorities' freedom of action in trying to achieve growth and employment objectives.

Fiscal deficit

The *fiscal deficit* summarises the balance between the amount of money the government collects from taxes and other revenue sources, and what it spends on goods and services and transfer payments. If it spends more than it receives, it has to borrow to make up the difference. From time immemorial governments as well as households have found it hard to live within their means, and have been tempted to run deficits. In times of recession, with unemployment rising and tax revenues falling, governments come under pressure to spend more in order to get the economy growing. During the 1970s most governments around the world gave in to this temptation and incurred major fiscal deficits.

As we shall see in more detail in Chapter 5, successive Irish governments borrowed very heavily during the 1970s and 1980s. The result of this borrowing was an accumulation of debt. The total *national debt* at the end of December 1990 stood at IR£26,447 million. Of this, IR£12,754 million was *external debt*, that is, it was owed to foreigners or non-residents.

The problem with debt is that it has to be *serviced*. Interest must be paid on the outstanding balances. In 1991 Ireland paid IR£2,194 million in interest on public debt. This is equivalent to two-thirds the yield of income tax. In addition, large amounts of debt *mature* each year and either have to be *redeemed* or *rolled over* (that is, new loans taken out to replace the maturing debt). Even if no further foreign borrowing takes place, the burden of servicing our debt will remain very heavy into the next century. With so much money committed to debt service, the burden of taxation is heavy and the government's ability to spend in other areas, such as education or job creation, is severely constrained. In subsequent chapters we shall examine in greater detail the dynamics of debt and the limits to the amount of borrowing that can be undertaken by the state.

The balance of payments

The *balance of payments* is a record of a country's transactions with the rest of the world. A balance of payments deficit, that is, an excess of imports over exports, has to be paid for by borrowing from the rest of the world or by running down assets held abroad. There are limits to the extent to which foreigners are willing to lend to countries that are experiencing balance of payments difficulties. This imposes a constraint on domestic policy and forces policy-makers to pay attention to the implications of their actions for the balance of payments.

In particular, an attempt to sustain a high growth rate may result in a rapid growth in imports without a corresponding expansion of exports. The result would be a balance of payments crisis, demanding that sharp corrective measures be taken. This possibility is of particular concern in Ireland, because the country is a classic example of a *small open economy*. In this context, "small" relates to the very small share of Irish firms in relation to the overall world market, and "open" refers to the importance of international trade to the economy. One measure of "openness" is imports and exports as a percentage of GNP. Figure 1.6 shows that using this yardstick, Ireland is considerably more open than Germany, the UK, the US and, perhaps surprisingly, Japan.

The international dimension of macroeconomic theory and policy is therefore very important in an analysis of the Irish economy.

1.8   Long-term Growth

Traditionally, macroeconomic textbooks place greater emphasis on short-run economic management (stabilisation theory) than on the issues of longer-term growth and development. The present book is no exception, but in the concluding chapter we discuss the question of the long-run performance of the Irish economy

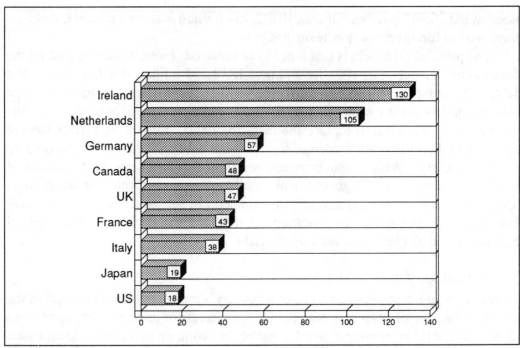

Figure 1.6 Exports + imports as a percentage of GNP, 1990

in some detail, and throughout the book we point to several links between the short and long run.

In the short and medium term, macroeconomic management in a small, open economy such as Ireland consists primarily of trying to reconcile the domestic goals of stable growth, low unemployment and moderate inflation, with the constraints imposed by the need to maintain the fiscal and balance of payments deficits within manageable limits. In the longer term, the central issue is: how can the potential growth rate of the economy be raised? This question takes us into the area of economic development, which is concerned with the analysis of the problems facing less developed countries and the policies that will lift them out of poverty. The lessons of economic history are also relevant, because there is much to be learned from the history of the countries that are rich today, about how they reached this privileged situation.

While there is no conflict between the goals of long-term growth and short-term stabilisation, when dealing with the issue of long-term growth the emphasis switches from the demand to the supply side of the economy. In the long run countries do not become richer because the level of demand increases, but because the productive powers of the population and its ability to compete internationally increase. In the long run what matters are the skills and motivation of the labour force, the capital equipment and the natural resources they have to work with. A stable monetary framework is also important. (We have noted that a high rate of inflation is

16

incompatible with growth in the longer run.) Finally, in a small open economy it is also important that the rate of exchange is kept at a realistic level, relative to domestic costs. A *misaligned* exchange rate acts as a drag on the long-run growth of the economy.

1.9   Do Economists Take Too Narrow a View?

Economists are often criticised for taking a narrow, materialistic view of life. The emphasis they place on money income is believed by many non-economists to give a misleading picture of human well-being or happiness. In fact economists are conscious that money is not everything and have tried to incorporate wider considerations into their measures of economic progress. A recent attempt is to be found in the United Nations Development Programme's (UNDP) *Human Development Report*, which presents a "Human Development Index" (HDI). The HDI tries to measure a country's success in providing its citizens with "the options to lead a long and healthy life, to be knowledgeable and to find access to the assets, employment and income needed for a decent standard of living".[7] The HDI is calculated by adding together a country's ranking on three basic variables: life expectancy, educational attainment and per capita income. However, the importance attached to income is progressively reduced as the level of income rises, reflecting the concept of diminishing marginal utility of income.

Note:
Utility refers to the satisfaction derived from income. Marginal utility is the extra satisfaction derived from an extra unit of income.

The HDI was calculated for 160 countries in 1990. Japan ranked first, Sierra Leone last. Ireland was in 23rd place, compared with 29th in terms of income per person. Table 2.1 shows how Ireland's HDI compares with that of the countries included in Figure 1.2, which was based on income. Note that the gap between the countries is much narrower in Table 1.2. Ireland is only 5 per cent below Japan on the HDI, but our per capita income is only 58 per cent of the Japanese. Undoubtedly the HDI gives a more meaningful picture of the relative levels of well-being throughout the world than a simple comparison of per capita incomes, but none the less, it is reassuring to note that there is a very close correlation between a country's rank on the HDI and its rank in terms of per capita income.

Table 1.2
Human development index, 1990

~~~~~~

Japan	99.3
Switzerland	98.1
USE	97.6
Australia	97.3
France	97.1
UK	96.7
West Germany	95.4
Italy	95.5
Spain	95.1
Ireland	94.5
Greece	93.4

Source: UNDP, *Human Development Report, 1991*, New York/Oxford, Oxford University Press, 1991.

1.10   Conclusion

In this chapter we

- Introduced the main topics to be dealt with in a course on macroeconomics

- Outlined the concepts of gross national product (GNP) and national income

- Provided data on the level and trend of Irish national output and some international comparisons

- Discussed the principal goals of macroeconomic policy, which are to maintain over the long run an as high as possible growth rate of real output and income and an as low as possible rate of unemployment

- Discussed the manner in which the fiscal deficit and the balance of payments act as constraints on policy-makers in a small open economy such as Ireland

- Introduced a wider measure of well-being known as the Human Development Index.

Notes:

1. As we shall see in Chapter 3 two estimates of real GNP are published by the CSO, one derived from the income approach, the other from the expenditure approach. We have used the average of the two series. Our data was obtained from the Department of Finance's *Databank of Economic Time Series* (1987) and *National Income and Expenditure*, published by the CSO.

2. We discuss the concept of Gross Domestic Product (GDP), which is closely related to GNP, in Chapter 3. In making international comparisons, it is necessary to convert domestic currencies into a common currency (usually the US dollar). However, exchange rates fluctuate widely and the data from different countries will vary according to what exchange rate is used. For example, at the beginning of February 1991 an Irish pound was worth $1.81, but by mid-June it had fallen to $1.48. If these exchange rates were used to calculate the level of Irish GDP in dollars, it would be implied that we were 18 per cent worse off in June than in February. In order to avoid misleading comparisons of this type, the OECD has calculated what are called *purchasing power parity* (PPP) exchange rates. The idea behind PPP is that exchange rates should reflect the relative cost of a bundle of goods and services in the different countries. We discuss this topic in greater detail in later chapters. The data used in Figure 1.2 was obtained from the OECD, *Main Economic Indicators*, April 1991, p. 173.

3. D. F. Hannan, J. J. Sexton, B. M. Walsh and D. McMahon, *The Economic and Social Implications of Emigration*, National Economic and Social Council, Report No. 90, May 1991.

4. A recent study found that the unemployed were five times more likely to suffer high levels of psychological distress than people at work, and that this distress increased with the duration of unemployment: see Christopher Whelan, Damian Hannan and Sean Creighton, *Unemployment, Poverty and Psychological Distress*, Economic and Social Research Institute, General Research Paper, No. 150, January 1991.

5. For data on the Irish situation, see T. Callan, B. Nolan, B. W. Whelan, D. F. Hannan with S. Creighton, *Poverty, Income and Welfare in Ireland*, Economic and Social Research Institute, General Research Series, Paper No. 146, September 1989, and the collection of papers published in *The Economic and Social Review*, Vol. 20, No. 4, July 1989.

6. See International Monetary Fund, *World Economic Outlook*, May 1991, Chart 36, for a picture of unemployment and inflation in a sample of industrialised countries.

7. See UNDP, *Human Development Report*, 1991, New York/Oxford, Oxford University Press, 1991, p. 88.

Data appendix

Year	Real GNP growth rate %	Unemployment rate %	Inflation rate %
1963	4.0	5.0	2.5
1964	4.9	4.7	6.7
1965	2.4	4.6	5.0
1966	0.7	4.7	3.0
1967	4.8	5.0	3.1
1968	7.2	5.3	4.8
1969	4.7	5.0	7.4
1970	3.3	5.8	8.2
1971	4.3	5.5	9.0
1972	6.4	6.2	8.6
1973	4.4	5.7	11.4
1974	3.4	5.4	17.0
1975	0.2	7.3	20.9
1976	2.2	9.0	18.0
1977	5.6	8.8	13.6
1978	5.8	8.1	7.6
1979	3.0	7.1	13.2
1980	1.7	7.3	18.2
1981	2.0	9.9	20.4
1982	-1.7	11.4	17.1
1983	-1.8	14.0	10.5
1984	1.6	15.6	8.6
1985	0.9	17.3	5.4
1986	-1.1	17.4	3.8
1987	4.9	17.6	3.1
1988	2.5	16.7	2.1
1989	5.6	15.6	4.1
1990	7.5	13.7	3.3
1991	1.5^f	15.8	3.5

Note: f = forecast.
Sources:
Real GNP: Department of Finance *Databank of Economic Time Series* (1987) and *National Income and Expenditure*, various issues.
Unemployment rate: *The Trend of Employment and Unemployment* and *Labour Force Survey*, various issues.
Inflation: *Statistical Bulletin*, October 1991, Consumer Price Index, Table 4.

Chapter 2

Introduction to the Theory of Income Determination

2.1 Introduction

We saw in Chapter 1 that the primary objectives of macroeconomic policy are to achieve a high and stable growth rate in national income and to maintain a low level of unemployment. A low rate of inflation is also desirable, both in its own right and because it helps to achieve high and stable growth. In pursuing these objectives policy-makers are constrained by the need to avoid excessive fiscal and balance of payments deficits.

In this chapter we introduce a simple model of the economy. We outline two broad schools of thought, classical and Keynesian, and explain how they differ in regard to their conclusions about the workings of the economy and the scope for an active macroeconomic policy.

2.2 Macroeconomic Models

In Chapter 1 we stated that macroeconomic theory uses models to explain how the economy works. Model-building consists in setting out the way in which the main variables, such as, income, consumption, employment, the price level and so on, are inter-related. A model can be used to explore how *policy variables*, such as government expenditure, affect the economy's performance. It is important to keep testing a model against the facts of economic life to make sure it has not lost touch with reality. We should question the value of a model of the Irish economy if, for example, it predicted that unemployment would always be low.

Macroeconomic theory has developed at a rapid pace in recent years, but there is still no clear-cut consensus on some of the major issues. The most important disagreements relate to the causes of persistently high rates of unemployment and the scope for using an active macroeconomic policy to alleviate this problem.

There are two broad schools of macroeconomic thought: classical and Keynesian. Classical economics emerged gradually from the writings of the great eighteenth- and nineteenth-century British economists, such as David Hume, Adam Smith, David Ricardo and John Stuart Mill. It provided a strong intellectual justification for a non-interventionist, *laissez-faire* political economy. The classical economists believed that, in the long run at least, the economy tends *automatically* towards full employment, without the benefit of active macroeconomic management. The only sound policy was to avoid fiscal deficits: governments, like households, should always balance their books.

Keynesian economics is named after the British economist, John Maynard Keynes (1883-1946), whose most important book was *The General Theory of Employment, Interest and Money* (1936). Keynes felt that the classical model was unable to explain the reality of the Great Depression. He believed that it was obvious that very high rates of unemployment tended to persist beyond what could reasonably be called the "short run".[1] He questioned the efficacy of the mechanisms that were supposed to keep the economy at or near full employment. He proposed active management of the economy by government to supplement the self-correcting tendencies of the market.

Keynes remarked in the preface to the *General Theory*, that

The composition of this book has been for the author a long struggle to escape. . . The difficulty lies, not in the new ideas, but in escaping from the old ones, which ramify . . . into every corner of our minds.[2]

At the time he was writing, the industrial countries of the world were in the severest depression in modern history. In the US the unemployment rate increased from 3.2 per cent in 1929 to a peak of 25 per cent in 1933, before falling back to 17.2 per cent in 1939. By the time Franklin Delano Roosevelt (FDR) took office in 1933, the depression was much more severe than anything experienced in the past. Unemployment in Britain increased from 10.4 per cent in 1927 to a peak of 22.1 per cent in 1932, before decreasing to 2.4 per cent in 1942. In Ireland, unemployment increased from 22,858 in 1929 to a peak of 133,319 in 1933 and decreased to 83,963 in 1942.[3]

However, not all of the European countries remained mired in depression throughout the 1930s. In Italy, the Fascist regime had embarked on a public works programme in the 1920s and averted the worst effects of the Great Depression. After Hitler's accession to power in Germany in 1933, government expenditure was increased and there was a rapid expansion in output and employment. In Sweden a social-democratic government had maintained a high level of employment by expending public works programmes. Keynes, in a lecture delivered in University College, Dublin, in 1933, mentioned with approval the fact that European countries "have cast their eyes or are casting them towards new modes of political economy". He praised the protectionist policies of the recently installed Fianna Fail Government as an alternative to the *laissez-faire* recommendations of classical economics.[4]

Policy-makers in the English-speaking democracies at this time did not have a macroeconomic model that would have justified action by governments to move the economy out of the depression. Keynes's *General Theory* was devoted to developing such a model. At its crudest, what he proposed was relatively simple. If the economy is in a depression, with high unemployment and plenty of unused capacity, government should increase spending or reduce taxation. This would lead to a higher level of economic activity and lower unemployment.

In fact Keynes's ideas had little immediate impact on policy. The Establishment in America, as well as in Britain, remained intellectually committed to the tenets of orthodox (classical) economics, which predicted that in due course the economy would right itself. Their main concern was with balancing the budget. Taxes were raised and expenditure cut, which had the effect of exacerbating the unemployment problem. The Federal Reserve Bank (the US Central Bank) pursued contractionary or deflationary policies. Only when government spending on armaments soared and vast numbers were mobilised into active military service, as the Second World War loomed, did unemployment begin to fall rapidly.

After the Second World War Keynesian policy eventually became the new orthodoxy, especially in English-speaking countries. The appeal of the theory lay in the way it seemed to show governments how to minimise unemployment without enkindling inflation. At the theoretical level the whole profession debated the validity of Keynes's ideas and strove to refine his model and explain it within the basic classical framework. Textbooks incorporated elements of both Keynesian and classical economics in what was called a *neo-classical synthesis*.[5] In the 1970s, however, a classical counter-revolution gained ground. As economies began to experience both rising inflation and rising unemployment, there was increasing scepticism about the effectiveness of active macroeconomic policy in achieving lasting increases in employment and output. New, sophisticated versions of the classical model were developed, and found an increasingly receptive audience, first in academic circles and then among politicians, especially those of a conservative hue.

There is still a good deal of disagreement between adherents to classical (or New Classical) theories and followers of Keynes, especially in regard to the effectiveness of policies to alleviate the problem of unemployment. We shall return repeatedly to this continuing debate in the course of this book. In this chapter we present an overview of the main issues.

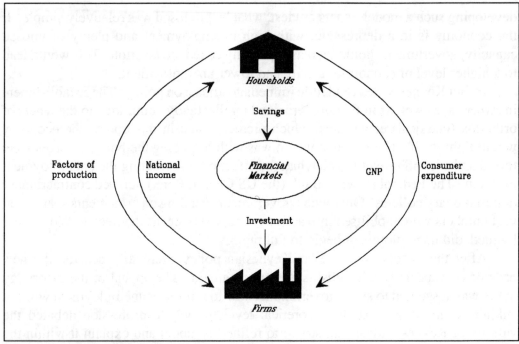

Figure 2.1   Circular flow of income

2.3   The Theory of Income Determination

In this section we develop the simple Keynesian model of income determination. The Keynesian theory is based on the *circular flow of income*, a model which was first described by a court physician to Louis XV, François Quesnay (1694-1774). A modern version is outlined in Figure 2.1.

Circular flow of income In this simple model we assume that the economy has no government or foreign trade sectors. We also assume that the price level is *fixed* or constant. These simplifying assumptions will be dropped later, and the model will be elaborated to correspond more closely to the real world.

There are only two kinds of *economic agent* in our simple economy, namely, *households* and *firms*. Consider the two loops on the left-hand side of the diagram. Households own the factors of production: land, labour, capital and natural resources. These factors of production are made available to firms in return for payments of rent, wages, interest and profit. Wages are paid for the use of labour, rent for the use of land, interest for the use of capital, and profits are received by the owners of firms. The sum of rent, wages, interest and profit equals *national income*.

Note:
If we ignore rent, interest and profits, the two loops on the left-hand side simply represent people going to work and receiving a salary or wage for their labour.

24

Consider now the two loops on the right-hand side. (Ignore for the moment the flows to and from financial markets.) Firms combine the factors of production to produce goods and services. We do not go into detail about the techniques of production. We shall just assume that inputs of land, labour and capital simply enter a "black box" called the *production function*, and outputs of goods and services emerge on the other side. We shall use the familiar term GNP (Gross National Product) to describe the aggregate output of goods and services. To close the loop, households, using the income they have earned (national income), purchase the goods and services produced by firms. We refer to this household expenditure as *private consumption expenditure* (C). Given that the two right-hand loops are equal, that is, expenditure equals output, it follows:

(1) GNP ≡ Expenditure

where the symbol ≡ denotes an identity or something that is true by definition.

Going a stage further, since all of the money received by firms is passed on to households in the form of wages, rent, interest and profit, it is also true that total expenditure equals national income. Hence:

(2) National income ≡ GNP ≡ Expenditure

The essential message of the simplified circular flow diagram given in Figure 2.1 is that, in the aggregate, we consume what we produce, and we spend what we earn. People go to work and get paid, and spend their income purchasing the goods and services produced by the firms.

Savings and investment Notice that in Figure 2.1 there are two additional flows relating to *savings* (S) and *investment* (I) which we have not yet mentioned. The flow of savings reflects the fact that households do not spend all of their income.[6] Some proportion of national income is saved. This represents a *leakage* from the circular flow. However, in the absence of a government or foreign sector, people must either spend or save their income. The sum of consumer expenditure and savings equals national income. That is:

(3) National income ≡ C + S

In the modern economy, household savings are channelled into the financial system (banks and building societies). Firms borrow from these institutions in order to finance investment. Investment refers to firms' expenditure on new machinery and buildings. Thus, households do not buy all of the goods and services produced by firms. Some firms produce machines and the materials to build factories, and

25

these goods are purchased by other firms. Total expenditure now equals consumer expenditure plus investment (I). Substituting into (2), above, we obtain:

(4) National income $\equiv$ GNP $\equiv$ Total expenditure $\equiv$ C + I

This relationship states that national income equals GNP, which in turn equals total expenditure, and that total expenditure is divided into households' consumer expenditure and firms' investment expenditure. Finally, substituting (3) into (4):

(5) C + S $\equiv$ GNP $\equiv$ Total expenditure $\equiv$ C + I

Note:
The letters or symbols we are using to describe macroeconomic variables have become standard.[7]

The government and foreign sectors Earlier we made the simplifying assumption that there was no government or foreign sector. The discussion of the national income accounts in the next chapter explains in some detail the exact relationship between households, firms, government and the foreign sector. At this stage we make the point that if government and a foreign sector are included, total expenditure expands to include government consumption expenditure (G), exports (X) and imports (M). Total expenditure now consists of five categories:

Private consumer expenditure	C
Investment	I
Government current expenditure	G
Exports	X
minus Imports	-M

In short:

(6) Total expenditure $\equiv$ C + I + G + X - M

Exports are expenditure by foreigners on Irish-produced goods and services; imports are expenditure by Irish people on goods produced in other countries. Imports are *deducted* from total expenditure to arrive at expenditure on domestically produced goods and services, which generate national income. C, I, G and X include both domestic and foreign goods and services. Subtracting M leaves us with expenditure on the *domestically* produced components of aggregate demand. (As we shall see, imports are a new leakage from the circular flow of national income and expenditure.) The difference between exports and imports (X - M) is referred to as *net exports*, NX, so we can rewrite (6) as

(7)   Total expenditure $\equiv$ C + I + G + NX

Inserting (7) into (4) gives:

(8)   NI $\equiv$ GNP $\equiv$ TE $\equiv$ C + I + G + NX

This relationship states that national income (NI) equals output which, in turn, equals total expenditure (TE). We use (8), above, to explain how the government can influence output and employment. Before doing so, however, we introduce two further concepts and we explain the role of stocks in macroeconomic analysis.

Aggregate demand and aggregate supply   Expenditure and demand are one and the same thing. If someone buys a cup of coffee, they contribute to the demand for coffee. Total expenditure is referred to as *aggregate demand* (AD). This is a particularly important concept in macroeconomic analysis. If the government has increased total expenditure, then it has increased the demand for goods and services in the economy.

The total amount of goods and services produced by firms, which we have labelled GNP, may also be referred to as *aggregate supply* (AS). The concepts of AD and AS are at the heart of all macroeconomic models. If AS equals AD, the economy is said to be in *equilibrium*. If AS exceeds AD, there is an *excess supply* of goods and services. If AS is less than AD, there is an *excess demand* for goods and services.

Stocks   An important role is played by changes in *stocks* or *inventories*. Changes in stocks are classified as part of investment. It is assumed that firms have a desired stock level, and plan to achieve this by setting aside some of the current period's output for stock-building. If, however, demand falls short of the level anticipated by firms, there will be *unplanned accumulation* of stocks: firms will have produced too much relative to the level of demand, and unsold current production will pile up in stocks. This will serve as a signal to firms to reduce production.

Alternatively, if firms under estimate the level of demand for their products, they will have to meet the unexpected demand from stocks accumulated out of past production. This unexpected *destocking* will mean that stocks are run down below the target level. An *unplanned reduction* in stocks will serve as a signal to firms to increase output in the next period. Thus, although small relative to total output, changes in stocks play a crucial role in modern economies, sending signals to managers on which they base their production plans. In short:

AS = AD	equilibrium	stocks are unchanged
AS > AD	excess supply	unplanned increase in stocks
AS < AD	excess demand	unplanned reduction in stocks

Determining equilibrium output To understand what is meant by the equilibrium level of output we need to examine carefully the relationship between investment and stocks. There can be *unplanned* as well as *planned* changes in stocks. Thus, the change in total stocks (ΔSK_t) over a particular period is comprised of a planned and unplanned component:

(9) $\Delta SK_t \equiv \Delta SK_p + \Delta SK_u,$

where the p and u subscripts refer respectively to planned and unplanned. ΔSK_u consists of the *unintended* accumulation/decumulation of stocks. This part of total stock changes is included in our definition of GNP, but *not* in investment or total expenditure. Planned changes in stocks are, however, included in the definition of investment. Now GNP is said to be in equilibrium with total expenditure *only* when there is no unintended change in stocks. We have, therefore, the equilibrium condition that

(10) $\Delta SK_u = 0$

Equation (8) can now be rewritten as:

(11) $NI \equiv GNP = TE \equiv C + I + G + NX$

The identity sign between GNP and TE has been replaced by an equals sign in order to allow for an equilibrium/disequilibrium relationship to exist between the two variables. If GNP exceeds TE, $\Delta SK_u > 0$ and firms are producing too much output. This is a signal to cut back on production until $\Delta SK_u = 0$. Similarly, if GNP is less than TE, $\Delta SK_u < 0$ and firms are producing too little output. This is a signal to increase production until $\Delta SK_u = 0$.

How does unemployment fit into the set of relationships given in (11)? An increase in real GNP or national income is associated with a fall in unemployment. In the *short run*, land and capital are relatively constant, so a firm that wishes to expand its output will tend to hire more workers. Assuming the labour force is relatively constant, an increase in employment will be associated with a fall in unemployment. Hence, changes in real output are inversely related to unemployment. We express this as follows:

(12) $U = f(GNP)$
$$\underset{-}{}$$

where the notation f( ) means "is a function of" and the negative sign underneath the variable in brackets indicates that the two variables are inversely related, so that as GNP increases, unemployment falls.

What can the government do if output and income are stagnant and there is a high rate of unemployment? In the Keynesian model, the emphasis is on the demand side of the economy. Government can alleviate the problem by boosting expenditure to create an additional demand for goods and services, . An increase in government expenditure (G) leads to an increase in total expenditure (TE). Given that the level of output is initially unchanged, the government has created an excess demand for goods and services. Firms will recognise the excess demand through falling levels of stocks, and respond by producing more. To do so, firms must hire more labour, so unemployment will fall. To compensate households for the extra labour they have supplied, more wages will be paid and national income will increase.

In short:

$$\uparrow G \quad \rightarrow \quad \uparrow TE \quad \rightarrow \quad \uparrow GNP \quad \rightarrow \quad \downarrow U \text{ and } \rightarrow \quad \uparrow NI$$

Note:
The symbols $\uparrow$ and $\downarrow$ indicate an increase and a decrease, respectively, and $\rightarrow$ means "leads to".

Conversely, a decrease in government expenditure would lead to an excess supply of output. As stocks build up, firms respond by reducing output and workers are laid off. Employment decreases and national income declines.

Note:
The government could also vary total expenditure by changing taxation. An increase in taxation would, for example, reduce personal income and lead to a fall in consumer expenditure. (Consumer theory is discussed in Chapter 4.) However, a considerable amount of tax revenue is recirculated in the economy in the form of *transfer payments*, that is, payments made to households that are not in return for a contribution to the production of GNP (therefore they are not *factor payments*). In Ireland in 1990, over IR£4.0 billion was spent by government on transfer payments. From the point of view of total expenditure, what matters is the *net* impact of government taxation less government transfer payments. We refer to the difference between these magnitudes as *net taxation*.

Fiscal policy consists in the use by government of its expenditure or/and taxation to influence total expenditure. An increase in expenditure is referred to as an *expansionary* fiscal policy and a decrease in expenditure as a *contractionary* fiscal policy. The active use of public spending and taxation in this manner raises a number of questions about the level of taxation, borrowing, and the manner in which the government spends its money. We discuss these issues at length in later chapters.

2.4   Aggregate Supply and Aggregate Demand

We now move beyond the simple circular flow diagram where prices were held constant to develop aggregate demand (AD) and aggregate supply (AS) schedules. A *demand schedule* shows the relationship between price and consumers' demand for a firm's product. The higher the price, the lower the demand for the product. This inverse relationship between price and quantity demanded for a good is depicted by a downward sloping demand curve. Similarly, a *supply schedule* shows the relationship between price and the firm's willingness to supply a product. More will be offered for sale, the higher the price. This positive relationship between price and the supply of goods is shown as an upward sloping supply curve.

The rationale behind supply and demand schedules for individual products is explained in courses in microeconomics. Similar but somewhat different considerations apply when we derive the AD and AS schedules in macroeconomics. At this stage we give a brief, intuitive explanation of why the AD and AS curves slope downwards and upwards, respectively. A full treatment cannot be presented until we have developed our knowledge of the money and labour markets more fully in later chapters.

Aggregate supply

Figure 2.2 shows an upward sloping aggregate supply (AS) curve. The price level (P) and real GNP are measured on the vertical and horizontal axes, respectively. An upward sloping AS curve indicates that an increase in P will lead to an increase in the supply of goods and services. Conversely, a decrease in the price level will lead to a fall in the supply of goods and services. We can easily accept that a rise in the price of its own product affects a firm's willingness to supply it, but why should a firm increase its output when all prices are rising? To answer this, consider the fact that a firm's profit is equal to total revenue minus total cost:

(13)   Profit = total revenue - total cost

In turn, total revenue equals the price of output (P_q) multiplied by the volume of output (Q). Total cost equals the price of inputs (P_z) multiplied by the volume of inputs (Z), such as raw materials and labour. (Wages are the price of labour.) Substituting into equation (13):

(14)   Profit = $(P_q \times Q) - (P_z \times Z)$

We assume that the firm's output price increases as the general price level rises. An increase in output prices will increase profits if input prices remain constant: the firm enjoys higher revenue for the same cost. Higher profits, in turn, act as an

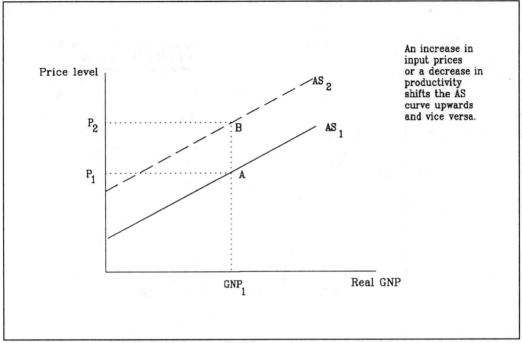

Figure 2.2   Aggregate supply curve

incentive for firms to increase the volume of output. This positive relationship between the price level and the volume of output supplied is reflected in an upward sloping AS curve.

This result depends crucially on the assumption that input prices, and wages in particular, remain constant as output prices change. The *real* wage (W/P) is defined as the *nominal* wage (W) divided by the price level (P). In the above example, W is constant so that the increase in P reduces (W/P). This means that workers have experienced a fall in real wages while the firm's profits have risen. The assumption that W is constant is certainly not valid in the long run. Hence, the AS schedule depicted in Figure 2.2 is a *short run* relationship.

Location of the AS curve The AS curve is drawn for a given level of input prices or total costs. If input prices (costs) change, the AS curve will shift. To see that this is the case, consider the point A in Figure 2.2, where the price level, P_1, corresponds to the real output level GNP_1. Suppose that costs increase and firms, in order to maintain profits, pass these higher costs on to customers in the form of higher prices for their products. In terms of equation (14), the increase in costs is reflected in an increase in input prices. Firms increase output prices in order to maintain profit levels. The increase in output prices is shown in Figure 2.2 as a movement from A to B. At B, real GNP is unchanged, but the price level has increased from P_1 to P_2. The supply schedule has shifted upwards to the left, from AS_1 to AS_2. By moving the AS curve upwards in this way, we can examine the relationship between the new,

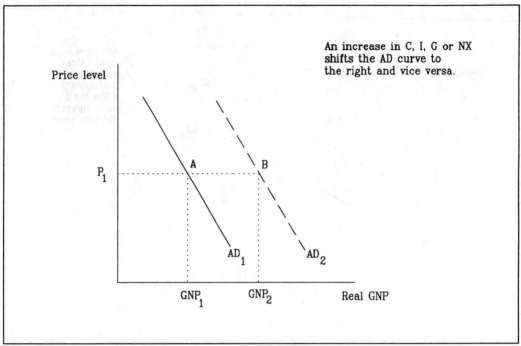

An increase in C, I, G or NX shifts the AD curve to the right and vice versa.

Figure 2.3   Aggregate demand curve

higher price level and the original level of real GNP. Conversely, lower input prices will be reflected in a shift downwards to the right of the AS curve.

An important influence on the location of the AS curve, which we have not yet mentioned, is *productivity*, defined as the ratio of output to inputs. (Total output divided by the quantity of labour employed is referred to as *labour productivity*.) If more output is obtained from the same, or fewer, inputs, productivity has increased. This occurs as technology improves. An increase in productivity reduces costs as more output can be produced with a given amount of inputs. Hence, an increase in productivity shifts the AS curve outwards to the right, whereas a decrease in productivity shifts the AS curve inwards to the left.

Aggregate demand

On the demand side of the economy there is an inverse relationship between the price level and real GNP. This is shown by a downward sloping aggregate demand (AD) curve. It is easy to understand why a change in the price of its product would affect the demand for a firm's output. If a firm lowers its price, consumers will switch their spending from alternative products with a higher price. The demand for the firm's product will increase and the demand for the substitute product will fall. But why should a change in the general price level P affect the aggregate level of spending?

One justification for drawing a downward sloping AD schedule is the *international substitution effect*. Assuming a fixed exchange rate, a fall in the domestic price level relative to the foreign price level will increase the *price competitiveness* of domestic firms. As a result, exporters will capture a greater share of foreign markets and exports will increase. Similarly, firms whose products compete with imports will also capture a greater share of the domestic market and imports will fall. Hence, a reduction in the average price level leads to an increase in exports and a fall in imports. In terms of equation (9), above, net exports (NX) rise, and this leads to an increase in aggregate demand and subsequently to an increase in real GNP. This justifies drawing a downward sloping AD schedule, but it is not the only reason for doing so.

A second way in which changes in the price level may affect real GNP on the demand side is through the *real balance effect*. This refers to the effect of the price level on the real value of assets denominated in current prices, and subsequently on the level of consumption. If you hold some of your savings in cash, a fall in the price level will increase the real value (or purchasing power) of your *wealth*. Because you are now richer, you are likely to feel that you can afford to consume more out of your income. A fall in the aggregate price level, P, increases households' wealth and may be expected to lead to a higher level of aggregate consumption expenditure (C). An increase in C is an increase in aggregate demand. This reasoning reinforces the inverse relationship between P and AD that we already showed exists because of the international substitution effect.

The real balance effect is sometimes known as the *Pigou effect* because it was first suggested by Keynes's contemporary at Cambridge, Arthur C. Pigou (1877 1959), who believed that this effect would tend to move the economy back towards full employment following a deflationary shock. It became an important component of classical macroeconomics.

A third important reason underlying the downward sloping AD curve is an *intertemporal substitution effect*. Briefly, the argument is that high interest rates (r) encourage consumers to postpone or abandon expenditure plans because of the high cost of borrowing money. For example, suppose you intend to finance the purchase of a CD player by borrowing from a bank. If interest rates increase, you may decide to make do with your old music system as the cost of finance is too high. On the other hand, low interest rates encourage people to spend as the cost of borrowing is cheap.

As explained in detail in Chapters 6 and 7, there is a relationship between the price level (P), the money supply (M^s) and the interest rate (r). Changes in P affect the *real value of the stock of money* (M^s/P). As P rises, the real money supply falls; as P falls, the real value of the money supply increases. Starting from an equilibrium situation, in which the public is holding its desired level of real money balances, a fall in P implies that the public is holding *excess real cash balances*. As discussed later, this leads to a fall in the rate of interest. The fall in the interest rate, in turn,

33

leads to increased spending on interest-sensitive components of AD, such as consumer expenditure (C) and investment (I). Conversely, a higher price level reduces the real money supply and increases the interest rate. The higher interest rate should lower C and I, and therefore aggregate demand.

Note that the intertemporal substitution effect differs from real balance effect. In the former case the source of the increased aggregate demand is the fall in interest rates caused by the excess supply of cash balances that emerges as the price level falls. In the real balance effect the increased aggregate demand is due to the increase in C as a result of a wealth effect.

Location of the AD curve   Let us consider now the factors that determine the location of the AD schedule. For a given price level, an increase in any component of AD, such as C, I, G or NX, will shift the AD schedule upwards to the right. A fall in any of the components of AD will shift the schedule downwards to the left. The government can therefore use fiscal policy to shift the AD curve. To see how, consider the point A in Figure 2.3, which corresponds to a price level P_1 and a real GNP level of GNP_1. An increase in G moves the AD curve out to the right. B is a point on the new aggregate demand curve, AD_2. At this point the level of output has risen to GNP_2.

Equilibrium

In Figure 2.4, the AS and AD curves are brought together, and we see that the equilibrium price (P_1) and real output (GNP_1) combination is at the point A. As we mentioned in connection with our discussion of the circular flow of income, changes in stocks act as a signal to firms as to whether production should be increased, reduced or left unchanged. At the point A, actual stock levels equal the planned (or desired) stock levels, and there are no unanticipated changes in stocks. This is the key to the concept of equilibrium in the market for goods and services.

If the price level is lower than P_1, as at P_2, AS is less than AD and there is excess aggregate demand. This excess demand will lead to an unplanned reduction in stocks which will fall below the desired level. In order to ration the available supply among those trying to buy it, firms will initially raise prices. They will subsequently increase production in order to meet demand from current production. Thus, the economy will tend to move quickly back to equilibrium.

Similarly, if the price level is greater than P_1, as at P_3, AS exceeds AD and there is an excess supply of goods and services. There will be an unplanned increase in stocks which will rise above the desired level. It seems logical to argue that, just as firms raised prices and production when they were too low to ensure equilibrium, they will lower prices in order to clear unwanted stocks, and cut production in order to bring current production into line with current demand. If this chain of events takes place, the economy will also move quickly back towards equilibrium, starting from a point of excess aggregate supply. However, to ensure that this will happen

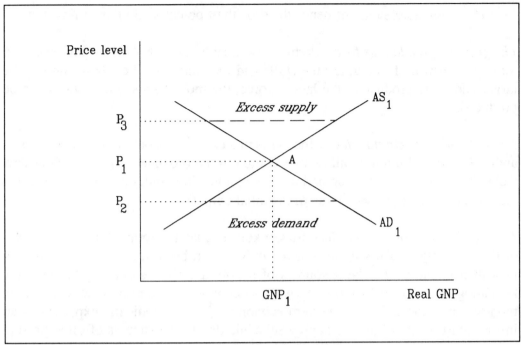

Figure 2.4 Equilibrium in the goods and services market

prices must be *flexible downwards*. If, in fact, prices are *sticky* or *downward rigid*, then the move back to equilibrium may be a slow process. We shall see that the behaviour of prices and costs of production in a situation of excess aggregate supply is one of the keys to the functioning of the economy, and one of the sources of disagreement between classical and Keynesian economists.

In this context we must be clear that "equilibrium" simply means that the market clears. It implies nothing about the level of unemployment. Point A in Figure 2.4 *does not necessarily correspond to the full employment level of output*. However, the classical economists believed that there were forces at work which tended to ensure that equilibrium would correspond to full employment; Keynes denied this. We turn to this issue now.

2.5　Classical Economics

Potential GNP is defined as that level of output that could be produced in the economy given the state of technology, the size of the labour force, and without accelerating inflation. If the economy is operating at this level, firms are operating at capacity and there is *full employment* in the labour market.

Note:
Capacity output is where a firm has maximised efficiency, and costs per unit of output are minimised. Also "full employment" does not imply zero unemployment. We discuss this concept in Chapter 9.

The main factors that influence the growth of potential GNP over time are:

The growth of the labour force Perhaps the most important of all the influences on long- run growth of output are the skills and motivation of the labour force. The larger and more productive the labour force, the more goods and services can be produced.

The growth of the capital stock Increases in a country's stock of productive assets and technological progress allow more output to be produced. In as much as new technologies are usually embodied in new equipment, a high level of investment is vital to sustain a high growth rate of potential output.

The supply of raw materials Scarcities of key raw materials could hinder the growth of the economy. Such scarcities have not,however, been much of a constraint on growth over the years. New sources of supply are always opening up and new technologies are constantly finding ways of economising on raw materials. None the less, since the 1970s the western economies have periodically experienced an inward shift of the aggregate supply schedule due to the success of oil exporting countries in restricting the supply of oil.

In addition to these supply-side considerations, it is obvious that a small economy could not specialise and expand its output of certain goods unless it had access to international markets. Historically, the quest for such markets has been very important. However, our discussion is at this stage primarily concerned with a closed economy in which aggregate supply expands in line with the demand of the domestic population. We shall return to these aspects of long-term growth at later stages in this book, but initially, our emphasis is on short-run fluctuations about the growth path.

The long-run aggregate supply schedule

We have seen that the economy will always tend towards equilibrium through firms reacting to unplanned changes in stocks. The really interesting question, however, is whether this equilibrium will correspond to the full employment or potential level of GNP. The distinguishing prediction of the classical model is that this will, in fact, be the case. Discussing what is meant by this prediction and how realistic it is will preoccupy us in several chapters of this book. In this chapter we provide a simple introduction to the basic issues.

In Figure 2.5 the price level (P) is represented on the vertical axis, and real GNP on the horizontal axis. The level of GNP corresponding to potential GNP is indicated as GNP*. If actual GNP is less than the potential level, firms are operating at less than full capacity and unemployment will increase. The classical model holds that the aggregate supply schedule (AS) is *vertical* at the point corresponding to potential

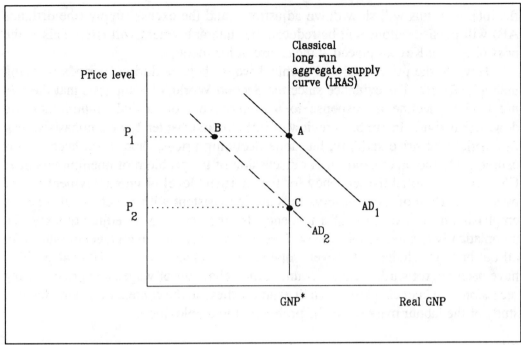

Figure 2.5   Classical model

GNP. According to this model there exists an *automatic adjustment mechanism*
which tends to drive the economy towards full employment. Thus, not only does
the economy tend towards equilibrium through the equality of actual to desired
stocks, but in the long run this equilibrium is always at the potential, or full
employment, level of GNP. (The distinction between long- and short-run is
discussed below.)

      To see how the automatic adjustment mechanism is supposed to function,
assume that the economy is initially at a point such as A in Figure 2.5. At this point,
GNP equals GNP* and the price level is P1. Suppose now that the economy is
subjected to a deflationary shock, that is, a leftward shift in AD from AD1 to AD2.
(This would occur if exports slumped, or if there was a decline in consumer or
investment spending, or a contractionary fiscal policy.) Initially, the price level
remains at P1 and output at GNP* so that an *excess supply* equivalent to the distance
between points A and B emerges. The classical model predicts that the price level
will quickly fall from P1 to P2, moving the economy down along the AD2 schedule
until aggregate demand once again equals the full-employment level of output, GNP*
at C. The AS schedule joins points such as A and C. The vertical AS curve indicates
that full employment output is maintained by the rapid adjustment downward of the
price level in the face of excess supply. Thus, excess unemployment proves to be a
short-run phenomenon that disappears quickly as the economy reverts, of its own
accord, back to GNP*. However, if input prices, (and wages in particular), are not

37

flexible, then this will slow down adjustment and the excess supply (the distance AB) will persist, output will be reduced and unemployment will rise. This is the possibility that Keynes placed at the centre of his model.

How do the price level and nominal wages behave during periods of rising unemployment? The evidence since the Second World War suggests that they do *not* tend to decline in response to unemployment or unsold output: they are downwards rigid. In our brief review of inflation in Chapter 1, we emphasised how few periods of price stability, let alone declining prices, there have been in this century. On the other hand, in our discussion of the problem of unemployment in Chapter 1, we noted the tendency for the "normal" level of unemployment to rise over time. Both of these observations are inconsistent with the classical school's emphasis on the existence of a tendency for the economy to adjust quickly and automatically to shocks, and to stay close to the full employment level of output for all but brief interludes. However, sophisticated defences of the classical position have been put forward, taking account of the behaviour of wages and prices during recessions. In later chapters we shall examine these in the context of a more detailed study of the labour market and the problem of unemployment.

The classical model and economic policy

The policy conclusion which emerges from the classical analysis is that there is no need for intervention on the part of the authorities. When the economy is at the point B in Figure 2.5, for example, it will revert, automatically, to the point A. There is no need for the government to intervene and shift the AD curve downward, as there would be if the price level remained at P_1.

Similarly, classical theory predicts that the government cannot increase real GNP beyond the potential level for any length of time. Suppose the economy is at the point A in Figure 2.6, and the government implements an expansionary fiscal policy either by increasing government expenditure or/and lowering taxes. The AD curve shifts outwards to the right, from AD_1 to AD_2, and the economy moves from A to B. At the point B there is an excess demand for goods and services and this puts upward pressure on the price level. As the price level rises from P_1 to P_2, the economy will move back along AD_2 until the point C is reached. At C the economy is once again in equilibrium on the AS schedule. The government's attempt to stimulate the economy has only resulted in a bout of inflation: there has been no long-run gain in output.

In the classical model, therefore, there is no scope for the government to influence, except in the short run, the level of output or employment. The only way to increase the level of output is by increasing potential GNP, which requires a rightward shift of the AS curve. This comes about through growth in the skills and expertise of the labour force, and investment in new and better capital equipment. Thus, classical economists place the emphasis on *supply-side* measures rather than

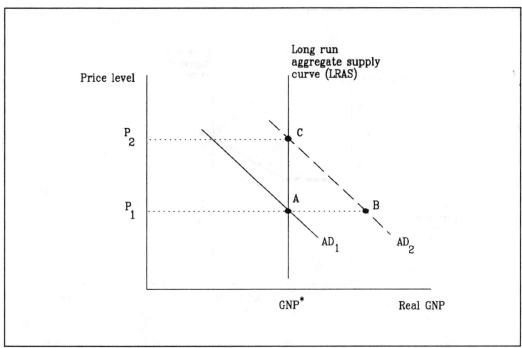

Figure 2.6   Expansionary fiscal policy

on the manipulation of aggregate demand, as the way to achieve lasting increases in the level of output.

2.6   Keynesian Economics

The Keynesian model

To understand how the Keynesian model justifies intervention by government to move the economy towards full employment, consider Figure 2.7. The diagram shows the classical AS curve and the downward sloping AD curve. However, we now include a short-run aggregate supply (SRAS) curve which, at certain levels of real GNP, is horizontal or positively sloped. Suppose the economy is at A and there is a shift of the AD curve from AD_1 to AD_2 (due to a fall in C, I or NX). The economy moves along the SRAS curve to the point B. Note that, in contrast to the classical model, both the price level *and* real GNP adjust following the shift of the AD curve. The relative sizes of the changes in P and real GNP depend on the slope of the SRAS curve. If the SRAS curve were relatively flat, a shift to the left of the AD curve would result in a large decrease in real GNP and a small decrease in the price level. In the classical analysis, there is no distinction between the short and long run AS curves. Both are vertical, and only the price level changes. The level of output remains at GNP*.

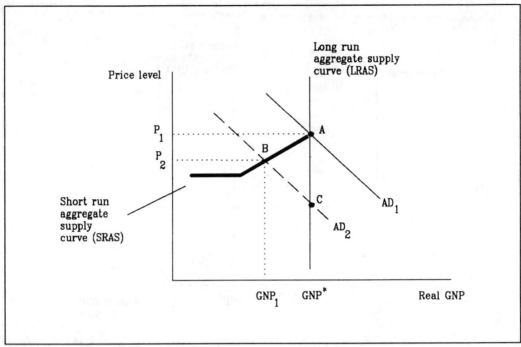

Figure 2.7 Keynesian model

At B the economy can be said to be in equilibrium because the level of output, measured along the horizontal axis, has been reduced to correspond to the level that is demanded. There is no unwanted or unintended accumulation of stocks. However, *actual* GNP is less than *potential* GNP, and unemployment over and above the full employment level emerges.

Note:
At B real wages (W/P) have increased. The output price level has fallen from P_1 to P_2, but nominal wages are unchanged. It follows that W/P has increased. As we explain in detail in Chapter 8, real wage and price expectations play a crucial role in the Keynesian analysis.

Keynes argued that the economy could remain at the point B in the long run and not merely for some brief period of time. He argued that output gaps could persist and that the economy could get stuck at levels of output below GNP*. We defer a discussion of this crucial issue until Chapter 8. For the moment, if we accept that this is the case, then it is possible that the SRAS curve shown in Figure 2.7 is *not* short run at all, but is in fact a segment of the LRAS. Put another way, it is possible that the slope of the LRAS curve is not uniform at all levels of real GNP. It is possible that when there is a great deal of excess capacity in the economy and the unemployment rate is high, the LRAS curve is likely to be horizontal. As GNP* is approached, the LRAS curve becomes steeper and eventually vertical.

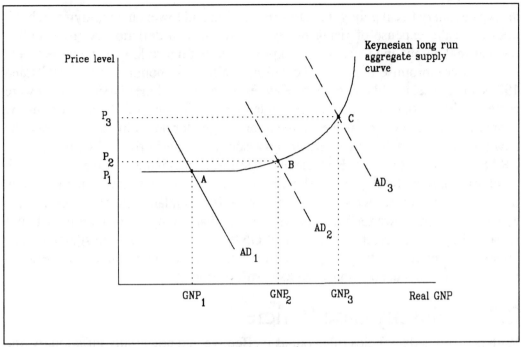

Figure 2.8 Keynesian long run aggregate supply curve

Figure 2.8 shows a *kinked* LRAS curve based on these assumptions. At low levels of real GNP (relative to GNP*) unemployment is high, there is a great deal of excess capacity, and the AS curve is relatively flat or elastic. A shift in the AD curve, from AD_1 to AD_2, leads to an increase in real GNP without a marked increase in the price level. As the economy approaches full employment, however, the AS curve becomes increasingly steep. Larger price increases accompany any expansion in real output. This is shown in Figure 2.8, when AD shifts from AD_2 to AD_3. At this stage on the LRAS curve, increases in AD simply increase prices and do not raise the level of output, and we are back in the classical world.

Thus Keynes argued that output gaps could persist and that the government should intervene and use fiscal policy to eliminate the resultant unemployment. Fiscal policy would be effective depending on where on the LRAS curve the economy is located. When it is on the flat segment, there are plenty of unemployed resources and aggregate supply will respond to an increase in demand. Fiscal policy will be highly effective in this situation. However, as the economy approaches the full employment level of output, GNP*, the response to increased aggregate demand comes more and more in the form of higher prices, and less and less in the form of additional real output. Fiscal policy, therefore, becomes less appropriate.

As mentioned, an expansionary fiscal policy leads to an increase in prices. This increase in the price level is referred to as *demand-pull inflation*, because aggregate demand is pulling up prices in the face of an inelastic supply. In terms of the policy objectives stated in Chapter 1 and at the beginning of this chapter, *trade-off* exists:

41

an expansionary fiscal policy increases real output and lowers unemployment, but it does so at the expense of rising prices. Conversely, a deflationary fiscal policy reduces real output and increases unemployment, but it also lowers the price level.

This compromise picture of economic reality was popular in the 1960s and 1970s: in a sense, it said that both the Keynesian model and the classical model were correct. Which one was relevant depended on how close to full employment the economy was. However, as we shall explain in greater detail in later chapters, the new classical revival has gone further and asserted that the horizontal segment of the LRAS curve is a figment of Keynesian economists' imagination: if it exists at all, it is relevant only in the shortest of short runs. Thus, there are today, as there were in the 1930s, economists who believe that there is a fundamental tendency for the economy to move towards full employment, and that attempts by government to use fiscal policy to increase the level of real GNP are fundamentally misguided. The issues are sharper now than they were in the 1930s, but the disagreement between rival views of how the economy works is still profound.

2.7   Supply-side Policies

With demand- side policies ruled out as ineffective and potentially inflationary, the classical model relies on policies designed to shift the AS schedule to the right in order to increase the level of real GNP. Examples are an increase in the efficiency of the labour force or a greater willingness to accept offers of employment at a given wage level (which is equivalent to an increase in the supply of labour). The shift in the AS curve results in higher output and a decline in the price level, which is a highly desirable outcome. When supply-side policies are successfully pursued, there need be no trade-off between inflation and unemployment. The improvement in real output is accompanied by a fall in the price level.

Events that shift the AS curve to the left have a harmful effect on the economy, resulting in rising prices and falling output, a combination that has been labelled *stagflation*. In Figure 2.9, a shift of the LRAS curve to the left increases the price level from P_1 to P_2 and reduces real output from GNP_1 to GNP_2. (Note here that we use the Keynesian version of the LRAS curve for illustrative purposes.) A leftward shift of the AS curve occurred when the price of energy inputs rose sharply in the 1970s, and again, although only briefly, during the Persian Gulf crisis of 1990 - 91.

Keynesian economics did not emphasise the supply side of the economy. This was understandable when the economy was operating at less than full capacity and unemployment was very high. However, concern over a tendency for inflation to emerge, even when the official indices of unemployment are quite high, led to a renewed interest in supply-side economics in the 1980s. Versions of the underlying model became popular in the US during the Reagan administration and in Britain during the Thatcher era. It was widely believed that the key to greater prosperity lay in shifting the AS curve to the right by increasing the incentives for the unemployed

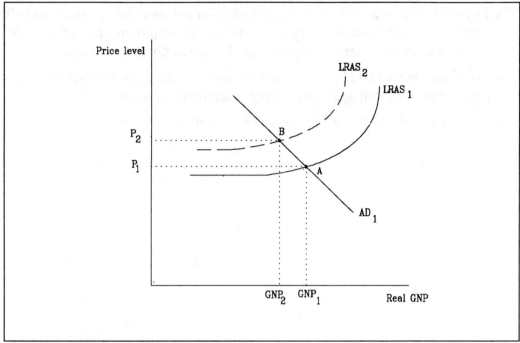

Figure 2.9 Shift in AS curve to the left

to accept whatever jobs were available (basically by making the welfare system more harsh) and encouraging people to work harder and take greater risks by lowering the top rates of income tax.[8] The possible contribution of aggregate demand to maintaining prosperity was minimised.

2.8   Conclusion

In this chapter we have introduced the broad themes of macroeconomics. These include:

- The idea of a macroeconomic model

- The circular flow of income and the relationship between expenditure, output and income

- The role of unplanned changes in stocks or inventories in maintaining the equilibrium level of production

- The theory of income determination and the concepts of aggregate supply and aggregate demand

- The classical macroeconomic model and the concept of an automatic mechanism tending to maintain the economy at the full employment level of output. The related idea that the long-run aggregate supply curve is vertical at full employment output

- Keynes's dissatisfaction with the contradiction between the classical model's prediction that the economy always tended to full employment and the reality of widespread, persistent unemployment during the Great Depression

- The Keynesian model of income determination and the scope for an active fiscal policy if the long-run aggregate supply schedule is not vertical

- The role of policies that affect the supply side of the economy.

Notes

1. Of course it all depends on how long the short-run is. Keynes quipped: "In the long-run we are all dead".

2. J. M. Keynes, *The General Theory of Employment, Interest and Money*, London: Macmillan, 1936, p. viii.

3. We use the numbers unemployed rather than an estimate of the unemployment rate because estimates of the labour force at this time are unreliable.

4. J. M. Keynes "National Self-Sufficiency" (the first Finlay lecture at University College, Dublin), reprinted in *Studies*, June 1993, p. 184. Keynes went on to decry "decadent international capitalism" which, he said, "doesn't deliver the goods".

5. This term was coined in the 1950s by the American economist Paul Samuelson, a Nobel prize winner in economics, who wrote the first modern textbook of economics aimed at university students. The book is now in its thirteenth edition.

6. According to Keynes, this is a "fundamental psychological law, upon which we are entitled to depend with great confidence both *a priori* from our knowledge of human nature and from the detailed facts of experience ...", *The General Theory of Employment, Interest and Money, op. cit.* p. 90.

7. It was not always so. In a paper entitled, "Mr Keynes and the Classics" *(Econometrica*, April, 1937) which reviewed the *General Theory*, the Nobel prize winning economist John Hicks (1904-1989) used the symbol *I* for national income. In a letter to Hicks, Keynes wrote, "I regret that you use the symbol *I* for income. One has to choose, of course, between using it for income and investment. But, after trying both, I believe it is easier to use *Y* for income and *I* for investment. Anyhow we ought to try and keep uniform in usage". This letter is reproduced in J.R. Hicks, *Economic Perspectives: Further Essays on Money and Growth*, Oxford University Press, 1977, p. 145.

8. These policies have been satirised as being based on the view that the poor won't work because they have too much money and the rich won't work because they have too little.

Chapter 3

Measuring the Country's Economic Performance

3.1   Introduction

In Chapters 1 and 2 we introduced the basic concepts of national output, income and expenditure. In this chapter we shall explore these in greater detail, focusing on issues that are important in assessing the performance of the Irish economy and illustrating them with data from the most recent edition of *National Income and Expenditure* (NIE).

3.2   Measuring National Output and Income

Circular flow of income   In Chapter 2 we presented a simplified diagram of the circular flow of income and expenditure. This showed the relationships between households and firms in the economy. Figure 3.1 shows an expanded diagram which includes four sectors, namely, firms, households, government and the rest of the world. Households provide firms with the *factors of production* (land, labour and capital). In return, firms pay households wages, rent, interest and profit, which add up to *national income*. These two flows are represented by the two loops on the left-hand side of the diagram. Firms combine the factors of production to produce *national product* sometimes referred to as *gross national product* (GNP). Households use most of their income to purchase the consumer goods which are the largest component of national product. They save some of their income and financial institutions such as banks and building societies lend this money to firms who use it to purchase the investment goods that constitute the rest of national product. These flows are represented by the two loops on the right-hand side and the flows in the centre of the diagram.

Consider first how the inclusion of a government sector affects the circular flow of income and expenditure. The government receives *taxes* (T) from households and makes *transfer payments* to households under various social welfare schemes. (We refer to these as B, for Benefits.) These payments are not in return

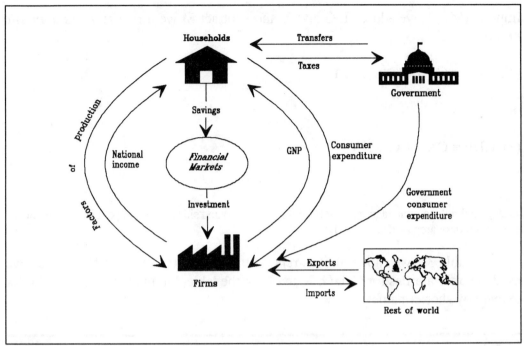

Figure 3.1 The circular flow of income and expenditure

for goods bought or services rendered, which is what distinguishes them from factor payments. The difference between what the government receives in taxes and what it transfers back to households is known as *net taxes*, NT = T - B. The government uses this net revenue to pay the people who work in the public sector and to purchase goods and services from firms. These purchases are shown by the arrow labelled *government consumption expenditure* on the far right of Figure 3.1. (To keep the diagram simple, we have omitted the transactions from firms to government.)

Consider now the relationships between the foreign sector (the rest of the world) and domestic firms. Irish firms sell goods and services to the rest of the world. These *exports*, X, are expenditure by foreigners on Irish-produced goods and services. On the other hand, Irish households and firms spend money on foreign goods and services. This expenditure is called *imports* (M). The flows of exports and imports are shown by the two arrows on the bottom right of Figure 3.1. The difference between exports and imports is *net exports*, NX = X - M.

Measuring output: the expenditure approach   In the circular flow diagram we referred to the flow of output as simply as GNP. We need to give more detail about how this is measured. In Figure 3.1 there are four expenditure arrows pointing towards firms. These refer to household consumption expenditure (C), investment[1] (I), government consumption expenditure[2] (G) and exports (X). There is one expenditure arrow pointing away from firms to the rest of the world, which represents imports (M). If we add C, I, G and X and subtract M we arrive at *gross domestic product* (GDP):

(1) $GDP \equiv C + I + G + X - M$

or

(1) $GDP \equiv C + I + G + NX$

Note:
The symbol $\equiv$ denotes an identity or definition. The right-hand side of (1) is expenditure on domestic production or aggregate demand (AD).

In Table 3.1 we show GDP as reported in the 1990 edition of NIE. We have used the official titles for C, I, G, X and M in the table, but in the text we shall refer to them by shorter names.

Table 3.1
Expenditure on GNP, £ millions, 1990

	£ millions	*as a % of GDP*
Personal expenditure on consumers' goods and services (C)	14,231	55.4
+ Net expenditure by public authorities on current goods and services (G)	4,021	15.7
+ Gross domestic physical capital formation (I)	5,363	20.8
+ Exports of goods and services (X)	15,940	62.0
- Imports of goods and services (M)	-13,861	-53.9
= *Gross Domestic Product* at current market prices (GDP)	25,693	100.0
+ Net factor income from the rest of the world (F)	-2,782	
= *Gross National Product* at current market prices (GNP)	22,911	

Source: *National Income and Expenditure*, 1990, Central Statistics Office, Dublin (1991), Table 5.

As Table 3.1 shows, C accounts for over half of GDP. X and M are individually very large relative to GDP, but net exports (X-M) are relatively small. G amounts to about 16 per cent of GDP. Total government expenditure is much larger than G because G excludes benefits, B, and government capital expenditure, which is included in I.

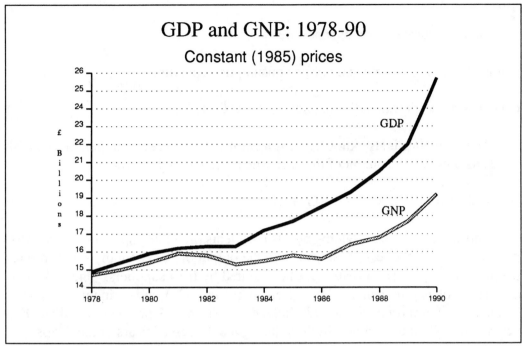

Figure 3.2 Gross national and domestic product

The significance of the word *domestic* in GDP is that it measures the value of all the production *occurring within the country*. When we wish to refer to the value of the production *accruing to residents of the country* we refer to gross *national* product (GNP). This is shown on the last line of Table 3.1. The difference between the GNP and GDP is *net factor income from the rest of the world* (F):

(2) $GNP \equiv GDP + F$

In Ireland, F is now a substantial *negative* figure due to the level of debt service payments to non-residents and of the profits repatriated by foreign-owned companies. These outflows grew more rapidly than GDP during the 1980s, to the point where they now equal more than 10 per cent of GDP. Figure 3.2 shows the trend of GDP and GNP between 1980 and 1990. It may be seen that the gap between GNP and GDP widened rapidly in the early 1980s.

The figure for GNP is more meaningful than that for GDP as a guide to the resources available to Irish residents to consume and invest, but GDP gives a better picture of the level of production within the country. GDP is generally used in international comparisons of economic activity.[3]

The following sub-totals of GDP are used in different contexts:

(3) Domestic consumption expenditure $\equiv$ C + G

that is, the sum of private and public consumption spending.

(4) Gross domestic expenditure, GDE $\equiv$ C + G + I

This aggregate is also known as *absorption* and measures total spending by Irish residents, both on the output of the domestic economy and on imports.

(5) Final demand, FD $\equiv$ C + I + G + X

This measures total spending by Irish residents (including spending on imports) plus spending by the rest of the world on the output of our economy. It represents the total potential market that might be captured by Irish suppliers. Thus, M/FD is a measure of *import penetration*. (Remember that C, I and G include imported components.) Import penetration in Ireland rose from 24.9 per cent in 1960 to 40.9 per cent in 1979, but declined slightly during the depressed years of the 1980s.[4]

Measuring output: the income approach In the version of the circular flow given in Chapter 2 households purchased output from firms and firms passed *all* of the proceeds back to households as payment for the use of the factors of production. Under these circumstances, national income and national production are equal.

This is an over-simplification. The government or public sector drives a wedge between the value of spending on output and the total paid to the factors of production. Taxes are levied on expenditure (these are called *indirect* taxes, T_i) and *subsidies* (S_u) are provided for some goods and services. Indirect taxes and subsidies drive a wedge between an item's market price and the factor payments embodied in it. For example, a pint of beer sells for about IR£1.60, of which about IR£0.80 represents excise duties and value added tax (VAT). Only IR£0.80 goes to pay for the production and distribution of the beer and this is all that enters into national income. The existence of taxes and subsidies therefore requires us to distinguish between magnitudes measured at *market prices* and *factor cost*. The factor cost measure includes only payments made to the factors used to produce goods and services.

(6) GDP$_{fc}$ $\equiv$ GDP$_{mp}$ - T_i + S_u

where the fc, mp subscripts refer respectively to factor cost and market prices.

Another complication arises from the distinction between *gross* and *net* investment. The significance of the word *gross* in gross domestic product and gross national product is that the measure of investment included, I, is gross investment.

50

No allowance has been made for the *depreciation* of the capital equipment used in the production process. This should not be included in national income, because it is not paid to a factor of production: it represents the cost of capital equipment from the past that is used up in the course of this year's production. Including it in this year's production results in an element of double counting. It is however difficult to estimate the value of the depreciation of capital that takes place in a year and this is why GDP and GNP, rather than their net counterparts, are so often used. In due course, the accountants make estimates of depreciation, D, allowing us to calculate the value of *net domestic product* (NDP) and *net national product* (NNP).

(7) $NDP_{fc} \equiv GDP_{fc} - D$

net domestic product is equal to gross domestic product minus depreciation. Adding F to NDP we obtain:

(8) $NNP_{fc} \equiv NDP_{fc} + F$

This identity states that met national product equals net domestic product plus net factor income from the rest of the world. NNP_{fc} includes everything that constitutes income of the factors of production. It therefore equals *National Income* (NI).

(9) $NNP_{fc} \equiv NI$

Table 3.2 shows the derivation of national income in 1990.[5]

Summary It is possible to calculate GDP and GNP by using the expenditure or income method. The former involves adding up all the expenditures in the economy. The latter involves calculating national income and then working back to derive GDP. These closely related definitions of economic activity can be confusing, but the student should remember three important principles:

1. The difference between *gross* and *net* magnitudes depends on whether investment, I, is measured gross or net.
2. The difference between *national* and *domestic* magnitudes depends on whether factor income from the rest of the world is included (national) or excluded (domestic); and
3. The difference between magnitudes measured at factor cost and at market prices is indirect taxes less subsidies.

Table 3.2
Gross Domestic Product, Gross National Product and National Income, 1990

£ millions

Gross domestic product at market prices (GDP$_{mp}$)	25,693
- Taxes on expenditure (T$_i$)	4,444
+ Subsidies (S$_u$)	1,803
= Gross domestic product at factor cost (GDP$_{fc}$)	23,051
- Provision for depreciation (D)	2,583
= Net domestic product at factor cost (NDP$_{fc}$)	20,469
+ Net factor income from the rest of the world (F)	-2,782
= Net national product at factor cost (NNP$_{fc}$) = National Income (NI)	17,687

Source: *National Income and Expenditure*, 1990, Tables 1 and 2.

A breakdown of NI by *sector of origin* is provided in *NIE*. Table 3.3 shows the trend in the relative importance of the main sectors since the early 1970s. Industry (which includes building and construction, public utilities, as well as manufacturing industry) is the largest sector followed by distribution, transport and communications. Agriculture now accounts for only 11 per cent of GDP.

NI is disaggregated by type of income (income from self-employment, profits, etc. and wages and salaries). Wages, salaries and employers' social security contributions ("remuneration of employees") constituted 73 per cent of national income in 1990. The other components, such as profits, interest and rents, are relatively small. However, changes in the share of profits in national income are important as an indication of the profitability of investment in the economy.

Table 3.3
National Income by sector of origin, 1972 and 1990

	1972 %	1990 %
Agriculture	18.7	11.1
Industry	37.3	44.3
Distribution, transport and communications	18.3	19.7
Public administration and defence	6.8	7.7
Other (including rent and interest)	23.5	27.8

Source: *National Income and Expenditure*, 1979 and 1990, Table 2.
Note: These proportions do not add to 100 per cent because three components of NDP are not distributed by sector, namely, the adjustment for financial services, the adjustment for stock appreciation and F.

Gross national disposable income   GNP is a comprehensive measure of the value of production accruing to the residents in the country, but it takes no account of *transfers* between the country and the rest of the world. (Transfers relate to payments and receipts not in exchange for any good or service.) These are significant in Ireland because of the scale of the grants and subsidies received from the European Community and the smaller amount of emigrants' remittances. (Ireland makes small transfers to international organisations and overseas development assistance.) In the *NIE* accounts there is a figure for *net* current transfers from the rest of the world (R).[6] When R is added to GNP$_{mp}$ we obtain *gross national disposable income* (GNDI):

Table 3.4
Gross national disposable income, 1972 and 1990

	1972 £ millions	% of GNDI	1990 £ millions	% of GNDI
Gross domestic product at market prices	2,237.8		25,693	
+ Net factor income from the rest of the world	29.6	1.2	-2,782	-11.4
= Gross national product at market prices	2,267.4		22,911	
+ Net transfers from the rest of the world	41.9	1.8	1,347	5.5
= Gross national disposable income	2,309.3		24,258	

Source: *National Income and Expenditure*, 1979 and 1990, Table 7.

(10) $\text{GNDI} = \text{GNP}_{mp} + \text{R}$

The figure for GNDI is the total amount available to Irish residents to consume and invest. From Table 3.4 it may be seen that the gaps between GDP, GNP and GNDI have grown markedly since the early 1970s due to the increases in F and R.

3.3   Macroeconomic Relationships

The national income accounts provide a frame of reference for the analysis of the key macroeconomic relationships. We discuss the most important of these in this section.

Absorption and the balance of payments

In a small, open economy, financial relationships with the rest of the world are very important. The *balance of payments* is a summary of these flows. We discuss the balance of payments in detail in Chapter 10. At this stage we wish to show the link between the balance of payments and the difference between national income and expenditure. Using definitions (1), (3), (4) and (10) it follows that:

(11) $\text{GNDI} \equiv \text{C} + \text{I} + \text{G} + \text{NX} + \text{F} + \text{R}$

Recall from definition (4) that $(\text{C} + \text{I} + \text{G})$ equals gross domestic expenditure (GDE) or Absorption. Hence rearranging:

(12) $\text{GNDI} - \text{GDE} \equiv \text{NX} + \text{F} + \text{R}$

This identity states that the difference between national income and national expenditure is net exports plus net factor payments and net transfer payments from the rest of the world. Now the sum of NX, F and R is *the current account of the balance of payments* (BoP). What identity (12) implies therefore is that when a country's expenditure exceeds its income, it is running a current account deficit. Conversely, when its income exceeds its expenditure, it is running a current account surplus.

Note:
A BoP deficit involves increasing the country's international indebtedness (or, equivalently, reducing its net international assets). Hence, the current account deficit is the same as the country's *net foreign borrowing*.

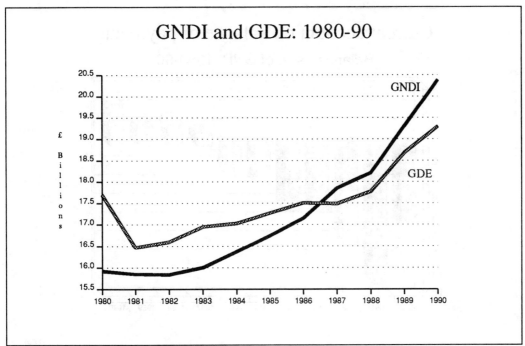

GNDI and GDE: 1980-90

Figure 3.3 GNDI and GDE, 1980-90

Figure 3.3 shows the trend of Irish GDE and GNDI during the 1980s. The sizeable excess of expenditure over income in the early years was reflected in record BoP deficits. The gap between expenditure and income closed in the mid-1980s as expenditure fell relative to income. By the end of the decade there was a small current account surplus. The reduction in expenditure was due to a sharp drop in the volume of C, personal consumption expenditure, which fell by 7.6 per cent in 1982 alone, and in I, investment, which was over 20 per cent lower in 1987 than in 1981. Government consumption expenditure (G), on the other hand continued to rise between 1980 and 1986. It was not until 1987 that there was a reduction in the volume of public consumption.

Savings, investment and the current account

In the circular flow diagram we showed that households pay taxes to the government and then either spend or save the rest of their income. At the national level, GNDI is either spent on consumption goods and services (private and public) or saved:

(13) GNDI $\equiv$ C + G + S

Note:
S $\equiv$ gross national savings and net national savings $\equiv$ S - D. Savings, S, is a *flow*: it represents an amount set aside out of income in each period. This flow should not be confused with the *stock* of savings that a person or country accumulates in the form of assets such as bank deposits or bonds.

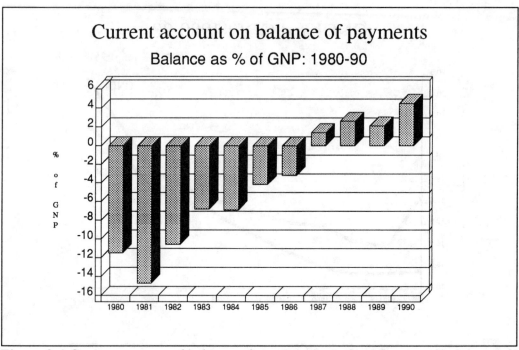

Figure 3.4 Current account of balance of payments

Hence,

(14) $S \equiv GNDI - (C + G)$

Now from (11) we know that $GNDI \equiv C + I + G + NX + F + R$. Substituting into (14):

(15) $S - I \equiv NX + F + R \equiv BoP$

The left-hand side term (S - I) is the difference between national savings and investment. This tells us that the excess of national savings over national investment is equal to the current account balance of payments surplus. Alternatively, if I exceeds S, there is a current account deficit. A current account deficit therefore allows the country to invest more than it is saving. Thus there are two sources from which a country can finance its capital formation, namely, from national savings, S, and from a current account deficit.

Figure 3.4 shows the trend in the current account of the balance of payments between 1980 and 1990. In the early 1980s as much as half of Ireland's capital formation was financed by a BoP deficit and only half from national savings. By 1990 the situation had changed to one in which national savings exceeded domestic capital formation by 12 per cent, which was reflected in a BoP current account surplus.

By disaggregating savings and investment by sector, this term can be broken down into a private sector and a public sector balance. The *public* sector's balance is equal to its revenue minus expenditure. This is the *Public Sector Borrowing Requirement* (PSBR), which we examine in detail in Chapter 5. The *private* sector's balance is the difference between private sector savings, S_{pr}, and private sector capital formation, I_{pr}. Inserting this disaggregation into (15):

$$(16) \quad (S_{pr} - I_{pr} + PSBR) \equiv NX + F + R \equiv BoP$$

The sum of the two internal balances (public and private) must equal the current account of the balance of payments, BoP.

Countries go through different phases in regard to the relationship between these balances. Table 3.5 illustrates some possible combinations. In case 1 the BoP and the PSBR are both zero. Under these conditions $(S_{pr} - I_{pr})$ must also equal zero and hence $S_{pr} = I_{pr}$. This is the situation in a closed economy with no public sector: private savings are the only source from which capital formation can be financed. This situation is often summarised by saying that in a closed economy *savings must equal investment*.

Table 3.5
Illustration of possible relationships between the current account of the balance of payments, and private and public sector balances

	$S_{pr} - I_{pr}$	PSBR	BoP
Case 1	0	0	0
Case 2	100	-50	50
Case 3	50	-100	-50
Case 4	-10	-150	-160
Case 5	-100	0	-100

In case 2, the surplus of S_{pr} over I_{pr} more than offsets the deficit in the government's budget and there is a surplus on the current account of the balance of payments. The country as a whole is saving more than it is investing domestically, and the surplus is invested abroad. This is the situation that Japan has been in for many years. In case 3, the public sector deficit more than offsets the private sector surplus. National savings (public plus private) are less than investment and the country is borrowing from the rest of the world through a current account deficit to finance some of its absorption. This has been the situation in the United States for some time now. In case 4, both the public and private sectors of the domestic economy are in deficit, leading to a large current account deficit. The situation in Ireland in 1981 resembled this. Finally, in case 5 there is a large excess of private sector investment over private sector savings and, even though there is no public sector borrowing, there is a large BoP deficit. This was the case in many New World countries in the nineteenth century as they drew in funds from Europe to finance large-scale private sector investment in the development of their economies.

The distribution of the deficits between the three sectors can give rise to concern. In the 1980s there was much discussion of the fact that US investment was being financed by a BoP deficit. The other side of this deficit was the Japanese BoP surplus, through which their investors are acquiring substantial ownership of foreign assets. This problem has remained with us in the 1990s, although somewhat reduced by the shrinking of the US BoP deficit. In Ireland in the early 1980s the exceptionally large current account deficit was cause for concern. The level of capital formation was exceptionally high relative to GNP but national savings had fallen to a low level. The BoP deficit bridged the gap. In this situation, the question of the *sustainability* of the current account BoP deficit has to be considered.[7] Sustainability requires that the extra investment that is financed by the current account BoP deficit must be *productive* enough to repay both the principal and interest on the foreign borrowing associated with it. In Ireland in the early 1980s, unlike the New World countries in the nineteenth century, the conditions for sustainability were not being met. Many of the investment projects were not productive and have not generated an adequate stream of income to match the debt that was incurred.

National savings

The discussion in the previous section implies that swings in the level of domestic savings have important implications for the balance of payments. In the early 1980s in Ireland net national savings fell to 3.5 per cent of GNP. As may be seen from Figure 3.5 this low level of national savings was primarily a reflection of the high level of public sector *dissavings* (the PSBR). In fact, personal savings reached over 15 per cent of GNP at this time. This is an extremely high savings/income ratio, implying that over 20 per cent of personal disposable income was being saved. Even now, when it has declined to about 13 per cent of personal income, the Irish personal savings ratio is high by international standards.[8] By 1990, despite the decline in personal savings, net national savings had risen to 14.9 per cent of GNP because of the sharp decline in the PSBR. It is clear from Figure 3.5 that there was an inverse correlation between personal and public sector savings in Ireland during the 1980s. A similar pattern has been noticed in other countries. The significance of this association will be discussed in Chapter 5.

The national income accounts provide details of the distribution of national savings within the private sector between companies and households. Net savings of companies have been relatively constant and amount to approximately 4 per cent of GNP. The main component of company savings is the *retained earnings* of the

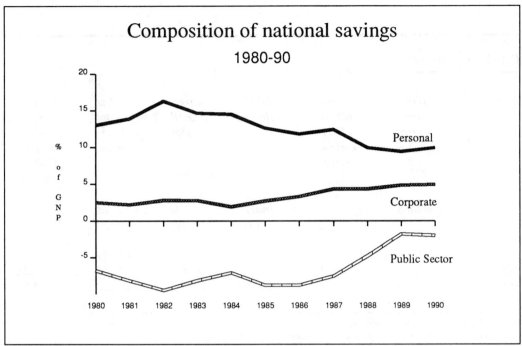

Figure 3.5 Personal, corporate and public savings

---

larger corporations. Like investment, savings can be measured either gross or net: gross savings include the depreciation allowances set aside by companies to replace the equipment used up in the course of the year. The provision for depreciation in many years during the 1980s exceeded net national savings.[9]

3.4   Adjusting for Inflation

In Chapter 1, in our discussion of the business cycle, we drew attention to the need to adjust certain macroeconomic variables for the effects of inflation. The national income data are presented in *current* market prices and *constant* market prices. The latter are also called "real" or "volume" series. When looking at the performance of an economy over time it is usual to concentrate on the trend in the constant price or volume series.

To calculate GDP in constant prices we need information on GDP in current market prices and on the price level. The constant price series equals the current price series *deflated* by the relevant price index or *deflator*. The rate of growth in GDP at current prices equals the rate of growth of GDP at constant prices *plus* the rate of inflation. Table 3.6 shows GDP in current market prices in Ireland for 1985, 1986 and 1987. The table also displays a price index, called the *GDP deflator*, which

Table 3.6
Calculating real GDP

Year	GDP at current prices	Growth rate in GDP current prices	GDP deflator	Change in GDP deflator	GDP at constant (1985) prices	Growth rate in GDP constant (1985) prices
	£ millions	%	Index	%	£ millions	%
	(1)	(2)	(3)	(4)	(5)	(6)
1985	17,789		100.0		17,789	
1986	18,877	6.1	106.6	6.6	17,707	-0.5
1987	20,262	7.3	109.4	2.7	18,516	4.6

Source: *National Income and Expenditure*, 1990.
Note: Only columns (1) and (2) are published; the others are derived.
Column (2) = column (4) + column (6)

is equal to 100 in the 1985, the *base year*. The *inflation rate* is the rate of increase in the deflator relative to the previous year. From Table 3.6 we see that the price level increased by 6.6 per cent between 1985 and 1986 and by 2.7 per cent between 1986 and 1987.

The data in Table 3.6 show that although GDP at current market prices was 6.1 per cent higher in 1986 than in 1985, constant price GDP fell by 0.5 per cent because the price level rose by 6.6 per cent. Between 1986 and 1987, on the other hand, GDP at current prices rose by 7.3 per cent, but the price level only rose by 2.7 per cent (that is, (109.4 - 106.6) as a percentage of 106.6) so that GDP at constant prices rose by 4.6 per cent.

Terms of trade adjustment   A further refinement has to be made to allow for the effects of changes in the *terms of trade*, that is the price of exports, P_x, relative to the price of imports, P_m. Recall from equation (11) that

(17) $GNDI \equiv C + I + G + X - M + F + R$

In the national income accounts, in order to adjust GNP for inflation each component is deflated using a different price index. C is deflated by the consumer price index, I by the price index for investment goods, G by an index based on rates of pay in the public sector and X and M are deflated by export and import price indices respectively.[10]   The figure thus obtained for GNP does not, however, take

60

account of the impact of changes in the terms of trade on living standards. Let us examine this effect in detail.

We export in order to import. Hence, what matters is how much our exports will buy in terms of imports. Think of Ireland as a country exporting dairy products and importing petroleum products. If the price of oil rises when that of milk is static, we have to export a larger quantity of milk to finance a given quantity of imported oil. Conversely, if the price of milk rises relative to the price of oil, we have to give up less milk in order to import a given quantity of oil. The terms of trade index is defined as the ratio of P_x to P_m:

(18) Terms of trade index = $(P_x/P_m) \times 100$

If the ratio P_x/P_m *increases*, the terms of trade are said to have *improved* because we have to export less in order to obtain a given amount of imports. If the ratio *falls* the terms of trade are said to have *deteriorated.*

A *terms of trade adjustment*[11] can be calculated as the difference between the value of exports deflated by the price of imports and exports deflated by the price of exports, that is:

(19) Terms of trade adjustment = $(X/P_m - X/P_x)$ or $X(1/P_m - 1/P_x)$

If $P_x = P_m$ this adjustment is equal to zero. If $P_x > P_m$ then it is *positive* because the terms of trade have improved, allowing the country to buy more imports with the proceeds of a given volume of exports. If $P_x < P_m$ then the adjustment is *negative* because the terms of trade have deteriorated and the country has to export more in order to purchase a given volume of imports. The terms of trade adjustment given in (19) has to be added to (17) in order to obtain GNDI adjusted for the terms of trade.

Note:
Some of the pioneering work on this topic was done by the Irish statistician R. C. Geary (1896 1983), who made important contributions to the theory of national income accounting and index numbers while Director of the Central Statistics Office in Dublin and of the United Nations Statistical Office in New York.

The terms of trade effect is measured with reference to the base year. Because both $P_x = P_m = 100$ in the base year, the terms of trade effect is zero in that year. If export and import prices change at different rates over time, a terms of trade effect will come into existence. For example, in 1986 the terms of trade effect was important because world oil prices collapsed, leading to a sharp improvement in Ireland's terms of trade. As Ireland is very dependent on imported oil, this improvement in the terms of trade meant that real living standards rose faster than

Table 3.7
The terms of trade effect, 1985-87

	1985 £ millions	1986 £ millions	1987 £ millions
GNP at constant (1985) prices	15,824	15,643	16412
+ Terms of trade adjustment	0	+ 480	+ 454
+ Net current transfers from abroad at constant (1985) prices	923	1,031	982
= GNDI at constant (1985) prices	16,748	17,155	17,850

Source: *National Income and Expenditure*, 1990, Table 8.

shown by the constant price GNDI figures. In Table 3.7 we show how this effect is taken into account as we move from GNP at constant prices to GNDI adjusted for the terms of trade.

We see from these figures that the terms of trade adjustment added 3 per cent to GNP in 1986. Without the terms of trade adjustment the volume of GNP would have declined by over 1 per cent, but with it the volume of GNDI grew by over 2 per cent. Between 1986 and 1987 this adjustment was negative but very small. (Note that the adjustment is cumulative from the base year 1985, so that the effect in 1987 was £454 million *minus* £480 million.)

Changes in the terms of trade have had large impacts on Irish GNDI. In the 1970s there was an enormous loss of income due to increases in world oil prices and unfavourable developments on the farm price front. There was a very significant gain as farm prices recovered and oil prices collapsed in 1986. Over the long run, the gains and losses have tended to cancel out. Many developing countries, however, have faced a steady deterioration in their terms of trade as the prices of the commodities they export have declined on world markets.

3.5   Taking Account of Population Growth

National income *per person* (or *per capita*) is usually taken as the best measure of living standards.[12] In most developed countries the rate of population growth is low and there is no need to worry about adjusting for population growth in the analysis of short-run economic performance. Ireland is unusual, however, in having had a very volatile rate of population growth. During the 1970s our population grew by about 1.5 per cent a year, the highest growth rate in Europe, while during the 1950s it declined by over 1 per cent a year. At the beginning of the 1980s the population

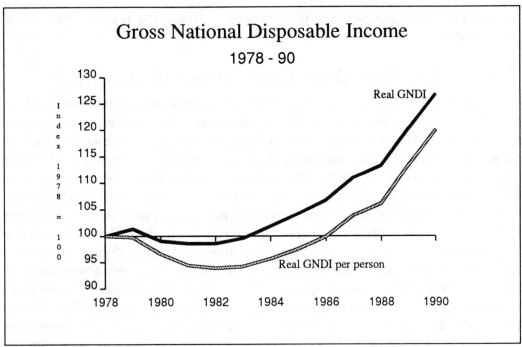

Gross National Disposable Income

1978 - 90

Figure 3.6 Gross national disposable income

was still growing rapidly but due to the resumption of large-scale emigration and the decline in the birth rate it has been static since the middle of the decade. Our view of the country's recent economic performance would be distorted if we did not take these fluctuations in the rate of population growth into account.

Figure 3.6 shows the trend in GNDI and in GNDI per person over the period 1980-90, both expressed as a volume index to base 1980 = 100. The severity of the recession of the early 1980s may be gauged from the facts that the level of real income per person dropped by 8 per cent between 1979 and 1982 and that it was not until 1986 that the level of the late 1970s was regained.

The early 1980s was one of the most depressed periods that has ever been experienced in Ireland. Income was falling due to the global recession and the population grew quite rapidly because emigration fell to a low level due to the lack of opportunities abroad. (In contrast, during the 1950s recession in Ireland led to massive emigration and a falling population: this at least protected the living standards of those remaining at home.)

The situation was transformed in the mid-1980s by three factors: first, the resumption of net emigration on a scale sufficient to avert further population growth; second, the dramatic improvement in the terms of trade in 1986 as world oil prices collapsed; and third, the spurt of growth in GNP in Ireland during the period 1988-90. (We examine in later chapters the factors that contributed to this growth.) Unfortunately, the pace of economic growth slowed in 1990 and this, combined with the low level of emigration due to the recession in Britain, led to a sharp increase in unemployment.

3.6   The Distribution of National Income

Indices such as GNDI per person are averages and provide no information about the *distribution of income*. One indicator of income distribution is the *rate of unemployment*. The unemployed have no earned income and hence a rise in the rate of unemployment implies an increase in the numbers dependent on transfer payments. This may not be apparent from the data on the trend in income per person. For example, during the 1980s the rate of unemployment soared from under 8 to over 15 per cent of the labour force. Even though the real value of unemployment benefits and assistance increased over the period, the standard of living of those who became unemployed fell sharply. The rate of unemployment declined during the spurt of rapid growth at the end of the 1980s, but it remained considerably above the level of the late 1970s. Thus even though income per person has now risen to a new peak, the *incidence of poverty* has remained much higher than it was in the 1970s. This is true especially when poverty is measured in *relative terms*, that is as the proportion of the population whose income falls below a certain fraction, say one third, of national income per person.

3.7   International Comparisons
of Economic Growth

In Chapter 1 we presented some comparisons of the level of income in Ireland relative to other countries. It is also of interest to compare Ireland's recent economic performance with that of other countries. As a small open economy, we are strongly influenced by external forces. In the past the main external influence on the Irish economy was the United Kingdom, but during the 1980s the links between the Irish and the UK economies were weakened by our full membership of the European Monetary System. For the purposes of a comparison of the relative performance of the Irish economy we have used GDP in the OECD, which gives a broad measure of the performance of the industrialised economies of the world. (We use GDP because this is the series mostly used by the OECD in its international commentaries.)

Figure 3.7 shows the growth rates in each of the years between 1978 and 1990. The broadly similar pattern of the business cycle in Ireland and the OECD is striking. There were, however, significant differences. Until 1983, the Irish growth rate exceeded that of the OECD, whereas in 1983 to 1986 our growth rate was considerably lower than that of the OECD. For the last four years growth in Ireland was again higher than in the OECD. Over the entire period 1978-90, Irish GDP increased by 44 per cent compared with only 39 per cent in the OECD as a whole. While this comparison is based on GDP and does not take account of population

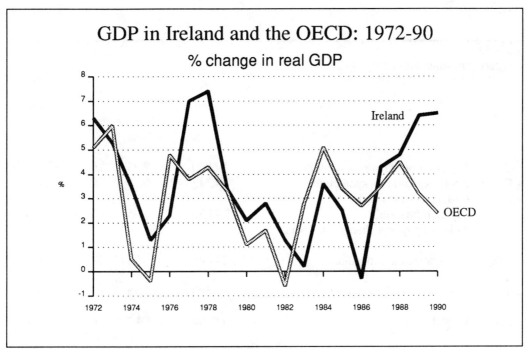

Figure 3.7 GDP in Ireland and the OECD

growth, it none the less points to a relatively strong performance by the Irish economy. We shall discuss some of the issues raised by these figures in Chapter 5 and return to the longer-term performance of the economy in the concluding chapter.

3.8 Short-term Forecasting

Government and business economists are mainly concerned with the very recent past and the prospects for the future. A great deal of effort is devoted to the preparation of estimates of the main macroeconomic variables for the current year and forecasts for the coming year. The Department of Finance, the Central Bank of Ireland, the Economic and Social Research Institute (ESRI) and a growing number of private sector firms prepare forecasts.

There is always a delay before official data for the main macroeconomic series become available. For example the 1990 *NIE* was not published until November 1991. Moreover, the data for 1990 and 1989 in this edition of *NIE* will be subject to significant revision in subsequent editions as more information on our recent economic performance becomes available.

A review of the track record of forecasting in all areas of economics and the social sciences reveals that estimates are strongly influenced by current conditions. Forecasters rarely anticipate *turning points* or even recognise them until some time

Table 3.8
Forecast expenditure on GNP, 1992

| | | 1991 | % change | | 1992 |
		£ m	volume	price	£ m
C	Personal consumption expenditure	14,860	2.75	3.0	15,745
+ G	Public net current expenditure	4,343	-0.25	7.0	4,633
+ I	Gross domestic fixed capital formation	4,872	1.5	3.0	5,105
+ S	Value of physical changes in stocks	420			150
= GDE	Gross domestic expenditure	24,495	0.75	3.75	25,633
+ X	Exports of goods and services	16,599	7.75	2.0	18,208
= FD	Final demand	41,094	3.5	3.0	43,841
- M	Imports of goods and services	14,613	6.0	2.5	15,872
= GDP	Gross domestic product at market prices	26,481	2.25	3.25	27,969
+ F	Net factor income from rest of world	-2,935			-3,139
= GNP	Gross national product	23,546	2.0	3.5	24,830

Source: Central Bank of Ireland, *Quarterly Bulletin*, Winter 1991, Table 1.

after they have occurred. A recent example was the failure of economists to anticipate the impact of the Iraqi invasion of Kuwait in mid-1990 on the world economy. A survey of 14 forecasts of Irish economic growth compiled in July 1990 depicted a "Rosy future, despite Saddam: Four more years of growth".[13] The consensus forecast for real GNP growth was 3.8 per cent for 1991 and 3.6 per cent for 1992. However, between August and the end of the year it became apparent that much lower growth would be recorded, and the typical forecast was reduced to under 1 per cent for 1991 and about 2 per cent for 1992.

The standard way of preparing forecasts for the macroeconomy is to build up to GDP through the expenditure components, C, G, I, X and M. A forecast of the growth in the *nominal* value of these components is prepared and disaggregated into *price* and *volume* components. Table 3.8 shows the forecast for 1992 published in this manner by the Central Bank towards the end of 1991 in its Winter 1991 *Quarterly*

Bulletin. At the end of 1991 there was great uncertainty about the prospects for the world economy and this made projections of the performance of the Irish economy very difficult. A useful exercise is for the student to compare the forecasts presented in Table 3.8 with the more up to date information that is now available and to try to account for the discrepancies in the light of international and domestic developments.

3.9   Conclusion

In this chapter we have examined the concepts of national income and product in some detail. We discussed the measures that are used in analysing the country's economic performance. Among the key concepts are:

- The circular flow of income including government and a foreign sector
- The measurement of national income and expenditure
- The distinction between national and domestic product and income
- The components of national output, expenditure and product
- The distinction between gross and net measures of investment
- The concept of absorption
- The relation between absorption and the balance of payments
- The relationship between savings, investment, the fiscal deficit and the balance of payments
- The role of the balance of payments in financing domestic investment
- The calculation of real output from data on nominal output and the price level
- The terms of trade adjustment
- The trend in real GNDI adjusted for the terms of trade and population growth
- International comparisons of recent economic performance
- The preparation of short-term forecasts.

Notes

1. Investment is referred to as "gross domestic physical capital formation" in *NIE*. It includes both private and government investment. The significance of the word "physical" is that the value of changes in stocks are included. A fall in the level of stocks is a negative contribution to investment, a rise is a positive contribution. Investment excluding changes in stocks is called *fixed* capital formation. See also note 9.

2. This is called "net expenditure by public authorities on current goods and services" in *NIE*. Thus it does not include transfer payments (B), national debt interest paid to Irish residents (which are treated as transfers) or government capital spending.

3. Because F, net factor payments from the rest of the world, are volatile, it is generally believed that GDP provides a better measure of short-term economic performance and the business cycle than GNP. In 1991 the US switched to using GNP, leaving Japan and Germany as the only important exceptions still using GNP. See "Grossly distorted picture", *The Economist*, 14 December 1991, p. 73.

4. John D. FitzGerald, *The Determinants of Irish Imports,* The Economic and Social Research Institute, Research Paper 135, October 1987.

5. The Central Statistics Office start from obtaining data on agricultural income and details of non-agricultural income (wages and salaries, the income of the self-employed, profits, interest payments and rents) obtained from the Revenue Commissioners and other sources. In this way they build up a picture of the value of what is being produced in the country and what types of income are being received by those producing it. This income measure is taken as the *definitive* GDP figure. The expenditure figure is then reconciled to the income figure by taking consumer expenditure (C) as a *residual.*

6. Account should also be taken of capital transfers from the rest of the world, which are not included in R, but are part of BoP. We have ignored this in the text.

7. These ideas were discussed by the National Planning Board in their report *Proposals for Plan* published in April 1984 against the background of the extraordinary balance of payments deficits of the early 1980s.

8. A high proportion of income is also saved in Japan, but in the US the savings/GNP ratio is now below 4 per cent and in the UK it fell from 16 per cent in 1980 to a mere 2 per cent in 1988.

9. Account has to be taken of the effect of changes in the value of stocks attributable to price changes. The increase in the value of existing levels of stocks due to inflation is not included in the figure for physical capital formation or in national savings. See note 1.

10. The export price index is used to deflate F in years when the net flow is *negative*. This is on the grounds that a net outflow can be used to purchase imports and ultimately has to be paid for with increased exports. The import price index is used to deflate F in years when the net flow is *positive*.

11. For a detailed discussion of alternative approaches to adjusting for the terms of trade see Aidan Punch, "Real Gross National Disposable Income Adjusted for the Terms of Trade: 1970-84", ESRI *Quarterly Economic Commentary*, April 1986.

12. The phrase "per capita" is firmly embedded in economics, even though it does not mean "per person" but refers to a legal method of transferring property. The correct Latin for "per person" is per caput!

13 See *Finance: The Journal of Ireland's Money and Capital Markets*, August 1990, pp. 8-14.

Data appendix

Year	GDP at current market prices	GDP at constant (1985) prices	GDP deflator	Rate of inflation based on GDP deflator	Growth in GDP at constant (1985) prices
	(1) £ millions	(2) £ millions	(3) = (1)/(2)	(4) % change in (3)	(5) % change in (2)
1978	6,757	14,977	45.1		
1979	7,917	15,438	51.3	13.7	3.1
1980	9,361	15,914	58.8	14.7	3.1
1981	11,359	16,274	69.8	18.7	2.3
1982	13,381	16,339	81.9	17.3	0.4
1983	14,683	16,397	89.5	9.3	0.4
1984	16,407	17,258	95.1	6.2	5.3
1985	17,790	17,790	100.0	5.2	3.1
1986	18,877	17,707	106.6	6.6	-0.5
1987	20,263	18,516	109.4	2.6	4.6
1988	21,815	19,341	112.8	3.1	4.5
1989	24,307	20,577	118.1	4.7	6.4
1990	25,693	22,041	116.6	-1.3	7.1

Source: *National Income and Expenditure*, 1990 and earlier editions.
Note: GDP and GNP are from expenditure tables.

Data appendix (continued)

Year	GNP at constant (1985) prices	GNDI at constant (1985) prices	Population (thousands)	GNDI at constant (1985) prices per person	Growth in GNDI at constant (1985) prices per person
	(6)	(7)	(8)	(9) = (7)/(8)	(10 =
					% change
	£ millions	£ millions	£ millions	in (9)	
1978	14,677	16,071	3,314	4,849	
1979	15,081	16,310	3,368	4,843	-0.1
1980	15,485	15,929	3,401	4,684	-3.3
1981	15,889	15,850	3,443	4,604	-1.7
1982	15,778	15,847	3,480	4,554	-1.1
1983	15,373	16,007	3,504	4,568	0.3
1984	15,567	16,379	3,529	4,641	1.6
1985	15,824	16,748	3,540	4,731	1.9
1986	15,619	17,155	3,541	4,845	2.4
1987	16,436	17,850	3,543	5,038	4.0
1988	16,784	18,214	3,538	5,148	2.2
1989	17,728	19,318	3,515	5,496	6.8
1990	19,196	20,385	3,503	5,819	5.9

Source: *National Income and Expenditure*, 1990 and earlier editions.
Note: GDP and GNP are from expenditure tables.

Chapter 4

Fiscal Policy: An Introduction

4.1   Introduction

In Chapter 2 we discussed the role of aggregate demand or total expenditure in determining output and employment in the economy. In this chapter we examine in some detail two important components of aggregate demand, namely, consumer expenditure and government expenditure. The aim of the chapter is to introduce the reader to the essentials of fiscal policy in a simplified model of the economy.

The first part of the chapter is concerned with *consumer theory*. We discuss a key relationship in macroeconomics, namely, that between consumption and disposable income. This relationship is referred to as *the consumption function*. The second half of the chapter is concerned with fiscal policy, that is, how the government, through changes in expenditure and taxation, can influence the level of output and income. We outline the concept of the *multiplier* and explain how this affects the ability of the government to smooth the business cycle. This is followed by a discussion of the limitations of fiscal policy in a small open economy such as Ireland. The concluding section of the chapter discusses the implications for the economy of a rising national debt and introduces the concept of a *sustainable fiscal policy*.

4.2   Disposable Income, Consumption and Savings

It was pointed out in Chapter 3 that *personal consumption expenditure* (C) in Ireland accounts for about 57 per cent of total expenditure or aggregate demand (AD). The study of consumption is therefore important not just in its own right but for our understanding of the determination of output, income and employment.

The determinants of personal consumption expenditure, that is, the factors which cause it to vary over time, are of great importance in macroeconomics. A number of different variables have been identified as having a potentially important influence on consumer expenditure. In this section we concentrate on the most important, which is *disposable income* (Y^d). The link between income and consumption is intuitively easy to understand. If a household receives an increase in income it will normally spend more on consumption goods and services. However, it will not normally spend all of its increased income: some will be saved.

At the level of the whole economy, if the nation's income increases, personal consumption, C, will also increase, but so too will personal savings, S.

Disposable income is equal to gross personal income minus income taxes. Since people must either spend or save their disposable income it follows that $Y^d = C + S$. The relevant data for 1989 are shown in Table 4.1.

Table 4.1
Personal income, consumption and savings, 1989

		£ millions
	Personal income	20,060
-	Income tax	4,324
=	Disposable income (Y^d)	15,736
of which		
	Personal Consumption Expenditure (C)	13,728
	Personal Savings (S)	2,008

Source: *National Income and Expenditure*, 1990, Table 9, Central Statistics Office, Dublin, 1991.

Although we are primarily concerned with consumption expenditure aggregated over all types of consumer goods and services, it is of interest to look at the composition of this expenditure. Table 4.2 shows the breakdown of personal consumption between the different categories of expenditure. The largest components are food, transport and communications, and alcoholic beverages. (Irish households spend an unusually large proportion of their income on alcoholic beverages and tobacco.) The data given in Table 4.2 are an average for all the households in the country. When households are classified by income group important differences in consumption patterns are apparent. In particular, people on low incomes spend a higher proportion of their income on necessities such as food. As income increases, the proportion of income spent on clothing, transport and leisure activities rises. High income households buy better quality food but they spend a smaller proportion of their income on it.

The relationship between Y^d, C and S is shown in Table 4.3 for a hypothetical *cross section* of households. Household A has zero income and consumption of £3,000 per annum. Household B has an income of £5,000 and spends £6,000. These two households are *dissaving*. Dissaving has to be financed from the sale of assets, by using up previous savings or by borrowing. The richer households in the table, C to G, all manage to save some of their income.

Table 4.2
Composition of personal consumption expenditure, 1989

Category	£ millions	%
Food and non-alcoholic beverages	3,027	22.1
Alcoholic beverages	1,595	11.7
Tobacco	553	4.0
Clothing and footwear	976	7.1
Rent	811	5.9
Fuel and power	671	4.9
Household equipment	1,161	8.4
Transport and communication	1,752	12.7
Recreation, entertainment and education	1,441	10.5
Miscellaneous	1,739	12.7
Consumer expenditure	13,726	100.0

Source: *National Income and Expenditure*, 1990, Table 13, Central Statistics Office, Dublin, 1991.

The main point illustrated in Table 4.3 is that as disposable income increases, households spend less and save more as a proportion of income. This point can be made more formally by calculating the *average propensity to consume* (APC) and the *average propensity to save* (APS) for each household. The APC is defined as being equal to consumption expenditure divided by disposable income, C/Y^d. For example, the APC for household D is calculated as follows:

(1) $APC = C/Y^d = £12,000/£15,000 = 0.8$

An APC of 0.8 indicates that the household spends 80 per cent of its disposable income on consumption goods and services. The APS is defined as being equal to savings divided by disposable income, S/Y^d. Again for household D:

(2) $APS = S/Y^d = £3,000/£15,000 = 0.2$

An APS of 0.2 indicates that 20 per cent of disposable income is saved. Because disposable income is either spent or saved, the APC and the APS must sum to 1:

(3) $APC + APS = 1$

Table 4.3 shows the APC and the APS for each household. It can be seen that as disposable income increases, the APC declines and the APS rises. The low income households dissave or save very little of their income whereas the high income groups save a large proportion of income.

Table 4.3
Household disposable income, consumption and savings

	Disposable Income (Y^d) £	Consumption (C) £	Savings (S) £	APC	APS
A	0	3,000	-3,000		
B	5,000	6,000	-1,000	1.20	-0.20
C	10,000	9,000	1,000	0.90	0.10
D	15,000	12,000	3,000	0.80	0.20
E	20,000	15,000	5,000	0.75	0.25
F	25,000	18,000	7,000	0.72	0.28
G	30,000	21,000	9,000	0.70	0.30

The consumption function

Figure 4.1 plots the relationship between disposable income and consumption given in Table 4.3. Consumption expenditure is shown on the vertical axis and disposable income on the horizontal axis. Point B in Figure 4.1 corresponds to consumption expenditure of £6,000 and income of £5,000. The remaining points in Figure 4.1 correspond to the other households in Table 4.3.

The line joining the points A, B, C etc. is the *consumption function*. This function plays a central role in modern macroeconomic theory. The importance of this relationship was stressed by Keynes.[1] Using the notation we introduced in Chapter 2, the consumption function may be written as:

$$(4) \quad C = f(Y^d)$$
$$+$$

Equation (4) reads "consumption expenditure is an increasing function of disposable income". Changes in Y^d cause changes in C. For this reason, the variable inside the bracket is referred to as the *explanatory* (or independent) variable and the variable on the left-hand side as the *dependent* variable.

Figure 4.1 also includes a 45° line. This line has the property that at every point on the line consumption expenditure equals disposable income. This is because the vertical and horizontal axes are measured in the same units (thousands of pounds). The 45° line is a reference line which enables us to determine how a household disposes of its income. For example, the point B in Figure 4.1 is above the 45° line

74

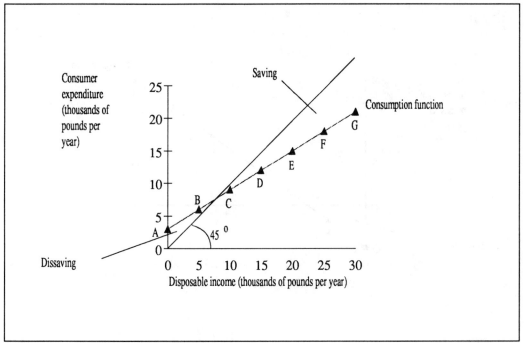

Figure 4.1 Consumption function

and this indicates that household B is spending more than its income. In other words, household B is dissaving. When the consumption function lies above the 45^0 line, the vertical difference to the 45^0 line measures the amount of dissavings. The point F, on the other hand, is below the 45^0 line. Household F is spending less than its income, it is saving. When the consumption function lies below the 45^0 line the vertical distance between the two lines measures the amount of saving.

Savings function

We have seen how consumption expenditure and saving sum to disposable income. Because C depends on Y^d, it follows that S also depends on Y^d. The relationship between S and Y^d is referred to as the *savings function*. Mathematically the relationship may be written as:

(5) $S = f(Y^d)$
       $+$

Increases in Y^d lead to increases in S and decreases in Y^d lead to decreases in S. Figure 4.2 is a graphical representation of the savings function based on the data in Table 4.3. Savings is measured on the vertical axis and disposable income on the horizontal axis. Point A corresponds to household A in Table 4.3 and so on. As already mentioned, households A and B are dissaving and this gives two negative

75

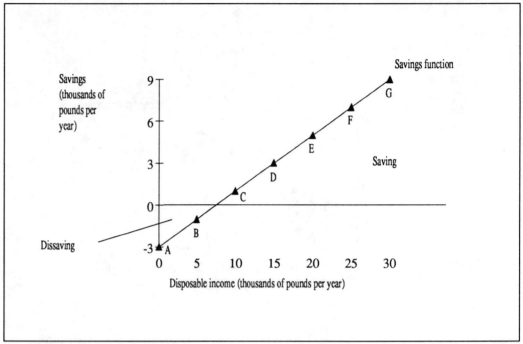

Figure 4.2 Savings function

---

values for savings in Figure 4.2. As household income increases, savings increase. This is reflected in the upward sloping savings function.

The marginal propensity to consume and save

An important question in macroeconomics is how consumer expenditure reacts to a change in disposable income. The *marginal propensity to consume* (MPC) tells us by how much a household's consumption will increase as a result of a given increase in income. (In economics, the word "marginal" means "extra" or "additional".) Hence:

(6) $\Delta C = MPC \times \Delta Y^d$

where Δ denotes change. Equation (6) states that the change in C is equal to MPC multiplied by the change in Y^d. The MPC is a positive number equal to or less than one: $0 < MPC \leq 1$. An MPC of 0.9 means that for every £1 increase in income, spending increases by £0.90.

Rearranging, (6) may also be written as:

(7) $MPC = \Delta C / \Delta Y^d$

that is the MPC equals the ratio of the change in C to the change in Y^d. The

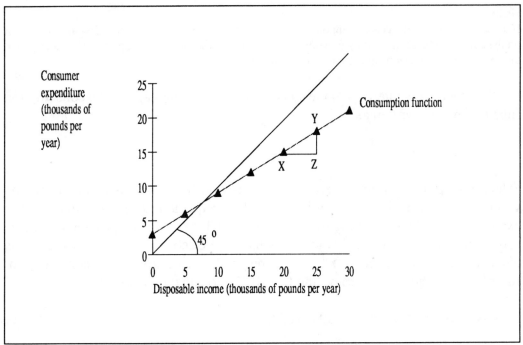

Figure 4.3 Marginal propensity to consume (MPC)

hypothetical data on income and consumption in Table 4.3 may be used to calculate the MPC. As household income increases from £10,000 to £15,000, consumption expenditure increases from £9,000 to £12,000. The MPC is therefore 0.6.

(8) $MPC = \Delta C / \Delta Y^d = (12{,}000 - 9{,}000)/(15{,}000 - 10{,}000) = 0.6$

Similarly, as income increases from £20,000 to £25,000, consumption increases from £15,000 to £18,000. Hence the MPC is again equal to 0.6.

The MPC may also be represented graphically as the *slope* of the consumption function. In Figure 4.3 the triangle labelled XYZ measures the MPC. The distance XZ represents the change in disposable income and the distance ZY represents the change in consumption expenditure. The slope of the consumption function XY is the ratio ZY/XZ and equals $\Delta C/\Delta Y^d$, which we defined as the MPC.

Note that because the consumption function in Figures 4.1 and 4.3 is *linear* the MPC is the same at all points on the line. (The reader can confirm this by calculating the MPC for the range of income and expenditure given in Table 4.3.) We have presented a linear consumption function simply for illustrative purposes. In reality, it is possible that the MPC would decrease at higher levels of income because the richer a household becomes, the larger the proportion of any further increase in income it is likely to save.

Note:
If a line is non-linear then each point on the line has a different slope. The slope at a particular point on the curve can be calculated by drawing a line tangent to the curve at that point. The slope of the tangent line gives the slope of the curve at that point.

If we write the intercept of the consumption function as a, then the consumption function may be written as:

(9) $C = a + MPC \times Y^d$

(The intercept is the point where the consumption function cuts or intercepts the vertical axis.) If Y^d is zero, then it follows from equation (9) that C equals a. For example, in Table 4.3 and Figure 4.1, C equals £3,000 when disposable income is zero. The intercept can be thought of as the level of consumption spending that is independent of the level of Y^d, and is referred to as *autonomous* consumption. Inserting household D's income and the MPC into equation (9) we have:

(10) $C = 3,000 + 0.6 \times 15,000 = 12,000$

The same procedure may be applied to calculating the other households' consumption expenditure.

Marginal propensity to save

Closely related to the MPC is the *marginal propensity to save* (MPS). The MPS is equal to the change in saving for a given change in disposable income. That is:

(11) $MPS = \Delta S / \Delta Y^d$

To calculate the MPS consider again the data in Table 4.3. Suppose that household D's income increases from £15,000 to £20,000. Its savings increase from £3,000 to £5,000. Hence, the MPS for this household is 0.4.

$MPS = (5,000 - 3,000)/(£20,000 - £15,000) = 0.4$

The MPS shows how household saving changes for a given change in disposable income. Rearranging (11):

(12) $\Delta S = MPS \times \Delta Y^d$

The change in saving equals the MPS multiplied by the change in disposable income. Earlier in equation (5) the savings function was written as $S = f(Y^d)$. This function may now be written:

78

(13) $S = -a + MPS \times Y^d$

where a is, as before, the intercept of the consumption function. Savings for each household may be derived by inserting the values for the intercept, the MPS and income. For example, in the case of household F in Table 4.3:

(14) $S = -3,000 + 0.4 \times 25,000 = 7,000$

Because income is either spent or saved, the MPC and the MPS must also sum to one.

(15) $1 = MPC + MPS$

If the MPC equals 0.8, then the MPS must equal 0.2. That is, if a household receives one extra pound in income, 80 per cent is spent and 20 per cent is saved.

The consumption and savings functions are very important building blocks in macroeconomic theory. As we shall see later in this chapter the consumption function partly determines the effectiveness of fiscal policy. Before we turn to a discussion of this, however, we round out the theory of consumption with a brief discussion of two more sophisticated theories of consumption and a look at the Irish aggregate consumption function.

4.3   Theories of Consumer Behaviour

Keynes argued, on the basis of his own intuition rather than a detailed study of the data, that as income rose the average propensity of consume (APC) declined. He was influenced by the fact that the rich appear to save much larger proportions of their income than the poor. This led him to worry about the problem of absorbing the growing stream of savings that would be siphoned off the circular flow of income and expenditure and for which it would be difficult to find profitable investment outlets. In a famous passage he praised the ancient Egyptians for building pyramids and the people in the Middle Ages for building cathedrals because these activities used up their savings and provided employment. Furthermore, there was no tendency for the returns from these activities to fall: "Two pyramids, two masses for the dead, are twice as good as one; but not so two railways from London to York."[2]

The evidence for a declining APC was, however, shaky. In the mid-1940s Nobel Prize winner Simon Kuznets (1901-85) presented evidence, based on aggregate data for very long time periods, that the APC remained constant over time. He found that the APC for the period 1880 to 1910 was the same as that for 1910 to 1940.

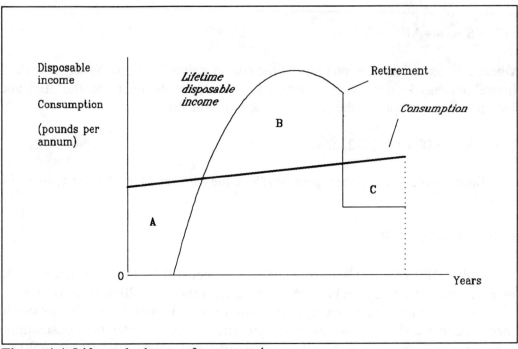

Figure 4.4 Life-cycle theory of consumption

This apparent conflict between Keynes's intuition and Kuznets's data led to the refinement of theories of consumer behaviour. Two of the most influential contributions have been, first, the *life-cycle hypothesis* and, second, the *permanent-income hypothesis*. We now turn to a brief discussion of these two theories.

The life-cycle theory of consumption

The life-cycle theory of consumption was developed by Nobel Prize winning economist Franco Modigliani.[3] He argued that a household's consumption does not depend only on its *current* disposable income, as in the Keynesian consumption function, but rather on its *life-time* income.

The life-cycle hypothesis assumes that people prefer to maintain a constant or slightly increasing flow of consumption over their life-time to one where consumption depends completely on current income. They can achieve this if they are willing to save at those periods in their life when their earnings are high and to dissave when their income falls. Disposable income changes over the life cycle. Typically an individual has no income in the first eighteen years of life, while at school. Once he or she starts work, income rises rapidly reaching a peak in mid-life. On retirement at, say, sixty there is a sharp decline in income as the individual has to live on a pension. In order to smooth out the consumption stream, the individual can dissave early and late in life, and save during the peak earning years.

This is depicted in Figure 4.4. The upward sloping consumption line depicts a steadily rising expenditure stream, the inverted U-shaped disposable income line depicts how the typical individual's income might vary over his or her life-time. Areas A and C in Figure 4.4 are associated with dissaving. In area B the individual saves a proportion of income. The savings of one period are used to finance consumption in other periods so that over the life cycle consumption equals life-time income. The dissaving in areas A and C should equal the savings in area B. This theory predicts that changes in current disposable income have much less influence on consumption than would be expected from the cruder consumption function we introduced above. Individuals are supposed to take a long view of their income and to set their consumption targets in line with this rather than simply adjusting consumption to day-to-day fluctuations in income. In a steadily growing economy, each generation enjoys a higher life-time income than its predecessor, but it sets its consumption sights higher, too. This averts the decline in the APC that Keynes feared.[4]

The permanent-income hypothesis

The permanent-income hypothesis was developed by Milton Friedman, 1976 Nobel Prize winner in economics.[5] The permanent-income hypothesis is similar in many respects to the life-cycle hypothesis. The permanent-income hypothesis argues that current consumption depends on *permanent-income* (YP):

(16) $C = f(YP)$

In Friedman's original exposition of the theory, no precise definition of permanent-income was given. However, we can think of permanent-income as being equal to a *weighted average* of current and past incomes. A simple example is:

(17) $YP_t = 0.6Y^d_t + 0.3Y^d_{t-1} + 0.1Y^d_{t-2}$

where Y^d_t is disposable income in time t, Y^d_{t-1} is disposable income in time t-1 and Y^d_{t-2} is disposable income in time t-2. Equation (17) says that today's permanent-income is equal to 60 per cent of this year's disposable income plus 30 per cent of last year's income plus 10 per cent of income two years ago. Note that the weights used in the calculation tend to get smaller the further we go back in time. The basic idea underlying equation (17) is that people use their past incomes as a means of calculating *expected* future income. Because permanent-income is based on long-run average income it is similar to life-time income. The permanent-income hypothesis does however have the advantage in that it can easily be applied to aggregate time series data for income, whereas the concept of life-time income is difficult to measure using aggregate data.

Friedman's basic hypothesis was that there is a constant proportional relationship between consumption and permanent-income, in other words, the APC out of permanent income is constant. This would imply, for example, that 90 per cent of permanent-income is consumed *regardless of the level of permanent-income*. However, actual income is highly variable and the proportion of it that is consumed also varies. Income which is not expected to be repeated in the future is referred to as *transitory income* (YT). A good example of such income would be a win on the Lottery. In Friedman's theory income of this type is expected to have a weak effect on consumption; most of it is saved. If you think about this proposition, and especially if you recall that purchasing consumer durable goods such as a car or a house should be treated as investment rather than consumption, the theory squares well with what we observe people doing.

4.4 The Irish Aggregate Consumption Function

Figure 4.5 shows the data for personal disposable income and personal consumption expenditure for the Irish economy over the period 1958-88. As expected there is a close relationship between the two variables. Towards the end of the 1980s, however, there was a noticeable widening of the gap between income and consumption, indicating an increase in savings as a proportion of income.

Figure 4.6 presents a *scatter diagram* of the two variables. Consumption expenditure is represented on the vertical axis and disposable income on the horizontal axis. Both income and consumption have been adjusted for inflation. Each point in Figure 4.6 corresponds to the combination of income and consumption in a particular year. A scatter diagram like this can be used to estimate the consumption function. The best fit to the data is the dotted line in Figure 4.6. All points are very close to this line in the period up to the mid-1970s. The deviations from it increase in the 1980s, reflecting the widening of the gap between consumption and savings mentioned above. The estimated consumption function is:

(18) $\quad C = 0.24 + 0.74Y^d$

The estimate for the marginal propensity to consume (MPC) is 0.74 which is low compared to other countries.[6] The equation states that a 10 per cent change in disposable income leads to a 7.4 per cent change in current consumption. The implied marginal propensity to save (MPS) is 0.26. A 10 per cent change in disposable income leads to a 2.6 per cent change in savings.

This consumption function is a very simple one. It does not take into account any of the influences on consumption other than current year's income. Yet it gives

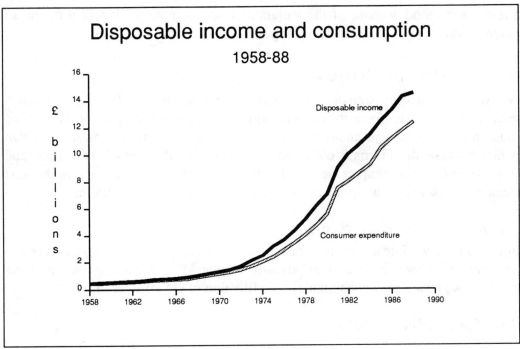

Figure 4.5 Disposable income and consumption

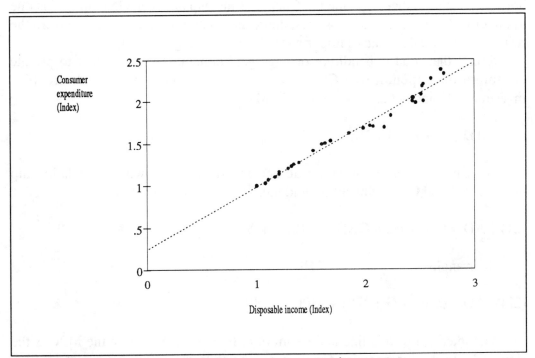

Figure 4.6 Scatter diagram of income and consumption

a reasonably good account of the variations in consumption. It will serve as an introduction to our discussion of fiscal policy, to which we now turn.

4.5 Fiscal Policy

We now turn to a discussion of the effectiveness of fiscal policy. Fiscal policy refers to attempts by government to influence aggregate demand, output and income by changing its expenditure and/or taxation. This is also referred to as *stabilisation policy* because the ultimate objective is to stabilise the growth of output and employment. In this chapter we present the theoretical background and in the next chapter we discuss fiscal policy as practised in Ireland in recent decades.

The Keynesian cross diagram

In section 4.2 we introduced the consumption function as a relationship between consumption expenditure and disposable income, Y^d. Retaining our previous notation, we now depict consumption as a function of GNP rather than Y^d.

(19) $C = a + MPC \times GNP$

Figure 4.7 shows the consumption function with GNP rather than Y^d on the horizontal axis. As we explained in Chapter 3 the gap between GNP and Y^d is due to direct and indirect taxes, subsidies, depreciation and net factor income from the rest of the world, the relative importance of which changes over time.

Recall that total expenditure or aggregate demand (AD) is equal to private consumption expenditure (C), government consumption expenditure (G), investment (I) and net exports (NX = X - M):

(20) $AD = C + I + G + NX$

We can now derive an aggregate demand function showing the relationship between AD and GNP. Substituting identity (19) into (20) we have:

(21) $AD = (a + MPC \times GNP) + I + G + NX$

Rearranging:

(22) $AD = (a + I + G + NX) + MPC \times GNP$

The intercept of this line is the sum of a, I, G and NX, while the MPC is the slope. Hence the consumption function and the aggregate demand line are parallel. This is because I, G and NX are all assumed to be independent of the level of GNP,

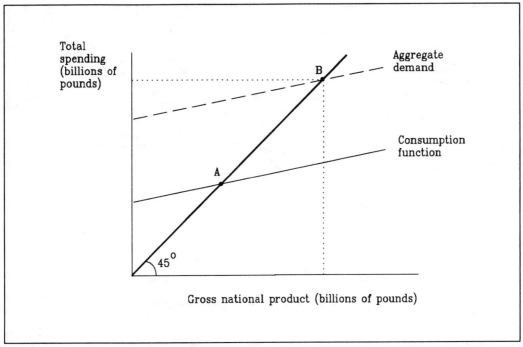

Figure 4.7 Aggregate demand

that is, they are *autonomous* or *exogenous*. The AD line lies above the consumption function reflecting the contribution of I, G and NX to aggregate demand.

What we have in effect done in this diagram is to take the consumption function diagram of Figure 4.1 and, by adding the remaining components of total expenditure to the consumption function, obtained a diagram depicting the relationship between AD and GNP. Because GNP represents the supply of goods and services, this diagram brings together aggregate demand and aggregate supply. At the point were the AD line cuts the 45° line, aggregate demand equals aggregate supply.

This diagram is known as the *Keynesian cross diagram* and has proved very popular in textbooks since it was first introduced by the American Keynesian economist Alvin Hansen (1887 1975) in his exposition of Keynes's theory in 1946.[7] It is important to note that in this model *the aggregate price level* (P) *is fixed* and all variables are measured in real terms. In other words, it is assumed that the entire effect of a change in AD is on the volume of GNP: there is no impact on the price level. In terms of the aggregate demand-aggregate supply model of Chapter 2, this is equivalent to assuming that we are on the horizontal segment of the AS line. This may be realistic in a situation where there are considerable unemployed resources in the economy, and demand-pull inflation is not a factor to be reckoned with, which of course was the case when Keynes was writing in the 1930s, but is less obviously true for later periods.

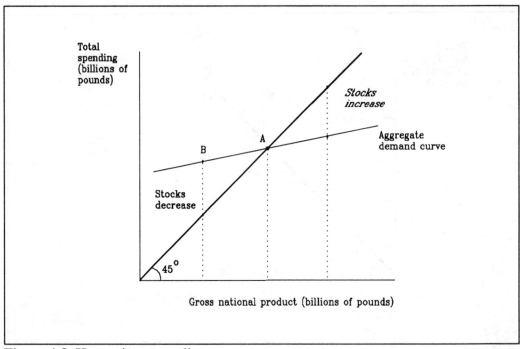

Figure 4.8 Keynesian cross diagram

The point where the AD curve intersects the 45° line, point A in Figure 4.8, is the *equilibrium level of GNP*. At this point AD equals GNP: the level of spending on the economy's output is equal to the level of output that firms plan to produce. This implies that firms' *actual* stock levels are equal to their *desired* stock levels. At points to the left of the equilibrium point, such as B, the level of AD is higher than GNP. Spending on the economy's output exceeds the level of output being produced. As a result, firms' stocks fall below desired levels. Faced with this situation, firms will expand production and move GNP towards the equilibrium level. At points to the right of the equilibrium point, such as C, the level of AD is less than GNP: less is being spent than is being produced. There is unintended accumulation of stocks. In this case, firms cut production and GNP moves back towards its equilibrium level. Hence, changes in stocks send signals to firms to increase or decrease output and this moves the economy towards equilibrium.

Note:
Another way of thinking of the equilibrium point A is that only at this level of output does planned *(or ex ante) investment* equal *actual investment*. At all other points there are unplanned or unintended changes in stocks, which are part of *ex post* or actual investment.

Let us now apply this model to the analysis of fiscal policy. Figure 4.9 gives an example of an expansionary fiscal policy. Initially, the economy is at point A and output corresponds to GNP_1. An increase in government expenditure shifts the

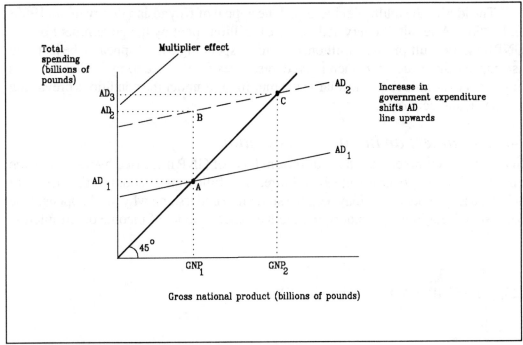

Figure 4.9 The multiplier

aggregate demand curve from AD1 to AD2 and aggregate demand increases along the vertical axis. The economy moves from A to B. Point B is a *disequilibrium* point as AD is above GNP and there is an unplanned reduction in stocks. This encourages firms to increase output, so GNP increases along the horizontal axis and, after a time, equilibrium is eventually regained at the point C.

Figure 4.9 highlights an important point. The initial increase in government expenditure is from AD1 to AD2 but by the time equilibrium is re-established at the point C, aggregate demand has increased to AD3. In moving from B to C, aggregate demand increases from AD2 to AD3. Thus the final change in GNP is greater than the initial increase in government expenditure. This phenomenon is referred to as the *multiplier*. Let us now examine this concept in some detail.

4.6 The Multiplier

The concept of the multiplier theory is an integral part of Keynesian economics. The basic idea is that an increase in any of the components of total expenditure, C, I, G or NX, will raise equilibrium GNP by a *multiple* of the initial increase in expenditure. The multiplier is simply a number that relates the initial change in expenditure to the ultimate change in equilibrium GNP. In general:

Change in equilibrium GNP = Initial change in expenditure × multiplier

The idea of the multiplier increased the appeal of Keynesian theory in the 1950s and 1960s. After all, if every additional £1 million spent by the government boosts GNP by some multiple of £1 million, additional spending would appear to be justified as long as there are any unemployed resources in the economy. Clearly, it is important to be able to say how large the multiplier is under the conditions prevailing in a particular economy.

The multiplier: an intuitive explanation

In Figure 4.9 we noted that the equilibrium level of GNP increased by more than the initial increase in government expenditure. The following account of the effects of an increase in expenditure may help the student to understand why this happens. The basic set of relationships underlying the Keynesian model of income determination is:

$$\overset{4}{NI} \equiv \overset{3}{GNP} = \overset{2}{AD} \equiv \overset{5}{C} + I + \overset{1}{G} + NX \qquad (23)$$

where NI is national income and all the other variables are as before. The numbers in the top row indicate the sequence of events. The objective is to show the ultimate effect on output of an initial increase in government expenditure (G). An increase in G (step 1) raises aggregate demand (step 2) by definition. This results in an excess demand for goods and services. Assuming the aggregate supply curve is horizontal, firms respond to the higher level of demand by producing more goods and services at unchanged prices, and GNP (step 3) and NI (step 4) both increase. At the end of this first round GNP has increased by exactly the amount of the initial increase in G.

That, however, is not the end of the process. In the second round we take account of the fact that the increase in NI raises C (step 5) and this further increases AD and GNP. The link between income (NI) and consumption expenditure (C) is, of course, the consumption function. This function is of crucial importance in the multiplier process. This process will continue into third, fourth and successive rounds because the economy has entered into a rising income-consumption spiral. Every increase in income induces a subsequent increase in consumption which in turn increases income and so on. The process does however eventually come to an end because the MPC is less than 1. In each successive round the increase in consumption is the MPC *times* the increase in income. If the MPC is equal to 0.8, an increase of £1 million in income will lead to a £0.8 million increase in consumption. In the next round, NI rises by £0.8 million and C rises by a further £0.64 million (that is, the £0.8 million increase in NI *times* the MPC). Thus the increases in consumption taper off in successive rounds. The expansion therefore comes to a halt sooner, the smaller the MPC. Conversely, it lasts longer the higher the MPC.

Calculating the multiplier formula

In order to derive the multiplier formula consider the following equations:

(24) $GNP = AD$ Equilibrium condition
(25) $AD \equiv C + I + G + NX$ Aggregate demand
(26) $C = a + MPC \times GNP$ Consumption function

To derive the multiplier formula substitute (25) into (24) to obtain:

(27) $GNP = C + I + G + NX$

Now substitute (26) into (27):

(28) $GNP = a + MPC \times GNP + I + G + NX$

Bring the $(MPC \times GNP)$ term over to the left-hand side:

(29) $GNP (1 - MPC) = a + I + G + NX$

divide both sides by $(1 - MPC)$ to obtain:

(30) $GNP = [1/(1 - MPC)](a + I + G + NX)$

We see that if any of the terms (a, I, G or NX) changes, the level of equilibrium GNP changes by $1/(1 - MPC)$ *times* this change. The multiplier therefore equals $1/(1 - MPC)$. For example, if the MPC equals 0.8, the multiplier is:

Multiplier $= 1/(1 - MPC) = 1/(1 - 0.8) = 5$

An increase in G of £1 million would raise GNP or national income by £5 million. If the MPC were 0.9, the multiplier would be 10. We see immediately that the higher the marginal propensity to consume, the larger the multiplier.

We know from our earlier discussion that the MPC and the MPS must sum to 1 (see equation 15 above). It follows that $(1 - MPC)$ is equal to MPS and the multiplier formula can be rewritten as:

Multiplier $= 1/MPS$

An MPC of 0.8 implies an MPS of 0.2. Inserting this value for the MPS into the above formula, the multiplier again equals 5. The higher the MPS, the lower the multiplier; the lower the MPS, the higher the multiplier.

We know from Chapter 3 that savings is only one of the three possible leakages from the circular flow of income and expenditure. The other two leakages, which we have ignored in this section, are taxes and imports. It is the sum of these leakages that determines the size of the multiplier. We now turn to a more generalised version of the multiplier formula that takes all three leakages into account.

Generalising the multiplier

The size of the multiplier depends on how much of an initial increase in AD is passed on through an increase in C. In the very simplified model we have just presented, there was only one possible leakage out of domestic expenditure, namely, the amount of an increase in income allocated by households to savings. However, in a more complete model of income determination, in which we allow for (i) a foreign sector and (ii) a public sector, there are other important leakages.

In an open economy, much of any increase in income will leak abroad in the form of additional imports (M), that is, spending on the output of some other economy. Clearly this does nothing to stimulate further increases in the level of output in the domestic economy. Similarly, in a country with a large public sector, taxes (T) divert a sizeable proportion of any additional consumer income to the government and are another leakage from the circular flow of income. These additional leakages tend to bring the multiplier process to a halt sooner than would be the case in the simple model we discussed above. We now consider how these leakages affect the value of the multiplier.

Taxation If there is a single, flat rate of tax on income, the relationship between tax revenue (T) and GNP is given by the following equation:

(31) $T = MPT \times GNP$

where MPT is the *marginal tax rate* or "marginal propensity to tax", and $0 < MPT < 1$. The MPT gives the flat rate of income tax. Hence, if there was a flat rate of tax of 30 per cent, the MPT would equal 0.3. Allowing for a tax of this type, the multiplier formula becomes:

Multiplier $= 1/(MPS + MPT)$

This formula is derived in Appendix 1. Note that the formula has the sum of the "marginal propensities to leak" in the denominator. Hence, the larger these leakages from extra income, the smaller the multiplier. This general principle holds true even for the most complicated models.

90

Imports   The third possible leakage is due to the relationship between national income and imports. The relationship may be expressed as:

(32) $M = b + MPM \times GNP$

where b is an intercept term, and MPM is the *marginal propensity to import,* and $0 < MPM < 1$. If, for example, MPM equals 0.2, then equation (32) states that 20 per cent of any increase in GNP will be spent on imports. As shown in Appendix 1 the multiplier with savings, taxation and import leakages is:

Multiplier $= 1/(MPS + MPT + MPM)$

Once again, the denominator is the sum of all the leakages from the circular flow of income.

Summary   The conclusions of the above section are that any change in the level of investment (I), government expenditure (G), net exports (NX) or the intercept terms of the consumption and import functions affects the equilibrium level of GNP and national income and that the change in equilibrium income will be greater than the initial change in AD. The ratio between the two depends on the multiplier. The larger the leakages from the circular flow of income and spending, the smaller the multiplier and, conversely, the smaller the leakages the larger the multiplier.

The inclusion of G and T in the list of variables that can set the multiplier process in motion highlights the relevance of the multiplier when we are assessing the scope for using fiscal policy to stabilise the level of income and output.

Multiplier formulae depend on the structure of the macroeconomic model with which we are working. We derive a number of examples in Appendix 1. However, all of these are based on models that lack a money market, which we have not yet discussed. When the model is expanded to include a money market, the multiplier formula becomes more complex.

The multiplier in the Irish economy

Ireland is a small economy that is extremely open to international trade. Furthermore, the marginal rate of income tax and the indirect tax rates applied to discretionary spending are very high. These considerations would lead us to expect that the multiplier would be very low. A survey of the available research confirms this. There is widespread agreement that $MPS = 0.26$, $MPT = 0.24$ and $MPM = 0.4$ are realistic values for the parameters that enter into the calculation of the multiplier. Inserting these values into the formula given above yields the following result:

Multiplier $= 1/(0.26 + 0.24 + 0.4) = 1.11$

This implies that an increase in G, C, I, or X, or a reduction in M of £1 million would raise GNP by £1.11 million. Under these conditions "multiplier" is somewhat of a misnomer. The leakages are so large that GNP only increases by marginally more than the initial increase in aggregate demand itself. Thus one of the alluring features of the simple Keynesian model, the idea that an increase in government spending results in an increase in the equilibrium level of GNP equal to a multiple of the original stimulus, does not hold under Irish conditions. But while this conclusion may dampen our enthusiasm for the concept of the multiplier somewhat, it is none the less true that increased aggregate demand *does* increase the equilibrium level of national income. However, in recent years, simple multiplier analysis of the type presented here has lost much of its prominence in the economic literature. In addition to the belief that large tax and import leakages give rise to small multipliers, there are other considerations, which we shall explore in subsequent chapters, that suggest that fiscal policy will not have any long-lasting effect on GNP.

4.7   Stabilisation Policy

As we saw from Figure 1.1 in Chapter 1, the growth of Irish GNP has been very erratic over the years. One of the principal tenets of Keynesian economics is that fiscal policy can be used to eliminate the business cycle by stabilising the behaviour of GNP over time. In particular, Keynes argued that fiscal policy should be used to keep the *actual* level of GNP close to the *potential* or full employment level.

Note:
The concept of potential GNP was discussed in Chapter 2. It is that level of output the economy could produce given the state of technology and the size and education of the labour force without accelerating inflation.

In Figure 4.10 the growth rate of potential GNP is indicated by the horizontal line. It assumes that the Irish economy is capable of growing by about 3 per cent a year. A higher growth rate would not be sustainable due, for example, to the emergence of shortages of skilled labour. However, *supply-side* policies (e.g. retraining of unskilled unemployed workers, investment in more and better capital equipment) would raise the growth rate of potential GNP over time.

The actual growth rate of GNP is shown crossing and re-crossing the potential growth rate line. When the actual growth rate is above the potential GNP line firms are operating at above full capacity and there is pressure to increase prices. Hence, *demand-pull inflation* occurs if the actual growth rate remains above the potential rate for any length of time. Conversely, when the actual growth rate is below the potential rate firms find they have excess capacity and workers will be laid off.

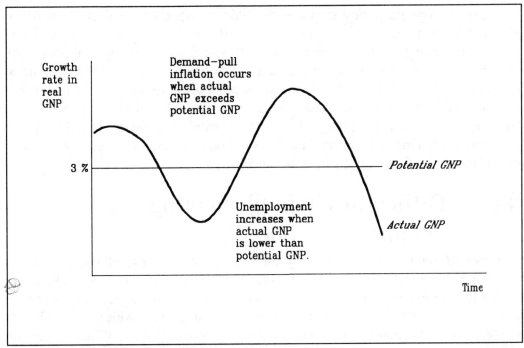

Figure 4.10 Stabilisation policy

Employment decreases and *cyclical unemployment* increases. The objective of stabilisation policy is to keep actual GNP as close as possible to its potential or full employment level and thereby minimise inflation and unemployment.

Recall that in the short run, if there are unemployed resources, we can assume that GNP is demand-determined. Aggregate demand (AD) is broken down into: C + I + G + X - M. A recession or boom can be triggered by a change in any of the components of AD. Stabilisation policy is an attempt by government to offset the instability caused by fluctuations in the other components of AD by altering its own contribution. For example, if the economy begins to move into a recession because of a fall in exports, the government could counter this fall in demand in a number of different ways. It could increase its own consumption expenditure (G), or stimulate personal consumption expenditure (C) by reducing taxes or increasing transfer payments, or it could provide increased incentives to investors in order to stimulate investment spending (I).

If the government implements this type of policy GNP will be kept closer to its full employment level than would be the case if the government did not intervene in the economy. Similarly, if prices are rising because of an excess demand for goods and services, the Keynesian prescription is for government to cut expenditure or raise taxes, thereby dampening down the inflationary pressure. This type of fiscal policy is called *counter-cyclical* because it acts against the business cycle.

The appropriate policy response depends on whether the decline in AD is believed to be *permanent* or *temporary*. If a shock is temporary the government should do nothing because after a while AD will revert to its normal level. An example of a temporary shock is the short-lived rise in oil prices which occurred during the 1990/91 Gulf crisis. Because the price of oil quickly fell to its pre-war level it would have been destabilising if governments had tried to counteract the rise by an expansionary fiscal policy. On the other hand, if a country is suddenly and permanently excluded from an important export market, there is a case for an expansionary fiscal policy to offset this shock.

4.8 Difficulties in Implementing a Stabilisation Policy

The idea of stabilising the economy through appropriate use of fiscal policy is appealing, but experience has shown that it is in practice very difficult, if not impossible, to *fine tune* the economy in this manner. There are several reasons for this, which we shall discuss under the following headings: (1) inside and outside lags (2) determining the magnitude of the appropriate response (3) the political dimension to budgetary decisions, and (4) the uncertain effect of changes in aggregate demand on output.

Inside and outside lags

It takes time for the government to respond to movements in the business cycle. First there is the delay arising from the time required to recognise turning points in the business cycle. Timely economic data are not easily obtained: data on key variables are not issued until months after the event. Forecasters are not good at predicting the turning points of the business cycle. As a result it may be some time before the government is aware that the economy is beginning to overheat or to move into a recession. For example, in framing its 1991 budget, the Irish government assumed that GNP would grow by 2.25 per cent during 1991, but during the year this forecast was revised down to 0.5 per cent, although it subsequently became clear that the growth rate was somewhat higher.

Note:
As noted in Chapter 3 in the middle of 1990 the consensus was that the Irish economy would grow by at least 3 per cent in 1991. In fact recession set in after the invasion of Kuwait in August 1990. None of the forecasters recognised that the economy was at a turning point in mid-1990 and they all tended to extrapolate the strong growth of the previous year too far into the future. This is a problem with sophisticated models as well as back-of-the-envelope projections. Forecasters should always keep in mind Keynes's dictum: "The inevitable never happens, the unexpected always does."

Second, there is a *decision lag*. Government has to decide whether to increase expenditure and, if so, how to spend the extra money: should it go on health, education, social welfare or roads? These deliberations take time.

Third, there is an *implementation lag*. Social welfare rates can be increased quickly, but capital projects have long *lead times*. If the government decides to increase expenditure on roads, for example, project documents have to be drawn up, contractors vetted, and tenders approved. If it is decided to influence aggregate demand through tax changes, these are usually introduced only once a year, at budget time, and do not take effect until they have been passed into law.

These three types of lags are referred to as *inside* lags and can result in considerable delays. There is also an *outside* lag. That is the time between implementing a policy and when it affects aggregate demand. For example, there is a relatively long delay before income tax changes affect people's disposable income and consumption expenditure. Moreover, the impact of fiscal policy on the economy will not be confined to a single year but will be spread out over several years, by which time the underlying conditions may well have changed and made the policy inappropriate.

The upshot of these lags is that the policy could be inappropriate by the time it becomes effective and end up *destabilising* instead of stabilising the economy. This would happen if the economy were already changing direction when the policy was introduced. For example, if a fall in exports were superseded by a consumer boom, recession could give way to boom before the policies designed to deal with the recession had begun to take effect.

Quantifying the appropriate response

A second problem is deciding *how much* additional demand the government should inject or withdraw. The appropriate amount to spend to counter a fall in investment can only be calculated on the basis of an exact knowledge of the investment and fiscal multipliers. But calculating multipliers entails estimating a model of the economy, which is a far from exact science. Even minor differences between models can result in different policy prescriptions. Consequently, it is difficult to prescribe the appropriate response to a demand-side shock.

The political business cycle

There is a constant temptation for politicians to use increases in public expenditure and tax cuts to curry favour with the electorate. As a result, the timing of elections tends to influence fiscal policy. In Ireland in 1978, for example, the major political parties vied with one another in their extravagant promises to the electorate. After the general election an expansionary fiscal policy was implemented when the economy was already moving into a boom under its own steam. Furthermore, there is a ratchet effect in government expenditure: governments find it easy to increase expenditure but very difficult to reduce it. This makes it impossible to adhere to the basic principle of stabilisation policy, which requires a balance between strategic surpluses and deficits over time.

Keynesian theory should not be interpreted as justifying creating thousands of unproductive jobs in the civil service or subsidising unproductive state firms, although he himself, in the passage we quoted earlier in this chapter, favoured wasteful expenditure in the private sector because, unlike productive investment, it is not subject to diminishing returns. (Diminishing returns to labour relates to the productivity of an individual worker. As more and more labour is applied to a fixed amount of land and capital, output per worker or labour productivity eventually declines.) He also stated that

"if the Treasury were to fill old bottles full with banknotes, bury them at suitable depths in disused coal mines. . .and leave it to private enterprise ... to dig the notes up again ... then there need be no more unemployment."[8]

Passages like this may have contributed to the wasteful public expenditure that was justified in the name of job creation in the 1970s. However there is now a greater awareness that government expenditure financed by borrowing should be *productive*, in the sense of yielding a return to the community adequate to warrant the burden that the servicing of the debt will impose on taxpayers for years to come.

Uncertain effect of changes in demand on output

We now discuss two other issues which may further undermine the effectiveness of fiscal policy. A budget deficit can be financed from four sources. The government can borrow from (1) abroad (2) the central bank (3) the commercial banks and (4) the non-bank public. If the government borrows from sources (1), (2) or (3), the money supply in the economy is increased. This form of borrowing is referred to as *government monetary financing* (GMF). If the government borrows from the non-bank public the money supply is not affected. Borrowing from this source is called *domestic bond financing*.

The impact of an expansionary fiscal policy on aggregate demand depends crucially on whether the deficit is financed through an expansion of the money supply or by selling bonds. Monetary financing will be examined in Chapter 7 in the context of monetary policy. Here we mention two issues that arise when domestic bonds are issued to finance a government deficit.

First, there is the problem of *crowding out*. When the government sells bonds to the public, the result can be higher interest rates: as we shall discuss in more detail in Chapter 7, increasing the supply of bonds tends to drive their price down and this raises the rate of interest. Higher interest rates may in turn reduce private sector investment. Thus government expenditure may crowd out private sector spending. If the fall in I equals the increase in G, there is complete crowding out. The result is a change in the composition of AD, with no change in its level. If this is the case, the overall impact of fiscal policy on aggregate demand is even smaller than is suggested by the multiplier we calculated above.

The second issue relates to the effect of debt financing on consumption expenditure. In an influential article published in 1974, the Harvard economist Robert Barro proposed the idea that increases in government debt could result in a fall in private sector consumption. It was subsequently pointed out that the classical economist David Ricardo (1772-1823) appeared to have entertained the same idea, hence it is now known as the *Barro-Ricardo Equivalence Proposition*. At its simplest, this theory can be explained as follows. Suppose the government lowers taxes and finances the deficit by selling bonds to the public, which must be redeemed (with interest) at some time in the future. Households' current disposable income rises due to the tax cut, but future disposable income will fall by an equivalent amount because of the necessity of repaying the debt. Thus, households' long-run or permanent income is not increased by the tax cut and hence their consumption should not be affected. It follows, therefore, that if households have the foresight and prudence to worry about the long-run implication of a tax cut, it will have no effect on consumption. We discuss the evidence of the existence of this effect in Ireland in Chapter 5.

4.9   Full Employment Budget

In modern economies, there are two important *built-in stabilisers* which have a cushioning effect on the business cycle. First, the amount paid in income tax increases as nominal income rises. A progressive income tax code, where a higher tax rate is applied at higher levels of income, intensifies this effect. As incomes increase, people who were previously liable at the lower rate become liable at a higher rate as their money income increases. This is referred to as *bracket creep*. As a result, as the economy expands, the government *automatically* withdraws more money from the circular flow of income. This phenomenon tends to dampen the growth of the economy and is known as "fiscal drag". Conversely, during a recession consumers are cushioned from some of the fall in national income due to the even more rapid fall in the amount of income tax they have to pay. A similar effect operates through the indirect tax system, as high rates of excise taxes and VAT are levied on extra spending.

Second, government transfer (social welfare) payments automatically change as economic activity and the level of unemployment change. For example, as the economy moves into a recession, people who lose their jobs become entitled to unemployment benefits. As a consequence, their expenditure need not fall as sharply as would otherwise be the case. This will also tend to dampen the business cycle.

The effect of the income tax system and transfer payments on the government's budget is illustrated in Figure 4.11. The diagram shows government expenditure,

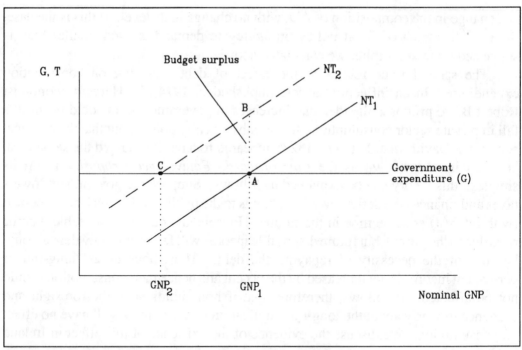

Figure 4.11 Discretionary and automatic budget deficits

G, and *net taxes* (tax revenue minus transfers) along the vertical axis. Nominal GNP is shown on the horizontal axis.

Government expenditure is assumed to be constant at all levels of GNP and is therefore represented as a horizontal line. The net taxes line (NT), on the other hand, is positively sloped. This is because more tax revenue is collected and less is paid out in transfers as GNP increases. NT therefore increases. Conversely, as GNP falls, less is collected in tax and more paid out in transfers and NT decreases.

At the point A in Figure 4.11, which corresponds to GNP_1, government expenditure equals net taxes and the budget is balanced. To the left of GNP_1 there is a budget deficit (expenditure exceeds revenue) and to the right a budget surplus (expenditure is less than revenue). It is clear from the diagram that changes in budget deficits or surpluses *automatically* follow from changes in GNP. This is shown as a movement along the NT line in the diagram. We wish to distinguish these automatic changes in the budget balance from *discretionary* changes. Discretionary budget changes arise when the government changes tax rates, the level of social welfare benefits or the level of its expenditure on goods and services, G. In terms of Figure 4.11, a tax increase or a reduction in transfer payments shifts the NT curve to the left. Conversely, lower tax rates or higher transfer payments shift the NT curve down to the right. Similarly, changes in the level of government consumption, G, alter the budget balance. An increase in G shifts the government expenditure curve upwards and widens the deficit, while a decrease in G shifts the curve downwards and closes the deficit.

Suppose for example that the government decides to raise taxes. This is shown in Figure 4.11 as a shift to the left in the NT curve from NT_1 to NT_2. Assuming for the moment that GNP remains unchanged at GNP_1, there is now a budget surplus as measured by the distance AB. This budget surplus was brought about by discretionary government policy. If the government had lowered taxes, the NT curve would shift downwards and a discretionary budget deficit would have arisen.

When there is a discretionary change in any of the budgetary variables, the level of GNP at which the budget will be balanced will change. A tax increase or spending cut will lower the level of GNP at which the budget is balanced, and a tax cut or expenditure increase will raise it. For example, following the increase in taxes shown in Figure 4.11, the level of GNP consistent with a balanced budget falls from GNP_1 to GNP_2. A balanced budget is restored because as we move from B to C, the government collects less in tax revenue and pays out more in transfer payments.

It can be argued that the relevant budget from a policy perspective is the *full employment budget* (also referred to as the *structural*, *high-employment* or *cyclically adjusted* budget). That is, the government should choose a combination of tax rates and levels of expenditure that would result in a balanced budget *if the economy were at full employment*. At other levels of national income the government should allow for the effect on the budget of the built-in stabilisers. A policy of balancing the full employment budget is consistent with surpluses and deficits due to the fact that over the course of the business cycle the economy does not remain at the full employment level of output. By accepting the deficits and surpluses that arise due to the operation of the built-in stabilisers, government will dampen the business cycle.

4.10   Taxation and the Supply Side of the Economy

Up to this point, our emphasis has been on how taxation affects the demand side of the economy by influencing private consumption and investment expenditure. However, economists have for a long time recognised that taxation also affects the supply side of the economy. The reason is that taxation affects the incentives to work and save and this in turn affects the level and composition of output and income. This line of argument can lead to the attractive proposition that tax cuts may increase rather than decrease, tax revenue. An extreme form of this argument has been put forward by the University of Southern California economist Arthur Laffer, who reputedly first drew the *Laffer Curve* on a napkin in a Washington restaurant to explain the point to a reporter.[9]

The Laffer curve depicts the relationship between the average tax rate (vertical axis) and the yield of the tax (horizontal axis) (Figure 4.12). There are two points

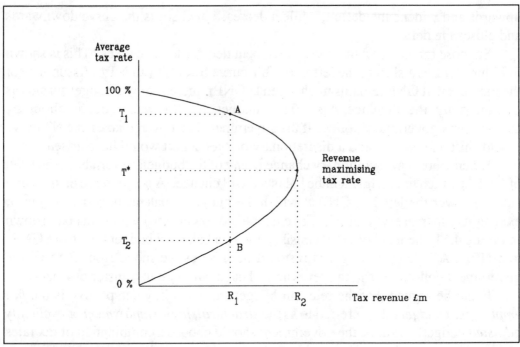

Figure 4.12 Laffer curve

on the vertical axis where the tax yield is zero, corresponding to the zero and the 100 per cent tax rates. In the first case, there is no tax and therefore no revenue. In the second case, all income is taken in tax so that there is no incentive to work and, as a result, tax revenue is zero. Between these two extremes, it is argued, tax revenue first increases and then decreases as the tax rate is raised.

The diagram indicates the tax rate (T^*) which maximises tax revenue. If the tax rate is above this rate, *lowering* it will generate *extra* revenue. For example, if the tax rate were lowered from T_1 to T^*, revenue would increase from R_1 to R_2. Note that the same amount of tax revenue can be obtained at high or low tax rates: T_1 and T_2, for example, generate the same revenue, R_1. It follows, therefore, that government could cut the tax rate from T_1 to T_2 without suffering any loss of revenue. Furthermore, it may be argued, this reduction in tax rates would have a stimulating effect on the economy, encouraging people to work harder and to save and invest more, leading to a rise in national income.

Note:
Higher taxes can distort people's economic behaviour and this entails *deadweight losses*. For example, higher taxes might encourage Irish people to work less in the formal economy and more in the informal or "black" economy, to shop in Northern Ireland, to take their money out of the country and place it in foreign tax havens, and even to emigrate. These responses are consistent with Laffer's hypothesis that at very high rates of taxation the economy begins to shrink.

While the effect of taxation on incentives gained increased recognition during the 1980s, the ideas underlying the Laffer curve remain controversial. There are a number of reasons why tax cuts may not have the dramatic effects predicted by this theory. It is possible, for example, that lower taxes might encourage people to work *less* because after the tax cut they can obtain the same level of take-home pay with less effort; they may decide to enjoy more leisure rather than more income. To the extent that they do so, the effects predicted by Laffer will not materialise.

Moreover, for the Laffer curve to bend back on itself, the reduction in taxes has to boost output by an amount sufficient to more than compensate for the initial loss of tax revenue. Suppose, for example, that national income is £10,000 million. With a tax rate of 35 per cent total tax revenue is £3,500 million. If the government lowers the tax rate to 30 per cent, total tax revenue will initially fall to £3,000 million. National income would have to increase to £11,667 million before tax revenue would return to its initial level (30 per cent of £11,667 million = £3,500 million). This is a 16.7 per cent increase in national income, and this large an expansion may not be forthcoming in response to a reduction of 5 percentage points in the tax rate. While there may be particular sectors of the economy where tax cuts increase tax revenue, it is by no means certain, even at very high levels of taxation, that this will hold for the economy as a whole.

However the openness of the Irish economy does imply that we cannot afford to move too far out of line from the tax rates that obtain in European countries and, in particular, the UK. This was illustrated by the manner in which high excises and VAT rates on spirits, petrol and electrical goods led shoppers from the Republic to purchase these items in Northern Ireland in the mid-1980s. When the tax rates were cut towards the end of the decade, more was spent in the Republic and revenue rose. Similarly, emigration of qualified people to the UK and the US is encouraged by the relatively low rates of income taxation in those countries. These effects of high tax rates are consistent with the basic idea underlying the Laffer curve.

4.11   Financing the Deficit

We have seen how Keynesian theory assigns an important role to budget deficits as an instrument of stabilisation policy. To finance a deficit the government has to borrow. (We listed in section 4.9 the main sources from which governments borrow.) Thus, an increase in debt is a consequence of running a fiscal deficit. If deficits outweigh surpluses over the years, the amount owed by government will rise.

It is evident that the debt/income ratio cannot go on growing without limit. Taxes have to be raised from the working population to service the debt. We have mentioned the danger that a high level of taxation will give rise to large deadweight losses. (A deadweight loss arises when there is a reduction in output due to the economy departing from its optimal or most efficient equilibrium point.) This is the case even when the tax receipts are being used to pay interest to Irish residents (many of whom are, of course, themselves taxpayers). But to service the externally held debt a surplus of exports over imports has also to be generated. There are limits to the capacity and willingness of an economy to accept these burdens. The present generation of taxpayers may feel that it benefited little from the spending which gave rise to the debt. *Debt fatigue* can easily set in, leading to pressure on the government to default on its obligations to its creditors. Thus, a steadily rising debt/income ratio will sooner or later result in a *debt crisis*.

Following the second oil price increase in 1979, the oil exporting countries generated high balance of payments surpluses. Much of this money was deposited in western banks, who were eager to on-lend it. The bankers believed they were safe in lending money to developing countries and to countries in eastern Europe as long as the borrowing was guaranteed by their governments. However, early in the 1980s there was a sharp rise in arrears in debt service among the debtor countries. This culminated in a panic in August 1982 when Mexico announced it would no longer pay interest on its massive outstanding loans. It became apparent that many other countries, particularly in Latin America and Sub-Saharan Africa, were about to default. At the same time, the economies of many of the communist countries of eastern Europe, notably Poland, were stagnating and incapable of servicing the enormous debts they had incurred from western banks. The problem was so large that it threatened the stability of the western world's banking system. The political economy of *debt rescheduling* and *debt forgiveness* has preoccupied the international financial community ever since. We shall see that in the early 1980s Ireland also came close to undergoing a debt crisis.

The dynamics of debt accumulation

The dynamics of debt accumulation was studied by the Polish-American economist Evsey Domar (born in 1914) who analysed the implications of the US war-time borrowing in an article written in 1944, which has provided the foundation of the recent literature on *sustainable fiscal policy*.[10] A key concept in this context is the *primary deficit*. To define this, consider that the fiscal deficit may be classified into two components interest payments on outstanding debt and the non-interest deficit. The primary deficit is the total deficit exclusive of interest payments. That is:

(33)   Total deficit = non-interest expenditure + interest payments - total revenue

and

(34)   Primary deficit = non-interest expenditure - total revenue

The primary deficit (surplus) is therefore the excess (shortfall) of government spending, exclusive of interest paid on the national debt, over revenue. If there is a primary deficit, that is, if borrowing is greater than interest repayments, then the government is not raising enough in revenue to cover its spending exclusive of debt service. It is borrowing more than is needed simply to service past borrowing.

We shall use the following definitions:

r	=	the rate of interest
D	=	the national debt at the start of the year
d	=	(D/GNP) = debt to GNP ratio
P	=	primary ratio = total borrowing - interest payments (rD)
p	=	(P/GNP) = primary deficit to GNP ratio
y	=	rate of growth in nominal GNP

Domar showed that the change in the debt to GNP ratio, Δd, is given by:

(35) $\Delta d = p + (r - y)d$

Equation (35) shows that the change in the debt/GNP ratio depends not just on the primary deficit (p) but also on the interest rate payable on borrowings (r), the growth rate in the economy (y) and the stock of debt outstanding (d). This equation is derived in Appendix 2.

It is now possible to obtain the conditions under which the debt/GNP ratio is stabilised. If equation (35) is set equal to zero (so that the debt/GNP ratio is stabilised) then we can calculate the primary deficit required to meet the condition of stability.

(36) $-p = (r - y)d = 0$

Equation (36) states that in the long run the debt/GNP ratio will be stabilised if the primary *surplus* (a negative value for p indicates a primary surplus) is equal to (or greater than) the product of the debt/GNP ratio and the difference between the rate of interest and the rate of growth of nominal GNP. Applying this formula to the Irish economy in 1991, the debt/GNP ratio is 1.03, the growth rate of nominal GNP is about 0.5 per cent and the rate of interest on national debt is about 9 per cent. Inserting these values into equation (36):

(37) $p = -(9.0 - 0.5)1.03 = -8.25$

Hence a primary surplus of 8.25 per cent of GNP is necessary in order to stabilise the debt/GNP ratio. A primary surplus greater than this will lead to a fall in the debt/GNP ratio and, conversely, a lower primary surplus will lead to a rise in the debt/GNP ratio. The primary deficit/surplus for the Irish economy is discussed in greater detail in Chapter 5.

The importance of equation (35) is that it defines a sustainable fiscal policy. If the deficit exceeds the level indicated by this formula, in the long run the ratio of debt to income will rise and this is unsustainable because it implies that less and less will be available for purposes other than debt service.

4.12 Conclusion

The main points discussed in this chapter are:

- The relationship between household disposable income, consumption and saving
- The average and marginal propensities to consume and save
- The consumption and savings functions
- Life-cycle and permanent-income theories of consumption
- The aggregate consumption function for the Irish economy
- The Keynesian cross diagram
- The role of unplanned changes in stocks or inventories in arriving at the equilibrium level of production
- The multiplier effect and how its size depends on the savings, tax and import leakages
- Other factors tending to reduce the size of the multiplier
- Keynesian stabilisation policy and the difficulties in the way of implementing such a policy
- The concept of a sustainable fiscal policy and the conditions under which the debt/income ratio will stabilise.

Notes

1. J. M. Keynes, *The General Theory of Employment, Interest and Money*, Macmillan, 1936.

2. See J. M. Cheyennes, *The General Theory of Employment, Interest and Money*, London: Macmillan, 1964, p. 131.

3. The life-cycle hypothesis was developed by Modigliani in conjunction with Richard Brumberg and Albert Ando. See F. Modigliani and R. Brumberg, "Utility Analysis and the Consumption Function", in K. Kurihara (ed), *Post-Keynesian Economics*, New Brunswick, N.J., Rutgers University Press, 1954.

4. Another way of thinking of this is to allow consumption to be a function of income *and* wealth. Wealth has increased significantly over the long run and this shifts the short-run consumption function upward. Thus, even if each short-run consumption function displays a declining APC, the long-run consumption function cuts through a series of upward shifting short-run consumption functions and is much steeper than they are.

5. M. Friedman, *A Theory of the Consumption Function*, Princeton, Princeton University Press, 1957.

6. Many estimates of the MPC have been published. Michael Moore, "The Irish Consumption Function and Ricardian Equivalence", *The Economic and Social Review*, Vol. 19, No. 1, October 1987, estimates an MPC of 0.67 and Brendan M. Walsh, "Ricardian Equivalence and the Irish Consumption Function: A Comment", *The Economic and Social Review*, Vol. 20, No. 1, October 1988, estimates an upper value for the MPC of 0.855. The consumption function estimated by both authors is more elaborate than the simple version given here.

7. Alvin Hansen, *A Guide to Keynes*, New York: McGraw-Hill, 1953.

8. Keynes also pointed out that the "form of digging holes in the ground known as gold-mining" was quite acceptable to those who deplored "wasteful" public spending! See *General Theory*, Book III, Chapter 10.

9. It has been said of the Laffer curve that you can explain it to a politician in half an hour and he can talk about it for six months.

10. E. Domar, "The Burden of the Debt and National Income", *American Economic Review*, Vol. 33, 1944.

Deriving multiplier formula when savings is the only leakage   In order to simplify the notation we shall denote the marginal propensity to consume (MPC) as c, the marginal propensity to save (MPS) as s, the marginal propensity to tax (MPT) as t and the marginal propensity to import (MPM) as m. The basic model consists of an equilibrium condition and the consumption function:

(1) $GNP = C + I + G$

(2) $C = a + c\,NI$

where a is the intercept term. Substitute (2) into (1).

(3) $GNP = (a + c\,NI) + I + G$

Assume GNP = NI (recall from the circular flow diagram that only depreciation and indirect taxes separate these two variables).

(4) $GNP = (c\,GNP) + a + I + G$

Bring the term in brackets over to the lefthand side.

(5) $GNP - (c\,GNP) = a + I + G$

or

(6) $GNP(1 - c) = a + I + G$

Divide both sides by (1 - c).

(7) $GNP = [1/(1 - c)] \times (a + I + G)$

The term $[1/(1 - c)]$ is the multiplier. Given that the marginal propensity to save (MPS), $s = 1 - c$, the multiplier formula could also be written as $[1/s]$. An increase in a (the intercept term in the consumption function which represents an increase in consumption not brought about by an increase in income), I or G will raise GNP by the multiplier. Conversely, a fall in a, I or G will reduce GNP by the multiplier.

Deriving the multiplier formula with savings, taxation and import leakages

Again the notation c, s, t and m is used to denote the marginal propensity to consume (MPC), the marginal propensity to save (MPS), the marginal propensity to tax (MPT) and the marginal propensity to import (MPM) respectively. The equilibrium condition is:

(1) $\text{GNP} = \text{C} + \text{I} + \text{G} + \text{X} - \text{M}$

The behavioural relationships underlying the equilibrium condition are:

(2) $\text{C} = a + (c\ \text{NI}) - \text{T}$ Consumption function
(3) $\text{T} = t\ \text{NI}$ Taxation function
(4) $\text{M} = b + m\ \text{NI}$ Import function

The letters a and b denote the intercept term in the consumption and import equations respectively. The coefficients c, t and m show how C, T and M react to changes in NI. The consumption function here differs from the over-simplified multiplier formula given above in that consumer expenditure is determined by gross income and by taxation. Previously, consumer expenditure depended only on gross income. Here the consumption function states that a change in gross income affects consumer expenditure via c whereas a change in taxation has a *direct* effect on consumer expenditure. In the next section we examine the case where consumer expenditure depends on disposable income, that is, gross income minus taxation.

Substitute equation (3) into equation (2).

(5) $\text{C} = (a + c\ \text{NI}) - (t\ \text{NI})$

or

(6) $\text{C} = a + (c - t)\text{NI}$

Substitute equations (6) and (4) into the equilibrium condition (1).

(7) $\text{GNP} = a + (c - t)\text{NI} + \text{I} + \text{G} + \text{X} - b - (m\ \text{NI})$

Bring the terms involving NI over to the left-hand side and assume GNP = NI.

(8) $\text{GNP} - (c - t - m)\text{GNP} = a - b + \text{I} + \text{G} + \text{X}$

or

(9)   GNP(1 - c + t + m) = a - b + I + G + X

Recall that s = 1 - c

(10) GNP(s + t + m) = a - b + I + G + X

Divide both sides by the term in brackets:

(11) GNP = [1/(s + t + m)] × (a - b + I + G + X)

The term [1/(s + t + m)] is the multiplier formula when savings, taxation and import leakages are allowed for. Note the minus sign on the import intercept term, b, indicates that an increase in imports, not brought about by a change in national income, will decrease GNP via the multiplier formula. As before, an increase in a, I, G or X will increase GNP via the multiplier formula and vice versa.

Deriving the multiplier formula when consumer expenditure depends on disposable income Again the notation c, s, t and m is used to denote the marginal propensity to consume (MPC), the marginal propensity to save (MPS), the marginal propensity to tax (MPT) and the marginal propensity to import (MPM) respectively. The equilibrium condition is:

(1) $GNP = C + I + G + X - M$

The behavioural relationships underlying the equilibrium condition are:

(2) $C = a + c(NI - T)$ Consumption function
(3) $T = t\,NI$ Taxation function
(4) $M = b + m\,NI$ Import function

As before, the symbols a and b denote the intercept term in the consumption and import equations respectively. The coefficients c, t and m show how C, T and M react to changes in NI. The consumption function indicates that consumer expenditure is determined by *disposable income*, NI - T. Unlike the consumption function in the previous section, changes in taxation now affect consumer expenditure via the C.

Substitute equation (3) into equation (2).

(5) $C = a + c(NI - t\,NI)$

or

(6) $C = a + c(1 - t)NI$

Substitute equations (6) and (4) into identity (1).

(7) $GNP = a + c(1 - t)NI + I + G + X - b - (m\,NI)$

Bring the terms involving NI over to the left-hand side and assume GNP = NI.

(8) $GNP - c(1 - t)GNP + (m\,GNP) = a - b + I + G + X$

Rearrange

(9) $GNP[1 - c + (ct) + m] = a - b + I + G + X$

Recall that MPS = 1 - c

(10)   GNP[s + (ct) + m] = a - b + I + G + X

Divide both sides by the term in square brackets:

(11)   GNP = [1/(s + (ct) + m)] × [a - b + I + G + X]

The term [1/(s + (ct) + m)] is the multiplier formula when savings, taxation and import leakages are allowed for and when the consumption function depends on disposable income. Note the minus sign on the import intercept term, b, indicates that an increase in imports, not brought about by a change in national income, will decrease GNP via the multiplier formula. As before, an increase in a, I, G or X will increase GNP via the multiplier formula.

Many more complex multiplier formulae can be derived. One that is of some interest is the *balanced budget multiplier* which shows that an equal increase in tax revenue and government expenditure has a multiplier of 1, and not zero as might be expected. Some textbooks elaborate multiplier formulae, presumably in the belief that a bit of algebra is good for the soul! However, it is far more important that the student understands the basic concepts, and the issues at stake, in the application of the Keynesian model, than that he or she spends a lot of time refining the multiplier formulae.

Appendix 2

Conditions under which the debt/GNP ratio is stabilised

In Chapter 4 we used the following notation:

r	=	the rate of interest on the national debt
D	=	the level of the national debt at the start of the period
GNP	=	gross national product in current prices
NT	=	net taxes, that is, the excess of tax revenue over transfer payments
G	=	government consumption expenditure
P	=	G - NT = the primary deficit
$g = \Delta$ GNP/GNP	=	the growth rate of nominal GNP
d = D/GNP	=	the initial debt/GNP ratio

Now, ignoring for simplicity the government's borrowing for capital purposes, the fiscal deficit equals the change in the national debt,

$$(1) \quad \Delta D = G - NT + rD$$

The change in the national debt is equal to government expenditure minus net taxes plus the interest on the national debt. Given that the primary deficit is equal to G - NT, substitute into (2) to obtain:

$$(2) \quad \Delta D = P + rD$$

Multiply and divide P by GNP to obtain:

$$(3) \quad \Delta D = [(P/GNP) \times GNP] + rD$$

Let p = P/GNP, that is , the primary deficit as a proportion of GNP. Hence:

$$(4) \quad \Delta D = p \times GNP + rD$$

Divide both sides by D to obtain:

$$(5) \quad \Delta D/D = p \times GNP/D + r$$

or

$$(6) \quad \Delta D/D = p/d + r$$

Now the rate of growth of D/GNP, d, is equal to the difference between the rates of growth of Y and D, that is,

(7) $\Delta d/d = \Delta D/D - \Delta GNP/GNP)$

Substitute (6) into (7) and using g to denote $\Delta GNP/GNP$:

(8) $\Delta d/d = p/d + r - g$

Now a *sustainable* fiscal policy is one consistent with a stable or declining debt-to-income ratio, that is, $\Delta d/d \leq 0$. It follows, therefore, that a sustainable policy implies:

(9) $p/d + r - g \leq 0$

Rearranging we obtain

(10) $-p \leq (r-g)d$

In words this says that for a fiscal policy not to lead to an ever increasing burden of taxation to service an ever growing national debt, it is necessary that there be a primary budget *surplus* (that is, -p) equal to or greater than the difference between the rate of interest and the rate of growth of income multiplied by the initial ratio of debt to income.

Chapter 5

The Public Finances and Fiscal Policy in Ireland

5.1   Introduction

As we saw in Chapters 2 and 4, the Keynesian theory of fiscal policy suggests that the public sector contribution to aggregate demand may be used to offset fluctuations in private consumption, investment and export demand. If successfully pursued, this approach will move output closer to the full employment level and help to keep it growing in line with its potential. In this chapter we examine the record of fiscal policy in Ireland over the years since 1972 and try to establish whether it has contributed to the goal of maintaining a high level of output and employment. We start with an examination of the trend in public spending, taxation, and borrowing. Then we examine the impact of fiscal policy on the economy and conclude by discussing the outlook for fiscal policy in Ireland.

5.2   The Growth of Government Spending and Taxation

In Ireland, the government's budget is divided into a current and a capital account. Current expenditure is of a day-to-day nature and no fixed assets are created. Details of this expenditure are presented each year prior to the budget in the book of *Estimates for the Public Services*. Current revenue is income from taxes and state-owned enterprises. Details of receipts from the individual taxes are published each year immediately before the budget in the *Estimates of Receipts and Expenditure*. A current budget deficit (CBD) arises if current expenditure exceeds current revenue.

Capital expenditure involves the creation of assets such as schools, hospitals and roads. The details of the government's capital spending are set out each year in the *Public Capital Programme* (PCP), which is published prior to the budget. Capital revenue consists of interest on stocks owned by government, loan repayments and capital grants received from the EC. Details are published in the pre-*Budget Estimates*. The excess of the central government's capital expenditure over capital revenue is called *exchequer borrowing for capital* purposes.

Table 5.1

The government's budget and the public sector borrowing requirement

	1972	*1981*	*1992*
		(per cent of GNP)	
A1. Current expenditure	29.4	44.0	38.9
A2. Current revenue	29.1	36.6	37.5
A = A2 - A1. Current budget deficit	0.3	7.4	1.4
B1. Exchequer capital expenditure	6.5	17.4	6.6
B2. Exchequer capital revenue	0.1	8.9	5.6
B = B2 - B1. Exchequer borrowing for capital purposes	7.2	8.5	1.0
(C) Exchequer borrowing requirement (EBR), (A + B)	7.4	15.9	2.4
(D) Borrowing by state-sponsored bodies and local authorities	2.0	4.4	1.2
(E) Public sector borrowing requirement (PSBR), (C + D)	8.6	20.3	3.6

Source: *Budget Book*, 1990.

Note: These data are on a budgetary classification and differ from NIE data in Table 5.2. Social security revenue and expenditure and other "extra-budgetary funds" are not included in the budget but are treated as government revenue and expenditure in the NIE tables.

Table 5.1 presents a summary of the government's current and capital budgets for 1972, 1981 and 1992. The sum of the current and capital budget deficits (subtotals A and B) is the *exchequer borrowing requirement* (EBR). This is the total amount of money the central government must borrow to cover the excess of its spending over revenue. When borrowing by state-sponsored bodies and local authorities is added to the EBR we obtain the *public sector borrowing requirement* (PSBR). Details of all these are published in the tables that accompany each year's budget. (The classification of government revenue and expenditure in the budget differs somewhat from the way these are treated in the national income accounts.)

The PSBR is the widest measure of the public sector's contribution to aggregate demand, and changes in the PSBR are a broad indicator of the stance of fiscal policy. Later in this chapter we shall look at more refined indicators. We turn now to an examination of the trends in government expenditure, revenue, and borrowing.

Current expenditure From Table 5.1 it is clear that current spending rose very sharply relative to GNP during the 1970s and then stabilised during the 1980s. In Table 5.2 we summarise the trend in the main components of government current expenditure. In this table we use the national income rather than the budget classifications, because the former correspond more closely with the components of aggregate demand we introduced in Chapter 4. The largest proportional increases occurred in national debt interest, followed by transfer payments (which we labelled B in Chapter 4). The share of current expenditure on goods and services (labelled G in Chapter 4) in GNP also increased, but less dramatically. There was a marginal decrease in subsidies relative to GNP after 1980.

Table 5.2
Public sector current receipts and expenditure: percentage of GNP

	1962	1972	1980	1989
Current receipts				
Taxes on income	7.2	11.9	18.1	21.9
Taxes on expenditure	14.9	18.4	16.4	19.1
All other current income	4.0	4.2	5.0	5.4
Total	26.1	34.5	39.5	46.4
Current expenditure				
Current subsidies	3.6	4.2	4.0	1.6
National debt interest	2.8	3.7	6.8	9.8
Transfer payments	6.2	9.3	13.4	16.5
Expenditure on goods and services	12.8	15.9	21.7	19.2
Total	25.4	33.1	45.9	47.1

Source: *National Income and Expenditure*, 1990, Central Statistics Office, 1991, and Department of Finance databank of economic time series.

Although the growth of government consumption, G, was not as dramatic as that of national debt interest and transfer payments, none the less some heads of expenditure grew very rapidly. For example, between 1977 and the early 1980s total public sector employment rose by 17 per cent, and employment in the health services and in education increased by 27 per cent and 22 per cent, respectively. There is a ratchet effect in public sector employment: once it has been increased it is extremely difficult to reduce it. Table 5.3 looks at the trends in some "big ticket" heads of current spending between 1986 and 1990, both years expressed in 1990 prices. These years are chosen for comparison because over this period the current budget deficit was reduced from 8.3 to 0.7 per cent of GNP and the volume of current government expenditure declined by 8.5 per cent. But despite the widespread impression that there were savage cuts in spending on health and education over this period, both actually rose in real terms. Much of this increase was due to higher levels of pay: the numbers employed in these sectors declined. The sharp increase in debt service in real terms is also notable. Spending on other items fell by over a quarter in real terms: the Departments of Agriculture, Labour, the Environment and the smaller ministries experienced significant reductions in current spending over this period.

Table 5.3
Principal heads of government current expenditure: constant 1990 prices

| | 1986 | | 1990 | |
	£ m	%	£ m	%
Service of the public debt	2,240	24.6	2,300	27.3
Social welfare	1,728	19.0	1,487	17.6
Health	1,232	13.5	1,253	14.9
Education	1,028	11.3	1,122	13.3
Garda Siochana	296	3.2	294	3.5
Defence	285	3.1	283	3.3
Other	2,299	25.2	1,682	20.0
Total current expenditure	9,108	100.0	8,421	100.0

Source: *Budget Booklet*, 1986 and 1990.

Despite the attempt to cut government current spending after 1986, the level of employment in the public sector declined by only 9,682 or 5.6 per cent between 1986 and 1990 (Table 5.4), while the public sector wage bill as a percentage of GNP only fell from 15.5 per cent in 1986 to 15.0 in 1992. Moreover, a high price had to be paid for the modest reduction in the numbers employed. The cost of voluntary redundancy or early retirement in the public service was £12,658 per employee over the period 1986-89. (In 1990 this soared to £31,847 per employee, but the level of redundancies fell.)

Capital spending We can see from Table 5.1 that government capital spending increased very dramatically relative to GNP during the 1970s and then declined during the 1980s. In 1981 over 17 per cent of GNP was being invested by the public sector, an exceptionally high proportion by international standards. Unfortunately, much of this investment was in loss-making state companies and in projects that did not yield an adequate return to the country. The scale of public capital spending was sharply reduced during the 1980s, due to the completion of many of the large projects started in the early 1980s, such as the Moneypoint power station, the Dublin Cork gas pipeline and the Dublin Area Rapid Transit (DART), and the reduction in capital injections into ailing state-sponsored bodies. Allowing the PCP to shrink proved to be a more palatable way of reducing the overall PSBR than curbing the current budget deficit.

Table 5.4
Public sector employment and redundancy

	Public service pay bill £ m	Public service numbers	Numbers voluntarily leaving the public sector	Average cost per early leaver £
1986	2,625	184,717		
1987	2,759	179,578	1,190	7,072
1988	2,845	170,827	7,332	13,071
1989	2,914	170,742	1,003	17,832
1990	3,160	172,750	157	31,847
1991	3,444	n.a.	n.a	n.a.
1992	3,726	n.a.	n.a	n.a.

Source: *Estimates for the Public Services*, 1991, and *Budget Booklet* 1990.
Note : NA denotes not available.

Changes in the PCP have a disproportionate effect on the level of activity in the building and construction sector. The numbers at work in the building industry rose by 23 per cent between 1976 and 1980 and then fell by 32 per cent between 1980 and 1988. Clearly, those employed in this sector do not enjoy the degree of job security that exists in the public sector. The construction sector is inherently prone to wide cyclical fluctuations and changes in the government's capital budget during the past two decades amplified these fluctuations.

Current revenue When we turn to the revenue side of the public sector's accounts, the growth in the burden of taxation relative to GNP is striking. The basic data are shown in Tables 5.1, 5.2 and 5.5 and summarised in Figure 5.1. There has been a persistent increase in the ratio of taxation to GNP since the early 1960s, and this trend accelerated after 1977. From Table 5.2 it may be seen that the proportion of GNP taken in *taxes on income and wealth* (including social security contributions) more than trebled between 1962 and 1989. This led to a very heavy burden of taxation on employees liable to PAYE, who contributed almost 61 per cent of all income and wealth tax paid in 1989. Although the proportion of GNP taken by *taxes on expenditure* or *indirect taxes* rose over the period, their share in total taxation fell. They have been overtaken by income taxes as the major source of revenue to the government. Part of the reason for this is the declining revenue from customs duties with the dismantling of protectionism over the 1970s and 1980s. The abolition of rates on residential property in the late 1970s also contributed to the reduced importance of indirect taxes.

Table 5.5 compares the yield of the three largest heads of taxation in 1972 and 1991 using constant 1991 prices. The fastest growth has been recorded in the yield of the corporate profits tax. Many of the tax concessions given to firms in the 1970s are now being phased out. Revenue from VAT has also been very buoyant. This is an *ad valorem* tax, levied as a percentage of the price of the taxed items, whose yield rises automatically with inflation. In addition the rates of VAT were increased repeatedly from its introduction in 1972 until the mid-1980s. The yield of income tax has also increased impressively in real terms. Income tax receipts rise automatically as incomes increase if the tax allowances and bands are not adjusted to compensate for inflation. During the 1970s and 1980s failure to adjust fully for inflation increased the real burden of income tax dramatically. Social insurance contributions (which are treated as a tax in the National Accounts but not included in the budget) have increased very rapidly as more and more income has been made subject to this levy and higher rates of contribution have been introduced. *Excise duties* are mostly specific taxes (that is, levied in terms of so much per unit) and have to be adjusted to prevent inflation eroding their real value. It is clear from the growth of the yield of this tax that successive ministers for finance have imposed higher excises on the "old reliables" (tobacco, drink and petrol) in their budgets.

Table 5.5
Yield of the major taxes, 1972 and 1991 (both at 1991 prices)

	1972 £ millions	1991 £ millions	% increase
Income tax	1,153	3,184	176
VAT etc.	671	2,090	211
Excise duties	690	1,750	153
Social insurance contributions	386	1,529	296
Corporate profits tax	141	527	274
Customs duties	773	125	-84

Source: Budget Booklets and *NIE*.

Taxation: international comparisons The burden of taxation must never be lost sight of in discussions of macroeconomic policy in Ireland. The high level of taxation and its uneven pattern impose a considerable deadweight burden on the economy and entail serious welfare losses.[1] During the 1980s the reduction in

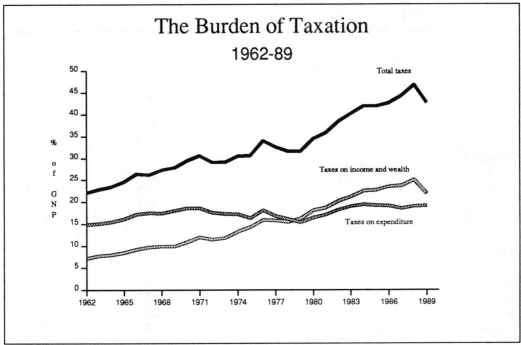

The Burden of Taxation

1962-89

Total taxes

Taxes on income and wealth

Taxes on expenditure

Figure 5.1   Taxes as a percentage of GNP

disposable income due to higher taxation fuelled inflationary wage claims and impaired the country's international competitiveness.

A trend towards heavier taxation was widespread throughout the western world during the 1970s and 1980s. However, the burden of taxation rose more rapidly in Ireland than in most other countries, with the result that we moved up the international taxation "league table". Table 5.6 compares the level of taxation, relative to GNP, in Ireland with that in other OECD countries in 1965 and 1988. Over this period Ireland moved from below to above the average of the OECD countries. Furthermore, it is striking that the countries whose burden of taxation was as heavy as Ireland's in 1988 were all much wealthier. By comparison with other countries at a similar income level, such as Spain, Greece and Portugal, the burden of taxation in Ireland is exceptionally heavy.

From the perspective of incentives to work and save *marginal* tax rates are more relevant than the aggregate measure of the burden of taxation presented in Table 5.6. In Ireland in 1992 a single worker becomes liable to the higher rate of income tax (48 per cent) on income in excess of £9,575. In addition, social insurance contributions must be paid at the rate of 7.5 per cent. A single man earning the average industrial wage (£270 weekly) is consequently liable to a marginal tax rate of 55.5 per cent. Such a high marginal income tax rate does not apply at a comparable income level in any other OECD country.

119

Table 5.6
Total tax revenue as a percentage of GDP

	1965	1988
Sweden	35.4	55.3
Denmark	29.9	52.1
Netherlands	33.2	48.2
Norway	33.3	46.9
Belgium	30.8	45.1
France	34.5	44.4
Austria	34.7	41.9
Ireland	*26.0*	*41.5*
Germany	31.6	37.4
Italy	25.5	37.1
Greece	20.6	35.9
Portugal	18.4	34.6
Canada	25.4	34.0
Spain	14.5	32.8
Switzerland	20.7	32.5
Japan	18.3	31.3
Australia	23.2	30.8
US	25.9	29.8
Turkey	15.0	22.9
Unweighted average:		
OECD Total	26.7	38.4
OECD Europe	27.5	39.9

Source: OECD, *Revenue Statistics*, 1989, Table 4.
Note: Tax revenue includes social security contributions.

Moreover, in addition to this high rate of income tax, the level of indirect taxes in Ireland is now significantly above the OECD average. In the EC, Denmark is the only country where rates of VAT and excise duties are generally higher than in Ireland. One consequence of the widening of the gap between Irish and UK rates of indirect taxation during the 1980s was large-scale cross-border smuggling and importation from Northern Ireland.

The high level of taxation relative to the EC countries has made it difficult for the government to finance the growth in expenditure we outlined in the previous section by increasing tax revenue. As a result, during the late 1970s and early 1980s, recourse was had to borrowing on a large scale. We now examine the implications of this.

5.3 Borrowing and the Growth of the National Debt

Government borrowing Before 1973 Ireland government budgets were framed so as to "balance the books". However, this was interpreted as requiring only that current revenue should match current expenditure; borrowing for capital purposes was condoned on the grounds that it resulted in the creation of valuable assets. As a result we had accumulated a significant national debt by the early 1970s. However, due to a combination of fairly rapid growth in GNP and low real rates of interest, the ratio of debt to GNP declined from over 70 per cent in the early 1960s to 54 per cent in 1972. (In Chapter 4 we discussed the parameters that determine the trend in this ratio.) We saw from Table 5.1 how the growth of current and capital spending outstripped the growth of revenue from taxation and other sources during the 1970s. As a result very large current and capital budget deficits were incurred. Table 5.7 shows the trend in the current budget deficit (CBD), the exchequer borrowing requirement (EBR) and the public sector borrowing requirement (PSBR) since 1972. (The difference between the CBD and the EBR is government borrowing for capital purposes.) It may be seen that the CBD rose from less than 1 per cent of GNP in 1972 to over 7 per cent in 1981, when borrowing for capital purposes was at a record level of 8.5 per cent of GNP, and borrowing by state-sponsored companies amounted to 4.4 per cent. The PSBR totalled a record 20 per cent in this year, more than double what it had been ten years earlier.

Borrowing for capital purposes and by stated sponsored companies was at a peak in 1981, and declined from 12.9 per cent of GNP in 1981 to less than 1.9 per cent in 1989. This was made possible by a scaling down of the PCP, by the increased contribution of the European Regional Development Fund to infrastructure projects and by bringing the losses of the state-sponsored companies under control. It took longer and proved harder to bring the CBD under control. We examine the reasons for this later in the chapter.

As a result of the high level of government borrowing, the level of its debt (excluding borrowing by state-sponsored bodies) rose from £1,251 million in 1972 to £25,400 million in 1992. Relative to GNP it reached a peak of 129 per cent in 1987 (Table 5.8 and Figure 5.2). The interest on this debt reached 12.5 per cent of GNP or 93.5 of the yield of the income tax in 1985. Since the mid-1980s both the debt and debt service have declined slowly relative to GNP.[2] However, heavy interest payments will continue to be required to service the national debt well into the next century.

Table 5.7

The public sector borrowing requirement and its components, 1972-91

	Current budget deficit		Exchequer borrowing requirement (EBR)		Public sector borrowing requirement (PSBR)	
	£ m	% of GNP	£ m	% of GNP	£ m	% of GNP
1972	6	0.3	151	6.6	197	8.6
1973	10	0.4	206	7.5	248	9.0
1974	93	-	334	-	385	-
1975	259	6.8	601	15.8	672	17.7
1976	201	4.4	506	11.0	595	12.9
1977	201	3.6	545	9.7	697	12.5
1978	397	6.1	810	12.4	973	14.9
1979	522	6.8	1,009	13.2	1,230	16.1
1980	547	6.1	1,218	13.5	1,559	17.3
1981	802	7.4	1,721	15.9	2,204	20.3
1982	988	7.9	1,945	15.6	2,466	19.8
1983	960	7.1	1,756	12.9	2,277	16.7
1984	1,039	7.0	1,825	12.4	2,375	16.1
1985	1,284	8.2	2,015	12.8	2,444	15.5
1986	1,395	8.3	2,145	12.8	2,506	14.9
1987	1,180	6.5	1,786	9.9	2,056	11.4
1988	317	1.7	619	3.3	751	4.0
1989	263	1.3	479	2.3	667	3.2
1990	152	0.7	462	2.0	681	3.0
1991	300	1.3	510	2.1	816	3.5
1992	339	1.4	592	2.4	884	3.6

Source: Various *Budget Books*.

Notes:

(1) Data for 1988 includes once-off tax amnesty receipts. If these receipts are excluded the current budget deficit, the EBR and the PSBR equal 4.3, 5.9 and 6.6 of GNP respectively.

(2) Data for 1991 are the provisional out-turn and for 1992 the post-budget estimate.

(3) 1974 was a nine-month period as the accounts switched from a calendar to a financial year.

(4) Debt service consists primarily of interest paid on outstanding debt. It also includes the small amount paid to a *sinking fund* from which some of the principal is repaid. This is subtracted from current spending when the borrowing requirement is calculated.

Table 5.8
Government debt and debt service, 1972-1991

	Government debt £ m	Government debt to GNP ratio	Annual debt service £ m	Debt service as a % of GNP	Debt service as a % of income tax
1972	1,251	54.7	100	4.3	n.a.
1973	1,421	51.8	109	3.9	n.a.
1974	1,622	64.4	126	4.1	n.a.
1975	2,651	69.8	195	5.1	n.a.
1976	3,612	80.1	278	8.2	60.2
1977	4,229	79.2	334	6.3	64.0
1978	5,167	79.1	418	6.4	69.1
1979	6,540	85.7	514	6.7	70.2
1980	7,896	87.7	661	7.3	65.2
1981	10,195	93.9	885	8.2	71.2
1982	11,669	93.7	1,249	10.0	85.6
1983	14,392	105.9	1,456	10.7	87.5
1984	16,821	113.7	1,705	11.5	86.7
1985	18,502	117.9	1,967	12.5	93.5
1986	21,611	128.0	1,989	11.9	83.3
1987	23,691	129.0	2,118	11.7	78.1
1988	24,610	128.0	2,141	11.4	76.8
1989	24,828	117.1	2,141	10.3	76.2
1990	25,100	110.0	2,300	10.0	76.1
1991	25,400	107.0	2,409	10.3	74.6
1992	n.a.	n.a.	2,411	9.7	70.8

Source: Various *Budget Books*.
Notes: 1. Debt service includes interest and payments to sinking.
2. The data do not include debt incurred by local authorities and state-sponsored bodies.
3. "1974" was a nine-month period as the accounts were changed from a calendar to a financial year.
n.a. = not available.

Figure 5.3 compares the Irish debt/GNP ratio with that prevailing in some other OECD countries. It is clear that Ireland's situation is quite exceptional. Only Belgium approaches the Irish level of indebtedness relative to income.

Note:
National debt interest payments are part of current expenditure, while principal repayments are capital expenditure. In the national accounts tables, national debt interest paid to Irish residents is classified as a transfer payment, whereas interest paid to non-residents is classified as a factor payment.

The composition of the national debt in 1990 is shown in Table 5.9. Government bonds and stocks issued in Irish pounds account for 50 per cent of the

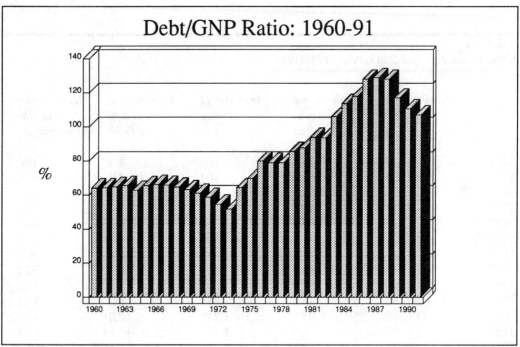

Debt/GNP Ratio: 1960-91

Figure 5.2 Debt/GNP ratio

total debt, short term exchequer bills account for 3.5 per cent, and stocks issued in foreign currencies account for a further 34 per cent. Various types of small savings schemes (of which the most important are Savings Certificates) account for the remainder.

It is the convention to divide this debt into "domestic" and "external" with reference to the currencies in which it is denominated. "Domestic" debt is issued in, and will be redeemed in Irish pounds; "external" debt is denominated in, and has to be redeemed in, foreign currencies. To obtain a complete picture of the government's external liabilities, however, account should also be taken of the "domestic" debt that is owned by non-residents. In recent years foreign investors, Germans in particular, have purchased sizeable amounts of Irish government securities because the yield on them was attractive relative to that obtainable in other countries. When the £3,859 million held in this manner and the external liabilities of the state-sponsored bodies are added to the government debt denominated in foreign currencies a figure for the total external liabilities of the public sector of £14,919 million is obtained for 1990. Paying the interest on this externally held debt involves a transfer of income abroad. Furthermore the Irish government is vulnerable to the effects of exchange rate changes on the debt that is denominated in foreign currencies. (However, about one third of this external debt is in deutsche marks (DMs), a currency with which we are linked through the European Monetary System.)

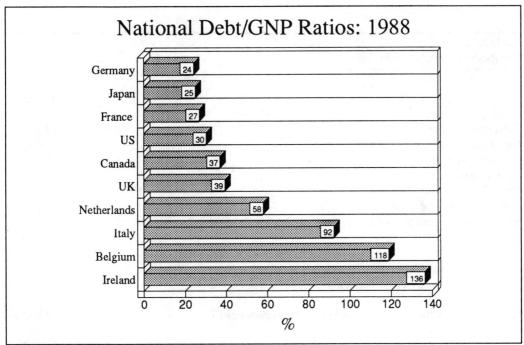

National Debt/GNP Ratios: 1988

Country	%
Germany	24
Japan	25
France	27
US	30
Canada	37
UK	39
Netherlands	58
Italy	92
Belgium	118
Ireland	136

%

Figure 5.3 Debt to GNP ratio for selected countries

From Table 5.10 it may be seen that government external debt increased from £107 million or 4.7 per cent of GNP to a peak of £9,693 million or 53.7 per cent of GNP in 1987. Between 1987 and 1990, debt denominated in foreign currencies decreased to £8,861 million, equivalent to 33 per cent of total debt or 38 per cent of GNP. However, during these years there was an increase in the externally held domestic debt, from £830 million in 1984 to £4,110 million in 1991, so that the external liabilities of the government are now at an all-time high of £12,990 million. Interest on the externally held debt increased from £7 million in 1972 to £795 million, or 4.9 per cent of GNP, in 1985. It continued to grow in absolute terms to reach £1,009 million in 1990, but declined to 3.2 per cent of GNP.

Note:
In order to minimise the cost of servicing the national debt, the government established the National Treasury Management Agency (NTMA) in 1990. A separate unit within NTMA is responsible for the management of the exchange rate risk related to the debt.

Table 5.9
Composition of public debt, 1990

	£ millions
Government stocks (i.e. bonds)	13,198
Exchequer bills	928
Savings certificates	1,112
Prize bonds	86
Index-linked savings bonds	309
National instalment saving	142
Exchequer overdraft at the Central Bank	0
Other	1,810
(A) Total domestic debt	17,585
(A1), of which, held by non-residents	3,859
(B) External government debt (stocks in foreign currencies)	8,862
(C = A + B) Total government debt	26,447
(D) External liabilities of state-sponsored bodies	2,198
(E = C + D) Total public sector debt	28,645
(F = A 1 + B + D) Total external liabilities of the public sector	14,919

Source: Central Bank of Ireland, *Quarterly Bulletin* Autumn 1991, Tables D1, D2 and D8.

The burden of a country's external debt can be roughly gauged by studying the ratio of interest paid on external debt to GNP. This ratio rose from virtually zero in the early 1970s to a peak of 4.9 per cent in 1985. By the end of the 1980s it had fallen to about 3 per cent. By comparison with many of the debt-distressed developing countries, this ratio has remained low in Ireland because exports have continued to grow rapidly over the years. As a result there is no uncertainty about our ability to honour our international debt service obligations.

Table 5.10
Government external debt, 1972-90

	External debt £ m	External debt as a % of total debt	External debt as a % of GNP	Interest on the external debt £ m	Interest on the external debt as a % of GNP
1972	107	8.6	4.7	7	0.3
1973	126	8.9	4.6	9	0.0
1974	311	8.9	4.6	9	0.0
1975	471	17.7	12.4	33	0.1
1976	1,040	28.8	23.0	53	1.1
1977	1,039	24.6	19.4	95	1.4
1978	1,064	20.6	16.3	131	1.4
1979	1,542	23.6	20.2	154	1.3
1980	2,207	28.0	24.5	193	1.8
1981	3,794	37.2	34.9	266	2.3
1982	5,248	45.0	42.1	526	4.1
1983	6,899	47.9	50.7	597	4.2
1984	8,740	59.0	53.4	720	4.7
1985	9,022	48.7	51.7	795	4.9
1986	10,337	47.8	61.1	761	4.2
1987	11,451	48.3	62.5	804	3.9
1988	12,163	49.4	63.1	894	3.6
1989	12,790	51.5	60.1	973	3.4
1990	12,720	48.0	55.5	1,009	3.2
1991	12,990	51.1	52.4	n.a.	n.a.

Source: *Budget Book*, 1990; the Central Bank of Ireland, *Annual Report,* 1991, Table D2; and Michael Somers, "The Management of Ireland's National Debt", paper read to the Statistical and Social Inquiry Society of Ireland, 13 February 1992, Table 4. Interest on the external debt from 1977 onwards taken from *NIE* Balance of Payments tables.
Note: "External" debt includes all debt held by non-residents, regardless of currency denomination.

5.4   The Stance of Fiscal Policy

Against the background of these trends in revenue we now examine how fiscal policy has been conducted in Ireland since the beginning of the 1970s.[3]   Initially we shall assess the *stance of fiscal policy* primarily by looking at changes in borrowing. In a later section we shall discuss more refined measures.

1972-77   The year 1973 was a watershed in western economic history.   The Organisation of Petroleum Exporting Countries (OPEC) raised crude oil prices from $3 to $12 a barrel. This was a severe shock to both the demand and the supply sides

127

of economies dependent on imported energy. On the demand side, the enormous price rise greatly increased expenditure on imports because there was little scope in the short run for reducing dependence on imported energy. An increase in imports reduces aggregate demand and has a deflationary impact on the economy. On the supply side, the dramatic increase in the cost of a basic input had the effect of shifting the aggregate supply schedule to the left, leading to a fall in output and a rise in prices. Moreover the increase in the *relative* price of energy rendered a large amount of the western world's existing capital equipment inappropriate and made investment in new, energy-efficient processes a matter of urgency. Governments were quicker to recognise and respond to the deflationary implications of the oil price shock than to its implications for the supply side of the economy. In fact it was not until after the second oil price shock, at the end of the 1970s, that investment in energy conservation began in earnest.

In Ireland the immediate reaction to the increase in oil prices in 1972-73 was to try to maintain the level of aggregate demand in the face of a sharp increase in the level of imports by increasing government spending without any corresponding increase in the level of taxation. We have seen that the PSBR increased from 8.6 per cent in 1972 to 17.7 per cent of GNP in 1975. Much of this deterioration in the public finances was due to the growth of the current budget deficit, which rose to 6.8 per cent of GNP in 1975. Increased borrowing for capital purposes and a growing current budget deficit were justified as a Keynesian response to a demand-side shock. However, in 1975 the government recognised the need to dampen the inflationary pressures that were building up. Food subsidies and tax cuts were introduced in a mini-budget in mid-1975 in the hope that this would moderate wage inflation. In fact it increased the current budget deficit and added to the inflationary pressures. In a reversal of policy in 1976 the Minister for Finance (Richie Ryan) raised taxes and curbed expenditure as the economy began to recover. (This earned him the title "Minister for Hardship" and "Red Richie" in the media.) The measures announced in the 1976 Budget, together with the unexpectedly rapid growth of the economy during the year, reduced the PSBR to 12.9 per cent and the current budget deficit to 4.4 per cent of GNP. By 1977 the PSBR and the current budget deficit had fallen to 12.5 per cent and 3.6 per cent of GNP, respectively.

By 1977 the economy had weathered the first oil crisis and the public finances were at least moving in the right direction. But in fact the structural problems created by the oil price shock remained unresolved and Ireland, like those of most other OECD countries, was still vulnerable to further shocks due to its continued dependence on imported oil and the failure to eliminate the fiscal deficit that had emerged for the first time in the early 1970s.

1977-81 The General Election of 1977 destroyed the chances of further progress towards restoring order to the public finances. The political parties vied with one another in promising to cut taxes and raise expenditure. (Both major parties claim credit for having promised to abolish rates on private houses and put nothing in their place.) The incoming Fianna Fáil government exceeded their Manifesto commitments to cut taxes and increase expenditure. The measures introduced by the Minister for Finance, George Colley, in the 1978 budget added about 1.5 per cent of GNP to the current budget deficit and increased the projected EBR to 13 per cent of GNP. (In the course of the budget speech the minister pointed out that this was "exactly as specified in the [election] manifesto".) A total of 11,250 new posts were authorised in the public sector between mid-1977 and the end of 1978. This occurred at a time when the economy was already growing at an unsustainable rate: real GNP expanded by 7.0 per cent in 1977 and was forecast to continue to grow rapidly in 1978 even if there had been no fiscal stimulus. The numbers at work increased by 1.8 per cent from April 1977 to April 1978, real earnings grew by 3.3 per cent in 1977 and 6.5 per cent in 1978, and for the first time ever there was substantial net *immigration* to Ireland.

The expansionary fiscal policy implemented in the 1978 budget was justified by reference to the need to reduce unemployment, which, although falling, was still above its 1973 level. This illustrates how important it is to have a working definition of the concept of "full employment", a point we shall take up again in a later chapter. It was argued that the increase in the fiscal deficit would only be a temporary expedient. It would lead to increased private sector investment which would then sustain the economic expansion. The policy was compared with launching a two-stage rocket, because it was hoped that private sector investment would rise on the back of the initial increase in government expenditure, leading to a sustained increase in the growth rate. According to this view, the higher tax revenue that would be generated by the faster growth would quickly lead to the elimination of the budget deficit without the need to raise tax rates. It was claimed that the fiscal stimulus would turn out to be self-financing over the medium term. Terms such as "pump-priming" and "self-financing fiscal boost" were used to describe this policy.[4]

Events between 1978 and 1980 confounded the hope that the budget deficit would be quickly eliminated. Real GNP grew by 5.5 per cent in 1978 but the rate of growth fell to 2.7 per cent in 1979 and remained at that level in 1980 (see Figure 5.4). The current budget deficit remained above 6 per cent of GNP and a high level of borrowing for capital purposes was maintained, bringing the PSBR to 17.3 per cent of GNP in 1980. Of even greater significance was the fact that the current account balance of payments deficit rose to 11 per cent of GNP in 1980. The Irish economy was plunging into a crisis. But even when it became clear that the logic behind the strategy adopted in 1978 was flawed, no serious attempt was made to restore balance to the public finances through tax increases or cuts in expenditure. We were therefore particularly ill-prepared to cope with the second oil price shock, which occurred in 1979, when the price of crude oil rose to over $40 a barrel. The fiscal deficit was already so large and the level of the national debt was growing so rapidly, that no scope remained for trying to offset the deflationary impact of the oil

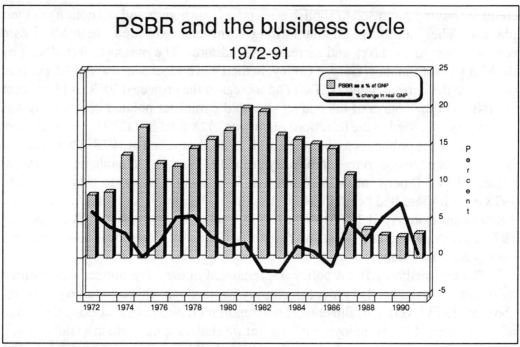

Figure 5.4 PSBR and the business cycle

price increase through an expansionary fiscal policy. The budget deficits incurred after 1973 and our resort to external borrowing to finance them had turned us into a *net debtor country* by 1980: the level of our external public debt had reached £2,207 million, whereas our official external reserves were only £1,346 million.

Note:
As we discuss in a later chapter the external reserves consist of gold, foreign currencies and credits with the International Monetary Fund and the European Monetary Cooperation Fund held by the Central Bank of Ireland. These reserves are used to stabilise the exchange rate of the Irish currency in foreign exchange markets.

In 1979 and 1980 there was little general awareness of the speed with which the country was being plunged into debt and the implications of this for the tax burden on future generations. Some economists argued that there was no need to worry about further external borrowing because our credit rating was still sound on international financial markets and additional borrowed money could be used to generate employment and create valuable assets in Ireland. But in reality much of the money that was borrowed in the 1970s was used to finance day-to-day expenditure or projects with a rate of return that was much lower than the rate of interest that had to be paid on the borrowed funds. Further borrowing for such purposes was not warranted, regardless of the willingness of international bankers to lend to the country. Moreover, as we saw in Chapter 4, the growth of public sector debt throughout eastern Europe, Africa and Latin America was to trigger off an international crisis in 1982 which completely changed the attitude of international creditors to countries in Ireland's situation.

Note:
At this time the Irish banks were eager to lend to farmers to buy additional land at very inflated prices. The bankers believed that the security of the whole farm shielded them from the speculative investments being made by their customers. In a similar fashion, international bankers seemed to draw comfort from the idea that their loans to sovereign countries were backed by the taxpayers of the countries, rather than the quality of the investments on which the money was spent. In both cases the bankers incurred significant bad debts.

1981-86 In July 1981 the new Coalition government introduced a mini-budget to try to correct the deteriorating fiscal situation. The emphasis was placed on tax increases, rather than cuts in expenditure, to reduce the deficit. This set the pattern for several subsequent attempts to restore order to the public finances. However, due to the absence of revenue buoyancy during the year the current budget deficit actually increased to 7.4 per cent of GNP, bringing the PSBR to 20.3 per cent of GNP, the highest level it ever reached. This outcome (higher taxation leading to larger rather than smaller current budget deficits) was to be repeated in subsequent years.

The financial and economic crisis continued to intensify in the course of 1981 and 1982. The balance of payments deficit reached almost 15 per cent of GNP in 1981, while government external debt doubled between the end of 1980 and the middle of 1982. Despite this extraordinary increase in foreign debt, unemployment increased by 38 per cent between April 1980 and April 1981 and by an additional 17 per cent in the next year. By the time of the general election of November 1982 (the third within 18 months) awareness of the gravity of the fiscal crisis facing the country had become widespread. The main political parties were agreed that the need to restore order to the public finances had to take precedence over other objectives, such as trying to reduce the level of unemployment. The only disagreement concerned the speed with which the current budget deficit would be phased out and the appropriate balance between higher taxation and lower expenditure to achieve this objective.

The Coalition government tried to tackle the problem over the period 1982-86 primarily by raising the level of taxation and reducing current expenditure. However, they failed to make any significant progress towards the objective of restoring balance to the public finances. They were unable to control current spending because a ban on public sector recruitment did not bring the wage bill under control and the momentum of rising unemployment and accumulating debt caused transfer payments and national debt interest to increase more rapidly than GNP. Higher tax rates did not yield more revenue due to the lack of growth in the economy and the Laffer-type effects we discussed in Chapter 4. The most striking example

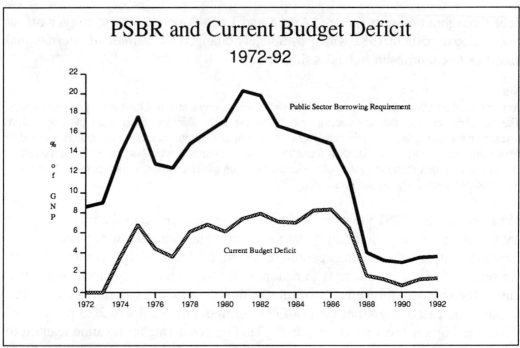

Figure 5.5 PSBR and the current budget deficit

---

of the failure of the strategy of trying to reduce the deficit by increasing the tax burden was provided by Minister for Finance Alan Dukes' 1983 budget, which set a record for the tax increases it contained, but produced hardly any reduction in the current budget deficit.

In the government's White Paper on the economy *Building on Reality 1985-87*, published at the end of 1984, the target for fiscal rectitude was changed from the elimination of the current budget deficit to the *stabilisation of the debt/GNP ratio*. While the latter is an economically more meaningful objective, the switch of goals entailed an admission that the ambitious targets that had been espoused during the 1982 election campaigns would not be attained in the foreseeable future. In fact, between 1983 and 1986 virtually no progress was made towards either goal. The PSBR only decreased from 16.7 per cent to 14.9 per cent of GNP, while the current budget deficit rose from 7.1 per cent to 8.3 per cent and the debt/GNP ratio rose from 105 per cent to 129 per cent.

During the third quarter of 1986 disappointing exchequer returns led to a loss of confidence in the economy's prospects, which was manifested in nervousness on the foreign exchange markets and a 3 per cent increase in Irish relative to UK interest rates. This episode marked the beginning of the end of the attempt to reduce the level of borrowing through higher taxation. It had become clear to all but a small minority that this strategy was proving self-defeating. The economy was shrinking under the rapidly growing burden of taxation; unemployment was continuing to rise despite the fact that emigration had resumed on a massive scale, and capital was fleeing the country for more benign tax environments. (It is estimated that the private capital outflow reached over £1 billion in 1986.)[5] The public finances were on a downward spiral due to falling revenue and rising transfer payments. It was now generally accepted that the budget deficit had to be tackled through drastic cuts in expenditure rather than further tax increases. However the Coalition government split and eventually fell on this issue. The cuts in current expenditure proposed by the Minister for Finance, John Bruton, in the draft Book of Estimates in October 1986 were not acceptable to his Labour Party partners in government, who still favoured maintaining a high level of expenditure and trying to reduce the deficit by increasing taxation.

1987-91 The formation of a minority Fianna Fáil government in January 1987 increased the uncertainty about the future course of economic policy. While in opposition the party had vehemently attacked what they had labelled the "monetarist" or "Thatcherite" policies of the Coalition government and fought the election with promises of increasing government spending. However, once in office the new government changed its policy and, with the support of the main opposition parties, tackled the problem of curbing government expenditure head-on. In the 1987 budget, the Minister for Finance, Ray MacSharry, reduced current government spending *below* the level that had been proposed by Fine Gael in the draft Book of Estimates that had led to the downfall of the Coalition government. Several factors contributed to a recovery that helped the government achieve its fiscal targets. These included the collapse of world oil prices, higher farm prices, and the accelerating growth in the UK economy, which were external in origin, and lower interest rates and an improvement in our international competitiveness which were due to the successful devaluation of the Irish pound in 1986.

The move towards fiscal rectitude gained momentum with the publication of the *Estimates for the Public Services* for 1988 in the autumn of 1987, which proposed a 3 per cent reduction in current government spending. These estimates were incorporated in the January 1988 budget, which was passed by the Dáil due to the support or abstention of the main opposition parties. As a result, in the course of 1988 the level of public expenditure declined in money terms for the first time since the 1930s.

The 1987 budget also proposed a tax amnesty (known as the Tax Incentive Scheme), with the objective of collecting £30 million in unpaid taxes. In fact during 1988 over £500 million was raised from this source and from the application of a new system of self-assessment of income tax to the self-employed. These amounts far exceeded the most optimistic forecasts. Furthermore, other sources of revenue (VAT and excises) were buoyant, and expenditure was held below the level projected in the budget. As a result of these developments the PSBR fell to 4.0 per cent and the current budget deficit to 1.7 per cent of GNP in 1988. The unexpectedly rapid progress towards restoring order to the public finances and the rise in sterling relative to the currencies of the European Monetary System (EMS) facilitated further reductions in rates of interest in Ireland even as they rose sharply in Britain. The improvement in the public finances was continued in 1989 and 1990 with the PSBR and the current budget deficit falling to 3.0 per cent and 0.7 per cent of GNP, respectively, in 1990.

In January 1991, the government and the other social partners (employers, trades unions and farmers) agreed on a *Programme for Economic and Social Progress* (PESP). The main fiscal target contained in PESP is to reduce the debt/GNP ratio to 100 per cent by 1993 while achieving a broad balance on the current budget deficit. (It also contained commitments on increasing the level of employment.) During 1991 the slow-down in economic growth led to an unplanned rise in the fiscal deficit and made the attainment of the programmed reduction in the debt/GNP ratio unlikely.

Recent developments   The performance of the Irish economy during the period 1986 to 1990 was extraordinary. Between 1986 and 1988 the PSBR as a percentage of GNP was reduced by over 10 percentage points, while the rate of growth of GNP increased markedly. This might seem to refute the Keynesian belief that the government's contribution to aggregate demand is the key influence on short-term performance of the economy. A number of alternative explanations of these developments have been put forward.

Some commentators have described this phenomenon as an *expansionary fiscal contraction* (EFC).[6] For a contraction in the fiscal deficit to have an expansionary effect on the economy it would be necessary that private sector components of aggregate demand, such as C and I, increase by *more* than the initial fall in the budget deficit. In other words, an EFC entails a multiplier effect operating in reverse. This could come about through the operation of "crowding in", the opposite of "crowding out" which we shall discuss in detail in Chapter 7. "Crowding in" could occur if lower government spending and reduced deficits led to lower interest rates which, in turn, stimulated private sector spending. However, the "crowding in" that occurs would have to be on a scale that more than offsets the reduction in aggregate demand due to the fiscal contraction and this is a very strong version of the theory.

This explanation may seem plausible in the light of the exceptional situation that obtained in Ireland in the mid- 1980s. As we have seen, the economy was facing a crisis arising from the lack of credibility of the government's commitment to restoring order to the public finances. This had led to capital flight and a widening interest rate differential between Ireland and Britain. It could be argued that once the financial markets became convinced that the government was intent on reducing the borrowing requirement, the capital outflow from Ireland subsided and this facilitated a reduction in domestic interest rates. The increased confidence and lower interest rates led to a recovery in private sector investment and consumption, which helped offset the contractionary effects of fiscal retrenchment. Another possibility is that a strong Ricardo-Barro effect (see Chapter 4) also operated, meaning that the improvement in the public sector finances led to an increase in private sector consumption as households realised that their future tax liabilities were not going to grow as calamitously as they had feared.

However, doubts may be raised about the accuracy of this version of what happened in Ireland after 1986. The proponents of this explanation tend to lose sight of the other factors that are also relevant to explaining the recovery in the Irish economy in the late 1980s. As we shall argue in a later chapter in the context of our discussion of Ireland's membership of the EMS, there was an improvement in Ireland's competitive position following the devaluation of the currency in August 1986. This contributed to an upsurge in net exports in 1987. The increase in net exports after the devaluation of 1986 can largely explain the rise in the real growth rate in 1987, without reference to the change in the stance of fiscal policy. Also the fall in real interest rates began *before* the deflationary budget of 1987. It is possible to argue that these developments induced an increase in consumer expenditure in 1988 and helped the economy to maintain the momentum of growth in 1989 *despite* the deflationary effects of the 1987 budget.

The commitment to fiscal adjustment that was evident in the period 1987-90 weakened in 1991. The Minister for Finance, Mr Albert Reynolds, in his 1991 budget provided for significant increases in public sector spending, due primarily to large special pay awards to public servants, doctors and teachers. These awards, in addition to the general pay increases agreed in the PESP, increased the public sector pay bill by more than 8 per cent in a year when inflation was running at less than 3 per cent and the numbers employed in the public sector were falling. Moreover, the 1991 budget was based on a set of macroeconomic assumptions that turned out to be over-optimistic. The projections of revenue and expenditure were based on the assumptions of 2.5 per cent growth in GNP and that the numbers on the Live Register would not rise above the December 1990 level. In fact by January 1991 it was clear that the economy was sliding into recession. This triggered higher than projected expenditure on social welfare and led to lower revenue from taxes, with the result that the current budget deficit increased to 1.5 per cent of GNP, the highest recorded since 1988.

The budget of 1992 was marked by a willingness to accept a rise in the deficit due to the high level of unemployment and the operation of the automatic stabilisers we discuss below. An attempt to reduce the growth in public sector pay by renegotiating the terms of the PESP resulted in the postponement of some of the increases until December 1992, but public sector pay has continued to increase rapidly due to the effect of special pay awards in addition to the PESP. The projected EBR of 2.4 per cent of GNP is higher than in any year since 1988.

5.5 Problems in Measuring the Stance of Fiscal Policy

So far we have taken little account of the issues we raised in Chapter 4 in our discussion of the theory of fiscal policy. While the PSBR is a comprehensive measure of the public sector's contribution to aggregate demand, we have to be cautious in drawing conclusions directly from changes in the PSBR about the stance of fiscal policy. We turn now to some of the other considerations that should be taken into account in assessing the stance of fiscal policy.

Discretionary versus automatic changes in revenue and expenditure In Chapter 4 we made the point that the PSBR is an *ex post* magnitude, that is, it reflects the impact of changes in the level of economic activity on the level of government receipts and expenditure. In assessing the stance of fiscal policy, it is desirable to net out the *automatic* effects and to isolate the changes in the deficit that are due to *discretionary* fiscal policy. An automatic deficit occurs when a slow-down in the economy leads to an increase in government spending on social welfare and lower tax revenue as people become unemployed. A discretionary budget deficit arises when the government deliberately implements a policy to change spending and taxation. It is the discretionary effects which give the best indicator of the stance of fiscal policy. It is difficult, however, to separate these effects.

In 1976, for example, the government raised taxes in order to reduce the current budget deficit, but at the same time the economy enjoyed the stimulus of renewed growth in the world economy. It is difficult to say what proportion of the reduction in the PSBR in 1976 was due to the measures included in the budget and what proportion was due to favourable external developments. Similarly, the deflationary 1983 budget was implemented at a time when the economy was moving deeper into recession. The tax increases introduced in the budget did not yield additional revenue due to the down-turn in the economy, with the result that only a slight reduction in the PSBR was achieved. Moreover, some of the decline in the level of economic activity during 1983 was itself due to the measures contained in the budget. Thus the extent to which fiscal policy was deflationary from 1981 onwards is not apparent from the unadjusted level of the current budget deficit, which continued to increase until 1987 as the recession caused interest and social welfare payments to increase and tax revenue to decline.

None the less it is possible to obtain some indication of the stance of fiscal policy from the budget. The "opening deficit" is the current budget deficit projected on the basis of existing tax rates and the levels of spending announced in the Book of Estimates. During the budget speech the minister announces changes in taxation, social welfare and other expenditure and concludes with a "post-budget estimate" of the current budget deficit. The difference between the opening and closing deficits gives some idea of whether the budget itself is expansionary or contractionary. Table 5.11 shows the figures for two important budgets, Mr Colley's expansionary one in 1978 and Mr Dukes' contractionary one in 1983. It may be seen that Mr Colley added 2.3 per cent of GNP to the projected deficit, while Mr Dukes reduced his projected deficit by a similar proportion.

A more systematic attempt to measure the stance of fiscal policy over the period 1979-83 was published in *Proposals for Plan*.[7] The approach taken was to see how built-in stabilisers such as expenditure on social welfare and tax revenue changed the level of the deficit compared with its level in a reference year (1979). The deficit adjusted for built-in stabilisers is referred to as the *structural* or *cyclically adjusted deficit*. This analysis showed that between 1979 and 1983 the structural deficit *fell* from 7.1 per cent to 3.8 per cent whereas the actual current budget deficit *increased* from 6.8 per cent to 7.1 per cent of GNP. Thus built-in stabilisers added 3.3 per cent of GNP to the current budget deficit over these years and disguised the deflationary nature of budgetary policy.

Table 5.11
Effect of budget on deficit

	Budget 1978 (% of GNP)	Budget 1983 (% of GNP)
Opening deficit	3.9	8.9
Post-budget estimate	6.2	6.6

Note: The difference between the opening and closing balances in 1983 takes account of the indirect tax increases introduced early in January, ahead of the budget.

Adjusting for the effect of inflation During periods of inflation the real value of the government's outstanding debt declines. If, for example, the inflation rate is 20 per cent and the government is paying a 23 per cent nominal rate of interest (3 per cent real return plus 20 per cent for expected inflation), then a large part of government's interest payments (which are classified as current spending) represents compensation of holders of government debt for the fall in its capital value. This is tantamount to advance repayment of principal and should be subtracted from the amount borrowed to obtain a figure for the change in real indebtedness. If this inflation adjustment had been applied to the Irish situation during the early 1980s, it would have reduced the PSBR by over 10 per cent of GNP. However, while this adjustment is of interest from the perspective of getting an accurate measure of changes in the real level of government indebtedness, it is a hypothetical exercise and not directly relevant to the measurement of the impact of the deficit on aggregate demand.[8]

Interest payments abroad   Another possible refinement to the data on the PSBR is to take into account the outflow from the economy caused by interest payments to non-residents. An increase in the deficit due to interest payments abroad clearly does not have an expansionary effect on aggregate demand in Ireland. We have seen that the growth of foreign borrowing by the Irish public sector led to a very rapid increase in interest payments to foreigners up to 1982. Although the level of foreign borrowing slowed down in the mid-1980s, the external debt and external interest payments continued to increase. In assessing the impact of fiscal policy on the economy, it should be noted that the current budget deficit *minus* interest payments to non-residents began to shrink as early as 1981. Since interest payments abroad have no effect on domestic aggregate demand, the fact that the deficit excluding these payments was falling is yet another indication of the deflationary stance of fiscal policy. In a later section we explore the trend in the borrowing requirement net of all interest payments, which has important implications for the sustainability of fiscal policy.

5.6   Evaluation of Fiscal Policy in Ireland

The first point that should be made about the experiment with fiscal activism in Ireland extending from the early 1970s to 1981 is that it did not work. While it is likely that the growth of GNP in the late 1970s was boosted above the rate that would otherwise have been achieved, this improvement proved to be short-lived. Despite, to some extent even because of, the enormous expansion of government spending and borrowing, the economy fared very badly during the 1980s. As we have noted in Chapter 3, the recession of the early 1980s was more severe and prolonged in Ireland than it was in other OECD countries. In part this was due to the need to correct the fiscal imbalances that emerged in the late 1970s and in part to the deep-seated structural problems of the Irish economy. Although there was disagreement among Irish economists at the time as to the merits of the expansionary policy that was pursued in the late 1970s and at the beginning of the 1980s, with the benefit of hindsight there is now unanimity that this episode was a very costly mistake.

There have been a few systematic attempts to evaluate Irish fiscal policy, taking account of some or all of the refinements we have just discussed. In a study of fiscal policy over the period 1972-81 based on a large-scale econometric model published by the Economic and Social Research Institute (ESRI) in 1982, the authors concluded:

Policy appears to have tended to operate in a pro-cyclical fashion during periods of expansion. For example, in 1973 and again in 1977 and 1978 it seems that fiscal policy was reinforcing the autonomous growth that was already underway. During the down-turn of 1974/75 policy was strongly counter-cyclical as it has been in the most recent recession.[9]

A similar assessment is contained in a subsequent analysis by Bradley and others,[10] which presents measures of the extent to which each budget over the period 1972-80 deviated from *fiscal neutrality* or *fiscal indexation*, that is, the level of the deficit that would have occurred if all rates of taxation, social welfare benefit and other types of spending had been held at the real levels that obtained in the base year (1967). Comparing the actual level of receipts and expenditure with these hypothetical indexed amounts provides a measure of the stance of fiscal policy: if actual expenditure was higher, or tax receipts lower, than the hypothetical level, discretionary fiscal policy is deemed to have been expansionary. Using this criterion the authors characterise the stance of fiscal policy as follows:

pre-1974	relatively inactive and neutral
1974-75	fiscal activism, counter-cyclical
1976	counter-cyclical contraction
1977-79	"an unbridled fiscal expansion which was strongly pro-cyclical"

These studies concur in giving low marks to the *timing* of the major fiscal stimulus in 1978. They believe that it tended to destabilise the economy. We have seen that discretionary fiscal policy became strongly deflationary after 1981, when the economy was contracting due to the world recession, so that once again it was strongly pro-cyclical.

We have already mentioned the way in which deficit spending leads to higher levels of taxation because of the need to service the growing national debt. In their evaluation of fiscal policy in Ireland, Bradley and others describe how increased government spending led to higher levels of taxation, which were passed on in the form of higher wages and prices because of the tendency of workers to bargain in terms of net-of-tax income. Wage and salary earners sought compensation for the fall in their disposable income through increases in pre-tax income. (Recall that because much of the additional spending went on increased debt service and transfer payments during the 1980s, the public did not see improvements in the level of public services commensurate with the higher level of taxation they had to shoulder.) The result of the higher taxation was, therefore, a reduction in the competitiveness of the traded sectors of the Irish economy, which reduced the level of employment it could provide. As a result, the expansionary fiscal policy generated no lasting increase in the level of employment. This sequence of events could be called *taxation crowding out*.

A summary analysis of the impact of fiscal policy on real output is contained in Walsh (1987).[11] He attempted to explain the growth of real GNP in Ireland in terms of the following variables: the rate of growth in GNP in the EC (a measure of world demand) and various definitions of the stance of fiscal policy in Ireland. The results indicate that changes in the structural budget deficit (that is the budget deficit adjusted for the effect of the built-in stabilisers) had a significant effect on the rate of economic growth and the level of unemployment. However, these effects were relatively small: the net effect of a reduction in the structural budget surplus of 1 per cent of GNP was to lower the rate of unemployment by only 0.4 (e.g. from 19 per cent to 18.6 per cent), while it raised the rate of growth of GNP by about 0.7 per cent. These are estimates of the short-run effects; in the longer run the expansionary effect of fiscal policy is likely to be even smaller as crowding out of one type or another occurs.

There is, therefore, a consensus that the impact of fiscal policy in Ireland is slight and that the timing of policy changes has been perverse, with the result that they have tended to accentuate rather than dampen the business cycle since the 1970s.

5.7   Sustainable Fiscal Policy

The high level of the debt/GNP ratio highlights the importance of meeting the conditions under which it will stabilise. In our discussion of the dynamics of the debt in Chapter 4, we saw that the key determinant of whether this will be attained is the primary deficit, defined as the exchequer borrowing requirement (EBR) less interest payments. The level of the primary deficit is shown in Table 5.12 and Figure 5.6. It may be seen that it reached a peak in 1981 at 13.4 per cent of GNP. In 1988 a small *surplus* was recorded which grew to over 7 per cent of GNP in 1989.

We saw in Chapter 4 that the growth of the debt/income ratio depends on (i) the initial debt/GNP ratio, D, (ii) the rate of interest on the national debt, r, (iii) the rate of growth of GNP in current prices, Δ GNP, and (iv) the primary deficit as a ratio of GNP, p. Under current Irish conditions the following ranges of values are relevant in order to calculate the p required to stabilise d:

d	=	1.1	(that is, 110 per cent of GNP)
Δ GNP	=	0.03 to 0.075	(that is, 3 to 7.5 per cent growth, comprising, say, 0 to 3 per cent growth in real GNP and 2 to 4 per cent inflation)
r	=	0.075 to 0.085	(that is, interest rates of between 7.5 and 8.5 per cent)

Using these ranges, Table 5.13 shows the primary surpluses or deficits (as a percentage of GNP) required to stabilise the debt/GNP ratio.

Comparing these required primary surpluses with the actual levels in recent years, it is clear that the condition for stabilising the debt/GNP ratio was comfortably met in 1988, 1989 and 1990. Even in 1991, when growth in GNP fell sharply and interest rates rose, a primary deficit of about 4.4 per cent of GNP would have been required to prevent the debt/income ratio from increasing. The actual projected primary deficit of 7.0 per cent exceeded what was required to prevent a rise in the debt/GNP ratio. Similarly, despite the relatively lax budget introduced in 1992, the projected primary deficit of 6.4 per cent of GNP will ensure that the ratio continues to decline.

None the less, Ireland remains vulnerable to a rise in world interest rates and/or a slow-down in economic growth due to the overhang of debt inherited from the 1970s and 1980s. The rate of decline in the debt/GNP ratio has slowed since the late 1980s and it is unlikely that we shall reach the target set out in the PESP to bring it down to 100 per cent by 1993. Some slippage from this target, arising from the operation of the automatic stabilisers during a recession, can be condoned provided the lost ground is made up during the recovery.

Table 5.12
The primary budget deficit

	£ millions	% of GNP		£ millions	% of GNP
1972	66	2.9	1983	413	3.1
1973	105	3.9	1984	307	2.1
1974	217	7.2	1985	218	1.4
1975	430	11.6	1986	353	2.1
1976	265	5.9	1987	-99	-0.5
1977	237	4.4	1988	-1,358	-7.0
1978	428	6.6	1989	-1,562	-7.3
1979	535	7.0	1990	-1,645	-7.2
1980	620	6.7	1991	-1,637	-7.0
1981	973	8.9	1992[f]	1,593	-6.4
1982	766	6.1			

Budget Book 1991 and Central Bank of Ireland, *Annual Report*, 1990.
f= forecast
Note: The primary deficit equals the EBR minus interest paid on the national debt. A minus sign indicates a primary *surplus*.

While in recent years Irish budgetary policy has been tight enough to meet this condition comfortably, and as a consequence the debt/GNP ratio has been declining, a sudden rise in interest rates or a slow-down in the rate of growth could result in the deficit rising again to an unsustainable level.

We shall see in Chapter 11 that the debt/GNP ratio will have to fall to 60 per cent (or be falling rapidly towards that level) if Ireland is to participate in the European Economic and Monetary Union when it starts in 1998 or 1999. It will be

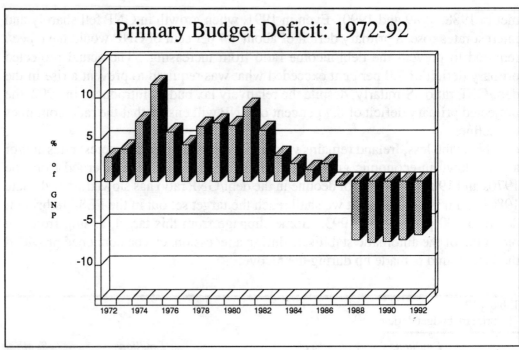

Figure 5.6 Primary budget

difficult, in the time available, to reduce the debt/GNP ratio to this level. (The debt/GNP ratio in 1991 was 107 per cent.) This objective leaves little scope for an active fiscal policy in Ireland from now on.

Table 5.13
Primary budget surplus required to stabilise the debt/GNP ratio

		r (%)	
	7.5	8.0	8.5
Δ GNP (%)			
3.0	4.95	5.5	6.05
4.0	3.85	4.4	4.95
5.0	2.75	3.3	3.80
6.0	1.65	2.2	2.75
7.0	0.50	1.1	1.65
7.5	0.00	0.5	1.10

5.8   Summary

There is now widespread agreement that under Irish conditions the scope for effective Keynesian fiscal policy is very limited. Moreover, fiscal policy was implemented in a very ill-judged manner over the period since 1972. This was due to a combination of analytical errors and the use of tax and spending decisions as an adjunct of party politics. Towards the end of the 1970s the mistake was made of stimulating the economy during a period when it was already growing at a satisfactory pace. This necessitated aggravating an externally caused recession by prolonged fiscal retrenchment after 1981. A consequence was that the recession of the 1980s was much more prolonged in Ireland than in other western countries. By the end of the 1980s, however, the major imbalances in the public finances had been corrected and a period of growth was enjoyed without the benefit of fiscal stimulus. However, some of the distortions in the structure of the economy introduced by the policy mistakes of the 1970s remain with us in the 1990s and the need to reduce the debt/GNP ratio dictates that we shall have to maintain a tight rein on spending and accept a heavy burden of taxation for many years to come. The goal of participating in the European Economic and Monetary Union before the end of the 1990s places very tight constraints on the conduct of fiscal policy in Ireland in the future.

5.9   Conclusion

In this chapter, we have reviewed the following topics:

- The growth of government spending and taxation

- The rise of the national debt and debt servicing

- The measurement of the stance of fiscal policy 1970 to 1992

- The effect of fiscal policy on the economy

- The conditions needed for fiscal policy to be sustainable.

  We showed that:
- The share of the public sector in GNP increased sharply during the 1970s and 1980s

- The burden of taxation increased dramatically and remains heavy by international standards

- An expansionary fiscal policy was not effective as a means of maintaining a high level of output and employment

- The timing of fiscal policy since 1978 was strongly pro-cyclical, that is, it has tended to amplify rather than dampen the business cycle

- The most conspicuous effect of deficit spending has been to increase the burden of the national debt

- The fiscal expansion of the late 1970s distorted the structure of the economy

- To prevent the debt/GNP ratio from increasing it is necessary to maintain a primary budget surplus. Recent Irish budgets have been consistent with this long-term objective

- Fiscal policy is now tightly constrained by the target of joining the EMU before the end of the decade.

Notes

1. This topic is explored by Patrick Honohan and Ian Irvine, "The Marginal Social Costs of Taxation in Ireland", *The Economic and Social Review*, Vol. 19, No. 1, 1987, p. 15-42.

2. For a discussion of the management of the national debt and related issues, see Michael Somers, "The Management of Ireland's National Debt", paper read to the Statistical and Social Inquiry Society of Ireland, 13 February 1992.

3. For an insider's account readers should consult T. K. Whitaker, "Fiscal Turning Points", in *Interests*, Dublin: The Institute of Public Administration, 1983.

4. This period in economic policy has been the subject of much criticism, some of it quite colourful. For example, Kevin Myers, in a profile of the civil servant Tom Barrington, wrote, "Fortunately for his mental health, his retirement came in 1977, the year in which Irish politics lurched from mere slovenly venality and genial incompetence to outright criminality. The economy of the country was debauched and local government effectively destroyed: the most brilliant civil service cannot stop credulous electorates choosing recidivist delinquents to represent them, nor prevent the consequences of malfeasant policy." *Irish Times*, 20 April 1991.

5 This was indicated by the magnitude of the persistent negative residual on the balance of payments. The amount of money recorded as held by Irish non-bank depositors in foreign banks rose from \$1.24 billion at the end of 1984 to \$3.27 billion at the end of 1987: see International Monetary Fund, *International Financial Statistics*, data on "Cross-border Bank Deposits of Non-banks by Residence of Depositor". This figure is a lower estimate because many Irish depositors presumably use foreign addresses.

6. The phrase "Expansionary Fiscal Contraction" was first coined by F. Giavazzi and M. Pagano, "Can Severe Fiscal Contraction be Expansionary? Tales of Two Small European Countries", National Bureau Economic Research, *Macroeconomics Annual*, 1990, O. Blanchard and S. Fischer, editors. Its chief exponent in Ireland has been Dermot McAleese in "Ireland's Economic Recovery", *Irish Banking Review*, Summer 1990; Dermot McAleese, "Expansionary Fiscal Contraction", paper to the Dublin Economics Workshop, Kenmare, October 1990. A review of the literature is given in Patrick T. Geary, "Ireland's Economic Recovery: A Preliminary Review of the Evidence", conference on *Ireland's Successful Stabilisation? Achievements and Prospects*, Trinity College, Dublin, September 1991.

7. See *Proposals for Plan*, April 1984, Chapter II.2, Table A.

8. This statement should be modified to the extent that the capital loss suffered by the private sector holders of public sector debt leads to a fall in their consumption spending through a wealth effect.

9. Peter Bacon, Joseph Durkan and Jim O'Leary, *The Irish Economy: Policy and Performance 1972-81*, Dublin, The Economic and Social Research Institute, 1982, p. 58.

10. John Bradley, Connell Fanning, Canice Prendergast and Mark Wynne, *Medium Term Analysis of Fiscal Policy in Ireland: A Macroeconomic Study of the Period 1967-80*, Dublin: The Economic and Social Research Institute, Research Paper 122, 1985.

11. Brendan M. Walsh, "Why is Unemployment So High?", in *Perspectives on Economic Policy*, 1, 1987, Centre for Economic Research, University College, Dublin, p. 19. This study uses a reduced-form model to assess the impact of fiscal policy. This means that instead of trying to estimate a full model of the whole economy, a single equation was used with the rate of growth in real GNP as the dependent variable and a few explanatory variables on the right-hand side.

Chapter 6

Money and Banking in Ireland

6.1   Introduction

In this chapter we introduce the student to the subject of money and banking in an Irish setting. The initial sections discuss the functions of money and the types of money used in a modern economy. We then outline the role of the banking system in a modern economy and the evolution of money and banking in Ireland. The chapter concludes with an account of the role and functions of a central bank.

The material in this chapter provides the background to the incorporation of money into the Keynesian macroeconomic model, which we undertake in Chapter 7 and to our discussion of monetary policy in Ireland in subsequent chapters.

6.2   What is Money?

Money performs four basic functions in an economy. The most important of these is its role as a *medium of exchange*. The other functions performed by money are that it serves as a *unit of account*, a *standard of deferred payment* and a *store of value*. We discuss each of these functions in turn.

Medium of exchange Without money an economy would have to operate on a *barter system*: all transactions would involve the exchange of goods and services directly for other goods and services. A farmer, for example, would have to exchange the output of his farm for clothes and other necessities. A doctor, in return for medical services, would receive goods or services from his patients. Such a system would be highly inefficient because it involves high transaction costs in the form of looking for a *double coincidence of wants*. That is, in order to complete a transaction, each party must want the other party's good or service. A hungry doctor and a sick farmer would be able to do business. However, in practice most people would find it extremely difficult to locate another party to a transaction. As a result, a third or fourth party would tend to become involved. For example, a sheep farmer in need of a horse might find a horse dealer in need of a suit of clothes. The sheep farmer, therefore, would swap his sheep for clothes in order to obtain the horse. He would then have to search for a tailor in need of sheep. Clearly, things would get complicated very quickly.

Adam Smith in *The Wealth of Nations* (1776) opened with a famous illustration of the benefits of the *division of labour* based on the working of a pin factory. By specialising in the production of a single item, the work force had become very efficient. However, people could not work all day making pins unless they were able to sell them for money and use the money to buy the things they wished to consume. Under a barter system the costs of transactions would deter people from specialising. They would be forced to be self-sufficient and prevented from concentrating on a particular skill or trade. Occupations requiring a high degree of specialisation such as engineering, accountancy and teaching would not come into existence. As a consequence, productivity would remain low.

In a money economy, goods and services can be sold for money which can be used to purchase other goods and services. Thus money is an invention that serves as a medium of exchange and greatly reduces the cost of doing business. This encourages people to specialise and trade. People can specialise in what they do most efficiently, selling the output that is surplus to their needs and buying what they want with the proceeds. This is an infinitely more efficient arrangement than a barter system.

Unit of account   Once people get involved in trading on a large scale they need a *unit of account* in which to do business. Using this unit of account, prices can be quoted and people can compare whether something is dear or cheap relative to other items. Normally prices are quoted in the local currency. It is possible, however, to use different units of account. The EC, for example, uses the ECU (European Currency Unit) in its contracts. A number of multinational firms operating in Ireland use dollars as their unit of account. In horse racing in Ireland and Britain, the guinea is still used as a unit of account worth £1.05, but there are no guineas in circulation any more.

Standard of deferred payment and store of value   These functions allow us to link the present with the future when doing business. Loans, leases and other contracts can specify amounts of money to be paid in the future. People can save some of their income as cash and use it to purchase things in the future. This is useful, but there are risks involved. How much will today's money be worth in a year's time? In inflationary periods, money loses its value quickly. If inflation gets out of control, people will learn to specify contracts in a manner that takes account of inflation (this is called *indexation*). Similarly, people will look to other assets (foreign currencies, land, works of art, old stamps) to use as a store of value. However, all these ways of coping with inflation involve costs. Thus inflation is a threat to the efficiency of a modern economy.

6.3   Types of Money

Over the centuries, money has taken many forms. Whales' teeth were used in Fiji, dogs' teeth in the Admiralty Islands, silk and salt in China, cowrie shells in Africa, and cattle in many countries including ancient Ireland. In fact, the Latin word for cattle is *pecu* and for money *pecunia*, which is the origin of the English word "pecuniary". Writing about Gambia in West Africa at the end of the eighteenth century, the Scottish physician and explorer Mungo Park gave a clear account of how a valuable commodity can serve as a unit of account:

In their early intercourse with Europeans, the article that attracted most notice was iron. Its utility in forming the instruments of war and husbandry, made it preferable to all others; and it soon became the measure by which the value of all other commodities was ascertained. Thus, a certain quantity of goods, of whatever denomination, appearing to be equal in value to a bar of iron, constituted, in the trader's phraseology, a *bar* of that particular merchandise. Twenty leaves of tobacco, for instance, were considered as a bar of tobacco; and a gallon of spirits (or rather half spirits and half water), as a bar of rum; a bar of one commodity being reckoned equal in value to a bar of another commodity. Mungo Park, *Travels in the Interior of Africa*, Eland, London, 1983, p. 19.

There are two basic types of money, namely, commodity money and token money.

Commodity money   When a commodity which is *intrinsically valuable* such as gold or silver, or iron in the above example, is used as money, then this is referred to as commodity money. (It is sometimes called "full bodied money".) Over the centuries, gold and silver have been preferred as commodity money because of their durability, divisibility and stable intrinsic value. The disadvantage of commodity money is that it ties up the commodity itself and diverts it from other uses. When silver is used to make coins the supply of silver to jewellers and other users is reduced.

Token money   This is money which does not have any intrinsic value. The notes and coins in circulation in Ireland today fall into this category. Their intrinsic value is very small compared to their value as a medium of exchange. For example, the paper in an Irish £100 pound note is almost valueless *as paper*. Our so-called silver coins are in fact made from a cheap cupro-nickel alloy. No silver is wasted in making them. The use of token money instead of commodity money generates a very large saving to society. The excess of face value of token money over what it costs to produce it is called *seigniorage* because this profit accrues to the *seigneurs* or rulers who issued currency. Today it generally accrues to central banks.

In the past, bank notes were *convertible* into something of intrinsic value, such as gold or silver, but this generally is no longer the case. Today inconvertible notes and coins made from cheap metals are issued by governments, which decree that they are the only *legal tender* that may circulate in their country. (Legal tender refers to the currency that must be accepted in payment of debts and taxes.) Because they derive their value ultimately from a government decree, they are known as *fiat money*.

Whatever commodity or paper or coin is used as money, it must first achieve a *circularity in its acceptance*. The only reason people accept paper money is because they are certain that they can use it to purchase goods and services at a later stage. If people had the slightest suspicion that paper money could not be spent, they would not accept it as payment. If token money is to be accepted it must not be easily reproduced or *counterfeited*.

Note:
Forged currency can be very sophisticated and bear a close resemblance to the real thing. In 1987 because of the number of counterfeited £10 notes in circulation in Ireland shopkeepers became suspicious of £10 notes offered to them. But not all forged money is so sophisticated. One of the authors discovered in his change a 10 pence coin battered down to look like a 50 pence coin. The forged coin has, however, six sides instead of the normal seven. Someone made 40 pence profit but it took him several hours of hard work.

Counterfeited currency is a potentially extremely serious problem for any government. If people become suspicious of the currency in circulation, they will no longer accept it as a medium of exchange and the economy would either revert to barter or begin to use some other currency. Vladimir Lenin asserted that the best way to bring down a government was to debauch the currency. In the Second World War, there was an attempt by the Germans to flood Britain with forged currency.

Note:
When gold and silver coins were in circulation, debasing them in one way or another was brought to a fine art. *Clipping* referred to clipping small pieces off the edges of coins. The authorities responded by milling the circumference of coins. A second practice was *sweating*. People put gold coins into a bag and shook the bag vigorously. The dust at the bottom of the bag that flaked off the coins was the profit. The issuers of coins themselves were not above cheating by adding a cheap metal alloy to the precious metals in the manufacture of the coins.

The English financial expert Thomas Gresham (1519-1579) asserted that bad money will always drive out good. This is known as *Gresham's Law*. To understand why this is generally true, consider what would happen if two types of coins with the same face value were in circulation and the public realises that one type had been debased. People would try to pass off the debased coins and hoard the good ones. A recent example of this occurred in 1979 following Ireland's entry into the European Monetary System. The Irish pound depreciated against sterling. Whereas formerly both currencies were equally acceptable in Ireland, after the change in the exchange rate people began to extract sterling coins from their change and cash them in at the banks, claiming the premium in Irish money. Sterling coins (the "good money") quickly disappeared from circulation in Ireland. However, Gresham's law only applies to the medium of exchange function of money: people prefer good money as a store of value. It makes sense to hoard good coins and spend bad ones.

In modern economies legal tender is supplemented by claims on money or IOUs. *Bank money* consists of the debts of banks that are used as money. A cheque may be written against a bank account to transfer money from the person writing the cheque to the payee. This is a very efficient way of transacting business, because it eliminates the need to go to the bank, withdraw money, give it to the payee, and for the payee to go to the bank and lodge it in his account. (Of course the person accepting the cheque should satisfy himself that there are sufficient funds in the account on which the cheque is drawn to honour it.) Any amount of business can be transacted for the charge the bank makes for clearing a cheque (about 30 pence in Ireland today). Because they are so convenient to use, bank cheques constitute the largest component of the money supply in modern economies.

6.4   A History of Currency in Ireland

Early history

Gold and silver were used in Ireland as a medium of exchange in ancient times, although the units took the form of rings and bracelets rather than coins.[1] Money, however, took many other forms as the following quote suggests:

... the Annals of the Four Masters, originating from a.d. 106, state that the tribute (Boroimhe meaning literally "cow-tax") paid by the King of Leinster consisted of 150 cows, 150 pigs, 150 couples of men and women in servitude, 150 girls and 150 cauldrons.[2]

The first coinage in Ireland can be traced to the Norse settlement in Dublin in the 990s.[3] The amount of coinage in circulation was relatively small and largely confined to the main trading areas such as ports and towns. The coinage increased at a steady pace after the arrival of the Normans in 1169. In 1460 the Irish Parliament that met in Drogheda established the first separate Irish currency and devalued it relative to the English currency: 15 Irish pence was worth 12 English pence (or one English shilling) so the exchange rate was 15:12.[4] In the sixteenth century the English monarchy allowed the so-called *Harp coinage* (sometimes referred to as "white money") to be issued. In doing so the monarchy acknowledged the existence of a separate Irish currency unit. This was followed in 1601 by an issue of copper coinage by Queen Elizabeth I.

By the 1680s, when banking-type activities first began to emerge, the currency situation in Ireland was unsatisfactory for a number of reasons. First, there was a general shortage of coins and the economy still operated partly on a barter system. James II had melted down cannons to manufacture coins. This was the so-called "gun money" which gave rise to the expression "not worth a brass farthing". The coinage in circulation consisted of a mix of Spanish, French, Portuguese and English coins, which were of different quality and design, and this lack of uniformity impaired their ability to function as a medium of exchange.

In the early 1720s a Mr Wood received a patent to issue coinage (Wood's half-pence) which would have increased the copper coinage in circulation by about a quarter. However, this patent was withdrawn two years later, partly because of the argument used by Jonathan Swift in *The Drapier's Letters* that the increase in currency would raise prices. (This idea is consistent with the Quantity Theory of Money, which we discuss in Chapter 7.) A general shortage of coinage continued in Ireland, but as the poorer people in the country areas still lived in a subsistence and semi-barter economy this had little effect on them. The merchants issued their own coins in order to facilitate trade.

From the eighteenth century to Independence

Throughout the eighteenth century, the Irish currency was at a discount of about 8 per cent relative to the English currency: 13 Irish pence equalled 12 English pence. In 1797, during the turmoil of the Napoleonic wars, the convertibility of Irish and British specie (that is, coins) to gold was suspended. This did not result in any immediate change in the exchange rate between Irish and English currencies, but in 1803 the Irish currency depreciated sharply. A parliamentary inquiry was established which issued a report known as the *Irish Currency Report* (1804). This Report argued that excessive credit expansion caused the 1803 depreciation and that the exchange rate could be stabilised if the growth of credit were controlled.

In the years after 1804, the Irish currency gradually stabilised at a 13:12 exchange rate with sterling. By the time gold convertibility was resumed in 1821, this rate was sufficiently firmly re-established for the Bank of Ireland to accept responsibility for maintaining the Irish currency at this rate. Following the implementation of the monetary provisions of the 1800 Act of Union, in 1826 full political and monetary union was established between Ireland and Great Britain and the Irish currency was abolished. Thereafter British coins and notes circulated in Ireland and could be obtained on demand from London.

Note:
The Irish Currency Report influenced thinking in the "bullionist controversy" in England (1796-1821) and is an important document in the history of monetary economics. The key issue it addressed was whether there could be an "excessive" growth in the money supply. The Report explained what came to be the orthodox view that an "excess" increase in the money supply would lead to an increase in the price level and this, in turn, would make exports less competitive and cause the exchange rate to depreciate. This was important in the development of the modern Quantity Theory of Money.

Developments since Independence

Following the foundation of the Irish Free State in 1922, the Coinage Act of 1926 was passed in order to enable the Minister for Finance to issue new Irish coins. These coins were used in Ireland until 1971 when a new design was introduced and the coinage decimalised.[5]

A Banking Commission was set up in 1926 to advise the government on the establishment of an Irish pound. (This was known as the *Parker-Willis Commission*, after its chairman, Professor Henry Parker-Willis (1874-1937) of Columbia University, a former secretary of the Federal Reserve Board (the US Central Bank). The Commission's final report was signed in January 1927. It recommended that a new currency unit, the Saorstat pound, be created. In order to ensure public confidence in the new currency, it should be backed 100 per cent by sterling reserves, British government stock and gold reserves and freely convertible into sterling. The exchange rate with sterling could not be changed without the introduction of additional legislation. Thus the new currency would in effect be sterling with an Irish design. This would ensure that it would be acceptable alongside sterling as a medium of exchange. The Commission also recommended the establishment of a new body, confusingly to be called the *Currency Commission*, to oversee the issue of the new legal tender notes.

The recommendations of the Parker-Willis Commission were incorporated into law in the 1927 Currency Act. The Currency Commission was established and remained in existence until 1942, when its powers were transferred to the new Central Bank. Its only chairman was Joseph Brennan (1887-1976), who became the first governor of the Central Bank of Ireland. The first Irish notes were issued in September 1928.

Note:
Under the new arrangements the commercial banks were allowed to issue a certain amount of private bank notes which bore the banks' name. This was called the Consolidated Bank Note issue and the notes were known as ploughman notes because of their design. These notes were finally withdrawn from circulation in 1953.

The main function of the Currency Commission was to supervise and regulate the issue of the new currency in exchange for suitable sterling assets. The Currency Commission did not exercise any of the other functions of a Central Bank.

The share of Irish legal tender notes in the total supply of money in circulation is believed to have reached about two-thirds by the beginning of the Second World War. This ensured that the benefits of seigniorage were captured by the Irish authorities. (The seigniorage on the British currency circulating in Ireland accrued to the British authorities.) It has been estimated that the value of the seigniorage amounted to about 0.2 per cent of national income at the time.[6]

Over the centuries, the exchange rate between the Irish and English currencies has varied considerably, but coincidentally has now settled in the region of 92.5 pence, almost the same as the 12:13 rate that prevailed throughout the eighteenth century. A summary of the fortunes of the Irish pound is given in Table 6.1.

Table 6.1
The exchange rate of the Irish currency in terms of sterling

Date	Exchange rate	Movement of Irish currency in terms of sterling relative to previous date
1200	Par	
1487	IR 1.5 silver coins/ UK 1 silver coin	Depreciation
1561	IR 1.3 silver coins/UK 1 silver coin	Appreciation
1601-1602	IR 4 silver coins/UK 1 silver coin	Depreciation
1603	IR 1.3 silver coins/UK 1 silver coin	Appreciation
1650	Par	Appreciation
1689	IR 13 pence/UK 12 pence	Depreciation
1797-1826	Irish currency floated against UK currency	Depreciation
1826	Abolition of independent Irish currency	Par
1927	Creation of Saorstat pound	Parity with sterling
1979	The Irish currency depreciated following Ireland's entry into the Exchange Rate Mechanism (ERM) of the European Monetary System.	Depreciation followed by appreciation
1990	Entry of Britain into the ERM	Stability at about IR£ = STG £0.92

6.5 The Banking System in a Modern Economy

The importance of bank money

We have seen that bank money is the most important component of the money supply in a modern economy. To understand how money is created, and its supply controlled, we must examine more closely the nature of modern banking. A key feature of modern banks is that they are *deposit taking institutions*. They accept funds from the public and place them in *current* and *deposit accounts*. In general, no interest is paid on a current account but cheques can be drawn on it. On the other hand, interest is paid on deposit accounts but cheques cannot be drawn on it and some notice may be required before money can be withdrawn from it. (In America, these accounts are known as *checking accounts* and *savings accounts*, respectively, which brings out the relevant distinction more clearly.) Accounts on which cheques can be drawn are clearly a component of the money supply; it is less clear how to classify other types of accounts.

Table 6.2
Money supply June 1991

	£ m
Currency	1,303.7
+ Current accounts	1,711.4
= M1	3.015.1
+ Deposit accounts	9,496.8
= M3	12,511.9

Source: Central Bank of Ireland, *Quarterly Bulletin*, Autumn 1991.
1. In 1983 the Central Bank redefined M3. The main change was the exclusion of non-residents' deposits from the new definition. Previously a definition of money called M2 was used but this is no longer published.
2. M3 does not include cash held by the licensed banks, but it does include foreign currency deposits held by residents at within-the-state offices of licensed banks.

In Ireland two measures of the money supply are used: the *narrow* and the *wide* money supply, referred to as M1 and M3 respectively. M1 is equal to notes and coins in circulation plus current accounts in banks. It is noticeable that notes and coins make up only a small component of the total money supply (10.4 per cent of M3). While cheques cannot be written on deposit accounts, funds can often be withdrawn from them without notice and used as payment. The broad money supply, M3, is therefore defined by adding deposit accounts to M1. Any definition of the money supply is somewhat arbitrary because it is very hard to draw a borderline between "cash" and "non-cash". Deposits with building societies and credit cards can readily be used to purchase things, but neither is included in M3.

Figure 6.1 shows the annual percentage change in M1 and M3 between 1966 and 1990. The variability of both series is striking. It is also noticeable that the two series have not always moved in tandem. In 1974, for example, M3 increased as M1 declined. This poses the question: which measure of the money supply should the Central Bank try to control? Before bank money became so important, controlling the money supply was simply a matter of not issuing too many notes or coins. With the widespread use of bank accounts as money, it has become a much more complicated matter. Early in the 1980s, the UK government placed great emphasis on controlling the money supply, which was defined as M3. However, in October

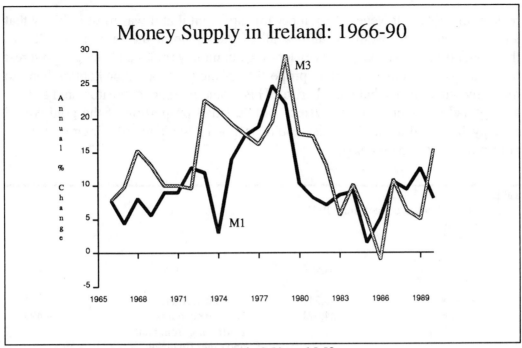

Figure 6.1 Annual percentage change in M1 and M3

1985, M3 was replaced by a very narrow measure of money, M0 (currency in circulation), as the key policy instrument.

The fractional reserve banking system

Banks act as *financial intermediaries*, that is, they channel funds from savers to borrowers. This function allows them to play a key role in the money creation process. To see that this is the case, consider the balance sheet of a typical bank (Table 6.3). The liability side contains current and deposit accounts and borrowing by the bank from other financial institutions. The money in current and deposit accounts is owed to depositors and hence is a liability from the banks' perspective. On the asset side, there are entries for bank reserves, loans and advances. Reserves consist of the banks' holdings of currency, deposits with the Central Bank of Ireland and government stock. Deposits with the Central Bank can be converted into cash immediately and used to meet depositors' demands. Government stock can be sold at short notice. Loans and advances consist of bank lending to the private sector, the government and other financial institutions. These loans cannot be called at short notice: the banks have to wait for them to mature in order to obtain cash for them.

Modern banking is based on a system of *fractional reserves*. This system was developed by the goldsmiths of the Middle Ages. People used to place gold and other valuables with them for safe keeping. At first, they simply stored the gold in a vault for a small fee and issued receipts which could be used at a later stage to reclaim the gold. However, it soon became apparent that it was most unlikely that all of the depositors would withdraw all of their gold at the same time. It was therefore possible to make profits by lending out money (gold) and charging interest on the loans. Of course, a certain proportion of the gold had to be kept on hand to meet any withdrawals that would arise. This would reassure depositors and as long as they had confidence in the system, only a small proportion of the gold would actually be withdrawn. The rest could be put to work to earn interest for the goldsmiths turned bankers.

Table 6.3
Licensed banks' balance sheet, June 1991
(vis-ä-vis residents)

	Assets		*Liabilities*
Reserves	1,217	Current accounts	1,711
Lending	24,021	Deposit accounts	9,497
		Borrowing from banks and other financial institutions	8,225
Other	1,476	Other	2,605
	26,714		22,038

Source: Central Bank of Ireland, *Quarterly Bulletin*, Autumn 1991, Table C4, page 34.
Note: Assets do not equal liabilities as we are only considering the balance sheet vis-ä-vis residents of the Republic of Ireland. When non-residents are included the two sides of the balance sheet are equal. Because the Irish banks operate in Northern Ireland, dealings with non-residents are very important.

Similarly, modern banking operates on the basis that it is not necessary to keep 100 per cent of deposits in cash. When £1 is deposited, the bank need keep only a fraction in reserve and can either lend out the rest or use it to purchase interest-bearing securities such as government stock or corporate bonds. Over a period such as a week or a month, new deposits are likely to match withdrawals so that all that is really necessary is to keep a small amount of "till money" to meet occasional net outflows. If a bank has sufficient reserves to meet normal requirements, the public's confidence in it will remain high and the fractional reserve system will work well. The bank will earn interest from its loans and advances, and the public will enjoy the convenience of having money on deposit.

However, if some contingency arises, such as the possibility of a bank strike or rumours that the bank has made unsound loans, a large proportion of depositors are likely to converge on the bank and ask to withdraw their money. If that happens, the bank on its own will not be able to meet depositors' demands and will have to close its doors while it tries to convert its loans and other assets into cash. If it cannot do so, it may have to cease trading. When a bank fails like this the depositors only receive a certain proportion, if any, of their money back. As we shall see, one of the functions of a central bank is to be ready to provide banks that are in trouble with the funds they need to tide them over a liquidity crisis.

Bank failures were rare in the 1950s and 1960s, but have become almost commonplace recently. In 1984 the Continental Illinois Bank of Chicago, one of America's largest banks, collapsed as a result of losses on its loans, especially in the area of property development. Even support from the Federal Reserve Bank failed to prevent deposit flight. The Savings and Loan Associations (the equivalent of Ireland's building societies) had to be collectively bailed out by the government in 1989. In 1991 the Bank of Credit and Commerce International (BCCI) had its banking licence revoked first in the United States then in Britain. Depositors world-wide lost billions of pounds in the largest bank collapse in history. Although fraud and illegal dealing played a part in the collapse of BCCI, the basic problem was the familiar one of lending depositors' money for risky projects that failed.

In Ireland the most recent bank failures were the Irish Trust Bank and Merchant Banking which closed in 1976 and 1982, respectively. Depositors with these banks lost a significant proportion of their money. Following the Central Bank Act of 1989, a *deposit protection account* has been established to protect bank depositors' money up to a certain limit in the event of a bank failure.[7]

Note:
The insurance industry is closely related to banking, taking in the public's money in return for a promise to pay out if certain events (accidents, death) occur. If an insurance company invests its money imprudently, it may not be able to meet claims when they arise. The Equitable Insurance Company was wound up in 1963, and the Private Motorists Protection Association (PMPA) and the Insurance Corporation of Ireland (ICI, a wholly owned subsidiary of Allied Irish Banks) were placed under administration in 1983 and 1985, respectively. It is believed that in the ICI case losses of around £100 million were incurred. These large losses were paid for by a levy on other insurance companies and by subventions from the Irish taxpayer.

Bank reserves

To minimise the risk of default and failure, in most countries banks are required by law to keep minimum reserves in relation to deposits. They can keep excess reserves if they wish, but since they earn less on their reserves than on other assets, they tend not to do so.

In Ireland the Central Bank of Ireland sets *required liquidity ratios*. There are at present two types of liquidity ratios, *primary* and *secondary*. These ratios stipulate the proportion of the banks' liabilities that must be covered by liquid assets. In March

1992 the liquidity ratios relating to the associated banks, namely, Allied Irish Banks, Bank of Ireland, National Irish Bank and the Ulster Bank, were as follows:

Primary liquidity ratio = 6 per cent of "relevant resources"

Secondary liquidity ratio = 25 per cent of "relevant resources"

Primary liquid assets consist of banks' holdings of notes and coins and deposits at the Central Bank. "Relevant resources" comprise mainly current and deposit accounts. Secondary liquid assets consist of government stocks. Thus, for every £100 they have in current and deposit accounts, the banks must keep a minimum of £6 as notes and coins plus deposits at the Central Bank and a further £25 worth of government stock. The purpose of this requirement is to ensure that the banks will have adequate liquid assets to meet demands for cash by their depositors. Because the specified liquid assets do not earn as high a return for the banks as would loans and advances, and the required ratio is much higher than the banks would voluntarily hold for prudential reasons, these requirements are like a tax on the banks.[8]

Bank profits

The rate of interest paid by banks on deposits is lower than the rate they charge on loans. Table 6.4 shows the lending and deposit rates for a number of financial institutions in Ireland in 1991. The associated banks paid 3.0 to 5.25 per cent on deposits less than £5,000 and charged 15.25 per cent to category A borrowers (i. e. personal and retail borrowings) on term loans. This interest differential is the main source of bank profits. (Banks charge for all transactions to cover their day-to-day operating costs. There are nearly thirty different types of charges relating to a current account.)

Bank profits can be very significantly reduced by bad debts, that is, borrowers defaulting on loans. In the financial year ending March 1991, Allied Irish Banks, Ireland's largest banking group, made pre-tax profits of £178.8 million despite bad debts of £174 million. Profits in Ireland were £143.3 million despite bad debts of £35 million. In the US, where bad debts amounted to £75 million, a profit of only £6.7 million was made. In the UK bad debts of £50 million were associated with a loss of £11.7 million. Obviously the lower the provision that has to be made for bad debts the higher bank profits will be.

Table 6.4
Selected bank deposit and lending rates, July 1991

	%
Lending rates	
Associated banks: overdrafts and term loans	15.25
Building societies	10.75 - 11.95
Trustee savings banks	10.75 - 19.00
Deposit rates	
Associated banks: deposit accounts	
Under £5,000	3.0 - 5.25
£5,000 to £25,000	4.75 - 5.25
£25,000 to £100,000	5.25 - 6.5
£100,000 and over	6.75 - 7.5
Building societies	5.5 - 8.35
Trustee Savings Bank	4.0
Post Office Savings Bank	6.25

Source: Central Bank of Ireland, *Quarterly Bulletin*, Autumn 1991, Table B1 and B2, pp. 16-18.
Note: The lending rates apply to category A borrowers. Rates are slightly lower for AA and AAA borrowers. (AAA category includes government and local authority borrowings, AA category includes manufacturing and service sectors and the A category includes personal borrowings).

To minimise bad debts banks screen and monitor borrowers very carefully. Yet bankers are influenced by the psychology of the moment, and when a boom in property or land starts, they lend to speculators to buy at prices that are unjustified by the underlying value of the assets being bought. When boom turns to bust, the value of the assets used as collateral falls and even if a bank forecloses it cannot realise its loans. There has been much criticism of bankers world-wide for the role they played in the boom of the 1980s which in many cases ended in bail-outs (at taxpayers' expense) and bankruptcy (at depositors' expense).

Money creation in a modern economy

In a modern economy, where bank money is the most important type of money, and the banks operate on fractional reserves, an inflow of cash will cause a multiple expansion in the money supply. This process is illustrated with a simplified example in Table 6.5. It is assumed that (A) there is only one bank in the country, (B) that the primary reserve requirement is 10 per cent, (C) there is no secondary reserve requirement, and (D) that the bank does not keep any excess reserves. On the liability side of the balance sheet are deposits. On the asset side, there are entries for bank reserves and bank lending.

Table 6.5
Money creation with fractional reserve banking

Licensed banks' balance sheet

				Assets			Liabilities			
Increases in round:		1	2	3			1	2	3
	Reserves	100	90	81		Deposits	1,000	900	810
	Loans	900	810	729					

Let us explore what happens when there is a net inflow of reserves (cash) to the bank. Suppose someone takes £1,000 in cash from under the mattress and deposits it in the bank. The bank immediately gains excess reserves, because the new deposit is 100 per cent backed by cash. It lends out as much as it can, which in view of the assumed 10 per cent reserve requirement is £900. Suppose the loan of £900 is used to purchase a car. A local garage receives £900 in exchange for the car and lodges it with its bank. Hence the car loan has, in the second round, resulted in the creation of a deposit of £900, fully backed by cash reserves. The bank again keeps 10 per cent (£90) of the new deposit in reserve and loans out the remainder (£810). The process need not end there. The borrower of £810 from the bank pays someone by drawing a cheque on his account and this cheque is, in turn, deposited with the bank. A deposit of £810 is created, fully backed by reserves, and once again the bank will keep 10 per cent in reserves and lend out the rest. This process will go on, but the amount loaned out at each successive stage dwindles.

Table 6.6 shows what happens to M3 as this process unfolds. As bank deposits increase in each round, so too does the money supply. Given a primary reserve ratio of 10 per cent, the initial £1,000 deposit will eventually lead to a £10,000 increase in the money supply. However, if somewhere along the line, someone hoarded the money and kept it out of the banking system, then the expansion of the money supply would halt. Of course, the process also works in reverse. If a bank loses reserves, there will be a multiple contraction of credit.

Table 6.6

The process of money creation with fractional reserve banking

Round	$\Delta M3$	$= \Delta$(Currency + Current and deposit accounts)
		£
1		1,000
2		900
3		810
4		729
.		.
n		.
Total		10,000

Note: The symbol Δ denotes the change.

Money multiplier The final increase in the money supply can be calculated using a formula for the *money multiplier*.

Money multiplier (m) = 1/reserve requirement

In the above example, m = 1/0.1 = 10, so that

Change in M3 = (m) × *(initial increase in reserves)*
£10,000 = 10 × £1,000

Note that the higher the reserve requirement, the lower the money multiplier. A reserve requirement of 20 per cent, for example, gives a money multiplier of 5, but a reserve requirement of 5 per cent gives a money multiplier of 20. The less money that has to be held in the form of reserves, the greater the final increase in the money supply. Bear in mind that this example is based on very unrealistic assumptions about the economy: in Appendix 1 to this chapter a more realistic example is worked out.

The money multiplier should not be confused with the fiscal multiplier, discussed in Chapter 4. The fiscal multiplier relates increases in aggregate demand to increases in the equilibrium level of income, whereas the money multiplier relates a change in a bank's reserves to the final change in the money supply.

6.6   The Evolution of Banking in Ireland

A key date in Irish banking history is 1783 when the Bank of Ireland was founded by Royal Charter. This bank operated on a commercial basis while simultaneously, but in a limited way, performing some of the functions of a central bank. It issued notes, managed the government's account and acted as (a reluctant) lender of last resort at various times. The other Irish banks both relied on and resented the special role of the Bank of Ireland.

The size of the banks was limited by legislation passed in 1783 which restricted the number of partners in a bank. Moreover, the banks were not limited liability companies: partners whose banks failed lost their town houses and country mansions.[9] The banks were, in fact, very vulnerable in times of crisis because of an over-reliance on land as collateral. In 1820, for example, the end of the Napoleonic wars and the withdrawal of the British navy from Cork coincided with a general fall in agricultural prices and this led to a number of merchants going bankrupt. This, in turn, led to speculation that certain local banks were in trouble owing to bad debts and that their assets were not adequate to cover their note issue. The result was a run on the banks, as depositors tried to withdraw their money. In one month in 1820, thirty private banks failed in Munster alone.[10] The run on the Cork banks set off a run on other banks throughout the country. By the time the crisis was over only ten private banks remained solvent outside Dublin.

In nineteenth-century Ireland there was no central bank to act as a "lender of last resort" in times of crisis and provide the liquidity that would have stopped a run on the banks. The banks did, however, turn to the Bank of Ireland, which because of its size and resources was able to lend money to banks that were in distress. It helped banks that were in trouble at the end of the eighteenth century and during the Great Famine, but it was not always willing or able to provide enough support to avert bank failures.

It was unlikely that the Bank of Ireland would have evolved into a fully fledged central bank because following the Act of Union in 1801 and the abolition of the Irish currency in 1826, the Bank of England was given some responsibility for supervising banking in Ireland. Also, greater competition in the banking sector following the Bankers' (Ireland) Act of 1845 forced the Bank of Ireland to evolve along commercial lines. There is a conflict of interest between acting as a central bank (helping other banks to remain solvent) and competing with them as commercial rivals. It was recognised in the 1920s that a serious conflict of interest would have emerged if the Bank of Ireland were asked to act as the central bank in the Free State.

None the less, Michael Collins, the Minister for Finance in the new provisional government, asked the Bank of Ireland to continue managing the government's account. The Banking Commission which reported in 1927 did not intend that the

Currency Commission would become a fully fledged central bank. It was not given the power to act as a lender of last resort, nor could it set reserve requirements for commercial banks. It did not gain control over the commercial banks' sterling assets, which continued to be kept in London. Furthermore, the Commission did not manage the government's account nor did it advise the government on monetary matters.

Perhaps the main reason a central bank was not established in the 1920s was that there was little such an institution could usefully do. Despite gaining political independence, we had remained in a monetary union with Great Britain. There was a fixed exchange rate between the Irish currency and sterling and there was no money market in Ireland. Under these circumstances, as we shall explain in detail in subsequent chapters, a central bank could not control the money supply or use monetary policy to influence the price level, output or employment and its role would be very limited. These issues are once again topical as the role of national central banks is a subject for discussion as economic and monetary union approaches in western Europe.

Another possible reason why a central bank was not established after Independence was:

a conviction that . . . central banks were being promoted as antidotes to backward or unduly risk-adverse commercial banking systems. Accordingly, creating an Irish central bank might be seen as both a slight and a threat to the long-established commercial banks. [11]

When in September 1931 the UK terminated the gold standard and sterling was devalued by 25 per cent against gold, there were misgivings in some quarters in Ireland that the Irish currency was automatically devalued due to the link with sterling. The Fianna Fáil government established a second Banking Commission in 1934 to report on money and banking in Ireland. The new Commission included Joseph Brennan (Chairman of the Currency Commission), George O'Brien (Professor of National Economics at University College, Dublin) and the Swedish economist Per Jacobsson who later became president of the International Monetary Fund. (John Maynard Keynes was considered but was not invited, possibly because of his support for the Irish government's protectionist policies in a lecture in Dublin in the previous year.)[12] A bishop was included but:

. . . Dr McNeely, was "unaware of any reasons why he should have been appointed, except to add an atmosphere of respectability to the conference."[13]

This second Banking Commission deliberated for nearly four years and reported in 1938. As one commentator put it:

"the opinion of the majority report on the system of banking and currency may be summarised as a recommendation to leave things as they were".[14]

The creation of an Irish central bank, as such, was not recommended but it was suggested that the Currency Commission be allowed to engage in open market operations. In fact

the government chose to ignore the Report, and used the threat of war to produce central banking legislation. In the end, the Central Bank Act of 1942 was a compromise between, on the one hand, Brennan and the Department of Finance [who did not wish to establish a Bank], and the majority of ministers [who did] on the other.[15]

In the days before the start of the Second World War, the Bank of Ireland approached the Bank of England to see if it would act as a lender of last resort to the Irish banks in an emergency. The Bank of England replied that it was not in a position to provide assistance and suggested that "as Eire was a separate political entity it should have a central bank of its own".[16] In the light of this rebuff, perhaps the Irish commercial banks, who had been heavily represented on both Banking Commissions and had staunchly opposed the creation of a central bank, had second thoughts on the issue.

The Central Bank Act was passed in 1942 and soon afterwards the Central Bank of Ireland was established, with Joseph Brennan, the former chairman of the Currency Commission, as the first governor. The primary function of the new Central Bank was to "safeguard the integrity of the currency". The powers of the new Central Bank were, however, limited. It could act as lender of last resort and use open market operations to influence liquidity in the money market. However, it could not set reserve requirements or act as a banker to either the government or the commercial banks. The government continued to hold its account with the Bank of Ireland and the commercial banks held most of their reserves in the London money markets. Thus little changed in Irish banking immediately following the establishment of the Central Bank.

The 1960s, however, were a period of rapid development in Irish banking. A number of new banks began operations in Ireland. The Bank of Ireland acquired the Hibernian Bank in 1958 and the National Bank in 1965. The Allied Irish Bank group was formed with the merger of the Munster and Leinster Bank, the Provincial Bank and the Royal Bank of Ireland in 1966. Appendix 2 to this chapter discusses the structure of the banking sector in Ireland today.

In 1965, the Central Bank of Ireland first issued "letters of advice" (or credit guidelines) to the banks telling them to restrain credit expansion in order to curtail the growing balance of payments deficit. The Central Bank began to promote new markets in foreign exchange, government stocks and money. Because of these developments, it was becoming increasingly clear that the 1942 Central Bank

164

legislation was inadequate. In response the Central Bank Act, 1971, was passed. This Act significantly increased the powers of the Central Bank. Its main features were:

1. The Central Bank became the licensing authority for banks.
2. The government's account was transferred from the Bank of Ireland to the Central Bank.
3. The commercial banks were required to keep their reserves with the Central Bank.
4. The Central Bank was given the power to issue primary and secondary reserve ratios (these were first issued in August 1972).
5. The new legislation made it possible to break the sterling link by government order. This power was exercised in March 1979, following Ireland's entry to the European Monetary System.

The Central Bank Act of 1989 brought money brokers, financial futures traders and companies associated with the new International Financial Services Centre (IFSC) under the supervision of the Central Bank. In addition, commercial bank charges were brought under its control and, as mentioned earlier, a deposit protection scheme was established to protect the savings of small depositors. Under the Building Society Act, 1989, and the Trustee Savings Bank (TSB) Act, 1989, the Central Bank gained responsibility for supervising the building societies and the TSBs.

6.7   The Functions of a Central Bank

Consider first the liabilities side of the balance sheet of the Central Bank (Table 6.7). There is £1,410 million Irish currency in circulation which is a liability of the Central Bank. The main asset in the Central Bank's balance sheet is the *official external reserves*. These are the country's official holding of foreign currency, gold and other reserves and they are what backs the currency. The Central Bank stands willing to exchange foreign currency, such as sterling, dollars and yen, for Irish pounds, and it is this convertibility which maintains confidence in the Irish currency and stabilises the exchange rate. The interest earned on these reserves is modern-day seigniorage. The surplus of this income over the Bank's operating expenses is turned over to the Department of Finance. In 1991 Finance received £127 million from this source.

The other two main Central Bank liabilities are the licensed banks' and the government's deposits. The government keeps accounts with the Central Bank, just as individuals do with commercial banks. On the asset side, in addition to the external reserves, there is Central Bank lending to the banks and the government. The Central Bank both accepts deposits and makes loans to the government and in this sense acts as banker to the banks and the government. (In fact, the government did not have any borrowing outstanding from the Central Bank as of June 1991.)

Banks normally borrow from the Central Bank only if they are short of reserves to meet the legal primary and secondary reserve ratios. Because it is willing to provide reserves to the banks in this manner, the Central Bank is referred to as *lender of last resort*. The "lender of last resort" function is important because it ultimately ensures that the banks can operate on fractional reserves and still obtain cash to meet any unexpected withdrawal of funds. The banks have to pay interest on borrowed reserves and repay them fairly quickly. It is important that the existence of a lender of last resort and an insurance scheme for depositors should not encourage the banks to lend out recklessly.

Table 6.7
Central Bank of Ireland balance sheet: £ m, June 1991

	Assets		*Liabilities*
External reserves	3,422.1	Currency	1,410.4
Loans:		Licensed bank reserves	1,128.3
Banks	213.2		
Government	0.0	Government deposits	317.5
Other	314.1	Other	1,093.2
Total	3,949.4	Total	3,949.4

Source: Central Bank of Ireland, *Quarterly Bulletin*, Autumn 1991
Note: Currency includes cash reserves held by the licensed banks. The figure is therefore larger than the figure given earlier in Table 6.2.

In summary, the main functions of the Central Bank are, first, to issue and control the currency; second, to act as banker to both the commercial banks and the government; third, to supervise the operation of the financial system; fourth, to maintain the integrity of the currency by adopting appropriate monetary policies.

6.8   Instruments of Monetary Policy

An important function of a central bank is its responsibility for the control of the money supply. It can use the following *instruments* for this purpose.

Setting reserve requirements   The Central Bank sets the reserve requirements that apply to all the banks in the country. They have to comply with these requirements or they will be penalised by the Central Bank. The primary reserve ratio is set well above the level deemed prudent from the banks' point of view and it ensures that they have sufficient liquid assets on hand to meet day-to-day withdrawals. The secondary reserve requirement, which obliges the banks to hold sizeable amounts of government stock, is designed to support this market. If the Central Bank increases the primary reserve ratio the banks have to realise some of their loans in order to raise the reserves needed to meet the new requirement. This leads to a contraction of credit. A large increase in the reserve requirement would have a drastic effect on the liquidity of the economy. In fact, apart from a relaxation of the ratio to accommodate the outflow of cash from the banks at Christmas time, reserve ratios are rarely changed in Ireland. The last occasion was in February 1992 when the primary ratio was reduced from 8 per cent to 6 per cent.

Open market operations Open market operations consist in buying and selling government stocks on the "open market" in order to influence the money supply. If the Central Bank buys government stock it pays for them with a cheque drawn on itself and the seller's bank account receives an inflow of reserves. In effect, the Central Bank injects money into the system and the money supply increases. On the other hand, when a central bank sells government stocks, the purchaser draws a cheque in favour of the Central Bank, and when this clears through his bank, bank reserves decrease. The Central Bank withdraws money from the economy and the money supply declines. By buying or selling government securities the Central Bank can increase or decrease its liabilities and assets which leads to a monetary expansion or contraction.

Credit guidelines A central bank can try to dictate to the banks by how much they can increase their lending over a specified period of time. If the banks exceed the guideline then they can be subject to penalties. Credit guidelines are asymmetrical in the sense that banks can be restrained from exceeding the ceiling but cannot be forced to go up to it. If the demand for credit is weak, banks will not be able to reach the ceiling. Credit guidelines were first used in Ireland in the mid-1960s and have now been abandoned. We discuss credit guidelines in detail in a later chapter.

The discount rate The interest rate a central bank charges on its lending to the commercial banks and the government has different names in different countries. In Britain it used to be known as the Bank Rate, then the Minimum Lending Rate, but now the only rate set by the Bank of England is the Bill Discounting Rate. In the US the rate charged by the Fed to the commercial banks is known as the Discount Rate. In Germany the Bundesbank sets the Lombard Rate. In Ireland the key rate is that charged on the *short-term credit facility* (STCF), which is an overdraft facility for the banks at the Central Bank. The banks can only use this facility to top up their reserves to meet the reserve requirement. They cannot borrow from the Central Bank and on-lend the money to the public. When the banks draw funds under this facility they are charged the STCF interest rate. As this is higher than the rate they earn on their reserves they are in effect being penalised for having to resort to the STCF to meet the reserve requirement. An increase in this rate discourages the banks from borrowing from the Central Bank and thus restricts lending throughout the economy. Moreover, the banks will tend to pass an increase in the STCF rate through to their customers. This allows the Central Bank to influence the whole structure of interest rates in the economy.

More often than not, a central bank uses the discount rate to indicate its intentions (or "send a signal") to the commercial banks. When the bank rate rises, this is taken as a signal by the commercial banks to curtail credit. However, Irish interest rates are strongly influenced by interest rates abroad, especially in Germany because of our exchange rate link with that country.

Many textbook accounts of how a central bank conducts open market operations and interest rate policy are based on the American banking system. The principal asset of the US Central Bank, the Fed, consists of US government securities and purchases and sales of these through the Open Market Committee is the main instrument of monetary policy in the US. Interest rates in the US economy have a major influence on interest rates all over the world, but foreign interest rates do not have much effect on US rates, so the Fed is relatively free to conduct an independent policy in this area.

In Ireland the context of monetary policy is very different. As we shall see in a later chapter, the Central Bank of Ireland tries to stabilise the Irish exchange rate by buying and selling foreign exchange from the market. Open market operations are used to control the liquidity of the commercial banks, which is strongly influenced by flows across the foreign exchanges. We are moving towards a monetary union with our European neighbours and this will severely curtail the ability of the Central Bank of Ireland to operate an independent monetary policy. In fact it can be argued that in a complete monetary union the national central banks will become redundant and could be dispensed with, as was in fact done during the early years of Irish independence when we remained in a monetary union with the United Kingdom.[17]

6.9   Conclusion

In this chapter we introduced the subject of money and banking and reviewed the development of banking in Ireland. The main points discussed include:

- Money performs a number of functions. The most important is its role as a medium of exchange

- The evolution of currency and banking in Ireland

- Fractional reserve banking

- How bank lending results in an increase in bank deposits

- Because of the fractional reserve banking system and because loans create deposits, an inflow (outflow) of reserves leads to a multiple expansion (contraction) of the money supply

- The money multiplier

- The origins of the Central Bank of Ireland

- The role of a central bank

- The instruments of monetary policy used by central banks include open market operations, changes in the reserve requirements, discount rates and credit guidelines.

Notes

1. P. Nolan, *A Monetary History of Ireland*, London, 1926.

2. P. Einzig, *Primitive Money*, New York: Pergamon, 2nd edition, 1966, p. 239.

3. See P. McGowan, *Money and Banking in Ireland: Origins, Development and Future*, Institute of Public Administration, 1990, for an extended analysis of money and banking in Ireland.

4. See J. Moore McDowell, "The Devaluation of 1460 and the Origins of the Irish Pound", *Irish Historical Studies*, xxv, No. 97 (May 1986), pp. 19-28.

5 Until the 1950s the "silver" coins minted for Ireland in fact contained significant amounts of silver. Some of them became very valuable as the price of silver rose. The two shilling and half crown coins from the early 1940s are now worth hundreds of pounds. Hence, following Gresham's law, they have entirely disappeared from circulation.

6. Cormac O Grada, *Ireland 1780-1939: A New Economic History*, Oxford University Press, forthcoming 1992, p. 42.

7. See McGowan, *op. cit.* for a discussion of the supervision of banks by the Central Bank.

8. The Central Bank pays an undisclosed interest rate on these two accounts. The rate is believed to be approximately 3 per cent below market rates.

9. McGowan notes that the banks ". . . were primarily concerned with facilitating the transfer of agricultural output from the countryside to Dublin and abroad and placing the proceeds of the sale of that output at the disposal of the landlords" (P. Mc Gowan, *op. cit.*, p. 10). Merchants borrowed from the banks to pay farmers for their crops which were sold on the domestic market and exported. The farmers used the bank notes to pay the landowners rent and the landowners returned the notes to the private banks in exchange for gold, silver or foreign currency. Hence the private banks facilitated a transfer of resources from tenant farmers to landowners. The private banks were superseded by joint stock banks following the banking crises in the early 1820s. In contrast to the private banks, joint stock banks had at least six major shareholders (who accepted unlimited liability) and they were therefore better able to withstand crises.

10. Eoin O'Kelly, *The Old Private Banks and Bankers of Munster*, Cork University Press, 1959. See also Kevin Hannon, "The Limerick Savings Bank", *Old Limerick Journal*, No. 3, 1980.

11. O Grada, *op. cit.*, p. 27. In the same vein, when government asked the commercial banks to underwrite a flotation of government stock in the 1930s, the banks were reluctant and wished to know how the government intended to spend the proceeds.

12. See John Maynard Keynes, "National Self-Sufficiency", the first Finlay lecture delivered at University College, Dublin, April 1933, reprinted in *Studies*, June 1933.

13. O Grada, *op. cit.*, p. 42.

14. James Meenan, *The Irish Economy since 1922*, Manchester University Press, 1970, p. 222.

15. O Grada, *op. cit.*, p. 39.

16. O Grada, *op. cit.*, p. 44.

17. This topic is discussed by Patrick Honohan in "Regional Autonomy in Central Banking", *Irish Banking Review*, forthcoming 1992.

The sum of the Central Bank's liabilities is referred to as *high-powered money* or the *monetary base*. The reserves of the commercial banks are included in this total. It is called high-powered because, as we have seen, changes in reserves have a multiple or expanded impact on the money supply. Ignoring, for simplicity, government deposits and "other liabilities" on the liability side of the Central Bank balance sheet (see Table 6.7), high-powered money (H) is equal to currency (CU) plus licensed bank reserves at the Central Bank (RE).

(1) $H = CU + RE$

　　　Using this definition we can now present a more complete version of the money multiplier than the simple one introduced earlier in section 6.5. We assume that people hold currency in proportion to their current and deposit accounts (D):

(2) $CU = c_p D$

where $0 < c_p < 1$. If c_p was equal to, say, 0.1, this means that for every £1 held in current and deposit accounts, the public holds ten pence in currency. Because of the primary liquidity ratio, licensed bank reserves at the Central Bank are also related to current and deposit accounts.

(3) $RE = r_b D$

Again, $0 < r_b < 1$. If the primary reserve ratio were 10 per cent, r_b would be at least 0.1. The banks can, however, keep excess reserves if they wish. If equations (2) and (3) are inserted into equation (1), we obtain:

(4) $H = (c_p + r_b)D$

Recall now that M3 is equal to currency plus current and deposit accounts.

(5) $M3 = CU + D$

Substitute equation (2) into equation (5):

(6) $M3 = (c_p + 1)D$

The final step in deriving the relationship between M3 and H is to take the ratio of equation (6) to equation (4):

(7) $M3/H = (c_p + 1)/(c_p + r_b)$

or

(8) $M3 = (c_p + 1)/(c_p + r_b)H$

This version of the money multiplier relates high-powered money to the overall money supply and allows for currency leakages. If $c_p = 0$ (the public does not increase currency holdings as deposits increase) we obtain the earlier version of the multiplier.

We can calculate the money multiplier in the Irish economy for June 1991 using the data in Tables 6.2 and 6.7.

$c_p = CU/D = 1,303.7/11,208.2 = 0.116$

$r_b = RE/D = 1,128.3/11,208.2 = 0.10$

The money multiplier is equal to

$(c_p + 1)/(c_p + r_b) = (0.116 + 1)/(0.116 + 0.10) = 5.16$

This means that an increase of £1 in high-powered money would lead to an increase of £5.16 in the money supply. An increase in currency holdings in relation to deposits (c_p) will reduce the money multiplier. For example, if c_p increased from 0.116 to 0.2, the money multiplier would fall to 4.0. Similarly, as we noted earlier, an increase in r_b will decrease the money multiplier.

High-powered money is increased whenever the Central Bank increases its assets or its liabilities. It follows therefore that if the Central Bank can control currency in circulation and bank deposits with the Central Bank it should be able to control the money supply. In practice, however, controlling the money supply has proved to be a very difficult task. During the early 1980s UK economic policy relied heavily on trying to control sterling M3 by controlling the stock of high-powered money. However, control of high-powered money did not translate simply into control of the money supply. It was found that the money multiplier was very unstable, perhaps because the UK banking system was undergoing a profound transformation under deregulation. None the less, international experience shows that it is not possible to have a sustained expansion of the money supply without an increase in the monetary base. Hence the Central Bank's balance is at the centre of the stage of monetary policy.

Although small, the Irish financial sector is quite complex. For historical reasons, a variety of different categories of banks exist and different regulations, including reserve requirements, are applied to them. The various types of financial institutions specialise in different segments of the market, attracting their deposits from different types of depositors and lending to different types of borrowers. The main categories of financial institutions are as follows:

Associated banks (Allied Irish Bank, Bank of Ireland, National Irish Bank and the Ulster Bank). These are public quoted companies which provide a full range of lending and deposit facilities and together they constitute the backbone of the Irish *retail banking* system, which meets the banking needs of the general public. The term "associated banks" comes from the Central Bank Act of 1942 and indicates that a special relationship exists between these banks and the Central Bank. It should be noted that the associated banks have important subsidiaries operating in other segments of the banking market and in hire purchase finance. The Irish retail banking system is characterised by a few large banks with hundreds of branches. In this it resembles the British and Canadian systems. Banking in the US, on the other hand, is still characterised by thousands of small, independent and localised banks, although regional and national banking networks are being established.

Non-associated banks This category is subdivided into:
1. Merchant and commercial banks (Allied Irish Investment Bank, Algemene Bank Nederland, Guinness and Mahon, The Bank of Nova Scotia, Citibank, etc.). These banks cater to the wholesale end of the market, which includes large personal and corporate accounts. They also provide investment management and consultancy services.
2. Industrial banks (Allied Irish Finance, Bank of Ireland Finance, Bowmaker Bank, Lombard and Ulster, UDT Bank, etc.). These specialise in providing fixed interest loans to the personal sector for consumer durables and to industry for machinery and other equipment.

Note:
The associated and non-associated banks comprise the *licensed banks*.

State-sponsored financial institutions (The Industrial Credit Corporation and the Agricultural Credit Bank). These are state-owned banks which were established to act as development banks in industry and agriculture, respectively. They are likely to be privatised in the near future.

The Post Office Savings Bank This is a government-owned savings bank. All deposits are used to purchase government securities. The Post Office also administers an instalment savings scheme and issues savings certificates.

Trustee savings banks Approximately 80 per cent of the deposits of these banks are lent to the government and the remainder is lent to the public. These banks are owned by trustees on behalf of their depositors.

Building societies (First National Building Society, Educational Building Society, Irish Permanent Building Society, etc.). Building societies now act very much like banks, but they were founded as mutual societies to help small savers acquire money for house purchase against the security of the property. The 1989 legislation has brought them more into line with ordinary banks.

Hire purchase finance companies (Allied Finance, Advance Finance, etc.). These companies are similar to the industrial banks in that they provide fixed interest loans for the purchase of consumer durables and machinery for industry. Many of them are subsidiaries of the associated banks.

Credit unions Credit unions are localised, cooperative banks whose main business is lending to their members on a non-profit basis.

In recent years the main insurance companies have launched a number of schemes to attract savings. These offer attractive returns by taking advantage of the favourable tax treatment of life insurance premia. They compete with the banks and other financial institutions for the public's savings.

Bank profits were the subject of much criticism in the 1920s. The Irish Banks' Standing Committee (IBSC) was set up in 1920, comprised of representatives of both southern and northern banks, to agree common interest rates and bank charges. This suggested that a cartel had been formed with the objective of making supranormal profits from bank customers. Criticism focused, in particular, on the spread between deposit and lending rates. It was pointed out that deposit rates were *lower* and lending rates *higher* than similar rates in the UK. The concern at the outflow of large deposits from Ireland to the UK added weight to this argument. The IBSC continues to exist but it no longer sets interest rates for the banks, and its influence has been eroded by the entry of new financial institutions into the banking market. Despite this growth, the Irish financial sector remains small by international standards. The London clearing banks (the counterpart of our associated banks) have combined deposits totalling almost £300 billion, compared with the £7 billion in the Irish banks.

The interest rate charged by the industrial banks is roughly double that charged by the associated banks. In October 1991, the associated banks' overdraft and term loan rate to A borrowers was 15.25 per cent. In contrast, the *annual percentage rate* (APR) charged by the industrial banks varied from 21 per cent to 28 per cent and the rates charged by hire purchase finance companies were at least as high. (The APR must now be displayed on all advertisements for loans, hire purchase arrangements, etc. This requirement was resisted by the financial institutions.) The reason for the higher interest rate charged by finance houses is that their loans are riskier and involve higher administration costs than those entered into by the banks. The hire purchase finance companies do not take deposits from the public but borrow from banks and other sources and on-lend this money at much higher interest rates to the public.

Table 6.8 shows the relative shares of the various financial institutions in the market for deposits The associated banks have 40 per cent of the market, followed by the building societies with 21 per cent and the non-associated banks with 19 per cent.

Over the years, a significant shift in market share has occurred. In 1966 the associated banks and the building societies had approximately 80 per cent and 6 per cent of the deposit market, respectively. The building societies and other financial institutions have gained at the expense of the banks. The building societies' gain was partly due to increased demand for housing, and, up to 1986, the confidentiality and favourable tax treatment of their interest payments. The Finance Act of 1986, however, moved some way towards creating a "level playing field" for all financial institutions. Since 1986 all have to deduct the *deposit interest retention tax* (DIRT) at the standard rate from deposit interest paid, which is not disclosed to the Revenue Commissioners.

Despite the smallness of the Irish financial market, in the past the number of *regulatory bodies* responsible for it was quite large. The situation was rationalised in the Central Bank Act, 1989, when the building societies, the trustee savings banks and hire purchase finance companies were all brought under the control of the Central Bank, which was already responsible for the licensed banks. The Department of Finance regulates the Post Office Savings Bank. The Department of the Environment in conjunction with the Registrar of Friendly Societies controls credit unions. The Department of Industry and Commerce is responsible for insurance companies and firms operating under the Money Lenders' Acts.

The years ahead will see further important changes in Ireland's financial services. The opening of the IFSC has created a new layer of activity which, however, is largely off shore, that is, dealing with non-Irish deposits and transactions, and subject to special regulations and enjoying special tax concessions. Tax harmonisation and the abolition of exchange controls within the European Community will allow Irish residents a wider choice in regard to where they place their money or from whom they borrow. At the same time, Irish banks will continue to seek to diversify internationally, so that the Irish banking sector will become increasingly closely integrated with other centres abroad.

Table 6.8
The distribution of deposits between the financial institutions, June 1991

	£ m	%
Associated banks		
Current and deposit accounts	7,712.4	39.0
Non-associated banks		
Current and deposit accounts	3,805.9	19.2
Post Office and Trustee Savings Banks		
Deposits	1,211.7	6.1
State-sponsored financial institutions		
Deposits	757.0	3.9
Building societies		
Shares and deposits	4,163.5	21.0
Government savings schemes		
Savings	2,123.2	10.8
Credit Unions		
Deposits	NA	
Higher purchase finance companies		
Deposits	0.0	0.0
Total	19,773.7	100.0

Source: Central Bank of Ireland, *Quarterly Bulletin*, Autumn 1991, Table A3. Note: NA denotes not available.

Chapter 7

Interest Rates and Money in a Closed Economy

7.1   Introduction

We begin this chapter by outlining the Quantity Theory of Money. This is the classical theory of how the price level or inflation is determined in a closed economy. This is followed by a discussion of the Keynesian theory of money. In particular, we examine the Keynesian demand for money and show how, in the Keynesian model, the supply and demand for money determine the rate of interest. This analysis of the money market is then incorporated into the simple Keynesian model developed in earlier chapters and the key relationship between the rate of interest and the level of investment is highlighted. Using the expanded Keynesian model, issues such as the relative effectiveness of fiscal and monetary policy as instruments of economic policy are discussed. We emphasise at the outset that much of what we say in the course of the chapter has to be modified to take account of the environment of a small, open economy, such as Ireland. We undertake these refinements in later chapters.

7.2   The Quantity Theory of Money

The Quantity Theory is essentially a theory of the price level and hence of the rate of inflation. In its simplest form it states that the larger the quantity of money in the economy, the higher the price level, or, alternatively, that the more rapid the rate of increase in the money supply, the higher the rate of inflation.

Note:
The discovery of large silver mines in Mexico, Bolivia and Argentina led to a vast increase in the stock of silver coins in circulation in Europe from the sixteenth century onwards. The rise in the price level experienced at the same time was attributed by many observers to the increase in the quantity of money. This is the origin of the modern Quantity Theory.

The *velocity of circulation of money* (V) is defined as nominal GNP divided by the stock of money:

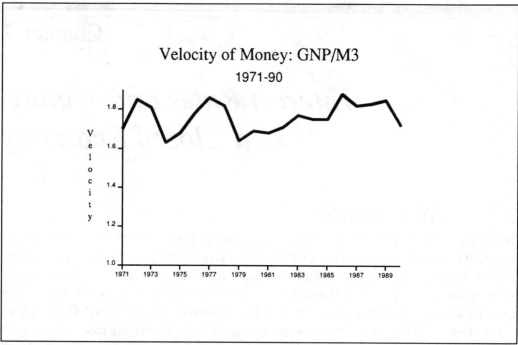

Figure 7.1 The velocity of circulation of money

---

(1) $V \equiv GNP/M^S$

Using the M3 definition of money, the 1990 figures for Ireland are:

$V \equiv$ £22,911 million/£12,635 million = 1.8

This means that the average monetary unit or £1 (notes and coins, current and deposit accounts in banks) financed £1.8 worth of expenditure on final goods and services. In other words, the average monetary unit was used less than twice during the year. This is what is meant by "velocity". Figure 7.1 shows the velocity of circulation of money in Ireland over the period 1971 to 1990 (data are not available for 1970 due to a bank dispute). Velocity has varied within a fairly narrow range over the years, never exceeding 1.9 or falling below 1.6.

If nominal GNP is divided into the price level (P) and real GNP, identity (1) can be written:

(2) $V \equiv (P \times \text{real GNP})/M^S$

Multiply both sides of (2) by M^S:

178

(3) $M^S \times V \equiv P \times \text{real GNP}$

Identity (3) can be used to explain the price level if we assume (i) that V is relatively stable (as it has in fact been in Ireland) and (ii) that output is at or close to the full employment level. Given these assumptions, what happens if the money supply, M^S, is increased? By assumption neither V nor real GNP will change and the brunt of the adjustment must come through increases in P, the price level. This, in a nutshell, is the explanation of inflation that follows from the Quantity Theory of Money: increases in the money supply lead to higher prices.

The Quantity Theory is a cornerstone of that school of economics that has come to be known as *monetarism*. The monetarists argue that V is constant and they add to this the assumption that the economy always tends to full employment. (See the discussion of classical economics in Chapter 2.) Monetarists believe that monetary policy should *not* be used to try to influence the level of GNP or to dampen the business cycle. They argue that an increase in the money supply will be translated into an increase in nominal GNP. Since real GNP tends to the full employment level, any increase in the money supply will cause the price level, rather than real GNP, to rise. Hence attempts to use monetary policy to stabilise the economy are doomed to failure. On the basis of these arguments, monetarists believe there should be no *discretionary* use of monetary policy. Instead, given the role of money as a medium of exchange, the authorities should maintain the growth in the money supply in line with the predicted growth in real GNP. This is the so-called *monetary rule*. If this rule is followed, the growth in the money supply will support the growth in the real economy and will not create inflation.

Note:
The exact mechanism by which increases in the money are transmitted into a higher price level is not specified. The Quantity Theory is a kind of "black box" theory.

As support for the Quantity Theory, monetarists point to the close correlation between inflation and the growth in the money supply in different countries and at different periods of time. Milton Friedman's *A Monetary History of the United States: 1867-1960* (written with his wife Anna Schwartz)[1] finds support for the monetarist point of view in the experience of the United States. Friedman also finds support for the Quantity Theory in inflation-prone countries such as Brazil, Bolivia and Israel. These countries have had high growth rates in their money supplies and rapid inflation. This has led Friedman to conclude: "Inflation is always and everywhere a monetary phenomenon."

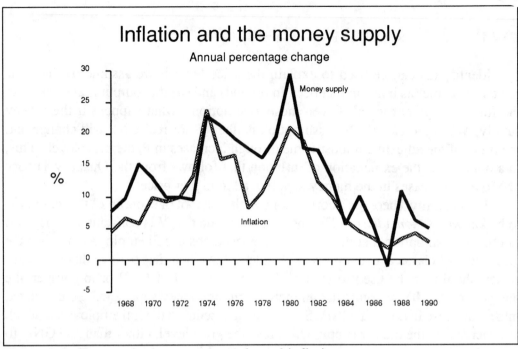

Figure 7.2 Changes in the money supply and inflation

Figure 7.2 shows the relationship between changes in the Irish money supply (M3) and Irish inflation over the period 1966 to 1990. The money supply series has been *lagged* one period in order to allow for the time it takes for changes in the money supply to translate into inflation. (For example, we are saying that the change in the money supply in 1979 caused the increase in inflation in 1980.) It can be seen that there is a close relationship between the two series. This is particularly evident during periods of high inflation such as the early 1970s and early 1980s. The relationship between the two variables is not so close in the mid-1980s. Also note that as changes in the money supply *preceded* changes in the price level, causation is clearly running from money to inflation and not the other way around. Thus the evidence for Ireland provides some support for the Quantity Theory of Money. However, a number of refinements have to be made before discussing the determinants of inflation in an open economy such as Ireland.

7.3   The Demand for Money

In the next few sections we outline the Keynesian theory of money. We begin by discussing the demand for money. We then show how changes in the money supply affect aggregate demand and output in the Keynesian model.

At first sight, the concept of the demand for money (M^d) may appear rather odd. If you ask someone what is her "demand for money", the answer is likely to be "infinite" or something to that effect. However, the term "demand for money" is used by economists in a rather special way and does not refer simply to the desire to be rich.

To understand what economists mean by the demand for money, we start from the consideration that people have a choice as to how to store their wealth. Wealth can be stored in many forms; money, government stocks, company shares, works of art, houses and so on. The essential difference between money and the alternatives is that money is *liquid*, that is, its value can be easily and quickly realised and converted into purchasing power. Unlike other assets, however, money does not give a *return* over time. Government stocks, company shares and other stores of value give a return but they are in varying degrees *illiquid*, that is, they cannot be immediately converted into a medium of exchange. The question we wish to address is why people forgo the return available on other assets and keep some of their wealth in money or cash.

Note:
The borderlines between the different categories of assets are not rigid. There is a spectrum ranging from the very liquid to the totally illiquid. Some liquid assets such as deposit accounts and some current accounts earn interest.

Transaction and precautionary motives

Keynes developed a theory called *liquidity preference* to account for people's desire to hold cash.[2] He analysed the reasons for holding cash under the headings of the *transaction*, *precautionary* and *speculative* motives. Let us now examine each of these in turn.

People need cash for *transaction* purposes, that is, to do their shopping, buy lunch, pay bus fares, etc. No matter how rich one is, it is hard to purchase a meal or a suit of clothes without paying with cash or something very close to cash (such as a credit card). Keynes described the transaction motive for holding money as the need "to bridge the interval between the receipt of income and its disbursement".[3] The more frequently people are paid, the smaller this interval and hence the smaller the demand for cash balances for this purpose. Also, improvements in the banking system have made it easier to transfer money between accounts and hence to minimise the amount of actual cash that has to be held for transactions purposes.

The *precautionary* motive is the desire to hold money to cater for unexpected contingencies (accidents, illness, etc.) or opportunities that may arise. According to Keynes, people hold cash to "provide for contingencies requiring sudden expenditure and for unforeseen opportunities of advantageous purchases".[4] It is reasonable to assume that the amount of money demanded for transactions and precautionary reasons depends on the level of income. The richer a person is, the more expensive her lifestyle and the more money she needs for transaction and precautionary reasons.

The same is true at the macro level. As national income or GNP increases, there is an increase in the demand for money for transaction purposes. An increase in GNP leads to an increase in the demand for money and a fall in GNP reduces the demand for money. The transaction and precautionary motives for holding money may therefore be written as:

(4) $M^d = f(GNP)$
        +

Equation (4) states that the demand for money is *a function of* nominal GNP. The + sign under the variable in brackets indicates that an increase in GNP results in a higher demand for money.

Note:
Recall from Chapter 4 that causation runs from the variable inside the brackets to the variable on the left-hand side (and not the other way). As a result, the variables inside the bracket are referred to as *explanatory* variables and the left-hand side variable as the *dependent* variable.

The speculative demand for money

In addition to the desire to hold money to finance day-to-day transactions and eventualities, Keynes believed that people hold money with the "object of securing profit from knowing better than the market what the future will bring forth".[5] He called this the *speculative motive*. He was referring to the bond market and to understand the speculative motive we need to look at the workings of the bond market.

Bond market Bonds issued by a company differ from shares in the company in a number of important ways. Shareholders own a proportion of the company and have voting rights, which gives them some control over the operations of the company. This ownership entitles them to an uncertain dividend which depends on the profits of the company. In contrast, bondholders lend money to a company for a specific period of time and do not have any control over the company's affairs; bonds pay a fixed monetary return (*coupon*) until the maturity date, so the bondholder knows with certainty how much income she will receive from the bond. For example, a bond with a face value of £2,000 and a coupon of £100 that matures in the year 2010 entitles the bondholder to a sum of £100 every year until 2010 and repayment of the £2,000 principal in 2010. A bond which is never redeemed but which pays an income indefinitely is known as a *perpetuity*.

In fact the government is the largest issuer of bonds in most modern economies, and government bonds provide a convenient medium for speculators trying to make *capital gains*. To see how this may be done, we need to consider what determines bond prices and bond yields. Consider the data in Table 7.1. Line 1 displays three rates of interest on bank deposits. Line 2 shows the *yield* on a government bond. The yield on a bond is defined as the coupon divided by the price of the bond. If the coupon is £10 and the price of the bond is £100 then the yield is 10 per cent.

Arbitrage ensures that the yield on the bond is roughly equal to the interest rate obtainable from a bank deposit. (In reality, risk, transaction costs and other factors have to be taken into account, and strict equality between the yields on different types of assets will not exist.)

Note:
Arbitrage is defined as buying a commodity or a currency in one market and selling it in another with a view to making a profit. The effect of arbitrage is to equalise prices across markets. For example, if the price of gold was lower in London than in New York speculators could make a profit by buying in London and selling in New York. But the increased demand for gold in London would drive up the London price, while simultaneously the increased supply in New York would drive down the New York price. In a short space of time the two prices would converge. Arbitrage is particularly effective in financial markets because information on prices and yields all over the world can be readily obtained. As a result, investors will buy and sell comparable assets until their yields are equal.

Table 7.1
The relationship between interest rates and bond prices

1. Interest rate on bank deposit	20%	10%	5%
2. Yield on bonds	20%	10%	5%
3. Fixed return on bonds	£10	£10	£10
4. Price of bonds	£50	£100	£200

Line 3 in Table 7.1 shows the coupon or fixed income from the government bond. In the example this is assumed to be £10. The only way for the yield on bonds to change, given that the coupon is fixed, is for the price of the bond to vary. (We assume that it is a perpetuity, so that what matters to an investor is its current and future yields rather than its value at maturity.) Line 4 shows the bond price that will equalise yields between bonds and money on deposit. For example, a coupon of £10 (line 3) and a price of £50 (line 4) gives a bond yield of 20 per cent (line 2). Notice now from Table 7.1 what happens when the interest rate falls from 20 to 10 to 5 per cent. Arbitrage will ensure that the yield on government bonds also falls from 20 to 10 to 5 per cent. For this to happen, the price of the bond must rise from £50 to £100 to £200. Therefore, as interest rates fall, bond prices rise and, conversely, as interest rates increase, bond prices fall.

Note:
There are many different interest rates, for example, the rates on short- and long-term government stocks, on low and high risk company bonds (the latter became known as "junk bonds" during the 1980s), as well as the rates charged by the banks on loans and paid on deposits. All these rates tend to move together so that we can refer to an average or representative interest rate as "the" interest rate.

Speculation The inverse relationship between interest rates and bond prices means that bondholders stand to make a capital gain when interest rates fall and a capital loss when interest rates rise. Investors should therefore buy bonds if they expect interest rates to fall and sell if they expect interest rates to rise. This strategy provides the basis of the Keynesian speculative motive for holding cash.

Keynes assumed that there exists a "normal" rate of interest and argued that departures from this rate are viewed as temporary. If interest rates rise above the normal rate, the expectation will be that they will eventually fall. Similarly, if interest rates fall below the normal rate, the expectation will be that they will rise. Suppose, for example, that the normal rate of interest is considered to be 10 per cent and interest rates increase from 10 per cent to 11 per cent. Investors holding bonds suffer a capital loss. However, the expectation is now that interest rates will fall back to the normal level of 10 per cent. Investors should therefore reduce their money holdings and purchase bonds in anticipation of making a capital gain sometime in the future. When interest rates are expected to fall, the demand for money will fall because investors will move their wealth from cash into bonds in the hope of making a capital gain.

The relationship between the interest rate (r) and the demand for money can be written:

(5) $M^d = f(r)$

where the minus sign indicates that an increase in the interest rate causes a fall in M^d and vice versa.

Opportunity cost The inverse relationship between the interest rate and the demand for money could also be explained in terms of the *opportunity cost* of holding cash. As we saw above, wealth held as cash does not earn a return, whereas wealth held as stocks or bonds or in other assets does. By holding cash, a person is therefore forgoing the interest that could have been earned on bonds, for example. In periods of inflation, cash balances actually decline in value and the holder receives no compensation for this, whereas a bondholder is paid an interest rate that tends to reflect the anticipated rate of inflation. When the interest rate is high, the opportunity cost of holding cash balances is also high and it is to be expected that the public will economise on their holdings of cash. It is therefore only realistic to include the rate of interest among the determinants of the demand for money.

Combining the transaction, precautionary and speculative motives

Combining equations (4) and (5) we can account for all the motives for holding money and write the demand for money function as:

(6) $M^d = f(GNP, r)$
$\qquad\quad + \quad -$

Equation (6) states that the demand for money is a function of nominal GNP and the interest rate. As before the signs indicate how the explanatory variables influence the dependent variable. Separating nominal GNP into its real and price components, equation (6) can be rewritten as:

(7) $M^d = f(\text{real GNP}, P, r)$
$\qquad\qquad\quad + \quad\; + \;\; -$

Equation (7) states that the demand for money is positively related to both real GNP and the price level (P), but negatively to the rate of interest. Rearranging:

(8) $M^d/P = f(\text{real GNP}, r)$
$\qquad\qquad\quad\; + \quad\; -$

Equation (8) expresses the demand for money in real terms or the demand for *real money* or *real cash balances* (M^s/P). This is a function of real GNP and the rate of interest. An increase in real GNP increases the demand for real cash balances and a rise in the rate of interest reduces it.

Graphical representation The demand for money schedule is drawn in Figure 7.3. The downward sloping line shows the inverse relationship between the rate of interest, on the vertical axis, and the demand for money, on the horizontal axis. An increase in the interest rate reduces the demand for money and conversely, a fall in the interest rate increases the demand for money. Note that the slope of the demand for money curve is not linear. At low interest rates the curve is flat or horizontal. The reason for this is that at low interest rates there may be unanimity among investors that interest rates will rise in the future and if this happens bond prices will fall. In order to avoid speculative losses in the bond market investors therefore keep their wealth in cash balances. Therefore, as the rate of interest falls to a low level, the demand for money increases very rapidly. This is reflected in the diagram in the flat portion of the demand for money curve.

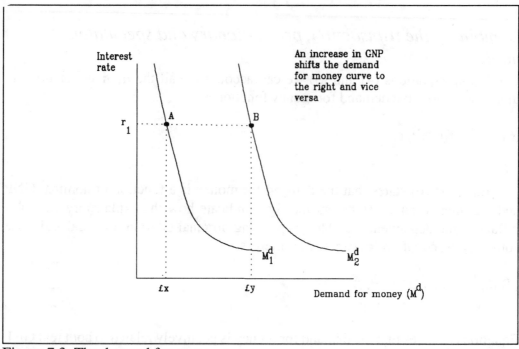

Figure 7.3 The demand for money curve

Nominal GNP on the other hand determines the *position* (or location) of the demand for money schedule. Whereas the relationship between the interest rate and the demand for money is shown by movements *along* the line, the relationship between GNP and the demand for money is shown by *shifts* of the line. An increase in GNP shifts the M^d schedule to the right, a fall in GNP shifts it to the left.

7.4 Money Market Equilibrium

In Figure 7.4 the money supply (M^s) schedule is combined with a demand for money (M^d) schedule. The money supply is shown as a vertical line which indicates that changes in the interest rate do not affect the supply of money. This assumes that the money supply is completely controlled by the monetary authorities or Central Bank. Put another way, we are assuming that the money supply is exogenous. (If changes in interest rates had a positive effect on the money supply, the M^s curve would slope upwards to the right.)

The important point here is that the interaction of the supply and demand for money determines the interest rate (r). In other words, the rate of interest is the price of money and, like other prices, it is determined by the forces of supply and demand. At an interest rate of r_1, the supply and demand for money are equal. The money market is in equilibrium. At interest rate r_2, however, there is an excess supply of money and the interest rate will fall towards the equilibrium rate. At interest rate r_3,

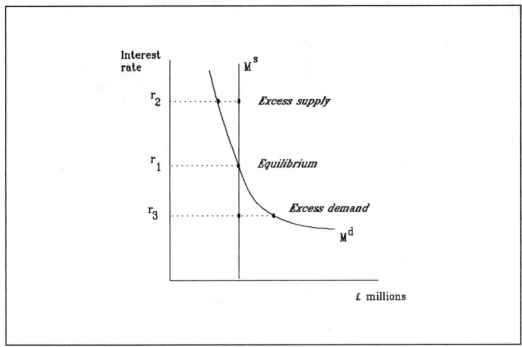

Figure 7.4 Equilibrium in the money market

there is an excess demand for money and the interest rate will rise to the equilibrium rate.

Note:
To understand how the rate of interest moves towards equilibrium bear in mind that an excess demand for money implies an excess supply of bonds. When the interest rate is below the equilibrium rate, the public is holding too many bonds. They will therefore sell bonds, which drives down the price of bonds and raises the rate of interest. This process continues until the equilibrium rate is reached.

Figure 7.5 illustrates what happens to the interest rate when the central bank increases the money supply, through, for example, open market operations. The money supply (M^s) line moves out to the right and the interest rate falls from r_1 to the new equilibrium level, r_2. An increase in the money supply therefore reduces the interest rate. Conversely, a reduction in the money supply leads to an increase in the interest rate.

As mentioned in the previous section, the demand for money schedule is horizontal at low interest rates. An increase in the money supply along the flat portion of the demand for money curve would not lower interest rates and, as we shall see, monetary policy would be ineffective. This situation is known as the *liquidity trap*.

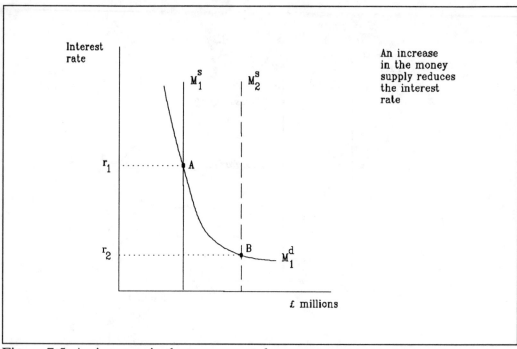

Figure 7.5 An increase in the money supply

Figure 7.6 illustrates the case where the demand for money (M^d) curve shifts upwards to the right following an increase in nominal GNP. The resulting excess demand for money increases the interest rate from r_1 to r_2. Similarly, a fall in nominal GNP will shift the M^d curve downwards and interest rates will fall.

7.5   Monetary Policy in a Closed Economy

Let us now incorporate our model of the money market into the model of the economy we developed in earlier chapters. We shall not assume, as is done in the Quantity Theory of Money, that the economy is at full employment: instead we assume that there are unemployed resources and that the level of real output can change in response to changes in aggregate demand and/or the supply of money. We also assume for the moment that the price level remains constant in the short run.

The expanded model of the economy contains two markets: the goods or product market and the money market. In the goods market, equilibrium occurs when aggregate supply (GNP) is equal to aggregate demand (or total expenditure). The demand side of a closed economy can be broken down in its components, private and public consumption expenditure and investment (C, G and I). In the money market, the supply and demand for money determine the interest rate. Now the authorities have two *policy instruments,* government expenditure and taxation (*fiscal*

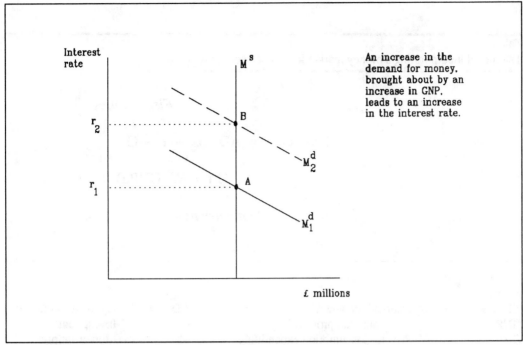

Figure 7.6 An increase in the demand for money

---

policy) and the money supply and interest rates (*monetary policy*), with which to influence output, income and prices.

Table 7.2 outlines how these instruments affect the level of economic activity. An increase in government expenditure (G) increases aggregate demand (AD) directly. If the economy is initially in equilibrium, the increase in G leads to an excess demand for goods and services. Firms recognise this excess demand as stocks fall and they respond by producing more goods and services. The resulting increase in GNP leads to an increase in national income (NI) and a reduction in unemployment (U).

Changes in the money supply affect GNP and NI via the interest rate (r) and investment (I). The sequence is as follows: an increase in M^s creates a disequilibrium in the money market because there is an excess supply of cash. This drives down the interest rate, which in turn increases I for reasons we explore in detail below. Some components of consumer spending may also respond to the reduction in the interest rate, the most obvious possibility being spending on durable goods that are bought on credit. Fiscal policy is much more direct in its effects than monetary policy: an increase in G increases aggregate demand directly, whereas an increase in M^s operates indirectly, through its effect on the rate of interest.

Table 7.2
The model incorporating a money market in a closed economy

$$Fiscal\ policy$$
$$\downarrow$$
$$NI \equiv GNP = AD \equiv C + I + G$$

$$M^s = M^d(GNP, r)$$
$$\uparrow$$
$$Monetary\ policy$$

where

NI	=	National income	AD	=	Aggregate demand
GNP	=	Gross national product	I	=	Investment
C	=	Private Consumption expenditure	M^s	=	Money supply
G	=	Government consumption expenditure	r	=	Interest rate
M^d	=	Demand for money			

Note: Because we are discussing policy in a closed economy, imports and exports are omitted from the components of aggregate demand.

The effect of changes in the money supply on output can be depicted as follows:

$$\uparrow M^s \rightarrow \downarrow r \rightarrow \uparrow I \rightarrow \uparrow AD \rightarrow \uparrow GNP \rightarrow \uparrow NI \rightarrow \downarrow U$$

The symbols, $\uparrow$, $\downarrow$ and $\rightarrow$ indicate increase, decrease and "leads to", respectively. Figure 7.7 makes use of the money market diagram and the Keynesian cross diagram (developed in Chapter 4) to illustrate the effect of an increase in the money supply. In the lower diagram, the Central Bank increases the money supply from M^s_1 to M^s_2. The interest rate falls from r_1 to r_2. The fall in the interest rate leads to an increase in investment, which shifts the aggregate demand schedule upwards and the economy moves from the point A to the point B in the upper panel of the diagram. Firms recognise the excess demand as stocks fall and they respond by increasing output. Real GNP increases from GNP_1 to GNP_2 along the horizontal axis and equilibrium is re-established at the point C. This increase in real output should lead to lower unemployment. Thus, the link between the money market and the goods market is the rate of interest through its effect on the level of investment. We now explore in more detail this key relationship in the Keynesian model.

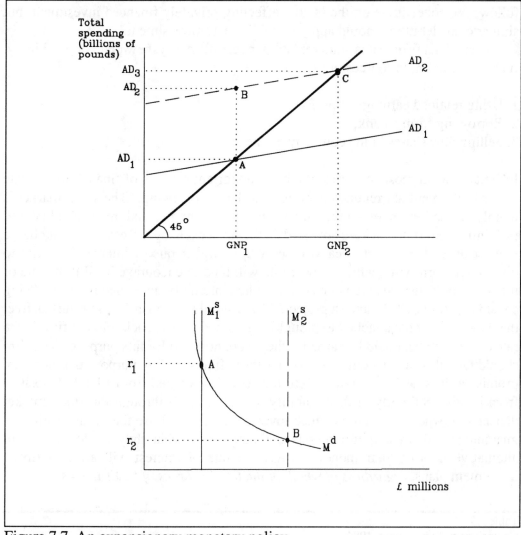

Figure 7.7 An expansionary monetary policy

7.6   Investment and Interest Rates

Investment consists of building roads, factories and houses, and purchasing plant and equipment. In the National Income and Expenditure accounts, the magnitude corresponding to what we have labelled I is referred to as *gross domestic physical capital formation*. This totalled £4,337 million in 1989. Table 7.3 shows its components. Some of this investment is undertaken directly by the public sector, some of it is financed in part by state grants, and the rest is privately financed. (The Public Capital Programme in 1988 totalled £1,406 million so more than one-third of all investment was financed directly or indirectly by the public sector.) In what follows we concentrate on the factors affecting privately financed investment, but similar considerations should apply to public sector investment.

Consider a firm that is contemplating investing in, say, new plant or machinery. It has three possible sources of finance:

1. Using retained earnings or profits;
2. Borrowing from a bank;
3. Selling new shares in the company on the stock exchange.

In Ireland, as in most countries, the most important sources of finance for private sector investment are retained earnings and bank borrowing. The stock market is mainly a market in existing, rather than new, shares, and most smaller and medium-sized companies are not listed on the stock exchange. Because banks charge interest on their loans, it is easy to see why a higher rate of interest will tend to discourage borrowing, while a lower rate will tend to encourage it. But the rate of interest should also be taken into account when internally-generated funds are being considered for use to finance a project. Firms should not regard these funds as free: the opportunity cost attached to ploughing retained profits back into the firm is the rate of interest that could be earned if they were not used for this purpose. The firm should take this into account and not use these funds for any purpose that does not promise at least as high a rate of return as could be earned from a bank deposit or from bonds. Similarly, a firm's ability to raise money through the stock market depends on whether it can convince investors that it will use the funds profitably, guaranteeing them a return that is comparable to what they could earn from alternative uses of their money. Thus, the rate of interest will affect a firm's investment plans, *regardless of which of the three sources of funds it uses.*

Table 7.3
Composition of investment, 1989

	£ m	%
Plant and equipment	1,252	28.9
Building and construction	962	22.2
Dwellings	965	22.2
Transport equipment	847	19.6
Roads	182	4.2
Agricultural machinery	129	2.9
Total investment	4,337	100.0

Source: The *National Income and Expenditure*, 1990, Table 15, Central Statistics Office, Dublin, 1991.

Net present value The effect of changes in the rate of interest on the profitability of an investment plan can be shown by employing the concept of the *net present value* (NPV), which is now routinely used in the evaluation of projects by firms, banks and governments.

To illustrate its use, let us suppose that you have the opportunity of investing in a project that is forecast to generate the following flow of income over a three-year period:

Year	Net income at end of the year: £
1	100,000
2	150,000
3	200,000

For simplicity, assume that no assets remain at the end of the three-year project. How much would you be prepared to pay to buy into this project? To answer this, we must *discount* the projected income stream to calculate its *(net) present value* (NPV).[6]

Discounting is the inverse of the more familiar concept of *compounding,* according to which a sum of money, £x, invested today at r per cent is worth £x(1+r) at the end of the year. Discounting inverts this process and asks: How much is £x to be paid at the end of a year worth today? What is its present value? The answer is £x/(1+r). Extending this logic, the same sum paid at the end of two years has a present value of $£x/(1+r)^2$.

Assuming an interest rate of 10 per cent (r = 0.10), Table 7.4 calculates the net present value of the numbers given above.

Table 7.4
Calculating the net present value

Year	Net income at end of year £	Discount factor £	Present value £
1	100,000	$1/(1.10) = 0.9091$	90,910
2	150,000	$1/(1.10)^2 = 0.8264$	123,967
3	200,000	$1/(1.10)^3 = 0.7513$	150,263
	Total = £450,000		Project's NPV = £365,140

These calculations tell us that while this project yields a total (undiscounted) income of £450,000, the discounted value or NPV of this income stream is £365,140.

The NPV can be thought of as the demand price of an investment project: it is the maximum that a person would be willing to pay to buy into it. If more than £365,140 has to be paid to invest in the above project, the investor would be better off putting his money in the bank and earning 10 per cent interest on it. If he can get in on the project for less than £365,140, then he should accept the opportunity as he will make more from the project than from the alternative use of the money.

Table 7.5 shows how the NPV of the hypothetical investment project falls as the interest rate increases. The higher the rate of interest the lower the value of the project to a prospective investor.

As a consequence, a rise in the interest rate can make a previously profitable project unprofitable. A fall in the interest rate can make an unprofitable project profitable. The interest rate has a greater effect on the NPV of projects that are long-lived: some very capital intensive investments that have a very long life, such as electricity generating projects, can only be profitable at low rates of interest.

Table 7.5
NPV and the interest rate

Interest rate %	NPV £
5	404,060
10	365,140
15	331,881
20	303,241

Marginal efficiency of investment It follows from this that an increase in the rate of interest will reduce the number of investment projects that people will want to undertake, and choke off the demand for funds for investment, while a fall in the rate of interest will increase the number of projects it is worth undertaking and increase the demand for investment funds. There is, therefore, an inverse relationship between the interest rate and the demand for funds for investment. This relationship is known as the *marginal efficiency of investment* (MEI) schedule and it is illustrated in Figure 7.8. The interest rate is measured along the vertical axis and the level of investment along the horizontal axis. If changes in the rate of interest have a weak effect on investment then the MEI curve will be steep. If, on the other hand, changes in the rate of interest have a strong effect on investment the curve will be flat. The

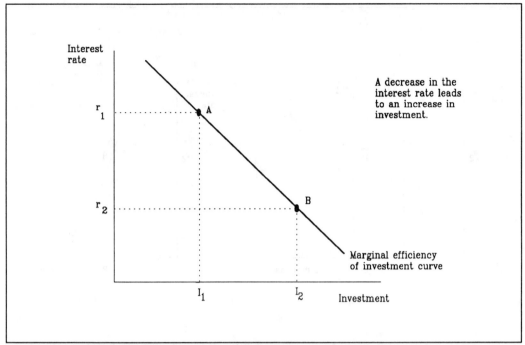

Figure 7.8 The marginal efficiency of investment

magnitude of the effect depends on the type of projects being considered: if they are mainly capital-intensive, long-lived projects, then the MEI will be very flat (elastic).

The MEI depicts the relationship between the interest rate and investment on the assumption that other relevant factors remain constant. It is very important to bear in mind that the MEI shifts as other factors change. In fact it is often argued that the rate of interest is not the most important influence on the demand for investment funds: factors such as changes in the level of business confidence and in expectations about the growth in national income could easily swamp the influence of the rate of interest. Keynes tended to dismiss the importance of the rate of interest as a factor in the investment decision: during a recession, for example, he felt little good would come from lowering interest rates in the hope of stimulating investment. He compared this approach to a starving man hoping to get fat by loosening his belt! He emphasised the importance of confidence in the future and sheer "animal spirits" as factors affecting the level of investment.

7.7   Fiscal and Monetary Policy in the Enlarged Model

We shall now explore the effects of fiscal and monetary policy on the economy, taking account of the complications introduced by the operation of the money market. Basically, the extreme Keynesian position is that fiscal policy is *effective* and that

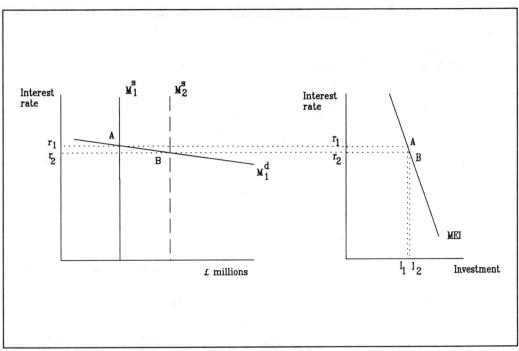

Figure 7.9 Monetary policy: the Keynesian position

monetary policy is *ineffective* in influencing GNP. In contrast, neo-classical economists and monetarists such as Milton Friedman argue that fiscal policy is *ineffective* and monetary policy has a *strong effect* on nominal GNP.

The disagreement between Keynesian and neo-classical economists essentially revolves about two relationships. The relationship between:

1. the interest rate and the demand for money (technically referred to as the *interest elasticity of the demand for money*)
2. the interest rate and investment (the *marginal efficiency of investment curve*).

Keynesians argue that the demand for money curve is relatively *flat*. This means that the interest rate is an important determinant of the demand for money. Second, Keynesians believe that the MEI curve is relatively *steep* (*inelastic*). Changes in the interest rate have a weak effect on investment. A flat M^d curve and a steep MEI curve are depicted in Figure 7.9.

In the left-hand side diagram, because the M^d curve is flat, an increase in the money supply leads to a small decrease in the interest rate. This change in interest rate, in turn, leads to a small change in investment because the MEI curve is assumed to be steep. Going one stage further, a small change in investment means that aggregate demand, output and income will not change very much. (In terms of the Keynesian cross diagram, which is not shown, there would be a small shift upwards

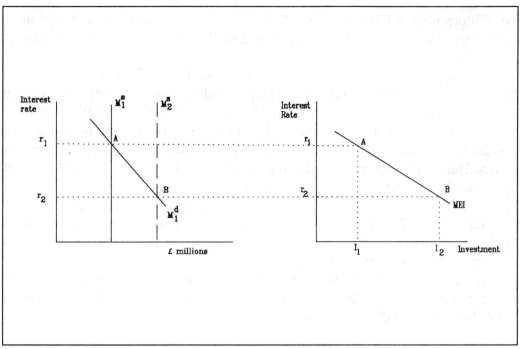

Figure 7.10 Monetary policy: the monetarist position

in the aggregate demand curve.) Overall, monetary policy has a weak effect on output and employment.

Note:
If the demand for money curve is horizontal at low interest rates, an increase in the money supply along this portion of the M^d curve will have no effect on the interest rate. In this case, monetary policy cannot be used to increase output and employment. This is known as the *liquidity trap*.

Neo-classical economists, on the other hand, argue that the demand for money curve is *steep*. Changes in the interest rate have a weak effect on the demand for money.[7] The interest rate is not an important determinant of the demand for money. Second, monetarists argue that the MEI curve is relatively *flat* (or elastic). Changes in the interest rate have a strong effect on investment. This is illustrated in Figure 7.10. Under these conditions a given increase in the money supply leads to a *large* fall in the interest rate. The lower interest rate, in turn, leads to a relatively *large* change in investment. The implication is that monetary policy (changes in the money supply) will have an important effect on aggregate demand and nominal output. This outcome is in accordance with the conclusions of the Quantity Theory of Money discussed in section 7.2.

Neo-classical economists also believe that fiscal policy has little or no effect on GNP. At first sight this appears rather odd. After all, an increase in government expenditure (G) boosts aggregate demand and GNP. Hence changes in government expenditure must influence GNP. Neo-classical economists, however, point to *crowding out* as a reason why fiscal policy is ineffective. We examine this issue in the next section.

A number of authors, including Pratschke and O'Connell (1973), Browne and O'Connell (1978), Browne (1984) and Hurley and Guiomard (1989), have studied the demand for money function for Ireland.[8] Browne and O'Connell (1978) estimate that the interest elasticity of the demand for money is - 0.18. This means that a 1 per cent increase in the interest rate leads to 0.18 per cent decrease in the demand for money. Hurley and Guiomard find a weak relationship between the interest rate and the demand for money (in fact the interest rate sometimes appears with a positive rather than a negative sign). These two studies therefore tend to offer support for the monetarist case. The demand for money curve for Ireland appears to be steep (inelastic). What evidence there is for Ireland indicates that interest rates have a weak effect on investment, that is the MEI is steep.[9]

The evidence on the effects of interest rates on the Irish economy is therefore mixed, tending towards a Keynesian view of its effects on the demand for investment funds, but towards a classical view of its effects on the demand for money.

7.8 Crowding Out

Neo-classical economists accept that changes in government expenditure lead to changes in aggregate demand and therefore GNP but, they point out, that is not the end of the story. An increase in GNP increases the demand for money (M^d) and, if there is no increase in the money supply, this will push up interest rates (see Figure 7.6). The rise in interest rates will, in turn, lower the level of investment. The initial increase in government expenditure thus leads to a reduction in private sector spending. Investment has been crowded out by government expenditure. In short:

$$\uparrow G \quad \rightarrow \quad \uparrow AD \quad \rightarrow \quad \uparrow GNP$$

However,

$$\uparrow GNP \quad \rightarrow \quad \uparrow M^d \quad \rightarrow \quad \uparrow r \quad \rightarrow \quad \downarrow I$$

If $\uparrow G = \downarrow I$, there is 100 per cent crowding out. In this case, AD and GNP revert back to their original level and fiscal policy is completely ineffective. This is the extreme neo-classical position.

Figure 7.11 illustrates the crowding out effect. The expansionary fiscal policy increases GNP. The increase in GNP, in turn, shifts the demand for money curve upwards from M^d_1 to M^d_2 (left-hand diagram). The interest rate rises from r_1 to r_2 along the vertical axis. In the right-hand diagram, the increase in interest rates reduces investment. In terms of the components of aggregate demand, the fall in

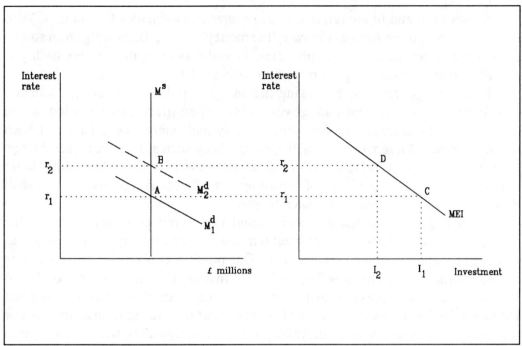

Figure 7.11 The crowding out effect

investment offsets the initial increase in government expenditure and aggregate demand may revert back to its initial level.

The elasticity of the MEI schedule is what determines the degree of crowding out. The neo-classical contention that the MEI is flat (elastic) at the current interest rate means that a small increase in the interest rate will have a relatively large effect on investment. If this is the case, crowding out will be important. If, however, as the Keynesians argue, the MEI curve is steep (inelastic), crowding out will not be important, as changes in interest rates have little or no effect on investment.

Monetary financing It is important to note that the crowding out effect only occurs when the money supply remains unchanged in the face of a fiscal expansion. If the money supply increases as the demand for money rises, the interest rate need not rise and crowding out need not occur. In this context, the method of financing government expenditure is important. Recall from Chapter 4 that the government can finance its borrowing requirement from four sources:

i.   Abroad
ii. From the Central Bank
iii. From the commercial banks
iv. From the domestic non-bank public.

Sources i, ii and iii are referred to as *government monetary financing (GMF)*. Borrowing from these sources increases the money supply. Borrowing from source iv does not affect the money supply. (In a closed economy, the first possibility is ruled out, thereby increasing the risk of crowding out.)

In Ireland government borrowing has relied heavily on monetary financing. Consequentially, increases in government expenditure have tended to be accompanied by increases in the money supply and interest rates have not been unduly affected. Moreover, in a small open economy such as Ireland, higher interest rates tend to attract capital inflows from the rest of the world. Both these considerations reduce the risks of crowding-out. These are points that we shall develop more systematically in a later chapter.

In the course of our discussion of Ireland's economic performance during the second half of the 1980s it was pointed out that a contractionary fiscal policy was followed by a period of increased growth. One possible explanation of this episode is that a form of "reverse crowding out" or "crowding in" occurred. According to this view, the reduced pressure on the domestic money market due to the lower deficit led to a reduction in interest rates, which stimulated private sector investment. For this interpretation of events to be valid private sector spending would have had to increase by *more* than the reduction in public sector spending. This is more extreme than the case of complete crowding out on which the classical case for the ineffectiveness of fiscal policy is based.

7.9   The IS-LM Model

The model outlined in Table 7.2 can be represented graphically using what are called IS-LM curves. These show the combinations of income and the rate of interest which simultaneously achieve equilibrium in the goods market and the money market. The IS-LM graph was first developed by the Nobel Prize winning English economist John Hicks (1904-1989).[10] The "I" in IS stands for investment and "S" for savings. The "L" in LM denotes liquidity preference (demand for money) and "M" the money supply. In this section, we develop the IS-LM model and use it to illustrate the issues we have introduced in earlier sections. In a later chapter we use the IS-LM model to evaluate fiscal and monetary policy in an open economy under fixed and flexible exchange rates.

The IS curve

Consider first the relationship between the interest rate and GNP in the goods market. The equilibrium condition in this market in a closed economy is:

(9) $GNP = AD \equiv C + I + G$

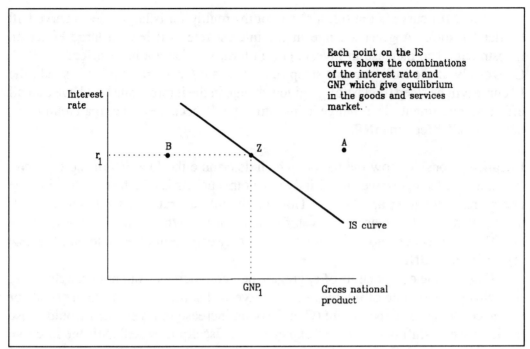

Figure 7.12 The IS curve

Spending on output equals planned production. As we have seen, an increase in interest rates leads to a fall in investment, and this in turn decreases aggregate demand and hence the equilibrium level of GNP. In short:

$\uparrow r \rightarrow \downarrow I \rightarrow \downarrow GNP$

Hence, in the goods market, there is an *inverse* relationship between the interest rates and the levels of GNP consistent with equilibrium. This is shown in Figure 7.12 as a downward sloping curve, labelled IS. Each point on the IS curve is a combination of the interest rate and GNP consistent with equilibrium in this market.

Slope The *slope* of the IS curve indicates how a change in the interest rate affects GNP. If the IS curve is flat (or elastic) a given change in the interest rate leads to a large change in GNP. Conversely, a steep (or inelastic) IS curve means that changes in the interest rate have little effect on GNP. The slope of the IS curve depends on:

i. The link between the interest rate and investment (the MEI schedule); and
ii. The link between investment and GNP (the multiplier).

201

If the MEI curve is flat (elastic) and/or the multiplier is large, the IS curve will be flat (elastic). A given change in the interest rate will have a large effect on investment. The increase in investment, in turn, will have a large effect on GNP. Conversely, if the MEI curve is steep (inelastic) and/or the multiplier is small, the IS curve will be steep (inelastic). A given change in the interest rate will have a small effect on investment. The change in investment will, because of the small multiplier, have a small effect on GNP.

Location Consider now the factors which determine the *location* of the IS curve. In Figure 7.12 suppose we are initially at a point such as Z which is on the IS curve and corresponds to r_1 and GNP_1. Holding the interest rate constant, suppose that aggregate demand increases. This shifts the IS curve to the right. Point A is on the new IS curve, which shows the relationship between the interest rate and the new higher level of GNP.

If any of the components of aggregate demand increase, but not brought about by a change in the rate of interest, the IS curve will shift. An increase in private or public consumption expenditure (C or G) or an increase in investment would cause the IS curve to shift out. Thus an expansionary fiscal policy will shift the IS curve to the right and a deflationary fiscal policy will shift the IS curve to the left. In an open economy, changes in the level of net exports, the difference between exports and imports, will also cause the IS curve to shift.

The LM curve

Consider now the relationship between the interest rate and GNP as reflected in the *money market*. The equilibrium condition in the money market is:

(10) $M^s = M^d(GNP, r)$

That is, the money supply equals the demand for money. The demand for money, in turn, is determined by the level of GNP and the interest rate. For a given money supply (M^s), an increase in GNP leads to an increase in the demand for money (M^d) and this in turn pushes up interest rates. In short:

$\uparrow GNP \rightarrow \uparrow M^d \rightarrow \uparrow r$

Hence, in the money market there is a *positive* relationship between the levels of GNP and the interest rate that is consistent with equilibrium and this is represented in Figure 7.13 by an upward sloping curve, labelled LM.

Each point on the LM curve is consistent with money market equilibrium. To see this consider two points not on the LM curve. At the point A in Figure 7.13, GNP and therefore the demand for money (M^d) is greater than that consistent with equilibrium so that there is an excess demand for money. At point B, GNP and M^d

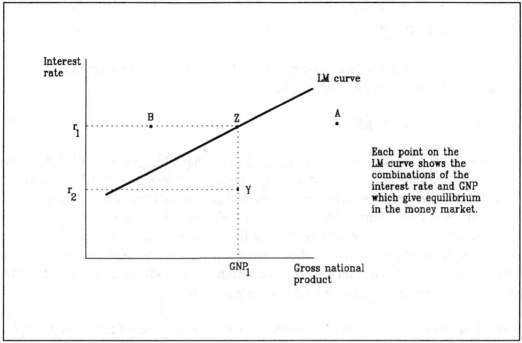

Figure 7.13 The LM curve

are lower than is consistent with equilibrium and there is therefore an excess supply of money. Only points on the LM curve are consistent with money market equilibrium.

Slope Consider now the factors which determine the *slope* of the LM curve. A steep LM curve means that a given change in GNP has a large effect on the interest rate. Conversely, a flat LM curve means that a given change in GNP has a small effect on the interest rate. Perhaps the easiest way to identify the determinants of the LM curve is to first write out the demand for money function in full. Earlier, equation (6) stated that the demand for money (M^d) was a function of nominal GNP and the interest rate. That equation may be written explicitly as:

(11) $M^d = \alpha \, GNP - \beta \, r$

The term α is a coefficient which shows how changes in GNP affect M^d and is known as the income elasticity of the demand for money.[11] The larger the coefficient α the greater the effect GNP has on M^d. The coefficient β shows how changes in the interest rate affect the demand for money and is referred to as the interest elasticity of the demand for money. Substituting equation (11) into the money market equilibrium condition, equation (10), we have:

203

(12) $M^S = \alpha\, GNP - \beta\, r$

We now want to see how changes in GNP will affect the interest rate. Solving equation (12) for the interest rate we have:

(13) $r = 1/\beta\, (\alpha\, GNP - M^S)$

An examination of equation (13) indicates that changes in GNP affect the interest rate via the coefficients α and β. Hence it is these two coefficients which determine the slope of the LM curve. A given change in GNP will have a *large* effect on the interest rate (steep or inelastic LM curve) if α is *large* and/or β is *small*. In other words, the LM curve will be *steep* if the income elasticity of the demand for money is large *(elastic)* and/or if the interest elasticity of the demand for money is small *(inelastic)*. Conversely, if the coefficient α is small (inelastic) and/or the coefficient β is large (elastic) the LM curve will be flat.

Location   The *location* of the LM curve depends on the level of the money supply. An increase in the money supply shifts the LM curve to the right and a decrease to the left. For example, in Figure 7.13, suppose the economy is at the point Z which is on the LM curve. Holding GNP constant, an increase in the money supply reduces the interest rate from r_1 to r_2 and the economy moves to the point Y. The point Y is one point on the new LM curve. Once the LM curve is shifted downwards, we can examine the relationship between GNP and the new lower interest rate which was brought about by the higher stock of money.

Equilibrium in the goods and money markets

Figure 7.14 combines the IS and the LM curves. Recall that points on the IS curve are consistent with equilibrium in the goods market and points on the LM curve are consistent with equilibrium in the money market. Hence, at A, where the two curves intersect, there is equilibrium in both the goods market and the money market. At the point A, and only at this point, aggregate demand equals planned production and the stock of money equals the desired holdings of cash balances by the public.

If a disequilibrium situation should arise, either because the interest rate or GNP is too high or too low, then it can be shown that the economy will adjust back to equilibrium. To establish this, we divide the non-equilibrium points in the diagram into four regions. Points in region I correspond to an excess supply of goods and of money. If the economy were at a point such as B in this region, the effect of the excess supplies in both the goods and money markets would be to drive the interest rate and GNP down until equilibrium is re-established at A. If the economy is at a point in region II, there will be an excess supply of goods but an excess demand for money. In this situation, the interest rate will rise and GNP will fall until equilibrium

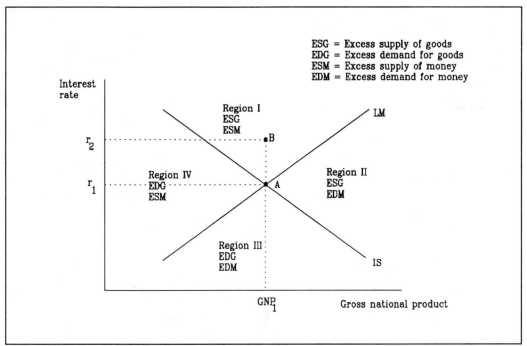

Figure 7.14 Equilibrium in the goods and money markets

is re-established. If the economy is at a point in region III, there is excess demand for goods and for money. Both GNP and the interest rate will rise until equilibrium is re-established. Finally, if the economy is in region IV, there is excess demand for goods and excess supply of money. GNP will rise and the interest rate would fall until equilibrium is re-established.

Thus the combination r_1 and GNP_1 represents a stable equilibrium to which the economy will return if for some reason it is displaced from it. However, we must not exaggerate the merits of this equilibrium: it is simply the combination of interest rates and GNP that results in *market clearing* in the goods and money markets. We leave to later chapters a discussion of whether it is consistent with other goals of macroeconomic policy such as balance of payments equilibrium or full employment.

7.10 The IS-LM Model and the Keynesian/Neo-classical Debate

The IS-LM framework can be used to illustrate issues raised earlier in this chapter concerning the relative effectiveness of fiscal and monetary policy.

Fiscal policy An expansionary fiscal policy shifts the IS curve to the right. As the two diagrams in Figure 7.15 illustrate, the resulting increase in GNP depends on the slope of the LM curve. In the upper panel, the LM curve is relatively flat and a shift

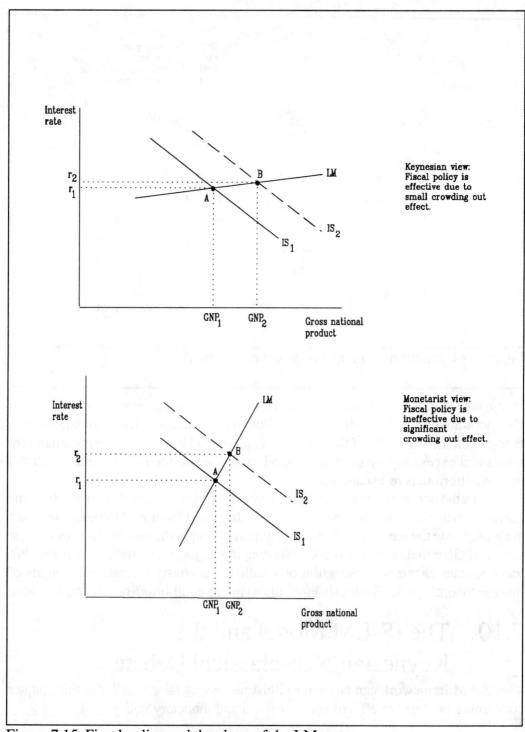

Figure 7.15 Fiscal policy and the slope of the LM curve

of the IS curve to the right leads to a large increase in GNP. In the lower panel, the LM curve is steep and a similar shift of the IS curve has a small effect on GNP.

The reason for this difference in the change in GNP is the crowding out effect. When the LM curve is horizontal, there is a small increase in the interest rate on the vertical axis and the crowding out effect is insignificant. On the other hand, if the LM curve is steep, there will be a large increase in the interest rate and the crowding out effect will be significant.

In our expanded model, therefore, the effectiveness of fiscal policy depends not only on the determinants of the multiplier we discussed in Chapter 4, but also on the crowding out effect.

Monetary policy Figure 7.16 examines the case of an expansionary monetary policy (shift of the LM curve to the right). In the upper panel, the IS curve is relatively flat and a shift of the LM curve to the right has a large effect on GNP. The reason is that the decrease in the interest rate on the vertical axis has an important effect on investment. As a result, monetary policy has an important effect on the level of output and employment.

In the lower panel, the IS curve is steep and an expansionary monetary policy has a small effect on GNP. In this case, investment is not very sensitive to interest rate changes. As a consequence, a change in the money supply has a weak effect on GNP.

The Keynesian, classical debate In terms of the IS-LM diagram, the Keynesian view is represented by a *steep* IS curve and a *flat* LM curve (upper diagram in Figure 7.15 and the lower diagram in Figure 7.16). Fiscal policy has a significant effect on GNP and monetary policy has little or no effect on GNP.

The neo-classical view is just the opposite, namely, that the LM curve is *steep* (lower diagram in Figure 7.15) and the IS curve is *flat* (upper diagram in Figure 7.16). In the classical case, an increase in government spending crowds out private sector investment and fiscal policy is ineffective as a means of influencing GNP. In contrast, changes in the money supply will have an important effect on the level of nominal GNP. This conclusion is in accordance with the Quantity Theory of Money discussed in section 7.2. However, bear in mind the monetarist conclusion that changes in the money supply will, in the longer term, be reflected in an increase in the price level rather than real GNP. Therefore, they argue that the government should not pursue an active or discretionary monetary policy. We examine these issue in greater detail in Chapter 8.

As is often the case, it is possible to compromise and to suggest that the truth lies between the extremes represented by the Keynesian and classical views. When interest rates are low, for example, an increase in interest rates may not crowd out investment and the Keynesian view that fiscal policy is effective may be valid. On the other hand, when interest rates are relatively high any further rise in interest rates

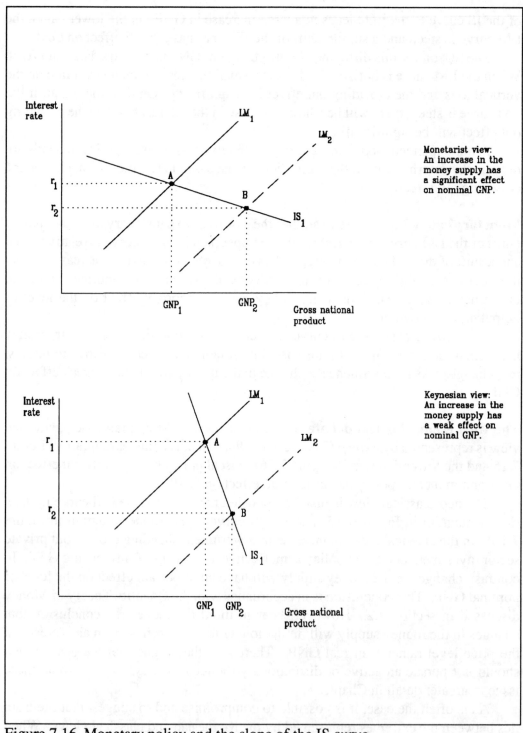

Figure 7.16 Monetary policy and the slope of the IS curve

may lead to significant crowding out of investment. In this case, the classical view that fiscal policy is ineffective may be valid. Over a half a century since Keynes launched his *General Theory* the economics profession is still far from unanimous on controversies it provoked.

The macroeconomic model developed so far has to be significantly modified to take account of the special factors affecting small, open economies. We shall discuss these factors in later chapters.

7.11   Conclusion

In this chapter we have extended our basic macroeconomic model by incorporating a money market. The extended model consists of a goods market and a money market. The authorities can influence aggregate demand by changing government expenditure or taxation (fiscal policy) or by changing the money supply (monetary policy). The key points or concepts covered in this chapter include:

- The Quantity Theory of Money as a theory of inflation

- The demand for money

- Changes in nominal GNP and interest rates affect the demand for money

- The interaction of the supply and demand for money determine the interest rate

- Changes in the money supply affect aggregate demand and GNP via the rate of interest and its influence on the level of investment

- The link between interest rates and investment is known as the marginal efficiency of investment schedule (MEI) and reflects the effect of changes in the rate of interest on the net present value (NPV) of investment projects

- A fiscal expansion leading to a rise in GNP increases the demand for money. This raises interest rates. Higher interest rates tend to crowd out investment.

- The extent to which crowding out occurs depends on how sensitive investment is to the rate of interest

- An increase in the money supply results in a reduction in interest rates. The amount of this reduction depends on the interest elasticity of demand for cash balances

- Keynesians argue that fiscal policy has a large effect on GNP and monetary policy a small effect because an increase in the money supply results in only a small drop in interest rates which has little effect on investment spending

- Classical economists argue that monetary policy has a large effect on nominal GNP but fiscal policy has a small effect because increased government borrowing leads to higher interest rates which depresses private sector investment

- The IS-LM model shows the combinations of GNP and interest rates that give a simultaneous equilibrium in the goods and money markets and allows us to illustrate these points about the relative effectiveness of fiscal and monetary policy diagramatically.

We have left to later chapters the task of modifying this analysis to allow for the special factors that influence a small open economy.

Notes

1. M. Friedman and A. Schwartz, *A Monetary History of the United States: 1867-1960*, Princeton University Press, 1963.

2. J. M. Keynes, *The General Theory of Employment, Interest and Money*, London: Macmillan, 1936.

3. J. M. Keynes, *op. cit.*, p. 195.

4. J. M. Keynes, *op. cit.*, p. 196.

5. J. M. Keynes, *op. cit.*, p. 170.

6. The significance of the "net" in NPV is that the income stream is net of costs; we are calculating the net income or profit from the investment.

7. An early exposition of the classical position is given in Irving Fisher, *The Purchasing Power of Money*, New York: Macmillan, 1911. A very influential paper which argued that the interest rate had a weak effect on the demand for money is: Milton Friedman, "The Quantity Theory of Money: A Restatement", in Milton Friedman (ed), *Studies in the Quantity Theory of Money*, University of Chicago Press, 1956.

8. J. L. Pratschke and T. O'Connell, "The Demand for Money in Ireland, 1948-60, A preliminary Report", mimeo, Central Bank of Ireland, 1973. F. X. Browne and T. O'Connell, "The Demand for Money Function in Ireland: Estimation and Stability", *The Economic and Social Review*, April, Vol. 9, 1978. F. X. Browne, "The Short Run Demand for Money with Exogenous Money Creation in a SOE", *Technical Paper*, 10/RT/84, Central Bank of Ireland, 1984. M. Hurley and C. Guiomard, "Determinants of Money Demand in Ireland 1971 to 1988: Rounding-up the Usual Suspects", *The Economic and Social Review*, Vol. 21, No. 1, October 1989.

9. F. X. Browne, "Loan Market Price and Quantity Effects in a Production Smoothing Model of Inventory Investment", Central Bank of Ireland, *Technical Paper*, 11/RT/84, November 1984. A. Leddin , "The Impact of Credit Control on Consumer Durable Expenditures and Fixed Investment in the Irish Economy", *Irish Business and Administrative Research*, Vol. 8, No. 20, 1986.

10. J. R. Hicks, "Mr. Keynes and the 'Classics': A Suggested Interpretation", *Econometrica*, Vol. 6, p. 147-159, April 1937.

11. These coefficients are elasticities if the variables are expressed as logarithms.

Chapter 8

Unemployment and Inflation

8.1   Introduction

The problem of unemployment is central to macroeconomic policy. There is little need to emphasise this in a country such as Ireland, where the rate of unemployment has been unacceptably high since the recession of the early 1980s and shows little sign of declining to a tolerable level. But while minimising the rate of unemployment is among the principal goals of macroeconomic policy, it cannot be pursued without regard to other considerations, such as maintaining a stable price level. In the long run, rampant inflation is incompatible with economic growth and an unrealistic target rate of unemployment would prove self-defeating if it led to a rising rate of inflation.

In previous chapters we assumed that the economy had unemployed resources and that supply would readily respond to increases in aggregate demand. We did not explore how unemployment and inflation are inter-related. In this chapter we explore this issues in detail. Our approach is first to expand the AS-AD analysis of Chapter 2 by showing how the AS schedule is derived from a production function and the interaction of the supply and demand of labour. We then use this expanded model to show how different assumptions about the underlying schedules lead to different conclusions about policy towards inflation and unemployment. While the theoretical framework we use is mainly that of a closed economy, towards the end of the chapter we examine some evidence relating to Ireland.

8.2   The Aggregate Production Function

On the supply side of the economy, land, labour and capital are the three basic *factors of production*. These are the three factors used as inputs in the production of goods and services. The *aggregate production function* shows the relationship between these three inputs and the output of goods and services for the economy as a whole. It can be written as

(1)   GNP = f(C, L, N)

where N = employment (or labour), L = land, and C = capital (plant and machinery). Because land and capital are constant in the short run, we can hold these two variables constant and examine the relationship between output and employment. In the upper

212

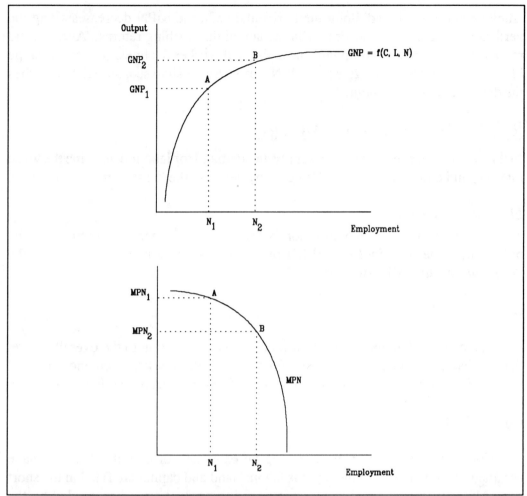

Figure 8.1 The production function and MPN

diagram in Figure 8.1 an increase in employment along the horizontal axis leads to an increase in output on the vertical axis. For example, an employment level of N_1 is associated with an output level of GNP_1. However, it will be observed that the curve relating these two variables becomes *flatter* as the level of output increases. This means that as more and more labour is hired, output continues to increase but at a diminishing rate. In Figure 8.1, the increase in employment from N_1 to N_2 leads to a less than proportional increase in GNP. The reason for this is *diminishing returns* to labour. As more and more labour is applied to a fixed amount of land and capital, labour becomes less productive. Output continues to increase, but it does so at a diminishing rate.

The lower diagram in Figure 8.1 shows the *marginal product of labour* (MPN). The MPN measures the extra output produced by hiring one extra worker. In other words, it is the productivity of an additional worker. It can be seen that as employment is increased along the horizontal axis, the MPN decreases along the vertical axis. This again accords with the law of diminishing returns. As more and more labour is hired, the output of the additional worker declines. In fact, the slope of the production function gives the MPN curve. As we shall see, the MPN underlies the demand curve for labour.

8.3   The Labour Market

In this section we explain how the supply and demand for labour determine the wage rate (W) and employment (N). We begin by deriving the demand for labour curve.

Demand for labour

The basic rule for profit maximisation is that a firm will increase output up to the point where the *marginal cost* (MC) of producing an extra unit is equal to the *marginal revenue* (MR) from selling it:

(2) $MC = MR$

In a competitive market, each firm is so small in relation to the overall market that increases in its output will have no effect on the market price and marginal revenue is therefore equal to output price (P). The profit maximising rule becomes:

(3) $MC = P$

Consider now the cost of producing an extra unit of output, MC. We have assumed that the only variable input is labour: land and capital are fixed in the short run. MC is therefore equal to the cost of hiring one extra worker divided by the number of units of extra output he produces. The cost of the worker is the wage rate (W) and the output of the worker is the marginal product of labour (MPN). Hence:

(4) $MC = W/MPN$

If, for example, the wage rate is £100 and an additional worker produces 20 units of output, the MC of a unit of output is £5. Substituting equation (4) into (3), a firm maximises its profits when:

(5) $W/MPN = P$

Rearranging, the profit maximisation rule can be written as:

(6) $W/P = MPN$

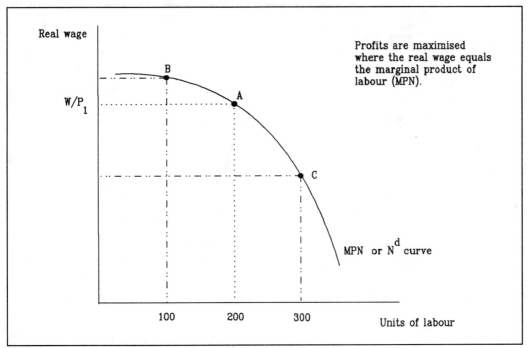

Figure 8.2 The MPN and the demand for labour

Equation (6) states that a firm's profits are maximised when the real wage rate (W/P) is equal to the marginal product of labour, MPN. Figure 8.2 shows the MPN schedule and the real wage on the vertical axis and the level of employment on the horizontal axis. If the real wage is $(W/P)_1$ the profit maximising level of employment is 200 workers. If the firm hired only 100 workers the MPN would exceed the real wage and profits could be increased by hiring additional labour. Similarly, if the firm hired 300 workers then the MPN is less than the real wage and the firm is incurring a loss on the last 100 workers hired. The firm could increase profits by reducing its work force to 200.

It follows that the point A in Figure 8.2 is one point on the *demand for labour schedule*. In fact, the demand for labour curve coincides with the MPN curve. For any level of (W/P) we can read off the profit maximising level of employment by moving horizontally over to the MPN curve and then vertically down to the X-axis. Each point where W/P cuts the MPN curve corresponds to a point on the demand for labour schedule. Because the MPN schedule is downward sloping, due to diminishing returns, the demand for labour schedule is also downward sloping.

If the MPN curve in Figure 8.2 is re-labelled the demand for labour (N^d) curve, it can be seen that there are two variables which determine the demand for labour, namely, the real wage and MPN. First, an increase in the real wage reduces the demand for labour *along* the N^d curve. Conversely, a decrease in the real wage increases the demand for labour along the N^d curve. Second, an increase in MPN

215

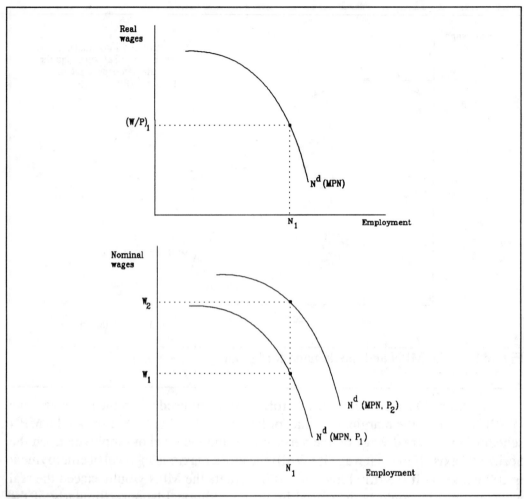

Figure 8.3 The demand for labour

---

*shift*s the N^d curve upwards and, for a given real wage, the demand for labour increases. Conversely, a decrease in MPN shifts the N^d curve downwards and, for a given real wage, the demand for labour decreases. An improvement in technical progress, the accumulation of capital equipment and the education and training of the labour force are the main sources of increased labour productivity (MPN). An improvement in all of these will increase productivity and shift the demand for labour curve upwards to the right.

The upper diagram in Figure 8.3 reproduces the demand for labour curve. The real wage is given along the vertical axis and employment along the horizontal axis. The relationship between W/P and demand for labour is shown by movements along the N^d curve. The curve is now labelled N^d(MPN) to indicate that a change in MPN will shift the N^d curve.

216

Alternatively, the demand for labour can be plotted as a function of the *nominal* wage. Rearranging, equation (6) can be written:

(7) $W = P \times MPN$

Using this rule, firms hire workers up to the point where the nominal wage equals the *value* of the output produced by workers.

Note:
The term $P \times MPN$ is the value of workers output and is referred to as the marginal *revenue* product (MRP).

The demand for labour now depends on the nominal wage, the price level and MPN:

(8) $N^d = F(W, P, MPN)$

This is drawn in the lower diagram in Figure 8.3. The relationship between W and demand for labour is shown by movements along the N^d curve. The N^d curve is labelled $N^d(MPN, P)$ to indicate that a change in MPN and/or P will shift the N^d curve. An increase in either of these variables shifts the N^d curve to the right. This is illustrated in the lower panel of Figure 8.3. Conversely, a decrease in either variable shifts the N^d curve to the left. Throughout this chapter we use this version of the demand for labour equation because it allows us to highlight important issues.

Before concluding this section, an important qualification is necessary. An employer hires labour with a view to producing additional output and selling it profitably. This is a *forward*-looking decision and involves expectations of the wages that will have to be paid to workers and the prices that will be obtained for selling the output. To simplify our analysis we will assume throughout this chapter that firms in fact have *perfect foresight* and know the exact future values of wages and prices. *This is equivalent to assuming that their expectations about the price level are always correct.* If we write P^e for the *expected* price level, then we are assuming that, for firms, $P^e = P$. Because of this assumption we use P through-out this chapter as the relevant variable affecting the demand for labour.

The supply of labour

The way in which the supply of labour is specified has major implications for inflation and unemployment. The basic assumption is that the supply of labour depends on the real wage, W/P. However, the real wage depends on the price level that prevails over the period for which the worker agrees to accept a given nominal wage. This is not known when the worker accepts the offer of employment. In effect, he makes the decision to accept the job offer on the basis of a nominal wage (W) and

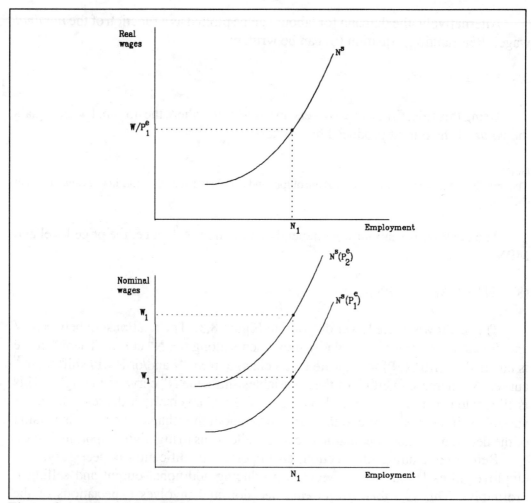

Figure 8.4 The supply of labour

the price level he *expects* (P^e) will prevail for the duration of the agreement on nominal wages. The relevant real wage is therefore (W/P^e). The question of how *inflation expectations* are formed is brought to the centre of the stage because of the influence it has on the supply of labour. The supply of labour function is written:

(9) $N^S = f(W/P^e)$

This relationship is shown in the upper diagram in Figure 8.4. The labour supply curve (N^S) is upward sloping, indicating that firms must offer higher real wages in order to encourage workers to supply more labour. The basic argument is that, after a time, leisure becomes increasingly important to workers and additional labour input to the economy will only be forthcoming if higher wages are offered. *Note that unlike the demand for labour case, we shall not assume that workers are always*

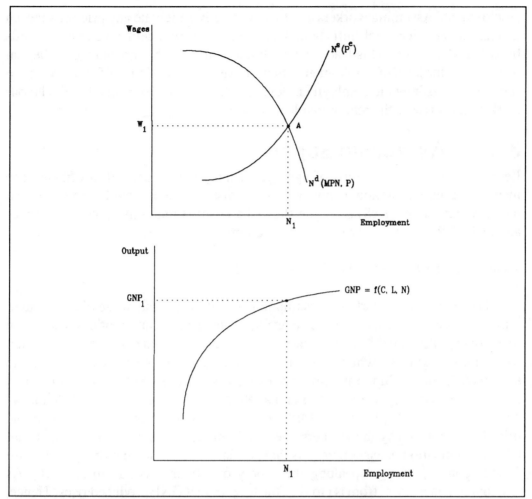

Figure 8.5 The labour market and the production function

correct if formulating price expectations. Hence the relevant variable affecting N^S is P^e and not the actual level P.

In the lower diagram in Figure 8.4, we separate out the price level and express the supply of labour as a function of the *nominal* wage. The relationship between the supply of labour and the nominal wage is shown by movements along the N^S curve. The curve is now labelled $N^S(P^e)$ to indicate that changes in P^e shift the N^S curve. If P^e rises, the N^S curve shifts to the left. Conversely, if P^e falls, the N^S curve shifts to the right.

Equilibrium in the labour market

The labour market and the production function describe the supply side of the macroeconomy. Figure 8.5 shows how they interact. In the upper diagram, the demand and supply of labour determine the nominal wage rate and the level of employment. Assuming workers and firms correctly anticipate any price change, an increase in the price level shifts both the labour supply and demand curves upwards by an equal amount. This leads to a high nominal wage but no change in the real wage rate or the level of employment. In the lower panel of Figure 8.5 the production function shows how the employment level (N_1), which is determined in the labour market, gives rise to the real output level GNP_1.

8.4   Aggregate Supply

Let us now expand the model of aggregate supply we introduced in Chapter 2 to incorporate these ideas about how the labour market operates. It will be recalled that the aggregate supply (AS) schedule showed a positive relationship between prices and real GNP on the supply side of the economy. The process was as follows:

$\uparrow$ Output Prices (P) $\rightarrow$ $\uparrow$ Profits $\rightarrow$ $\uparrow$ Real GNP

The important underlying assumption is that costs, and wages in particular, remain constant as P increases. As a result, an increase in output prices leads to an increase in profits and this, in turn, encourages firms to expand real output. Consider, for example, Figure 8.6 which shows the labour market and the associated aggregate supply (AS) curve. Suppose output prices increase from P_1 to P_2. We assume that firms are immediately aware of this and as a result there is a upward shift of the N^d curve (from N^d(MPN, P_1) to N^d(MPN, P_2). If, however, there is no change in the price level expected by the workers, the supply of labour does not shift. The result of this combination of assumptions is that nominal wages and employment increase as the economy moves up along the supply of labour curve from A to B. As employment increases (from N_1 to N_2), the level of real GNP produced rises. Hence, on the supply side of the economy there is a positive relationship between prices and real output. This is shown as a movement along the upward sloping AS curve, from C to D. Note, however, that to obtain this result it is necessary to assume that *workers' price expectations are incorrect.* Workers have supplied more labour in response to *higher* nominal wages but *lower* real wages (the change in the price level is greater than the change in the nominal wage). They are under the illusion they are being paid more but when inflation is allowed for, this is not the case. In a sense they have been tricked. This is known as *money illusion.*

If money illusion exists, the steepness of the AS curve depends on the slope of the labour supply (N^s) curve. The flatter (more elastic) the N^s curve, the flatter the AS curve. To see this point note that if the N^s curve is flat a given increase in the price level will lead to a large increase in employment and, via the production function, a large increase in real GNP. A large increase in real GNP indicates a relatively flat AS curve.

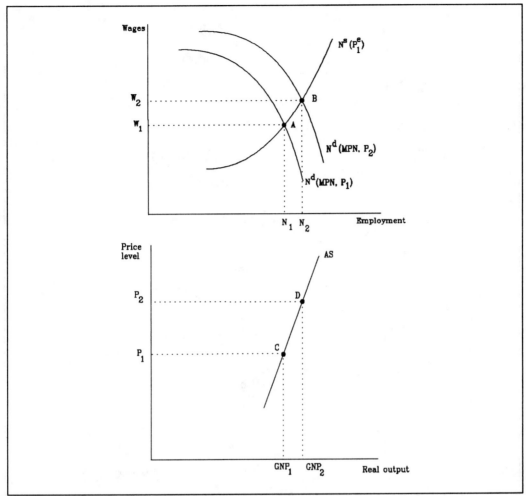

Figure 8.6   The labour market and the AS curve

Consider now what would happen when workers realise that real wages have fallen and demand an increase in money wages in line with the increase in output prices. This is shown in Figure 8.7 as a leftward shift of the labour supply schedule. Equilibrium in the labour market is now at point B. We have drawn the diagram so that the increase in W equals the increase in P and the real wage returns to its initial level. At point B employment falls to its original level. The increase in money wages also shifts the AS curve upwards. In the lower panel of Figure 8.7 this is shown as a shift from AS₁ to AS₂. Prices have increased but real GNP is unchanged. The economy moves from C to D. This means that the upward sloping AS schedule is only a short-run phenomenon. The AS schedule slopes upwards only for as long as workers suffer from money illusion. As soon as workers demand higher wages to compensate for higher output prices, the short-run AS schedule shifts to the left. The movement of short-run AS schedules enables us to map out the *long-run* AS

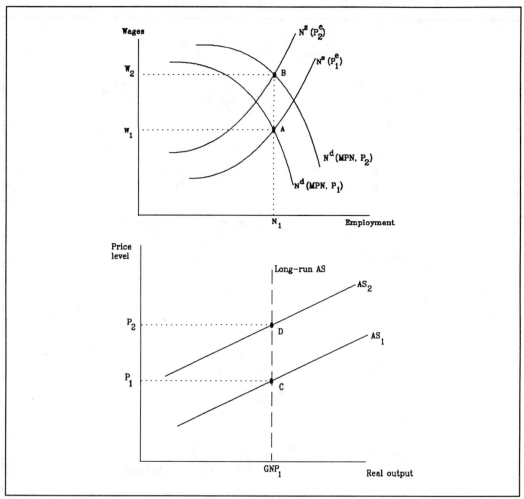

Figure 8.7   The labour market and the vertical AS curve

schedule. C and D are two points on the long-run AS curve, which is vertical. Increases in output prices do not lead to any increase in real output in the long term. This is because only N_1 workers are willing to accept employment at the original real wage level. Furthermore, at this real wage, N_1 is the full employment level of employment. *Any remaining unemployment is voluntary, reflecting an unwillingness to accept jobs at the prevailing real wage.* These ideas are crucial to the (neo-)classical model and its vision of an economy that always tends to full employment.

8.5   Aggregate Demand

In Chapter 2 we stated that on the demand side of the economy there is an inverse relationship between prices and real GNP. We explained this in terms of the link

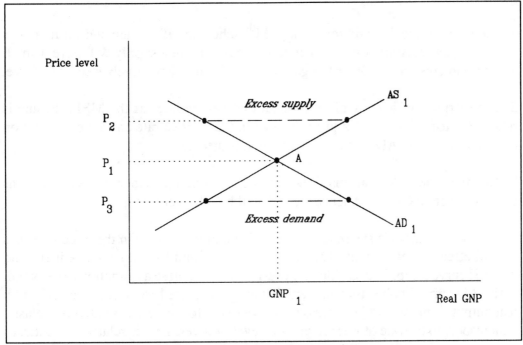

Figure 8.8 Equilibrium in the goods and services market

between the price level, international competitiveness and the trade account of the balance of payments. An increase in the domestic price level leads to a loss of competitiveness and this results in a decrease in exports and an increase in imports. A trade account deficit emerges which decreases aggregate demand and GNP.

In the expanded model of Chapter 7, an alternative explanation is given by the relationship between changes in the money supply and nominal GNP. Briefly, an increase in the money supply lowered interest rates which increased investment and this, in turn, increased aggregate demand and GNP. This allows us to derive a downward sloping AD curve without recourse to balance of payments effects. If we focus on the *real money supply* (M^S/P), the links between the price level and GNP on the demand side of the economy are as follows:

$$\uparrow P \;\rightarrow\; \downarrow (M^S/P) \;\rightarrow\; \uparrow r \;\rightarrow\; \downarrow I \;\rightarrow\; \downarrow AD \;\rightarrow\; \downarrow GNP$$
$$\qquad\qquad\; 1 \qquad\quad 2 \qquad\quad 3$$

An increase in the price level reduces the real money supply. The reduction in the real money supply increases interest rates and this reduces investment, aggregate demand and real GNP. Conversely, a decrease in the price level increases the real money supply and lowers interest rates. Investment, aggregate demand and GNP now increase. The steepness of the AD schedule depends on links 1, 2 and 3, namely:

1. The slope of the demand for money (M^d) schedule. If the demand for money is relatively flat (elastic), a given change in the real money supply will have a small effect on interest rates. Other things equal, this implies a relatively steep AD curve.

2. The marginal efficiency of investment (MEI) schedule. If the MEI schedule is relatively steep (inelastic), a given change in the interest rate has a weak effect on investment and the AD curve will be relatively steep.

3. The multiplier. A small multiplier means that a given change in investment has a small effect on GNP and hence the AD will be relatively steep.

If the AD curve is steep, this implies that a given change in the price level has a small effect on real output. This occurs if the demand for money curve is flat and the MEI curve steep. We saw that Keynesians believe these assumptions to be valid. A flat AD curve implies that a given change in the price level has a large effect on real output. This would be the case if the demand for money is relatively inelastic with respect to the rate of interest and the level of investment is relatively elastic, as is assumed by the classical economists.

The location of the AD line depends on the level of private and public consumption expenditure (C and G), investment (I), net exports (NX = X - M), and the money supply (M^s). An increase in C, I, G, NX or M^s (assuming no change in the price level) will shift the AD curve to the right. Thus an expansionary fiscal or monetary policy will shift the AD schedule outwards.

In Figure 8.8, the upward sloping short-run AS schedule derived in the previous section is combined with the AD schedule. The interaction of these two schedules determines the equilibrium price level (P) and the level of GNP. If the economy is not at point A it is assumed that firms will quickly adjust both prices and output so that equilibrium is re-established. This diagram is very similar to that discussed in Chapter 2. The main difference is that we have expanded the analysis underlying the two schedules. A labour market and a production function now underlie the AS schedule and the goods and money markets underlie the AD schedule. We shall use this framework to clarify some key issues in modern macroeconomics, particularly the relationship between the level of unemployment and the rate of inflation, as viewed by "Keynesians", "Monetarists" and "Classicals".[1]

8.6   The Keynesian Model

Figure 8.9 gives an outline of the Keynesian model, using the IS-LM diagrams developed in Chapter 4 and the aggregate supply-demand analysis outlined above. The Keynesian theory of aggregate demand is given by the IS-LM diagram in the lower right-hand corner. The IS curve is steep and the LM curve is flat representing

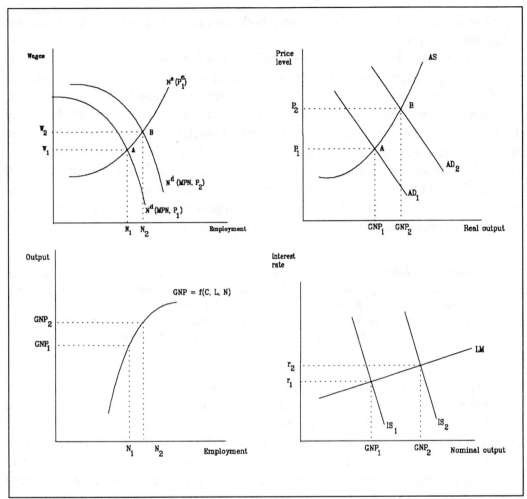

Figure 8.9   The Keynesian model

the Keynesian belief that fiscal policy is effective and monetary policy ineffective as a means of influencing output and employment.

On the supply side, Keynes emphasised the fact that most wage contracts are for periods of one, two or three years into the future. In order to maintain real wages, workers have to anticipate or forecast changes in the price level for the duration of the contract. Hence, given that the nominal wage is known, the supply of labour depends on the expected price level (P^e) rather than the actual price level.

Consider now the effects of an expansionary fiscal policy on output and employment. An increase in government expenditure shifts the IS curve from IS_1 to IS_2 (diagram bottom right). Nominal output rises along the horizontal axis and, because of the flat LM curve, there is only a small increase in the interest rate on the vertical axis. This means that the crowding out effect will be very small. The increase in government expenditure also shifts the AD curve from AD_1 to AD_2 and

225

because the AS curve is positively sloped both real output and the price level increase (diagram top right).

The increase in the price level shifts the N^d curve from $N^d(MPN, P_1)$ to $N^d(MPN, P_2)$ (diagram top left). However, because the supply of labour depends on the expected price level, the N^s curve does not immediately shift. In the Keynesian model, workers formulate price expectations by looking at the historical trend in prices. Price expectations are, in effect, backward looking. This is not an unreasonable assumption. If someone asks what the inflation rate in Ireland will be in 1993, your answer might be: It will be similar to the inflation rate in 1992. Of course if some kind of shock occurs, such as an increase in oil prices, then you will be wrong in your forecast. However, by and large we might expect inflation in one year to be similar to the inflation rate in the previous year.

Note:
This formulation of expectations is referred to as *static* expectations. People do not react to previous forecast errors in formulating forecasts. An alternative approach is known as *adaptive* expectations. In this case, forecasts are adjusted on the basis of previous forecast errors. *Rational expectations* are formed on the basis of all the knowledge available at the time, and on the basis of a knowledge of how the economy works. While not always right, rational expectations cannot be systematically wrong.

In the Keynesian model, the expansionary fiscal policy leads to an unexpected increase in the price level. Workers are not aware that the price level has increased and they supply more labour in response to a higher nominal wage. In reality, the price level has increased and the real wage has fallen. Workers are suffering from money illusion. Because the N^s curve does not immediately shift, employment increases and this enables firms to produce more goods and services. The failure of the N^s curve to shift to the left following an increase in the price level also explains why the AS curve is positively sloped.

In the longer term, workers will, of course, recognise that real wages have fallen and they will demand an increase in nominal wages to compensate. The N^s curve will now shift to the left and employment and output revert back to their initial levels. In the Keynesian model, government can influence the level of output and employment in the short run but not in the long run.

8.7   Monetarism

Monetarism is a variant of the classical school of thought that incorporated some of Keynes's ideas. The monetarist model in outlined in Figure 8.10. The theoretical structure of the monetarist model is not very different from the Keynesian model. On the supply side of the economy, the monetarists accept the Keynesian view that workers do not have perfect information on future price movements and that errors

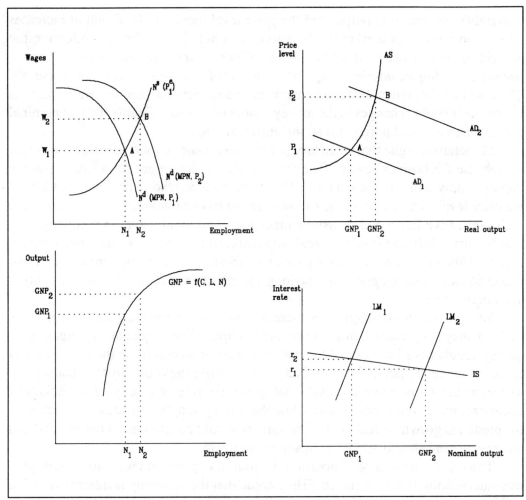

Figure 8.10 The monetarist model

are made in forecasting prices. As a result, the N^S curve is positively sloped and this, in turn, gives a positively sloped AS curve in the goods and services market.

The main difference between the monetarists and Keynesians lies in the slope of the IS and LM curves. Figure 8.10 shows the monetarist view that the LM curve is steep and the IS curve is flat. This means that fiscal policy has a relatively small effect on output and employment. For example, an increase in government expenditure would shift the IS curve upwards to the right (not shown). The large increase in the interest rate along the vertical axis would crowd out investment with the result that there is a small increase in real·output on the horizontal axis.

Monetary policy on the other hand has a very significant effect on nominal output. In Figure 8.10 (diagram bottom right), an increase in the money supply shifts the LM curve from LM1 to LM2 and nominal output increases along the horizontal axis. The increase in the money supply also shifts the AD curve from AD1 to AD2 (top right) and both real output and the price level increase. Real output increases because in the labour market the N^S curve does not shift to the left following the unanticipated increase in the price level. Workers are supplying more labour in response to a higher *nominal* wage but in terms of *real* wages they are worse off. The essential theoretical difference between the monetarists and the Keynesians is the proposition that changes in the money supply have a significant effect on nominal output whereas fiscal policy has an insignificant effect.

Monetarists argue that monetary policy should *not* be used to influence output or stabilise the business cycle. They reason that in the longer run increases in the money supply will, via the Quantity Theory of Money, lead to an equal increase in the price level. The process is as follows. In the labour market, workers realise that real wages have fallen and demand an increase in nominal wages in compensation. The N^S curve shifts to the left and real output and employment revert to their original levels. This means that in the long run, the AS and the N^S curves are vertical. An expansionary monetary policy has no long-run effect on real variables such as output and employment.

Second, monetarists argue that there is a *long and variable lag* between changes in the money supply and changes in nominal output. They argue that changes in the money supply have been one of the major sources of instability in the economy and an active monetary policy is more likely to destabilise the economy than stabilise it. The monetarists therefore conclude that, given the role of money as a medium of exchange, the government should allow the money supply to increase in line with the predicted growth in real GNP. The targets should be announced beforehand and the government should adhere to this *monetary rule.*

Thus the monetarists' position is that the government should adopt a non-interventionist policy stance. They argue that the economy is inherently stable and any output gaps which emerge will be eliminated automatically by market adjustments. To see this, note that in the Keynesian model, the AD curve is very steep and the price level has to fall significantly in order to return the economy to full employment GNP. However, in the monetarist model, because of the slopes of the IS and LM curves, the AD curve is flat. This means that only a small fall in the price level is necessary to restore the economy to full employment GNP. Output gaps tend to be closed quickly .

Note:
The monetarists also advocate legislation to abolish restrictive practices in the labour market. It is argued that closed shops, picketing, open ballots and trade union immunity to civil actions slow down wage adjustments and impede the process back to full employment GNP. If wages can be made more responsive to shifts in the supply and demand for labour, the adjustment process will be speeded up.

8.8   The Neo-classical Model

Neo-classical economists have come to the defence of the classical model that Keynes tried to discredit. They focus on the role of expectations. It will be recalled that in the Keynesian model price expectations are formulated by using past inflation to predict future inflation. This method of formulating expectations has been criticised as being naive because it allows people to be *systematically* wrong in their predictions. The neo-classical economists argue that people will use *rational expectations* in forecasting economic variables such as inflation. As we noted above, a rational forecast is based on all available information and a correct knowledge of what causes inflation. For example, if people believe in monetarism they will anticipate changes in the rate of inflation from increases in the money supply. If the economy is close to full employment and the government pursues an expansionary monetary policy, people will anticipate that the rate of inflation will increase. Similarly, if the government increases expenditure, people will expect an increase in taxes sometime in the future to pay for the spending.

The rational expectations assumption does not imply that people are correct all the time in their forecasts. It is likely that any particular forecast will be wrong, but *on average* forecasts will be correct. Errors will be random. The over estimates in one year will be cancelled by under estimates in the next year so that the average forecast error will be zero. There must be no discernible pattern which could be used to improve a forecast. (See also the discussion on forecasting in Chapter 16.)

Note:
According to the neo-classical economists, people will use information intelligently and the forecast they arrive at will be very similar to that offered by the professional economist who uses sophisticated economic models. How people arrive at their forecasts is not relevant. What is important is the consensus forecast and how it influences behaviour. In this regard, note that the consensus forecast can influence the outcome. If workers, for example, expect an increase in prices and demand an increase in nominal wages in compensation, that increase in wages will influence prices. The forecast influences the outcome. This is not the case in forecasting the weather. A forecast that it will rain tomorrow will not in any way affect the weather the next day.

The concept of rational expectations originated with John Muth in 1961.[2] The idea was subsequently taken up by Robert Lucas of the University of Chicago in the early 1970s and he, in turn, influenced Thomas Sargent of the University of Chicago and Robert Barro of Harvard University. These economists make a distinction between *anticipated* and *unanticipated* policies or shocks. Consider first the effect of an anticipated policy.

Figure 8.11 outlines the neo-classical model. Note that the structure of this model is the same as the monetarist and Keynesian models. There is the now familiar IS-LM diagram, the aggregate supply and demand curves, the labour market and the production function. The neo-classical economists agree with the monetarists on the

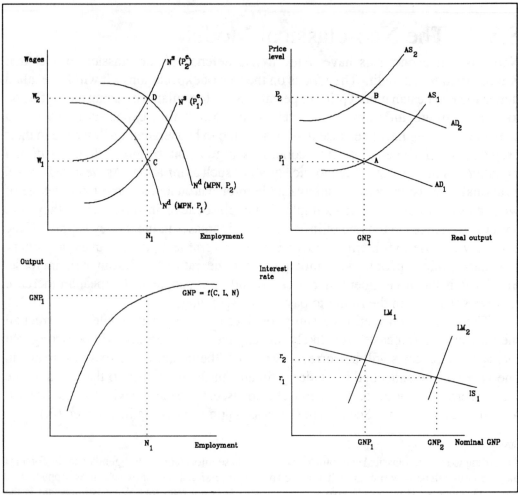

Figure 8.11 The neo-classical model

slopes of the IS and LM curves and on their conclusions regarding the ineffectiveness of fiscal policy.

The neo-classical innovation is largely concerned with the role of expectations in the labour market. Suppose the government implements an expansionary monetary policy. The LM curve shifts to the right and output increases. The aggregate demand curve also shifts to the right and both the price level and real output increase. In the labour market, the increase in the price level shifts the N^d curve to the right. So far the analysis is the same as in the monetarist model.

However, in the labour market, workers realise that the increase in the money supply will increase prices and they demand an immediate increase in nominal wages in compensation. In contrast to the Keynesian and monetarist case, workers do not suffer from money illusion. Because expectations are formed rationally, workers anticipate that prices will rise following the increase in the money supply. The labour supply (N^S) curve therefore shifts to the left and the real wage is restored. In the goods and services market, the aggregate supply (AS) curve also shifts to the left and both employment and real output revert back to their original levels. Once the policy or the shock is anticipated, the N^S and the AS curves are vertical and there is no trade-off between inflation and unemployment except in the very short run.

Note:
Both employers and employees forecast an increase in prices equal to the increase in the money supply. This forecast takes account of any secondary increases in the price level due to a shift of the AS curve.

The analysis of fiscal policy is similar except that fiscal policy is even less effective due to crowding out of investment. (The Barro-Ricardian Equivalence Proposition discussed in Chapter 4 is another reason why the neo-classical analysis believes that fiscal policy is ineffective.)

However, even in a neo-classical world it is possible to raise output above the level corresponding to full employment or the natural rate of unemployment. This can occur through an *unanticipated* increase in the price level, which in turn could come about as a result of a *surprise* fiscal or monetary expansion. As before the aggregate demand schedule will shift to the right and real output and the price level will increase (not shown). If, however, workers do not anticipate the increase in prices, neither the N^S curve nor the AS curve will shift to the left. Under these circumstances, real output and employment will rise. This conclusion is the same as in the Keynesian and monetarist models. Unanticipated policies or unanticipated shocks to the economy can result in changes in real output. The N^S and the AS curves are no longer vertical.

Note:
The neo-classical aggregate supply function can be written:

(10) $GNP = GNP^* + \alpha(P - P^e)$

where GNP* and GNP represent full employment GNP and actual GNP, respectively. It is clear from this equation that actual GNP can exceed full employment GNP only if the actual price level exceeds the expected price level.

However, neo-classical economists argue that there is no role for a Keynesian stabilisation policy to offset the instability in the private components of aggregate demand. Because shocks are unanticipated, the government cannot respond in time to offset their effects on output. Both the private and the public sector are caught unawares. Once the shock is identified or becomes known the private sector will use rational expectations to forecast its implications and will adjust price expectations accordingly. There is no need for the government to become involved as the private sector reaction will ensure the economy reverts to the natural rate of unemployment. In this regard, the neo-classical economists are very sceptical about the governments' ability to "fine tune" the economy. As Lucas comments about economists: "As an advice giving profession we are in way over our heads."[3]

8.9   The Original Phillips Curve

The previous discussion of the Keynesian, monetarist and classical schools of thought highlighted the role of price expectations. If workers price expectations are imperfect, an increase in the price level will lead to an increase in output and employment and a fall in unemployment. Hence there is an inverse relationship between movement in the price level (inflation) and unemployment.

The idea that there is a negative relationship between the rate of unemployment and inflation was first suggested by the New Zealand economist A. W. Phillips (1914-75), working at the London School of Economics in the 1950s. He noted that between 1862 and 1956 in Britain there was a tendency for periods of low unemployment to coincide with periods of rising wage rates.[4] He drew a diagram depicting this inverse relationship, which has come to be known as the "Phillips curve". Variants of it have appeared in macroeconomic textbooks ever since.

The Phillips curve can be written as:

$$(11) \quad \Delta P = f(U)$$
$${-}$$

where ΔP = the rate of inflation and U = the unemployment rate. Equation (11) states that the inflation rate is a function of the rate of unemployment. The negative sign under the U term indicates that we expect an increase in unemployment to lead to a fall in the rate of inflation and, conversely, a fall in unemployment to lead to an increase in inflation.

Phillips suggested that the best fit to the historical data was a non-linear one, as shown in Figure 8.12. As unemployment fell to very low levels, the rate of inflation accelerated more rapidly, while at very high levels of unemployment, inflation levelled off or even became negative.

The economic rationale underlying this relationship is the Keynesian belief that shifts of the AD curve to the right lead to increases in both inflation and real GNP. As the economy approaches full employment, the AS curve becomes increasingly steep and the price level increases more rapidly. (See the discussion on the kinked AS curve in Chapter 2.)

The thinking behind the Phillips curve was enormously influential in the 1960s. It led macroeconomic policy-makers to believe, in a phrase used by Paul Samuelson and Robert Solow (both Nobel Prize laureates teaching at the Massachusetts Institute of Technology) in 1960, that there exists a "menu for policy choice".[5] This led to the belief that there was a *trade-off* between the two evils of inflation and

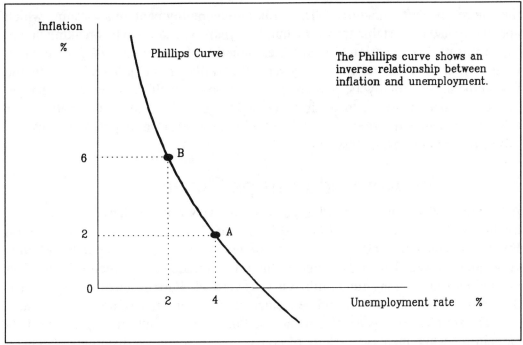

Figure 8.12   The Phillips curve

unemployment: it is not possible to enjoy a low rate of inflation *and* a low rate of unemployment at the same time, but it is possible to have less of one at the cost of more of the other.   Countries have to decide how much extra inflation they are prepared to tolerate in order to achieve a reduction in unemployment.

For example, suppose the economy is initially at point A in Figure 8.12 where an inflation rate of 2 per cent is combined with an unemployment rate of 4 per cent. If the government now uses fiscal or monetary policy to move the economy to point B, unemployment is reduced to 2 per cent but inflation rises to 6 per cent. The gain in terms of lower unemployment has been paid for in terms of a higher rate of inflation.   The choice between these two evils is essentially a political one. Conservatives might prefer low inflation and ignore the high unemployment which this entails whereas labour or left-wing parties might tend to opt for low unemployment and accept the consequences in terms of inflation.

Attempts to exploit the trade-off between unemployment and inflation during the 1960s led to increasing disillusionment. The emphasis during these years was on keeping the rate of unemployment low, and a fair degree of success was achieved in this regard, but in many countries it became evident that the rate of inflation associated with what was considered full employment was rising. Even worse was the experience of the late 1960s when the rate of inflation began to increase at a time of rising unemployment. This became known as *stagflation*. It appeared that the policies designed to move the economy *up* the Phillips curve were in fact causing

233

the curve to *shift outwards*. The inflation/unemployment relationship, which apparently had been stable for over a hundred years, appeared to be breaking down. There was much discussion of possible explanations for this: increased trade union militancy, a growing mismatch between the skills of the job seekers and the requirements of employers, a more generous social welfare system and so on. However, none of these explanations seemed to go to the heart of the matter. For this, a fundamental reformulation of the Phillips curve idea was required. We discuss this reformulation in a later section.

8.10   The Revised Phillips Curve

A fundamental critique of the Phillips curve analysis was advanced independently by the monetarist economists Edmund Phelps of Columbia University and Milton Friedman in the late 1960s.[6] They incorporated price expectations into the Phillips curve and showed that in the long run there is no trade-off between inflation and unemployment: the long-run Phillips curve is vertical. Furthermore they argued that this vertical Phillips curve would be located at the natural rate of unemployment.

The starting point is to reformulate the Phillips curve in terms of how workers bargain for wage increases. Here, of course, it is essential to distinguish between nominal wages (W) and real wages. Because wage contracts last into the future, workers will try to anticipate the rate of inflation in order to protect their real wages for the duration of the contract. For example, if inflation is expected to be 20 per cent over the coming year, workers will demand a 20 per cent increase in wages to compensate for anticipated inflation and maintain real wages at the present level. Hence the variable that matters in wage bargaining may be defined as ($\Delta W / \Delta P^e$), where ΔW is the change in wages and ΔP^e is the expected price inflation.

The second main strand in the Phelps-Friedman theory is to incorporate the natural rate of unemployment into the analysis. They argue that inflation depends on the *gap* between the actual unemployment rate (U) and the natural rate of unemployment (U_n). That is, inflation is influenced by ($U - U_n$), rather than U. If U is greater than U_n, there is downward pressure on inflation and, conversely, if U is less than U_n there is upward pressure on inflation. Unemployment does not affect inflation when U is equal to U_n.

The *revised or expectations-augmented* Phillips curve may be written:

(12) $\Delta P_t = \Delta P^e_t - \alpha (U - U_n)$

where α is a coefficient, $0 < \alpha < 1$, which indicates how the rate of inflation reacts to the difference between the unemployment rate and the natural rate ($U - U_n$). As in the original Phillips curve an increase in unemployment leads to a fall in inflation and vice versa. Equation (12) states that the inflation rate in time t (ΔP_t) depends

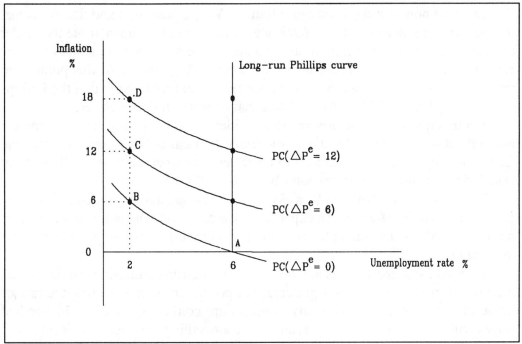

Figure 8.13 The long run (vertical) Phillips curve

on the expected rate of inflation (ΔP^e_t) plus an adjustment based on the difference between the actual rate of unemployment and the natural rate of unemployment.

In the Keynesian model, workers formulated expectations about inflation by assuming that this year's inflation rate will recur next year, that is, $\Delta P^e_t = \Delta P_{t-1}$, where the subscript t indicates the year. This assumes that if inflation is 3 per cent in 1991 the same inflation rate is expected for 1992. As already mentioned, this is a static, backward-looking approach to formulating expectations and in periods of high and volatile inflation it is likely to lead to systematic errors in the anticipated rate of inflation. Inserting this formulation of expectations into equation (12) we have:

(13) $\Delta P_t = \Delta P_{t-1} - \alpha (U - U_n)$

Equation (13) states that the inflation rate in time t depends on inflation in the previous year plus an adjustment based on the unemployment gap. The expectations-augmented Phillips curve is illustrated in Figure 8.13. The Phillips curve is again downward sloping indicating an inverse relationship between inflation and unemployment. We have also inserted a vertical line labelled the *long-run Phillips curve*. For reasons which we shall explain, the long-run Phillips curve is located at the natural rate of unemployment which for illustrative purposes may be taken to equal 6 per cent unemployment.

235

Suppose now that the expected inflation (Δp^e) equals zero and that the actual unemployment rate equals the natural rate. Phelps and Friedman argue that under these circumstances the inflation rate will also be zero. This means that in Figure 8.13 the Phillips curve cuts the horizontal axis at the point A. At this point, zero inflation is combined with a 6 per cent unemployment rate. Note that the Phillips curve is labelled $PC(\Delta P^e = 0)$ to indicate that expected inflation is zero.

Let us suppose that the government decides that 6 per cent is an unacceptably high rate of unemployment and uses monetary or fiscal policy to increase nominal GNP. Initially, inflation increases to 6 per cent and unemployment falls to 2 per cent and the economy moves to point B on $PC(\Delta P^e = 0)$.

The movement from A to B in Figure 8.13 is a satisfactory outcome from the government's point of view. An expansionary macroeconomic policy has increased real output and lowered unemployment to 2 per cent at the cost of a 6 per cent increase in inflation.

At point B the economy is not, however, in long-run equilibrium. Inflation has increased from 0 per cent to 6 per cent, but people are still expecting the rate of inflation to be zero. Consequently, workers are confusing increases in nominal wages with increases in real wages, and hence are willing to increase their supply of labour. This money illusion will not continue for ever. Workers will revise their inflation expectations upwards and as a result the Phillips curve will shift upwards and to the right, from $PC(\Delta P^e = 0)$ to $PC(\Delta P^e = 6)$, corresponding to an increase in price expectations from 0 per cent to 6 per cent. The upward sloping Phillips curves are in effect only *short-run* Phillips curves. Changes in inflation expectations cause these short-run curves to shift upwards or downwards.

Note:
When actual unemployment equals the natural rate, actual inflation is determined by expected inflation. In other words, the short-run Phillips curve intersects the long-run Phillips curve at the point on the vertical axis corresponding to the expected rate of inflation.

If, in the new situation, policy-makers persist in trying to maintain the rate of unemployment at 2 per cent, the economy will move to the point C on $PC(\Delta P^e = 6)$. At this point, 2 per cent unemployment is combined with an inflation rate of 12 per cent. Why has the inflation rate increased from 6 per cent to 12 per cent? Because the revision in price expectations from 0 per cent to 6 per cent resulted in an increase in wage demands and this added a further 6 per cent to the inflation rate.

However, as before, point C is not a long-run equilibrium point, because the expected inflation rate of 6 per cent falls behind the actual inflation rate of 12 per cent. Workers will eventually revise their inflation expectations upwards once again, from 6 per cent to 12 per cent, and the Phillips curve will shift upwards from $PC(\Delta P^e = 6)$ to $PC(\Delta P^e = 12)$. The economy now moves to the point D, where 2 per cent unemployment is combined with an 18 per cent inflation rate.

The crucial point is that as long as policy is dedicated to maintaining the rate of unemployment below its natural level, the economy cannot reach equilibrium. Inflation will have to go on accelerating in order to maintain the money illusion which is necessary to increase the level of output above the level corresponding to the natural rate of unemployment.

Note:
The above analysis could also be conducted in terms of the Phillips curve equation. Recall from equation (13) that:

$$\Delta P_t = \Delta P_{t-1} - \alpha (U - U_n)$$

The expansionary monetary policy reduced U below the natural rate of unemployment and this added 6 per cent to P_t in the first year. In the second year, this increase in inflation feeds back into the P_{t-1} term and this pushes the actual inflation rate to 12 per cent. In the third year the increase in inflation again feeds back into the P_{t-1} term and inflation again rises and so on.

The consequences of trying to lower the rate of unemployment below its natural rate would be very unsatisfactory. The price of the reduction in unemployment is an ever rising rate of inflation.[7] The expansionary macroeconomic policy has not just caused a once-off increase in inflation but has led to an accelerating rate of inflation. Eventually, workers will adjust their price expectations to take account of previous forecast errors. The increase in wages will catch up with inflation and the economy will revert back to the natural rate of unemployment. Equally, the policy-maker will come to view the inflation problem as more serious than the unemployment problem and policies will be introduced to stop inflation accelerating.

By joining points such as A and the point at which we return to the natural rate, we obtain the long-run Phillips curve. We can see that it is *vertical* because we started at the natural rate and ultimately we end up back at the natural rate. The inflation rate may differ, but the unemployment rate will in the long run be the same. Given that we started from the natural rate and that we have now ended back at this rate, what has been gained by the expansionary macroeconomic policy? The answer is "a *temporary* reduction in the rate of unemployment and a *permanent* increase in the rate of inflation". This is obviously less attractive than the permanent reduction in unemployment that was promised by the original version of the Phillips curve.

Note that if the cost of maintaining unemployment below its natural rate is accelerating inflation, the attempt to do so would eventually have to be abandoned in order to prevent the breakdown of economic life. Accelerating inflation would lead to *hyperinflation* of the sort experienced in central Europe after the First World War and in many Latin American countries in recent years. Such inflation is so disruptive that it undermines normal economic processes and leads to a sharp decline in living standards.

Note:
There are numerous stories of what hyperinflation does to an economy. Here are some examples.

Argentines went on a buying spree yesterday in a race against soaring prices. In a whirl of hyperinflation, supermarkets are sometimes marking up prices twice a day while the Argentine currency, the Austral, plunges in value. Customers overturned trolleys full of goods at one supermarket after the management announced over loudspeakers that all prices were being immediately raised by 30 per cent. (*Irish Times*, 26 April 1989).

In Germany in the 1920s inflation was running at 3,000 per cent per month. The story is told that if you went into a bar in Germany at that time it would be worth your while to buy two pints of beer rather than one. The reason was that the rate at which the second pint was going stale was slower than the rate at which the price was going up. A nice example of marginal cost analysis!

In Brazil four new currencies were introduced during the period 1985-91. One million 1986 cruzeiros were replaced by one new (1991) cruzeiro!

On the basis of their critique of the earlier Phillips curve analysis, therefore, Phelps and Friedman rejected the notion that in the long run unemployment could be reduced by accepting a higher rate of inflation. The *accelerationist theory* of inflation, as this theory has been called, left little or no room for expansionary macroeconomic policy as an instrument for lowering the rate of unemployment.

8.11 The Speed of Adjustment and the Persistence of Output Gaps

Beliefs about the nature of the aggregate supply schedule and the Phillips curve have a crucial bearing on the appropriate response to deflationary shocks and lie at the heart of modern controversies in macroeconomics. Figure 8.14 illustrates the implications of an adverse demand shock for the economy, using the familiar AS-AD framework. In the top diagram, a decrease in investment shifts the AD curve from AD_1 to AD_2 and the economy moves from point A to B. Both real output and the price level fall. In the labour market the decrease in the price level shifts the N^d curve to the left and the market moves from point X to Y. Employment decreases along the horizontal axis. The decrease in nominal wages is, however, smaller than the fall in the price level and as a result the real wage rises. The N^s curve is not immediately affected because the change in the price level was unexpected. The reason for the rise in unemployment is the increase in the real wage.

After a time, workers realise that the price level has fallen and they accept a cut in the nominal wage so as to restore the real wage. In the labour market, the N^s curve shifts to the right so as to intersect the N^d curve at the point Z. At this point, the fall in the nominal wage is equal to the fall in the price level and the original real wage

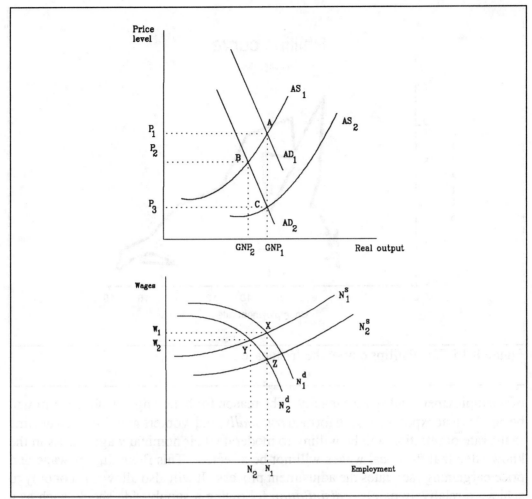

Figure 8.14 The persistence of unemployment

is restored. In the goods market, the fall in nominal wages causes the AS curve to move to the right and the economy moves to the point C.

Note:
The movement of the AS curve brings forth yet another fall in the price level from P_2 to P_3. This means that in the labour market, the N^d curve again shifts to the left (not shown) and employment falls. In order to restore the real wage, workers will again have to revise their price expectations downwards and this process, involving protracted unemployment, may continue for as long as workers fail to anticipate the changes in the price level. Eventually, workers will come to anticipate the effect of a shift of the AS curve on the price level and equilibrium will be achieved.

The key question is: How long will the unemployment that emerges as a result of a shock persist? Those who believe in a smooth-functioning, self-regulating economy claim that prices and wages will fall quickly in response to the emergence

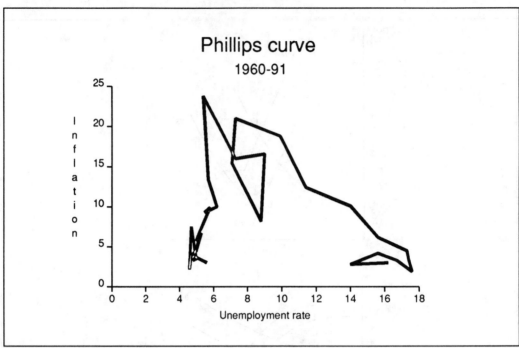

Figure 8.15 The Phillips curve: the Irish case

of unemployment and spare capacity. The reason for believing that adjustment will be rapid is that expectations are formed *rationally*, and workers anticipating a decline in the rate of inflation will be willing to moderate their nominal wage claims in the knowledge that their real wages will not be affected. This flexibility of wage and price bargaining facilitates the adjustment process. It will also allow an economy to achieve a relatively painless *disinflation* following a supply-side shock, such as a rise in oil prices.

Keynes, on the other hand, argued that wages and prices are *rigid*. As a result the price level will remain at P_1 for some time. Wages, too, will remain at their pre-recession level because workers have no reason to anticipate a fall in the price level that would lead them to accept cuts in nominal wages. Faced with these rigidities, Keynes argued that the government should intervene in the economy and pursue a stabilisation policy of the type discussed in Chapter 4. Hence, Keynes advocated an *interventionist* policy. Instead of waiting for possibly a very long time while prices and wages slowly and painfully adjust downwards, why not shift the AD curve back to its original location, AD_1, through an expansionary fiscal policy?

8.12 The Irish Experience

In our discussion of inflation in Chapter 1 we drew attention to the fact that in no year since the Second World War has the price level declined in Ireland. Similarly,

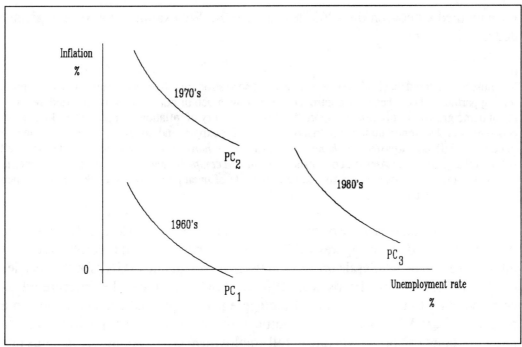

Figure 8.16 Shifts in the short run Phillips curve

in no year did the level of nominal wages decline, despite the fact that the rate of unemployment trebled over the period and is now at a historical peak. In Figure 8.15 we show the Phillips curve for Ireland over the period 1960 to 1991. The rate of inflation (based on consumer prices) is shown on the vertical axis and the unemployment rate on the horizontal axis. Apart from the points representing the decline in inflation from over 20 per cent to under four per cent between 1981 and 1986, which coincided with an increase in unemployment from 10 per cent to over 17 per cent, Figure 8.15 bears little resemblance to either the downward sloping short-run Phillips curve or the vertical long-run Phillips curve discussed above.

A possible explanation for this is that we are looking at a collection of short-run Phillips curves that shift over time. In the 1960s low unemployment was combined with low inflation. In the 1970s low unemployment was associated with high inflation. The Phillips curve representing this decade would therefore be above the curve for the previous decade. In the 1980s high unemployment was initially associated with very high inflation, but during the decade the rate of unemployment soared and the rate of inflation subsided. (Whether this was cause and effect is a moot point.) The Phillips curve for this decade would therefore be to the right of that for the previous decade. In Figure 8.16 we show a stylised version of these three short-run Phillips curves. If the short-run Phillips curves have in fact shifted in this manner then it would follow that the natural rate of unemployment in Ireland has risen markedly between the 1960s and the 1990s. We examine this issue in greater detail in Chapter 9.

Note:
We must bear in mind that Irish inflation has always been strongly influenced by inflation in our main trading partners. There has been controversy as to how much of our inflation is imported and how much home grown. If inflation is imported a different theory of inflation is appropriate. In an open economy it is also important to recall that the demand for exports and imports is affected by the rate of domestic inflation *adjusted for changes in the rate of exchange*. At a given rate of inflation, a fall in the exchange rate increases the country's *international competitiveness* and shifts the AD curve to the right, thereby at least temporarily reducing the rate of unemployment. We take up these open economy issues in later chapters.

A more detailed review of the behaviour of output and prices in Ireland since the war is provided by Figures 8.17 and 8.18. These show the combinations of inflation (based on wholesale prices) and the real growth rate in GNP for the decades of the 1950s, 1960s, 1970s and 1980s. Each point can be interpreted as corresponding to the intersection of the aggregate supply and demand curves in a particular year. We have inserted a vertical line at the 4 per cent growth rate, as a reference point for the growth rate in full employment GNP. Assuming that this rate had been maintained it would have kept the economy close to its potential level. Points to the left of this vertical line are associated with an *unemployment* and *output gap* and points to the right with an *inflationary gap*. We are interested in seeing, first, how long the economy remained above or below this trend growth rate, and second, whether the rate of inflation tended to moderate when there was an output gap.

It can be seen from the diagrams that in the 1950s and the 1980s the economy remained to the left of the vertical line for long periods of time. This is not supportive of the belief that output gaps are short-lived. There is no evidence that the economy adjusted rapidly back to full employment during these two decades. On the other hand, the evidence for the 1960s and the 1970s suggests that output gaps were not persistent. The upward sloping curve during the 1960s and the first half of the 1980s is what would be expected if inflation moderated in the face of a large output gap. The moderation in inflation that occurred in the face of a large output gap would help to restore full employment growth. However, during other periods there is little evidence of a positive relationship between the rate of growth of the economy and the rate of inflation. The persistence of a major output gap despite the moderation of inflation during the 1980s is particularly striking.

8.13   Conclusion

In this chapter we have discussed how inflation and unemployment are interrelated. The main topics discussed are:

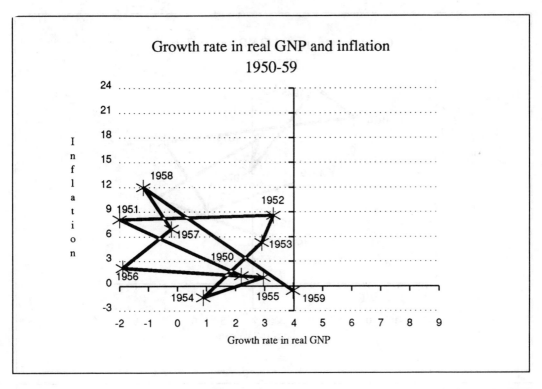

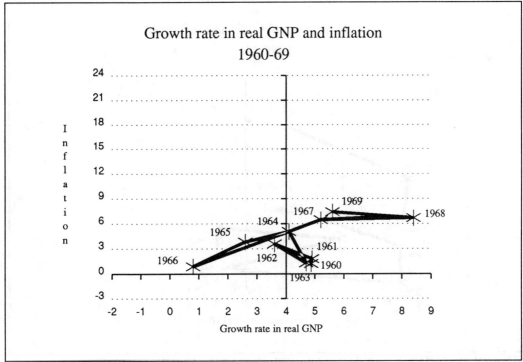

Figure 8.17 Inflation and the real growth rate

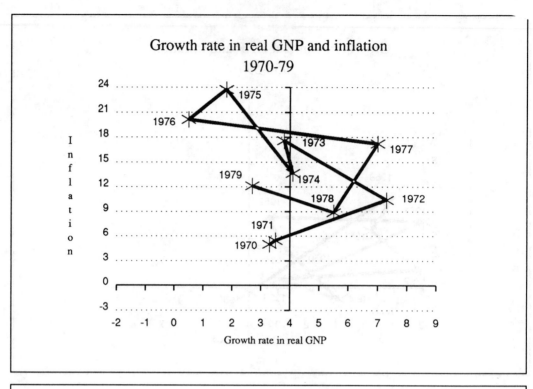

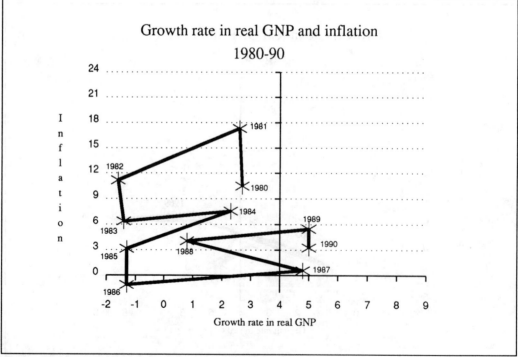

Figure 8.18 Inflation and the real growth rate

- The aggregate production function

- The supply and demand for labour, the wage rate and the level of employment

- The role of price expectations, the concept of money illusion and the aggregate supply schedule

- The Keynesian model and the Phillips curve

- Evidence from the Irish economy on the persistence of output gaps

- The monetarist model and the Phelps-Friedman critique of the Phillips curve analysis

- The long-run Phillips curve is vertical at the natural rate of unemployment. Holding the rate of unemployment below this rate will lead not just to a higher, but to a rising, rate of inflation

- The neo-classical model and rational expectations

- Unanticipated increases in the price level and the neo-classical aggregate supply schedule.

We left to later chapters an explicit discussion of how these models should be modified to fit conditions in a small open economy.

1. These terms mean different things to different economists. In fact the term "classical economist" was first coined by Karl Marx to describe orthodox nineteenth-century British economics. A representation of the classical model was given by Keynes in Chapter 2 of the *General Theory* in order that he could replace it with his own "Keynesian" model. Mark Blaug has commented that "perhaps the recent proliferation of definitely new but conflicting interpretations of the essential meaning of classical economics is simply an expression of the fact that modern economists are divided in their views and hence quite naturally seek comfort by finding (or pretending that they can find) these same views incorporated in the writings of the past". See "Classical economics" in *The New Palgrave: A Dictionary of Economics,* edited by John Eatwell, Murray Milgate and Peter Newman, (London, Macmillan, 1987).

2. The concept of rational expectations originated in a paper that attracted little attention when it was first published, John Muth, "Rational Expectations and the Theory of Price Movements", *Econometrica,* 29 July 1961. The idea was taken up by others in the 1970s. See Robert Lucas, "Rules, Discretion and the Role of the Economic Advisor", in Stanley Fischer (ed.), *Rational Expectations and Economic Policy*, University of Chicago Press, 1980.

3. Robert Lucas, "Rules, Discretion and the Role of the Economic Advisor", in Stanley Fischer (ed.), *Rational Expectations and Economic Policy*, University of Chicago Press, 1980. Lucas also argued that changes in policy changed the slope of the Phillips curve. These ideas are key parts of what is called "New Classical Economics" and were developed by University of Chicago economists Robert Lucas and Thomas Sargent, Neil Wallace of the University of Minnesota and Robert Barro of the University of Rochester and Harvard University. See R. E. Lucas, "Some International Evidence on Output-Inflation Tradeoffs", *American Economic Review* 63(3), September 1973, pp. 326-34, and T. J. Sargent and N. Wallace, "Rational Expectations, the Optimal Monetary Instrument, and the Optimal Money Supply Rule", Journal of Political Economy, 83(2), April 1975, pp. 241-54.

4. See A. W. Phillips, "The Relation Between Unemployment and the Rate of Change of Money Wages in the United Kingdom, 1861-1957", *Economica*, Vol. 25, November 1958. In fact Irving Fisher published a similar study for the United States in 1926: see Robert Barro, "I Discovered the Phillips Curve", *Journal of Political Economy*, April 1973.

5. Samuelson and Solow coined the phrase "the Phillips curve". They warned explicitly that their analysis was a short-run one and that the relationship between unemployment and inflation might shift under conditions of full employment. See P. A. Samuelson and R. M. Solow, "Analytical aspects of anti-inflation policy", *American Economic Review, Papers and Proceedings,* May 1960.

6. See E. Phelps, *Inflation Policy and Unemployment Theory*, Norton, 1973, and M. Friedman, "The Role of Monetary Policy", *American Economic Review*, March 1969.

7. The term "non-accelerating inflation rate of unemployment" (NAIRU) was introduced by James Tobin, of Yale University. This title has the merit of avoiding the moralistic overtones of the "natural" rate. However, it would be more correct to call it the *non-increasing* rate of inflation: acceleration is the second difference of the level of a variable.

Chapter 9

The Labour Market and the Problem of Unemployment in Ireland

9.1 Introduction

Unemployment is the most intractable economic problem facing Ireland and many other European countries today. After the recessions of 1974-75 and 1981-82 the rate of unemployment did not return to the level that prevailed in the 1960s and it rose again during the recession of 1990-91. The persistence of high rates of unemployment in Europe contrasts with the return to lower rates that occurred in the US during the 1980s. Furthermore, Ireland's unemployment rate, which is surpassed only by the Spanish rate in the OECD, would be even higher had not more than 200,000 people emigrated from the country during the 1980s.

In Chapter 8 we reviewed the relationship between unemployment and inflation. In this chapter we discuss the Irish labour market in some detail and summarise recent research on the problem of unemployment. We start with a review of trends in the labour force and the level and composition of employment and unemployment. We then examine some explanations for the high level of unemployment in Ireland and look at policies that might reduce it.

9.2 The Supply of Labour

In this section we examine how demographic factors affect the size and structure of the population. We then discuss the relationship between the population and the labour force.

Demographic factors

The rate of growth of the population is a key determinant of the growth of the labour force. Population growth in turn is determined by *natural increase* (the excess of births over deaths) and *net (external) migration*:

(1)   Rate of population growth ≡ rate of natural increase + net external migration rate

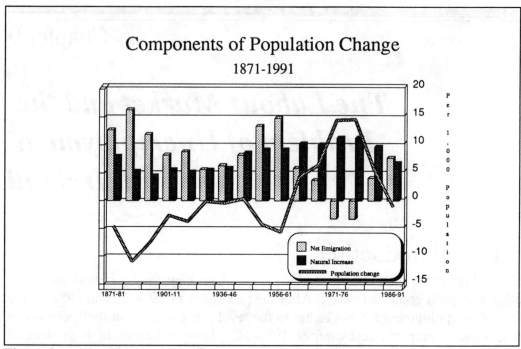

Figure 9.1   Population, natural increase and emigration

Figure 9.1 shows the rates of population growth, of natural increase and net external migration for the period 1871-1991.

Natural increase   The rate of natural increase is the difference between the birth and death rates:

(2)   Rate of natural increase ≡ birth rate - death rate

The annual rate of natural increase in Ireland rose from 0.5 per cent early in this century to a peak of 1.2 per cent in the 1980s. It had fallen to 0.7 per cent by 1991. The birth rate has been the main reason for these changes in the rate of natural increase. The birth rate peaked in 1980 and has fallen steadily since then.

Emigration   External migration has had an exceptional impact on Ireland's population history. During the 1950s we lost as much as 2 per cent of our population a year through net emigration and the population declined, while during the 1970s a net immigration of about 0.5 per cent a year raised the rate of population growth to over 1.5 per cent a year. Since the mid-1980s renewed large-scale emigration resulted in a stationary population.

The rate of emigration is determined mainly by the rate of economic growth in Ireland relative to Britain and the other countries to which Irish people emigrate. As a result, the supply of labour is extremely elastic, increasing rapidly during periods of economic growth and declining during recessions. As is clear from Figure 9.1, fluctuations in the emigration rate have been the main cause of year-to-year changes in the population. Under these circumstances population and labour force forecasting is difficult. In the early 1980s, before the resumption of large-scale emigration, it was projected that the population would exceed 4 million by the end of the century. More recent projections suggest that it will remain at its present level of 3.5 million.

The structure of the population The convention is to refer to the "under fifteen" and "sixty-five and over" age groups as *inactive*, while those aged fifteen to sixty-four are called the *population of active age*. A traditional feature of the Irish population age pyramid is the relatively high proportions in the inactive age groups. The proportion of the population in the under-fifteen age group reached a peak of 31.3 per cent in 1971, which was extremely high by European standards and reflected the high birth rate. By 1991 the proportion aged under 15 years had fallen to 27.3 per cent due to the decline in the birth rate during the 1980s. A continuation of this trend will ease pressure on the educational system and eventually reduce the numbers entering the labour force. The proportion aged sixty-five and over has remained stable in the region of 11 per cent. This too is relatively high by comparison with other European countries, but most developed countries are now experiencing a sharp rise in the proportion of elderly people in their population, whereas in Ireland this proportion will remain stable until well into the twenty-first century.

Labour force participation

In an age of prolonged schooling and flexible retirement patterns the traditional classification of the population into the "active" and "inactive" age groups is no longer very meaningful. It is therefore important to examine the *labour force participation rates* (LFPR). The LFPR is the proportion of the population that is in the labour force (whether employed or unemployed).

(3)   Labour force ≡ numbers at work + numbers seeking work

(4)   LFPR ≡ Labour force/population

The LFPRs in various population groups in 1979 and 1990 are shown in Table 9.1. The most important trends revealed are:[1]

- The LFPR has fallen quite sharply among those aged fifteen to twenty-four, as young people stay on longer in the educational system.

249

- There has been a marked move towards earlier retirement among men.

- The LFPR has increased among women aged twenty-five to forty-four. This has been due primarily to the increase in the proportion of married women who are working outside the home.

These trends in LFPRs can be understood as responses to economic factors. High unemployment undoubtedly encouraged young people to postpone entry into the labour force. Many older men were offered early retirement by firms that were anxious to reduce their labour force. The increasing participation of married women in the paid labour force reflects the fall in the birth rate and higher levels of educational attainment and potential earnings among women. It has also been encouraged by the fact that, despite the decline in total employment in recent years, more job opportunities have become available in the occupations where women are traditionally employed (notably in the service sectors). Despite these changes, women's LFPRs are still much lower than men's at each age group and low by European standards.

Table 9.1
Labour force participation rates (per cent)

Age	15-24	25-44	45-64	65+
Males				
1979	66.1	96.4	84.7	26.0
1990	52.8	96.1	81.3	15.9
Females				
1979	54.2	28.9	22.1	4.6
1990	44.9	43.8	23.4	3.1
Married Women				
1979	26.9	17.3	12.8	n.a.
1990	46.0	32.9	21.4	n.a.

Source: *Labour Force Survey* 1979 and 1990.
n.a. = not available.

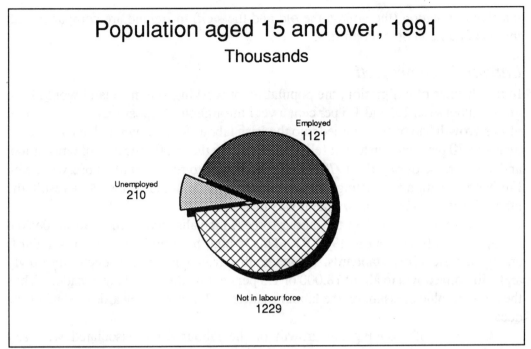

Population aged 15 and over, 1991

Thousands

Employed
1121

Unemployed
210

Not in labour force
1229

Figure 9.2 Population aged 15 and over, 1991

Working and non-working population   We noted above that in Ireland over 40 per cent of the population is either under 15 or over 64 years old. We can see from Table 9.1 that the LFPRs of those in the "active" age groups, especially women, are quite low. As a result of these two factors, in 1991 out of a population of 3,523,000 only 1,331,000, or 38 per cent, were in the labour force. Moreover, because we also have a very high rate of unemployment, the ratio of non-employed to employed is exceptionally high. There were 1,121,000 people at work in 1991, compared with 2,402,000 not at work: or 214 not working for every 100 working. While the largest single category in the "non-working" population is children aged under 15 years old, there are over 1.2 million people aged 15 and over who are classified as neither employed nor unemployed but fall into various categories of the "inactive" population. Figure 9.2 shows the distribution of the population aged 15 and over between those who are employed, unemployed and not in the labour force.

We have one of the lowest proportions economically active in the OECD. At the other extreme is a country like Sweden, where 52 per cent of total population is in the labour force and there are only 96 not working for every 100 working. Thus, our burden of dependency is over twice that of Sweden, and much higher than that in most other OECD countries. This is a fact that should never be forgotten when the levels of benefits and services that are provided for the various categories of the inactive population (the young, the old and the sick) in Ireland are compared with those available in other countries.

Labour force projections

In the absence of emigration, the population of working age in Ireland would have grown at between 1.0 and 1.5 per cent a year throughout the post-war period.[2] If all of this growth had been absorbed into the Irish labour force, it would have increased by about 80 per cent. Instead it fell sharply during the 1950s because of emigration, and the increase during the 1970s was only enough to restore it to its pre-war level. Further emigration and falling LFPRs reduced it again in the 1980s. As a result, the labour force is no larger now than it was in 1926.

The potential growth of the labour force (in the absence of emigration) peaked at 25,500 or 1.9 per cent in 1990-91. This is high both by international standards and by historical Irish standards. However, this growth rate is now declining slowly and will come down to about 18,000 or 1.3 per cent by the end of the decade.[3] Thus the demographic pressure on the labour market will diminish towards the end of the decade.

One way of reducing the growth of the labour force associated with any underlying rate of population growth is by lowering the labour force participation rate (LFPR). This could happen through early retirement, raising the school-leaving age, more liberal use of the disability category of social insurance, etc. However, this approach would increase the burden of dependency and threaten our ability to maintain the level of support for those not in the labour force (pensioners, school-children etc.). Moreover, a reduction in the LFPR does not permanently affect the growth rate of the labour force. To see that this is the case rearrange identity (4) above:

(5)   Labour force $\equiv$ population $\times$ LFPR

It follows that:

(6) Δ Labour force $\equiv$ Δ population $+$ Δ LFPR

where the symbol Δ denotes rate of change. Thus, if the aggregate LFPR were stable, the rate of growth of the labour force would be equal to the rate of growth of the population of working age. A reduction in the LFPR lowers the rate of growth of the labour force below that of the population, but once the LFPR stabilises again, it reverts back to the underlying population growth rate. Reducing the LFPR therefore results in only a temporary reduction in the growth rate of the labour force. This point is often overlooked by those who advocate early retirement or prolonged schooling as ways of reducing the rate of growth of the supply of labour. These strategies cause a once-off reduction in the *size* of the labour force, but have no

252

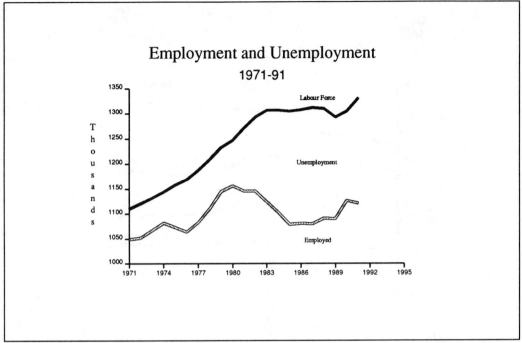

Figure 9.3 Labour force, employment and unemployment

---

long-run effect on its underlying *growth rate,* which will only decline when the growth rate of the population of working age declines.

9.3 The Trend of Employment

Figure 9.3 shows the labour force and its two components, employment and unemployment, over the period 1971-91. Employment grew rapidly during the 1970s, although the labour force expanded even more rapidly due to the net return flow of population to Ireland. As the level of employment turned down in the early 1980s, and emigration was curtailed by rising unemployment abroad, the labour force continued to grow and unemployment rose very sharply. However, large-scale emigration started up again in the mid-1980s, siphoning off the potential growth of the labour force. This had the effect of stabilising the level of unemployment. With over 270,000 unemployed and the labour force still expanding by over 20,000 a year, it is natural to wonder whether the additional jobs needed to absorb the growth of the labour force and reduce unemployment are likely to materialise or whether the prospect is for further large-scale emigration and higher unemployment.

Looking back at Ireland's record of employment creation gives little grounds for optimism. Figure 9.4 shows the level of employment in each sector over the period 1961 to 1991. We can see the following trends:

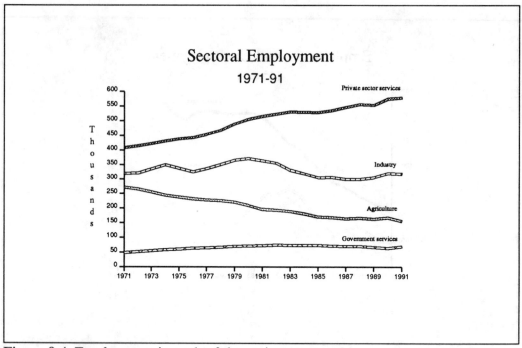

Figure 9.4 Employment in each of the main sectors

Agriculture There has been a long-run decline in employment in agriculture that accelerated in recent years. In view of the major restructuring of agricultural policy that is now occurring as the Common Agricultural Policy is scaled down under pressure of the EC's budget problems and the GATT negotiations, this trend is likely to continue. Despite the long-run reduction in numbers in this sector, many farmers are underemployed and the number of farms will continue to fall.

Industry There was sustained, if modest, growth from 1961 to 1979, but since 1981 the numbers employed in this sector have declined by over a quarter. The small number of successful large Irish firms have all reached the maximum employment that can be sustained by the Irish market and are expanding by investment abroad. Employment in new foreign-owned firms has grown steadily, but not rapidly enough to offset the losses in Irish-owned and in the older foreign-owned firms. Ireland no longer seeks to attract low-wage, labour intensive industries. The amount of employment created by more capital intensive projects is relatively small.

Public sector services In Ireland, as in most countries, there was a major expansion of public sector employment after the Second World War. The rate of expansion accelerated in the 1970s, but the state of the public finances necessitated a reversal of this trend in the 1980s. There was a drop of about 9 per cent in the numbers employed in the public sector between 1987 and 1991. In view of the budgetary problems discussed in Chapter 5, there is little prospect of renewed expansion in the immediate future.

Private sector services This sector has recorded steady long-run growth, which accelerated in the 1980s. The new jobs that are being created in this sector range from highly skilled occupations in computer software and consulting to low-paid posts in personal services. (Other occupations, such as domestic servants, have virtually disappeared.) It is expected that employment in services will continue to be an important growth area in the 1990s. This sector can act as an "employer of last resort" when no other employment opportunities are available. This is very apparent in low-income countries where there is rapid population growth. Many young people are only able to find jobs like selling cigarettes or polishing shoes on the street corners. In the United States, much of the recent employment growth has been in relatively low-wage service jobs. In Ireland, however, emigration is preferred by many young people to low-wage employment at home.

If we extrapolate these sectoral employment trends, it is hard to see how the economy will generate the 1.5 to 2 per cent annual growth rate in employment that is necessary to absorb the potential growth of our labour force into employment during the 1990s. However, it should be borne in mind that the growth rate of employment in the US consistently exceeded 1.5 per cent a year throughout the post-war period. Many developing countries have recorded even higher growth rates of employment. Moreover, Ireland's own record of job creation outside agriculture has been quite impressive: non-agricultural employment grew by 44 per cent over the thirty-year period 1961-91, an annual average growth rate of 1.2 per cent. As the agricultural sector shrinks in importance, the overall growth rate will be closer to that of the non-agricultural sector. Under favourable conditions, the rate of employment creation could accelerate in Ireland.

9.4　Unemployment in Ireland

Definition and measurement

Unemployment is surprisingly difficult to define and measure. Our statistics come from two sources, the annual *Labour Force Survey* (LFS) and the monthly *Live Register* (LR) statistics. In the LFS, a sample of about 45,000 households is interviewed. The questionnaire used has been constructed in accordance with EC and International Labour Organisation (ILO) methodologies. Each member of the household is classified by "Principal Economic Status". To be classified as unemployed a person has to be (1) not working and (2) actively seeking work. People who are not looking for work because they believe that no jobs are available are not recorded as unemployed, but they constitute a type of *hidden unemployment*. Estimates from the Labour Force Survey show that the level of unemployment in Ireland would increase by about 5 per cent if "discouraged workers" of this type were enumerated as unemployed.[4] As is clear from Figure 9.2, which is based on LFS data, the numbers classified as *unemployed* are relatively small compared with the total who are *not at work*: only 29 per cent of males, and 4 per cent of the females, aged 15 and over, who were not at work were classified as unemployed.

The LR, on the other hand, is a record of those who qualify under the rules and regulations of the Department of Social Welfare for either unemployment benefits or unemployment assistance ("the dole"). The LFS data are regarded as more reliable than the LR numbers and are used as the basis of the official estimates of employment and unemployment and for international comparisons. The LR data, however, attract widespread attention when they are published at the end of each month and they are useful in monitoring the short-term trend in unemployment.

In 1991 the LR figure for total unemployment was approximately 3 per cent higher than the LFS figure. The unemployment rate according to the LFS was 15.8 per cent, compared with 18.6 per cent according to the LR. The main reason for the discrepancy is that many more women now register as unemployed than are recorded as unemployed in the LFS. This is only partly offset by the larger number of young people recorded as unemployed in the LFS.

Note:
International evidence shows how easily the population moves between labour force categories in response to changing social patterns and changes in the social welfare regulations. In the Netherlands, after the revenue from North Sea gas began to flow in the 1970s, a very generous national disability system was introduced. The numbers classified as disabled doubled between 1975 and 1980. By 1989 15 per cent of the population aged 15-64 were classified as "permanently disabled". The comparable percentage in West Germany was only 5 per cent.

The structure of unemployment

Different population groups experience different rates of unemployment. Men are generally more likely to be unemployed than women. The unskilled, the young, those in building trades and those living in Dublin experience relatively high rates of unemployment. Table 9.2 summarises the most important differentials in unemployment rates in Ireland today.

The existence of such differentials does not establish that there is a serious *structural* unemployment problem. For this it is necessary to show that there has been a *widening* of differentials over time, due for example to the failure of some sectors to benefit from a general reduction in unemployment. There is no strong evidence that such a deterioration in the operation of the labour market has occurred, in fact the differentials have been relatively stable over the years.

The structural dimension of the Irish labour market that received most attention in the early 1980s was the demographic one. Great concern was expressed about the rapid rise in youth unemployment when emigration was choked off by recession in Britain and America. A Youth Unemployment Levy of 1 per cent on all incomes was introduced in 1981 as a response to this problem. The proceeds were used to help fund the Youth Employment Agency whose task it was to create employment for those aged under twenty-five. This agency was merged into the National Employment and Training Agency (FAS) in 1988. The income levy remains in place.

Table 9.2
Unemployment differentials

	High unemployment rate	Low unemployment rate
Occupations	Unskilled	Skilled, Professional
Industries	Building & Construction	Public sector, Banking, Insurance
Demographic groups	Youths	Adults
Regions	Dublin, The North West (males)	The West (both sexes)

Note:
Taxing the employed to fund job creation for the unemployed is not a sensible policy. Pay-roll taxes tend to increase the cost of hiring workers and discourage employment. Moreover, singling out one category of the unemployed for special aid puts others at a disadvantage. It should only be done where there is a clear need to overcome a particular problem, such as lack of skills or employer discrimination.

The rate of unemployment among young people is much higher than the adult unemployment rate in all countries. In the early 1980s the ratio of the rate of youth to adult unemployment was about 2:1 in Ireland, not exceptional by international standards. The resumption of large-scale emigration siphoned off thousands of young people from the Irish labour market, but had relatively little effect on the older population. As a result by 1990 the ratio of youth to adult unemployment rates had declined to 1.6:1. The emphasis formerly placed on youth unemployment is now giving way to a concern about the plight of.older workers who have been unemployed for a long time.

There is a tendency for shortages of skilled workers to emerge even when the overall unemployment rate is still very high. This happened during the 1970s and the resultant rise in skilled wage rates spilled over in a generalised wage inflation.

257

This feature of the labour market implies that structural rigidities are present which can lead to rapid wage inflation even when the overall rate of unemployment is relatively high.

9.5   Explaining Unemployment

This section looks at the problem of high unemployment in Ireland in the light of the research on the persistence of high unemployment in Europe since the 1970s.[5]

Okun's law

The Yale economist Arthur Okun (1928-80) showed that there is a close association between the rate of growth of real output (GNP) and the rate of unemployment in the US. This relationship is known as *Okun's law*. The US evidence suggests that the rate of unemployment will increase unless the rate of growth of GNP is above 3 per cent, and that every additional one per cent of GNP growth (above 3 per cent) lowers the unemployment rate by 0.5 percentage points. The statistical evidence for Ireland indicates that a similar relationship holds, but that our GNP has to grow by at least 3.8 per cent in order to avert an increase in unemployment, and that each additional one per cent of GNP growth reduces the unemployment rate by only 0.4 percentage points.[6]

Figure 9.5 shows a scatterplot of the change in the unemployment rate (horizontal axis) and the change in real GNP (vertical axis) for Ireland over the period 1977-91. Each point in the diagram represents the unemployment/real GNP combination for that particular year. The inverse relationship between the two variables is evident. However, the link between the two variables in Ireland is weaker than in the US, probably because of the major impact of external migration on the Irish labour market: in a year like 1981, for example, unemployment increased sharply even though GNP grew, because there was virtually no emigration from Ireland due to rising unemployment in Britain.

The Okun relationship highlights the impact of recession on Irish unemployment and the importance of trying to keep GNP close to its trend growth rate. However, as we have seen in previous chapters, few effective instruments are available to policy-makers for this purpose in an economy such as Ireland.

Earlier in this chapter we summarised the structure of the Irish labour force and drew attention to its relatively high potential growth rate. This is due to two factors. The first is the fact that Ireland had in the past a high birth rate and hence would experience a rapidly growing population in the absence of net external migration. The second is the relatively low rates of labour force participation in certain population groups (notably women). Accelerated economic growth leading to increased employment opportunities has a relatively weak effect on unemployment in Ireland *due to the tendency of the labour force to expand more rapidly as employment opportunities increase.*

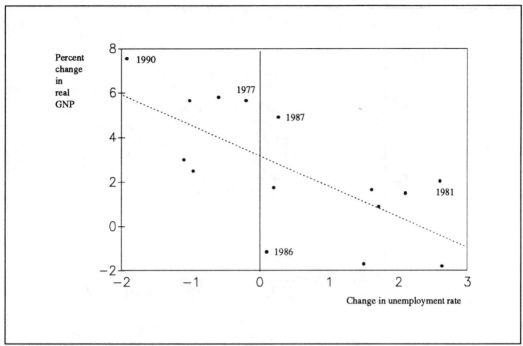

Figure 9.5 Unemployment and the growth rate in real GNP

For example, it may be seen from Figure 9.3 that employment grew rapidly during the 1970s. There were 10 per cent more people at work in 1980 than in 1971, yet the numbers unemployed *increased* by 50 per cent over the same period. Even over the period 1976-80, when non-agricultural employment grew by an unprecedented 115,000 or 13.8 per cent, unemployment fell by only 14,000. The additional jobs were filled by school leavers, returning emigrants, women returning to work and the outflow from the farm labour force. It has been estimated that for every 100 additional people employed in Ireland, unemployment only falls by about 50: the other 50 jobs are filled from the growth of the labour force.[7]

What is "full employment"?

In the past we thought we knew what we meant by "full employment" in Ireland. The National Industrial Economic Council in 1967 specified 2 per cent as the target rate for full employment. The National Economic and Social Council (NESC) published a study in 1975 using a rate of 4 per cent. In 1977 NESC used a rate of 5 per cent as equivalent to full employment. However, in a study of unemployment published in 1984, the Economic and Social Research Institute simply stated that the goal of economic policy should be ". . . to redistribute the benefits of growth to ensure viable employment for all who are willing and able to avail of it".[8] Similarly, recent official documents, including the Programme for National Recovery (1987) and the Programme for Economic and Social Progress (1990), have avoided

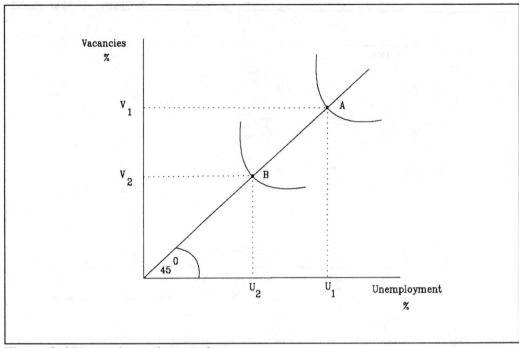

Figure 9.6 Vacancies and unemployment

specifying precise targets for employment or unemployment. In this subsection we discuss the definition of "full employment" and we examine the implications for policies designed to reduce unemployment.

The natural rate of unemployment In Chapter 8 we discussed Milton Friedman's *natural rate of unemployment*. A closely related concept advanced by James Tobin is called the *non-accelerating inflation rate of unemployment* (NAIRU). Both of these concepts are based on the idea that there is an equilibrium rate of unemployment at which, in the past, the rate of inflation has been stable. If unemployment is pushed below this rate the labour market will overheat and the rate of inflation will rise. The natural rate, therefore, is the economist's interpretation of "full employment".

The unemployment that exists at "full employment" is due to *frictions*, *imperfect information* and *job search*. It takes time and effort for job-seekers to find out about job openings. Employers have to invest in recruiting and screening employees. There is never a perfect match between the qualifications of the unemployed and the skills sought by employers. Also people who are looking for jobs do not take the first job that becomes available: they have *reservation wages* for the type of jobs they are seeking. If a person's reservation wage is above the wage that is being offered by employers for the type of work he wishes to do, he will continue searching until he is lucky enough to get a better than average offer or until he lowers his expectations.

Beveridge curve   The efficiency of the labour market can be depicted using the curve linking the combinations of unemployment and vacancies that coexist in an economy. This is known as the *Beveridge curve*, after the British economist William Beveridge (1879-1963) who is famous as the "father of the British welfare state". In Figure 9.6, vacancies and unemployment are given along the vertical and horizontal axis, respectively. A 45° line is inserted for illustrative purposes. At every point on the 45° line the number of vacancies equals the number of people unemployed. When the economy is operating below full employment, it will be to the right of the 45° line (unemployment exceeds vacancies); if there is overfull employment, it will be to the left of it (unemployment is less than vacancies).

Imagine two economies: one with an inflexible labour force, a poor match between the qualifications of the unemployed and those sought by employers, and a generous social welfare system; the other with a flexible labour force, a good match between the qualifications of the unemployed and those sought by employers, and a harsh social welfare system.

The first economy would have a high natural rate of unemployment, the second a low rate. In the first economy both the number unemployed and the number of vacancies (U_1, V_1) are much higher than in the second (U_2, V_2). The labour market in the second economy is more efficient than in the first, so it has a lower natural rate of unemployment. A central objective of labour market policy is to shift the Beveridge curve inwards, thereby lowering the equilibrium rate of unemployment.

Note:
This analysis assumes that the size of the labour force is the same in both countries, and that there is full employment in the sense that the number of vacancies equals the number of unemployed people.

Numerous influences have been suggested to account for why the natural rate of unemployment differs across countries and, within a country, over time. Among these influences are:

- The wage bargaining process. The more sensitive wages are to the rate of unemployment, the lower the rate of unemployment consistent with price stability. If wages are indexed to inflation and there is a lack of willingness on the part of workers to accept a fall in living standards as a result of an adverse external shock, then it will require a large rise in the rate of unemployment to bring the rate of inflation under control.

- The level of unionisation of the labour force. This is related to the previous point because unions tend to bargain for indexation and reduce the flexibility of real wages.

- The match between the skills of the labour force and those sought by employers. A mismatch of skills will lead to shortages in key occupations even when the overall rate of unemployment is high.

- The social welfare system. A relatively generous social welfare system tends to raise people's reservation wages and encourage job search. This increases the natural rate of unemployment.

- The mobility of the labour force. If unemployed workers are reluctant to move in search of jobs, the natural rate of unemployment will be high. Mobility can be reduced by the difficulty of obtaining housing in growing areas or the desire to retain a subsidised council house in an area of high unemployment.

Hysteresis in the labour market

The natural rate hypothesis implies that there is a *stable* equilibrium rate of unemployment. However, in many countries when unemployment rose following the oil shocks of the 1970s, it tended to remain high even after economic growth resumed. *There seems to be no tendency for unemployment to return to its former "natural rate"*. The persistence of high unemployment in the 1980s has been very pronounced in Europe, but even in the US it has been noted that the level of unemployment at the peak of each successive business cycle is rising. This calls into question the notion that there is some underlying, constant, "natural" rate of unemployment.

Note:
In Ireland the *average* rate of unemployment during the 1960s was 5.0 per cent, it was 6.9 per cent during the 1970s, 14.3 per cent during the 1980s and over 17 per cent by early 1992. (A graph of the rate of unemployment was shown in Figure 1.3 in Chapter 1.)

Hysteresis is the concept that has been developed to explain the phenomenon of a natural rate that changes over time in response to changes in the *actual* level of the variable. It is a concept borrowed from physics to describe a kind of inertia, where the past history of a variable influences its present level.

Note:
Think of what would happen if every time you got a high temperature there was a tendency for your body's normal temperature to rise. As your fever subsided, your temperature would not return to 37^0 Celsius, but would settle down at a higher level. Your temperature would be exhibiting the phenomenon of hysteresis. It sounds unpleasant!

Hysteresis means that if the rate of unemployment rises due to an adverse shock, the longer it remains above the natural rate, the more likely it is that a new, higher natural rate will be established. Conversely, the longer the actual rate of unemployment can be held below the natural rate, the lower the natural rate will become. In this area nothing succeeds like success, and nothing fails like failure.

Robert Solow has questioned the usefulness of the concept of natural unemployment:

A natural rate that hops around from one triennium to another under the influences of unspecified forces, including past unemployment rates, is not natural at all.[9]

However, while taking this criticism into account, we cannot dispense with the concept of an "equilibrium", "natural" or "non-accelerating inflation" rate of unemployment. Some such concept has to be used when we try to define what we mean by "full employment" and when policy-makers set goals in this area.

Econometric research supports the view that the natural rate of unemployment has been rising. In Ireland the evidence indicates that the natural rate has drifted up from 6.1 per cent in 1961 to 9.7 per cent in 1981 to 14.4 per cent in 1991. A more elaborate approach in a recent study of unemployment yielded a very similar estimate.[10] The results for several countries are reproduced in Table 9.3:

Table 9.3 Actual and equilibrium unemployment

	Equilibrium unemployment rate		Actual unemployment rate	
	1960-8	1980-8	1960-68	1980-88
Ireland	6.1	13.1	5.0	14.1
Spain	4.6	15.0	2.4	17.7
Belgium	3.8	7.0	2.3	11.1
Germany	0.5	4.0	0.7	6.1
UK	2.6	7.9	2.6	10.3
USA	5.0	6.4	4.7	7.4
Japan	1.6	2.1	1.4	2.5
Sweden	1.6	2.4	1.3	2.2

Source: R. Layard, S. Nickell and R. Jackman, *Unemployment: Macroeconomic Performance and the Labour Market*, Oxford University Press, 1991, p. 436.

The authors attribute the rise in the equilibrium rate of unemployment, and the differences between individual countries, to the factors we listed above. They stress in particular the importance of the wage-bargaining process, the skills mismatch problem and the structure of the social welfare and tax systems.[11]

In view of their importance in discussions of the problem of unemployment, we turn now to a more detailed examination of these factors.

9.6   Wages, Employment and Unemployment

Real wage resistance In the typical microeconomic setting, an excess supply in any market should lead to a fall in the price until the market clears. High unemployment should therefore lead to a fall in the real wage rate so as to restore full employment. If there is resistance to a fall in real wages then excess unemployment will persist in the wake of a demand shock. What should have been temporary, disequilibrium unemployment is converted by *real wage resistance* into a permanently higher rate of unemployment.

Table 9.4
Real earnings, employment and unemployment rates

		1960	*1990*
Real earnings (index)			
	US	100	145
	EUR-12	100	251
	Ireland	100	275
Employment (index)			
	US	100	176
	EUR-12	100	109
	Ireland	100	107
Unemployment rate (%)			
	US	5.7	5.5
	EUR-12	2.5	8.4
	Ireland	5.6	13.7

Source: Commission of the European Communities, *European Economy*, No. 50 (Dec. 1991), Tables 2, 3 and 29.

The experience of the US and European economies since 1960 may be used to illustrate this point. Table 9.4 shows that between 1960 and 1990 *real wages* grew by only 45 per cent in the US while they increased by 151 per cent in Europe and 175 per cent in Ireland. Over the same period *employment* grew by 76 per cent (1.9 per cent a year) in the US, but by only 9 per cent (0.3 per cent a year) in Europe and by a mere 7 per cent (0.2 per cent a year) in Ireland. The *unemployment* rate rose more than threefold in Europe, and more than doubled in Ireland, but showed no upward trend in the US. Only over the last five years, from 1985 to 1990, has Europe performed better: real wages fell, employment rose and the unemployment rate

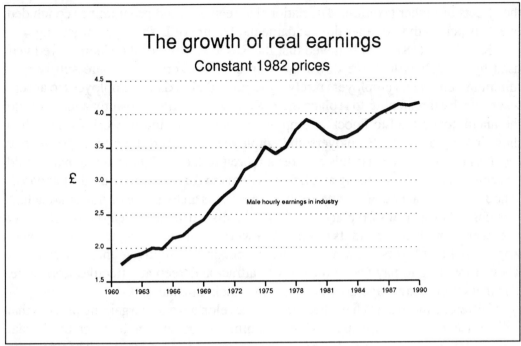

Figure 9.7 The growth of real earnings

decreased. The simple correlation between the growth of employment and the moderation of real wages over time is very striking.

In Ireland, nominal wage rates increased in every year since 1961. This is hardly surprising in a period of high inflation. Of greater interest is the behaviour of real wages, shown in Figure 9.7. It may be seen that real wages increased steadily until 1973, and again between 1975 and 1980, and between 1982 and 1990. There has been only a weak tendency for higher rates of unemployment to slow down the growth of real wages.[12]

The wage-bargaining process There are many possible explanations for this lack of responsiveness of real wages to labour market conditions. Trade unions exist in part to ensure that real wages *are* rigid. By combining together, workers try to prevent their wages from being reduced by the forces of supply and demand. In inflationary periods unions look for indexation of wages, that is, automatic increases in nominal wages to compensate for rises in the cost of living. The type of money illusion we discussed in the previous chapter in conjunction with the Keynesian model did not last long when inflation increased during the 1970s and 1980s. Wage bargaining quickly focused on *real* rather than *nominal* wages and, as the tax wedge between gross and net earnings grew, the key variable became real *take-home* pay: trade unions sought to protect their members not only from inflation but also from the effects of higher taxation. The national agreements and programmes concluded over this period did not alter this fundamental feature of Irish wage bargaining.

Karl Marx (1818-83) believed that the Reserve Army of the Unemployed was used by capitalists to force down the wages of workers to the bare subsistence minimum, but in fact employers rarely try to force their existing employees to accept wage cuts by threatening to replace them with new recruits at lower wages. Nor do the unemployed tend to knock at employers' doors offering to work for less than those in employment. Employers and employees enter into long-term (*explicit* or *implicit*) *contracts* because this ensures a more productive labour force than would be achieved by ruthless hiring and firing as demand for the firm's output fluctuated. The Japanese practice of "hiring for life" (*nenko*) is an example of this approach.[13] It is costly for a firm to replace *insiders* (established workers, enjoying relatively high wages) with new entrants or *outsiders* who might be willing to work for lower wages. All employers use wages to recruit, retain and motivate the best workers. They are willing to pay above the odds to attract and keep an effective workforce. The market clearing wage does not enter into their calculations.

Different approaches have been tried to develop a wage-bargaining process that will reduce real wage resistance. One possibility is cooperation between the "social partners" (that is, unions, employers and government) or *corporatism*. There is some evidence that countries with a high degree of corporatism (such as Sweden and Austria) or those with a low degree (such as Japan and the US) have achieved a better economic performance compared with those where a number of relatively powerful, but uncoordinated, unions and employer organisations, negotiate wage bargains on behalf of their members.[14]

National wage agreements The Irish version of corporatism has taken the form of national agreements or understandings or programmes. These were introduced during the 1970s to try to establish an orderly system of wage bargaining that would avoid the very disruptive strikes and industrial unrest that had occurred during the 1960s. These involved employer organisations, trade unions and government agreeing on rates of increase for wages. They were followed by broader National Understandings which involved government commitments relating to taxation, employment creation, social welfare and spending on headings such as health and education. It was widely felt that by the time of the Second National Understanding (1980) government pressure to reach a settlement (in order to avert industrial unrest) resulted in *higher* rates of wage inflation than would have been recorded under a system of decentralised wage bargaining. A national consensus on pay moderation in the interest of job creation, along the Austrian or Scandinavian lines, was not achieved.

Between 1981 and 1987 there were no national wage agreements. Wages were set by a process of decentralised wage bargaining. As may be seen from Figure 9.7, during this period the rate of growth of real wages moderated significantly.

However, a Programme for National Recovery (PNR) was negotiated in October 1987, which provided for pay increases of 2.5 per cent in each of the years 1988, 1989 and 1990. Pay increases were in general held to this guideline, and industrial peace was preserved with the aid of low inflation and tax reductions. However, numerous arbitrations in pay in the public sector resulted in major "special" pay awards, which resulted in very rapid increases in public sector pay in 1991. A new Programme for Economic and Social Progress (PESP) was ratified in February 1991. This provides for overall pay increases of 4 per cent in 1991, 3 per cent in 1992 and 3.75 per cent in 1993 and contains commitments by government to create additional employment, to lower rates of income taxation and grant substantial further "special" pay increases in a wide range of public sector jobs. Following the deterioration in the public finances during 1991, however, government argued that the pay increases were conditional on the availability of resources, a view that was rejected by the public sector unions. Under threat of widespread industrial action, a compromise was reached which postponed part of the 1992 increases until the end of the year.

Thus when economic growth slowed down in 1991, the priority was the continued improvement in the living standards of those at work in the sectors of the economy covered by the national agreement, rather than wage moderation to create additional employment. It could be argued that centralised agreements have protected the pay and conditions of work of those who have jobs in the public sector and the unionised private sector at the expense of the outsiders who would work for less. This has the effect of increasing the supply of labour to the unprotected sectors of the economy (which include the informal or "black" economy) where pay and conditions of work for young job-seekers have probably deteriorated, and raising the level of unemployment and emigration.

International competitiveness The problem of unemployment in a small open economy cannot be divorced from that of international price and cost competitiveness. In principle a small country like Ireland should be able to sell enough on world markets at prevailing prices to ensure full employment. In practice, this requires a competitive cost structure. The main component of domestically controlled costs are wages. Thus in a small open economy the problem of maintaining a high level of demand for the sectors producing internationally traded goods and services comes back to the question of the wage structure and the exchange rate. We have discussed the issue of wage flexibility above and we return to the role of the exchange rate as a determinant of competitiveness in a later chapter.

9.7　The Social Welfare System

The *replacement ratio* measures the proportion of after-tax income that is replaced by social welfare payments to which an unemployed person is entitled:

(7)   Replacement ratio ≡ unemployment benefit/after-tax income

A single man whose best employment opportunity offers a gross wage of £175 a week (about two-thirds the average weekly earnings of an adult male industrial worker in 1992) will have to pay £30 a week in PAYE and a further £14 a week in PRSI, leaving £131 a week in after-tax income. When unemployed he would be entitled to £53 a week in unemployment benefit. Thus the replacement ratio in this situation is 35 per cent (£53/£131 = 0.4). However, several other factors may increase the real income of the unemployed, depending on family circumstances. In reply to a Dail question, the Minister for Finance estimated that in 1991 an entitlement to social welfare payments of £58 a week could be worth more in net terms than a gross income from employment of £231. This conclusion was reached on the basis of entitlement to the Family Income Supplement, a medical card, and a subsidised local authority rent. We lack evidence on how widespread such "social welfare traps" are. Calculations by the OECD show that in 1990 very high replacement ratios applied to (i) single persons on low incomes, and (ii) married couples with several children. [15] We also know that as the rate of unemployment has risen, successive governments have raised the rates of assistance for the long-term unemployed faster than the take-home pay of those at work was increasing. The average value of the replacement ratio rose from 46 per cent in 1978 to 58 per cent in 1985. [16]

Note:
The financing of the social welfare system has implications for the demand for labour because it increases the *tax wedge* between the cost of hiring a worker and his take-home pay. A person earning gross pay of £175 costs his employer at least £196 a week because of the 12.2 per cent employer PRSI levy. Thus, it costs the employer £196 to give an employee take-home pay of £131. When the employee spends this £131, about 30 per cent of it will be taken in indirect taxes (VAT, excise taxes, etc.). Thus, the net-of-all-taxes income left from the £196 paid gross by the employer is only £92, less than 50 per cent. Moreover, since marginal income tax rates are higher than average, it would take more than £1 of additional income to secure an extra 50p of net-of-tax purchasing power for the employee. The tax wedge between gross and net pay increased by about 30 per cent between 1979 and 1986. Because workers resist reductions in their real after-tax earnings, the growth of this wedge tends to lower the level of employment and raise the level of unemployment.

The other relevant dimension of the social welfare system is the *duration of benefits*, that is, how long claimants are entitled to draw unemployment benefits. In Ireland, the duration of benefits was extended from a maximum of six months in the 1960s to 15 months at present. After that, if a person is still unemployed, he moves down to the means-tested unemployment assistance. Assistance may be drawn indefinitely provided the claimant meets the conditions. Rates of assistance are lower than benefits, but the gap between the two has narrowed over the years. Thus, although the replacement ratio is higher in the earlier months of a spell of unemployment, there is almost indefinite entitlement to income maintenance as long as a person remains unemployed. (Recently, in recognition of the growing incidence of long-term unemployment, special higher rates of long-term unemployment assistance were introduced.)

The key issue is whether, and by how much, the level of the replacement ratio and the duration of benefits affect the level of unemployment. The evidence of the importance of these effects in Ireland is not extensive because relatively little econometric work has addressed the issue. However, it has been shown that higher levels of the replacement ratio tend to lengthen the typical spell of unemployment in Ireland. The long-run improvement in Ireland's social welfare system from the 1950s to the 1980s is likely to have caused a significant upward drift in the equilibrium rate of unemployment. An unemployed person is no longer compelled by economic hardship to grab the first job offer or to emigrate. The alternative of remaining unemployed in Ireland has become more acceptable over the past generation.

There is also evidence that countries with extended entitlement to unemployment benefits, such as Ireland, have higher incidences of *long-term* unemployment than countries where there is a fixed-term entitlement to benefits. Layard *et al.* report that "the role of benefit duration is clear-cut" throughout their study of the unemployment-inflation trade-off in 19 OECD countries.[17] They conclude that economies perform well in response to exogenous shocks if social welfare benefits have a fixed duration. In the US, for example, there is no Federal unemployment insurance system, and most state and occupational systems do not provide benefits after six months' unemployment. The risk of unemployment looms large before a sizeable proportion of the labour force.

In Sweden those who have been out of work for over six months are required to undergo intensive counselling and retraining and, when they have completed these courses, steps are taken to place them in employment. The idea of simply paying the long-term unemployed income maintenance is not part of the Swedish social insurance system. The result is a low level of long-term unemployment.[18] The contrast between Ireland, Sweden and the US is clear from the statistics in Table 9.5. In Ireland and Europe generally as unemployment has risen it has become more concentrated among the long-term unemployed and most workers disregard the risk of unemployment when they are bargaining for wage increases. Thus the structure of unemployment tends to raise the equilibrium rate of unemployment.

Table 9.5
Short- and long-term unemployment rates, 1987

	Short-term unemployment rate %	Long-term unemployment rate %
Ireland	10.4	8.3
Sweden	1.7	0.2
US	5.7	0.5

Note: Long-term = one year and over.
Source: OECD, Employment Outlook, 1988, Tables 1.7 and M. Note that the OECD uses LFS data on the duration of unemployment, which yields a much higher proportion of long-term unemployed than the LR data.

9.8 Policies to Reduce Ireland's Unemployment Rate

Numerous policies have been suggested by economists studying Europe's problem of high unemployment and a fair degree of consensus has emerged as to what will and what will not work. In this concluding section the main approaches to reducing unemployment are related to the Irish situation.

Maintain a high and stable growth rate

A high and stable growth rate is the single most important factor in reducing unemployment and keeping it low. Throughout this book we have emphasised the need to keep the economy as close as possible to its long-run trend growth path, but we have also seen that the scope for domestic policy in this area is limited. In a small and open economy the main determinant of the growth rate is the growth rate of the world economy and the main reason for sudden rises in unemployment has been adverse external shocks, such as the recessions caused by the oil price increases in the early and late 1970s. Relatively little can be done at the domestic macroeconomic policy level to ward off the effects of the cycle in world business. Fiscal policy is of limited effectiveness and is constrained by the need to reduce the debt/GNP ratio. The scope for an independent monetary or exchange rate policy is virtually ruled out by our commitment to join the European Economic and Monetary Union by the end of the decade.

Incomes policy is, however, an area that will be unaffected by these moves and it is one that offers scope for alleviating the unemployment problem. In our review of the reasons for the relatively weak effect of high unemployment on the growth of real wages, we saw that it is not evident that national wage agreements along the

270

lines of the PNR and the PESP have been very effective in this regard. An incomes policy that will ensure the international competitiveness of the Irish economy has a crucial role to play in ensuring the growth of employment and output.

Reform the tax and social welfare systems

Earlier in this chapter we discussed the way taxation drives a wedge between the cost of employing a person and that person's take-home pay. This reduces the level of employment. We also drew attention to the traps created by the social welfare system, as a result of which in certain circumstances there is little incentive to accept employment in the formal economy. Reform of the tax and social welfare system is required to eliminate these obstacles to increasing employment. In regard to the social welfare system various proposals have been published, including the possibility of replacing the existing elaborate patchwork quilt with a single *negative income tax* or *social dividend* approach.[19] These alternatives might reduce the labour force by providing an incentive for many who are now working only part-time or in poorly paid employment to withdraw from the labour force, while providing others with increased incentives to take full-time employment.

Another possibility is the use of *incremental employment subsidies*, such as forgoing (employers') PRSI levies on additional employment or providing grants to those willing to recruit additional workers. These lower the cost of taking on additional workers without any loss of exchequer revenue from those already in employment. A number of schemes of this type have been tried in Ireland, notably the *Employment Incentive Scheme*, but all have been on a very small scale. Evaluations have concluded that they have achieved relatively little *net additional* job creation, although they have been relatively costless to the exchequer. The problem is that these schemes mainly encourage employers to bring forward jobs that they would have created eventually without the subsidy.[20] None the less their net contribution is positive. In view of the small size of the existing programmes relative to the resources devoted to job creation through capital grants to industry, the presumption is that they should be expanded.[21]

Another possibility is to link the payment of unemployment benefits to the contribution of a certain amount of community work. The *Social Employment Scheme* exists as a prototype. Under the scheme those on unemployment assistance contribute a 20-hour week in return for a wage of £72 (married) or £55 (single) per week. Participation in this scheme is voluntary. Also workers can work part-time in their off-days without suffering a loss of pay. Schemes of this type play a major role as alternatives to unemployment in countries such as Sweden.

Special issues arise with regard to the long-term unemployed, who now constitute such a high proportion of total unemployment in Ireland. The incidence of long-term unemployment increases sharply with age and lack of skills. These workers are not attractive to training agencies anxious to show high placement rates for their graduates. In other countries, notably Sweden and the Netherlands, many

271

in this situation are classified as disabled or retired. While this does not solve the problem, it may result in a more realistic picture of the true availability of job-seekers. Recently some similar schemes have been introduced in Ireland, as a result of which in 1991 over 11,000 persons aged under 65 were on pre-retirement schemes instead of being classified as unemployed.

The key policy issue is, however, how to prevent additional unemployed workers from moving into long-term unemployment. A strategy of intervention in the earlier stages of unemployment, so that the inflow into the long-term category is staunched, is urgently needed. The following is an outline for a reformed social welfare scheme designed to achieve this objective: in the early stages of unemployment, say the first three months, unemployment benefits would continue to be paid unconditionally. After three months further payments would be conditional on participation in an intensive training programme, at the end of which active placement measures would be used to help find suitable employment. If these efforts were unsuccessful, further income maintenance would be dependent on participation in schemes such as the social employment scheme. Those who are unable to participate in such schemes would be assessed with a view to be reclassified as disabled or retired. The unconditional right to indefinite income maintenance would be discontinued. The additional costs which this more active approach to the long term would be in large measure met from the EC Social Fund, whose support for measures to help the long-term unemployed is particularly generous.

Intensify education and training

We have seen that during the past two decades there has been a significant reduction in the LFPR of those in the 15-24 year age group. This reflects a marked increase in educational participation by young people, which has brought our general educational standards above the European average. Spending on general education is also high relative to national income. However, the relevance of some of this education to the requirements of the economy is debatable. It is often asserted that we have over-expanded second and third level education of a general, non-vocational nature and steered too high a proportion of each generation of students into academic courses that do little to enhance their employment prospects. There is some evidence of this in the poor employment experience in Ireland of recent cohorts of school-leavers, although those with higher educational attainment have a better chance of finding employment than those with low attainment.

Educational policy is rarely included in discussions of the unemployment problem, although "manpower policy" always is, yet public spending on second and third level education is three times as high as that on training. However, in recent years there has been a marked expansion of training programmes, which have been coordinated since 1988 by a single authority, FAS, whose budget in 1992 will be in excess of £200 million. It is estimated, however, that when account is taken of savings on social welfare spending and contributions from the EC Social Fund, the net cost of these programmes to the exchequer is only about 30 per cent of the gross total.[22]

An idea of the relative scale of spending on labour market programmes is provided in Table 9.6, which shows the proportion of GDP spent by various countries on "active" measures and income maintenance measures in selected OECD countries. Not surprisingly, in view of our high unemployment rate, we spend more than any other country on unemployment compensation (3.7 per cent of GDP compared with 2.6 in Denmark, the next highest). Our spending on "active" measures such as labour market training, special job creation schemes and schemes for the young, is also high, in fact second only to Sweden. (We actually spend proportionately more than Sweden on adult labour market training but Sweden, along with the Netherlands, spends very heavily on special measures for the disabled.) The persistence of high unemployment despite this high expenditure points to the need to increase its effectiveness.

Table 9.6
Public expenditure on labour market programmes in 1987 as a percentage of GDP

	"Active" measures	Income maintenance	Total
Ireland	1.5	3.7	5.2
Austria	0.4	1.1	1.5
Belgium	1.1	3.3	4.4
Denmark	1.1	3.9	5.0
France	0.7	2.3	3.0
Germany	1.0	1.3	2.3
Italy	0.5	0.8	1.3
Japan	0.2	0.4	0.6
Netherlands	1.1	2.9	4.0
Sweden	1.9	0.8	2.7
UK	0.9	1.7	2.6
USA	0.2	0.6	0.8

Source: OECD, *Employment Outlook*, 1988, Table 3.1.
Note: "Active" measures include employment services, training, special employment schemes and subsidies. "Income maintenance" refers to unemployment compensation and special early retirement schemes.

Review development policies

Since the 1960s a very extensive range of measures have been implemented to try to increase the rate of industrial policies in Ireland. It is estimated that up to £600 million was spent by government in 1991 to assist industry on a broad definition of this concept. However, despite the very high level of subsidy, the level of employment in industry is now no higher than it was in the early 1970s. Although the EC is making strong efforts to reduce the subsidisation of industry on a Community-wide basis, the need to compete with other locations to attract footloose direct foreign investment to Ireland remains a reality. With wage levels in industry that are similar, if not higher, than those obtaining in Britain and the US, and levels of other (transport, communications and energy) costs that are higher that those in many other developed countries, Ireland's main advantage is a ready supply of skilled labour and a package of subsidies that is attractive to investors seeking a location within the EC.

The cost of the various industrial programmes operated by the Industrial Development Authority is estimated at £713 million over the period 1989-93, of which 51 per cent will be borne by the EC.[23] The main policy issue in this area is whether subsidies to industry have been overextended when the alternative of subsidising unemployed labour does not seem to have been pushed to the point where the marginal return equals the marginal social cost. Moreover, the EC provides a higher rate of subsidy to employment and training than to industry and it will undoubtedly intensify its efforts to reduce the overall level of industrial subsidies in the context of a Single European Market. The review of industrial policy published early in 1992 was highly critical of the failure of this policy to generate any sustained net increase in industrial employment.[24] It recommended that policy should concentrate on lowering costs to industry by improving infrastructure, minimising and rationalising taxes on labour and on other inputs, and increasing the efficiency of the services on which industry depends. The traditional approach of subsidising the acquisition of fixed assets should be replaced by increased equity participation by the state in join ventures. These recommendations have received widespread support from economists and it is believed that their implementation would increase the effectiveness of Irish development policy.

Summary

There is no simple prescription that will dramatically reduce the level of unemployment in Ireland. However, a combination of the policies discussed in this section would, we believe, make a significant contribution to this goal. Assuming a favourable external economic environment, and prudent domestic macroeconomic policies within the constraints placed on our action by EC commitments, there are several steps that could be taken to reduce unemployment. These include: greater flexibility in the wage-bargaining process to allow market forces more scope to operate and to reduce the gap between the pay and conditions of those employed in the privileged sectors of the economy and other job-seekers; a reform of the tax and social welfare system designed to remove anomalies and increase the incentives to accept job offers; a switch in expenditure from industrial grants to employment subsidies; and a restructuring of the general educational system to align it more closely to producing the qualifications and skills required by the economy and an intensification of training expenditures, especially with a view to preventing any growth in the numbers in the long-term unemployment category . We presented a proposal for reforming the social welfare system, with a view to averting the transition from short- to long-term unemployment. An integrated package along these lines would, in our view, make a significant impact on the current unacceptably high level of unemployment in Ireland.

9.9   Conclusion

The main topics discussed in this chapter are:

- The growth of population, the labour force and employment

- The nature and structure of employment and unemployment in Ireland today and the main differentials in unemployment rates

- Factors, such as the wage-bargaining process, the social welfare system, the structure of the labour force, that affect the equilibrium rate of unemployment

- The reasons why the equilibrium rate of unemployment has risen over time. The concept of hysteresis

- Policies that will reduce the level of unemployment include maintaining the economy near its trend growth path; reform of incomes policy in favour of greater decentralised wage bargaining; reforms of the social welfare and tax system to reduce the incidence of long-term unemployment; reforms of the educational and training systems aimed at increasing the employability of school-leavers and the long-term unemployed and, finally, a more effective industrial policy.

Notes

1. Most of the labour force data in this chapter come from the LFS.

2. See Brendan Walsh, "The Impact of Demographic Variables on Unemployment", *Administration*, Vol. XXXV, No. 3 (1987)

3. See National Economic and Social Council, *The Economic and Social Implications of Emigration*, March 1991, Table 4.6.

4. OECD, *Employment Outlook*, 1987, Table 6.1.

5. This section has drawn on several recent books in particular: Peter Fallon and Donald Verry, *The Economics of Labour Markets*, Philip Allen, 1988; Peter Sinclair, *Unemployment: Economic Theory and Evidence*, Basil Blackwell, 1987; and R. J. Gordon, *Macroeconomics*, Little, Brown and Company, third edition, 1984; and Richard Layard, Stephen Nickell and Richard Jackman, *Unemployment: Macroeconomic Performance and the Labour Market*, Oxford University Press, 1991.

6. Calculations of Okun's law in Ireland are reported in Walsh, "Why is Unemployment So High?", *op. cit.*, Table 5. The version used in the text is based on the result for the US presented by N. Gregory Mankiw, *Macroeconomics*, New York: Worth Publishers, 1992, p. 36.

7. See Brendan Walsh, "Why is Unemployment So High?", *Perspectives on Economic Policy*, 1, 1987, (Department of Political Economy, University College, Dublin).

8. Denis Conniffe and Kieran A. Kennedy (eds), *Employment and Unemployment Policy for Ireland*, Dublin: The Economic and Social Research Institute, 1984, p. 299.

9. Robert Solow, "Unemployment: Getting the Questions Right", *Economica*, 1986 (Supplement), p. S54.

10. See Layard, Nickell and Jackman, *op. cit.*; Walsh, *op. cit.;* and George Lee, "Hysteresis and the Natural Rate of Unemployment in Ireland", *Journal of the Statistical and Social Inquiry Society of Ireland*, 1989/90.

11. James Tobin has suggested the following reasons why the natural rate might change:

Among the mechanisms that produce [hysteresis] are improvements in unemployment compensation and other benefits enacted in response to higher unemployment, loss of on-the-job training and employability by the unemployed, defections to the informal and illegal economy and a slower rate of capital formation as business firms lower their estimates of needed capacity.

See James Tobin, "Stabilization Policy Ten Years After", *Brookings Papers on Economic Activity*, 1:1980, p. 60.

Another important consideration is the *duration* of unemployment. In Ireland in 1990, 45 per cent of the unemployed had been out of work for a year or more, compared to less than one-third in 1979 and only one-fifth in the 1960s. A high duration of unemployment may lead to a less active job search by the unemployed and less downward pressure on wage rates. Thus a rise in the duration of unemployment could be expected to generate an upward drift in the equilibrium rate of unemployment.

12. If the difference of the log of real wages is regressed on the log of the unemployment rate, the following result is obtained:

log (change in real wages) = 0.1 - .03 × log (rate of unemployment)

Solving this equation for the level of unemployment that would stabilise real wages yields a value of 22 per cent. However, the fit to the data is poor and for the period since 1980 there has been a *positive* association between the growth real wages and the rate of unemployment.

13. This practice applies only to the elite workers hired by the big corporations. The conditions of those working for smaller firms and subcontractors to the big companies are far less secure.

14. See Lars Calmfors and John Driffill, "Centralisation of Wage Bargaining and Macroeconomic Performance", *Economic Policy*, OECD, April 1988.

15. See OECD, *Economic Survey: Ireland*, Paris, 1991, and *The Irish Times*, 7 March 1991. See also Paul Tansey, *Making Irish Labour Markets Work*, Dublin: Gill and Macmillan, 1991. For a review of the international evidence on the effects of unemployment compensation on the labour market see Anthony B. Atkinson, "Unemployment Compensation and Labor Market Transitions: A Critical Review", *Journal of Economic Literature*, Vol. XXIX (December 1991), pp. 1679-1727.

16. B. Nolan, "More on Actual Versus Hypothetical Replacement Ratios in Ireland", *Economic and Social Review*, April 1988.

17. See J. G. Hughes and Brendan M. Walsh, "Unemployment Duration, Aggregate Demand and Unemployment Insurance", *The Economic and Social Review*, January 1984, for the Irish experience and Layard *et al., op. cit.,* p. 417, for the international evidence.

18. In Sweden a relatively large proportion of the working age population is classified as handicapped. The OECD estimates that the true unemployment rate in Sweden is about 5 per cent, compared with the 1.6 per cent rate used in official statistics. See OECD, *Economic Survey: Sweden*, 1988/89, p. 62.

19. The issue has been debated at great length in several NESC reports and by the Commission on Taxation and the Commission on Social Welfare. None the less, the anomalies to which the 1991 OECD report on Ireland drew attention remain.

20. See R. Breen and B. Halpin, *Subsidising Jobs: An Evaluation of the Employment Incentive Scheme*, The Economic and Social Research Institute, 1989.

21. F. Barry, "Pay-Roll Taxes, Capital Grants and Irish Unemployment", *The Economic and Social Review*, Vol. 21, No. 1, October 1989, p. 107-121.

22. This figure was reported in *The Irish Times*, 30 December 1991, in an account of a study by the economic consultants Davy Kelleher McCarthy.

23. See Frances Ruane, "The Traded Sectors: Industry", Chapter 11 of *The Economy of Ireland: Policy and Performance*, edited by John O'Hagan, sixth edition, Dublin: Irish Management Institute, 1991, Table 11.6.

24. Report of the Industrial Policy Review Group, *A Time for Change: Industrial Policy for the 1990s*, Dublin, 1992.

Chapter 10

The Foreign Exchange Market and Exchange Rates

10.1 Introduction

In this chapter we introduce the student to open economy macroeconomics. We take up topics arising from trade and other transactions between countries that have been neglected in earlier chapters. We begin by discussing in section 10.2 the balance of payments and the terms of trade. Section 10.3 examines the foreign exchange market in Ireland. Section 10.4 examines the trend in the exchange rate of the Irish currency in recent years. Section 10.5 identifies some of the main factors influencing exchange rates over time. The concluding sections discuss the role of central banks in foreign exchange markets and outline the case for and against flexible and fixed exchange rate systems.

10.2 The Balance of Payments

The balance of payments is a record of a country's economic transactions with the rest of the world. The basic rule in drawing up the balance of payments accounts is that *receipts* of foreign exchange (such as exports) are denoted by a *positive* (+) sign and *payments* of foreign exchange (such as imports) by a *negative* (-) sign.

Note:
The balance of payments records flows, that is, transactions that occur over a period of time. On the other hand, foreign exchange reserves are a stock, measured at a point of time.

Table 10.1 presents a simplified version of the Irish balance of payments for 1990. There are four main subheadings: the *current* account, the *capital* account, changes in the official *external reserves*, and the *net residual*.

Table 10.1
The balance of payments, 1990

	£ millions	£ millions
1.1 Merchandise trade		1,814
1.2 Services		281
1.3 Trading and investment income		- 2,798
of which		
1.3.1 Net profit, dividends, interest and royalties	- 2,145	
1.3.2 National debt interest	- 1,009	
1.3.3 Net inflows (other)	356	
1.4 International transfers		1,567
1 *Balance on current account*		864
2.1 Private capital		- 1,814
2.2 Official capital		59
of which		
2.2.1 Government foreign borrowing	- 115	
2.2.2 Government securities sold abroad	64	
2.2.3 Other	110	
2.3 Banking transactions		727
2 *Balance on capital account*		- 1,028
3 *Change in official external reserves*		- 513
(Increase = -)		
4 *Net residual* = (1) + (2) + (3)		677

Source: Central Bank of Ireland, *Quarterly Bulletin*, Autumn 1991, Table B7.
Note: Normally both receipts (or credit items) and payments (debit items) are given for each entry in the balance of payments accounts. In the simplified version given above, we show the balance or *net* receipts under each of the main headings.

Consider first the *current account* of the balance of payments. Within this account there are, in turn, four sub-accounts: merchandise trade, services, investment income and transfers. Merchandise trade records exports and imports of *goods* only. In 1990, merchandise exports exceeded imports by £1,814 million. The services account records transactions such as international freight, tourism and travel. This sub-account was approximately balanced in 1990. The investment income sub-account records profits, dividends, interest and royalties paid and received by Irish residents during the year, including interest paid by the government on foreign debt. There was a substantial deficit on this account in 1990. Finally, the international transfers sub-account relates to payments or receipts not in return for any goods or service, such as, for example, transfers to Ireland from the European Regional and Social Funds, remittances from emigrants and Irish aid to less developed countries. Current transfers of funds into the country exceeded payments by £1,567 million in 1990. In 1990 there was an overall surplus on the current account, equal to £864 million. The large deficit on the "trading and investment income" sub-account, due to profit repatriation by firms and interest payments by the government on foreign debt, offset much of the combined surplus on the other three accounts.

The *capital account* records payments and receipts relating to the purchase and sale of assets, such as land, government stock, company shares or works of art. Foreign borrowing by the government, banks or the private sector is a capital account item because it results in an increase in indebtedness. (However, as we have seen, interest payments on that debt is a current account entry.) As shown in Table 10.1, the capital account is subdivided into private sector transactions, government transactions and banking sector transactions. In 1990, the government sub-account had a small net inflow, even though the government repaid some of its foreign borrowing (which is shown as an outflow). The surplus on the banking sub-account was more than offset by a deficit in the private sector sub-account. As a result, there was a deficit of £1,028 million on the capital account in 1990.

Consider now the entry for the change in the *official external reserves*. The official external reserves are the Central Bank of Ireland's holdings of foreign currencies such as deutsche marks (DM), dollars and yen. An increase in these reserves involves a use of foreign exchange and is therefore recorded as a negative item in the balance of payments. The Central Bank is pursuing a fixed exchange rate policy by maintaining the value of the Irish pound in the European Monetary System (EMS) and, as we shall explain in the course of this chapter, it *intervenes* in the foreign exchange market to stabilise the exchange rate of the Irish pound. Intervention entails the purchase and sale of foreign currency by the Bank and this leads to changes in the official external reserves. If the Central Bank did not intervene in the foreign exchange market and the exchange rate were allowed to float freely, the external reserves would be more stable. The current and capital accounts of the balance of payments would tend to sum to zero because any imbalance between the supply and demand for Irish pounds on the foreign exchanges would cause the exchange rate to move so as to clear the market. We return to this point below.

The *net residual* is a reconciliation of the other three components of the balance of payments sub-accounts. The difference between the current and capital account balances *should* equal changes in the official external reserves. In fact, it does not and the discrepancy is labelled the net residual. It reflects unrecorded transactions, and errors and omissions in the current and capital accounts. (The residual includes money that is being moved illegally into and out of the country and similar "hidden

280

economy" transactions.) In 1990 the evidence available to the Central Statistics Office (CSO) indicated a current account surplus of £864 million and a capital account deficit of - £1,028 million, giving an overall balance of payments deficit of - £164 million. To finance this, the official external reserves should have *decreased* by this amount. However, they actually *increased* by £513 million. To reconcile these estimates it is necessary to assume that an unrecorded net inflow of £677 million occurred. This compares to a residual of - £147 million in 1988 and the record - £908 million in 1986. There has been a significant turn-around, from net outflows to net inflows, in unexplained transactions in recent years.

Note:
The distinction is frequently made between *autonomous* and *accommodating* transactions. An autonomous transaction is an "ordinary" transaction, such as an export or an import or purchases of land or government stock by private individuals. If the net autonomous transactions result in an overall deficit, the Central Bank has either to finance that deficit or allow the exchange rate to depreciate. If the Central Bank is pursuing a fixed exchange rate policy, the deficit can be financed by running down the official external reserves or by borrowing foreign currency abroad. The change in the external reserves plus government foreign borrowing are referred to as accommodating or financing transactions. The accommodating transactions ensure that the overall balance of payments adds to zero. The balance of accommodating transactions is sometimes referred to as the "official settlements balance".

The trade account

Exports and imports of goods and services are of immense importance in a small open economy such as Ireland. They have a major impact on aggregate demand, output and income. A deficit on the trade account reduces aggregate demand and a trade surplus increases aggregate demand.

Figure 10.1 shows the level of Irish imports, exports and net exports (exports minus imports) over the period 1950-90. It can be seen that Ireland's trade account was in deficit up to 1985. In fact, between 1928 and 1985, there were only three years, 1941, 1943 and 1944, when Ireland had a surplus on its trade account. Since 1985, however, exports have exceeded imports.

When discussing trade flows it is important to distinguish between *price* changes and *quantity* changes. We can write:

$$X = P_x \times Q_x$$
$$M = P_m \times Q_m$$

where X and M denote the *value* of exports and imports respectively, P_x and P_m denote the price of exports and imports and Q_x and Q_m indicate the quantity of exports and imports respectively.

What matters for domestic production and employment are quantity changes. Firms hire more workers to produce a greater quantity of goods and services.

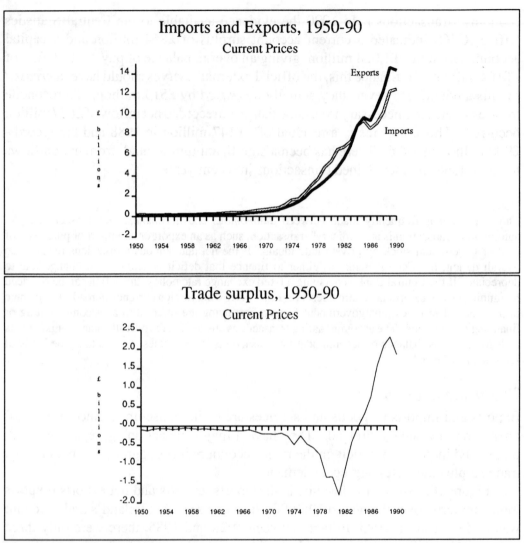

Figure 10.1 Trade account

However, price changes have a direct effect on the balance of payments. Starting from an equilibrium position, an increase in P_x relative to P_m will result in a trade account surplus because the value of exports increases relative to the value of imports. (This is a short-run effect; over time, the quantities traded will respond to the change in relative prices.) The *terms of trade* are defined as P_x/P_m. An increase is this ratio is referred to as an *improvement* in the terms of trade. When such an improvement occurs, we need to export fewer goods and services to import a given quantity of imports.

Figure 10.2 shows the terms of trade index (1975 = 100) for Ireland over the period 1975-90. This index is strongly influenced by changes in the price of petroleum products, on the import side, and of agricultural products, on the export

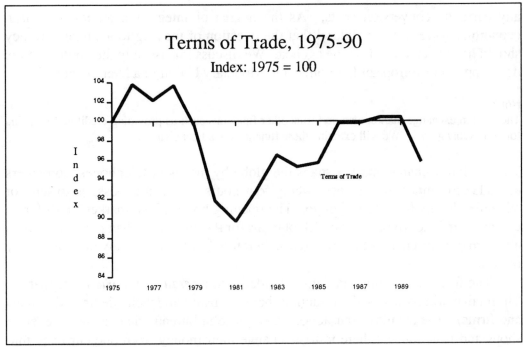

Figure 10.2 Terms of trade

side. There was an adverse movement in the terms of trade between 1978 and 1982, but this was reversed between 1982 and 1986. In 1990 there was a deterioration in the terms of trade, due mainly to the fall in agricultural export prices. We explored the impact of these movements in the terms of trade on the population's standard of living in Chapter 3 and saw how important it has been in the case of Ireland.

10.3 The Foreign Exchange Market

The foreign exchange market is a market for currencies. It facilitates trade between countries that use different currencies. If, for example, an Irish co-operative sends a shipment of beef to France, the French importer probably pays the Irish exporter in francs, which are sold for Irish pounds on the foreign exchange market. This completes the transfer of purchasing power from the French importer to the Irish co-operative. If there were only one currency in Europe, there would be no need for a foreign exchange market. The US economy operates with a single currency; but the European Community (EC), whose economy is about as large as that of the US, uses eleven different currencies. A considerable volume of resources is tied up dealing in pounds, francs, escudos and so on in Europe. The necessity of changing money from one currency into another adds to the cost of doing business. This cost has been estimated to be in the range £50-£100 million in Ireland. On the other hand, American businesses can buy and sell from Maine to California without incurring any currency conversion costs. As the degree of integration among European economies increases it is natural that the question of moving to a single currency should have been placed on the agenda. We discuss this issue in the context of the development of European Economic and Monetary Union in a later chapter.

Note:
The foreign exchange market also performs other functions such as providing credit and reducing foreign exchange risk. We will examine these functions in a later chapter.

The foreign exchange market spans the globe by means of telephones, computers and telex machines, and is open twenty-four hours a day. It is possible to sell, for example, dollars for DM in Tokyo. The opening hours of the markets in different centres round the world overlap. Quotations for the current exchange rates between all the major currencies of the world can therefore be obtained at any time of the day or night.

The foreign exchange market is divided into a *retail* and a *wholesale* market. The retail market consists of transactions between banks and their clients (individuals and firms). The smallest transactions take place in bureaux de change, or even in shops and restaurants, where tourists change their money from one currency into another. The wholesale market is an inter-bank market where banks buy and sell foreign exchange in large amounts.

Exchange rates An exchange rate is the price of one currency in terms of another. If a currency falls in value relative to the foreign currency, it is said to have *depreciated*; if it rises, it is said to have *appreciated*. The US dollar, which is the most important single currency in the world for international transactions, is *floating* against the currencies of Europe, including the Irish pound. In September 1989, when the US dollar was very strong, the Irish pound/US dollar exchange rate was IR£1 = $1.37. Over the following five months the US dollar depreciated steadily on the foreign exchanges. On 10 February 1991 it fell to a low point and the dollar/Irish pound exchange rate reached IR£1 = $1.83. Thus between September and February the Irish pound appreciated by 34 per cent relative to the dollar or, alternatively, the dollar depreciated by 25 per cent relative to the Irish pound. The gyrations of the dollar against the European currencies over this period provide a good illustration of the *volatility* that is a major disadvantage of floating exchange rates.

Note:
In the above example, the Irish pound/dollar exchange rate is expressed as dollars per Irish pound. This is known as an *indirect quote*. The alternative is to express the exchange rate in units of the foreign currency, for example, $1 = IR£0.546 (0.546 = 1/1.83). This is known as a *direct quote* because it gives the Irish price of a dollar. In Ireland, the UK and Australia, exchange rates are expressed as indirect quotes. Most other countries use direct quotes. The reason for this difference is that the old pound, shilling and pence (*£. s. d.*) used up to the early 1970s made it cumbersome to express the pound price of foreign currencies. Also we use the phrases "appreciate" and "depreciate"

to refer to movements of a floating exchange rate, and "revaluation" and "devaluation" to refer to movements of a fixed or pegged rate.

Spreads In addition to commission charges, banks earn a profit by quoting different exchange rates for buying and selling foreign currency. These rates are known as the *bid rate* (the rate at which banks will buy Irish pounds or sell foreign currency) and the *offer rate* (the rate at which banks sell Irish pounds or buy foreign currency). The difference between the bid and offer rates is known as the *spread*. Table 10.2 shows bid and offer $/IR£ rates quoted by the banks for November 1991.

As an example of how a bank earns a profit on foreign exchange transactions consider the case of two different firms, one selling $1 million to the bank and the other buying $1 million from the bank. The bank is willing to buy dollars from firm A at an exchange rate of IR£1 = $1.6890 and pays IR£592,066 to the firm in return for $1 million. The bank then sells the $1 million to firm B at an exchange rate of IR£1 = $1.6550 and receives £604,229. The profit to the bank from the two transactions is IR£12,163 or 2 per cent.

Table 10.2
Bid and offer rates for the Irish pound, dollar exchange rate: November 1991

Bid	Offer
1.6550	1.6890

Source: Allied Irish Banks, International Department.
Note: Exchange rates quoted relate to transactions less than £1,000. The spread decreases on transactions greater than £1,000.

Bureaux de change and banks charge hefty commissions or fees for small transactions in foreign currencies, in addition to having a spread between their buying and selling rates. As a result, converting small amounts of currency is expensive. If, for example, you had IR£1,000 and you converted it into sterling, francs, pesetas etc. until you had done the rounds of the EC currencies and ended up back in Irish pounds, you would be left with only about IR£750! The missing IR£250 would have gone to the foreign exchange dealers.

The structure of the foreign exchange market It is important to distinguish between banks that act as *price-takers* and those who act as *price-makers*. Price-taking banks are simply intermediaries. If a customer wishes to buy dollars, the bank finds someone willing to sell them. The price-taking bank does not take a *position* in the market. That is, it does not hold a portfolio of foreign currency. The spread between the bid and offer exchange rates provides it with its profit from foreign exchange transactions. On the other hand a price-making bank keeps a portfolio of foreign exchange and takes a position in the market by being ready to quote prices for foreign currencies. Depending on which way the exchange rate moves, the price-making bank can make profits or incur losses on foreign exchange transactions.

As an example, suppose a bank buys $1 million at an exchange rate of IR£1 = $1.4500 at a cost of IR£689,655. The bank now holds $1 million. If during the course of the day the Irish pound fell to IR£1 = $1.4400 the bank would exchange the $1 million for IR£694,444 and make a profit of IR£4,789. However, if the exchange rate rose to IR£1 = $1.4600 the bank would receive only IR£684,932 and incur a loss of IR£4,723. It should be noted that most banks are not trying to make a profit from this kind of speculation; their interest lies in the profit to be made from the spread between the bid and offer prices.

At present there are 20 banks authorised to act as market-makers by taking a position in foreign exchange in Ireland. Since 1 April 1990 all financial institutions can deal in foreign exchange on a price-taking basis. The five largest banks account for nearly 90 per cent of all business transacted.

Up to the early 1970s there was virtually no foreign exchange market in Ireland. The sterling/Irish pound exchange rate was fixed at a one-to-one parity, a very large proportion of Irish trade was with the UK and the commercial banks held their reserves in sterling in London. Such Irish demand as there was for third currencies (dollars, francs, etc.) was easily met on the London foreign exchange market. In 1969, the Money Market Committee set up by the Central Bank of Ireland under the chairmanship of Professor W. J. L. Ryan issued a report which became known as the *Money Market Report*. One of its recommendations was that the Central Bank should take steps to develop a foreign exchange market. In line with this recommendation, in the early 1970s the licensed banks' reserves were transferred from London to the Central Bank of Ireland and the banks were requested to conduct their foreign exchange business directly with the Central Bank. In 1976 the Central Bank ceased quoting for small amounts of foreign exchange and this encouraged the banks to hire and train dealers and to conduct more of their business directly between themselves and on world foreign exchange markets.

Table 10.3
Transactions on the Irish foreign exchange market: 1990
(Purchases *or* sales)

	IR£ millions	%	IR£ millions	%
1. Irish pound turnover			84,000	(8.9)
2. Non-Irish pound turnover			859,000	(91.1)
of which				
$/DM	240,520	(28)		
Sterling/$	223,340	(26)		
Sterling/DM	206,160	(24)		
ECU/DM	103,080	(12)		
Other	85,900	(10)		
3. Total turnover (1 + 2)			943,000	(100)

Note: ECU denotes European currency unit. The ECU is discussed in a later section.
Source: Allied Irish Banks, International Department.

Before 1979 the Irish pound was pegged to sterling. In March of that year, Ireland entered the exchange rate mechanism (ERM) of the European Monetary System (EMS) but the pound sterling did not. Following the termination of the sterling link, the foreign exchange market in Ireland came of age and the associated banks moved from being price-takers to price-makers. The banks began to quote a sterling/Irish pound exchange rate, something that had not been required before. (The first deal in sterling was done for STG£500,000 at an exchange rate of IR£1 = STG£0.9975 on 30 March 1979. Many firms with large sterling borrowings lost heavily as the Irish pound unexpectedly depreciated against sterling.) The banks coped very well with the new arrangements.

It might be expected that most of the business conducted on the Irish foreign exchange market involves Irish pounds. This is not the case, however. Table 10.3 shows that in 1990 only 9 per cent of total turnover involved Irish pounds. The vast majority of deals involve sterling, DMs and dollars, but not the Irish pound.

One reason for the large foreign currency turnover in Ireland is that the Irish pound market has little "depth". Dealers are unwilling to act as price-makers and take a position on the Irish pound when they cannot spread the risk with other dealers or banks and, of course, foreigners have little interest in buying and selling Irish pounds, other than the small amounts needed to finance foreign trade. As a result, dealers find it easier and safer to deal in foreign currencies.

10.4   Exchange Rates

Figure 10.3 shows the three most important *bilateral* exchange rates for the Irish pound over the period 1977-91. Since 1979 the Irish pound/sterling exchange rate has moved fairly widely in both directions without showing any clear long-run trend. There was a sustained depreciation of the IR£ relative to the DM until 1987 but since then the rate has been virtually unchanged in the region of IR£1 = DM2.67. The US$/IR£ exchange rate has varied very widely since the 1970s, reflecting the movement of the dollar against the EMS currencies. The dollar was weak in 1980 but climbed to a peak in 1985 (when for a brief period IR£1 was worth less than $1). Since 1985 the dollar has lost much of the ground it gained in the first half of the 1980s, so there has been no clear trend over the period since 1977.

Trade-weighted exchange rate index

Clearly it would be useful if a single statistic could be derived that summarised the pound's external value. The summary statistic that is most widely used for this purpose is the *trade-weighted exchange rate index*, sometimes referred to as the *effective exchange rate index*. This is an index of the average cost of foreign currency in terms of the Irish pound. The index is based on the bilateral exchange rates weighted in accordance with the importance of various currencies in the country's international trade.

In Table 10.4 we show how the trade-weighted exchange rate index is calculated. Column 1 lists Ireland's trading partners according to their share in Ireland's imports and exports. (Only nine countries are used in compiling the index because they account for virtually all our trade.) Column 2 shows the trade weight for each country. The UK has the largest weight of 0.43 (43 per cent of Ireland's trade is with the UK), Germany has a weight of 0.14 and so on down to Denmark which has a weight of 0.02. These weights sum to 1.0.

The first step in deriving the trade-weighted exchange rate index is to express the bilateral exchange rates as indices. The exchange rates are set equal to 100 in a base year and the index for subsequent years calculated with reference to this base. For example, if the $/Ir£ exchange rate was IR£1 = $1.60 in 1991 and IR£1 = $1.50 in 1992, the dollar exchange rate index would be 100 in 1991 and 93.75 in 1992. Hypothetical exchange rates for two years are given for several countries in columns 3 and 4 of Table 10.4. It is assumed that over the year the Irish pound depreciated against the UK, German, Dutch and Belgium currencies but appreciated against the other currencies on the list.

The trade-weighted exchange rate index is calculated by multiplying each exchange rate index by its trade weight and summing for all countries. This is done in columns 5 and 6 for 1991 and 1992 respectively. Column 6 shows that in 1992 the trade-weighted exchange rate index had fallen to 99.4. This indicates that, on

288

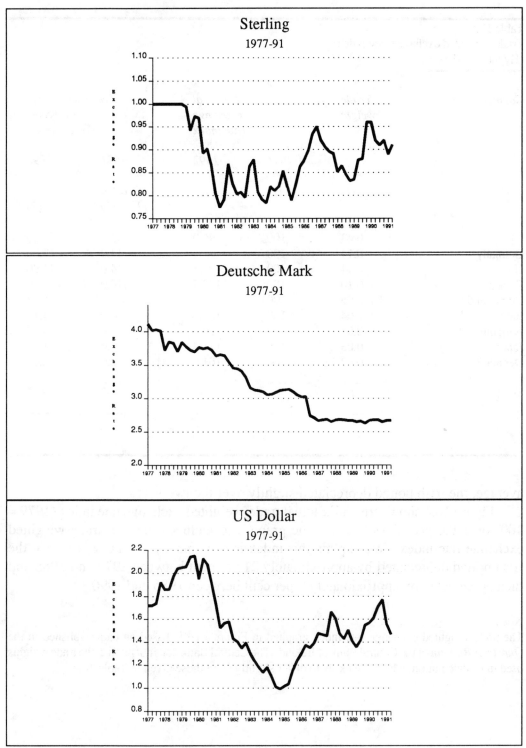

Figure 10.3 Irish pound exchange rate: Sterling, DM, $

Table 10.4
Trade-weighted exchange rate index
(Hypothetical data.)

Country	Trade weight	Bilateral exchange rate index		Trade-weighted exchange rate index	
		1991	1992	1991	1992
	(1)	(2)	(3)	(4) = (1)× (2)	(5) = (1)× (3)
UK	0.43	100	96.0	43.0	41.30
Germany	0.14	100	97.4	14.0	13.60
US	0.14	100	106.8	14.0	14.90
France	0.10	100	100.7	10.0	10.10
Netherlands	0.06	100	99.5	6.0	5.97
Italy	0.04	100	104.4	4.0	4.17
Belgium	0.04	100	99.5	4.0	3.98
Japan	0.03	100	111.4	3.0	3.34
Denmark	0.02	100	101.9	2.0	2.04
Total	1.0			100	99.4

average, the Irish pound depreciated slightly over the two years.

Figure 10.4 shows Ireland's actual trade-weighted exchange rate index (1979 = 100) over the period 1979-91. (The graph also includes the *real* trade-weighted exchange rate index. We explain this index in a moment.) It can be seen that the Irish pound depreciated by approximately 21 per cent between 1979 and 1985 and then appreciated by approximately 9 per cent between 1985 and 1990.

Note:
The trade-weighted exchange rate index graphed in Figure 10.4 is based on data published in the *Quarterly Bulletin* of the Central Bank of Ireland. The Central Bank does not publish the trade weights used in its calculation, which are likely to differ slightly from those given in Table 10.4.

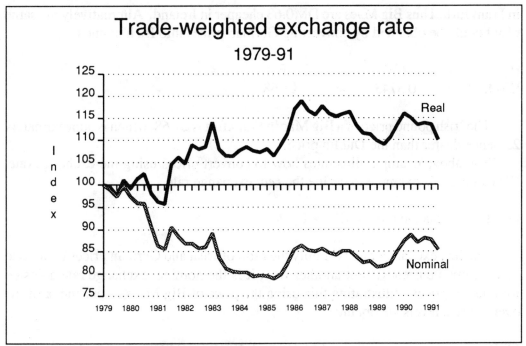

Figure 10.4 Trade-weighted exchange rate

Real exchange rates

So far we have discussed movements in exchange rates without regard to movements in the price levels in the different countries. Thus, we were dealing with *nominal* exchange rates. We will now take account of changes in the purchasing power of the currencies.

If we wish to compare the cost of living in two countries we must compare price levels converted by means of exchange rates. For example, we cannot compare the price of food in Dublin and Frankfurt without taking account of the DM/IR£ exchange rate. In 1992, a Big Mac cost IR£1.45 in Dublin and DM4.5 in Frankfurt. Are Big Macs more expensive in Ireland or Germany? The exchange rate in April 1992 was IR£1 = DM2.6713. We can compare the two prices by converting the Irish price to DMs or alternatively converting DMs to Irish pounds using this exchange rate. Consider first converting Irish prices into DMs.

$$P_{irl} \times E = P_g$$
$$£1.45 \times 2.6713 = DM3.87$$

where P_{irl} is the Irish price, E is the DM/IR£ exchange rate and P_g is the Irish price in DM. This says that a Big Mac in Dublin costs DM3.87, whereas it costs DM4.50

in Frankfurt. Thus Big Macs are DM0.63 cheaper in Ireland. Alternatively the same result could be obtained by converting German prices into Irish pounds:

$$P_g \quad \times \quad (1/E) \quad = \quad P_{irl}$$
$$DM4.50 \quad \times \quad 0.3743 \quad = \quad \pounds 1.68$$

The Irish pound price of a Big Mac in Frankfurt is £1.68, which is approximately 23 pence dearer than the Dublin price.

The above example illustrates how to convert prices using the exchange rate. We can use this example to define the *real* exchange rate.

(1) Real exchange rate $= (P_{irl} \times E)/P_g$

The real exchange rate is simply the ratio of Irish and German prices expressed in a common currency. Put another way, it is the nominal exchange rate adjusted for relative prices. Illustrating this using the price of Big Macs as our index of the overall price levels we obtain:

(2) Real exchange rate index $= (2.6713 \times 1.45)/4.5 = 0.8607$

If in the following year P_{irl} increased to Ir£1.60, and both the nominal exchange rate and P_g remained unchanged, the real exchange rate would be:

(3) Real exchange rate index $= (2.6713 \times 1.60)/4.5 = 0.9498$

The rise in Irish relative to German prices has caused the real exchange rate index to rise. If we set the index equal to 100 in year 1, it would have risen to 110.3 in year 2.

The real exchange rate index is a measure of whether a country is becoming more or less *price competitive* relative to its trading partners over time. A rise in the real exchange rate implies a loss of competitiveness because either domestic prices have risen relative to foreign prices and/or the nominal exchange rate has appreciated. Conversely, a fall in the real exchange rate implies a gain in competitiveness. Note that prices (expressed in a common currency) do not have to be equal in the base year. The index monitors movements in competitiveness relative to the base year: it is not necessarily the case that the economies were equally competitive in that year.

Note:
The concept of the real exchange rate is closely related to that of purchasing power parity (PPP) which we discuss in a later chapter, where we also discuss the effects of changes in competitiveness on output, income and unemployment.

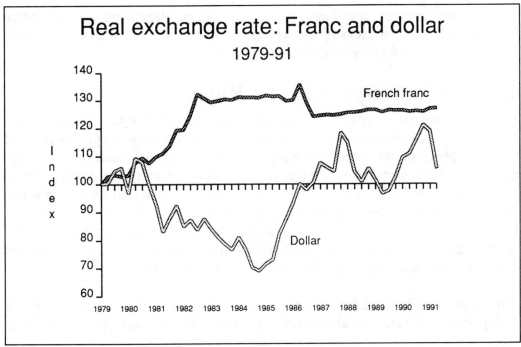

Figure 10.5 Irish pound real exchange rate: $ and Franc

Figure 10.5 shows Ireland's real exchange rates for the dollar and the French franc over the period 1979 to 1991 based on indices equal to 100 in 1979. Ireland lost competitiveness relative to France between 1979 and 1983 and there was little change in the following years. We gained competitiveness against the US between 1979 and 1985, but by 1991 all of this gain had been lost again. In Chapter 13 we discuss in detail the effects of joining the EMS on our real exchange rate with the DM and the other currencies in the System.

In Figure 10.4 we showed Ireland's *real trade-weighted exchange rate index* over the period 1979 to 1991. This index is calculated by trade-weighting real exchange rates over time. This is identical to the calculation in Table 10.4 except that nominal exchange rates have been replaced by real exchange rates.[1] The real trade-weighted exchange rate index appreciated between 1979 and 1991. This means that Ireland suffered a sustained loss in competitiveness against the average of our main trading partners over the period. The real trade-weighted exchange rate index peaked at 118.9 in 1986 and then declined to 110. Appendix 1 shows the data for the nominal and real exchange rate of the Irish pound against sterling, the deutsche mark and the dollar. Also included is the nominal and real trade-weighted exchange rate index.

In deriving the real exchange rate index, the choice of the price index to be used poses some problems. It is possible to use an index of consumer prices, of manufacturing output prices or of wholesale prices. These usually move closely together but sometimes a different picture can emerge depending on which price index is used. The real exchange rates given in Figures 10.4 and 10.5 and Appendix 1 were calculated using the consumer price index.

10.5   Floating Exchange Rates

What causes the exchange rate to appreciate or depreciate? Why are exchange rates so volatile? In this section we discuss these topics in terms of the supply and demand for Irish pounds on the foreign exchange market. We shall assume that exchange rates are floating, that is, they are free to move up or down in response to shifts in the supply and demand for currencies. In fact it is difficult to find a situation where exchange rates are allowed to float completely free of central bank intervention. Even when currencies are not part of a fixed exchange rate system, such as the EMS, central banks buy and sell foreign exchange in order to stabilise the market or to hold their currencies at a target rate. This is known as "dirty floating".

The supply and demand for Irish pounds   In deriving the demand and supply for Irish pounds (IR£) on the foreign exchange market, the following points should be noted:

1. Any transaction that gives rise to a *receipt* of foreign currency leads to a *demand* for Irish pounds. For example, if an exporter sells goods in the UK and receives sterling in return, when the sterling receipts are exchanged for Irish pounds in a bank, the exporter is demanding Irish pounds.

2. Any transaction that gives rise to a *payment* by Irish residents leads to a *supply* of Irish pounds. If an Irish importer needs to obtain sterling to pay his UK supplier, Irish pounds are exchanged for sterling in a bank and the importer supplies Irish pounds to the foreign exchange market.

A graphical representation of the supply and demand for Irish pounds is given in Figure 10.6. The exchange rate, E, is expressed as the foreign currency price of an Irish pound on the vertical axis and the number of Irish pounds supplied/demanded is on the horizontal axis. The demand curve is downward sloping and the supply curve is upward sloping.

We need to examine more closely the justification drawing these curves in this manner. A downward sloping demand schedule implies that a depreciation (appreciation) increases (decreases) the demand for Irish pounds. For example, a depreciation makes Irish goods and services more competitive by enabling exporters to reduce prices abroad. As a result, more goods are exported and the demand for Irish pounds increases. As an example, suppose the exchange rate were IR£1 = $2. Ignoring transport costs, taxes and other factors, if the price of an Aran sweater is

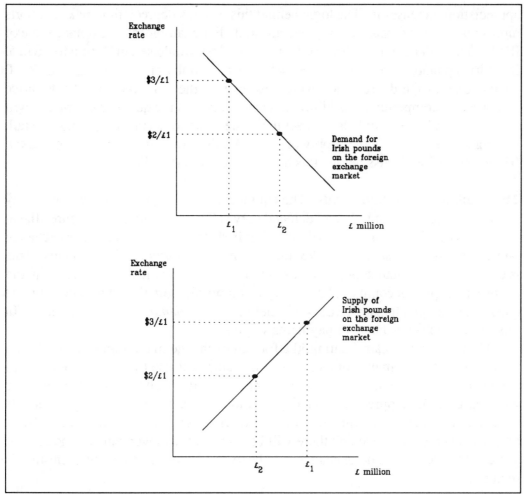

Figure 10.6 The foreign exchange market

IR£40 in Dublin, the price in New York at this exchange rate would be $80. Suppose now the Irish pound depreciates to IR£1 = $1.50 and the sweater still costs IR£40 in Dublin. The exporter could afford to lower the New York price to $60. The lower price in New York would make the item more competitive and more sweaters would be sold. Any increase in the quantity sold at $60 would increase the demand for Irish pounds. Alternatively, the exporter could decide to leave the New York price at $80 and allow her profits to absorb the full benefit of the depreciation. Assuming no change in the number of sweaters sold, the demand for Irish pounds would still increase because the Irish pound equivalent of $80 would rise from IR£40 to IR£53.33. Thus a devaluation *must increase the value of exports denominated in the home currency*. Hence the demand curve for the home currency slopes downwards.

An upward sloping supply curve for Irish pounds indicates that a depreciation reduces the supply of Irish pounds on the foreign exchange market and an appreciation increases it. The logic behind this is that a depreciation makes imports more expensive and consequently less are sold. For example, at an exchange rate of IR£1 = $2, a pair of jeans selling for $30 in New York would sell in Dublin for IR£15. If the Irish pound depreciates to IR£1 = $1.50, the Dublin price would rise to IR£20 unless some of the depreciation were absorbed by the US exporter. As the price increases the competitiveness of imports is reduced and the quantity of imports will fall. In general, we would also expect the value of imports (in Irish pounds) to fall, leading to a reduction in the supply of Irish pounds to the foreign exchange market. (However, as we discuss below, this does not *necessarily* follow.)

The equilibrium exchange rate The equilibrium exchange rate is determined by the intersection of the supply and demand curves for Irish pounds. In Figure 10.6 at a rate of IR£1 = $2 the supply and demand for Irish pounds are equal. At an exchange rate higher than this, say, IR£1 = $3, there is an *excess supply* of Irish pounds. This is equivalent to a balance of payments deficit on the combined current account and the private capital accounts. The country is importing more than it is exporting. At a lower exchange rate, say IR£1 = $1, there is *excess demand* for Irish pounds. In this case, there is a balance of payments surplus.

If exchange rates are floating, the foreign exchange market must clear. When there is an excess demand for a currency, its value will rise (the exchange rate will appreciate) and when there is an excess supply, its value will fall (the exchange rate will depreciate). Appreciation or depreciation will continue until supply equals demand. Hence under floating the current and private capital accounts of the balance of payments must balance and there will be no need for movements on the official settlements account. The exchange rate bears the brunt of any adjustment that is required.

The J-curve Will the foreign exchange market always adjust in the well-behaved manner depicted in Figure 10.7? The answer is "yes" if the supply curve slopes upwards, as in Figure 10.7. But consider now Figure 10.8 where the supply curve slopes down. This would be the case if a depreciation *increases* the Irish pound value of imported goods and services. Recall that the value of imports = $P_m \times Q_m$, where P_m and Q_m are the price and quantity of imports respectively. A depreciation will tend to increase P_m and as P_m increases, Q_m will fall. However, for the fall in imports to be sufficient to reduce the overall value of imports the *price elasticity of demand for imports has to be greater than one*. If a large proportion of imports are goods for which there are no domestically produced substitutes, this may not be the case. For example, in Ireland petroleum products constitute a large proportion of imports. These products are price inelastic in the short run at least. If the overall demand for imports is inelastic, then as P_m increases due to a depreciation, Q_m will fall less than proportionately. In this case, following a depreciation the value of imports, $P_m \times$

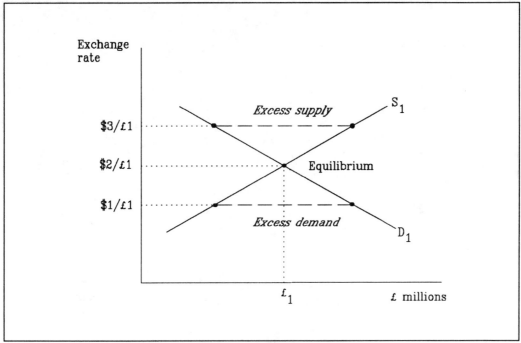

Figure 10.7 Equilibrium in the foreign exchange market

Qm, will *increase* and so too will the supply of Irish pounds on the foreign exchange market.

Thus if the demand for imports is inelastic, the supply curve of Irish pounds is *downward* sloping and the foreign exchange market is unstable. This is illustrated in Figure 10.8. The market is initially in equilibrium at an exchange rate of $2/IR£1. A depreciation of the exchange rate to $1/IR£1 results in an excess supply of Irish pounds and the exchange rate moves away from the equilibrium rate. Similarly, exchange rate appreciation leads to an excess demand for Irish pounds and moves the foreign exchange market away from equilibrium.

The slope of the supply curve for the domestic currency has implications for the effect of a depreciation or devaluation on the balance of payments. If there is a downward sloping supply curve for the home currency, as in Figure 10.8, then a depreciation will lead to a deterioration, rather than an improvement, in the balance of payments. In Figure 10.9 the balance of payments is shown along the vertical axis and time along the horizontal axis. We have also inserted a line labelled BP = 0. Along this line the balance of payments is in equilibrium. Points above the line are associated with a balance of payments surplus and points below with a balance of payments deficit. The country is experiencing a balance of payments deficit and the government decides to devalue the currency in order to correct this. Because the supply curve of domestic currency is downward sloping, the devaluation will lead to a deterioration in the balance of payments. In due course, however, the price

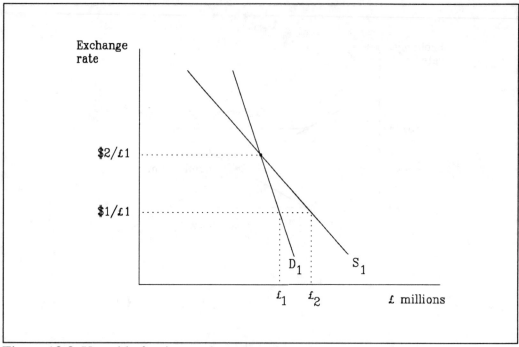

Figure 10.8 Unstable foreign exchange market

effects work and the long-run elasticity of demand for imports is greater than one, so there is eventually an improvement in the balance of payments. The curve which maps out how the balance of payments reacts to a devaluation under these assumptions is known as the *J-curve*.

Note:
In international trade theory, the student learns that the *Marshall-Lerner condition* must be met for a depreciation to improve the trade balance. This condition states that the sum of the import and export elasticities must be greater than one. If the supply curve of domestic currency slopes upward, this condition will be met. Note that we assumed that domestic production of exports would expand in response to increased demand, that is, we are assuming there are unemployed resources. A difficulty with depreciation as a means of correcting a balance of payments deficit is that it leads to higher import prices which eventually feed into the domestic cost structure, causing the price of exports to rise, eroding the initial impact of the depreciation on relative prices. We return to this topic later in the chapter.

Speculation Our discussion of the exchange rate up to this point has been in terms of the demand and supply of foreign exchange that arises because people wish to import and export goods and services. However, the reality of foreign exchange markets today is that they are dominated by *speculative flows*, that is, by the supply and demand that arises from individuals and institutions trying to make capital gains by anticipating movements in exchange rates. It is estimated that global imports and exports amounted to $5.8 trillion in 1989, but that total foreign exchange transactions

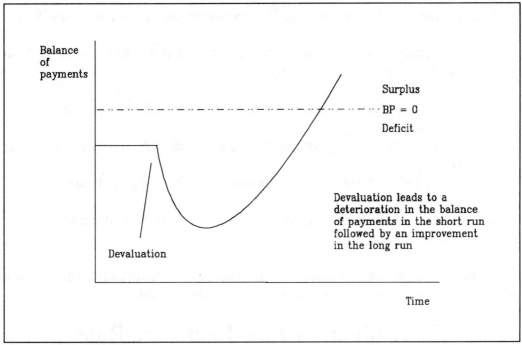

Figure 10.9 The J-curve

amounted to $150 trillion or 26 times the value of trade.[2] Thus foreign exchange transactions amount to about $600 billion per working day, the preponderance of which are not trade-related. Speculative demand for currencies accounts for most of the non-trade-related transactions and they can shift vast amounts of money from one currency to another in the course of a day. As a result, exchange rates move up and down on the basis of all sorts of news and rumours. For example, on 17 January 1991, when the war started in the Persian Gulf, the US dollar bounded up on the foreign exchange markets. Dealers, who suddenly seemed to be experts in military matters, read the results of the first day of air strikes as an indication that Saddam's forces could not put up any real resistance. As the week went on and the battlefield situation became less clear, the dollar lost all its gains. Later in the month, as the military defeat of Iraq became inevitable the dollar began to rise back to its pre-war level. Thus, if exchange rates are allowed to float freely, the prices of the different currencies will tend to be extremely *volatile*.

Shifts in the supply and demand curves Changes in the flow of imports or exports, not brought about by changes in the exchange rate, shift the supply and demand schedules. In Figure 10.10 an increase in imports due, for example, to higher oil prices shifts the supply schedule of Irish pounds to the right. If the exchange rate is floating it will depreciate from IR£1 = $3 to IR£1 = $2. The lower panel shows an increase in the demand for Irish exports brought about, for example, by a successful marketing campaign for Irish exports. The exchange rate appreciates from IR£1 = $2 to IR£1 = $3.

A wide variety of events can affect the supply and demand curves for Irish pounds. The following are some examples.

1. A decrease in exports due to a global recession would shift the demand curve for Irish pounds to the left.
2. An increase in debt service payments abroad would shift the supply curve of Irish pounds to the right.
3. A rise in sales of Irish land to foreigners would shift the demand curve for Irish pounds to the right.
4. An increase in foreign borrowing by Irish banks would shift the demand curve for Irish pounds to the right.

If the exchange rate is floating, the first two events would cause the exchange rate to depreciate, the second two would cause an appreciation.

10.6   Determinants of the Exchange Rate in the Longer Term

We now examine the factors influencing the exchange rate in the medium or long term. This amounts to asking: What determines the *location* of the supply and demand for foreign exchange curves? Over time the balance of payments and therefore the exchange rate are influenced by three main factors: inflation differentials, interest rate differentials and differentials in growth rates. Let us examine these in turn.

Inflation differentials   In our illustration of how the real exchange rate is constructed, above, we showed that if one country's rate of inflation exceeds that of its trading partners, it will suffer a loss of competitiveness. The demand for its exports will fall and the demand for its imports will rise. The demand curve for its currency shifts to the left and the supply curve shifts to the right. Under a floating exchange rate system, the currency will depreciate.

The theory that explains changes in exchange rates in terms of differentials in inflation between countries is referred to as the theory of *purchasing power parity* (PPP). This is the most important theory of exchange rate determination. It is due to the Swedish economist Gustav Cassel (1866-1944).[3] In its simplest form, PPP theory states that prices in different countries (expressed in a common currency) should be the same. Recall from section 10.4 that the real exchange rate was defined as $(P_{irl} \times E)/P_f$, where P_{irl} and P_f are Irish and foreign prices respectively. This version of PPP predicts that the real exchange rate will be constant over time because

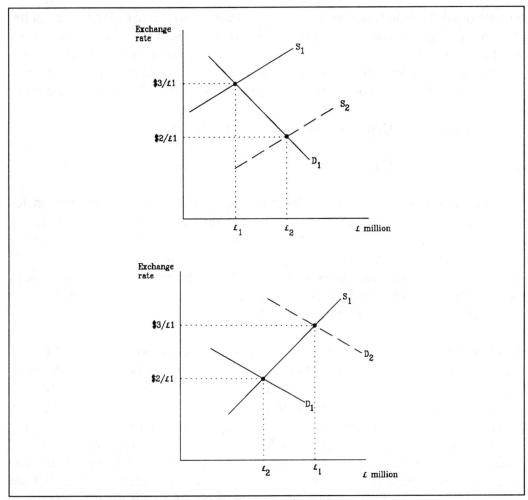

Figure 10.10 Shifts in the supply and demand curves

changes in the nominal exchange rate, E, will offset changes in the ratio of domestic to foreign prices, P_{irl}/P_f. This implies that increases in P_{irl} relative to P_f will *cause* the nominal exchange rate, E, to depreciate until the real exchange rate reverts back to its initial level. Conversely, a rise in P_f relative to P_{irl} will cause E to appreciate. Hence, PPP predicts that the main determinant of the nominal exchange rate is a country's rate of inflation relative to that of its trading partners.

We saw, however, in Figures 10.4 and 10.5 that Ireland's real exchange rate has *not* been constant over the last twenty years. This raises questions about the validity of this version of PPP. In a later chapter we shall develop PPP theory and review the evidence in more detail.

Interest rate differentials   As we noted above, speculative flows, rather than trade-related flows, dominate movements across the international exchanges.

Internationally mobile funds are very responsive to interest rate differentials. In the absence of exchange controls, money is free to move from one country to another and high interest rates in one country will lead to an inflow of funds. As a consequence, a fall in domestic interest rates relative to those prevailing in the rest of the world will lead to a depreciation of the currency, and a rise to an appreciation.

$$r_{irl} > r_{foreign} \Rightarrow \text{Capital inflow} \Rightarrow \text{appreciation}$$

$$r_{irl} < r_{foreign} \Rightarrow \text{Capital outflow} \Rightarrow \text{depreciation}$$

On a day-to-day basis, movements in interest rates are the main reason for sudden movements in exchange rates. The weakening of the dollar in the second half of 1991 was mainly due to the decline in US short-term interest rates at a time when German interest rates were rising. The US authorities wished to "kick start" their economy by an expansionary monetary policy, whereas the German authorities used a tight monetary policy to curb the inflationary pressures. The result was a depreciation of the dollar relative to the DM.

Speculation   In comparing the return to placing money on deposit in different countries, as well as taking account of interest rate differentials, investors consider the *expected* movement in the exchange rate over the investment period.   If speculators expect a currency to depreciate they will move funds out of it in anticipation of making a capital gain. For example, the dollar exchange rate at the beginning of 1992 was STG£1 = $1.87.   Some believed that the dollar was undervalued.   They would have hoped to make profits by buying dollars and converting them back into pounds after the dollar had appreciated.   If in fact the dollar rises, to £1 = $1.70 for example, then a profit of 10 per cent [= 100(1.87 - 1.70)/1.70], less commissions, could be made simply by buying and selling the two currencies. If the deals are well timed this return would be made over a short period of time, so that it would represent an enormous annualised rate of return. Moreover, if enough speculators were to move money in this manner, the supply of sterling to the foreign exchange market would increase significantly, thereby exerting pressure on the exchange rate. Hence speculation can act as self-fulfilling prophecy.

Countries sometimes introduce *exchange controls* in order to try to prevent speculative inflows or outflows, but this is no longer permissible between EC states that are participating in the EMS. Moreover, speculation is very difficult to stop as it can take different forms. For example, *leading* and *lagging* by companies has been an important factor in Ireland. It works as follows: if an exporter to the UK expects the Irish pound to depreciate relative to sterling in the near future, he will delay (lag) converting his sterling receipts into Irish pounds because they will be worth more after the depreciation has taken place. Similarly, an importer may speed up (lead) payments to his UK supplier in order to avoid paying more after the depreciation.

302

Because of the size of Ireland's trade in relation to GNP, leads and lags in payments and receipts can put tremendous pressure on the exchange rate. This was very apparent during 1986 and resulted in a large drop in the Central Bank of Ireland's external reserves.

Exchange rate expectations are therefore a crucial influence on exchange rate movements in the short run. In the longer run, however, expectations should be related to the underlying "fundamentals", such as whether a currency is over- or under-valued. Views about this will depend on the level of the real exchange rate, which in turn depends on the price levels in one country relative to another. We discuss in a later chapter the formation of expectations about exchange rate movements.

Growth rate in real GNP Increases in GNP lead to higher levels of imports through the marginal propensity to import. As the economy expands we import more raw materials, capital equipment and final goods. It would be expected then that countries with a relatively high rate of growth in real GNP will tend to run a balance of payments deficit with slow-growth countries. The increased flow of imports will be reflected in a shift of the supply curve to the right and the exchange rate will depreciate. However, these expectations may not materialise. Faster growth in GDP, may stimulate more rapid technical progress and thereby boost the country's productivity, causing its exports to grow faster than its imports. An example is the case of Japan, which has consistently grown more rapidly than the US, but equally consistently has achieved a balance of payments surplus with the US.

10.7   Fixed Exchange Rates

As we shall see in greater detail in a later chapter floating exchange rates are the exception rather than the rule in international economic relations. Various systems of fixed exchange rates have been constructed to facilitate international trade and investment. The European Monetary System (EMS) is an example of a regional system of fixed exchange rates. The basic objective of such systems is to avoid the disadvantages associated with floating exchange rates. Proponents of fixed exchange rates believe that freely floating exchange rates create uncertainty and discourage international trade and investment. Under floating exchange rates, speculative flows may drive exchange rates significantly above or below their equilibrium levels. When exchange rates are fixed, so the argument goes, uncertainty is reduced and trade and investment between member states are promoted. This in turn should increase output and employment.

In order to operate a system of fixed exchange rates, central banks must be prepared to *intervene* on the foreign exchange markets to support a currency at the target levels. Before explaining how the Central Bank intervenes, we must first explain what is meant by the official external reserves.

Official external reserves

The official external reserves are central bank holdings of foreign exchange and assets that can be converted into foreign exchange. Table 10.5 gives a breakdown of Ireland's official external reserves as of July 1991.

Table 10.5
Ireland's official external reserves, July 1991

	£ millions	%
Foreign exchange	3,039.3	87.3
Ecu	188.9	5.5
SDR	115.6	3.3
Reserve position at IMF	82.5	2.3
Gold	56.9	1.6
Total	3,483.0	100.0

Source: Central Bank of Ireland, *Quarterly Bulletin*, Autumn 1991, Table A1.

In addition to foreign currencies and gold, the reserves consist of assets created by international agencies like the International Monetary Fund (IMF). *Special Drawing Rights* or SDRs, sometimes referred to as "paper gold", are reserve assets created by the IMF and issued to member countries in return for subscriptions in their own currencies. The SDR is a basket of the currencies of the main industrial nations. An SDR was worth IR£0.88 in July 1991. The IMF first began issuing SDRs in 1970 to supplement international reserves. If a central bank needs to borrow foreign currencies in order to stabilise the exchange rate, its SDR allocation at the IMF can be used for this purpose. The IMF simply debits one SDR account and credits the other.

The *European Currency Unit* or *ecu* is the numèraire of the EMS, based on a basket of European currencies. One ecu was worth IR£0.77 in July 1991. The ecu is similar to the SDR in that it is used by European central banks as a reserve currency. Any borrowing or lending involving ecus is supervised by the *European Monetary Co-operation Fund* (EMCF) which is the European equivalent of the IMF.

The external reserves are held by the Central Bank and may be used to purchase Irish pounds from the foreign exchange market and stabilise the exchange rate. This operation is called *intervention*.

Central bank intervention

Figure 10.11 illustrates the principles underlying central bank intervention to stabilise an exchange rate. Participating central banks agree on a *central exchange rate* and on *upper* and *lower limits* within which the exchange rate should be maintained. For example, a central exchange rate of DM2.67 = IR£1 might be agreed, with a maximum range of 2.25 per cent around this rate. The upper limit to this band would be DM2.71 = IR£1 and the lower limit DM2.63 = IR£1. The Irish and German Central Banks would be committed to intervene if these limits are about to be breached.

In Figure 10.11 the market is in equilibrium at DM2.67 = IR£1. If the supply schedule for Irish pounds shifts to the right (S_1 to S_2), the new equilibrium is at B and the IR£ would start to depreciate to DM2.50 = IR£1, below the agreed lower limit. The Central Bank of Ireland and the Bundesbank would respond by *buying* Irish pounds and *selling* DMs on the foreign exchange market. The Central Bank of Ireland would have to use up some of its external reserves for this purpose, whereas the Bundesbank would acquire additional reserves in the form of Irish pounds. This intervention would have the effect of shifting the demand curve for Irish pounds to the right (D_1 to D_2). The new equilibrium would be at C and the exchange rate would have been kept within the agreed band.

This process may be a waste of taxpayers' money if fundamental forces are operating to drive the Irish pound below the central rate in the longer run. If the Irish pound continues to depreciate, the two central banks involved in the intervention have been selling appreciating DMs and buying depreciating Irish pounds, which is not what a smart speculator would do. Similarly, the central banks can intervene by selling pounds to keep the exchange rate from rising above the upper limit of the agreed band.

A central bank can create an artificial demand for its own currency only within the limits of its holdings of reserves of foreign exchange. When these reserves fall below the minimum level believed to be prudent (often expressed as a multiple of the country's monthly import bill), the bank will be unable to continue to support the exchange rate. The options open to it then are either to borrow foreign currency from other countries or from the IMF, or to allow the exchange rate to depreciate. Other central banks could help by buying the currency that is under pressure, but there are limits to the amount of such a currency they will wish to acquire. It is easy to see that the Central Bank of Ireland could quickly exhaust its reserves of foreign exchange defending the Irish pound, and it is also clear that the Bundesbank would not want to go on buying Irish pounds indefinitely.

An exchange rate appreciation does not put nearly as much pressure on a central bank as does depreciation: an inflow of foreign exchange can be bought by a central bank using its own currency. This creates an artificial supply of the domestic currency on the foreign exchange market, which helps to stabilise the exchange rate.

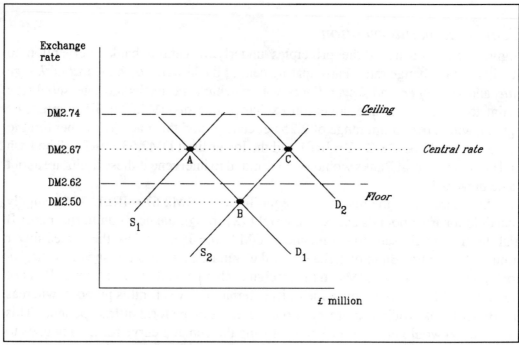

Figure 10.11 Central Bank intervention

Its reserves of foreign exchange increase. However, there is also an expansion of the domestic money supply, which generates inflationary pressures.

Note:
Sterilisation is a way of breaking the link between increases in the external reserves and the domestic money supply. This consists of open market sales of bonds to reduce the domestic money supply. We discuss sterilisation in a later chapter.

Foreign borrowing and the external reserves

Since joining the EMS, the Central Bank of Ireland has intervened heavily to maintain the exchange rate of the Irish pound. Some idea of the extent of this intervention can be got by considering that between 1971 and 1990 the government borrowed approximately IR£10 billion abroad, but the external reserves only increased from IR£381 million to IR£2.9 billion over the same period. Figure 10.12 shows the trend in government foreign indebtedness and the level of the external reserves. The difference between the growth in foreign indebtedness and the increase in the level of external reserves, which was most marked over the period 1979-1986, gives an indication of the degree of Central Bank intervention in the foreign exchange market.

When the government borrows foreign currency abroad, it is exchanged at the Central Bank for domestic currency. The Central Bank adds the foreign currency to its external reserves and credits the government's account with Irish pounds. If the Central Bank were not intervening in the foreign exchange market, the external reserves would rise by an amount equal to government foreign borrowing. The fact that Irish reserves did not increase by the amount of government borrowing during the 1980s shows that the Central Bank of Ireland used a large proportion of the proceeds of this borrowing to stabilise the exchange rate. It would not have been possible to have maintained the exchange rate of the pound at the level that actually prevailed over this period had the Central Bank not used the inflows of foreign exchange that resulted from government external borrowing for this purpose.

In this sense, the Irish pound could be said to have been *over-valued* for much of the period. (This is also the conclusion that would be drawn from the appreciation of the real exchange rate shown in Figures 10.4 and 10.5.) An over-valued exchange rate impairs the competitiveness of domestic firms. Exporters and firms competing with importers find it difficult to maintain market share and a fall in output and employment in the traded sectors of the economy can result.

It is also clear that without government foreign borrowing, Ireland's external reserves would have been depleted a long time ago. In fact, it was to prevent this that the government borrowed abroad in the first place. However, as we discussed in Chapter 5, external borrowing on the scale that was incurred early in the 1980s could not have continued indefinitely and the exchange rate would have eventually depreciated. Central bank intervention is therefore not a substitute for corrective action in the form of deflationary fiscal policy.

In fact, despite central bank intervention, the value of the Irish pound has fallen over the years (see Figures 10.3 and 10.4 and Appendix 1). Hence the Central Bank has been using appreciating foreign exchange to buy depreciating Irish pounds. Irish taxpayers are now saddled with the burden of servicing this external debt in more expensive foreign exchange. Moreover, to the extent that the result has been an over-valued exchange rate, the Irish economy has grown less, and unemployment has increased more than would have been the case if the exchange rate had not been supported in this manner.

In summary, whilst intervention in foreign exchange markets may seem reasonable as a way of smoothing out short-term fluctuations in exchange rates, it can easily become an expensive and futile exercise if a central bank tries to halt a fundamental adjustment in exchange rates.

10.8 Fixed Versus Floating Exchange Rates

In principle, countries have a choice between fixed exchange rate systems or floating or various compromises between these two systems. Orthodox economic opinion has varied as to the relative merits of the alternatives. In this section we examine some of the arguments.[4]

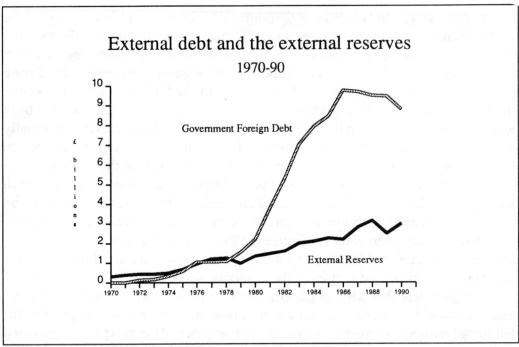

Figure 10.12 Foreign borrowing and the external reserves

Floating The basic argument in favour of floating is that the foreign exchange market should be allowed to function free of government intervention and find its own equilibrium through the interaction of the forces of supply and demand. Attempts by governments to set targets and peg exchange rates are, according to this view, as misguided in this market as they would be in the markets for apples or shoes. How do governments know what the "correct" exchange rate is? How can they tell a temporary fluctuation in the supply and demand for foreign exchange (which should be smoothed out) from a fundamental adjustment (which should not be resisted)? How can they avoid handing speculators sure bets by merely delaying a realignment?

Under fixed exchange rate systems, governments fix exchange rates and this can result in *misalignments*. This gives rise to problems of adjustment. If, for example, a balance of payments deficit indicates that the exchange rate is over-valued, and the government is committed to maintaining a pegged rate, it has to introduce measures to reduce domestic costs and prices. However, deflationary policies inevitably have an adverse effect on output, incomes and employment, and are politically difficult to implement. If the government fails to take appropriate action, the result will be a prolonged balance of payments disequilibrium.

An over-valued exchange rate can also be a fundamental cause of excess unemployment. Domestic firms may be unable to compete with foreign firms because an over-valued currency has rendered all domestic costs too high relative to the international competition. Under these circumstances it is unrealistic to expect employees and trade unions to understand that they should accept cuts in nominal wages so as to restore the country's international competitiveness. The best that can be hoped for is to hold domestic costs down while foreign costs rise, but this will take a long time to yield the desired result. A more realistic approach would be for the authorities to devalue the currency while trying to ensure that there is no offsetting rise in domestic money wages and costs.

Another advantage of flexible exchange rates is that, in principle at least, as there is no need for central banks to intervene to stabilise rates, they need not hold large external reserves. Consequently, liquidity problems should not arise, as periodically occurs in fixed exchange rate systems.

Fixed rates   Left to its own devices the foreign exchange market tends to be dominated by speculative flows, based on the anticipated capital gains from moving into currencies that are expected to appreciate. However, speculators' expectations at times appear to lack an anchor and it is possible for exchange rates to fluctuate wildly and to move away from equilibrium over long periods. The gyrations of the $/IR£ exchange rate over the last ten years, which were shown in Figure 10.3, illustrate this point. A basic argument in favour of fixed exchange rates is that they avoid the uncertainty and volatility that occur under floating. However, there is surprisingly little evidence that this volatility actually reduces the level of international trade and investment.

A further potential disadvantage of flexible exchange rates is that depreciation may provoke a *depreciation-inflation spiral*. This occurs when an initial depreciation increases domestic costs and output prices, which in turn generates pressure for further depreciation and so on. Why do we have such high inflation? Because the exchange rate is depreciating. And why is the exchange rate depreciating? Because we have high inflation. The experience of a number of South American countries illustrates how difficult it can be to stop this inflation-depreciation spiral.

Note:
In Chapter 8 we illustrated the problem of *hyperinflation* with reference to Argentine's recent woes. Soaring inflation has undermined the value of the country's currency in terms of foreign currencies. The austral was introduced in 1985 when it was worth $1.25. By mid-1991, there were 10,000 australs to $1 and the government announced plans to replace it with a new currency, which will be called the (new) peso. This was only the most recent in a series of new currencies introduced as inflation undermined the old ones: one new peso will be worth 10,000 *billion* of the old pesos that were in use in the 1960s. To avoid the uncertainty about future purchasing power people tend to use a foreign currency, such as the dollar, in preference to the local one. This process is called *dollarisation*. Pegging the exchange rate to a hard currency is a way of breaking the inflation-depreciation spiral.

For a fixed exchange rate system to succeed the chosen rates must accurately reflect the relative costs of doing business in the participating countries. It is essential that fundamental misalignments be avoided if the system is to endure. It is also essential that the participating countries pursue similar macroeconomic policies, so as to avoid the emergence of misalignment over time. If the currencies are misaligned to start with, or divergent policies create misalignments with the passage of time, persistent balance of payments deficits and surpluses will arise, as will a tendency for some countries to experience excess unemployment. These symptoms of disequilibrium will eventually lead to realignments and the possible breakdown of the system of fixed exchange rates.

An example of the tensions caused by uncoordinated policies is provided by the early years of the EMS. In 1983 France was pursuing an expansionary fiscal policy while Germany was implementing a deflationary monetary policy, while both were committed to maintaining stable exchange rates within the EMS. The result was an increasing balance of payments deficit in France and surplus in Germany. Speculators anticipating a devaluation of the French franc converted large amounts of money from francs into DMs. Eventually the French franc was devalued, rewarding the speculators. It was only after France abandoned its expansionary fiscal policy that the speculation subsided. The lesson to be learned is that fixed exchange rate systems can only reduce exchange rate uncertainty if there is *consistency of macroeconomic policy* between member states, based on explicit or implicit *coordination*. Another example of the consequences of misaligned exchange rates and the failure to coordinate policies is provided by Ireland's experience of prolonged high unemployment following the stabilisation of its currency within the EMS in the late 1980s. We discuss this case in detail in a later chapter.

The complete renunciation of separate currencies, as is now being contemplated within the EC, requires that the member states sacrifice an instrument of policy that could be used to help a country adjust to shocks such as an external recession or a domestic resource boom. For example, if the UK had been linked to the European currencies when North Sea oil began to flow, the pound sterling would not have been allowed to appreciate and the strain of adjustment to a balance of payments surplus would have been greater than it was during the 1980s. The rise and fall of sterling in line with world oil prices eased the strain of adjustment. Oil-exporting states such as Texas or Oklahoma in the US are subject to very wide cycles in income and employment as oil prices fluctuate. This is because the US$ does not fluctuate in line with oil prices, as would separate Texas or Oklahoma currencies

As Europe moves towards adopting a single currency, we should be aware of the problems this will create if external shocks have differential impacts on different regions of the currency union. A boom in luxury car exports and orders for machine tools would benefit Germany more than Portugal, but Portugal would have to adjust to the resultant strengthening of the common European currency. We shall return to this issue in a later chapter.

Despite the problems involved in renouncing the exchange rate as an instrument of macroeconomic policy, the instability of floating exchange rates has convinced many economists of the merits of some arrangement whereby rates are fixed or pegged. We seem to be moving into an era when there will be only three independent currencies in the world; the dollar, the yen and the European currency.

10.9 Conclusion

In this chapter we have discussed a number of topics relating to the balance of payments, exchange rates and the international financial system. The main issues and concepts covered include:

- The balance of payments is a record of a country's economic transactions with the rest of the world. The current and capital accounts are the main sub-accounts within the balance of payments

- The foreign exchange market in Ireland

- Nominal and real exchange rates

- Trade-weighted exchange rates

- How supply and demand for foreign exchange determine the exchange rate

- The main factors influencing exchange rates are inflation and interest rate differentials and the economy's growth rate

- The effects of devaluation on the balance of payments

- The official external reserves held by the central banks consist of foreign exchange, gold and other reserves such as ecus and SDRs

- Intervention or the use of official external reserves by the central banks to stabilise the exchange rate

- The advantages and disadvantages of floating and fixed exchange rates.

Note

1. The weights in Table 10.4 were used to derive the real trade-weighted exchange rate index. All of the data relating to exchange rates used in this chapter are period averages taken from the Central Bank of Ireland, *Quarterly Bulletins*. The price indices are based on consumer prices obtained from the OECD, *Main Economic Indicators*.

2. Robert A. Mundell, "Do Exchange Rates Work? Another View", International Monetary Fund, Research Department, WP/91/37, April 1991.

3. Gustav Cassel, "Abnormal Deviations in International Exchanges", *Economic Journal*, 28, December 1918. J. M. Keynes, *A Tract on Monetary Reform*, Macmillan and St Martin's Press, 1971, Chapter 3, suggests that purchasing power parity theory can be traced to the writings of David Ricardo in the nineteenth century.

4. An early discussion on the advantages and disadvantages of fixed and flexible exchange rates is given by Milton Friedman, "The Case for Flexible Exchange Rates", in Milton Friedman, *Essays in Positive Economics*, Chicago: University of Chicago Press, 1953. The reader should also consult: Jacques Artus and John Young, "Fixed Versus Flexible Exchange Rates: A Renewal of the Debate", *IMF Staff Papers*, 26, December 1979, and Rudiger Dornbusch, "Exchange Rate Economics: Where Do We Stand?", *Brookings Papers on Economic Activity*, No. 1, 1980.

Data appendix
Real and nominal exchange rates: 1979-91
(Based on consumer prices and period averages.)

Year		Nominal sterling exchange rate	Nominal deutsche mark exchange rate	Nominal dollar exchange rate	Nominal trade-weighted exchange rate
		index	index	index	index
1979	1	100.0	100.0	100.0	100.0
	2	96.2	101.7	99.3	98.8
	3	92.4	100.7	102.9	97.4
	4	97.3	99.1	104.0	99.8
1980	1	92.7	99.0	103.8	97.4
	2	90.3	99.7	102.3	95.9
	3	89.0	100.6	105.2	95.8
	4	82.3	100.0	97.4	90.8
1981	1	76.9	98.9	88.1	86.3
	2	77.3	97.7	79.7	85.5
	3	81.8	97.6	74.6	87.1
	4	84.1	94.9	78.5	89.0
1982	1	81.2	94.1	74.4	86.9
	2	81.7	92.4	72.1	86.9
	3	80.2	91.8	68.6	85.9
	4	81.8	90.3	66.9	86.2
1983	1	89.4	88.1	67.9	89.2
	2	81.7	84.4	63.0	83.6
	3	78.9	84.2	59.1	81.3
	4	78.9	83.0	57.6	80.6
1984	1	79.5	82.4	56.6	80.4
	2	80.9	81.9	56.1	80.3
	3	81.4	82.4	52.5	79.4
	4	83.5	83.0	50.5	79.6
1985	1	85.9	83.3	47.5	79.5
	2	80.7	83.7	50.3	78.9
	3	79.6	83.4	54.3	79.8
	4	83.2	82.6	59.3	82.3
1986	1	89.7	81.1	64.0	85.5
	2	89.7	81.2	67.3	86.5
	3	91.5	76.0	67.6	85.3
	4	94.9	72.8	67.3	85.0
1987	1	94.2	71.4	72.0	85.7

	2	90.2	71.5	73.5	84.8
	3	89.9	71.6	72.2	84.2
	4	89.1	71.2	77.5	85.1
1988	1	88.4	71.2	78.8	85.1
	2	85.1	71.5	77.7	83.8
	3	84.8	71.8	71.4	82.5
	4	84.2	71.5	74.8	82.8
1989	1	82.6	71.4	69.9	81.5
	2	85.0	71.4	68.5	81.7
	3	86.9	71.4	68.8	82.4
	4	92.1	70.8	72.4	85.1
1990	1	94.8	70.9	77.9	87.4
	2	95.4	71.7	79.3	88.3
	3	90.4	71.7	83.5	87.1
	4	91.5	71.5	88.0	88.1
1991	1	89.9	71.4	77.6	87.7
	2	91.1	71.5	73.3	85.5

Source: Central Bank of Ireland, *Quarterly Bulletins*, various issues.

Year		Real sterling exchange rate	Real deutsche mark exchange rate	Real dollar exchange rate	Real trade-weighted exchange rate
		index	index	index	index
1979	1	100.0	100.0	100.0	100.0
	2	96.2	104.4	99.5	100.0
	3	89.1	105.9	103.3	98.3
	4	95.0	106.8	105.2	101.8
1980	1	89.7	109.2	105.5	100.3
	2	89.1	115.9	107.9	102.8
	3	88.8	119.3	112.2	104.1
	4	82.8	120.9	104.2	100.0
1981	1	79.4	123.8	97.0	98.4
	2	79.1	124.4	88.8	97.6
	3	87.1	130.4	85.8	102.6
	4	93.0	132.9	94.2	107.9
1982	1	90.4	132.2	90.6	106.6
	2	94.0	136.1	91.8	110.6
	3	92.7	136.0	87.4	110.3
	4	95.2	134.5	86.3	110.4
1983	1	106.8	134.4	90.1	115.6

314

	2	97.8	131.4	84.8	110.1
	3	96.1	133.1	80.6	109.2
	4	97.1	133.2	79.7	109.2
1984	1	99.7	134.3	79.7	110.7
	2	101.9	135.9	80.2	112.1
	3	102.5	138.3	74.9	112.1
	4	104.4	139.3	72.0	112.5
1985	1	108.1	140.9	68.7	114.1
	2	99.7	142.6	72.7	111.7
	3	99.1	144.4	79.2	113.0
	4	103.4	142.9	85.9	114.9
1986	1	112.5	142.3	93.9	119.9
	2	112.7	144.8	100.4	121.9
	3	114.7	136.4	100.3	119.3
	4	117.7	131.4	99.8	118.7
1987	1	117.6	130.4	107.4	119.7
	2	111.9	131.0	108.8	117.4
	3	111.5	131.8	106.3	117.2
	4	109.4	131.2	113.2	117.0
1988	1	109.4	131.4	115.3	117.4
	2	103.2	131.8	112.8	114.4
	3	102.1	133.2	103.1	112.9
	4	99.7	133.1	107.7	112.5
1989	1	97.7	132.7	100.9	110.7
	2	98.7	132.7	98.2	110.6
	3	101.2	134.6	99.2	112.4
	4	106.1	133.9	104.4	115.3
1990	1	108.4	133.7	111.4	117.6
	2	104.7	134.8	112.8	116.5
	3	98.1	135.5	117.8	114.4
	4	98.4	134.6	122.7	114.8
1991	1	97.1	134.4	108.4	112.3
	2	97.0	134.5	102.5	111.2

Source: Central Bank of Ireland, *Quarterly Bulletins*, various issues, and OECD, *Main Economic Indicators*.

Chapter 11

From the Gold Standard to European Monetary Union

11.1   Introduction

We reviewed the history of the Irish monetary system in Chapter 6. We saw that almost complete integration of the Irish and British banking systems was maintained for many decades after Independence. The Central Bank of Ireland did not come into existence legally until 1942 and it had little scope to conduct an independent monetary policy until we joined the European Monetary System (EMS) in 1979. The decision to join the EMS was the most important event in the monetary history of the Irish state. In this chapter we explain how the EMS evolved and examine the proposals to extend it and create an economic and monetary union (EMU) in Europe. In a later chapter we examine the Irish experience in the EMS.

In order to appreciate the problems and strains facing the global economy today it is necessary to look briefly at the history of earlier international financial systems. The next three sections therefore contain an account of the gold standard, the Bretton Woods system and the Snake. This is followed by a discussion of the EMS and the proposals to create an EMU in Europe. We discuss the costs and benefits of EMU for a country like Ireland and the prospects for a convergence of living standards within the Community.

11.2   The Gold Standard

In the nineteenth century the international financial system operated on the gold standard, which was in full force from 1870 to the outbreak of the First World War in 1914.[1] Under this system, the value of the world's major currencies was fixed in terms of gold and this determined their values relative to each other. For example, a US dollar was worth 23.22 grains of gold and a pound sterling 113 grains, so the parity between the pound and the dollar was £1= $4.8665 (= 113/23.22). As there are 480 grains in a Troy ounce, an ounce of gold was worth $20.66 or £4.25.

The gold standard incorporated an automatic mechanism which corrected current account surpluses and deficits in the balance of payments. If, for example, a country was experiencing a deficit, gold would flow out of the country. This would reduce its money supply and lower the price level, as predicted by the Quantity Theory of Money. Lower prices would, in turn, improve competitiveness, increase exports and reduce imports. The incipient balance of payments deficit would be eliminated. Similarly, a country with a balance of payments surplus would experience an increase in its money supply and rising prices. The loss in competitiveness would choke off the balance of payments surplus. The monetary authorities in these countries should not intervene to prevent these flows or their effects on the price level: this was an essential "rule of the game".

Note:
This automatic mechanism is behind the modern *Monetary Approach to the Balance of Payments* (MAB) which we discuss in a later chapter. Versions of it were outlined by Richard Cantillon, who was from County Kerry, in his *Essai Sur la Nature du Commerce en General* (published in 1755 but written 20 years earlier) and by David Hume in *Political Discourses* (1752).

Under the full-blown gold standard, current account surpluses or deficits would not last indefinitely: factors of production (labour and capital), as well as money, would flow from the deficit to the surplus country, and there would be rapid adjustment as the level of economic activity declined in the former and rose in the latter. This is what happens today between the regions of a country which are linked by the use of a common currency: when there is an improvement in Texas' trade balance due to a boom in oil prices, it runs a balance of payments surplus, money and resources flow into the state and the level of activity picks up; when there is a decline in Michigan's trade balance due to a decline in its automobile sales, it runs a balance of payments deficit and resources flow out of the state and activity declines. This adjustment process gives rise to fears about the implications of full monetary union for the less developed regions of Europe in the future.

The factors that brought the gold standard to an end were:

1. As international trade increased there was an associated increase in the demand for gold to act as reserve backing for currencies. Increases in the gold supply, however, depended on new discoveries and these occurred erratically in the course of the nineteenth century, in California, South Africa and Australia. Consequentially there was a tendency for periodic shortages of international liquidity to develop.

2. Governments were not willing to tolerate the prolonged deflationary or inflationary effects on their economies of outflows or inflows of money as balance of payments disequilibria were corrected. In the United States the Federal Reserve System, created in 1914, did not abide by the rules of the gold standard in the inter-war period. In order to avert inflation it tried to prevent gold inflows from increasing the US money supply.

3. One of the major partners in world trade, Britain, adopted an over-valued exchange rate in terms of gold after the First World War. The adjustment to this mistake was slow and painful.

4. Finally, the system could not withstand the shock of the Great Depression and the downward spiral of world trade.

During the First World War France and Britain suspended convertibility of their currencies into gold, and, although the US maintained a limited form of convertibility of the dollar, this marked the end of the gold standard as it had operated in its heyday. However, at the time the suspension of convertibility was regarded as temporary, like the suspension of gold payments during the Napoleonic wars. A major aim of British post-war policy was to return to the gold standard at the pre-war value of sterling. Winston Churchill, as chancellor of the exchequer, re-established the pre-war parity in 1925. Orthodox financial opinion in Britain was gratified at the thought that the pound was once again worth $4.8665, but as Britain had experienced considerably more inflation since 1914 than the US, sterling was over-valued at this parity. France went back on the gold standard in 1928 but at a realistic, lower exchange rate that more than compensated for the inflation that had occurred since 1914.

The Great Depression brought these attempts to restore the gold standard to an end. The fixed exchange rates to which the gold standard committed countries meant that recession was quickly transmitted from the US to Britain and around the world, coming back to the US as world trade spiralled downwards. Britain suspended convertibility in 1931 and in 1933 dollar convertibility was suspended, to be restored in 1934 at the higher gold price of $35 an ounce.

Keynes regarded Mr Churchill's decision to re-establish the pre-war gold value of sterling in 1925 as a quixotic blunder that imposed a severe deflation on the economy. In fact he regarded the financial world's obsession with gold as a "barbarous relic". When, in September 1931, Britain abandoned the gold standard, Keynes wrote: "There are few Englishmen who do not rejoice at the breaking of our gold fetters. We feel that we have at last a free hand to do what is sensible. The romantic phase is over, and we can begin to discuss what policy is for the best."[2] However, Mundell points out that the magnitude of the over-valuation was estimated by Keynes to be 10 per cent and "it seems silly to observers in an age accustomed to wild gyrations of major currencies to blame so many of the ills of the world on this little event".[3] Mundell believes that the fundamental problem was not the over-valuation of sterling but that the entire post-war monetary system was unstable due to the under-valuation of gold. According to him, the pound may have been over-valued relative to the dollar, but the dollar itself was about 35 per cent over-valued relative to gold. This meant that there was a deflationary bias in the world monetary system that asserted itself with a vengeance in the 1930s.

318

After the abandonment of fixed exchange rates during the 1930s country after country implemented "beggar thy neighbour" devaluations in an attempt to gain a competitive advantage. Countries devalued in order to boost output and employment, but the countries that were adversely affected retaliated by devaluing in turn. The net result was that no country gained a lasting advantage. Because of the instability of the floating exchange rate system during the 1930s, a high priority was attached to re-establishing a fixed exchange rate system as the Second World War drew to a close.

11.3 The Bretton Woods System: 1945-71

Bretton Woods is a small resort town in New Hampshire. It was here that representatives of the major allied countries met in 1944 to discuss the arrangements for the post-war world monetary system. They hoped that when the war ended there would be no going back to the chaotic international financial system that had prevailed in the 1930s. They believed that only a system of fixed exchange rates could provide the stable framework required for economic reconstruction. As a result of its role in financing the war, the US held most of the western world's gold reserves by 1945. Consequently it was natural that the dollar should assume the role of the new reserve currency for the western world. It was agreed that the dollar would remain fixed at its 1934 value of $35 to an ounce of gold, and that all other currencies would be pegged to the dollar. Only central banks would be able to convert their holdings of dollars into gold. This *dollar exchange standard* was, therefore, an attenuated form of the old gold standard.

Note:
The principal architects of the new system were John Maynard Keynes and an American economist, Harry Dexter White. This was Keynes's last contribution to public affairs before his death in 1946.

The International Monetary Fund (IMF) and the International Bank for Reconstruction and Development (IBRD or the World Bank) were set up to provide funds to countries experiencing balance of payments difficulties and to assist in post-war reconstruction. (The IMF and World Bank are still known as the "Bretton Woods Institutions".) Central banks could borrow foreign exchange from the IMF and use it to support their currency on the markets. If, however, a country was experiencing a "fundamental disequilibrium" in its balance of payments, it was expected to devalue. This provision marked a crucial difference between the new system and the old gold standard. No longer did countries have to suffer the protracted deflation of the automatic adjustment mechanism in order to correct a balance of payments problem. Instead they could obtain international agreement on a devaluation and assistance in adjusting their economies.

The Bretton Woods system worked well during the 1950s and into the 1960s. The major currencies held to fixed exchange rates for long periods of time. For example, between 1949 and 1967, sterling was worth $2.80 (and, of course, the Irish pound was fixed at one-to-one parity with sterling). This was a fact of economic life and no one bothered to look up the newspapers to see if there had been any change. Trade and investment between the nations of the western world expanded rapidly under this arrangement.

Strains began to be felt as the 1960s wore on. The rising rate of inflation in the US, which was printing money to fight a War on Poverty at home and a War on Communism in south-east Asia, led to massive US current account deficits and undermined confidence in the dollar. The other main industrial countries were unwilling to revalue their currencies to help to eliminate the US deficit. For a while, central banks accepted additional dollars to augment their reserves, but the loose US monetary policy soon created an excess supply of dollars. This led to a demand that the US convert surplus dollars into gold, which it was no longer willing to do. German and Japanese Central Banks became reluctant to continue to absorb the dollars flooding on to world foreign exchange markets. (In 1969 the German money supply grew by 25 per cent in a week due to the inflow of dollars.) By the end of the decade they held so many dollars that if they had been allowed to obtain gold in exchange for them, American gold reserves would have been completely depleted. Something had to give.

In 1968 a two-tier gold price was established, with the market price rising far above the official price. The major nations decided to discontinue suppling their gold reserves to the world gold markets at the official price. Thus most of the world's gold was immobilised. Finally, in August 1971 President Richard Nixon officially terminated the convertibility of the dollar into gold, which in fact had already ceased to operate. In December 1971, at the Smithsonian Agreement (which was concluded at the Smithsonian Institution [Museum] in Washington, DC) the dollar was devalued by almost 8 per cent, raising the price of gold to $38 an ounce. Most of the other major currencies also devalued in terms of gold. This final attempt to patch up the Bretton Woods system did not succeed. There was a further devaluation of the dollar in terms of gold in February 1973 (which raised the price of gold to $42.22 an ounce), but this did not restore confidence in the dollar. Instead it encouraged the countries of Europe to terminate their links with the dollar and to float their currencies independently of the US currency.

The instability of the international payments system and the decline in the value of the dollar in terms of gold opened the way for the greatest monetary inflation in the history of the world. There was a direct link between the fall of the dollar and the decision of the Organisation of Petroleum Exporting Countries (OPEC) to quadruple the dollar price of oil when the opportunity presented itself during the Arab-Israeli war late in 1973. The rise in oil prices in turn fuelled the massive global inflation that occurred between 1973 and 1985. The Irish price level rose *fivefold* over this period.

Note:
The price of gold at the beginning of 1992 was $350 an ounce. Thus the dollar is now only 6 per cent of its nineteenth-century value in terms of gold. Sterling is worth just over 2 per cent of its former value.

11.4 Towards a New World Monetary System

The major currencies of the world (the dollar, the yen and the German mark) were floated in the spring of 1973. However, politicians in the larger countries were unwilling to allow the value of their currencies to be determined by market forces, where speculation plays the dominant role, so central banks intervened frequently in order to stabilise exchange rates, without openly declaring target rates. The new system came to be known as *dirty floating*. (See Chapter 10 for a discussion of central bank intervention.)

An important change in policy took place in 1985 when the world's seven main industrialised nations (known as G-7) met in the Louvre to "coordinate" a depreciation of the dollar against the other currencies. Since then there have been periodic meetings of this exclusive club to coordinate exchange rates. These meetings restore stability to the foreign exchange markets for a while, but do not remove the potential for further tensions. Because of its importance in world trade, the dollar always occupies centre stage. For example, at the London meeting of G-7 in mid-1991 the rise in the dollar was the focus of attention. By the beginning of 1992 the weakness of the dollar was a cause for concern. However, there is no agreement as to its equilibrium level. Thus, there is an uneasy compromise between floating and pegged exchange rate systems for the world's major currencies. The search continues for a system that will combine the merits of greater stability with the degree of flexibility required to allow individual countries to adjust to external shocks.

Despite its periodic weaknesses and the long-run decline in its value relative to the DM and yen, the dollar remains the currency in which most of the world's trade is denominated and the most widely held reserve currency. The enlargement of the EMS has, however, led to a more important international role for the ecu, which is the only real alternative to the dollar as a world currency. Many smaller currencies are linked to the dollar or the German mark. We are moving to the situation where there will be only three currencies of any significance in international trade, the dollar, the yen and the ecu. There are only two independent exchange rates between three currencies, so the role of foreign exchange dealers will be greatly reduced.

In the following sections we outline in more detail the development of monetary union in Europe since the breakdown of the Bretton Woods system.

11.5   The Snake

In 1972 the countries of the EEC (as it was called then) agreed to intervene in the foreign exchange markets to prevent their currencies fluctuating widely against each other, while maintaining the dollar exchange standard. Participating countries were expected to hold their currencies in a band around a central rate. This was known as the "snake in the tunnel" because the European currencies wriggled around within the band as they followed the movements of the dollar. But in March 1973, when what was left of the dollar exchange standard finally collapsed, the tunnel no longer existed and the system of linking European exchange rates to each other became known as the Snake.

The Snake was led by France and Germany. It enjoyed limited success. The UK joined at the start, but left after two months because it proved impossible to maintain the value of sterling at the target level. (The Irish pound entered and left the Snake along with sterling.) France left and rejoined as the franc rose and fell against the German mark (DM). By the mid-1970s the Snake was dead. However, renewed currency instability increased the awareness of the need for a system that would stabilise exchange rates in Europe and led to the initiatives that culminated in the launch of the European Monetary System (EMS) in 1979.

The main reason for the failure of the Snake was the same as that which led to the downfall of the gold standard and the Bretton Woods system, namely, the lack of economic policy coordination between the participating countries. If countries do not have similar rates of inflation, they cannot hope to maintain their balance of payments in equilibrium under a system of fixed exchange rates. Chronic surpluses and deficits in the current account of the balance of payments will eventually lead to the breakdown of the original parities. During the Snake, France and the UK tended to pursue much more expansionary fiscal and monetary policies than Germany. It was inevitable that balance of payments deficits and surpluses arose and forced exchange rate changes so large as to make the whole arrangement pointless.

The lesson that should have been learned from this episode is that countries can not maintain fixed parities unless their economic policies are closely coordinated or at least very consistent. However, such consistency is difficult to achieve as long as national governments believe they can improve their countries' economic performance by pursuing independent monetary and fiscal policies. If a system of fixed exchange rates is to be successful, it requires that the participants surrender or at least curtail the independent use of fiscal and monetary policies to secure domestic policy objectives.

How significant a loss the surrender of independent macroeconomic policies is depends on how effective these policies are in promoting growth and employment. We reviewed the Irish experience in Chapter 5 and saw that very few lasting results were obtained from fiscal activism in the 1970s. The expansionary policies pursued by Britain and France in the 1970s which led to the break-up of the Snake resulted in higher inflation but no extra growth. Both countries have now accepted that on balance it is better to adopt the discipline of a European system of fixed exchange rates than to attempt to stimulate their economies through independent macroeconomic policies. (However, the British commitment to this doctrine was tested by the temptation to devalue in the hope of lifting the prolonged recession before the 1992 election.)

11.6   The European Monetary System

During the second half of the 1970s the Commission of the EC pressed ahead with plans for a European monetary union. The interim goal was to create a "zone of monetary stability" in Europe. After long and difficult negotiations, the EMS commenced on 13 March 1979. It has survived and to some extent flourished since then, confounding those sceptics who thought it would quickly suffer the fate of its predecessor, the Snake.

At the heart of the EMS is a system of quasi-fixed exchange rates, known as the *Exchange Rate Mechanism* (ERM). The central banks of the countries that participate in the ERM intervene to keep exchange rates within a narrow band. The

---

Table 11.1
The European currency unit (ecu): September 1989

		Units of currency	*Weight (%)*
1.	German mark (DM)	0.6242	30.1
2.	French franc (FF)	1.332	19.0
3.	Dutch guilder (HFL)	0.2197	9.4
4.	Belgian franc (BFR)	3.30 ⌉	⌉
5.	Luxembourg franc (LFR)	0.13 ⌋	⌋ 7.9
6.	Italian lira (LIT)	151.8	10.15
7.	Danish krone (DKR)	0.1976	2.45
8.	Irish pound (IR£)	0.0085	1.1
9.	Pound sterling (STG£)	0.0878	13.0
10.	Spanish peseta (PTA)	6.885	5.3
11.	Greek drachma (DR)	1.15	0.8
12.	Portuguese escudo (ESU)	1.393	0.8
		———	———
		1 ecu	100.0

Note:
Although the Greek drachma is used to calculate the ecu, this currency does not participate in the ERM.

participating countries are: Germany, France, Italy, the Netherlands, Belgium, Luxembourg, Denmark, Ireland, the United Kingdom, Spain and Portugal. Greece is also a member of the EMS but does not participate in the ERM. Many small countries that are formally outside the EMS have adopted a *de facto* peg to the System. These include Sweden, Norway, Austria and Switzerland.

At the centre of the system is the *European currency unit* (ecu) which is a weighted basket of currencies. (The original ecu was a medieval French coin.) Table 11.1 shows the weights of the currencies in September 1989, when the current weighting was adopted. The amount of each currency in the ecu is based on the country's GNP and intra-EC trade. The DM has by far the largest weight reflecting the size of the German economy and its dominant role in European trade. The Irish pound has a weight of only 1.1 per cent.

Note:
The ecu was first defined when the EMS commenced in 1979. Reflecting changes in each country's GNP and intra-EMS trade, it was re-defined in 1984 and 1989. A new weighting is expected in September 1994.

Table 11.2
Calculating the ecu exchange rate

	Basket	Exchange rate 25 October 1991	Converted to IR£
	(1)	*(2)*	*(3) = (1)/(2)*
DM	0.6242	2.6741	0.2334
FF	1.332	9.1261	0.1459
HFL	0.2198	3.0133	0.0729
BFR ⎤	3.301		
LFR ⎦	0.13	55.05	0.0623
LIT	151.8	1,999.14	0.0759
DKR	0.1976	10.3532	0.0190
IR£	0.008552	1	0.008552
STG£	0.0878	0.9194	0.0955
PTA	6.885	168.29	0.0409
DR	1.44	299.69	0.0048
ESU	1.393	229.81	0.0060
	Total = 1 ecu		0.7655

The Irish pound/ecu exchange rate is calculated by converting each currency in the basket to the Irish pound and then summing. In Table 11.2, the currencies are converted to Irish pounds using the exchange rates prevailing on 25 October 1991. The basket is worth IR£0.7655. Hence, 1 ecu = IR£0.7655 or IR£1 = ecu1.30225. A similar calculation can be performed for all other currencies.

When the ecu was defined in 1989, each currency was given a *central exchange rate* against the ecu. These central ecu exchange rates are used to calculate *cross rates* between individual currencies. For example, if the DM/ecu and IR£/ecu exchange rates are known, the DM/IR£ cross rate can be calculated. The matrix of central rates is known as the *parity grid*. The maximum permissible deviation between the strongest and weakest currencies in the *narrow band* of the grid is 2.25 per cent. The Spanish peseta, the Portuguese escudo and the pound sterling are, however, allowed a 6 per cent spread. (The EMS grid is shown in a graph in the Central Bank of Ireland's *Quarterly Bulletin* and the position of the various currencies in the grid is published weekly in the newspapers.) The *intervention margins* are the upper and lower levels beyond which intervention would be initiated to bring the currencies back towards the central rate and avoid them breaking out of the band. For example, the central rate of the Irish pound in the ERM implies an exchange rate of IR£1 = DM2.67. If the value of the Irish pound fell to IR£1 = DM2.60, the central banks of the European countries would cooperate and buy Irish pounds until it had moved back into the band. (See the note to Table 11.3.)

Incorporated into the system is a *divergence indicator*, which is an early warning device. The indicator is set at 75 per cent of the allowed intervention margins. Once an exchange rate has moved 75 per cent of the way to the ceiling or floor, there is a presumption that central banks will begin to intervene. This helps to take the limelight away from the strongest or weakest currency in the System.

Table 11.3
Central rates and intervention margins for IR£: January 1991

	HFL	B/LFR	DM	DKR	FF	LIT	PTA
Central Rate + 2.25%	3.08	56.49	2.73	10.44	9.18	2050.0	184.5
Central Rate	3.02	55.25	2.67	10.22	8.98	2004.9	174.1
Central Rate - 2.25%	2.95	54.00	2.61	9.98	8.77	1959.8	163.6

Notes:
1. If all the currencies in the system were at their central rates, the Irish pound could move by a maximum of 4.5 per cent. This would occur if the Irish pound was at the top of the band (+ 2.25 per cent) and fell to the bottom of the band (- 2.25 per cent). However, at any one time, no two currencies can be more than 2.25 per cent apart. Hence if any other currency were at the bottom of the band, the Irish pound could not move above any of its central rates.
2. The maximum margin of fluctuation for the peseta, the escudo and the pound sterling is +/- 6 per cent.

An important part of the EMS is the *European Monetary Cooperation Fund* (EMCF). In 1979 the EMCF received 20 per cent of all members' gold and foreign exchange reserves. In return, each member was credited with a similar amount of ecus. The objective of the EMCF is to make available reserves to countries experiencing balance of payments difficulties. Significant exchange controls were in operation between the participating currencies when the EMS was formed, but by 1992 these were almost completely dismantled.

Table 11.4
EMS realignments: per cent change in bilateral central rates

No.		Date	DM	B/LF	DKR	FF	IR£	LIT	HFL
1	1979	24/9	+2.00		-2.86				
2		30/11			-4.76				
3	1982	3/3						-6.00	
4		5/10	+5.50			-3.00		-3.00	+5.50
5	1982	22/2		-8.5	-3.00				
6		14/6	+4.25			-5.57		-2.75	+4.24
7	1983	21/3	+5.50	+1.5	+2.50	-2.50	-3.5	-2.50	+3.50
8	1985	22/7	+2.00	+2.0	+2.00	+2.00	+2.0	-6.00	+2.00
9	1986	7/4	+3.00	+1.0	+1.00	-3.00			+3.00
10		4/8					-8.0		
11	1987	12/1	+3.00	+2.0					+2.00
12	1990	6/1						-3.75	

Source: Commission of the European Communities.

The EMS contains important elements of flexibility. The first is the margin of variation around the central rates that we described above. A much more important provision is that finance ministers can agree to realign the central rates if it becomes clear that they are no longer appropriate. This is akin to the IMF notion of a "fundamental disequilibrium", but the procedure for agreeing on an EMS realignment is much less cumbersome than the one that was required to change the Bretton Woods parities in the 1950s and 1960s.

Realignments occurred frequently in the early years of the EMS. (Table 11.4 gives the details.) There were two in every year from 1979 to 1983, but since 1986 the System has enjoyed considerable stability. Most of the realignments were in response to the desire of smaller countries to devalue to offset the effects of high inflation and to reduce balance of payments deficits. One of the reasons the EMS has survived is that it permitted such corrections to be made quickly in the early years while avoiding changing exchange rates so frequently that the whole System was undermined.

Four of the realignments (numbers 4, 6, 7 and 9) were of fundamental importance as they arose from the differing performances of the German and French economies. Following the election of a socialist president and government in 1982, France pursued an expansionary fiscal policy that was incompatible with the conservative policies being pursued in Germany. The resulting additional inflation in France created major tensions in the ERM, which survived only because compromises were worked out that allowed the French franc to fall and the DM to rise. Gradually French and German economic policies came more into line as the French abandoned the attempt to stimulate their economy without regard for the repercussions on the exchange rate.

When sterling, the dollar or the yen weakened during the 1980s there was a tendency for speculative funds to flow into DMs, which was regarded as the strongest of the EMS currencies. The realignment in 1987 occurred because of the impact of the weakness of sterling on the ERM. This caused the DM to appreciate and put a strain on the parity grid. The same tendency was evident at the end of 1991, when the dollar weakened. This problem would be avoided if complete capital mobility existed between the currencies of the ERM and their exchange rates were permanently locked, so that they were perfect substitutes. This would remove the tendency to seek out the strongest currency in the ERM and all the participating currencies would move together against the non-participating currencies.

Note:
Speculators have on occasion anticipated EMS realignments and reacted by moving considerable amounts of money between countries in the hope of making a capital gain. Although it is generally clear which currencies are likely to be devalued, speculators have not always gained. In March 1983, the French authorities delayed a realignment against the DM and hoisted interest rates on the Euro-Franc market to unprecedented rates of five and six *thousand* per cent. Speculators who had borrowed on this market and converted their borrowings into DMs hoping to make a capital gain lost out badly. "Once speculators' fingers looked memorably burned, the (interest) rate was allowed to subside to a mere three to four hundred per cent." (*Irish Times*, 19 March 1983, p. 18)

At most realignments, the Irish pound went "through the middle", that is, its central rate was not changed as the DM rose and the French franc fell. However, the Irish pound was devalued on two occasions: 21 March 1983 and 4 August 1986. Both devaluations were provoked by a depreciation of sterling relative to the ERM currencies. As sterling depreciated, Irish traders and speculators took the view that sterling was a good buy and converted large sums of Irish pounds into sterling and other foreign currencies. This capital outflow led to a fall in the Central Bank's external reserves. In order to stop the outflow of funds, Irish short-term interest rates were raised, but eventually the Irish pound was realigned in the ERM. Speculators who converted Irish pounds into foreign currency and back to Irish pounds following the devaluation gained. The effects of devaluation on the Irish economy are discussed in a later chapter.

With the exception of the realignment of the lira in January 1990, which preceded its entry into the narrow-band of the ERM, there has been no realignment since January 1987. This stability has been facilitated by the fact that the countries participating in the narrow-band of the ERM have been implementing broadly consistent economic policies and their rates of inflation have been much lower and more uniform than was the case during the early 1980s.

One of the problems that bedevilled attempts at exchange rate unions in the past is known as the *nth country problem*. It arises from the fact that there is one fewer exchange rate than there are countries in a union. If there are two countries, as under the Irish pound-sterling link, the only exchange rate is that between the Irish pound and sterling. Under these circumstances, it is sufficient for one country's central bank to intervene to hold a target exchange rate. (If they both intervene, they have to coordinate their intervention so that they are working towards the same target rate.) In the EMS there has to be an nth country, whose exchange rate is passively determined as a result of the decisions of others. This country is free to pursue its own monetary policies and the other n - 1 countries have to intervene in foreign exchange markets to maintain the target rates of exchange. By intervening, they lose control of their own money supplies. Thus, their monetary policies come to be dictated by those of the nth country, just as British policy dominated Ireland under the sterling link. Under the "dollar exchange standard" that operated until 1971, the US was the nth country, but as it relaxed its grip on its money supply, other countries became increasingly unhappy at leaving it in this role. The reason why Germany is generally acceptable as the dominant country in the EMS is ultimately that other countries have more faith in the ability of the Bundesbank to control the German money supply than they have in the ability of their own central banks to control their money supplies. *The Economist* made this point in a characteristic passage: "Tory gentlemen may like appointing City gents as governors of the Bank of England, but Mr Karl Otto Poehl [governor of the Bundesbank at that time] would do a better job." (21 September 1988)

11.7   European Economic and Monetary Union

My annals have it so:
A thing my mother saw,
Nigh eighty years ago
With happiness and awe.

Sight never to forget:
Solemn against the sky
In stately silhouette
Ten emus walking by.[4]

The European Council at its meeting in June 1988 in Hanover decided to set up a committee with "the task of studying and proposing concrete stages leading towards (economic and monetary) union".[5] The committee was chaired by the EC Commission President Jacques Delors and consisted of the governors of the central banks of the twelve member states, an EC Commission representative and three invited experts. The committee published its report (known as the Delors Report) in April 1989.

The Delors Report envisaged Europe evolving rapidly towards an economic and monetary union (EMU). It argued that the two unions "form two integral parts of a single whole and would therefore have to be implemented in parallel".[6]

Monetary union Monetary union consists of:
- complete convertibility of currencies

- the complete liberalisation of capital transactions and full integration of banking and other financial markets

- the irrevocable locking of exchange rate parities.

The Delors Report noted that while a single currency was not strictly necessary for monetary union it was a "natural and desirable further development of the monetary union". Monetary union would also entail the need for a common monetary policy which would require the setting up of a new European institution. The "shift from national monetary policies to a single monetary policy is an inescapable consequence of monetary union and constitutes one of the principal institutional changes".

Economic union The principal features of an economic union as outlined in the Report are:
- a single market in which persons, goods, services and capital can move freely

- a common competition policy

- common policies aimed at structural change and regional development

- macroeconomic policy coordination, including binding rules for budgetary policies.

In addition economic union would involve a "large degree of freedom for market behaviour and private economic initiative with public intervention in the provision of certain social services and public goods".

Steps towards economic and monetary union

Table 11.5 gives a chronology of events leading to EMU. The goal of creating an EMU has been facilitated by two developments that pre-date the Delors Report. First, in June 1988 the Council of Economic Ministers adopted a directive to liberalise capital movements by July 1990. Greece, Ireland, Portugal and Spain were allowed until the end of 1992 to achieve this objective. Second, the Single European Act was passed in 1987 with the objective of *completing the internal market* by the end of 1992. This is to allow the free movement of persons, goods, services and capital between member states and dismantle all physical, technical and fiscal barriers within the Community. The removal of all exchange controls and the completion of the internal market will create the preconditions essential for realising EMU.

Note:
In Ireland, approximately 70 per cent of the 300 measures identified as preconditions for completing the internal market had been adopted by the end of 1991. Difficulties remain particularly with regard to the harmonisation of indirect taxes. The Department of Finance has estimated that the complete harmonisation of Irish indirect taxes (both VAT and excise duty) on Community rates would result in a loss of approximately IR£560 million a year in tax revenue. The Commission has modified its definition of the acceptable degree of harmonisation.

The Delors Report recommended that EMU be achieved in the following three stages.

Stage 1 During this stage a start would be made towards convergence of fiscal and monetary policies including new procedures for budgetary policy coordination, the completion of the internal market and the strengthening of Community competition policy. In line with this, the EC's structural funds have been increased and their administration reformed in order to reduce disparities in living standards between member states. A *single financial area*, allowing free access to banking services, stock exchanges and other financial services across member states will have been created by the end of 1992. All financial instruments will be freely tradeable and there will be no impediments to capital flows between member states. To complete this stage, all Community currencies should adhere to the ERM and there should be no impediments to the private use of the ecu.

Stage 2 Stage 2 was to be largely a transition period in which the progress achieved during Stage 1 will be consolidated. The most important step in this stage was to be the setting up of a European System of Central Banks (ESCB). The ESCB would begin the transition from coordination of independent national monetary policies to a common European monetary policy. A common monetary policy will not be fully implemented until Stage 3. In addition, the ERM bands were to be narrowed and a further 10 per cent of member states' external reserves will be pooled and managed by the ESCB. At the European Council meeting in Rome in October 1990 it was agreed that, subject to further progress on economic integration, Stage 2 would commence in January 1994.

Stage 3 During this stage rules relating to macroeconomic policy and government budgets should become binding. In particular, upper limits on government budget deficits are to be imposed and there will be no recourse by governments to monetary financing of budget deficits. This implies that governments will not be able to borrow from their central banks or from outside the Community. Structural and regional policies will be further strengthened. Exchange rates will be irrevocably fixed and the ESCB will assume responsibility for the implementation of a common monetary and exchange rate policy. All external reserves will be pooled and managed by the ESCB. Finally, the transition to a single Community currency will commence.

The Maastricht proposals

At the meeting in Maastricht in December 1991 between heads of state of the EC countries these proposals were brought a stage closer to realisation. Agreement was reached to make passage to EMU by 1999 irreversible. The framework for creating a single European currency was established along the lines proposed in the Delors Report. In Stage 2, which will last until 1997, a European Monetary Institute (EMI) (rather than the Central Bank envisaged in the Delors Report) is to be established. The EMI will have limited powers. Its president will be elected by the governors of member state central banks. There will be increased use of the ecu as a unit of account and governments will strive to lower budget deficits and debt.

The transition to Stage 3 and the creation of an new European currency will begin during 1996. Finance ministers will decide which member states have met the *convergence criteria* which we list below. If at least seven do, then a summit meeting will decide if these countries are ready for EMU and, if they do, when it should start. If seven member states do not meet the specified criteria another summit meeting will be held before July 1998 to decide which members are ready. *Those countries will automatically adopt the ecu as their single currency by January 1999.* During this Stage the EMI will be replaced by a European Central Bank which will have responsibility for monetary and exchange rate policy and for maintaining price stability in the Community. Rules relating to government budget deficits will become binding. The United Kingdom insisted on the right to opt out of the process of adopting a single currency.

As a result of the Maastricht agreement, the countries of the European Community are now embarked on the road that will lead to full-scale economic and monetary union by the end of the decade, barring some unforeseen economic or political upheaval. The Maastricht treaty provides for a two-speed procedure towards creating a single currency, with countries that do not meet the convergence criteria by 1998 not joining until a later date. The five criteria are:

- The rate of inflation must be within 1.5 per cent of the three lowest inflation rates in the Community

- The interest rate must be within 2 per cent of the two lowest interest rates in the Community

- The fiscal budget deficit must not exceed 3 per cent of GDP. However, a country may join if its deficit is above this limit, provided it is falling quickly or if there are exceptional or temporary reasons for a large deficit

- The currency must have been within the narrow band of the ERM and not devalued for at least two years

- The public debt/GDP ratio must be no more than 60 per cent or falling rapidly to that level.

At the end of 1991 only France and Luxembourg were fulfilling all five criteria. Britain had met all except the exchange rate criterion. Ireland failed only on the debt/GDP ratio. (The Irish ratio, according to EC definitions, was just over 100 per cent in 1991). We have, however, reduced this ratio significantly since the mid-1980s and it could be down to between 70 and 80 per cent by 1997, which might be sufficient to allow us to participate from the start in the single currency system. Belgium and Italy have unacceptably high debt/income ratios and are not showing much signs of lowering them. Greece and Portugal meet none of the criteria as yet.

A number of issues have yet to be resolved. The new European Central Bank is to be "independent of instructions from national governments and Community authorities" and will probably be modelled on the German Bundesbank. This raises the question to whom the governors of the new bank will be answerable. It is also not clear what role will remain for national central banks. We have seen that under the sterling link the functions of the Central Bank of Ireland were minimal: it will have less power in the EMU. It is therefore questionable whether fully fledged national central banks should continue to exist after the formation of the EMU. Finally, if reserves are pooled and the new single currency issued by the European Central Bank, the question of how to share the seigniorage arising from this currency will have to be resolved. A formula based on GDP, population and national reserves will probably be used.

Table 11.5

Chronology of events leading to European Monetary Union

- April 1951: France, West Germany, Italy, Belgium, the Netherlands and Luxembourg sign the Treaty of Paris which establishes the European Coal and Steel Community (ECSC).

- March 1957: These six countries sign the Treaty of Rome which establishes the European Economic Community (EEC). One of the objectives of the Treaty is to establish a customs union where there is free movement of goods, services and capital. The Treaty also refers to the desirability of achieving international monetary stability. The EEC and the ECSC constitute the European Communities (EC).

- March 1958: An EC Monetary Committee is formed to review the monetary situation in member states.

- January 1962: The EC Common Agricultural Policy (CAP) commences with the aim of establishing a common market and prices for agricultural produce.

- October 1962: A Commission report to the Council proposes to form a monetary union by 1971. Germany objects on the grounds that the Bretton Woods system is working well.

- February 1969: Barre Report on the coordination of economic and monetary policies is published.

- December 1969: At a conference of European governments in The Hague, the German Chancellor Brandt called for establishing economic and monetary union in stages. This followed the devaluation of sterling in 1967 and the realignment of the French franc and German mark in 1969. His proposal was based on the Barre Report and was adopted by the European Council and a working party chaired by Mr Pierre Werner (Prime Minister of Luxembourg) was set up to examine the issues.

- October 1970: The Werner Report is published. The Report calls for the creation of a monetary union, in stages, by 1980. Monetary union will entail (i) fixing European currencies irrevocably or introducing a single currency, (ii) free movement of capital, (iii) the establishment of a European central bank and (iv) coordination of macroeconomic policy. The Report called for "parallel progress" towards monetary union, involving coordination of fiscal and monetary policies at the same time as progress was being made towards fixing exchange rates. The Report suggested that economic policies be coordinated and exchange rate fluctuations reduced so that after a period of ten years exchange rates could be irrevocably fixed.

- March 1971: The Council adopts a resolution to achieve economic and monetary union by 1980.

- March 1972: As the Bretton Woods system collapses, European governments agree to maintain exchange rates within a + or - 2.25 per cent band relative to each other (the Snake) while the whole group will fluctuate in a + or - 4.5 per cent band against the dollar (the Tunnel). The Snake did not succeed in stabilising European exchange rates and the remaining stages proposed in the Werner report were postponed.

- January 1973: Denmark, Ireland and the UK join the EC.

- April 1973: European Monetary Cooperation Fund (EMCF) is established.

- 1975: European unit of account (EUA) based on a weighted basket of currencies is introduced.

- 1977: In Florence, the President of the Commission, Roy Jenkins, calls for a new initiative to create EMU.

- April 1978: At the European Council meeting in Cooperage, the German Chancellor Schmidt and the French President Giscard d'Estaing propose the creation of a European Monetary System (EMS). The EMS is intended to create a zone of monetary stability in Europe.

- July 1978: EC heads of state and governments meet in Bremen and agree on the structure of the EMS.

- December 1978: The European Council meeting in Brussels agrees on the mode of operation of the EMS. Ireland is committed to joining.

- March 1979: The EMS commences operation. All EC countries become members of the EMS but the UK does not join the exchange rate mechanism (ERM). Greece joins in 1981 and Spain and Portugal in 1986 but do not immediately join the ERM. Spain joins the ERM in June 1989, the UK in October 1990 and Portugal in April 1992. The ecu is based on the same basket of currencies as the EUA.

- June 1985: The EC Commission submits a report on completing the internal market. The report identifies measures to remove barriers to the free movement of goods, services, capital and labour (the four freedoms).

- February 1986: Signing of the Single European Act which came into force in July 1987, after its adoption by referendum in Ireland. Its aim is to complete the internal market.

- June 1988: Council of Ministers directive to liberalise capital movements by July 1990. Transition period extended for Ireland, Portugal, Greece and Spain.

- June 1988: A committee of central bank governors and other experts is formed at a meeting of the European Council in Hanover to study how economic and monetary union could be achieved. The committee is chaired by EC Commission president Jacques Delors.

- January 1989: Commission president Jacques Delors proposes that the EC and the European Free Trade Association (EFTA, which includes the Nordic countries, Austria and Switzerland) create a European Economic Area (EEA).

- April 1989: The Delors Report is published.

- June 1989: European Council at a meeting in Madrid agrees to implement the first stage of the Delors Report starting July 1990.

- 1989: EC and EFTA begin formal negotiations to create a European Economic Area (EEA).

- December 1989: European Council meeting in Strasbourg agrees to establish the institutional changes necessary to implement Stages 2 and 3 of the Delors Report.

- July 1990: Beginning of Stage 1 of the process leading to EMU.

- July 1990: After more than forty years of separation, the economically strong Federal Republic of Germany united with the economically weak German Democratic Republic in an economic, monetary and social union.

- October 1990: German economic integration made irreversible by political unification.

- October 1990: European Council meeting in Rome agrees to start the second stage of EMU in January 1994.

- October 1991: The twelve countries of the EC and the seven countries of the European Free Trade Association (EFTA) agree to create a European Economic Area (EEA) in which there will be free movement of goods, services, capital and labour starting January 1993. This will be the world's richest free trade area with a population of 380 million.

- December 1991: At a meeting in Maastricht, in the Netherlands, the heads of state of the EC countries agree to create a single currency by the end of 1996 provided seven member states meet criteria relating to a convergence of inflation, interest rates and government debt. Even if this condition is not satisfied in 1996, a single currency will be automatically introduced in January 1999. Britain retains the right to opt out of this agreement. A European Monetary Institute (EMI) will be created in 1994.

11.8   Optimum Currency Areas

In Chapter 10 we reviewed the arguments in favour of a system of fixed exchange rates. Earlier in the present chapter we pointed out that following the upheavals of the 1930s there was overwhelming support for a return to a system of fixed exchange rates and after the instability that followed the collapse of the Bretton Woods system in the 1970s there was a similar desire to form regional exchange rate unions. However, forming an EMU which operates with a single currency has much more far reaching implications for the participating economies that those that follow from simply agreeing to maintain fixed exchange rates. In particular, EMU entails the surrender of an independent monetary policy and places narrow limits on fiscal policy. Economists have explored the conditions under which it makes sense for regions (or countries) to agree to such an arrangement. This literature has led to the following criteria for an *optimum currency area.*[7]

Price and wage flexibility   A basic concern is how easily a region within a larger currency union (e.g. Ireland as part of the EMU) adjusts to shocks. An independent exchange rate is potentially a useful instrument to help the process of adjustment and prevent protracted deflation and unemployment in the aftermath of a shock, especially one that has a greater impact on some regions than on the area as a whole. A decline in Community support for agricultural production, for example, would have a disproportionate effect on Ireland and a depreciation of the Irish pound could help the country adjust. On the other hand, if wages and prices were flexible in all regions of the currency union it would be unnecessary to use exchange rates to help the adjustment to the changing pattern of economic activity: in the above example, the prices of agricultural products and the incomes of those in agriculture would decline, resources would be quickly reallocated to other sectors and full employment restored. However, in the absence of such flexibility external shocks may result in persistent unemployment and growing regional disparities in levels of economic activity. Exchange rate realignments could be used to speed adjustment in these circumstances. However, in a very small and open economy such as Ireland it is very difficult to implement a successful exchange rate policy. On the other hand, there is not much evidence that Ireland, or indeed Europe as a whole, has exhibited the degree of wage-price flexibility required to maintain full employment in the face of shocks (see the discussion in Chapter 9). It is therefore not clear whether the creation of a currency union will assist or hinder the restoration of full employment.

Financial market integration   If a group of countries is formed into a single currency area, it is important that regional balance of payments surplus and deficits should be easily financed. This is only possible if there is a high degree of integration between the regions. It is for this reason that the EC has insisted on the removal of exchange controls and related barriers to the movement of funds before the next stage of EMU can commence.

Factor mobility Ideally the area in which a single currency is used should fulfil the definition of a "country" used by the international trade theorists, that is an area within which there is complete mobility of the factors of production but between which and the rest of the world there is limited mobility. We have seen that EMU will require the establishment of free movement of all the factors of production between the member states. This condition is already largely fulfilled. The remaining barriers to the free flow of financial capital between member states will have been dismantled by the end of 1992. Freedom to acquire or create fixed assets across national borders is already established. Since the end of the 1950s Ireland has encouraged external investment from all sources. Mobility of labour across national borders is unhindered in theory. In reality difference in language and culture, rigidities in housing markets and ethnic discrimination present significant barriers to freedom of movement between members states. There is also a high level of mobility into the Community from the rest of the world. Because of our long tradition of emigration to the new world, Ireland's labour market is unusually open to extra-Community influences, but we also have a high degree of intra-Community mobility due to the close integration of the Irish and British labour markets.

The pattern of trade Ideally, a single currency area would be relatively self-sufficient *vis-à-vis* the rest of the world. The EC as a whole is relatively self-sufficient: extra-EC trade amounts to under 20 per cent of GDP. Ireland in isolation is one of the most open economies in the world, but over 66 per cent of our imports come from other EC countries and 75 per cent of our exports go to them. Extra-EC trade amounts to 34 per cent of our GDP, which is higher than the EC average primarily because of the importance of our trade with the US.

Fiscal federalism The viability of a common currency area depends on political and social solidarity as well as on economic considerations. The logic of the adjustment process outlined above is that shocks will cause major differences in the level of economic activity between regions. Changes in exchange rates could help to dampen these wide swings in economic activity and reduce regional disparities, but in a common currency area these are ruled out. To be successful, therefore, a common currency area made up of disparate regions must develop mechanisms that will dampen the effects of region-specific shocks. Within countries that share common tax and social welfare systems, localised shocks tend to be automatically offset by a fall in tax payments and an increase in transfers. A decline in the fishing industry, for example, leads to a fall in the taxes paid from Donegal to the Irish exchequer and an increase in the social welfare transfers from the exchequer to Donegal. This process is called *fiscal federalism* and it has been developing rapidly between the EC and the member states. The European Social Fund (ESF) was established under the original EC treaty and provides up to 60 per cent funding to finance training programmes and special projects to aid disadvantaged groups. The European Regional Development Fund (ERDF) was established in 1975 with the aim of developing and improving the infrastructure of the less developed regions. Grants of up to 75 per cent are available to governments in the peripheral areas of the Community from the ERDF to improve communications, sea- and airports and roads and for industrial projects. The guidance section of the European Agricultural Guidance and Guarantee Fund (EAGGF) provides funds to reorganise and improve agricultural structures including small farms. As what is called an "Objective One" (that is, poor) Region, the Republic of Ireland as a whole benefits from the highest rates of grants available. Under the Maastricht proposal, a new *Cohesion Fund* is to be established which will assist in improving telecommunications, transport, environment and help lower energy costs in the less developed regions.

The budget proposals brought forward by Mr Delors early in 1992 proposed a doubling of the money allocated to Greece, Portugal, Ireland and Spain from the structural funds, which will include the new Cohesion Fund. However, the funds will still amount to a mere 0.4 per cent of the Community's GDP and the enlargement of the budget is meeting with resistance from the richer member states. A shortcoming of the existing structural funds is that they are linked to specific projects and require matching funds from the recipient government. While it is now proposed to reduce the amount that countries will have to raise from their own resources to match structural funds from the Community, there will still be no automatic mechanism to increase the flow in response to a decline in the level of activity in a region. For fiscal federalism to reach the level that would be required to cement the EMU, much larger transfers would have to be made from rich to poor regions and these transfers should be more closely linked to cyclical conditions in the regions.

11.9 The Implications of EMU for Ireland

One of the principal declared goals of European EMU is to raise the living standards of the Community's regions and bring them closer to those of the richer regions. This is referred to as *real convergence*, to distinguish it from the *nominal convergence* criteria that will have to be met for the launch of the single currency. It is argued that in order to achieve real convergence countries must first achieve the intermediate goal of stabilising exchange rates and equalising prices and costs. In this section we review the broader debate on the likely effects of EMU on the Irish economy.

Trade   The elimination of exchange rate fluctuations should stimulate intra-Community trade and help maintain balance in this trade. The current account balances of all the member states (except Luxembourg) are now relatively small.

Only Greece and Spain are running significant deficits. But this was already true in 1979 (except in Ireland) and it is debatable how much of a stimulus to intra-EC the relative stability of exchange rates since 1979 has been. Between 1979 and 1990 trade between Britain and the rest of the EC grew more rapidly than, for example, trade between France and Germany, despite the volatility of sterling as a non-member of the ERM. The growth of real income has been a more important influence on the volume of trade than the exchange rate system.

EMU will eliminate currency-related transaction costs between member states. It has been estimated that these costs amount to about 1 per cent of Irish GNP. (While the public as a whole will gain from the elimination of these costs, banks and foreign exchange dealers will experience a significant fall in business.) The reduction in transaction costs, the elimination of exchange rate uncertainty and the increase in competition will increase efficiency and raise output. The contentious issue is how these gains will be shared between the member states. The reduction in transactions costs should increase exports from Ireland but it will also increase our imports by making the domestic economy more open to competition. The overall effect on the trade account is ambiguous. Significant imbalances have emerged in intra-ERM trade. For example, between 1986 and 1989 Germany's trade surplus with the ERM countries quadrupled, while France's deficit with the ERM countries increased by over a half and Italy's deficit doubled. The likely net effect of full EMU on Irish trade is far from clear.

Investment and interest rates   A single currency should lead to lower interest rates, particularly in the countries that previously suffered from high inflation and consequently high nominal interest rates. To the extent that it is locally financed, this should lead to higher investment in the regions. Furthermore, lower interest rates will reduce the costs of servicing the national debt, which will benefit Ireland disproportionately because our debt/GDP is second highest only to Italy's. However, what matters are *real* interest rates, and the effect of a currency union on real interest rates is not clear-cut. In chapter 13 we show that high real interest rates have been a consequence of our participation in the ERM.

Monetary policy   Monetary union means that it will no longer be possible for any member state to conduct an independent monetary policy. This represents a surrender of sovereignty from member states to the Community. The Central Bank of Ireland is of the view that the cost of this will not be very high, as is stated in the following passage.

Are the costs of this loss of autonomy (in exchange rates and interest rates) significant? The answer seems to be that while there may be some cost involved, it may not be as great as one might initially expect, since our ability to use our present policy freedom constructively is more limited than might appear to be the case. This is particularly true as regards exchange rate movements. However, our loss of interest rate autonomy may also be more apparent than real since, in practice, our present

338

ability to influence rate movements while maintaining the external value of the currency is quite limited.[8]

In Chapter 14 we review how monetary policy was conducted in Ireland since the 1960s and conclude that it was relatively ineffective and may have entailed serious costs. We would agree, therefore, with the view that surrendering the use of this instrument may therefore entail no costs.

Fiscal policy We have seen that binding rules will be applied to national fiscal policy as a condition for participation in the single currency area in 1997. Furthermore, national governments will be prohibited from borrowing from central banks to finance fiscal deficits. With the complete integration of financial markets and a single currency in the Community these deficits will have to be financed at the prevailing European interest rates. The scope for national fiscal policy will therefore be extremely limited. Moreover, the level of national debt and its distribution between domestic and foreign ownership will further constrain the effectiveness of domestic

Table 11.6
Domestic and foreign debt as a percentage of GDP, 1990

	National debt as a % of GDP	Foreign debt as a % of GDP	Interest by general government % of GDP
Belgium	127.3	19.6	10.9
Denmark	66.4	16.2	7.2
France	46.6	10.0	3.1
Germany	43.6	12.2	8.6
Greece	93.7	n.a.	12.0
Ireland	103.0	34.8	8.4
Italy	93.6	3.2	9.7
Luxembourg	7.3	2.8	0.7
Netherlands	78.3	0.0	5.9
Portugal	68.2	n.a.	8.2
Spain	44.5	n.a.	3.5
UK	42.8	1.4	3.3

Source: *European Economy*, No. 50, December 1991, and Eurostat, *Eurostatistics*, 11, 1991.
n.a. denotes not available.

fiscal policy. High interest payments on the national debt pre-empt tax revenue and limit the scope for a counter-cyclical expenditure. Interest on foreign debt is a claim on export receipts and a leakage from domestic demand. High unemployment leads to lower tax revenues and higher government expenditure on social welfare. Table

11.6 shows that Ireland's national, foreign debt and debt service payments all exceed the EC average. Table 11.8, below, shows that Ireland's unemployment rate is the second highest in the Community. The combination of high debt and unemployment means that the EMU fiscal rules will be particularly constraining in Ireland's case.

Competitiveness of peripheral regions The major worry in regard to the effects of EMU on Ireland is that the completion of the internal market will expose Irish firms to increased competition which they will not be able to withstand. It is feared that the loss of employment as inefficient firms go out of business will not be offset by the expansion of efficient firms and the inflow of new capital to take advantage of the opportunities presented by the unified European market. It is also feared that the completion of the internal market and the introduction of a single currency may encourage foreign firms to engage in takeovers and mergers, leading to the emergence of a small number of very large European firms. The headquarters of these firms are likely to be at the hub of the Community in the area between Berlin, Paris and London and not in peripheral regions such as Ireland. They may tend to direct future investment away from the peripheral regions.

The reasons why firms might choose not to invest in peripheral regions include the high costs of transporting raw materials to the regions and of shipping finished products to the main markets. These costs are raised by poor roads, ports and telecommunications. Location at the centre allows closer contact with suppliers, high-level decision makers, and research and development teams. Finally, labour markets are larger and the supply of highly trained and specialised workers is usually more plentiful at the centre than in peripheral regions.

If EMU speeds up the rate of economic growth in the Community but concentrates activity at the centre, the result is likely to be increased movement of labour and capital from depressed to prosperous regions. This might help to equalise living standards across the Community, but only by shrinking the populations and economies of the peripheral regions.

These arguments and the view that the well-established core regions will benefit disproportionately from EMU have been set up in an Irish context in the National and Economic Social Council (NESC) report on the subject[9] and summarised by the governor of the central bank as follows:

It is quite possible that ... efficiency gains (from EMU) will only be fully realised if *less* production actually occurs in the periphery. The exploitation of economies of scale, in particular, carries with it the danger of a movement of production towards the core. Anyone who doubts the inability of a purely monetary union to deliver convergence of living standards need not look too far to find an example of how weakly they are linked. Ireland had the experience of a century and a half of monetary union with the UK during which time a convergence of living standards did not emerge. As far as one can tell the relationship between Irish and British GDP per head at the dissolution of this link in 1979 was about the same as it was at the beginning of the twentieth century.[10]

340

These pessimistic views of the implications of EMU are disputed by the Commission in its report *One Market, One Money.*[11] The Commission argues that lower tariff barriers will give producers in the regions easier access to the main markets in the centre and offset the negative factors affecting industry on the peripheral. This and the planned increase in transfers to the regions will allow them to benefit fully from EMU. It is also relevant to note that there are *diseconomies* of scale, as well as economies. Some costs (e.g. office, factory and warehouse rents, housing for employees, and wage rates) are higher in the main industrial centres than in the remoter regions. The development of telecommunications and the fall in their cost have reduced the penalty associated with being on the periphery.

It is difficult to predict whether the balance of advantages will lie with the periphery or the established centres. A highly educated labour force, low rental costs, an attractive environment and low crime rates could offset the attractions of locating in the large, densely populated industrial centres. However, a poorly trained labour force, bad telecommunications, inefficient and expensive access transportation, pollution, crime and urban decay would prevent a peripheral region from benefiting from the dynamics of EMU.

Note:

The parallel between the slow convergence of Irish living standards (and the long-run decline of the population) when Ireland was in a monetary union with the United Kingdom and what will happen under the proposed European EMU is flawed. In the period before Ireland gained independence the degree of fiscal federalism in the UK was very small: taxes on income and expenditure were minimal and there were no significant transfer payments until the non-contributory old age pension was introduced in 1908. In the period following Independence, although the currency link with Britain was preserved until 1979, the relationship between the two countries cannot be compared with that between Ireland and the EC.

Table 11.7
The catching up process in the Community

| | GDP per head of population EC average = 100 | | | |
	Spain	Greece	Ireland	Portugal
1975	81.9	57.3	62.7	52.2
1980	74.2	58.1	64.0	55.0
1986	72.8	55.9	63.4	52.5
1991	79.0	52.5	68.9	56.3

Source: Commission of the European Community, Annual Economic Report 1991/92, "Strengthening growth and improving convergence", December 1991.

Convergence of living standards Some light may be shed on the issues raised in the previous section by studying the record since we joined the EC. Table 11.7 shows income per head of population in Spain, Greece, Portugal and Ireland relative to the average of the Community as a whole in selected years since 1975. There was no improvement in Ireland's relative position over the period 1975-86. Clearly, the EC as it has operated in those years did not produce real convergence[12]. Table 11.8 shows GDP per person in each of the twelve EC countries in 1990. Denmark, Germany and Luxembourg are the richest countries and Spain, Ireland, Greece and Portugal the poorest. Average income is over 50 per cent lower in Ireland than in Denmark. However, Ireland, Spain and Portugal all have real growth rates above the EC average. This indicates that some real convergence occurred in recent years. However, in the case of Ireland, we must bear in mind that our GDP figures are inflated by transfer pricing. Moreover, unemployment is also relevant as an indicator of the standard of living. Unfortunately, the improvement in relative income per capita in Ireland has not been accompanied by lower unemployment rates. As Table 11.8 shows, the Irish unemployment rate is the second highest, after Spain, in the EC. Furthermore, Ireland is now the only EC country experiencing net emigration.

Table 11.8
Income per capita in EC countries, 1990

	GDP per capita		Index of real GDP per capita 1980 = 100		Unemployment rate %
	$	1980		1990	
Belgium	19,343	100		119.5	8.1
Denmark	25,466	100		121.7	7.9
France	21,014	100		118.6	9.0
Germany	23,697	100		120.3	5.1
Greece	6,578	100		109.8	7.5
Ireland	12,360	100		132.1	15.6
Italy	18,857	100		122.6	9.8
Luxembourg	23,097	100		137.2	1.6
Netherlands	18,609	100		113.1	8.1
Portugal	5,748	100		123.8	4.6
Spain	12,621	100		128.2	16.1
UK	16,893	100		126.3	6.4
Eur 12					8.4

Source: *European Economy*, No. 50, Dec. 1991.
Note: Change in real GDP is based on constant 1985 prices and constant 1985 exchange rates.

Summary Given that there are no automatic forces operating within EMU to transfer resources to the poorer regions or to regions that experience a localised shock, the conclusion must be that convergence of Irish living standards to the EC average will depend very much on our success in availing of the opportunities presented by the formation of the EMU rather than any mechanisms built into the Maastricht proposals.

These considerations point to the conclusion that national macroeconomic policies will have an increasingly diminished role to play in determining Ireland's economic performance in the years ahead, while the country's competitiveness will play an increasingly important role. As the single European market becomes a reality, exporters and import-competing firms who can maintain or increase competitiveness will be able to expand and increase domestic output, income and employment. However, a loss of competitiveness would have an adverse effect on a whole range of key macroeconomic variables. The determinants of competitiveness in this context will be the productivity and efficiency of the labour force, the cost of inputs, the quality of the country's infrastructure and similar factors.

The net effect of the formation of the EMU on the Irish economy will be a matter for economic historians of the future to assess. In 1992 the choices open to Ireland are very limited. Following the ratification of the Maastricht treaty the EC is moving irreversibly towards a single currency and complete economic and monetary integration, the only uncertainty being how quickly it will reach these goals and how many of the member states will participate in the new arrangements from the start. Ireland is committed to being one of these and this is clearly preferable to the alternative of aiming only at joining at a later stage or opting out of the whole process. Our tactic now must be to try to maximise the size of the Cohesion Fund and our share of it, and to use the money that flows from it to best advantage.

11.10 Conclusion

In this chapter we have discussed:

- The gold standard and the Bretton Woods system

- The Snake and the origins of the EMS

- The evolution of the idea of economic and monetary Union in Europe from the 1950s to the 1990s and the operation of the European Monetary System

- The concept of an optimum currency area

- The cost and benefits of EMU for a country like Ireland

- The trend in relative living standards in the poorer countries of the Community and the prospects for convergence of real living standards following the adoption of a single currency

Notes

1. The account of the gold standard in the text draws the article on "Money" in the *New Encyclopaedia Britannica* (15th edition), which was contributed by Milton Friedman, and on Robert A. Mundell, "Do Exchange Rates Work? Another View", International Monetary Fund, Research Department, WP/91/37, April 1991.

2. J. M. Keynes, "The End of the Gold Standard" in *Essays in Persuasion*, London, Rupert Hart-Davis, 1952. Keynes was visiting Ireland, to give the Finlay Lecture in University College, Dublin, in March 1933 when the news arrived that the dollar's convertibility had been suspended. The lecture was followed by a dinner and some of the best-known wits of Dublin were invited. "The dinner was a total failure. Keynes was called to the telephone in the middle of the meal. When he came back, he said: "You may be interested to know that the United States has just left gold." The short silence that was felt appropriate was broken by [Oliver St John] Gogarty: "Does that matter?" See James Meenan, *George O'Brien: A Biographical Memoir*, Dublin: Gill and Macmillan, 1980, p. 171.

3. See Mundell, *op. cit.*

4. M. Fullerton, "Emus" in Douglas Stewart (ed.) *Poetry in Australia*, Vol. 1, University of California Press, 1965, p. 193.

5. Committee for the Study of Economic and Monetary Union, *Report on Economic and Monetary Union in the European Community*, Office for the Official Publications of the European Communities, 1989, (The Delors Report), foreword.

6. The quotations in the text are from the Delors Report, pp. 17-22.

7. See Robert A. Mundell, "A Theory of Optimum Currency Areas", *American Economic Review*, Vol. 51 (September 1961), pp. 657-65, and Masahiro Kawai, "Optimum Currency Areas", in John Eatwell, Murray Milgate and Peter Newman, *The New Palgrave: A Dictionary of Economics*, London: Macmillan, 1987, Vol. 3, pp. 740-42.

8. M. F. Doyle, "European Monetary Union: The Impact on Ireland", Central Bank of Ireland, *Quarterly Bulletin*, Autumn 1991, p. 42-3.

9. The National Economic and Social Council (NESC) in its report *Ireland in the European Community: Performance, Prospects and Strategy*, No. 88, August 1989, discusses Ireland's prospects in an integrated market at some length (557 pages). It is argued that the gains from market integration are unlikely to be evenly distributed so that regional *divergence* rather than regional *convergence* could take place. However, the report evaluates a number of alternatives for Europe including a customs union, a common market and EMU and concludes that EMU would be the best arrangement provided there is a substantial Community budget which would transfer resources to the regions and ensure real convergence.

10. M. F. Doyle, "Implications of Economic and Monetary Union for Ireland", Central Bank of Ireland, *Annual Report* 1990, p. 86. The reader should also consult M. F. Doyle, "European and Monetary Union: An Irish Perspective" Central Bank of Ireland, *Quarterly Bulletin*, Spring 1992, and T. O'Connell, "Do Regions Naturally Converge or Diverge in an Economic and Monetary Union?", Central Bank of Ireland, *Quarterly Bulletin*, Spring 1992.

11. *One Market, One Money.*

12. This may not be the most relevant way to look at the issue. Few Irish people compare their standard of living with that of a German or a Dane, but all are concerned about the absolute level of unemployment and income in Ireland. The net effect of participation in the EMU could be faster growth and lower unemployment in Ireland than would otherwise be achieved but *without convergence to the standards obtaining in the richer European countries.*

Chapter 12

Macroeconomic Policy in an Open Economy

12.1   Introduction

In this chapter we outline two types of open economy models: the Mundell-Fleming model and the open economy monetary model. The Mundell-Fleming model is a Keynesian-type model that assumes fixed or sticky prices. The open economy monetary model, on the other hand, is a classical-type model that assumes prices are flexible. We use both models to explore the effects of fiscal, monetary and exchange rate policies on output and employment in a small open economy.

In an open economy a key issue is how the policy-maker can achieve simultaneously both full employment (*internal balance*) and balance of payments equilibrium (*external balance*). We explore the policy dilemma that can arise due to conflicts between these objectives. We discuss the effectiveness of devaluation as a means of improving competitiveness and increasing output and employment in an open economy.

12.2   The IS-LM Model and the Balance of Payments

In Figure 12.1 we reproduce the IS-LM diagram developed in Chapter 7. The IS curve shows the combinations of GNP and the interest rate consistent with equilibrium in the goods market. The LM curve, on the other hand, shows the combinations of GNP and the interest rate that give money market equilibrium. At A the two curves intersect and there is, simultaneously, equilibrium in both the goods and money markets.

In the closed economy model of Chapter 7 changes in government expenditure or taxation (fiscal policy) shift the IS curve and changes in the money supply shift the LM curve. In an open economy we have to take account of the fact that net exports (NX = X - M) are an important component of aggregate demand and that the IS curve shifts as NX change. In Chapter 10 we saw that the real exchange rate (E × P/P*), is one of the determinants of NX. (P and P* are domestic and foreign prices respectively.) It follows, therefore, that changes in the real exchange rate affect the

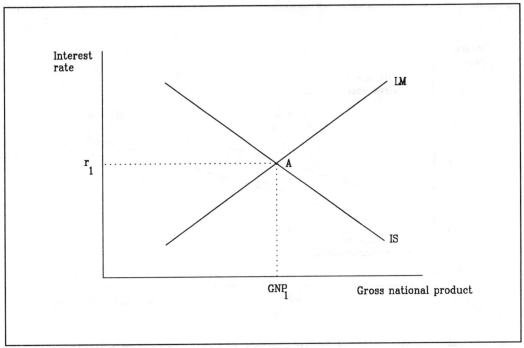

Figure 12.1 IS-LM model

position of the IS curve in an open economy. Similarly, in the closed economy the main influence on the position of the LM curve was the money supply, which in turn was determined by domestic monetary policy. In the open economy, on the other hand, the domestic monetary authorities (the country's central bank) have much less control over the money supply and the LM curve shifts as the Central Bank's external reserves rise due to changes in the balance of payments.

In an open economy macroeconomic policy cannot be exclusively concerned with *internal* targets such as maintaining full employment. Account has also to be taken of *external* goals, such as maintaining a sustainable position in the balance of payments. We now clarify this aspect of macroeconomic policy in an open economy.

External balance Definitions are important here. In Chapter 10 we pointed out that the balance of payments must always "balance" in the sense that the sum of the four sub-accounts must by definition be zero. By "external balance" we mean a situation where the Central Bank does not have to intervene in the foreign exchange market to stabilise the exchange rate. This implies that the sum of the current account and the private capital flows is zero. Overall balance could come about through a large current account deficit that is financed by an equally large private capital inflow. This would imply that the country is becoming increasingly indebted to the rest of the world, a trend that it might not want to continue indefinitely.

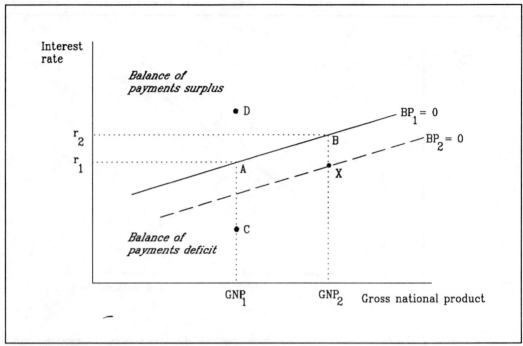

Figure 12.2 Balance of payments equilibrium

In Figure 12.2 we draw a reference line BP = 0 which shows the combinations of GNP and the interest rate which result in the overall balance of payments being zero. (Later in this chapter we shall look at the conditions required to achieve a balance on the current account, that is, NX = 0.) The BP = 0 line slopes upwards because increases in the interest rate and in GNP have opposing effects on the balance of payments. Consider first the effect of an increase in the interest rate. If the exchange rate is fixed, an increase in the domestic interest rate relative to the world rate leads to a capital inflow as investors move funds to the country that offers the highest return. This quickly restores domestic interest rates to the world level. (The rates that are most important from an Irish point of view are in Germany, the UK and the US.)

1. $\uparrow$ r (relative to the world interest rate) $\rightarrow$ $\uparrow$ capital inflows $\rightarrow$ surplus on the capital account of the balance of payments.

On the other hand, an increase in GNP leads to an increase in imports via the marginal propensity to import (MPM) and this results in a deficit on the current account of the balance of payments.

2. $\uparrow$ GNP $\rightarrow$ $\uparrow$ M $\rightarrow$ deficit on the current account of the balance of payments.

348

The BP = 0 line is drawn so that the positive effect of higher interest rates offsets the negative GNP effect and the balance of payments remains in equilibrium. In Figure 12.2, as the economy moves from A to B the interest rate increases from r_1 to r_2 and this leads to a capital account surplus. On the other hand, the increase in GNP from GNP_1 to GNP_2 leads to a current account deficit. If the economy is above the BP = 0 line, at a point such as D in the diagram, there is a balance of payments surplus. If it is below the BP = 0 line, at C for example, there is a balance of payments deficit.

Location of the BP line   The BP = 0 line is drawn for a given level of exports and imports, world interest rates and a fixed exchange rate. The position of the line changes if any of these variables change. An increase in exports or a fall in imports (not brought about by a change in GNP) will shift the BP = 0 line downwards to the right. To see why, suppose that exports increase. The point X in Figure 12.2 is on a lower BP = 0 line. At X the rise in GNP from GNP_1 to GNP_2 has increased imports sufficiently to offset the increase in exports and the balance of payments returns to equilibrium. A fall in world interest rates or an exchange rate depreciation would also shift the BP = 0 line downwards. A fall in exports, a rise in imports (not due to changes in GNP), an increase in world interest rates or an exchange rate appreciation would shift the BP = 0 line upwards to the left.

Slope of the BP line   The slope of the BP = 0 line depends on (1) the degree of capital mobility and (2) the marginal propensity to import (MPM). If capital flows are very sensitive to interest differentials then the BP line will be relatively flat. Only a small change in the interest rate (relative to the world rate) is necessary to attract sufficient capital to compensate for the increased imports due to a given increase in GNP and maintain the balance of payments in equilibrium. If there is *perfect capital mobility*, the BP = 0 line will be horizontal. A small change in the domestic interest rate would lead to unlimited capital inflows or outflows. In this case, only the world interest rate, r^*, is consistent with balance of payments equilibrium whatever the level of GNP. Changes in exports, imports and the exchange rate will *not* shift the BP = 0 line because enough capital will always flow in to finance the current account deficit. On the other hand, if capital flows are restricted by exchange controls the BP = 0 line will be relatively steep. A large change in interest rates would be needed to attract the capital inflows to finance the current account deficit due to a given increase in GNP.

A large MPM means that a given increase in GNP will lead to a relatively large increase in imports and interest rates will have to increase accordingly to compensate, hence the BP = 0 line will be steep.

In general:

If there is a high degree of capital mobility and the MPM is small then the BP line will be relatively flat.

If there is a low degree of capital mobility and the MPM is large then the BP line will be relatively steep.

At the present time the Irish economy is best described by a horizontal BP = 0 line because the degree of capital mobility between Ireland and the rest of the world is very high. It is true that the Irish MPM is relatively large but the increase in imports as GNP rises is likely to be dominated by the effect of an incipient rise in interest rates on the capital account. The BP = 0 line was horizontal in Ireland up to 1979 when the Irish pound was pegged to sterling and capital flowed freely between Ireland and the UK. Between December 1978 and December 1988 exchange controls restricted capital movements between Ireland and other countries. It is possible that during this period the BP = 0 line sloped upwards, allowing the Irish interest rate to deviate from r* (world interest rate). However with the approach of the complete abolition of exchange controls (due by the end of 1992) and the stability of the Irish pound in the EMS in recent years, it is likely that there is now near perfect capital mobility between Ireland and other countries.

Note:
We discuss capital mobility again in Chapter 14 when we discuss interest rate policy in Ireland. We explain how exchange rate expectations as well as interest rates are relevant in determining capital inflows or outflows.

From the foregoing discussion we can see that macroeconomic policy in an open economy has to take account of the situation with regard to the balance of payments as well as trying to achieve internal policy targets. The interaction of external and internal objectives is discussed in detail later in this chapter.

12.3　The Mundell-Fleming Model

Figure 12.3 is a graphical representation of the Mundell-Fleming model.[1] A horizontal BP = 0 reference line is amalgamated with the IS-LM model. At A the IS and LM curves intersect with the BP = 0 line. At this point the goods and money markets and the balance of payments are all in equilibrium. The model is based on several assumptions, which we now discuss.

First, and most important, the Mundell-Fleming model assumes that *the price levels in the domestic country and the rest of the world are constant.* (In the second part of the chapter we introduce an alternative open economy model which assumes flexible prices.) Second, the model assumes that there are no supply constraints curtailing or restricting the growth of real GNP. Third, we ignore "crowding out"

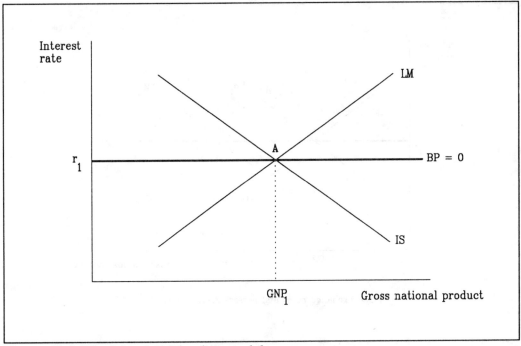

Figure 12.3 The Mundell-Fleming model

and the Ricardian Equivalence effect, which would undermine the effectiveness of fiscal policy in a closed economy. These three assumptions imply that the aggregate supply curve is perfectly horizontal and that changes in real output and employment are determined only by changes in aggregate demand. Fourth, we assume that an expansionary fiscal policy is financed in a non-monetary way and does not result in an increase in the money supply. Finally, we assume perfect capital mobility so that the BP = 0 line is horizontal. (Later in the chapter we show how imperfect capital mobility would alter the conclusions of the model.)

In the next section we use the Mundell-Fleming model to analyse the effects of fiscal and monetary policy on output and the balance of payments when the exchange rate is both fixed and flexible.

In what follows, it is important to bear in mind that under fixed exchange rates the Central Bank intervenes in the foreign exchange market to stabilise the exchange rate and as a result balance of payments deficits or surpluses are reflected in changes in the external reserves, which affect the domestic money supply and shift the LM curve. If, on the other hand, the exchange rate is floating and the Central Bank does not intervene in the foreign exchange market, balance of payments surpluses or deficits result in an appreciation or depreciation of the currency. As we will see, the effect of fiscal and monetary policy on output and employment is very different depending on whether the exchange is fixed or floating.

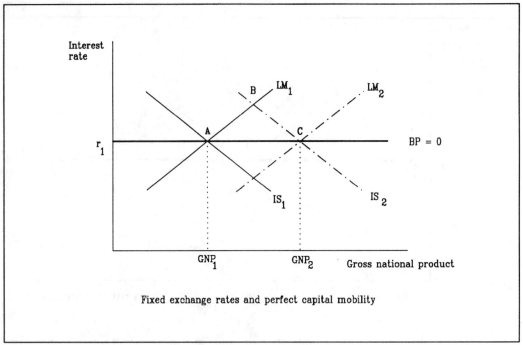

Figure 12.4 Expansionary fiscal policy

Fiscal policy: fixed exchange rates

In Figure 12.4 we show the effect of an increase in government expenditure on output when the exchange rate is fixed. An increase in government expenditure shifts the IS curve outwards from IS_1 to IS_2 and the economy moves from A to B. At B, GNP has increased and there is a balance of payments surplus as the economy is above the $BP = 0$ reference line.

An expansionary fiscal policy results in a balance of payments surplus because:

1. The increase in GNP leads to an increase in imports via the marginal propensity to import and this results in a deficit in the current account of the balance of payments.

$$\uparrow GNP \rightarrow \uparrow M$$

2. The increase in GNP increases the demand for money and therefore the domestic interest rate. This results in a capital inflow and a surplus on the capital account of the balance of payments.

$$\uparrow GNP \rightarrow \uparrow M^d \rightarrow \uparrow r \rightarrow \text{capital inflow}$$

352

Given perfect capital mobility, the second effect dominates the first with the result that there is an overall balance of payments surplus: the deficit in the current account is more than offset by the surplus on the capital account.

Point B in Figure 12.4 is not a final equilibrium. Because the exchange rate is fixed, the Central Bank must intervene in the foreign exchange market to stabilise it following the emergence of a balance of payments surplus. This intervention takes the form of selling Irish pounds and accumulating foreign currencies, which are added to the external reserves. The rise in the external reserves, in turn, increases the money supply and the LM curve shifts outwards from LM1 to LM2. The economy moves from B to C.

Note:
In appendix 1 to Chapter 6 we explained how a change in the external reserves leads to a change in the domestic money supply. If, however, the Central Bank engages in what is called *sterilisation*, changes in the external reserves will not affect the money supply. Sterilisation is discussed in a later chapter. We assume here that the Central Bank does not attempt to sterilise the impact of changes in reserves on the domestic money supply.

At C the domestic interest rate is again equal to the world rate and the overall balance of payments is zero. The current account is in deficit but this is offset by the capital account surplus. The level of GNP has risen as a result of the fiscal expansion. Fiscal policy is therefore effective when the exchange rate is fixed and capital is perfectly mobile. The magnitude of the impact of fiscal policy depends on the slopes of the IS-LM curves, as we discussed in Chapter 7.

Note:
If there is imperfect capital mobility the BP = 0 line will slope upwards. If the degree of capital mobility is such that the BP = 0 line is steeper than the LM curve, the reader can verify that an expansionary fiscal policy will result in a balance of payments deficit. The LM curve will then shift upwards to the left reflecting a fall in the Central Bank's external reserves and the increase in GNP will be smaller than when there was perfect capital mobility. The greater the degree of capital mobility, the more effective is fiscal policy.

Monetary policy: fixed exchange rates

Figure 12.5 shows the effect of an expansionary monetary policy when the exchange rate is fixed. The increase in the money supply shifts the LM curve from LM1 to LM2 and the economy moves from A to B. At B, GNP has increased but the economy is below the BP = 0 line, indicating that there is a balance of payments deficit.

The balance of payments deficit arises for two reasons.

1. The increase in the money supply leads to a fall in the domestic interest rate relative to the world interest rate and this results in a capital outflow and a deficit on the capital account of the balance of payments.

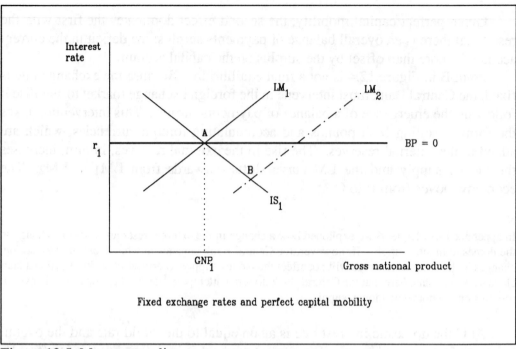

Figure 12.5 Monetary policy

$$\uparrow M^S \rightarrow \quad \downarrow r \quad \text{(relative to the world rate)} \rightarrow \quad \text{capital outflow}$$

2. The increase in GNP leads to an increase in imports (via the marginal propensity to import) and a current account deficit.

$$\uparrow GNP \rightarrow \uparrow M \rightarrow \text{current account deficit}$$

An expansionary monetary policy therefore results in a deficit in both the current and capital accounts of the balance of payments, giving rise to an overall balance of payments deficit.

The economy will not however remain at B. Because the exchange rate is fixed, the Central Bank must intervene in the foreign exchange market to offset the balance of payments deficit. It does this by buying Irish pounds with foreign exchange from the official external reserves. The fall in the reserves results in a contraction in the money supply. This is shown by the backwards shift in the LM curve, which continues until the economy returns to its original position at A. At this point, the domestic interest rate is again equal to the world rate and GNP has returned to its initial level. From this sequence of events we see that when the exchange rate is fixed the money supply is no longer controlled by the Central Bank. (We drew attention to this implication of fixed exchange rates in Chapter 11.)

354

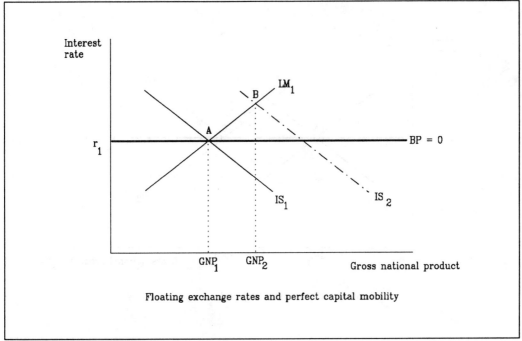

Figure 12.6 Expansionary fiscal policy

Because capital is perfectly mobile, the fall in the interest rate leads to an immediate capital outflow and the money supply and the interest rate quickly return to their original levels. Given the speed with which capital flows out of the country, the interest rate does not remain below the world rate long enough to have any effect on the level of domestic economic activity. Monetary policy is therefore ineffective when the exchange rate is fixed and capital is perfectly mobile.

Note:
The degree of capital mobility does not change the result that monetary policy is ineffective when the exchange rate is fixed. The reader can verify that even if the BP = 0 line is upward sloping, an expansionary monetary policy will again result in a balance of payments deficit and the economy will eventually return to the initial level of output. With imperfect capital mobility this will take longer.

Summary: fixed exchange rates
Our analysis shows that fiscal policy is effective, and monetary policy ineffective, when the exchange rate is fixed and capital is perfectly mobile.

Fiscal policy: floating exchange rates
In Figure 12.6, an expansionary fiscal policy shifts the IS curve outwards from IS_1 to IS_2 and the economy moves from A to B. At B, GNP has increased and there is an overall balance of payments surplus because the capital account surplus (brought

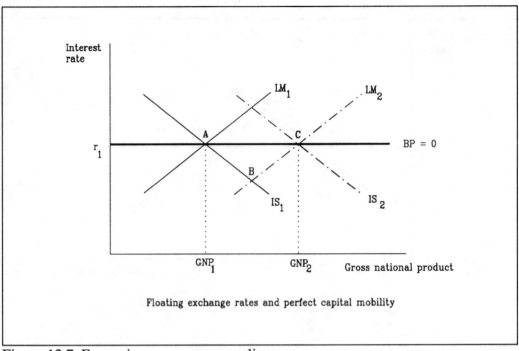

Floating exchange rates and perfect capital mobility

Figure 12.7 Expansionary monetary policy

about by higher interest rates) dominates the current account deficit (due to the increase in GNP).

However, if the exchange rate is floating and the Central Bank does not intervene in the foreign exchange market, the balance of payments surplus will result in exchange rate appreciation. The external reserves and the money supply remain unchanged. The LM curve is therefore not affected. But the rise in the exchange rate reduces exports and increases imports and the IS curve shifts backwards to the left. This process will continue until the economy reverts to point A. The increase in GNP was therefore only temporary. In effect, under floating exchange rates, an expansionary fiscal policy crowds out net exports (exports minus imports) through exchange rate appreciation. Fiscal policy is therefore ineffective when the exchange rate is floating and there is perfect capital mobility.

Note:
If the BP = 0 line is steeper than the LM curve due to imperfect capital mobility, an expansionary fiscal policy will result in an increase in GNP and a balance of payments *deficit*. In this case, the exchange rate depreciates and this results in a further increase in GNP. The reader can verify that under these circumstances fiscal policy will have a greater effect on output and employment than in the fixed exchange rate and perfect capital mobility case. But note that we are assuming there are no supply side constraints and that no domestic inflation follows from the exchange rate depreciation.

Monetary policy: floating exchange rates

Figure 12.7 illustrates the case of an expansionary monetary policy under floating exchange rates with perfect capital mobility. The increase in the money supply shifts the LM curve from LM_1 to LM_2 and the economy moves from point A to point B. At B, GNP has increased and a deficit has emerged on both the current and capital accounts of the balance of payments.

The exchange rate now depreciates and this increases net exports. The IS curve shifts outwards from IS_1 to IS_2 and the economy moves from B to C. GNP again increases and equilibrium is restored to the balance of payments. This implies that monetary policy is very effective when exchange rates are floating, capital is perfectly mobile and there are no supply-side constraints. This result is not changed if the BP = 0 line is upward sloping reflecting imperfect capital mobility.

Summary: floating exchange rates

Under floating exchange rates with perfect capital mobility, monetary policy is very effective and fiscal policy ineffective in terms of achieving increases in output and employment. This is a complete reversal of the conclusions we reached when the exchange rate was fixed. Moreover, under a floating exchange rate regime the effectiveness of monetary policy is not affected by the degree of capital mobility. However, imperfect capital mobility allows fiscal policy to be effective when the exchange rate is floating.

Table 12.1 summarises our conclusions for the fixed and floating exchange rate cases.

Table 12.1
The effect of fiscal and monetary policy on output

| | Exchange rate | |
	Fixed	*Floating*
Monetary policy	(regardless of degree of capital mobility)	
	Ineffective	Effective
Fiscal policy	*Capital mobile*	
	Effective	Ineffective
Fiscal policy	*Capital immobile*	
	Effective	Effective

12.4   Exchange Rate Policy

Devaluation, output and employment

In this section we examine the role of exchange rate policy. To do so, we have to abandon the assumption that the domestic and world price levels are constant.

Recall from the discussion in Chapter 10 that:

Value of Exports $= P_x \times Q_x$
Value of Imports $= P_m \times Q_m$

where P_x and P_m are export and import prices and Q_x and Q_m are the quantities of exports and imports sold. We saw that a devaluation must increase the value of exports $P_x \times Q_x$ measured in domestic currency. Similarly, a devaluation will increase P_m (measured in domestic currency), leading to a fall in Q_m. Provided the elasticity of demand for imports is large enough, the value of imports, $P_m \times Q_m$, measured in domestic currency, will also fall. Thus a devaluation will lead to an improvement in the trade balance and an increase in output and employment. Expenditure is switched from imports to domestically produced goods and services (i.e. exports). In short:

$$\text{Devaluation} \rightarrow \uparrow X \text{ and } \downarrow M \rightarrow \uparrow AD \rightarrow \uparrow GNP \rightarrow \downarrow U$$

Devaluation, by changing the price of exports relative to the price of imports, is an *expenditure switching* policy. However, it should be noted that the improvement in the home trade balance resulting from exchange rate devaluation has to be matched by an increase in some other country's trade deficit. An increase in Irish exports implies a rise in imports in some other country and a fall in our imports implies a drop in someone else's exports. Hence the gain in output and employment at home must be at the expense of a reduction in output and employment in some other country. This gives rise to the accusation that devaluation is a "beggar thy neighbour" policy in that the devaluing country is attempting to "export its unemployment" to other countries.

As happened in the 1930s, countries adversely affected by a devaluation are likely to retaliate by devaluing their currencies in order to restore competitiveness. This can result in a series of "competitive devaluations" with each country devaluing so as to maintain output and employment. If this happens, there will be no net increase in aggregate demand in the countries concerned. It is therefore frequently argued that if a number of countries are suffering from high unemployment, the best policy is not for them to try to solve the problem through competitive devaluations

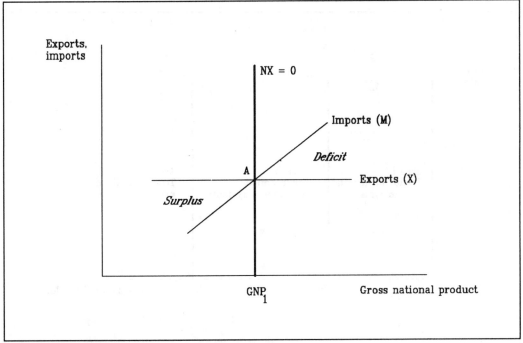

Figure 12.8 Exports, imports and trade balance

but instead to cooperate and implement a coordinated expansion in aggregate demand in all countries. This would result in an overall increase in output and employment.

Devaluation and the trade balance

An expansionary fiscal or monetary policy increases GNP but in doing so creates a *trade* deficit (or reduces a trade surplus). This happens because the increase in GNP leads to an increase in imports via the marginal propensity to import. Devaluation, on the other hand, increases GNP through an improvement in the trade balance. Devaluation is therefore a particularly useful policy instrument if there is a trade deficit and high unemployment. The policy dilemma that can exist between achieving a trade balance and full employment can be resolved by devaluation.

In Figure 12.8 we elaborate on this point by developing an NX = 0 reference line. The analysis is the same as it would be for the BP = 0 with zero capital mobility: we are now concentrating on the balance of trade because capital flows do not enter into aggregate demand. With GNP on the horizontal axis and exports and imports on the vertical axis, the import schedule is shown as sloping upwards. This reflects the fact that imports increase as GNP rises. The slope of this line is determined by the marginal propensity to import (MPM). The larger the MPM the steeper the imports schedule. The export schedule is shown as a horizontal line indicating that changes in GNP do not affect the level of exports, which are determined by aggregate demand in the rest of the world. At GNP_1, exports equal imports and the trade

359

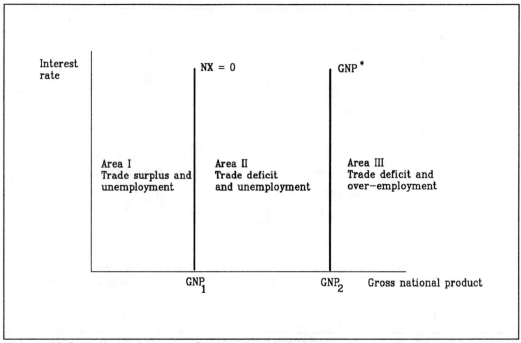

Figure 12.9 Full employment GNP and trade balance

account is balanced. We draw a vertical NX = 0 reference line to indicate this level of GNP. To the right of the NX = 0 line, there is a trade deficit and to the left there is a trade surplus. A devaluation will shift the import schedule down to the right and the export schedule upwards. The NX = 0 line will now shift to the right and the equilibrium level of GNP will move to the right along the horizontal axis.

Figure 12.9 shows an NX = 0 line which corresponds to a trade balance at GNP_1 and a full employment reference line denoted by GNP*. As drawn, the NX = 0 line is situated to the left of the GNP*. The economy can be in area I, II or III. These areas are characterised as follows:

Area I   Trade surplus and unemployment.
Area II   Trade deficit and unemployment.
Area III Trade deficit and over-employment.

If the economy is in area I or III there is no conflict between achieving a trade balance and full employment. For example, if the economy is in area I an expansionary fiscal or monetary policy can be used to reduce unemployment *and* reduce the trade surplus. Similarly, if the economy is in area III a deflationary fiscal or monetary policy can be implemented to reduce over-employment *and* reduce the trade deficit. A dilemma does however arise if the economy is in area II. An expansionary fiscal or monetary policy would aggravate the balance of trade deficit,

360

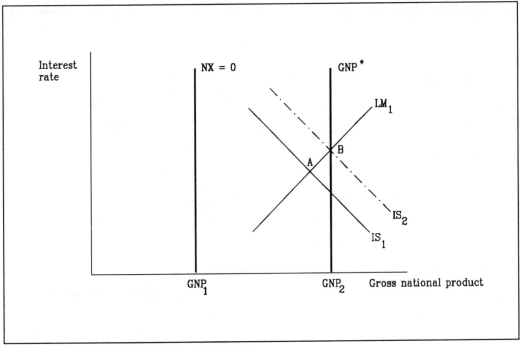

Figure 12.10 Devaluation and unemployment

whilst a contractionary fiscal or monetary policy would aggravate the problem of unemployment. In the early 1980s, when the balance of trade deficit was about 15 per cent of GNP and unemployment was high and rising, the Irish economy was clearly in area II. In the early 1990s, with a large balance of trade surplus and high unemployment, we are in Area I.

The dilemma between the internal and external policy objectives that exists when the economy is in area II can be resolved by introducing an additional policy instrument. Exchange rate policy is such an instrument. A devaluation could be used to resolve the policy dilemma. This is illustrated in Figure 12.10. A devaluation would shift the NX = 0 line towards GNP* and move the IS curve from IS$_1$ to IS$_2$ as NX increases. As a result full employment could be restored while at the same time maintaining a balance in the trade account.

Suppose however the economy is at a point such as A in Figure 12.11, which corresponds to full employment and a trade *deficit*. A devaluation would move the NX = 0 line towards GNP* but because of the shift to the right of the IS curve the economy moves to the point B. At the point B, there is over-full employment and the trade account continues to be in deficit. The reason the trade deficit increases is that the increase in GNP leads to an increase in imports. Overall devaluation should improve a trade account position but the increase in imports associated with the rise in GNP offsets some of the improvement. In this situation a deflationary fiscal or monetary policy is required to move the economy back to GNP*. This example

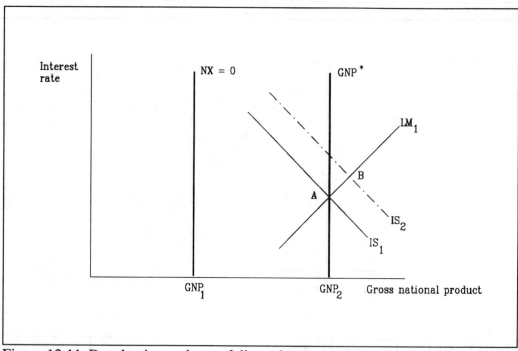

Figure 12.11 Devaluation and over-full employment

shows that if the economy is close to full employment, devaluation will have to be accompanied by an *expenditure reducing* policy if the objectives of internal and external balance are to be achieved simultaneously. Put another way, if the objective of devaluation is simply to improve the trade account without increasing output and employment, an expenditure reducing policy will have to accompany it.

12.5 How Effective is Devaluation as a Policy Instrument?

While a devaluation can increase output and employment in one country, it is not without its risks. The following points should be borne in mind:

- By decreasing P_x and increasing P_m a devaluation causes a deterioration in the terms of trade. The home country must now export more goods and services to import a given amount of goods and services. Thus a devaluation reduces domestic living standards in the short term so as to raise output and employment in the longer run. It is not a "soft option" that restores external balance without domestic sacrifice.

- By increasing import prices, a devaluation increases the domestic prices of imports. As prices rise, some of the competitive gain which exporters and import-competing firms initially enjoyed after the devaluation is eroded.

Eventually workers will seek compensation for the fall in their standard of living caused by the rise in the cost of living. If these claims are conceded, the domestic price level could eventually rise by the same proportion as the exchange rate has fallen, completely offsetting the initial gain in competitiveness. There would be no lasting gain in output and employment. The end result of the devaluation would be a higher price level and a lower exchange rate. It has been argued that in Ireland the benefits from a devaluation are relatively short-lived.[2]

■ Devaluation can result in a vicious cycle of rising inflation and a falling exchange rate. The sequence of events would be as follows: a lax monetary policy leads to a high rate of domestic inflation, which results in an over-valued real exchange rate and calls for a devaluation; the devaluation gives another twist to the inflationary spiral and if the stance of monetary policy is not changed, the underlying rate of inflation will continue to be high and further devaluations will be necessary to restore competitiveness once inflation has eroded the initial gain. When devaluations are frequent people will begin to anticipate them more and more rapidly until domestic prices adjust more or less instantaneously and there is no competitive advantage from the devaluation even in the short run. An inflation-devaluation spiral of this type, which is seen in many Latin American countries today, is very destabilising.

■ A devaluation increases the domestic value of foreign debt. This is an important consideration in Ireland. In August 1986, Ireland's foreign debt stood at approximately IR£9,753 million. Hence the 8 per cent devaluation in August 1986 automatically increased the foreign debt by IR£780 million. Foreign debt service is like an import with zero elasticity of demand. Additional export earnings have to be used to meet the higher debt service bill resulting from the devaluation, and this reduces the chances that the devaluation will improve the balance of payments. Countries with large external debt should therefore be particularly careful about resorting to devaluation.

12.6   Exchange Rates, Purchasing Power Parity and Inflation

In Chapter 10 we introduced the concept of purchasing power parity (PPP). We saw that in a system of floating exchange rates PPP is a theory of exchange rate determination. We shall now show that when exchange rates are fixed, PPP can be used to explain a country's rate of inflation.[3]

PPP relates the price level in one country to that in another via the exchange rate. The strong version of PPP, also referred to as *absolute PPP*, can be written:

(1) $P_{irl} \times E = P_f$

where P_{irl} and P_f are Irish and foreign price levels respectively and E is the nominal exchange rate expressed as the foreign currency price of an Irish pound. If we use the UK as the "rest of the world", we have:

(2) $P_{irl} \times E = P_{uk}$

Absolute PPP implies that the Irish and UK price levels expressed in a common currency will be equal. A reason for believing this is the *law of one price*. That is, the belief that internationally traded goods and services should have the same price in all countries. The operation of this law, in turn, depends on *arbitrage* and *price competition*. Arbitrage occurs when people spot an opportunity of making a profit by buying cheap in one market and selling dear in another. If, for example, shirts were $30 each in New York and £30 in London, and the exchange rate were £1 = $1.80, traders could make a profit by buying in New York and selling in London. If done on a large scale, the increased demand would drive up the New York price and the increased supply would drive down the London price. Arbitrage would thus ensure that the prices in the two centres would converge. Similarly, if two shops in the same street sell the same products, customers will switch their expenditure to the shop with the lower prices. The high price shop will be forced to cut prices or to go out of business. Competition will force a convergence of prices.

Note:
We saw the forces of arbitrage at work between Northern Ireland and the Republic in the 1980s. A whole range of goods, including petrol, drink and electrical appliances, was cheaper in the North than in the South when expressed in a common currency. Much of the discrepancy was due to the higher indirect taxes levied in the Republic. As people switched their expenditure to the northern side of the border, garages and supermarkets in the Republic, unable to cut their prices because of high taxes, went out of business and those in the North expanded. The Minister for Finance, Ray MacSharry, introduced a "48-hour rule" in 1987 to curtail shopping in Northern Ireland. This rule specified that people had to be resident outside the country for at least 48 hours before they could avail of the EC duty free allowances on returning to the Republic. The enforcement of this rule, combined with reductions in indirect taxes on selected items in the Republic, checked the flow of shoppers to the North. In June 1990 the European Court of Justice ruled that the 48-hour rule should be terminated, but in March 1991 the Council of the European Commission issued a directive that a 24-hour rule could be put in its place.

Many factors can weaken the operation of the law of one price. Tariffs and quotas limit the extent of international trade. Transport costs and indirect taxes drive a wedge between prices in different countries. Firms charge different prices in different markets and they do not adjust all their prices as exchange rates change. In fact the evidence against the absolute version of PPP is very strong: one economist concluded after a review of the literature:

the hypothesis that arbitrage quickly equates goods prices internationally has probably been rejected more decisively by empirical evidence that any other hypothesis in the history of economics.[4]

A weaker version of PPP theory may be formulated which expresses equation (2) in terms of rates of change. This version states that the rate of change in the exchange rate must equal the difference between the rates of inflation in the two countries:

(3) $\Delta E = \Delta P_{uk} - \Delta P_{irl}$

Note:
The symbol Δ denotes the *rate* of change so that ΔP_{irl} indicates the Irish inflation rate. (The student can confirm that (3) is implied by (2) for small changes by taking the natural log of (2) and differentiating.) Note that (3) can hold without (2) being valid.

Equation (3) is referred to as the *relative* or weak version of PPP and it states that nominal exchange rates will adjust to offset differentials in inflation rates between countries. If, for example, the rate of inflation in Ireland exceeds the British rate, the sterling price of an Irish pound, E, should fall. This will ensure that there is no tendency for the *gap* between the Irish and British price levels, expressed in a common currency, to widen or narrow.

The reasoning behind PPP applies primarily to internationally traded goods, but it can be extended to the whole economy by arguing that there cannot for long be a divergence between the rates of inflation in the traded and non-traded sectors of an economy. If the prices of one class of goods are rising consistently more rapidly than those of another, the pay and profits of those working in the production of the former would tend to rise more rapidly than that of the rest of the labour force. This trend could not continue indefinitely.

PPP and the real exchange rate Recall from Chapter 10 that the real exchange rate is defined as:

(4) Real exchange rate = $(E \times P_{irl})/P_{uk}$

It can be seen that equation (4) is simply a rearrangement of equation (2). It follows from equation (4) that if PPP holds, the real exchange rate will be *constant*. For example, if E is constant and P_{irl} increases in line with P_{uk}, PPP holds and the real exchange rate is constant.

The upper diagram in Figure 12.12 is a graphical representation of the PPP theory. The Irish price level and the exchange rate are measured on the vertical and horizontal axis respectively. A PPP line is drawn for a constant foreign (UK) price level. At all points on the PPP line the real exchange rate is constant. To see this

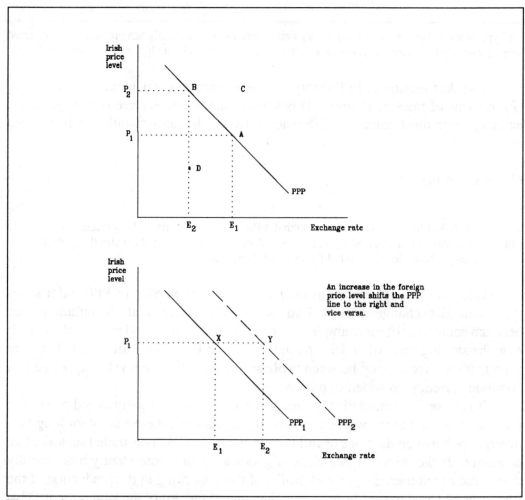

Figure 12.12 PPP: Flexible exchange rate

consider the movement from A to B. The increase in the Irish price level from P_1 to P_2 is exactly matched by a depreciation of the exchange rate from E_1 to E_2. As P_{uk} is constant, the real exchange rate is unchanged between the point A and B.

The real exchange rate is over-valued at all points above the PPP line. For example at the point C in the upper diagram, the Irish price level is higher than that consistent with PPP and the real exchange rate is over-valued. Conversely, the exchange rate is undervalued at all points below the PPP line. At the point D, P_{irl} is lower than the level consistent with PPP so the real exchange rate is undervalued.

An increase in P_{uk} shifts the PPP line out to the right. Conversely, a decrease in P_{uk} shifts the PPP line to the left. For example, in the lower diagram in Figure 12.12, an increase in P_{uk} shifts the PPP line to the right and the economy moves from the point X to the point Y. The nominal exchange rate appreciates from E_1 to

366

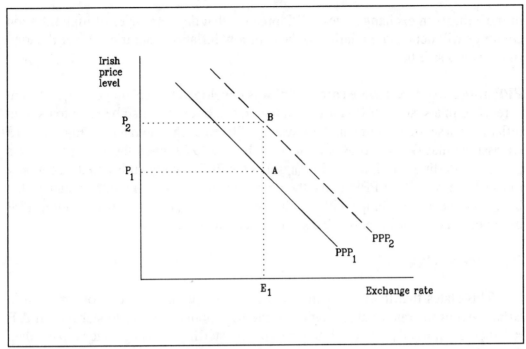

Figure 12.13 PPP: fixed exchange rates

along the horizontal axis and this offsets the rise in P_{uk} so that the real exchange rate is unchanged.

PPP under floating exchange rates According to PPP the most important determinant of the exchange rate is the price level in one country relative to that in the other. Arbitrage and price competition are the mechanisms that force exchange rates to adjust. If Irish prices represent good value at the going exchange rate, exports will boom and imports will slump, leading to a balance of payments surplus and a rise in Irish prices and/or an appreciation of the Irish pound.

The effects of inflation on the exchange rate are very evident in a hyperinflation. For example, in 1921 the dollar/German mark exchange rate was $1 = Mark 270. Following the hyperinflation in Germany, by October 1922 the mark had depreciated to $1 = Mark 25,000 million. As we saw in Chapter 10, massive depreciations occurred in Argentina and Brazil following their recent hyperinflations.

The problem of identifying the equilibrium exchange rate between the world's major currencies has been centre-stage since the collapse of the Bretton Woods system. In a world where the majority of foreign exchange transactions are driven by speculative, rather than trading motives, the real exchange rates of all the major currencies have fluctuated widely. PPP provides an anchor point or benchmark from which to judge whether a currency is under- or over-valued. It is widely used for this purpose by foreign exchange market analysts. It can be used to prepare forecasts of movements in exchange rates. PPP predicts that the currencies of high inflation countries will depreciate relative to those of low inflation countries. Over the long run, this is a safe bet.

PPP under fixed exchange rates PPP was developed to explain how equilibrium is reached in a system of floating exchange rates, but it can also be used to explain inflation in a small economy under a system of fixed exchange rates. In Figure 12.13 we assume that E is fixed as was the case before 1979 when the Irish pound was pegged to sterling. An increase in P_{uk} shifts the PPP line upwards and the economy moves from A to B. If PPP holds, the proportionate rise in P_{irl} will be equal to that in P_{uk} and the real exchange will remain constant. Thus, under these conditions PPP becomes a theory of inflation. To see this, rearrange equation (3) to obtain:

(5) $\Delta P_{irl} = \Delta P_{uk} - \Delta E$

This states that the rate of inflation in Ireland equals the rate of inflation in Britain *minus* the rate of appreciation of the Irish pound relative to sterling. If $\Delta E = 0$, then $\Delta P_{irl} = \Delta P_{uk}$, that is, if the Irish pound/sterling exchange rate is fixed, then the Irish and British inflation rates must be equal. Since Irish firms are in general price-takers with little or no market power, there is no question of Irish inflation causing British inflation. The causation must run in the other direction: Irish inflation is caused by British inflation. In the pre-EMS period, this led to the conclusion that, as long as our pound was pegged to sterling, we would experience the same rate of inflation as Britain.

Despite its theoretical appeal, the evidence in favour of even the looser version of PPP is not very strong. Persistent deviations from PPP have been documented in studies of the behaviour of the major exchange rates and national price levels since floating began in the 1970s. It is possible, however, to rescue PPP by redefining it as a tendency for the real exchange rate to fluctuate around some equilibrium value that is related to national price levels. (In an appendix to this chapter and in Chapter 13 we shall review the evidence relating to PPP for the Irish economy.)

12.7   The Open Economy Monetary Model

Building on the model of PPP developed above, in this section we outline an alternative to the Mundell-Fleming model, which we call the open economy monetary model. This model is essentially an open economy version of the classical model in which prices are assumed to be flexible and the economy quickly reverts back to full employment GNP following a disturbance. In contrast, the Mundell-Fleming model is in the Keynesian mould as it assumes constant or sticky prices and the persistence of output gaps. As we shall see, the open economy

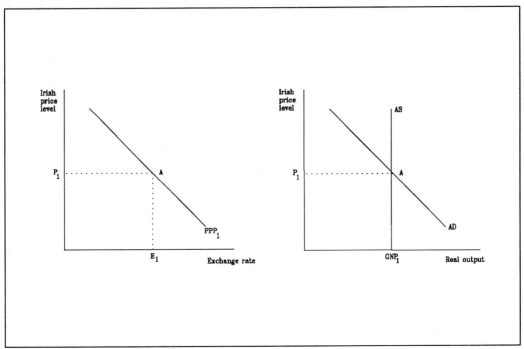

Figure 12.14 The open economy monetary model

monetary model appears to have formed the basis for monetary policy in Ireland in the late 1970s and 1980s and influenced the decision to join the EMS in 1979.

Figure 12.14 provides a graphical representation of the open economy monetary model. The diagram on the far right represents equilibrium in the goods market. The aggregate supply (AS) curve is vertical at full employment GNP. This outcome reflects the assumption that prices are flexible and all markets, including the labour market, clear. If unemployment or over-employment should emerge the real wage consistent with full employment GNP will be quickly restored. Superimposed on this vertical AS curve is the normal downward sloping aggregate demand (AD) curve. (The model can also be expressed in terms of rates of change, with inflation on the vertical axis and the change in the exchange rate and the growth rate in real GNP on the horizontal axis.)

Note:
The model outlined above accords with the neo-classical model given in Chapter 8. As pointed out in Chapter 8, if prices or nominal wages are sticky or there is imperfect information relating to future movement in prices, the AS curve will slope upwards.

The diagram on the left shows a PPP relationship between the Irish pound and sterling. The essence of the monetary model is that the inflation rate is determined in accordance with PPP, while the real economy remains at full employment. We

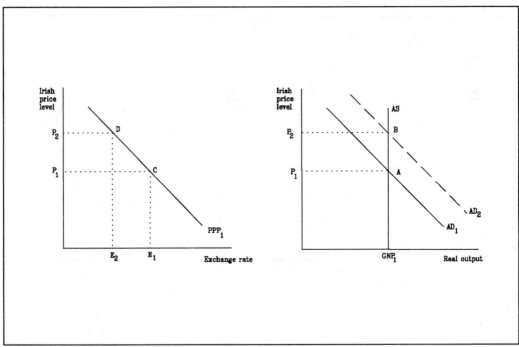

Figure 12.15 Monetary model: flexible exchange rates

now use this model to explore the effects of an expansionary fiscal and monetary policy under floating and fixed exchange rates.

Floating exchange rates

In the right-hand diagram in Figure 12.15, an increase in the money supply shifts the AD curve from AD_1 to AD_2 and the economy moves from A to B. In accordance with the Quantity Theory of Money, the increase in the money supply is matched by a rise in the price level. Any increase in real output is short-lived as workers anticipate the change in prices and demand an increase in nominal wages sufficient to restore the initial level of real wages.

In the left-hand diagram in Figure 12.15 the increase in the price level leads to the same proportionate depreciation of the exchange rate, from E_1 to E_2. This leaves the real exchange rate unchanged. Real output and unemployment are unaffected. Conversely, a decrease in the money supply will lead to an appreciation and leave the real economy unaffected.

An expansionary fiscal policy will have an effect similar to that of an expansionary monetary policy. In so far as the price level increases, it will be matched by a depreciation. However, a high degree of crowding out of investment may lead to a small increase in the price level. (See Chapter 7.)

Thus neither fiscal nor monetary policy is effective under these conditions. However, a supply-side policy which shifts the AS curve to the right (not shown)

370

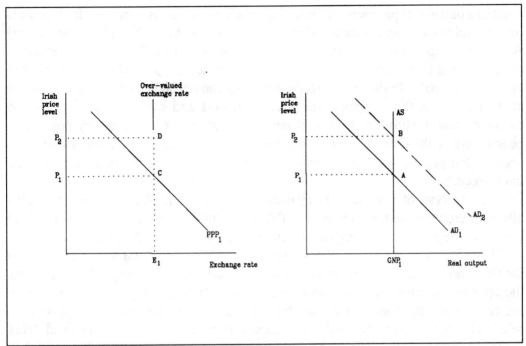

Figure 12.16 Monetary model: fixed exchange rates

would be particularly effective. As the AS curve moves out real output increases and the price level falls. The resulting fall in the price level causes the exchange rate to appreciate. Conversely, a policy or a shock to the economy that moves the AS curve to the left will reduce real output, increase the price level and cause the exchange rate to depreciate.

An increase in the *foreign price level* will shift the PPP line out to the right (not shown). The exchange rate will appreciate along the horizontal axis in the left-hand diagram and real output will be unaffected. Conversely, a decrease in the foreign price level will shift the PPP line downwards. For a constant domestic price level, the exchange rate will depreciate and again real output will be unaffected.

Fixed exchange rates

Figure 12.16 outlines the effect of an expansionary monetary policy according to the open economy monetary model when the exchange rate is fixed. In the goods market (right-hand diagram) the economy moves as before from A to B and the price level increases from P_1 to P_2. In the left-hand diagram, the exchange rate is fixed at E_1 and the economy moves from C to D. At D, which is above the PPP line, the exchange rate is over-valued because the nominal exchange rate has not been allowed to fall to offset the increase in domestic relative to foreign prices.

Consider now how the economy adjusts back towards equilibrium. The over-valued exchange rate makes exports more expensive and imports cheaper, and leads to a balance of payments deficit. This leads to an excess supply of Irish pounds on the foreign exchange market and in order to stabilise the exchange rate the Central Bank must mop this up by selling from its external reserves. The fall in the external reserves leads to a contraction in the domestic money supply, which shifts the AD curve downwards. In Figure 12.16 the economy moves back to its original position at A and C. As this happens, the price level falls and the over-valuation of the exchange rate is eliminated. The effect of the expansionary monetary policy has been to reduce the Central Bank's holdings of external reserves. All other variables, such as the price level, real output and the real and nominal exchange rate are unchanged.

The analysis of an expansionary fiscal policy is similar except that we must also allow for crowding out, which reduces the initial impact of the fiscal expansion. The higher the degree of crowding out the smaller the increase in the price level.

Consider now the effect of a supply-side policy which shifts the AS curve to the right (not shown). (We recommend that the reader redraws the graphs and inserts the appropriate movement of the curves.) A shift to the right in the AS curve increases real output and lowers the price level. As the domestic price level falls relative to the foreign price level, the real exchange rate becomes undervalued. This leads to a balance of payments surplus, an increase in the external reserves and in the domestic money supply. The AD curve shifts out to the right intersecting the new AS curve at the original price level. The overall effect will be to increase real output and employment and increase the Central Bank's external reserves, leaving the price level unchanged.

For the purposes of our discussion of the Irish experience in the EMS, it is particularly important to explore the effects of an increase in the foreign price level. This shifts the PPP line upwards (not shown). The exchange rate will become under-valued and a balance of payments surplus will emerge. The resulting increase in the external reserves will increase the money supply and the AD curve will shift upwards to the right. The effect will be to increase the domestic price level along the vertical axis. The increase in the domestic price level will continue until it equals the original increase in the foreign price level. Overall, the rise in foreign prices leads to an increase in the external reserves and an equal increase in the domestic price level.

12.8   Assessment

Extending the macroeconomic model developed in Chapter 8 to take account of the factors that are relevant in an open economy complicates life considerably. In addition to specifying whether prices and wages are sticky or flexible, it is necessary to spell out assumptions about the exchange rate system (fixed or floating) and the degree of capital mobility. The number of possible combinations of assumptions grows multiplicatively and radically different conclusions about the effectiveness of monetary and fiscal policy follow from different combinations of assumptions. In particular the appropriate way to deal with unemployment in a small open economy is far from clear.

The student may well wish for a "correct" model and a single answer to burning policy issues, but unlike the physical sciences, economics is not a subject in which hard and fast, well-established results have been derived by testing alternative models against the evidence. This is exasperating but it reflects our lack of knowledge about how real economies actually function.

Policy-makers have to make decisions and they use models, explicitly or implicitly, to guide them. The open economy monetary model that we presented in the previous section has been influential in the choice between fixed and floating exchange rate systems. In the next chapter we shall explain the anticipated benefits from Ireland's decision to participate in the EMS in terms of this model and assess whether the outcome lived up to the expectations. The Appendix to the present chapter contains a review of the evidence on PPP in Ireland. As will be clear to the reader, the evidence is not conclusive and a final assessment has yet to be made.

12.9   Conclusion

In this chapter we discussed fiscal, monetary and exchange rate policy in an open economy assuming fixed and flexible prices. Using the Mundell-Fleming model which assumed a fixed price level, we showed that:

- Fiscal policy is effective and monetary policy ineffective when the exchange rate is fixed and there is perfect capital mobility

- If the exchange rate is floating and capital perfectly mobile, fiscal policy is ineffective and monetary policy effective.

We then considered exchange rate policy. We pointed out that:

- Devaluation is an expenditure switching policy that increases output and employment by increasing the trade surplus. However this is a "beggar thy neighbour" policy which could lead to retaliation by other countries

- Devaluation must be accompanied by a deflationary fiscal or monetary policy if the objective is to remove a trade deficit

- There are severe limitations to devaluation as a way of increasing output and employment in a country like Ireland.

Finally, we discussed the open economy monetary model which assumes flexible prices. We discussed:

- How the open economy monetary model builds on purchasing power parity and a vertical AS curve

373

- How changes in fiscal and monetary policy are reflected mainly in changes in price level and the exchange rate

- When exchange rates are fixed, a small open economy imports its rate of inflation from the country to which its currency is pegged

- Even under fixed exchange rates, fiscal and monetary policy have no effect on real output or employment.

  Finally, we drew attention to the fact that

- A clear consensus on the appropriate way of achieving full employment in the face of a balance of payments constraint is lacking.

Notes

1. The model outlined here is known as the Mundell-Fleming model. See J. M. Fleming, "Domestic Financial Policies under Fixed and Floating Exchange Rates", *IMF Staff Papers*, 9, 1962, and R. A. Mundell, "The Appropriate Use of Monetary and Fiscal Policy Under Fixed Exchange Rates", *IMF Staff Papers*, 9, 1962. The reader may also consult R. A. Mundell, *International Economics*, New York: Macmillan, 1968. See also Rudiger Dornbusch, "Expectations and Exchange Rate Dynamics", *Journal of Political Economy*, 84, 1976, and P. J. K. Kouri and M. G. Porter, "International Capital Flows and Portfolio Equilibrium", *Journal of Political Economy*, 82, 1974. Surveys of the literature are given in P. B. Kenen, "Macroeconomic Policy: How the Closed Economy was Opened", in R. W. Jones and P. B. Kenen (eds), *Handbook of International Economics*, Vol. 2, North Holland, 1985, and A. O. Krueger, *Exchange Rate Determination*, Cambridge Surveys of Economic Literature, Cambridge University Press, 1983.

2. Flynn concludes that a 10 per cent devaluation will be fully reflected in an increase in import, output and export prices within one to two years. According to this paper, in the short term devaluation improves the trade balance but in the longer term this gain is eroded as prices rise. J. Flynn, "A Simulation Model of the Effects of Exchange Rate Changes on Inflation and the Trade Balance", Central Bank of Ireland, *Quarterly Bulletin*, 2, 1986.

3. Gustav Cassel first proposed PPP as a way of deciding the appropriate dollar/pound exchange rate after the inflation of the First World War. Other factors affect the equilibrium exchange rate: see J. Peter Neary, "Determinants of the Equilibrium Real Exchange Rate", *American Economic Review*, Vol. 78, March 1988. See also R. Dornbusch, "Purchasing Power Parity", *The New Palgrave: A Dictionary of Economics*, J. Eatwell, M. Milgate and P. Newman (eds), Macmillan Press, 1987, and L. C. Copeland, *Exchange Rates and International Finance*, Addison-Wesley, 1989.

4. John Williamson, *The Open Economy and the World Economy*, New York: Basic Books, 1983, p. 201. Recently, a US firm launched its products on the British market. Checking the advertised British prices against the US catalogue price showed that they were charging the same in pounds as in dollars: a shirt selling for $29.50 in the US was offered for £29.50 in Britain, even though the exchange rate at the time was £1 = $1.80!

Early econometric studies in Ireland supported the view that the Irish price level was determined by the UK price level as suggested by PPP theory.[1]   Oddly enough none of the papers published during this period actually estimated PPP, as for example specified in equation (1) or equation (5).   The estimated equations inevitably included a wage or productivity variable. The basic conclusion, however, was that Irish inflation was more or less equal to UK inflation. We shall show graphically that this is the case in Chapter 13. However, not everyone accepted that this proved that all our inflation was imported. During the 1960s and into the 1970s some economists maintained that a significant proportion of Irish inflation was due to internal factors. For example, an input-output study[2] of the causes of inflation concluded that "wage-push seems to be the major cause of inflation since 1966" and the Central Bank of Ireland commented in its 1973-74 Annual Report:

It is a fallacy, even for the open Irish economy, that inflation is due more to external than to internal causes and that it is beyond our power to curb or control it . . . The fact is . . . that even during 1973 when basic commodity and energy prices soared spectacularly and food prices continued to rise, imported inflation accounted directly for no more than half the rise in Irish retail prices . . .

Recent econometric studies have cast doubt on the ability of PPP theory to account for the short-run (quarterly) movements in Irish prices. Leddin (1988) tested for absolute PPP using quarterly data for both consumer and manufacturing output prices and found that in the short run PPP did not hold between Ireland and the UK and Ireland and Germany.[3] Surprisingly, PPP was found not to hold between Ireland and Britain even during the period of the sterling link. This finding that short-run PPP did not hold is supported by Callan and Fitzgerald (1989).[4] These authors also found that a long-run PPP relationship did hold between Ireland, on the one hand, and a weighted average of both the UK and Germany, on the other, after entry to EMS (1979-87) but not over the longer period 1976-87. They also find that a change took place in the pricing behaviour of Irish firms after 1979. According to these authors', changes in German prices have a stronger effect on Irish inflation than Germany's trade-weight would warrant. In fact, German and UK prices appear to have an equal influence on Irish prices.

Thom (1989) tested if there is a long-run equilibrium between the nominal exchange rate and the foreign/domestic price ratio.[5] His results suggest that PPP has *not* held between Ireland and the UK and the US (the results are not decisive in the case of Germany). More recently, Hodnett and Leddin (1992) have found that a long-run PPP relationship *did* hold between Ireland and the UK from 1945 to 1974 but not at any other time.[6] This study finds that a PPP relationship has been established between Ireland and Germany since 1988. Finally, economists working in the Central Bank of Ireland have produced the following apportionment of the blame for Irish inflation, 1977 to 1985: foreign inflation 52 per cent, domestic demand 26 per cent, exchange rate movements 9 per cent, indirect taxes 3 per cent and "drift" 9 per cent.[7]

In summary, there is a consensus that Irish inflation was strongly influenced by British inflation under the sterling link and that since we joined the EMS the influence of German inflation on the Irish price level has increased. While the short-run behaviour of the Irish price level cannot be explained simply in terms of changes in foreign prices and the exchange rate, there is evidence that in the long run PPP held between Ireland and the UK at certain times and that a PPP relationship now exists between Ireland and Germany.

References

1. See J. Bradley, "Lags in the Transmission of Inflation", *The Economic and Social Review*, Vol. 8 (1977), pp. 149-54; P. T. Geary, "World Prices and the Inflationary Process in a Small Open Economy: the Case of Ireland", *The Economic and Social Review*, Vol. 7, No. 4 (July 1976), pp. 391-400; P. T. Geary, "Lags in the Transmission of Inflation: Some Preliminary Estimates", *The Economic and Social Review*, Vol. 7, No. 4 (July 1976), pp. 383-89; P. T. Geary and C. McCarthy, "Wage and Price Determination in a Labour Exporting Economy: The Case of Ireland", *European Economic Review*, Vol. 8, No. 3 (April 1976), pp. 219-34.

2. R. C. Geary, E. W. Henry and J. L. Pratschke, "The Recent Price Trend in Ireland", *The Economic and Social Review*, April 1970, pp. 345-56.

3. A. Leddin, "Interest and Price Parity: The Irish Experience in the European Monetary System", *The Economic and Social Review*, Vol. 19, No. 3, April 1988.

4. T. Callan and J. FitzGerald, "Price Determination in Ireland: Effects of Changes in Exchange Rates and Exchange Rate Regimes", *The Economic and Social Review*, January 1989, pp. 165-88.

5. R. Thom, "Real Exchange Rates, Co-Integration and Purchasing Power Parity: Irish Experience in the EMS", *The Economic and Social Review*, January 1989, pp. 147-63.

6. D. Hodnett and A. Leddin, "Purchasing Power Parity: Evidence from the Irish Economy", mimeo, University of Limerick, March 1992.

7. T. O'Connell and J. Frain, "Inflation and Exchange Rates: A Further Empirical Analysis", Central Bank of Ireland, Research Paper 1/RT/89, April 1989.

Chapter 13

Exchange Rate Policy in Ireland: From the Sterling link to EMU

13.1 Introduction

In this chapter we examine Irish exchange rate policy and, in particular, the Irish experience in the European Monetary System (EMS).

13.2 Inflation and Exchange Rates pre-EMS

The open economy monetary model presented in the previous chapter predicted that Ireland would experience the same inflation rate as Britain as long as the Irish currency was pegged to sterling. Figure 13.1 shows the trend in the Irish and UK price levels from 1922 to 1991. It is evident that over the half century covered in this chart, the two price levels moved closely together. They diverged significantly only during the Second World War when rationing and price controls were in operation.

The upper panel of Figure 13.2 shows the rates of inflation in Ireland, the UK and Germany over the period 1964-78. It is clear that before 1979 inflation in Ireland and the UK was very similar and much higher than in Germany. The average difference between the annual rate of inflation in Ireland and the UK was only 0.35 per cent compared with a gap of 5.72 per cent between Irish and German inflation.

The analysis presented in Chapter 12 predicts that under a floating exchange rate system the higher inflation in the UK would lead to a fall in the DM/£ exchange rate. It may be seen from the lower panel of Figure 13.2 that in fact the pound fell from DM11 = £1 in 1964 to DM4 = £1 in 1978. (As the Irish pound was rigidly pegged to sterling, these rates apply to both sterling and the Irish pound.)

Early econometric studies used these trends as evidence that Irish inflation was determined by UK inflation, as predicted by the open economy monetary model under fixed exchange rates. However, this view of the causes of Irish inflation was not universally accepted. Some economists maintained that, although much of our inflation was imported, a significant proportion was still "our own fault". (See the discussion of PPP in the appendix to Chapter 12.)

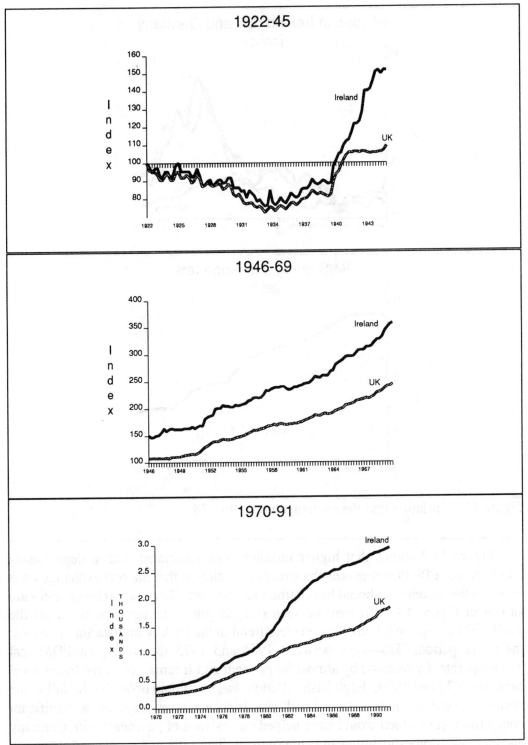

Figure 13.1 Consumer price index, 1922-91

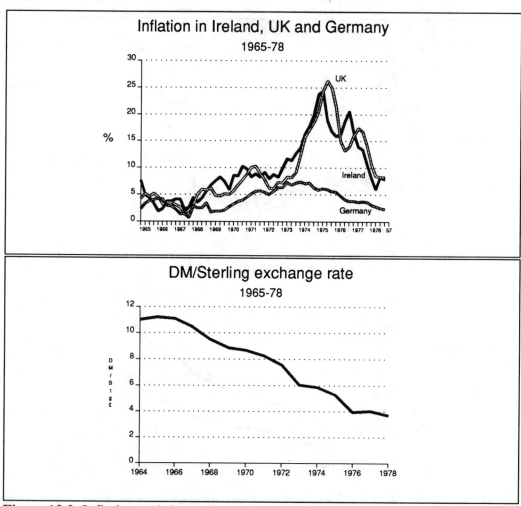

Figure 13.2 Inflation and the exchange rate, 1965-78

Figure 13.2 shows that higher inflation was associated with a depreciating currency, but PPP theory makes the stronger prediction that the real exchange rates between the currencies should have remained constant. The real exchange rates are shown in Figure 13.3. It may be seen that, despite a 10 per cent rise over the 1969-1975 sub-period, there was no clear trend in the Irish pound/sterling rate over the entire period. However, between 1964 and 1973 the Irish pound/DM real exchange rate *depreciated* by almost 30 per cent and it remained at the lower level between 1973 and 1979. High Irish inflation was more than offset by the fall in the nominal exchange rate. As a result the Irish economy enjoyed a significant competitive gain which would have helped our balance of payments with Germany and increased domestic output and employment. This outcome is not consistent with the predictions of PPP.

Figure 13.3 Irish pound real exchange rate, 1964-78

13.3   The Rationale for Joining the EMS

Benefits from EMS entry The Governor of the Central Bank of Ireland justified the decision to join the EMS and break the link with sterling under the following headings:[1]

- The inappropriateness of continuing the sterling link. He believed ". . . that a floating, unstable (but generally depreciating) pound [sterling], and a steady fall in (the relative importance of) Ireland's trade with the UK, had diminished the attractiveness and appropriateness of the link".

- The benefits in terms of a reduction in inflation to be obtained from adherence to a hard currency regime. "It would be prudent to assume that, in the longer run at any rate, membership of the EMS involves a harder currency regime than non-membership."

He also believed that Ireland should make a commitment to a major Community initiative, and that support would be forthcoming in the form of a "transfer of resources" from the Community. It was anticipated that the adjustment would not be instantaneous. In the White Paper published in December 1978 it was stated that:

. . . in the initial period of operation of the EMS, the parity of our currency might be higher than it otherwise would be. This could impose severe strain on Ireland's competitiveness, leading to a possible loss of output and employment (p. 9-10).

This temporary loss of competitiveness was the basis on which the Irish Government sought additional aid from the Community to finance an enlarged programme of infrastructural and industrial development. None the less, it is clear that the authorities expected the disinflation that would follow membership of the ERM would be relatively painless. For example, the Governor of the Central Bank stated:

. . . the Central Bank's calculations suggest that, given sensible domestic policies, the adjustment problems will be manageable and of *relatively short duration*.[2] (italics added)

Similarly an economist with the Central Bank stated:

After a decade of inflation, we can now contemplate the prospect of an *early* and sustained return to inflation rates comfortably back into single figures.[3] (italics added)

The belief that the disinflation would be relatively automatic was quite general at the time. As one author put it:

. . . so long as we are able to maintain a fixed exchange rate with the mark we will in the long run tend to have West Germany's rate of inflation. Indeed, so long as we maintain a fixed exchange rate with any major country with which there is relatively free trade, we will tend in the long-run to have that country's rate of inflation. (The reasoning amounts to little more than recognising that markets do exist.)[4]

These beliefs about the effects of changing our exchange rate peg can be illustrated with the help of the open economy monetary model developed in Chapter 12. To do so, however, we need to extend the model to include two countries in the "rest of the world", namely, the UK and Germany. (We use Germany as a proxy for the countries participating in the narrow band of the EMS exchange rate mechanism (ERM).) In Figure 13.4 the diagram on the right shows equilibrium in the goods market. The centre diagram shows a PPP relationship between Ireland and the UK and the diagram on the left hand shows a similar relationship for Ireland and Germany. The variables E_{dm} and P_{wg} indicate the DM/IR£ exchange rate and the German price level respectively.

The economy is initially at the points A, B and C. A PPP relationship exists between Ireland and both the UK and Germany and the Irish economy is at full employment.

This model provides a reasonable description of the experience of the Irish economy in the period leading up to EMS entry. P_{uk} was rising more rapidly than

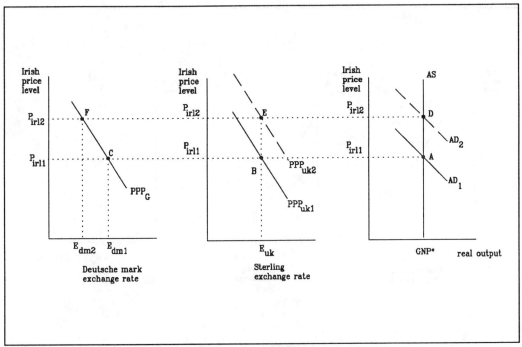

Figure 13.4 Adjustment under the sterling link

P_{wg}. This shifted the PPP_{uk} line upwards while leaving the PPP_{wg} unchanged. Because the Irish pound was pegged to sterling, the rapid inflation in the UK would have initially caused the real exchange rate to fall. The Irish pound would have been temporarily undervalued at B. This would have caused a balance of payments surplus in Ireland, an increase in the external reserves and in the domestic money supply which, in turn, would have shifted the AD curve upwards from AD_1 to AD_2. The economy would have moved from A to D, where the rise in the Irish price level would have matched the rise in the UK price level. By this process the over-valuation of the real exchange rate would have been eliminated and PPP maintained.

In the left-hand diagram, the DM/Irish pound (E_{dm}) exchange rate, and hence the DM/sterling exchange rate, depreciates to compensate for the higher Irish and UK prices and the economy moves from C to F. Overall, the increase in prices in Ireland and the UK is matched by a depreciation of the pound relative to the DM and PPP is maintained between all three countries.

Anticipated benefits from EMS membership The rationale for joining the EMS is depicted in Figure 13.5. In the left-hand panel, E_{dm} is fixed and a PPP relationship is assumed to exist between Ireland and Germany. A rise in the UK price level shifts the PPP line in the middle panel to the right and the Irish pound/sterling exchange rate rises. This is shown as a movement from B to C. Because of the EMS peg the rise in British prices does not affect the Irish price level or cause the Irish pound/DM

383

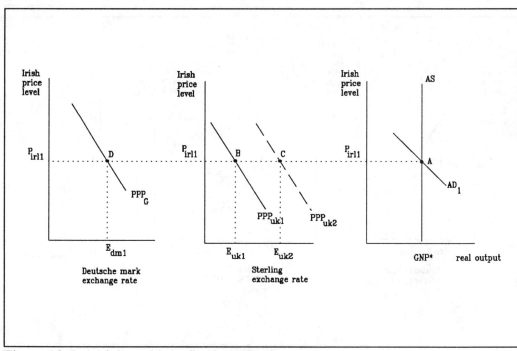

Figure 13.5 Anticipated benefits from EMS entry

exchange rate to change. PPP continues to hold between Ireland and the UK and between Ireland and Germany. The economy remains at full employment (point A in the right-hand panel). By joining the ERM, Ireland has traded rising prices and an exchange rate that was depreciating against the DM and stable against sterling for stable prices and an exchange rate that is stable against the DM and appreciating against sterling.

Adjustment path The hoped-for adjustment process is shown in more detail in Figure 13.6. In the short run, changes in Irish prices could be expected to continue to mirror UK prices. In the left-hand panel, because of the persistence of relatively high inflation in Ireland, the economy moves from A to B. The E_{dm} exchange rate is fixed in the ERM and the Irish price level increases along the vertical axis. At the point B the Irish pound is over-valued relative to the DM. In the centre diagram the economy moves from C to D. The Irish price level increases in line with the UK price level along the vertical axis but, because the DM appreciates relative to sterling, the Irish pound also appreciates. Hence, as E_{uk} rises from E_{uk1} to E_{uk2}, the sterling/Irish pound real exchange rate becomes over-valued at D.

Because the exchange rate is pegged and there is inertia in the rate of inflation, in the short run PPP breaks down between Ireland and the other two countries. The Irish pound will remain over-valued for as long as Irish inflation continues to mirror UK inflation and the E_{dm} exchange rate remains fixed in the EMS. Hence, a

384

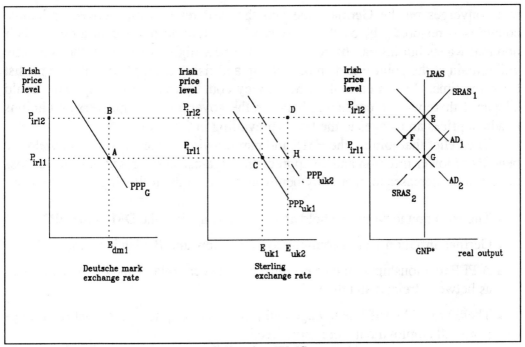

Figure 13.6 Adjustment process following EMS entry

temporarily over-valued exchange rate is part of the adjustment process. In the goods market we assume that the economy moves to a point such as E. To see why the economy moves to this point, the reader should review the discussion in Chapter 12, section 12.7, on how changes in the foreign price level are transmitted to the domestic economy.

To study the adjustment process, we introduce in the right-hand panel of Figure 13.6 a positively sloped short-run AS curves (SRAS). This reflects the view that in the short run some costs and prices are sticky and real output falls as the price level decreases. Now, in the short run, the over-valued real exchange rate results in a trade deficit which reduces the external reserves and the money supply. This shifts the AD curve from AD_1 to AD_2 and moves the economy along $SRAS_1$ from E to F. An output gap emerges and unemployment increases. The output gap also lowers Irish prices (or inflation) below the UK level as convergence towards the German inflation rate begins.

The degree of wage flexibility in the labour market is now of crucial importance. At the point F, *real* wages have increased because the price level has fallen relative to the nominal wage. If workers believe that lower price inflation will be maintained in the future, they will accept a decrease (or a smaller increase) in nominal wages and the real wage consistent with full employment will be restored. A decrease in nominal wages shifts the AS curve from $SRAS_1$ to $SRAS_2$. The economy moves from the point F to the point G and returns to full employment, the Irish inflation rate converges on the German rate and the PPP relationship between all three countries is restored. If, on the other hand, workers do not accept a cut in their nominal wages but instead try to maintain the new higher real wage, the economy will remain at the point F and an output gap and rising unemployment may persist for some time. In this case, the EMS policy could prove very costly. This could happen if there was no consensus between the government, employers and unions to adjust prices and wages to the levels prevailing in Germany.

The belief that joining the EMS and participating in the ERM would yield the benefits of lower inflation and an appreciation against sterling without serious loss of output or increases in unemployment was based on the following assumptions:

- The Irish pound would be held at a fixed rate against the DM in the ERM

- German inflation would continue to remain low and British inflation high

- A PPP relationship would be established between Ireland and Germany as well as between Ireland and the UK

- There would be sufficient wage and price flexibility to ensure that departures from full employment were short-lived.

As we have seen, a PPP relationship did not exist between the UK and Germany in the pre-EMS period. This should have served as a warning against firm predictions about the effects of joining the EMS. Moreover, even though the relationship between the Irish and British rates of inflation was a reasonable approximation to what was predicted by PPP, it was a major leap of faith to assume that by switching the currency peg to the DM a new PPP relationship between Germany and Ireland would quickly become established. Britain had been our main trading partner for centuries, the two banking systems were closely interwoven and there were no barriers to the movement of money between the two countries. In contrast, in 1979 our financial links with the EMS countries were relatively weak and exchange controls hindered their development, while the narrow-band EMS countries as a group accounted for only about one-third of our international trade.[5]

13.4   The Experience in the ERM

On 5 December 1978, the British Government announced that the UK would not participate in the exchange rate mechanism (ERM) of the EMS. The main reason for this decision was the fear that the commitment to a fixed exchange rate would involve loss of control over the domestic money supply, which was believed to be indispensable in the fight against inflation. Ten days later, the Irish Government announced that we would participate in the ERM and imposed exchange controls on movements of funds from Ireland to Britain. This signalled the end of the 153-year-old currency union between Ireland and Britain.

386

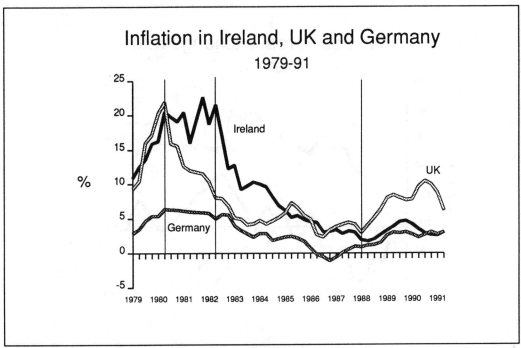

Figure 13.7 Inflation in Ireland, UK and Germany

With the coming into operation of the EMS on 13 March 1979, the Irish authorities were committed to holding the pound within the narrow band of the ERM, but sterling continued to float. If sterling had stayed close to the rate prevailing at the beginning of March 1979 it would have been possible for Ireland both to maintain the sterling link and participate in the ERM. However, during March, sterling strengthened sharply and it proved impossible for Ireland to ride both horses simultaneously. The actual break with sterling came on 30 March 1979, when the rise of sterling relative to the European currencies forced Ireland to choose between leaving the ERM or breaking the sterling link. We stayed with the ERM and for the first time since the Napoleonic wars the Irish pound and sterling diverged in value. Furthermore, for the first time ever Northern Ireland and the Republic were separated by an exchange rate.

Note:
One of the witnesses to the Banking Commission (1934-38) claimed that there were only two catastrophes that Ireland had been spared, earthquakes and an exchange rate. We got an exchange rate with sterling in March 1979. Five years later, on the morning of 19 July 1984, an earthquake measuring 5.4 on the Richter scale was recorded in Dublin!

Inflation Figure 13.7 shows the behaviour of Irish, UK and German inflation (based on the consumer price index) in the years following the launch of the EMS. The differential between the annual rate of inflation in Ireland and Germany *increased*

387

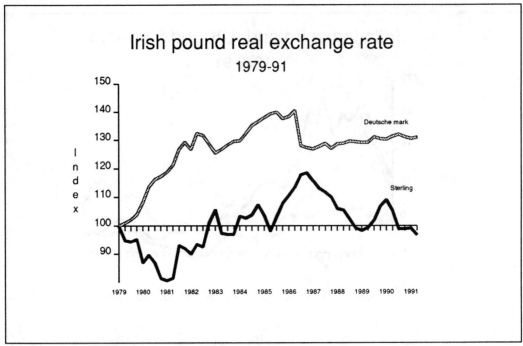

Figure 13.8 Irish pound real exchange rates

to 10.25 per cent in 1980. During the next two years Irish inflation remained relatively high while UK inflation *declined* towards the lower German rate. A significant gap emerged between Irish and UK inflation and the gap between Ireland and Germany remained as high as ever. Thus there was no tendency for Irish inflation to converge to the German level during the first three years of membership of the ERM and a gap opened up between Irish and British inflation which had never previously arisen.

After mid-1982 the Irish rate of inflation fell and the gap between Irish and German inflation gradually narrowed. By the third quarter of 1990 Irish inflation had fallen to the German level. However, in addition to participation in the EMS, other factors contributed to this development. These included a deflationary fiscal policy, an unprecedented rise in unemployment, and declining world oil prices. It is difficult to disentangle the contribution of individual factors to the Irish disinflation.

Interest rates The behaviour of interest rates following our entry into the ERM was similar to that of the rate inflation, with convergence to the lower German rates only becoming apparent towards the end of the 1980s. A fuller discussion of these developments in provided in Chapter 14.

The real exchange rate It was expected that the Irish pound would become temporarily over-valued relative to sterling and the DM following the decision to join the ERM. Figure 13.8 shows the real exchange rate of the Irish pound against the DM and sterling since the launch of the EMS, and Table 13.1 shows the real exchange rate against selected currencies in 1979, 1986 and 1991 (see also the data appendix to Chapter 10).

Between 1979 and 1986 there was a significant appreciation of the Irish pound against all the ERM currencies, the most pronounced being the 58 per cent real appreciation against the Belgian franc. Between 1979 and 1986 inflation remained so much higher in Ireland than in Germany that the DM/IR£ real exchange rate *appreciated* by almost 40 per cent despite a 30 per cent *fall* in the nominal exchange rate. This contrasts with the 25 per cent depreciation of the real DM/IR£ exchange rate over the period 1964-79. Moreover, the sizeable devaluation of 1986 only restored about one-third of the competitive loss of the previous six-year period. There has been no tendency for the real DM/IR£ exchange rate to return to the 1979 level. Relative to sterling, the Irish pound real exchange rate fell between the start of the EMS and the middle of 1981. This was followed by a long period, from 1981 to mid-1986, when the sterling real exchange rate rose significantly. After the devaluation of 1986 and the fall in Irish inflation relative to the UK, competitiveness with Britain has improved markedly, as is shown by the fall in the real exchange rate.

Table 13.1
Change in the Irish pound real exchange rate relative to selected currencies

	1979	1986	1991
Belgium	100	158	144
Netherlands	100	147	141
Germany	100	140	131
Denmark	100	147	130
France	100	136	127
US	100	100	105
Japan	100	147	100
UK	100	113	97
Italy	100	109	93
Weighted average	100	119	110

Source: Derived using consumer prices obtained from the OECD, *Main Economic Indicators* and nominal exchange rates obtained from the Central Bank of Ireland, *Quarterly Bulletin*.

The real trade-weighted exchange rate remained roughly unchanged during the first two years of membership of the EMS, the rise against the DM being offset by the decline against sterling, but it rose by 19 per cent between 1981 and mid-1986 due to the weakness of sterling. The devaluation of mid-1986 offset only half of this so that in mid-1991 the index was still 10 per cent above its level in 1979.

Note:
Given the stability of the real DM/IR£ exchange rate since 1987, it is tempting to choose this date as the base from which to monitor movements in competitiveness. To do so would entail ignoring the competitive loss that occurred in the period 1979-86. However, to restore the 1979 situation without another devaluation (which is now virtually precluded) would involve achieving a lower inflation rate than Germany for a number of years. Some progress was made in this direction in 1991, but the loss of competitiveness during the early years of our participation in the ERM have not yet been fully made up for.

13.5 Was there a Credibility Bonus?

The evaluation of Ireland's experience in the EMS forms part of a wider literature on the effects of the System. At the international level evidence is mixed.[6] In the following sections we look at several types of evidence on the question of whether there was a credibility bonus in Ireland.

The costs of disinflation

Different countries adopted different strategies to adjust to the inflation and recession of the late 1970s. In the UK the Thatcher government opted to curb inflation by controlling the money supply rather than by participating in the ERM. UK inflation fell from 18 per cent in 1980 to 4.5 per cent in 1983, but the cost of this disinflation in terms of lost output and unemployment was very considerable. Real output fell by nearly 3 per cent in the two years 1981 and 1982 and unemployment increased from 1.1 million in 1979 to 3 million in 1984. In Ireland it was hoped that participation in the ERM would confer a *credibility bonus* and help us to reduce inflation at minimum cost in terms of lost output and increased unemployment. This would have taken the form of rapid adjustment of wage and price increases to the rate consistent with maintaining a fixed exchange rate with the other countries in the narrow band of the ERM.

To see how this would work, bear in mind that the speed at which an economy returns to full employment after an adverse shock depends on how quickly firms reduce the rate of increase in output prices and workers reduce the rate of increase in nominal wage demands. If firms and workers believed in the government's commitment to the ERM, they would have immediately moderated their price increases and wage demands in anticipation of a rapid disinflation. The adjustment costs would have been small. (In terms of Figure 13.6, the movement from the point F to G would happen very quickly.) On the other hand, if the EMS policy lacked credibility, adjustment back to full employment would depend on the gradual operation of high unemployment on wage and price expectations and the deflationary effects of an over-valued exchange rate working their way through the economy.

These forces would take time to operate and the persistent output gap would prove costly in terms of unemployment. Hence, the success of the policy of joining the ERM depended very much on the credibility of the commitment to maintaining a fixed exchange rate.

Evidence that membership of the ERM did not bestow an immediate credibility bonus is provided by the level of the wage demands made in the early 1980s. In April 1979 the Central Bank of Ireland commented:

The industrial relations situation does not appear to have adjusted yet to the changed circumstances implicit in our adherence to the EMS. There have been several pay claims in excess of 20 per cent and some union leaders have suggested that 15 per cent would be an appropriate minimum. Such high settlements do not recommend themselves in a situation where *price inflation seems likely to decelerate well into single figures fairly quickly.*[7] [italics added]

Obviously the social partners did not share the Bank's view of the speed with which inflation would fall.

By the end of the 1980s Irish inflation had declined to under 3 per cent, compared with over 17 per cent at the start of the decade. However, inflation subsided earlier in the UK, which was not participating in the ERM. Moreover, the rise in unemployment in Ireland, from 8 per cent when the EMS was launched to over 18 per cent by the mid-1980s, was proportionally much the same as in Britain (from 5 per cent to 11 per cent). Thus neither the speed with which inflation fell nor the cost in terms of higher unemployment suggest that there was a credibility bonus from participating in the ERM. Of course, this is not conclusive evidence that there was no credibility bonus. Part of the rise in Irish unemployment was due to the increase in the labour force following the reduction in emigration as unemployment rose in Britain. Outside the ERM, Ireland might have experienced much greater difficulty in curbing inflation. However, the rise in the real exchange rate after 1979 was a consequence of adhering to the ERM during a period when our rate of inflation was still relatively high. The resultant loss of competitiveness contributed to the rise in unemployment,[8] but had only a limited effect in moderating the rate of wage inflation (see Chapter 9). The persistence of the higher real exchange rate for the Irish pound suggests that the model presented earlier in this chapter, which was the one underpinning our decision to participate in the ERM, may not have been appropriate for short-run policy analysis in Ireland.

The yield curve

Further evidence of the failure of membership of the ERM to bestow an immediate credibility bonus is provided by the behaviour of the *yield curve* over the period since 1979. Recall from Chapter 7 that the public holds bonds in order to obtain a yield. The yield on bonds of different *maturities* varies. Short-dated bonds, such as exchequer bills, need not pay the same yield as medium- or long-dated securities. If investors expect interest rates to increase in the future, bonds with long maturities will have to pay higher yields than those with short maturities in order to entice investors to purchase them. A graph showing yields on the vertical axis and maturities (from short to long) on the horizontal axis is called the *yield curve*. The yield curve reflects the *term structure* of interest rates. If longer-dated maturities have higher yields than short-dated ones, the yield curve will be positively sloped. This is considered the normal situation, because there is always some risk that the rate of inflation will rise over the longer run.

Note
To see why expectations of higher inflation result in a positively sloped yield curve, consider two investment strategies. Strategy A involves investing in a two-year government bond. In Strategy B funds are invested in a one-year government bond and then re-invested ("rolled over") for another year. The *expected* yields from strategy A and strategy B should be the same. If today the yield on a one-year bond is 7 per cent and on a two-year bond 8 per cent, then investors must expect that one year from now, when under Strategy B the time comes to buy the second one-year bond, the yield on one-year bonds will have risen to 9 per cent. This results in an upward sloping yield curve. A downward sloping yield curve suggests that interest rates are expected to fall in the future.[9]

Table 13.2 shows the yields on a range of Irish government stock in 1988 and 1989. It can be seen that in November 1988 the yield curve had an inverted U shape: the yield on a one-year bond was higher than that on a six-month bond, but yields on higher maturities were lower. In October 1989 yields were lower the longer the maturity, that is the yield curve was inverted or negatively sloped at all maturities.

Table 13.2
Irish government securities' yields: per cent per annum

Maturity	Yield November 1988	Yield October 1989
6 month	8.33	10.95
1 year	8.81	10.30
5 years	8.68	9.63
10 years	7.97	9.20
20 years	7.62	8.73

Source: Department of Finance

The slope of the yield curve provides information on the public's expectations about inflation. Throughout the 1970s Irish interest rates were consistently above German interest rates. One of the anticipated benefits of EMS membership was that Irish interest rates, in line with inflation, would converge to the lower German rates. Hence, if the EMS policy were credible, the expectation of lower interest rates should

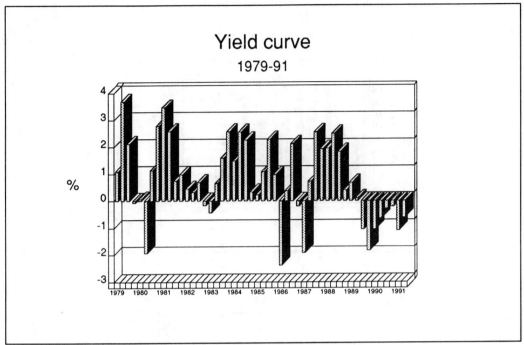

Figure 13.9 Long minus short interest rate differential

have led to a negatively sloped yield curve. The yield curve can be summarised by plotting the difference between long and short yields.

(1) X_t = long yield$_t$ - short yield$_t$

(Subscripts refer to the year.) If X_t is positive, the yield curve is upward sloping and interest rates are expected to rise. Conversely, if X_t is negative, interest rates are expected to decline. Figure 13.9 shows X_t for each quarter over the period 1979-91. Up to 1988, X_t was, with the exception of three quarters, either negligible or positive: the yield curve was either flat or positively sloped. Thus over the period 1979-88 the market expected interest rates either to remain unchanged or to rise. This indicates that investors did not believe that a sharp disinflation would follow from entry into the ERM. Only after 1988 did long rates fall below short rates. This was a clear indication of investors at last revising their expectations of nominal interest rates (and inflation) downward.

Capital flight

The public's confidence in the government's management of the economy can be gauged by flows of private capital into or out of the country. Anticipation of higher inflation and a loss of confidence in the currency will lead to a movement of funds out of the country, that is *capital flight*. To minimise these flows the government

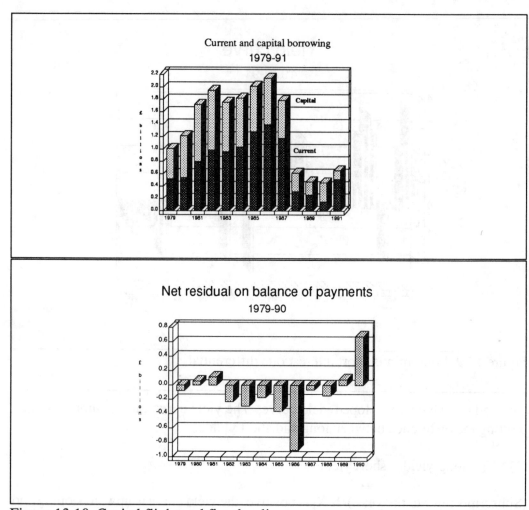

Figure 13.10 Capital flight and fiscal policy

imposed exchange controls on the movement of funds between Ireland and the UK following our entry into the EMS. (They already existed between Ireland and the rest of the world.) However, such measures are never watertight. As we explained in Chapter 10 the residual in the balance of payments reflects unrecorded flows across the foreign exchanges and tends to be dominated by illicit private capital flows. This residual rose to nearly £1 billion (equivalent to 6 per cent of GNP) in 1986, probably largely due to capital flight as investors contravened the exchange controls and moved money out of Ireland. This reflected a loss of confidence in the currency and a lack of credibility in the government's commitment to holding the value of the Irish pound in the ERM in the light of its continued failure to bring the public finances under control. (The weakness of sterling after 1983 aggravated the problem.) After 1986, following the devaluation of the Irish pound in the ERM and when a determination to restore order to the public finances became evident, capital flight subsided and by the end of the decade there was a net unexplained inflow across the foreign exchange (capital reflux), and even though exchange controls were relaxed there was no rush to move money out of Ireland. In Figure 13.10 we show the net residual on the balance of payments and the stance of fiscal policy (as measured by the exchequer borrowing requirement). The clear correlation between the two variables suggests the role of changes in the stance of fiscal policy, rather than membership of the EMS, in restoring confidence in the Irish economy among the financial community.

Assessment

The evidence does not support the view that EMS entry conferred a credibility bonus on Irish economic policy in the period up to 1986. Ireland's inflation rate did not converge rapidly to the German inflation rate. The Irish pound/EMS real exchange rate rose and remained above its 1979 level. The yield curve did not become inverted. There was evidence of large scale capital flight. None of these developments was consistent with the anticipated benefits of our participation in the ERM.

Studies of the Irish experience in the EMS The Irish experience in the EMS has attracted considerable attention and study. Unfortunately, no consensus has emerged from these studies. For example, Kremers concluded:

Ireland's disinflation policy has derived credibility from its participation in the exchange rate mechanism of the EMS. . . . Upon entry into the ERM (inflation) expectations soon reflected the expected price behaviour of ERM partners, and competitiveness became an important determinant of expected inflation in Ireland. *The process of gaining credibility seems to have taken place in various stages throughout the period 1979-82.*[10] [italics added]

While Kremers's study is based on rigorous econometric testing, he does not confront the issue of the adjustment of the Irish economy and the persistence of high unemployment in the wake of the disinflation of the 1980s. Dornbusch explores these issues and concludes that there was no credibility bonus:

A policy that uses a fixed exchange rate to disinflate and that at the same time requires fiscal consolidation can easily run into difficulties. The fixed exchange-rate policy stands in the way of a gain in competitiveness and in fact easily becomes a policy of over-valuation. The over-valued currency then needs to be defended by high real interest rates. The combination of budget cutting, high real interest rates and an overly strong currency creates unemployment on each score. There is no offsetting crowding-in mechanism unless money wages are strongly flexible downward or productivity growth is high. Neither was the case in Ireland and hence the country is locked into a high unemployment and high debt trap.

and

EMS membership has been portrayed as an important means of reducing the costs of disinflation. *We have seen that there is no evidence of such a credibility bonus from EMS membership . . .* Irish unemployment has increased sharply and remains stubbornly high: half the inflow into the labour force emigrates and the other half becomes unemployed! That experience is sharply at odds with the new classical model of the labour market . . . A major real depreciation at the outset of the program would provide the required offset to the budget cutting.[11] [italics added]

From this review of recent research we can at least conclude that the *a priori* economic theorising that was the main basis on which policy could be formulated in 1979 provided a poor guide to the effects of the major initiative that was undertaken. The models that were applied lacked realism and little empirical testing had been undertaken before they were used for predictive purposes. Unfortunately, the research that has been conducted on the experience since 1979 does not inspire confidence in the ability of economists, even when the evidence is in, to adjudicate between alternative models.

13.6   Factors Undermining Credibility

Several factors contributed to the disparity between the expected effects of membership of EMS and the outcome during the first half of the 1980s.

Fiscal and monetary policy   The failure of participation in the ERM to deliver the hoped-for benefits in terms of reduced inflation and interest rates until the second half of the 1980s was due above all to the inconsistency between the fiscal and monetary policies pursued during the years 1979-82 and the declared intention of bringing inflation down to German levels. The level of borrowing and the growth of debt during this period were incompatible with the declared goal of maintaining a fixed exchange rate with the low inflation countries of Europe and undermined the credibility of the strategy of our participation in the ERM. As we saw in Chapter 5, despite the belated reversal of policy in 1982, the level of debt and debt service continued to rise relative to GNP until 1986. By then discussion was rife of a deterioration in Ireland's international credit rating. If Ireland could not continue to borrow abroad, or could only do so at penal interest rates, the external reserves would have been rapidly depleted and maintaining the exchange rate within the ERM would have become impossible. These uncertainties undermined any credibility the government might have otherwise gained by participation in the EMS.

Exchange rate policy in the EMS   The benefits that were expected to follow from participation in the ERM depended on the credibility of the government's commitment to maintaining a fixed exchange rate with the low inflation DM in the face of temporary adjustment costs such as rising unemployment. As we saw in Chapter 11, however, during the early years of the operation of the EMS there were frequent currency realignments, usually involving a revaluation of the DM and a devaluation of the French franc and other weak currencies. Irish policy during the early years of the EMS was to "go through the middle" during realignments. We

396

resisted the opportunity to devalue at these realignments and our nominal exchange rate remained very stable against the average of the narrow-band EMS currencies until 1983. However, there was a significant fall in the value of the nominal Irish pound relative to the DM, which was the strongest currency in the group. (See the charts of the nominal exchange rate in Chapter 10.) The Irish pound was, however, devalued on two occasions, in 1983 and 1986. In this section we discuss briefly the reasons for these devaluations.

Reasons for the 1983 and 1986 devaluations During the first seven years of the operation of the EMS the Irish situation was anomalous. Our exchange rate was pegged to the currencies that participated in the ERM, yet they accounted for less than one-third of our total trade, whereas the UK, which remained outside the ERM, accounted for about 40 per cent of our trade. It is most unusual for a country to peg its currency to a group of currencies that account for such a small proportion of its trade and to float against its main trading partner.
Recall from Chapter 12 the real exchange rate:

(2) $(P_{irl} \times E)/P_{uk}$

Rearranging

(3) $E = P_{uk}/P_{irl}$

It is possible to illustrate the competitive position of the Irish economy *vis-à-vis* the UK by plotting separately the nominal exchange rate, E, and the price ratio, P_{uk}/P_{irl}. This presentation has the advantage of highlighting the dynamics of the real exchange rate. If these two series move together, the real exchange rate is constant. If P_{irl} increases faster than P_{uk}, the price ratio line will slope downwards. The exchange rate should now fall by an equal amount to compensate for this. If this does not happen there is a competitive loss. Hence if the Stg£/IR£ line rises above the P_{uk}/P_{irl} there is a loss of competitiveness and vice versa.
Figure 13.11 shows that during the first three years of EMS membership the Irish economy gained a competitive advantage relative to the UK. However this was reversed in 1983 and again in 1985-88. Consistent with the trend in the real exchange rate shown in Figure 13.8, the competitive gain in the late 1980s was more or less removed by a weakening of sterling in 1991.
The increase in the Irish pound exchange rate towards STG£0.90 = IR£1 reduced Irish competitiveness and forced a 3 per cent devaluation of the Irish pound in March 1983. A similar situation recurred in 1986. The Irish pound rose from STG£0.79 in February 1985 to STG£0.95 in July 1986. At the same time the dollar fell relative to the ERM currencies. The result was that our trade-weighted (effective) exchange rate index rose by 12 per cent in just over a year. It was against this background,

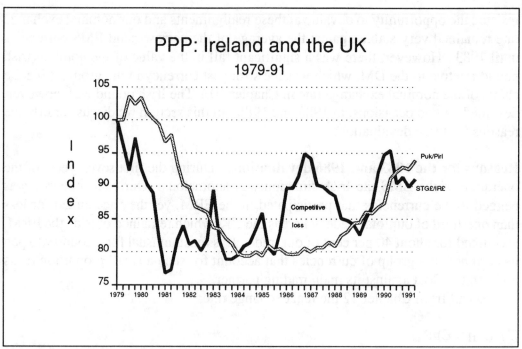

Figure 13.11 Competitiveness: Ireland and the UK

and particularly the growing loss of price competitiveness in the British market, that the decision to devalue the Irish pound by 8 per cent within the ERM was taken in August 1986. This was the largest devaluation of any currency in the ERM since its formation in 1979. It was reluctantly undertaken by the Irish authorities as a means of reconciling our participation in the ERM with the non-participation of our main trading partner, Britain.

The devaluation could have undermined the credibility of our commitment to the ERM. It gave a signal that if the Irish pound rose above STG£0.95 the authorities might devalue again. However, since August 1986 the Irish pound/DM exchange rate has remained within a very narrow range in the region of IR£1 = DM2.67. Maintaining this rate has been facilitated by the fact that during 1987 and 1988 sterling was "shadowing" the DM, that is, unofficially pegged in the range STG£1 = DM2.94 to DM3.00. (If sterling is pegged to the DM, then the STG£/IR£ exchange rate is more or less fixed through Ireland's adherence to the ERM.)

The devaluation of 1986 showed how important the sterling exchange rate remained to Ireland despite our adherence to the ERM. We had clearly not played the game according to the rules of the model outlined above and hence could not expect to enjoy the benefits predicted by it.

Note:
The sterling/DM exchange rate eventually proved unsustainable due to the excessive monetary

expansion that occurred in the last years of the Thatcher government, and by December 1989 sterling had fallen to DM2.80. This depreciation lead to pressure for sterling to formally join the ERM. Mrs Thatcher, however, remained entrenched in her view, stated at the Madrid summit in June 1989, that sterling would participate "only when the time is right". In this she was supported by her unofficial economic adviser, Professor Alan Walters. Disagreement on this issue eventually led to the resignation of the Chancellor of the Exchequer, Nigel Lawson, in October 1989. Mrs Thatcher finally brought sterling into the ERM, albeit only into the wide (6 per cent) band, on 8 October 1990. She argued that this would add credibility to the fight against inflation and she urged unions to accept modest wage increases in order to maintain UK price competitiveness. (This proved to be one of her last important decisions as Prime Minister. She resigned on 22 November 1990.) The British experience in the ERM has so far been impressive. Inflation fell from 10.8 per cent in October 1990 to 4.5 per cent in August 1991, and short-term interest rates fell from 15 per cent to 10.4 per cent over the same period. This occurred when both inflation and interest rates were rising in Germany. In contrast to Ireland's EMS policy, Britain placed greater importance on getting the preconditions for participation in the ERM right and the anticipated benefits appear to have materialised more quickly once the decision was taken to join.

13.7 How Appropriate was Exchange Rate Policy in the 1980s?

In view of the persistence of a very high level of unemployment, and the constraints placed on fiscal and monetary policy by the openness of the economy, it is important to consider whether the fixed exchange rate policy we have pursued since 1986 is appropriate. We have already discussed the question of the effectiveness of devaluation in Chapter 12. At this stage we simply add some additional points based on the evidence of the 1980s.

- A devaluation accompanied by an *incomes policy* which curtails subsequent wage increases could succeed in improving competitiveness. This point was made recently by the governor of the Central Bank of Ireland:

It is clear that the devaluation option will have the desired effect only if . . . real wages are flexible downwards, that is to say, if people are prepared to accept a reduction in their living standards. In a small open economy such as our own, the price rises due to devaluation penetrate the economy deeply and would be likely to prompt rapid claims for compensatory wage increases. The devaluation option may not, therefore, be particularly useful in an Irish context.[12]

- There are many examples of economies that have tried to use currency depreciation to offset a loss of competitiveness due to previous inflation, but have only reinforced the cost-price inflationary spiral by this strategy. At the end of this road lie the hyperinflation and worthless currencies of countries like Brazil (see Chapter 10). However, there are also examples where a depreciation has been used to achieve a cut in real wages and to offset a loss of competitiveness or to gain a competitive advantage. It is certainly *not* a universal law that a devaluation always leads to a proportionate increase in all domestic costs. A devaluation may be the only way to reduce unemployment by cutting domestic costs expressed in foreign currency. Devaluation was a part of several structural adjustment programmes in the 1980s, including those implemented in Sweden, Australia and New Zealand.

- The devaluation of the Irish pound in 1986 led to an improvement in the trade balance and had no discernible effect on the rate of inflation. It can be seen from Figure 13.7, above, that Irish inflation continued to converge on the German rate after the devaluation.[13]

- When an exchange rate is pegged it is important that it be at the appropriate rate. The adjustment of domestic costs and prices to an over-valued rate can be long and painful, as was the case in Britain in the 1920s. We argued in the previous chapter that in the period following Ireland's entry to the ERM the real exchange rate increased, indicating a loss of competitiveness which contributed to the persistence of very high unemployment. A misaligned Irish pound seems to have been part of the reasons for the country's low growth and persistent high unemployment between 1981 and 1986. Adjusting to an over-valued exchange rate can prevent the economy from attaining full employment.

Recent developments In Chapter 5 we discussed the remarkable turn-about in Irish economic performance in the second half of the 1980s. The annual average growth rate of real GNP was 0.6 per cent between 1980 and 1986, but 3.7 per cent between 1987 and 1991. (The contrast in *per capita* growth rates is even greater.) Inflation and interest rates have fallen to German levels. The exchange rate has been stabilised. The unemployment rate declined from 17.6 per cent in 1987 to 13.7 per cent in 1990. (It rose again in 1991 and 1992 as growth slowed and the supply of labour increased due to reduced emigration.)

One interpretation of the rapid improvement in the economy after 1986 is, as we saw in Chapter 5, that cuts in government expenditure and a reduction in the fiscal deficit led to an increase, rather than a decrease, in economic activity. The evidence for negative multipliers is, however, not convincing. Alternative factors can account for the change in the economy during these years.

Table 13.3 shows the contribution of the components of aggregate demand to the overall growth in the volume of GDP from 1986 to 1990. It is evident that the main impetus to higher growth in 1987 and 1988 was the increase in net exports. Domestic spending contributed very little to demand over the entire period. The volume of government consumption fell, private consumption grew slowly in 1986 and 1987, and investment spending remained flat until 1987. Net exports (NX), on the other hand, having declined in 1986 grew strongly in 1987 and 1988 due to the rapid growth of exports and the moderate increase in imports.

While the recovery in the world economy and trade was the main reason for the growth of exports, the behaviour of the real exchange rate should also be considered. Between 1979 and 1986 the real trade-weighted exchange rate index appreciated by 18.9 per cent. In contrast, between 1986 and 1989, it depreciated by 9.9 per cent. This was due to the devaluation of the Irish pound in August 1986 and the convergence of the Irish inflation rate on the German rate. The competitive gain that followed the devaluation allowed Ireland to capitalise on the recovery in the world economy.[14]

Another possible influence on the real growth rate may have been the *real interest rate*. (The real interest rate is the nominal interest rate adjusted for inflation, see Chapter 14.) During the recession years from 1981 to 1986, the real interest rate increased from - 8.3 per cent to 10.0 per cent. (A negative real interest rate occurs if inflation exceeds the nominal rate of interest.) However, between 1986 and 1989, the real interest rate *declined* by 5.4 per cent and this coincided with a modest recovery in investment. It is possible that the stabilisation of the real exchange rate against the EMS currencies (brought about by a continued narrowing of the Irish-German inflation differential) reduced exchange rate uncertainty, checked capital flight and made a fall in real rates possible.

Table 13.3
Contributions to the growth rate in real GDP: Annual percentage change

	GDP	C	G	I	X	M	(NX)
1986	-0.4	1.3	0.5	-0.4	1.7	-3.2	-1.5
1987	4.6	1.4	-0.8	-1.1	8.3	-3.1	5.2
1988	4.5	2.1	0.2	-0.2	5.9	-2.4	3.5
1989	6.4	2.2	-0.3	2.8	7.1	-6.7	0.4
1990	7.1	0.7	0.5	1.8	6.4	-3.9	2.5

Note: GDP = C + I + G + X - M. The change in each component is expressed as a percentage of the change in GDP.
Source: *National Income and Expenditure*, 1990, Table 6.

It can also be argued that the higher growth in income in 1987 induced the increase in consumer expenditure in 1988 and 1989. As the economy continued to grow this may have convinced firms to increase investment and this, in conjunction with the recovery in consumer expenditure, reinforced the recovery. Thus the economy generated its own momentum following the upsurge in net exports in 1987 and this more than offset the deflationary effects of fiscal policy. The export boom was, in turn, due to the belated operation of the benefits of participation in the ERM.

The stability of the Irish pound within the ERM since the devaluation of 1986, backed by prudent domestic fiscal and monetary policies, has firmly established the credibility of the government's commitment to maintaining low inflation and a strong currency. The main threat to this policy comes from the strains on the British economy of trying to keep sterling in the 6 per cent band around the central rate of £1 = DM2.95 at which it joined the ERM and the high real interest rates in Germany due to the large fiscal deficits incurred following reunification. A devaluation of sterling would raise once again the trade-off that Ireland faced in the mid-1980s between holding the value of the Irish pound in the ERM and suffering a loss of competitiveness against sterling. It is now much more likely that we would ride out the effects of the weakness of sterling rather than risk undermining the hard-won credibility of our commitment to the ERM by devaluing in its wake.

13.8   Conclusion

In this chapter we have examined the Irish experience in the EMS in the light of our earlier discussion of macroeconomic policy in an open economy. The topics discussed include:

- Inflation and the exchange rate prior to EMS entry

- The anticipated benefits from EMS entry

- The concept of a credibility bonus

- Evidence from inflation differentials, the real exchange rate and the yield curve on the credibility of the EMS policy

- The reasons why Ireland's commitment to the ERM lacked credibility until 1987

- The appropriateness of exchange rates policy in the 1980s.

Notes

1. C. H. Murray, "The European Monetary System: Implications for Ireland", The Central Bank of Ireland, *Annual Report*, 1979.

2. C. H. Murray, *op. cit.* p. 106.

3. C. McCarthy, "The European Monetary System and Irish Macroeconomic Policy", The Central Bank of Ireland, *Annual Report*, 1979, p. 109.

4. D. A. G. Norton, *Economic Analysis for an Open Economy: Ireland*, Dublin: The Irish Management Institute, 1980, p. 190.

5. Also, the assumption that sterling would remain a weak, inflation-prone currency, although widespread in 1978, proved invalid. The adoption of monetarist policies by the UK Labour government in 1978, the possibility of a Conservative Party victory under Mrs Thatcher in the 1979 election, and the effects of the rise in oil prices on an oil-producing country like the UK were not given due weight. The issue of what would happen to the sterling exchange rate if oil prices increased on world markets was raised by Patrick Honohan, "Some Effects of North Sea Oil on the Irish Economy", *The Economic and Social Review*, Vol. 9, No. 2, 1978.

6. See S. M. Collins, "Inflation and the European Monetary System", in the *European Monetary System*, F. Giavazzi, S. Micossi and M. Millar (eds), Cambridge University Press, 1988, and M. Russo and G. Tullio, "Monetary Coordination Within the European Monetary System: Is there a Rule?", *Policy Coordination in the European Monetary System*, International Monetary Fund, Occasional Paper No. 61 (1988) Part II. Collins does not find any evidence that the EMS contributed to the decline in inflation, but Russo and Tullio, on the other hand, find that the EMS had an important role to play in reducing inflation.

7. McCarthy, *op. cit.*, p. 119.

8. Some evidence is given in A. Leddin, "An Analysis of the Irish Unemployment Problem in the Context of EMS Membership", University of Limerick, January 1991.

9. M. Hurley, "The Information in the Term Structure Interest Rate Spreads: The Irish Case", Central Bank of Ireland, Technical Paper, 2/RT/90, May 1990 presents evidence which indicates that the term structure of interest rates in Ireland correctly predicts the future direction of both short and long interest rates. See also N. Mankin, "The Term Structure of Interest Rates Revised", *Brookings Papers on Economic Activity*, 1986. F. S. Mishkin, "What Does the Term Structure Tell Us about Future Inflation?", *Journal of Monetary Economics*, Vol. 25, No. 1, 1990.

10. Jeroen J. M. Kremers, "Gaining Policy Credibility for a Disinflation: Ireland's Experience in the EMS", *International Monetary Fund, Staff Papers*, Vol. 37, No. 1, March 1990, p. 138.

11. Rudiger Dornbusch, "Credibility, Debt and Unemployment: Ireland's Failed Stabilization", *Economic Policy*, April 1989, pp 174-209. Dornbusch shows a negative long-short interest rate differential in 1982-83 which conflicts with our evidence in Figure 13.9.

12. M. F. Doyle, "European Monetary System: The Impact on Ireland", Central Bank of Ireland, *Quarterly Bulletin*, Autumn 1991, p. 41.

13. See also Brendan Walsh, "Exchange Rate Policy and Competitiveness", Centre for Economic Research, University College, Dublin, PP88/1 (1988) where it is argued that in the early 1980s the relationship between changes in the Irish pound exchange rate and inflation was weak. However, J. Flynn argues in "A Simulation Model of the Effects of Exchange Rate Changes on Inflation and the Balance of Trade", Central Bank of Ireland, *Quarterly Bulletin*, 2, 1986, that the competitive gains from devaluation tend to be completely offset by higher inflation within two years.

14. Real interest rates started to decline *before* the government introduced a deflationary budget in 1987 so that the concept of an expansionary fiscal contraction cannot be the explanation. Moreover, the deflationary budget was *not* anticipated. The government had promised an *expansionary* fiscal policy and only changed its policy immediately before the budget. See our discussion of this topic in Chapter 5.

Chapter 14

Interest Rates and Monetary Policy in Ireland

14.1   Introduction

In earlier chapters we explained why, in the absence of exchange controls, there is virtually no scope for an independent monetary policy in a country whose currency is pegged to that of a larger country. The Irish pound was pegged to sterling until 1979. Between 1979 and 1986 it was in an adjustable peg in the ERM of the EMS. Since 1987 it has been Central Bank policy to keep the Irish pound very close to its central rate of IR£1 = DM2.67 in the ERM. We are committed to participating in the European EMU and adopting the single European currency towards the end of this decade. This will entail the end of an independent Irish currency and of exchange rates between this country and the countries participating in the EMU. When this happens, there will be absolutely no scope for an independent Irish monetary policy.

In Ireland monetary policy has consisted of two different types of policy: *interest rate policy* and *credit policy*. In this chapter we examine interest rate policy and in the following chapter we discuss credit policy. We begin by examining the role of exchange rate expectations in explaining differences in domestic and foreign interest rates. This is followed by a discussion of the trends in Irish, UK and German interest rates before and after our entry to the EMS. We then examine the factors which have a *short-run* influence on domestic interest rates. We conclude the chapter with an appraisal of the Central Bank's interest rate policy.

14.2   Interest Rates in an Open Economy

World interest rates are highly interdependent. Money flows instantaneously from New York to Tokyo to Frankfurt in search of the highest rate of return. For this reason, significant deviations between the expected returns from investing money in different countries are unlikely to persist.

In this context what matters is the *total* rate of return on this money. There are two components to this. The first is the interest earned on the money and the second is the effect of any change in the exchange rate on the value of that money. If the rate of exchange between two currencies is fixed, and there is no expectation that it will be broken, then deciding in which country to deposit money comes down to a comparison of the rates of interest available in the two countries. Furthermore, if the money market in one of the countries is very small relative to the other, and there are no legal restrictions on the movement of money, then any tendency for interest rates in the smaller country to diverge from those prevailing in the larger country would immediately lead to a capital inflow (if its rate rose) or outflow (if its rate fell). Hence, the small country's interest rate will tend to be determined by that prevailing in the large country.

This was the situation that existed in Ireland until we joined the EMS in March 1979. Our currency was rigidly pegged to sterling and, despite occasional academic discussions of the merits of this arrangement, there was no serious expectation that this link would be broken. The Irish money market is infinitesimal relative to the UK market. It was therefore inevitable that Irish interest rates were always very close to those prevailing in London.

Note:
There is a whole spectrum of interest rates in a country. Different rates are charged to different types of customers and on different types of loans. Short-term, medium-term and long-term rates differ. Moreover, even with perfect capital mobility and fixed exchange rates, Irish interest rates always tended to be a little higher than those in London, reflecting the narrowness of the Irish market and allowing some premium for the greater riskiness, from an outsider's perspective, of investing in Ireland.

This situation changed when we entered the ERM of the EMS in 1979 and Britain did not. As we saw in Chapter 10, between 1979 and 1990 the Irish pound/sterling exchange rate was quite volatile. An investor now had to take account of the effect of expected changes in the exchange rate when deciding whether to place money in Ireland or Britain.[1] However, when deciding where to invest money an investor does not know what is going to happen to exchange rates in the future, but *expectations* about the *future course of exchange rates* will play a crucial role in the investment decision.

The role of exchange rate expectations is illustrated in Table 14.1, where we compare Irish and UK interest rates under different assumptions of how sterling will move. In Case A, the Irish interest rate exceeds the UK rate by 5 per cent but the expected returns in the two countries are equivalent as the Irish pound is expected to depreciate by 5 per cent. For example, a UK investor could move funds to Ireland and receive an Irish pound return of 15 per cent. However, when the funds are converted back into sterling at the end of the investment period, a loss of 5 per cent is expected on the foreign exchange market. If this turns out to be correct, the net (sterling) return is only 10 per cent.

Table 14.1
Interest rate differentials and changes in the exchange rate

	r_{irl}	Expected change in the exchange rate	r_{uk}
	%	%	%
Case 1	15	-5	10
Case 2	15	-6	10
Case 3	15	-4	10

In Case 2, sterling is expected to depreciate by 6 per cent. If an Irish investor moves funds to the UK she receives an interest rate of 10 per cent and at the end of the period an additional gain of 6 per cent is expected because the Irish pound is expected to depreciate by this amount over the period. The total return, denominated in Irish pounds, would be 16 per cent. This exceeds the return available in Ireland by 1 per cent. In this case, capital will flow out of Ireland to the UK. This will tend to raise the rate of return in Ireland until, at 16 per cent, the expected return from lending money here is the same as that from moving it to the UK.

In Case 3, sterling is expected to depreciate by 4 per cent. Ireland now offers the better investment opportunity. A return of 10 per cent is available in the UK but the expected depreciation of sterling would result in only a 4 per cent gain on the foreign exchange market. This would give a total UK return (expressed in Irish pounds) of 14 per cent which compares unfavourably with the return available in Ireland. This will attract money to Ireland and drive the Irish rate of interest down.

These examples illustrate the importance of exchange rate expectations in comparing international interest rates. We shall return to the question of how exchange rate expectations are formed in Chapter 16 when we discuss the forward exchange rate and interest rate parity theory (IRPT).

14.3   Irish and UK Interest Rates Before 1979

Between 1826 and 1927 Ireland was in a monetary union with the UK and between 1927 and 1979 the Irish pound was rigidly fixed to sterling on a one-to-one, no margins basis. Exchange rate expectations did not enter into the comparison of Irish and UK interest rates during the period 1926 to 1979 because there was no possibility of the exchange rate link being terminated. In fact, as mentioned in Chapter 6, until the Central Bank Act of 1971 the government did not process the legal authority to break the sterling link. The only reasonable assumption was that the sterling exchange rate would remain at parity and there was no possibility of incurring a

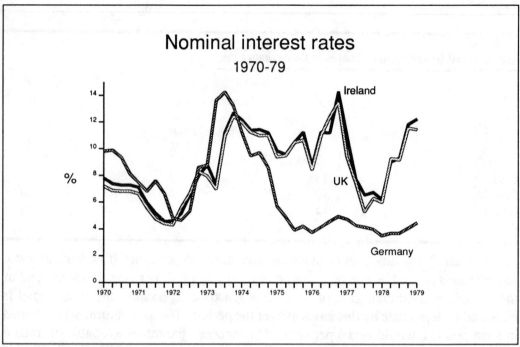

Figure 14.1   Nominal interest rates, 1970-79

capital loss or gain by moving money between Ireland and Britain. Some allowance for the greater riskiness of investing in the small Irish economy might be made, but otherwise a straightforward comparison of Irish and UK interest rates was appropriate in deciding whether to invest in Ireland or the UK.

Figure 14.1 shows the trend in Irish, UK and German interest rates between 1970 and 1979. It is evident that Irish interest rates were more or less the same as UK rates over the period. On the other hand, following the floating of the DM against sterling and the dollar in 1973, a significant gap opened up between Irish and British interest rates, on the one hand, and German rates, on the other. The average gap between Irish and UK rates over the period was 0.31 per cent compared with 2.14 per cent between Ireland and Germany. In late 1976 the Irish-German gap widened to 9.3 per cent. This differential reflected an expectation that sterling (and the Irish pound) would continue to depreciate relative to the DM. As we noted in Chapter 13 (Figure 13.2) the pound fell from about DM8 in the early 1970s to DM4 in 1976.

Under the sterling link, the size of the UK money market relative to the Irish and the fixed exchange rate between the Irish pound and sterling meant that Irish interest rates were dictated by UK rates. Ireland was in effect in a monetary union with Britain in much the same way as Wales or Scotland. The Irish authorities had no control over domestic interest rates or the money supply. If they tried to reduce the money supply and domestic interest rates rose above UK rates, money would flow into Ireland until such time that the domestic money supply and interest rates

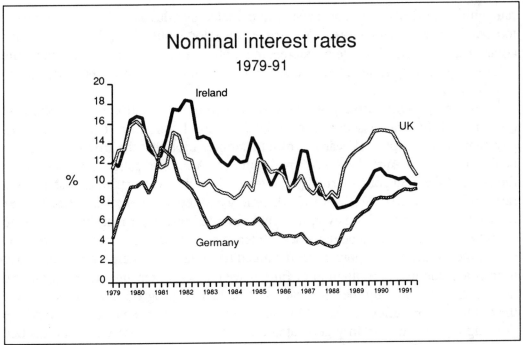

Figure 14.2   Nominal interest rates, 1979-91

were back to their initial levels. Conversely, an increase in the money supply would lower interest rates and lead to an immediate capital outflow until the money supply and interest rates reverted to their original levels.

14.4   Irish and UK Interest Rates Since 1979

Following Ireland's entry into the EMS and the termination of the sterling link in 1979, exchange rate uncertainty became an extremely important consideration for an investor comparing Irish and UK interest rates. The difference between Irish and UK interest rates now reflected exchange rate expectations. If the Irish pound was expected to appreciate over the period, Irish interest rates would be lower than UK rates. Conversely, if the exchange rate was expected to depreciate, Irish interest rates would exceed UK rates. Figure 14.2 shows Irish, UK and German interest rates for the period 1979 to 1991. On average, Irish interest rates exceeded UK rates by 0.3 per cent and German rates by 4.9 per cent over the period 1979 to 1991.

We saw in Chapter 13 that one of the arguments put forward in favour of Ireland's entry into the EMS was that Irish interest rates would quickly converge to the lower German rates. It was argued that given a fixed Irish pound/DM exchange rate, Irish interest rates could not remain above German rates without causing a capital inflow into Ireland. In fact this outcome did not materialise, at least until 1988. Markets were not convinced of the Irish commitment to holding the exchange rate within the EMS: they consistently anticipated devaluation. In fact, they were too pessimistic on this score. A German investor would have been more than compensated by the high rate of interest in Dublin for the loss on the exchange rate suffered by moving funds from Frankfurt to Dublin over most of the period from 1979 to 1987.

The sharp, but relatively short-lived, widening of the differential in the first quarter of 1986 was associated with leading and lagging of foreign exchange payments and receipts. This arose from the anticipation that the Irish pound might be devalued at the April 1986 EMS realignment. After the realignment, which left the value of the Irish pound virtually unaltered, there was a sharp fall in Irish interest rates and an increase in liquidity in Irish money markets as foreign exchange flowed back into the country. However, it became increasingly clear that the Irish pound would eventually have to be devalued. Interest rates rose again relative to the UK during the summer. The pound was devalued in August but interest rates continued to increase due to a combination of further weakness in sterling and the profound uncertainty provoked by the devaluation. The lack of progress towards correcting the public sector deficit, revealed in the autumn 1986 exchequer returns, and the growing political uncertainty generated a crisis atmosphere that was not dispelled until the second quarter of 1987, when the new government had successfully introduced a stringent budget and sterling had risen significantly relative to the EMS currencies, thereby reducing the pressure to restore competitiveness by means of another devaluation.

Developments during 1987 were remarkable. Irish money markets ignored the surge in UK interest rates in the middle of the year. For the first time ever, the level of interest rates in Dublin was more influenced by trends in Frankfurt than in London. By 1989 the fact that London short-term interest rates were almost 5 per cent higher than those in Dublin was no longer considered exceptional. The long-hoped-for decoupling of British and Irish money markets had become a reality due to the credibility of our commitment to maintain the value of our currency stable relative to the DM.

Note, however, that a relatively high UK interest rate is an indication that the market expects sterling to depreciate. When the exchange rate moves to what is regarded as a more sustainable level, money flows out to avail of the higher interest rate. In 1989, for example, the 5 per cent differential between UK and Irish interest rates in July was followed by an appreciation of the Irish pound from STG£0.87/IR£1 to STG£0.95/IR£1 by December. As sterling fell, the interest rate differential narrowed. The Central Bank of Ireland was forced to raise domestic interest rates by 1 per cent to stem the outflow of capital.

Since the beginning of 1991 the gap between the Irish and German short-term rates has been less than 1 per cent and following the entry of the UK into the ERM in October 1990 the UK interest rate has converged towards the German rate, which has reduced the pressure on Irish money markets from that source.

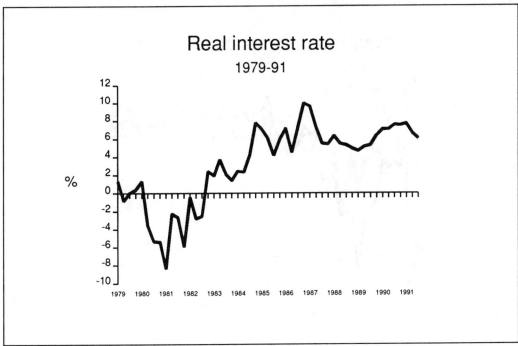

Figure 14.3 Real interest rate in Ireland, 1979-91

14.5   Real Interest Rates

So far the discussion has been confined to *nominal* interest rates. The *real* interest rate is the nominal interest rate adjusted for inflation.

(1) $r_{real} = r_{nominal} - \text{Inflation rate}$

Sometimes equation (1) is referred to as the *Fisher equation* after the Yale economist Irving Fisher. The original Fisher equation stated that the real interest rate is equal to the nominal interest rate minus *expected* inflation. If it is assumed that inflation expectations are realised, equation (1) is equivalent to the Fisher equation.

Figure 14.3 shows the real interest rate in Ireland between 1979 and 1990.[2] Between 1979 and 1991, the average real interest rate in Ireland was 3.0 per cent. The real interest rate has, however, varied quite considerably over the period, from a minimum of - 8.3 per cent in 1981 to a maximum of 10.0 per cent in 1986. The early 1980s were exceptional for the very large negative real rates that prevailed. On the other hand, the positive real interest rates now prevailing are unusually high.

Figure 14.4 shows the gap between Irish and UK and Irish and German real interest rates. On average, real interest rates in Ireland were 0.34 per cent and 0.73

411

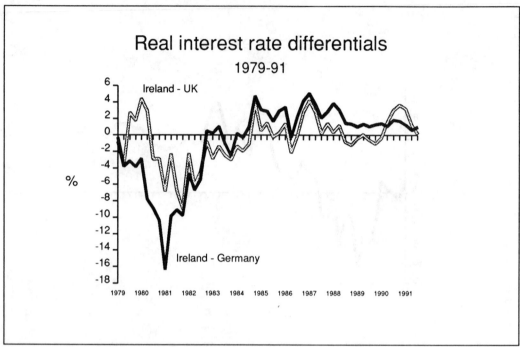

Figure 14.4   Differences in real interest rates

per cent *lower* than rates in the UK and Germany respectively.   Real interest rates were lower in Ireland because Irish inflation exceeded UK and German inflation by even more than the nominal interest rate differential.   While Ireland's nominal interest rates exceeded nominal rates in the UK and Germany, the differential has been more than offset by a relatively high Irish inflation rate.

14.6   Short-run Influences on Irish Interest Rates

We have seen that in the absence of exchange controls, the ability of a central bank to influence interest rates in a small open economy with a fixed exchange rate is very limited. The Central Bank of Ireland acknowledges this but none the less claims that it has an important role to play in regard to *short-term* fluctuations in interest rates:

Although the Bank may not attempt to affect the broad trend in interest rates, it does pursue . . . the important function of smoothing, within reason, short-run fluctuations and predictable seasonal patterns in interest rates.
T. F. O Cofaigh, "Observations on Interest Rates", Central Bank of Ireland, *Annual Report*, 1983, p. 102.

To understand how the Bank can influence interest rates, it is necessary to study the relationship between the balance sheets of the Central Bank and the licensed

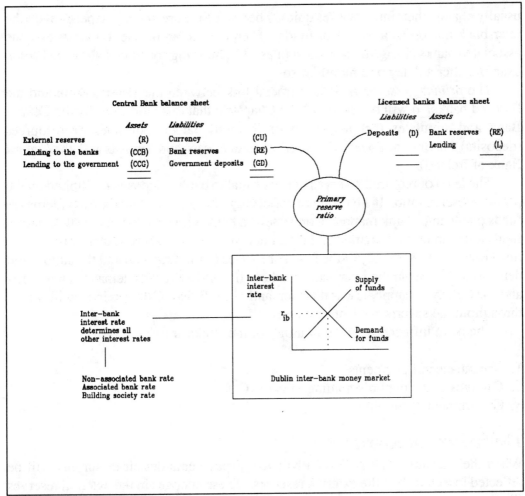

Figure 14.5 Interest rate determination in the short run

banks and the Dublin inter-bank money market. Figure 14.5 summarises the situation.

At the centre of the stage is the *inter-bank market*. This is a market where banks lend (supply) and borrow (demand) money from each other for periods ranging from a day to a year. The forces of supply and demand in this market determine the inter-bank interest rate (r_{ib}). The Central Bank exercises an important influence on the inter-bank rate through the rate at which it is willing to lend to the banks.

Note:
Although the inter-bank market is frequently referred to as the "Dublin" inter-bank money market it has no exact location. It is a market conducted through computers, telephones and telex machines.

The inter-bank interest rate is important because of its influence on all the other interest rates in the banking system. When r_{ib} changes, the non-associated banks

413

usually change their interest rates quickly because they are heavily dependent on the inter-bank market as a source of funds. Then after a lag of one to two weeks, the associated banks change their interest rates. The building societies follow the banks' example after a delay of a month or so.

The *primary reserve ratio* is a crucial link between the Central Bank and the licensed banks. It will be recalled from Chapter 6 that this ratio is set by the Central Bank and stipulates the proportion of licensed banks' liabilities or resources (deposits) that must be covered by reserves (that is, cash and deposits with the Central Bank of Ireland).

The level of required reserves (RE) is equal to banks' deposits multiplied by the primary reserve ratio. If a bank has a deficiency of reserves, it will borrow (demand) funds on the inter-bank market. Conversely, a bank with excess reserves will supply funds to the inter-bank market and earn interest on them. There is therefore a direct link between the adequacy of the banks' reserves (their *liquidity*) and the supply and demand for funds on the inter-bank market. If supply exceeds demand, r_{ib} will fall and conversely, if supply is less than demand, r_{ib} will rise. Changes in r_{ib} will spread throughout the spectrum of interest rates.

The main influences on the liquidity of the banks are:

1. The balance of payments
2. Changes in the public's holding of cash (CU)
3. Government borrowing.

The balance of payments

When the exchange rate is fixed a balance of payments deficit or surplus will be reflected in a change in the external reserves. These changes in the external reserves (R) have an important influence on domestic interest rates. In general, a change in the external reserves on the asset side of the Central Bank's balance sheet will be reflected in a change in licensed banks' reserves (RE) on the liability side. A fall in R will lead to a fall in RE and conversely an increase in R will lead to an increase in RE.

Consider a firm importing, say, £1 million worth of wine from France. We will trace through on the balance sheets the effect of an importer withdrawing £1 million from her account and then exchanging it for the equivalent in French francs. When the importer first withdraws money from her account, deposits (D) and reserves (RE) decrease on the licensed bank balance sheet. The importer is now holding £1 million in currency. On the Central Bank balance sheet, RE falls and CU increases. The importer now exchanges the domestic currency for French francs at the foreign exchange desk of the bank. The commercial bank holds only a small amount of foreign currency and is, in effect, only acting as an intermediary between the individual and the Central Bank. This foreign exchange transaction is reflected in the Central Bank balance sheet as a fall in CU and a fall in the external reserves (R)

414

on the asset side. Overall, on the Central Bank balance sheet, the fall in R is matched by an equal fall in RE (the change in CU was only temporary).

Suppose now that prior to the withdrawal of funds the banks had the correct reserves/deposit ratio to meet the primary reserve ratio. Following the drop of £1 million in its reserves the bank will have a deficiency of reserves and to redress the situation will borrow from the inter-bank market. This will put upward pressure on the interest rate (R_{ib}).

Note:
If a bank had £5 million in reserves and £50 million in deposit accounts and the required primary reserve ratio was 10 per cent, it has the correct amount of reserves: reserve/deposits = £50/£500 = 10 per cent. If an importer withdraws £1 million, the bank will have a deficiency of reserves. Reserves/deposits = £4/£49 = 8.1 per cent. In this case the bank will need to borrow £0.9 million on the inter-bank market in order to meet the reserve requirement.

Thus in general a balance of payments deficit will reduce licensed banks' reserves and lead to an increased demand for funds on the inter-bank market. Domestic interest rates will rise. Conversely, a balance of payments surplus will increase licensed banks' reserves and lead to an increase in the supply of funds on the inter-bank market and a reduction in interest rates.

As we pointed out in Chapter 10, the main factors influencing the balance of payments and therefore the level of the external reserves are relative inflation rates, changes in world interest rates, relative growth rates in GNP and speculation. For example, if speculators expect a depreciation of the Irish exchange rate, capital would be transferred from Irish pounds to foreign currencies in anticipation of making a capital gain. This will be reflected in the Central Bank balance sheet as a fall in R and RE and the banks will have a deficiency of reserves. The demand for funds on the inter-bank market will increase and domestic interest rates will rise. On the other hand, a fall in world (in particular, German) interest rates, a fall in Irish inflation and slower growth in Irish GNP would lead to a fall in inter-bank interest rates and therefore all other interest rates in the economy.

Changes in currency holdings

Net changes in currency holdings (CU) by the public tend to be seasonal and reasonably predictable. For example, there is always a significant increase in currency holdings in the weeks leading up to Christmas. In terms of the Central Bank's balance sheet in Figure 14.5, an increase in currency holdings will be reflected in an increase in CU and a decrease in RE on the liability side of the balance sheet. People simply withdraw money from their current and deposit accounts and hold it as currency. If the increase in CU was unexpected, and banks were maintaining only the exact amount of reserves in relation to deposits, the banks would be forced to borrow on the inter-bank market and interest rates would tend to increase. Conversely, a fall in currency holdings would tend to reduce inter-bank interest rates.

415

An increase in private sector *savings* (due for example to a decrease in currency holdings) tends to increase deposits. In the short-run, an increase in licensed bank deposits will lead to excess reserves and the supply of funds to the inter-bank market will increase. Interest rates will tend to fall.

Increased *bank lending*, not matched by an increase in deposits, can lead to a short-run increase in interest rates. The banks will find it necessary to borrow reserves on the inter-bank market and this will put upward pressure on domestic interest rates.

Government borrowing

The financing of the government's borrowing requirement (the EBR discussed in Chapter 5) has a major influence on the liquidity of the commercial banks. We have seen that the government can borrow from:

1. The non-bank public
2. The licensed banks
3. The Central Bank
4. Abroad.

The government borrows from the non-bank public by selling government securities. Purchases of government stock will lead to a fall in licensed bank deposits as they are drawn down to pay for the stock. When the government spends the money, a large part of it will find its way back to the banks and deposits will return to their original level. In the longer term, therefore, there will be little change in bank deposits, bank reserves or interest rates. On the other hand, an unexpected inflow of funds to the Government as happened in 1988, reduces liquidity in the banking system. (In an open economy with perfect capital mobility any tendency for an increased supply of government securities to drive interest rates up in the longer run will be offset by an inflow of funds. This is why an expansionary fiscal policy has no crowding out effect under these assumptions.)

If the government borrows from the licensed banks the effects are similar to what happens when a firm or individual borrows. Bank lending and deposits increase. If the banks had no excess reserves, there would be a deficiency in reserves following the increase in lending to the government. This would lead to an increased demand for funds on the inter-bank market and interest rates would rise.

Government borrowing from the Central Bank is the modern form of printing money and making it available to the government. Central Bank lending to the government (CCG) increases on the asset side of the balance sheet and government deposits (GD) on the liability side. When the government spends the money, GD will decrease and licensed bank reserves (RE) will increase. This will lead to excess reserves with the result that the supply of funds on the inter-bank market will increase and interest rates will fall. (Note that this method of financing government spending will no longer be permissible under the rules of the EMU.)

When the government borrows from abroad, it lodges the proceeds with the Central Bank. The result is similar to that of an increase in any other inflow across the balance of payments in that the Central Bank acquires additional reserves. The government, in turn, obtains additional balances with the Central Bank, just as it would if it had borrowed directly from the Bank. An internal monetary expansion will result.

Note that when the government borrows from abroad or from the Central Bank there is an increase in bank reserves which allows for a further rise in bank lending. Government borrowing from the banks on the other hand only leads to a once-off increase in the money supply. Furthermore, when the government borrows abroad, the Central Bank acquires additional external reserves.

14.7 The Central Bank of Ireland's Interest Rate Policy

In a small open economy, the main influences on bank liquidity are flows across the balance of payments. The Central Bank can try to break the link between these flows and short-term interest rates and the domestic money supply through its lending to the licensed banks. This is called *sterilisation*. Recall that an outflow leads to a decrease in R and in RE . This forces the licensed banks to borrow on the inter-bank market in order to observe the reserve requirement. If the Central Bank were to lend the required funds to the licensed banks (increase in CCB), the need for the banks to borrow on the inter-bank market would be avoided and interest rates would remain unchanged.

The objective is to smooth out the fluctuations in interest rates that would occur if the Central Bank stood back from the market and allowed interest rates to vary as the supply and demand for funds changed because of changes in bank liquidity. In so far as this intervention smooths predictable and temporary changes in interest rates it is desirable because fluctuations in interest rates can create uncertainty and discourage investment. The hoped-for effects of Central Bank intervention are shown in Figure 14.6.

The mechanics of Central Bank support for the market

If the Central Bank takes the view that the interest rates prevailing in the Dublin money market are sustainable, then its role is simply to smooth out the fluctuations in liquidity that would occur in the absence of intervention, as shown in Figure 14.6. To implement this policy the Bank must forecast changes in liquidity and then intervene to offset them. This type of intervention can be called *structural* intervention, and the Bank uses the following instruments for this purpose:[2]

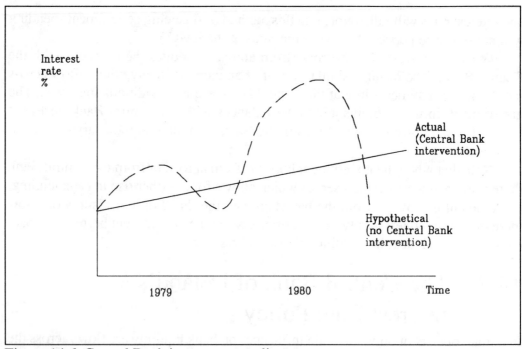

Figure 14.6 Central Bank interest rate policy

- Foreign currency swaps
- Sale and repurchase agreements (REPOs)
- Term deposits
- Changes in the primary reserve ratio.

We now provide a brief account of these.

Foreign currency swaps Licensed banks' holdings of foreign exchange are not included in banks' primary reserves. If a bank has foreign exchange for use at a later date and is short of reserves, the foreign exchange can be temporarily swapped for reserves at the Central Bank. This facility can be used both to inject liquidity into the market (the Central Bank swaps Irish pounds for foreign currency) or remove liquidity (the Central Bank swaps foreign currency for Irish pounds). Information on swap transactions is only published at the end of December and it only gives the average level of swaps during the year.

Sale and repurchase agreements (REPOs) This facility is similar to a foreign currency swap except that government securities rather than foreign exchange are exchanged for an agreed period at the end of which the transaction is reversed. The Central Bank lends money to the licensed banks at a fixed rate of interest for a fixed period. Government stocks are transferred to the Central Bank as security, with an agreement that the banks will buy back (repurchase) them at the end of the period. This provides the banks with temporary additional reserves. Both this arrangement and foreign currency swap are generally done at prevailing interest rates.

Term deposits The Central Bank may also withdraw liquidity from the inter-bank market by "quoting for funds", that is, quoting a specified interest rate for term deposits for specified periods. This instrument works only to withdraw funds from the market as the Central Bank does not keep deposits with the licensed banks and hence cannot inject liquidity by increasing these.

Changes in the primary reserve ratio A reduction in the primary reserve ratio increases the liquidity of the banking system, an increase in the ratio lowers it. The ratio is not changed frequently. Traditionally, it was lowered between November to January to help the banks deal with the large but temporary outflow of cash at Christmas time. In 1991/92 this seasonal reduction was not reversed. The standard primary ratio was lowered from 8 to 6 per cent of relevant resources.

In addition to using these instruments to influence the liquidity of the market in order to reduce interest rate volatility, the Bank can, within narrow limits, try to influence the *level* of interest rates. If, for example, it forms the view that Irish rates have fallen too low relative to the rates prevailing in Germany, and there is a risk of an outflow of funds as a consequence, it may wish to nudge interests up on the inter-bank market. If it wishes to *raise* interest rates it will try to create a liquidity shortage by supplying the market with *less* funds than it reckons will be required. This will force the banks to borrow and they will be accommodated through one of the following channels, rather than through any of the four listed above:

- The short term facility (STF)
- Secured advances
- Overnight deposits.

The short term facility (STF) This is similar to an individual's overdraft facility or authorisation at his bank. The licensed banks can use this facility to borrow from the Central Bank for up to seven days. Each of the licensed banks is given a quota which is determined by its size and participation in the inter-bank market. The quotas totalled £167 million in 1990. The banks are charged the *STF rate* on this borrowing and are penalised for frequent use of the facility by being charged a higher rate. By raising or lowering this rate, the Central Bank sends a signal about the direction in which it wishes interest rates to move throughout the economy. In December 1991, for example, the Central Bank of Ireland quickly responded to the increase of 0.5 per cent in the Lombard rate by the Bundesbank and raised the SFT by 0.5 per cent to 10.75 per cent.

Secured advances Banks can also borrow from the Central Bank on a longer-term basis against the security of government stocks. Banks tend to avail of this facility after they have reached their short-term facility quota. The terms on which the Central Bank lends are related to the STF rate.

Overnight deposits Banks can obtain funds from the Central Bank by placing funds on overnight deposit, but the rate paid on these deposits is unattractive.

These channels are used by the Central Bank to take the initiative and exert some influence on the level of interest rates in the inter-bank market, taking account of the rates prevailing abroad, especially in Germany.

The level of support offered to the inter-bank market through these instruments can be very high. By the end of 1989, for example the total came to £1.5 billion, which was then unwound over the following three quarters. During the second half of 1991 support climbed to over £800 million. The success or failure of the Central Bank's interventions depends crucially on how well it forecasts changes in liquidity in the market, and how accurate its view is of the "sustainable" or "appropriate" level of interest rates in Ireland relative to those in Germany. However, even a successful policy would now play a minor role relative to the external influences on the level and trend of Irish interest rates.

Central Bank intervention and the external reserves

There is a close link between Central Bank intervention in the Dublin money market and the level of the official external reserves. This can be clearly illustrated by what happened in the first two quarters of 1978. A speculative outflow of funds from the Dublin money market caused the external reserves (R) to fall. Central Bank lending to the licensed banks (CCB) was increased to offset the reduction in liquidity. This situation was reversed in the last two quarters, R increased and the banks repaid the Central Bank the money borrowed earlier in the year. In 1979, R fell over the first three quarters and the Central Bank provided funds to the banks. The banks reduced their indebtedness to the Central Bank in the final quarter. Thus during this period the Central Bank was providing or withdrawing funds from the market in order to offset the effect that changes in reserves would otherwise have had on bank liquidity and hence on interest rates.

Table 14.2
Changes in the external reserves and Central Bank credit: IR£ millions

		ΔR	ΔCCB			ΔR	ΔCCB
1978	q1	-45	34	1979	q1	-283	128
	q2	-194	115		q2	-43	177
	q3	150	-61		q3	-44	16
	q4	140	-45		q4	118	-252

Note: The CCB variable does not include foreign exchange swaps.
Source: Various Central Bank of Ireland, *Quarterly Bulletins*.

A number of points can be made with regard to this episode. First, Central Bank support of this type is supposed to be temporary, but in 1979 it lasted for over nine months. Secondly, as the support was extended it became clear that if the licensed banks were compelled by the Central Bank to repay their borrowings, interest rates on the inter-bank market would have increased significantly. The Central Bank was not prepared to allow this to happen. Instead it reduced the associated banks' primary reserve ratio from 13 per cent to 10 per cent and the secondary reserve ratio from 30 per cent to 25 per cent. As a result of this, the banks had excess reserves which they used to reduce their indebtedness to the Central Bank. This reduction in the reserve ratios facilitated the repayment of £252 million to the Central Bank in the final quarter of 1979.

Intervention had the effect of lowering the external reserves. If the Central Bank had not provided liquidity, domestic interest rates would have increased and capital would have flowed into the country. The capital inflow would, in effect, have financed the deficit on the current account of the balance of payments and the external reserves would have remained relatively stable. As the governor of the Central Bank commented at the time:

... there was a conscious decision to take action to prevent (interest) rates going even higher, in recognition of the burden this would have placed on the economy; it was, however, at the cost of a larger fall than we would have liked in the external reserves.
C. M. Murray, "Monetary Policy", Central Bank of Ireland, *Annual Report*, 1980, p. 117.

When we discuss the Bank's credit policy in Chapter 15 we shall see that at this time the Central Bank was trying to curtail bank lending by issuing credit guidelines. Yet at the same time it was lending hundreds of millions of pounds to the licensed banks so that they would not have to borrow on the inter-bank money market, which would have driven up interest rates. It is difficult to reconcile a policy of rationing credit with a policy that tried to avert an increase in interest rates.

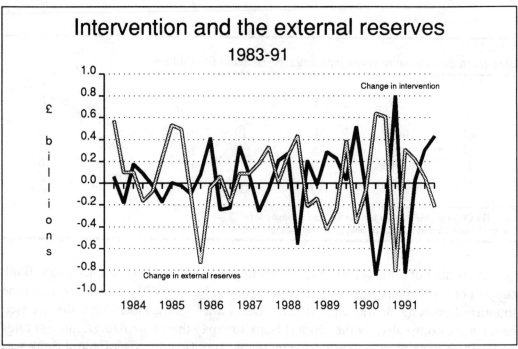

Figure 14.7 Sterilisation

Figure 14.7 shows the relationship between changes in the external reserves (ΔR) and the change in Central Bank lending (Δ CCB) over the period 1983 to 1991. CCB is defined here as the sum of REPOs and lending through the STF. The inverse relationship between the two series is evident. For example, in 1985 and again in 1989, sterling weakened on the foreign exchange market and this led to speculation that the Irish pound might be devalued in an EMS realignment in order to maintain price competitiveness with the UK. This led to a capital outflow and a fall in the external reserves. In order to stop domestic interest rates rising, the Central Bank provided support to the market.

The Central Bank also reacts to the other short-run influences mentioned above. The tax amnesty in 1987-88, for example, was expected to raise approximately £50 million whereas, in fact, £450-£500 million was actually collected. A large proportion of this money was transferred from deposit accounts in banks to the government's account at the Central Bank and was used to reduce government's borrowing requirement. There was, therefore, a net withdrawal of funds from the market. The Central Bank increased its support to the market in late 1987 and early 1988 to offset the effects of these developments on interest rates.

Evaluation of Central Bank sterilisation in Ireland

Econometric techniques can be used to indicate both the degree of Central Bank involvement in domestic money markets and the effectiveness of stabilisation policy. Consider the following equation:

(2) $\Delta \, CCB = \alpha - \beta \, \Delta \, R$

where α and β are coefficients and $0 < \beta < 1$. The coefficient β is known as the *sterilisation* coefficient. It measures how the Central Bank reacts to changes in the external reserves (R). A β coefficient of 0.7 would mean that for every £1 million fall in the external reserves, the Central Bank injects (notice the negative sign in the equation) £0.7 million into the money market.

In the following equation, the variables are reversed:

(3) $\Delta \, R = \chi - \delta \, \Delta \, CCB$

where $0 < \delta < 1$. The coefficient δ is known as the *offset* coefficient. It indicates what proportion of any injection or withdrawal of funds by the Central Bank is offset by a change in the external reserves. If, for example, δ were 0.4 this would mean that for every £1 million injected into the money market by the Central Bank, the external reserves would fall by £0.4 million. The offset coefficient indicates the effectiveness of Central Bank policy. A low offset coefficient suggests an effective interest rate policy. Conversely, a high offset coefficient suggests that injections of funds by the Central Bank will quickly disappear through changes in the external reserves.

If β and δ equal 1 and 0 respectively, then this would indicate complete sterilisation and no offset. In this case, interest rate policy would be very active and very effective. If, on the other hand, β and δ equalled 0.6 and 0.4, this means that for every £1 fall in the external reserves, the Central Bank injects 60 pence into the market and 40 per cent of this (24 pence) is immediately offset through changes in the external reserves.

Two studies have estimated the sterilisation and offset coefficients for the Irish economy. The first, using quarterly data, found sterilisation and offset coefficients of 0.01 and 1.0 respectively for the pre-EMS period (1972-79)[4]. This means that prior to EMS entry the Central Bank did not engage to any significant extent in an interest rate policy but when it did the policy was entirely ineffective due to complete offset through changes in the external reserves. In contrast, sterilisation and offset coefficients of 0.75 and 0.79 respectively were estimated for the period 1979-85. This means that for every £1 million fall in the external reserves, the Central Bank injected £0.75 million into the money markets, but that 79 per cent of this injection was offset through a subsequent fall in the external reserves. This suggests that, in contrast to the pre-EMS period, the Central Bank pursued an active interest rate policy after we joined the EMS. The reduction in the absolute value of the offset coefficient in the post-EMS period is probably a reflection of the exchange controls issued by the Central Bank in 1979. These were lifted in 1992. It is likely, therefore, that the effectiveness of intervention has decreased in recent years.

The second study,[5] based on monthly data over the period January 1980 to April 1985, estimated a sterilisation coefficient of 0.6. However, the offset coefficient was found to equal 1 over a period of five months. In other words, any injection (or withdrawal) of funds by the Central Bank was *completely* offset within five months by fall (rise) in the external reserves.

The results of these two studies are broadly consistent and suggest that there was a high degree of integration between Irish and foreign money markets both before and since we joined the EMS, with the result that there is very little scope for an independent interest rate policy in Ireland. Attempts to sterilise changes in the external reserves so as to stabilise domestic interest rates in the longer term could prove ineffective and costly.

Interest rate policy in the approach to EMU

We have noted that since 1987 the Irish pound has been virtually pegged at the rate of IR£ = DM2.67. There is not likely to be a change in this policy as we enter Stage II of the EMU, discussed in Chapter 13. The policy will therefore be limited to interpreting trends in German interest rates to the Irish market and signalling increases and decreases via the STF rate, as appropriate. If all goes as planned, and full monetary integration is achieved by 1997, there will be no further role for the Central Bank of Ireland to play in this area after that date.

14.8   Conclusion

In this chapter we examined interest rate policy in Ireland since the 1960s. The main points discussed were:

- The role of exchange rate expectations in comparing returns to foreign and domestic investment

- A comparison of Irish, UK and German interest rates before and after entry to the EMS

- Real interest rates in Ireland since entry to the EMS

- The short-run determinants of bank liquidity

- The goals of Central Bank intervention in the Dublin money market

- The instruments used by the Central Bank to intervene in the money market
- The link between Central Bank intervention and the level of external reserves
- By 1997, if the EMU is launched and Ireland is a participant, there will be no further role for the Central Bank of Ireland in regard to interest rates.

Notes

1. Another complication was the fact that exchange controls were extended to apply to dealing between Dublin and London in 1979, whilst the UK abolished all exchange controls in 1980. Investors were also affected by the introduction in Ireland of deposit interest retention tax (DIRT) in 1986.

2 The real interest rates described here are *ex post*, that is, they reflect actual rather than expected rates of inflation. The estimation of *ex ante* rates requires a model of how expectations are formed.

3. For a detailed discussion see K. Barry, "The Central Bank's Management of the Aggregate Liquidity of Licensed Banks", Central Bank of Ireland, *Annual Report*, 1983.

4. A. Leddin, "Portfolio Equilibrium and Monetary Policy in Ireland", *The Economic and Social Review*, Vol. 17, No. 2, January 1986.

5. F. X. Browne, "A Monthly Money Market Model for Ireland in the EMS", Central Bank of Ireland, *Annual Report*, 1986.

Chapter 15

Credit Controls and Monetary Policy in Ireland

15.1   Introduction

Credit controls were used intermittently as an instrument of monetary policy in Ireland between 1965 and 1982. The objective was to constrain the growth in bank credit with a view to influencing the level of nominal GNP and/or the external reserves. In the course of this chapter we outline the theoretical structures underlying credit policy, how the banks reacted to credit guidelines and we evaluate the effectiveness of this type of monetary policy.

15.2   Credit Guidelines

Credit guidelines may be issued by central banks as a means of curtailing the growth in bank credit. Typically, these guidelines stipulate by how much the banks can collectively increase their lending over a period such as a year. If the banks exceed the guideline they have *excess lending*, while if the growth of bank lending falls short of that specified by the guideline, they have a *deficiency in lending* relative to the guideline. Since loans are the principal component of the banks' assets, credit guidelines are equivalent to placing a ceiling on the assets of the banking system. If a borrower is refused a loan because of a credit guideline, he is said to have experienced *credit rationing*.

A credit guideline that attempts to control *total* credit is referred to as a *quantitative* credit guideline. Guidelines which relate to sub-sectors of total credit are referred to as *sectoral* credit guidelines. Table 15.1 shows the composition of licensed bank private sector credit as at February 1989. Lending to the personal sector (including loans for house purchase) is the largest single category.

Note:
Credit guidelines may not apply to all financial institutions. If a borrower is refused a loan at a licensed bank due to credit restrictions, it may be possible to obtain a loan at a bank or finance house not affected by the guidelines. Credit rationing could also lead to would-be borrowers reducing savings or selling assets to finance their spending. These responses circumvent the controls and reduce their effectiveness.

Table 15.1
Sectoral distribution of licensed bank lending to residents (excluding government), August 1991

	£ millions	%
Agriculture, fishing and forestry	1,418.7	10.2
Energy	181.5	1.3
Manufacturing	1,790.5	12.9
Building and construction	431.4	3.1
Distribution, garages, hotels and catering	1,732.1	12.5
Transport	366.2	2.6
Postal services and telecommunications	60.9	0.4
Financial	2,068.5	14.9
Business and other services	1,667.9	12.0
Personal	4,183.9	30.1
of which		
Housing	2,287.4	16.4
Total	13,901.8	100.0

Source: Central Bank of Ireland, *Quarterly Bulletin*, Winter, 1991.
The distinction between residents and non-residents is based on the customer's address and not on the location of the bank account.

Banks have a profit incentive to meet a demand for credit provided they have the necessary reserves, even if this involves breaching a credit guideline. As a result, central banks are normally obliged to accompany credit guidelines with some form of enforcement measure. The Central Bank of Ireland has imposed *special deposits* on the banks for this purpose. These try to ensure that a bank makes a loss on excess lending.[1]

15.3   Credit Policy in Ireland, 1965-77

Credit guidelines were first introduced in Ireland in 1965 as a means of curtailing the growth in the associated banks' lending to the private sector and to the government. Table 15.2 compares the growth in bank credit with the guidelines issued by the Central Bank over the period 1965-77. Column 1 shows the stipulated growth in credit and column 2 the actual growth in bank credit. As an indicator of the banks' compliance with the guidelines, column 3 expresses column 2 as a percentage of column 1.

Note:
Up to 1970, the credit guidelines applied only to the associated banks but in 1970 they were extended to non-associated bank lending (excluding instalment credit). These banks had grown dramatically

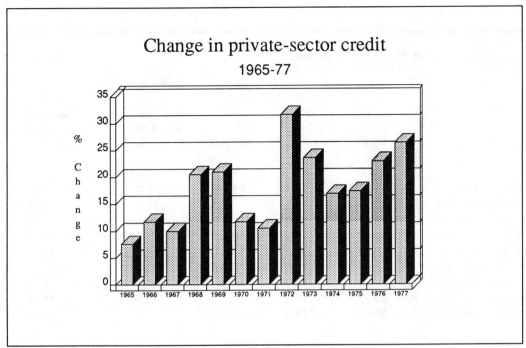

Change in private-sector credit
1965-77

Figure 15.1 Change in private sector credit, 1965-77

in previous years by finding profitable lending opportunities in Ireland and then financing the loans by borrowing on the London money market. From 1973 to 1976, the Central Bank abandoned credit guidelines as it was felt that the guidelines "hamper competition between banks and lead to inequities and possible misallocation of resources".[2] Credit guidelines were re-introduced in 1977.

Figure 15.1 shows the percentage change in licensed bank private sector credit over the period 1965-77. (The figures are affected by the bank disputes that occurred during 1970.) The rate of growth of credit followed the business cycle closely. It does not appear that credit guidelines smoothed the growth of credit over the period. While we would not expect exact compliance with the guidelines, column 3 of the table shows that the degree of adherence by the banks to the guidelines by the banks was low. The growth in bank credit was within 40 percentage points of the guideline stipulation on only three out of nine occasions. In 1967, 1968, 1970 and 1972 the actual growth in bank credit exceeded the guideline by 68 per cent, 65 per cent, 73 per cent and 60 per cent respectively. By any reasonable criterion, the guidelines could not be said to have succeeded in curtailing the growth of bank credit. It was not until 1978 that special deposits were introduced to enforce the guidelines. Before then compliance depended on moral suasion by the Central Bank and the goodwill of the banks. The outcome clearly indicates that these were not enough to ensure compliance.

429

Table 15.2
Credit guidelines and the growth in bank credit, 1965-77

Period	Credit guideline		Actual change in credit		Column (2) as a % of column (1)
	£m (1)	%	£m (2)	%	(3)
1. Mar. 1965-Dec. 1965	33.4	10.5	20.0	5.7	59.9
2. Mar. 1966-Mar. 1967	43.0	11.8	40.5	11.1	94.2
3. Mar. 1967-Mar. 1968	40.4	10.0	68.2	16.8	168.8
4. Apr. 1968-Apr. 1969	64.2	14.1	106.3	23.3	165.5
5. Apr. 1969-Apr. 1970	80.0	14.2	82.0	14.6	102.5
6. Apr. 1970-Apr. 1971	75.0	11.6	130.0	20.0	173.3
7. Apr. 1971-Apr. 1972	118.0	11.7	49.3	4.8	41.8
8. Apr. 1972-Apr. 1973	200.0	19.0	321.3	30.3	160.6
9. Jan. 1977-Dec. 1977	359.0	18.0	439.0	22.0	122.3

Source: Central Bank of Ireland, *Quarterly Bulletins*, various issues.
Notes:
1. Guidelines 1 to 6 relate to associated bank credit only. Guidelines 7 to 9 relate to licensed banks' credit.
2. With the exception of 1977, the controls relate to bank lending to the private sector and the government.
3. The guideline in 1966/67 was revised upwards from 6 per cent to 11 per cent and in 1972/73 from 15 per cent to 19 per cent.

Note:
A reading of the Central Bank statements accompanying the credit guidelines suggests that, on the whole, the credit guidelines were not particularly restrictive in the first instance (see Table 15.4). It is likely that if they had been more restrictive, the degree of compliance would have been even lower.

The objectives of credit policy Between 1965 and 1977 monetary policy in Ireland was formulated in two stages. The first stage involved using credit guidelines and reserve requirements to control bank credit and regulate the money supply. There is no statement outlining the theoretical foundations of monetary policy in these early years. We have to depend on indirect references in Central Bank publications in order to determine what theory provided the basis for monetary policy. The governor of the Central Bank commented:

Behind the innermost veil, there must still sit the notion of a Quantity! The Bank will still be aiming at controlling the aggregate lending of the banking system and, indirectly, the overall level of current and deposit accounts.[3]

The second stage involved estimating how changes in the money supply would influence prices and imports. The governor of the Central Bank, in discussing why changes in the money supply may not have the desired effect on imports, commented:

430

... the assumption that the parameters - that is, *income velocity* and the *marginal propensity to import* - are constant may be falsified by events, so that expenditure in general and expenditure on imports in particular may differ from what was expected.[4] (italics added)

The reference to the velocity of circulation of money implies that changes in the money supply determine total expenditure in accordance with the quantity theory of money. In turn, changes in total expenditure, via the marginal propensity to import, determine the level of imports.[5] The functioning of monetary policy would be roughly as follows. The credit guideline would control the growth in bank credit which in turn would regulate the money supply. Policy-induced changes in the money supply would influence total expenditure which, in turn, would determine the level of imports. At this time the Central Bank did not pay adequate attention to the difficulties of controlling the money supply in a small open economy with a fixed exchange rate.

The stance of monetary and credit policy over the period may be gauged from the Central Bank's policy statements. A reading of the statements (excerpts from which are contained in Appendix 1) indicates that monetary policy was in nearly all years aimed at accommodating the predicted growth in nominal GNP. There were only three years, 1965, 1969/70 and 1970/71, when policy could be said to have been clearly restrictive. (It might be argued that this was also the case in 1977.) Even when inflation and the balance of payments deficit were rising rapidly, as in 1974 and 1975, monetary policy was still designed to facilitate the projected growth in nominal GNP. The growth of nominal GNP is the main determinant of the growth of the demand for money and credit and hence it is difficult to assess whether a policy of accommodating the projected growth in nominal GNP has any effect on the outcome. Our assessment is that policy over these years was largely neutral, neither expansionary nor contractionary.

Summary

Over the period 1965-77 monetary policy in Ireland largely consisted of trying to regulate the money supply by issuing credit guidelines to control bank credit. This approach to monetary control was flawed because the Irish pound was pegged to sterling and the Dublin and London money markets were closely integrated. Moreover, due to weak enforcement, the credit guidelines did not succeed in constraining the growth of bank credit.

15.4   Credit Policy, 1978-84

In 1978 an important change was announced in the formulation of monetary policy in Ireland. The Central Bank acknowledged that it was not possible to control the money supply.[6] The Governor stated:

In an open economy such as Ireland's, it is generally accepted that the supply of money responds to the demand for it, so that monetary authorities cannot exercise a significant degree of control on the increase in money holdings . . .[7]

Monetary policy in Ireland after 1978 seems to have been based on the *monetary approach to the balance of payments* (MAB).[8] This theory provides a rationale for using credit guidelines to achieve an external reserves target. It is a modern-day version of the theory of international adjustment that operated under the old gold standard (see Chapter 11). The revival of the MAB dates from the work of the English Nobel Prize winning economist James Meade (b. 1907) in the 1950s. Under the influence of Jacques Polak this approach became the foundation of the International Monetary Fund's operational practices. Many countries that borrowed from the Fund are tied to policy programmes based on the MAB.

The MAB is based on the following identity which can be derived from the *consolidated balance sheet* of the banking system, which is known as the *monetary survey* by the IMF:

(1) $M^S \equiv DC + R$

where M^S = the supply of money, DC = domestic credit and R = external reserves. The money supply consists of cash and bank deposits, which are liabilities of the banking system; they equal the assets of the banking system, which consist of domestic credit and foreign reserves.

Note:
This identity is simplified for expositional purposes. In Appendix 2 to this chapter we derive the complete identity from the consolidated balance sheet of the Irish banking system.

Identity (1) can also be presented in terms of changes:

(2) $\Delta M^S \equiv DCE + \Delta R$

where DCE = domestic credit expansion, that is the change in domestic credit. This equals the change in bank lending to the private sector (BLP) plus bank lending to the government (BLG). Identity (2) can therefore be written:

(3) $\Delta M^S \equiv \Delta BLP + \Delta BLG + \Delta R$

One of the important assumptions underlying MAB is that the supply of money is determined by the demand for money (M^d). That is, the money supply is assumed to respond to demand. This assumption is consistent with the fact that the Central Bank cannot control the money supply in a small open economy when the exchange rate is fixed. However, the MAB suggests that it can influence the *composition* of the money supply by restricting domestic credit expansion. For any given growth in the demand for money, the slower the rate of domestic credit expansion, the faster the rate of accumulation of external reserves. This suggests that credit guidelines can be used to achieve an external reserves target.

Referring to identity (3) above, the following steps illustrate how a credit guideline can be used to achieve an external reserves target.

(1) Estimate the growth in the demand for money for the forthcoming year, which gives the target for the growth in the money supply. Typically this estimate is based on a forecast of the change in nominal GNP and the interest rate.

(2) Decide on the external reserves target. Usually some rule of thumb such as building up a certain number of months' import cover is used.

(3) Estimate the growth in Central Bank and licensed bank lending to the government $\Delta(BLG)$. Licensed bank lending to the government is largely determined by the secondary reserve ratio. Central Bank lending to the government is at the Bank's discretion.

(4) Issue a credit guideline to ensure that the change in bank lending to the private sector (ΔBLP) is consistent with the external reserves objective.

Suppose, for example, that the Central Bank predicts that the demand for money will increase by £100 million and that bank lending to the government will increase by £25 million. If the objective is to increase the external reserves by £25 million, from identity (3) the growth in licensed bank lending to the private sector should be restricted to £50 million. Given the various estimates and the external reserves objective, the credit guideline is in effect calculated as a residual.

Note:
MAB is a theory of the balance of payments because changes in the external reserves equal the overall balance of payments. A balance of payments deficit leads to a fall in the external reserves. Hence, an external reserves target is tantamount to a balance of payments target.

A credit guideline restricts the growth of bank credit and therefore curtails the growth in one of the counterparts of the money supply. If the demand for money exceeds this, an excess demand for money emerges which raises interest rates and reduces aggregate expenditure. This is expected to reduce expenditure on imports and lead to a capital inflow. As a result the balance of payments deficit falls and the external reserves increase. The Central Bank can thus achieve an external reserves target by pursuing a tight monetary policy. However, the capital inflow represents foreign borrowing, which will have to be repaid at a later stage.

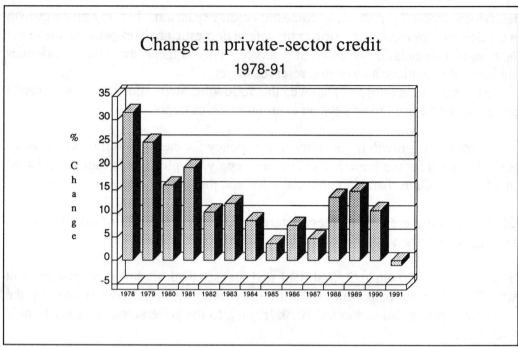

Change in private-sector credit

1978-91

Figure 15.2 Change in private sector credit, 1978-91

The influence of this theory on Irish monetary policy may be gauged from the following statement by the governor of the Central Bank :

The first step in determining credit policy is the estimation of the demand for money for the year ahead. Then, taking into account such features as the desired relationship between the level of reserves and imports and the new obligations which face us as members of the EMS, the Bank decides on the desired level of official external reserves. Given the projected increase in the demand for money this, in turn, yields the increase in total domestic credit which would be consistent with the reserves objectives. Taking account of the public sector's demand for credit, the amount of credit available to the private sector . . . is determined.[9]

It is important to note that a key assumption implicit in the MAB theory is that the demand for money is a *stable* function of a few variables such as nominal GNP and the interest rate. If, however, the demand for money fluctuates unpredictably over time, so too will the amount of additional money that can be absorbed by the economy and an identity like (3) will be of little value for policy purposes.[10]

15.5   Evaluation of Credit Policy

Figure 15.2 shows the growth in licensed bank credit to the private sector from 1978 to 1991. The growth rate slowed from 1978 to 1987 followed by a pick-up in 1988, but a *decline* of about one per cent was recorded in 1991. This was attributed to a lack of demand for credit due to the recession. As the growth of demand for credit decreased in the mid-1980s, credit guidelines became redundant. A central bank cannot implement a credit policy if the demand for credit falls short of the ceiling.

An important question is whether or not the credit guidelines achieved the desired external reserves target. Table 15.3 shows the guidelines, the external reserves objective and the external reserves outcome.

In 1978, a fall in the external reserves of up to £200 million was regarded as acceptable. (This was the only year the Central Bank published a specific target for the external reserves.) It was pointed out that

... the import cover afforded by the official external reserves is high at present by international standards and . . . some reduction can be tolerated.[11]

By the end of the year, bank lending exceeded the credit guideline by £320 million but, despite this, the external reserves *increased* by £50 million. The reason for this paradoxical outcome was that the Central Bank underestimated the increase in the demand for money by £348 million. This indicates a fundamental problem in implementing the MAB as an approach to policy, namely the assumption that the relationship between the growth in the demand for money and in nominal GNP is stable.

In 1979 the Central Bank's stated objective was ". . . little change in the external reserves", but in fact a decrease of £262 million occurred.

At the beginning of 1980 the economy was moving into a recession. The external reserves had fallen significantly during the previous year. The dilemma facing the Central Bank was to try to build up the reserves while at the same time to ". . . avoid introducing a deflationary element into economic policy . . ."[12] It resolved this dilemma by encouraging the banks to borrow abroad. This was achieved by issuing a restrictive credit guideline of 13 per cent and then exempting from the guideline any lending financed by foreign borrowing. If the banks borrowed abroad and then on-lent the money in Ireland, that lending would not be subject to the guideline.

The external reserves increased by £331 million in 1980, almost exactly equal to the £323 million borrowed abroad by the banks. The growth in the demand for money was underestimated by £302 million. This outcome was not expected by the Central Bank, whose goal was to achieve "a small increase" in the external reserves. In later years externally financed lending was included in the credit guidelines.

In 1981, credit policy aimed at maintaining the external reserves at "an adequate level". The outcome was more in line with intentions.

After 1981, the Central Bank became increasingly vague with regard to the external reserves objective. In 1982, the credit guideline was designed to "not . . . accommodate any slippage in the balance of payments" and, in 1983, to facilitate the "expected growth in nominal GNP". These guidelines did not act as a constraint: the growth in bank lending was less than that stipulated by the guidelines because there was a fall in the demand for credit as the economy moved into recession. The guidelines therefore could not have contributed to an external reserves target in these two years. In 1984 an "indicative" credit guideline of 10 per cent was issued. No credit guidelines have been issued by the Central Bank since then.

Table 15.3
Credit guidelines and the external reserves target

Period	Credit guideline	ΔR objective	ΔR outcome
Dec.1977- Dec.1978	20%	- £200m	+ £50m
Feb.1979 - Feb.1980	18%	"little change"	- £262m
Feb.1980 - Feb.1981	13%	"small increase"	+ £331m
Feb.1981 - Feb.1982	15%	"adequate level"	- £50m

Source: Central Bank of Ireland, *Quarterly Bulletin*, various issues.
Note:
The Central Bank abandoned the original credit guideline in the middle of 1978 and replaced it with a new six-month guideline for the period to March 1979.

In summary, the Central Bank would appear to have had only modest success in using credit guidelines to achieve external reserves targets in the early 1980s. Problems arose from estimating the demand for money and obtaining the banks' compliance with the guidelines. A more fundamental problem was, however, that while it is reasonable to expect that if the growth of domestic credit is held below the increase in the demand for money the external reserves will increase over time, this general relationship is not predictable enough to permit the use of the MAB framework to achieve a specific external reserves objective.[13]

15.6 The Costs of Credit Guidelines

The imposition of credit guidelines entails costs. Competition between banks is stifled. An efficient bank which is successful in attracting deposits is not allowed to increase its market share. This problem was mentioned by the Central Bank as one of the factors leading to the abandoning of credit guidelines in 1973.

More generally, credit guidelines are a form of non-price rationing that can cause a misallocation of resources. To illustrate this, in Figure 15.3 we show the supply of credit (C^s) and the demand for credit (C^d). On the vertical axis is the interest rate (r) and on the horizontal axis bank lending (Q). At A, the two curves intersect at the interest rate of r_1 and bank lending is Q_1. Suppose now the Central Bank imposes a credit guideline which curtails bank lending to Q_2. The market is now moved to X which is off the supply and demand curves. At the interest rate of r_1, the private sector demands Q_1 but because of the guideline the banks can only lend Q_2. There

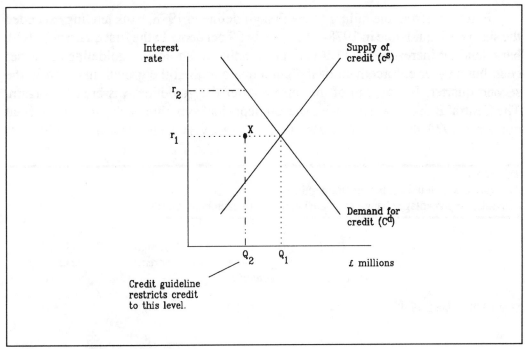

Figure 15.3 Credit rationing

is therefore an excess demand for credit equal to (Q_1 - Q_2) and the banks have to *ration* credit to customers.[14]

Rationing can result in a misallocation of resources. For example, banks may be more inclined to lend to old established customers rather than new customers even if, after allowing for risk, the projects proposed by new customers offer a higher return. The result may be that the banks do not allocate the available funds to the most productive uses. The interest rate is a more efficient way of allocating resources because, as the interest rate increases, low productivity projects will become unprofitable and will not be undertaken. Although the scope for an independent interest rate policy in an open economy with fixed exchange rates is limited, by controlling the growth of its assets the Central Bank can, as we saw in Chapter 14, have some influence on the liquidity of the banking system and hence the level of interest rates. If the interest rate were to rise to r_2 it would allocate the available funds to projects on the basis of their ability to service the borrowed money. This would be a more efficient way of controlling the expansion of credit than the imposition of credit guidelines.

Stop/go in the availability of credit Table 15.4 shows how the associated banks reacted to the quantitative and personal lending guidelines over the period 1978 to 1981. The data are presented as the *cumulative* percentage change from the introduction of each new guideline.

437

Following from the failure of the first guideline in 1978, bank lending exceeded the six-month guideline in 1978-79 by nearly 50 per cent. In the first quarter of 1979, bank lending increased by 11.9 per cent relative to an annual guideline of 18 per cent, but stricter enforcement of the guideline curtailed the growth in credit in the second quarter. By the end of the third quarter the guideline was breached again. The Central Bank now demanded special deposits from nine banks and, in the final quarter of 1979, the banks decreased lending to a level consistent with the guideline.

Table 15.4
Associated bank lending and the credit guidelines
(Cumulative percentage change from the beginning of each guideline)

Period	Total private sector credit	Quantitative credit guideline	Personal credit	Personal lending guideline
Sept 1978 - March 1979	14.7	10.0	- 3.0	5.0
1979 Q1	11.9		8.4	
Q2	14.6		0.4	
Q3	18.6		- 0.6	
Q4	17.5	18	- 1.4	10
1980 Q1	2.4		3.1	
Q2	- 0.5		3.6	
Q3	5.1		11.9	
Q4	12.7	13	5.7	6.0
1981 Q1	6.8		14.2	
Q2	6.8		3.8	
Q3	14.5		11.1	
Q4	16.3	15.0	13.5	Directive

Source: Central Bank of Ireland, *Quarterly Bulletin*, various issues.

Over the first nine months of the 1980 credit policy year, the cumulative increase in credit was only 5 per cent compared to a guideline of 13 per cent. It was only in the final quarter that lending was maximised relative to the guideline.[15]

This analysis suggests that there was a "stop/go" in the availability of credit as a result of the guidelines. When the banks expanded lending at a rate in excess of the guideline, the Central Bank sanctions led to a subsequent contraction in lending. It would have been difficult to obtain credit in the second quarter of 1979 and during the period from the fourth quarter of 1979 to the third quarter of 1980 but much easier in other periods. The odds of obtaining a loan therefore depended crucially on the *timing* of the loan application rather than on the profitability of the project for which the loan was sought.

A comparison of the growth in personal lending and the sectoral guideline in Table 15.6 shows that there was a decrease or slow-down in personal lending in several quarters. All of these were preceded by Central Bank requests to the associated banks to curtail lending.[16]

Discrimination Between November 1978 and February 1980, there was a cumulative *decrease* in personal lending of 10.9 per cent. However instalment credit, which was not subject to the personal lending guideline, *increased* by 25.9 per cent over the same period. As the interest rate on instalment credit is roughly double the interest rate on personal loans, this suggests that the banks discriminated against personal borrowers in order to maximise group profits.

Given that total credit was subject to a quantitative guideline, a reduction in personal lending made more money available for "productive" lending. Borrowers refused personal loans at the associated banks could be encouraged to avail of instalment credit which, although subject to higher interest rate charges, was at least available. Moreover, the associated banks have subsidiaries in the instalment credit business and disappointed borrowers could be channelled to these subsidiaries. The net effect of this manoeuvring would be to maximise the banks' group profits as "productive" borrowers were accommodated by the banks and personal borrowers by their subsidiaries at higher interest rates. Encouraging personal borrowers to switch to instalment credit was in effect a profitable way around the quantitative credit guideline. However, there is evidence to suggest that a significant proportion of rationed borrowers were not prepared to pay the higher interest rates which instalment credit entailed and instead abandoned their expenditure plans.[17]

15.7   The Future Role of Credit Policy

Credit guidelines were not an effective instrument of monetary policy over the years 1965 to 1984. Their impact was reduced by problems of enforcement and by the use of an inappropriate model of the economy in their formulation. The slow-down in the growth of the demand for credit during the mid-1980s rendered this approach to monetary policy redundant. Economists are now generally quite critical of the attempt to ration credit in this manner because of the distortions it creates in the economy.

It is difficult to see a role for credit rationing by the Central Bank in the future. If credit ceilings were imposed in one part of monetary union, borrowers could seek accommodation elsewhere. To the extent that any control can be exercised over monetary aggregates in Ireland in the future it is likely to be through indirect controls (that is, the supply of liquidity to the banking system) and their effect on interest rates, along the lines discussed in the previous chapter. However we saw that the scope for this type of monetary policy will be eliminated with the advent of irrevocably fixed exchange rates and complete capital mobility in Europe. We are, therefore, facing into an era in which the role of the Central Bank of Ireland will be reduced to a very minor one and its powers largely transferred to a European Central Bank.

15.8   Conclusion

In this chapter we examined credit policy in Ireland from 1965 to 1977 and from 1978 to 1982. We distinguished between these two sub-periods because of a fundamental change in credit policy after 1978.

With regard to the earlier sub-period, the main points are:

- Credit guidelines were designed to control the money supply
- The objective of controlling the money supply was to influence imports or the inflation rate
- The theoretical model underlying monetary policy appears to have been the quantity theory of money
- For the most part, the credit guidelines attempted to accommodate the predicted growth in nominal GNP
- The credit guidelines did not curtail bank lending in the first instance but even if they had it would still not be possible to control the money supply because of the fixed exchange rate and perfect capital mobility between Ireland and the UK.

The main points relating to the 1978-82 period are:

- The objective of the credit guidelines was to achieve an external reserves target
- The theory underlying credit policy was the monetary approach to the balance of payments (MAB)
- The evidence indicates that the Central Bank had only limited success in achieving its external reserves targets
- The quantitative credit guideline did not, on the whole, unduly constrain total private sector credit
- The Central Bank also issued sectoral credit guidelines to curtail banks' personal lending
- The credit guidelines involved costs in the form of misallocation of resources.

Notes

1. A bank that exceeds the credit guideline has to place special deposits, on which it earns no interest, with the Central Bank. Special deposits are not *sufficient* to remove profits on excess lending because excess lending increases a bank's lending base which, in turn, is used to calculate next year's credit allocation. Banks that breach a credit guideline therefore have an unfair advantage. In order to remove this incentive to breach the guideline, the Central Bank must make some adjustment to a bank's lending base in calculating the second year's credit allocation. This type of measure is referred to as a *market base deduction*. The effect is to return a bank to its "correct" lending base by the end of the second year. In this way, no advantage is gained over banks which comply with the guidelines.

2. Central Bank of Ireland, *Annual Report*, 1970/1971, p. 32.

3. T. K. Whitaker, "The Central Bank and the Banking System", Lecture to the Cork Centre of the Institute of Bankers, November 1971, p. 71.

4. T. K. Whitaker, "Banking and Credit in Ireland To-day", Central Bank of Ireland, *Quarterly Bulletin*, Geimhreadh, 1969, p. 114.

5. The research work of J. S. Oslizlok was used to formulate monetary policy. Although no formal model is outlined by Oslizlok in his published papers, he argued that the money supply could affect nominal output and that the Central Bank could exert some degree of control over the money supply: see: T. K. Whitaker, "Monetary Policy", Central Bank of Ireland, *Quarterly Bulletin*, Geimhreadh, 1969, p. 104; J. S. Oslizlok, "Surveys of Sources of Monetary Supplies in Ireland", *Journal* of the Statistical and Social Inquiry Society of Ireland, 1962/63; "Towards a Monetary Analysis of Aggregate Demand", Central Bank of Ireland, *Quarterly Bulletin*, November 1967; and "Towards a Monetary Analysis of Aggregate Demand - 2: The Circulation of Active Money", Central Bank of Ireland, *Quarterly Bulletin*, February 1968. The paper by T. F. Hoare, "Money, Autonomous Expenditure and Aggregate Income", Central Bank of Ireland, *Annual Report*, 1972/73, was the first published attempt to model the monetary sector in Ireland. The model was based on the quantity theory of money and assumed that the velocity of circulation of money was constant. The paper illustrated how to calculate the expansion in credit consistent with a nominal output target.

6. It is possible that the change in the Central Bank's view with regard to money supply control was influenced by the results in F. X. Browne and T. O'Connell, "A Quantitative Analysis of the Degree of Integration between Irish and UK Financial Markets", *Economic and Social Review*, Vol. 9, No. 4, 1978. The evidence presented by these two Central Bank economists indicated that there was perfect integration between Irish and UK financial markets in the period up to 1978. Under these circumstances it is not possible to control the money supply in the Irish economy.

7. C. H. Murray, "Monetary Policy", Central Bank of Ireland, *Quarterly Bulletin*, 4, 1979, p. 71.

8. For a collection of essays on MAB theory see J. A. Frenkel and H. G. Johnson (eds), *The Monetary Approach to the Balance of Payments*, London, Allen and Unwin, 1976. A useful survey of the early literature is given in M. E. Kreinin and L. H. Officer, The Monetary Approach to the Balance of Payments: A Survey, *Princeton Studies in International Finance*, No. 43, Princeton University Press, 1978.

9. C. H. Murray, "Monetary Policy", Central Bank of Ireland, *Quarterly Bulletin*, 4, 1979, p. 72.

10. The results presented in F. X. Browne and T. O'Connell, "The Demand for Money Function in Ireland: Estimation and Stability", *The Economic and Social Review*, Vol. 9, April 1978, indicated that the demand for money in Ireland is a stable function of a few variables. This result is supported

by the findings in M. Kenneally and M. Finn, "The Balance of Payments as a Monetary Phenomenon: A Review and Consideration of Irish Evidence, 1960-1978", *The Economic and Social Review*, Vol. 17, No. 1, October 1985. The implication of these results is that MAB theory could be used in Ireland for policy purposes.

11. Central Bank of Ireland, *Annual Report*, 1978, p. 25.

12. Central Bank of Ireland, *Annual Report*, 1980, p. 13.

13. Both R. Kelleher, "Recent Trends in Monetary Policy", *Quarterly Economic Commentary*, ESRI, 1980, and the National Planning Board, *Proposals for Plan: 1984-1987*, National Planning Board, Dublin, 1984, point to the inappropriateness of the external reserves as a policy target. The point is that the external reserves do not take account of foreign indebtedness and as such is an inadequate measure of the Central Bank's ability to maintain the Irish pound exchange rate in foreign exchange markets. Both papers argue that *external finance*, defined as the change in the external reserves minus foreign borrowing, is the more relevant policy objective. It can be shown that if the Central Bank's objective was to stabilise external finance over the period, no additional credit would have been available to the private sector.

14. This type of rationing is referred to as *guideline credit rationing* as it is the credit guideline which causes the excess demand for credit. Other forms of rationing have been identified in the literature. For example, a theory of *equilibrium credit rationing* is given in J. E. Stiglitz and A. Weiss, "Credit Rationing in Markets with Imperfect Information", *American Economic Review*, Vol. 71, No. 3, 1981. A third type of credit rationing is known as *disequilibrium* (or dynamic) *credit rationing*. This type of rationing arises when the interest rate fails to move instantaneously to its equilibrium level following some disturbance to the supply or demand curves for credit. See for example, F. X. Browne, "Empirical Estimates of Dynamic Credit Rationing in the Market for Associated Bank Private Sector Loans", Central Bank of Ireland, Technical Paper, 2/RT/84, January 1984.

15. The surge in the extension of credit towards the end of the year may have owed something to the scope for increased lending within the guideline; this, in turn, may have been attributable partly to the pursuit by the banks of conservative lending policies earlier in the year in order to avoid the danger of breaching the guideline (Central Bank of Ireland, *Annual Report*, 1981, p. 23, 24).

16. For example, starting with 1980 Q4:

. . . the increase (in personal lending) for the nine months to November was somewhat in excess of the 6 per cent guideline . . . The Central Bank has been in communication with banks in breach of the 6 per cent guideline, with a view to taking appropriate action in the light of subsequent developments. Central Bank of Ireland, *Quarterly Bulletin*, 4, 1980, p. 24.

. . . the increase in (personal) lending . . . was not consistent with the objectives of monetary policy. Accordingly, the banks concerned have been contacted with a view to securing compliance with the intent of monetary policy.
Central Bank of Ireland, *Quarterly Bulletin*, 2, 1981, p. 16.

. . . in view of this rapid increase (in personal credit), the Central Bank informed a number of banks that the intent of monetary policy was not being complied with and advised these banks . . .
Central Bank of Ireland, Quarterly Bulletin, 4, 1981, p. 24.

. . . growth in lending to the personal sector was relatively rapid and banks have been contacted with a view to securing compliance with the sectoral guideline of 7 per cent . . .
Central Bank of Ireland, *Quarterly Bulletin*, 2, 1982, p. 15.

The close relationship between Central Bank enforcement of the personal lending guidelines and the decrease in bank lending suggests that the banks rationed personal loans at certain times over the period.

17. See, for example, A. Leddin, "The Impact of Credit Controls on Consumer Durable Expenditures and Fixed Investment in the Irish Economy", *Journal of Irish Business and Administrative Research*, Vol. 8, No. 2, 1986.

Appendix 1 Objectives of monetary policy, 1965-77

Mar. 1965 - Dec. 1965. ". . . the Central Bank has had regard to the many difficulties both for the banks and for the economy in the way of slowing down the expansion in credit".
Central Bank of Ireland, *Annual Report*, 1964/65, p. 17.

Mar. 1967 - Dec. 1968. ". . . any slackening in the growth of bank credit is neither desirable nor necessary . . ."
Central Bank of Ireland, *Annual Report*, 1966/67, p. 22.

April 1968 - April 1969. ". . . the Board . . . have formed the opinion that a moderately liberal attitude towards the growth of credit is appropriate . . ."
Central Bank of Ireland, *Annual Report*, 1967/68, p. 20.

April 1969 - April 1970. ". . . the aim of credit policy must be to reduce the pressure of inflation . . . A lower rate of increase in total bank lending . . . than actually occurred last year . . . is indicated".
Central Bank of Ireland, *Annual Report*, 1968/69, p. 47.

April 1970 - April 1971. In 1970 monetary policy was designed to exert "some degree of internal demand restraint" (Central Bank of Ireland, *Quarterly Bulletin*, Spring, 1970, p. 11) with the objective of reducing the balance of payments deficit from a projected £80-90 million to £50 million. This entailed reducing the growth in nominal GNP from a projected 13 per cent to 10.5 per cent and the real growth rate from 5 per cent to 3 per cent. The Central Bank's view was that "both public expenditure and credit can be powerful inflationary forces through their influence on the level of expenditure and . . . there is no doubt that excessive income and price increases are vacillated by liberal fiscal and monetary policies."
Central Bank of Ireland, *Quarterly Bulletin*, Spring, 1970, p. 9.

April 1971 - April 1972. "In providing for the year ahead, it would not be advisable to envisage a degree of credit restriction which would adversely affect business liquidity and therefore, investment, production and employment."
Central Bank of Ireland, *Annual Report*, 1970/71, p. 31.

April 1972 - April 1973. ". . . monetary policy . . . is not restrictive. It is designed to facilitate the maximum sustainable growth in output and employment . . ."
Central Bank of Ireland, *Annual Report*, 1971-72, p. 31.

April 1973 - April 1974. "It would be most undesirable that credit expansion should itself generate inflationary spending . . ."
Central Bank of Ireland, *Quarterly Bulletin*, 2, 1973, p. 17.

1974 "The general effect is to allow bank credit . . . to be increased at about the same rate as the prospective increase in Gross Domestic Expenditure."
Central Bank of Ireland, *Quarterly Bulletin*, 2, 1974, p. 14.

1975 "It is expected that Gross Domestic Expenditure will increase by about 22 per cent in 1975. To support this increase, it is the intention of the Central Bank that the growth in the money supply should be of the same order . . . (and) . . . bank lending should increase at a somewhat higher rate . . ."
Central Bank of Ireland, *Annual Report*, 1975, p. 3.

1976 ". . . monetary policy will aim at accommodating the reasonable demands of the private sector".
Central Bank of Ireland, *Annual Report*, 1976, p. 10.

1977 " . . . monetary policy should contribute to the achievement of a further reduction in the rate of inflation . . ."
Central Bank of Ireland, *Annual Report*, 1977, p. 24.

Appendix 2 The monetary approach to the balance of payments (MAB)

Consider the following consolidated balance sheet of the banking system.

Consolidated balance sheet of banking system.

	31 Dec. 1991 £ millions
Liabilities	
1. Capital employed	2,464
2. Government deposits at the Central Bank	1,248
3. Currency	1,381
4. Current accounts	1,817
5. Deposit accounts	9,830
6. Accrued interest	234
$M^3 = 3 + 4 + 5 + 6$ (Money supply)	13,260
7. Net external liabilities of licensed banks	3,311
8. Acceptances	75
9. Other liabilities	991
Total liabilities	21,349
Assets	
10. Non-government credit	13,723
11. Accrued interest	137
12. Government credit	3,075
13. Official external reserves	3,256
14. Fixed assets	613
15. Other assets	545
Total assets	121,349

Source: Central Bank of Ireland, *Quarterly Bulletin*, Spring 1992, Table C1.
Note: Capital employed is calculated as a residual.

Assets = Liabilities. Hence:

$$M^3 \equiv 10 + 11 + 12 + 13 + 14 + 15 - (1 + 2 + 7 + 8 + 9)$$
$$\equiv (10 + 11) + (12 - 2) + 13 - 7 - (1 + 8 + 9 - 14 - 15)$$
$$\equiv NGL + BLG + R - NEL - NNDL$$

where

NGL	=	Bank lending to the non-government sector
BLG	=	Bank lending to the government
R	=	External reserves
NEL	=	Net external liability of domestic banks
NNDL	=	Net non-deposit liabilities of domestic banks

Consider changes over a period of, say, one year.

$$(1) \quad \Delta M^3 \equiv \Delta NGL + \Delta BLG + \Delta R - \Delta NEL - \Delta NNDL$$

Now from the balance of payments (see Chapter 10, Table 10.1):

$$(2) \quad \Delta R = BOP + GEB + PCI + \Delta NEL$$

where

BOP	=	Balance of payments on current account (deficit -, surplus +)
GEB	=	Government external borrowing
PCI	=	Private capital inflow
ΔNEL	=	Change in net external liabilities of banks

Substitute (2) into (1):

$$\Delta M^3 \equiv \Delta NGL + \Delta BLG + BOP + GEB + PCI + \Delta NEL - \Delta NEL - \Delta NNDL$$
$$\equiv \Delta NGL + \Delta BLG + GEB - \Delta NNDL + BOP + PCI$$
$$\equiv DCE - \Delta NNDL + BOP + PCI$$

where DCE is *domestic credit expansion* in the economy i.e. the increase in bank lending to the private sector (ΔNGL), plus monetary financing of the government ($\Delta BLG + GEB$). If $\Delta NNDL$ and PCI are both assumed to be zero, this accounting identity states that:

$$\Delta M^3 \equiv DCE + BOP$$

or

$$\Delta M^3 - DCE \equiv BOP$$

If we consider M^3 to be equivalent to the growth in resources in the banking system, this states that if resource growth is less than the growth of claims on resources (DCE) there will be a balance of payments deficit and vice versa.

Chapter 16

Foreign Exchange Markets, Interest Rates and International Finance

16.1 Introduction

In this chapter we discuss the workings of the foreign exchange market and we explain the links between this market and domestic and foreign interest rates. This is followed by a discussion of some aspects of international financial theory. This material will deepen the student's understanding of the issues relating to financial convergence discussed in Chapters 11 and 13.

16.2 The Forward Exchange Market

Individuals or firms engaging in commercial or investment transactions find it desirable to minimise *foreign exchange risk*. *Hedging* techniques help them to do so. As an example of exchange rate risk consider the case of an exporter who expects to receive STG£1 million in one month's time and anticipates that the exchange rate will be STG£0.92/IR£1. At this exchange rate, Irish pound receipts will be IR£1,086,957 (Stg£1,000,000 × 1/0.92) and the exporter calculates that he will make a normal profit on the transaction. Suppose, however, that the Irish pound unexpectedly appreciates to STG£0.94/IR£1. The exporter's receipts will translate into only IR£1,063,830. This is IR£23,127 less than was originally anticipated and could render the deal unprofitable. This shows how changes in exchange rates can reduce or eliminate profits from international transactions.

A number of different hedging techniques have been developed to avoid or eliminate exchange rate risk. These may be grouped into *internal* and *external* techniques. In this section we describe one of the most widely used external hedging techniques, the *forward exchange market*.

It is important to note at the outset that while a hedging strategy minimises exchange rate losses, it also removes any possibility of making windfall profits from exchange rate movements. In the above example, if the exchange rate had depreciated the exporter would have profited. In practice, firms' treasury managers and other individuals concerned with international cash flows do not always attempt to eliminate exchange rate risk because taking risks (or speculating) on foreign exchange movements can be profitable. However, most firms wish to concentrate on making money out of their trading activities and prefer to leave speculation on the foreign exchange markets to specialists.

Forward exchange contract

A forward contract consists of agreeing to buy or sell a specified amount of foreign currency *for delivery some time in the future* at an exchange rate agreed today. Payment and delivery are not required until the maturity date. For example, consider the case of an Irish firm importing cars from Germany. The cars will arrive in three months' time and the Irish importer will be required to pay, say, DM2,670,000 at that time. If the current *(spot)* exchange rate is DM2.67/IR£1, the importer's bill will be IR£1 million. The importer however may be worried that over the next three months the Irish pound could depreciate against the DM and not be prepared to take the exchange rate risk. (If the Irish pound fell to DM2.5/IR£1 the importer's bill would increase by IR£64,000.) To remove this uncertainty the importer could enter into a contract which provides *forward cover* and removes his *exposure* to exchange rate risk. For example, he could arrange today to have DM2,670,000 delivered in three months' time at an exchange rate *(the three-month forward rate)* agreed today. Once the importer enters into a forward agreement he is no longer exposed to any exchange rate risk.

Forward exchange rates are quoted for one, two, three, six and twelve months and contracts can be arranged for longer periods. The rates are available from the banks and are published in the financial newspapers. Table 16.1 shows the spot and six-month forward exchange rates for the Irish pound against sterling and the dollar in March 1992.

The spot rates given in Table 16.1 indicate that a bank dealer will sell sterling for STG£0.9325 per Irish pound and buy sterling for STG£0.9335 per Irish pound. Recall from Chapter 10 that the *bid* rate is the rate at which banks buy Irish pounds (or sell foreign currency) and the *offer* rate is the rate at which the banks sell Irish pounds (buy foreign currency). The difference between the bid and offer rates is referred to as the "spread" and it provides the banks' profit from foreign exchange transactions.

The six-month forward rates in Table 16.1 are the rates at which sterling and the dollar can be purchased or sold forward. Suppose, for example, an Irish importer wishes to obtain sterling six months from now. The bank will sell sterling forward to the importer (delivery is in six months' time) at an exchange rate of STG£0.9334/IR£1. Similarly, an exporter who is due to receive a certain amount of dollars in six months' time can eliminate exchange rate risk by selling dollars to the bank. The bank will buy dollars at a forward exchange rate of $1.5675/IR£1.

Table 16.1
Spot and forward exchange rates, March 1992

| | STG£/IR£ | | $/IR£ | |
	Bid	Offer	Bid	Offer
Spot	.9325	.9335	1.6120	1.6130
6 month forward	.9334	.9355	1.5655	1.5675

Source: AIB International Department.

The forward exchange rate is normally at a *premium* or a *discount* relative to the spot exchange rate. Using indirect quotes (i.e. STG£/IR£), which is the convention in Ireland, if the forward exchange rate is *lower* than the spot rate the Irish pound is said to be at a *discount* relative to the foreign currency. Conversely, if the forward rate is *higher* than the spot rate, the Irish pound is said to be at a *premium* relative to the foreign currency. (If the Irish pound is at a discount relative to sterling then sterling is at a premium relative to the Irish pound.)

Comparing the spot and forward rates in Table 16.1, more sterling can be obtained per Irish pounds delivered in the future than delivered today and hence the Irish pound is at a premium. Fewer dollars can be obtained in the future per Irish pounds and hence the Irish pound is at a discount relative to the dollar. If the spot and forward rates are exactly the same, the forward price is said to be *flat*.

Options contract A variation on the forward currency contract is the *forward currency options contract*. This gives the holder the right, but not the obligation, to buy or sell currency in the future. For this right, the holder will be charged a fee expressed as a percentage of the total amount of money involved. The right to *sell* a currency is referred to as a *put* option and the right to *buy* a currency is known as a *call* option. The distinctive feature of option contracts is that while the holder can avoid exchange rate losses (downside risk) she can benefit from any favourable movements in the exchange rate (upside potential), or vice versa.

For example, take the case of an Irish exporter who expects to receive $1 million in three months' time. To avoid exchange rate risk she enters into an options contract to convert dollars to Irish pounds at an exchange rate of, say, $1.6/IR£1. If the spot dollar exchange rate depreciates (Irish pound appreciates) to $1.7/£1, the exporter should exercise her option contract in order to avoid incurring an exchange rate loss. If however the spot dollar exchange rate appreciates (Irish pound depreciates) to, say, $1.5/IR£1, the exporter should allow the options contract to lapse and instead convert the dollars receipts to Irish pounds on the spot market. In this case she will gain from the exchange rate movement. If the exporter had used a normal forward currency contract, she would have avoided any exchange rate loss but would also have forgone any gains. The option contract will be used by people who are more worried about one type of risk than the other. Of course, a fee or commission is charged on these contracts, otherwise they would be clearly superior to using the forward market.

Speculation and the forward exchange rate

While the forward exchange rate is normally used to eliminate exchange rate risk, it can also be used for speculative purposes. This is because the forward exchange rate and the *future spot exchange rate* are rarely the same. Suppose for example that the six month sterling forward rate is currently STG£0.93/IR£1 and that a speculator anticipates that the spot exchange rate in six months' time will be STG£0.92/IR£1. On the assumption that in six months' time the speculator's expectations with regard to the future spot exchange rate prove correct, she could profit from the situation. The speculator could:

1. Contract to buy, say, STG£1 million forward at STG£0.93/IR£1. The Irish pound cost would be IR£1,075,269.

2. Then in six months' time sell the STG£1 million on the spot market at STG£0.92/IR£1 and receive IR£1,086,956.

3. Her profit on the transaction would be IR£11,687.

In general, if the speculator expects the future spot exchange rate to be lower than today's forward exchange rate, she should buy the foreign currency forward today and sell it on the spot market in the future. Conversely, if the expected future spot exchange rate is higher than the current forward exchange rate, the speculator should contract to sell the foreign currency on the forward market today and purchase it in the future on the spot market.

The profit on such a deal cannot be expressed in percentage terms as no capital is actually invested when the speculator enters into the forward contract. The profit is simply the return from risk taking. The amount that can be invested in this type of speculation will be limited by the amount of credit the speculator can draw down. There is, therefore, considerable scope for profitable speculation on the foreign exchange markets. A key question is: Can any rule be devised to be used to ensure that such speculation is profitable, or is it as random as playing roulette in a casino? We explore this issue in relation to the Irish experience with regard to sterling, the DM and the dollar in the following section.

It is important to note that the type of speculation discussed above is not permitted under Irish exchange controls. Up to January 1988 firms could only buy or sell currency forward if the transaction was *trade related*. Service industries had to use some alternative hedging technique or accept the exchange rate risk. However, the exchange controls were relaxed in January 1988 to allow service industries access to forward cover and in January 1992 to allow capital transactions and debt repayments cover. Speculative capital flows continue to be excluded from forward cover.

The exclusion of service industries from forward cover in the 1980s encouraged the development of alternative hedging techniques. One method of circumventing the controls was to use a *forward contract between two foreign currencies*. Consider the case of an exporter who expects to be paid in dollars in the future but who cannot obtain forward cover because of exchange controls. The exporter might observe that the Irish pound is much more stable relative to the DM than it is to the dollar because of Ireland's participation in the ERM. Hence the exporter could enter into a forward contract to convert dollars to DM and then re-convert the DM to Irish pounds on the spot market. (Irish exchange controls do not extend to contracts between two foreign currencies.) The stability of the Irish pound in the ERM would remove most of the exchange rate risk.

16.3 The Forward Exchange Market for Irish Pounds, 1979-91

Figures 16.1, 16.2 and 16.3 show the three month forward exchange rate (F_t) and the future spot exchange rate (E_{t+1}) for sterling, the DM and the dollar respectively. The forward rate today is compared with the spot rate three months from now. It is evident from the three graphs that the two variables do not coincide. In particular, it is noticeable that, for all three currencies, the forward rate consistently *fails to predict turning points* in the future spot exchange rate.

As mentioned in the previous section, if the forward exchange rate and the future spot exchange rate are not equal, it is possible to profit from speculation on the forward market. Consider the relationship between F_t and E_{t+1} from the perspective of exporters and importers. Suppose an exporter expects to receive STG£1 million in three months' time. The exporter has a choice as to whether to sell sterling forward and avoid exchange rate risk or sell sterling spot in three months' time and accept the exchange rate risk. Using data for 1980 quarter 4 the alternative outcomes would have been as follows:

1. If the exporter had sold STG£1 million three months earlier at a forward exchange rate of $(1/Ft) = (1/.8710)$, his receipts would have been IR£1,148,106.

453

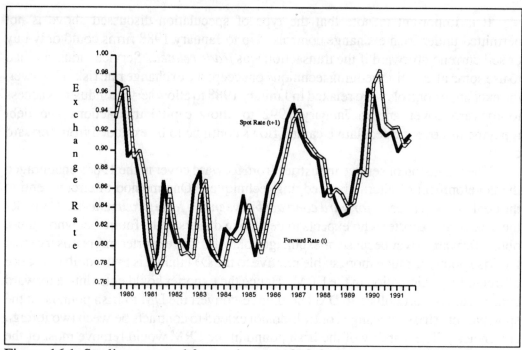

Figure 16.1 Sterling spot and forward rates, 1979-91

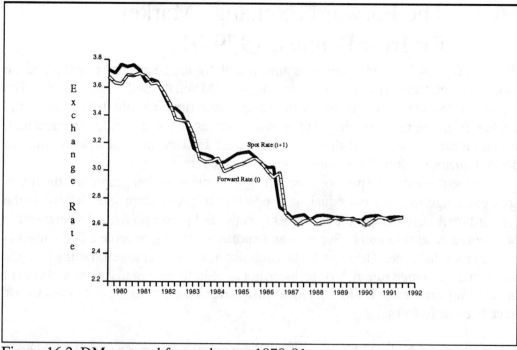

Figure 16.2 DM spot and forward rates, 1979-91

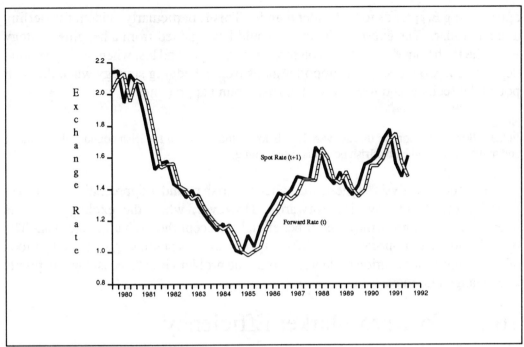

Figure 16.3 Dollar spot and forward rates, 1979-91

---

2. If the exporter accepted the exchange rate risk and sold STG£1 million on the spot market at $(1/E_{t+1}) = (1/.8038)$, Irish pound receipts would have been IR£1,244,091.

It is clear from this example that because F_t was not equal to E_{t+1}, the exporter's receipts differed significantly depending on which option he chose. If the exporter had decided to hedge, his receipts would have been IR£95,984 *lower* per STG£1 million transaction (or almost one per cent) than if he had accepted the exchange rate risk and sold sterling on the spot market. This illustrates how hedging can entail forgoing a significant profit. Thus exchange rate risk should not be avoided as a matter of course. For this reason, currency management is an integral part of treasury management in any large firm whose business involves extensive foreign exchange dealings.

In the above example the exporter would have forgone a profit by contracting forward. However, an importer would have gained by entering into a forward contract. The reason is that the importer is buying foreign currency when the exporter is selling: the two cases are mirror images of the same transaction.

Are there any indicators of when a trader should or should not engage in hedging? As in the previous example an exporter *loses* from a hedging strategy if E_{t+1} is *lower* than F_t. Referring to Figures 16.1, 16.2 and 16.3, note that when the Irish pound is depreciating, E_{t+1} is less than F_t and when the Irish pound is appreciating E_{t+1} tends to be greater than F_t. This is particularly evident for sterling and the dollar. The exporter therefore would have gained from a hedging strategy when the Irish pound appreciated on foreign exchanges and lost when the Irish pound depreciated. Conversely, the importer gains from a hedging strategy when the Irish pound depreciates and loses when the Irish pound appreciates.

Note:
In the following section we discuss why E_{t+1} is lower than F_t when the Irish pound is depreciating and higher than F_t when the Irish pound is appreciating.

The above analysis suggests that when the Irish pound is appreciating, exporters would profit from covering forward. However, when the exchange rate is depreciating, exporters may find it beneficial to accept the exchange rate risk. The opposite holds for importers. The difficulty, however, is predicting sustained periods of Irish pound appreciation or depreciation. The problem is to forecast turning points in exchange rate movements.

16.4   Forward Market Efficiency

The unbiased predictor hypothesis (UPH)   The forward exchange rate is said to be an *unbiased* predictor of the future spot rate if, over time, the forward rate is equal to the future spot rate plus or minus a random error. Mathematically, the unbiased predictor hypothesis (UPH) may be written:

(1) $E_{t+1} = \alpha + \beta F_t + u_t$

where E_{t+1} is the spot exchange rate in time $t+1$, F_t is the forward exchange rate in time t and u_t represents the forecast error. This error should be random with a mean of zero and a constant variance. If F_t is an unbiased predictor of E_{t+1}, the coefficients α and β will equal 0 and 1 respectively. F_t will equal E_{t+1} *on average*.

If the UPH holds, today's forward rate is the *best* indicator of what the spot exchange rate will be in the future. But this does not mean that it is an *accurate* predictor. It simply means that the forecast error (or prediction error) tends to be random and cannot be explained, and that no better rule can be devised for predicting E_{t+1}. For example, the six month dollar forward rate was \$1.3915/IR£1 at the end of June 1989. This could have been taken as a forecast of what the dollar spot rate would be in six months' time. In fact, the spot rate turned out to be \$1.4795/IR£1 at the end of December, giving a forecast error of 6.3 per cent. While this is an extreme example it does illustrate that, on occasions, the forward rate can be well wide of the mark. However, if UPH holds no better rule can be devised for predicting the future spot rate than using today's forward rate.

Similarly, note from Figures 16.1, 16.2 and 16.3 that the E_{t+1} and F_t curves rarely coincide and that F_t consistently fails to predict the turning points in E_{t+1}. In fact, the series E_t (the current spot rate) and F_t are much more closely related than E_{t+1} (the future spot rate) and F_t, which suggests that F_t merely embodies information on current spot rates and contains little or no additional predictive power not contained in the spot rate. However, even if this is true, F_t can still be an unbiased predictor of E_{t+1}. This is because the unbiased hypothesis does not require F_t to be a good predictor of E_{t+1}, it simply requires that F_t is *on average* right in its predictions. However, the unbiasedness criteria does imply that all other forecasting techniques are even worse predictors of the future spot rate. For example, a *lucky* guess would be better, but guessing will not perform systematically better than using the forward rate. (As the forward rate is closely related to the spot rate, the reader may infer that "the best predictor of tomorrow's exchange rate is today's rate". In fact, this is not far wide of the mark.)

Forward market efficiency   Related to the UPH is the issue of *forward market efficiency*.[1] A market is said to be efficient if prices fully reflect all available information. If this is not the case, unexploited profit opportunities are available and the stock market is said to be inefficient.[2]

The same idea can be applied to the forward exchange market. Forward market efficiency requires that, first, investors are rational in the sense that they process all available information and use it to prepare forecasts of the future exchange rate. Market efficiency requires that the forecast of a currency in time t+1 formulated in time t (which we shall write as $_{t+1}E^e_t$) equals its mathematically expected value denoted $EV(E_{t+1})$. The expected value is a *weighted average* of all possible outcomes, where the weights are determined by the probability of the outcome.[3] $EV(E_{t+1})$ is, in effect, the most likely outcome given current available information and will, on average, be correct. This, in turn, means that the forecast errors are randomly distributed about a mean of zero.

(2) $_{t+1}E^e_t = EV(E_{t+1})$

where $_{t+1}E^e_t$ is the expected exchange rate in time t+1 and $EV(E_{t+1})$ is its expected value.

The second criterium for market efficiency is that exchange rate expectations are reflected in the forward exchange rate. For example, suppose the expected future spot rate in six months' time ($_{t+1}E^e_t$) is equal to STG£0.92/Ir£1 and suppose that the current forward rate (F_t) is equal to STG£0.93/IR£1. Assuming expectations prove correct, a speculator could make a profit by purchasing sterling forward and then, in six months' time, selling it on the spot market (see section 16.2 above). However, if a sufficient number of speculators share this view about the future spot exchange rate, the forward rate will change. The sales of Irish pounds (purchases of sterling) on the forward market will drive F_t downwards towards $_{t+1}E^e_t$ and, as profit opportunities disappear, speculation will tend to diminish.

In summary, if the forward market is efficient, all available information will be accurately processed by investors in calculating the expected value of the future spot rate. Because of arbitrage, the forward rate will converge towards $_{t+1}E^e_t$, which will embody all the currently available information about the future spot exchange rate. If this happens, the forward market is said to be efficient. What is called the *simple market efficiency hypothesis* may be stated as:

(4) $_{t+1}E^e_t = EV(E_{t+1})$ and $F_t = {}_{t+1}E^e_t$

Exchange rate expectations prove correct on average and the forward exchange rate equals the expected future spot rate.

UPH and market efficiency If the simple market efficiency hypothesis is correct then it follows from condition (4) that:

(5) $_{t+1}E^e_t = F_t$

Subtracting E_{t+1} from both sides:

(6) $_{t+1}E^e_t - E_{t+1} = F_t - E_{t+1}$

or

(7) $V_t = F_t - E_{t+1}$

where $V_t = {}_{t+1}E^e_t - E_{t+1}$ is the forecast error in time t. Rearranging (7):

(8) $E_{t+1} = F_t - V_t$

When coefficients representing the intercept and slope are inserted into (8) we obtain the UPH equation given in (1) above. (V_t is an error term equivalent to U_t. Because of the zero mean the sign change is of no consequence.) Hence, the unbiased predictor hypothesis is closely related to the forward market efficiency hypothesis. If UPH holds then it is likely that the forward market is efficient.[4]

Risk premium Even if UPH does *not* hold the foreign exchange market may none the less be efficient. The explanation could be that the market allows a *risk premium* on forward contracts. In the previous example, speculators, in an attempt to make profits, drive F_t towards $_{t+1}E^e_t$. In practice, F_t need not exactly equal $_{t+1}E^e_t$ because at some point speculators may demand a risk premium in order to compensate them for the possibility of being wrong. Market efficiency now requires that

(9) $\quad F_t = {}_{t+1}E^e_t + RP_t$

where RP_t is the risk premium demanded by investors. (The simple market efficiency hypothesis can be restored by assuming that investors are risk neutral so that the risk premium does not enter into the analysis.) This is known as the *general efficiency hypothesis* and it requires that the forward rate embody all publicly available information on the future exchange rate (through ${}_{t+1}E^e_t$) as well as the market's attitude towards risk (given by RP_t). The important point to emerge from this discussion is that the relationship between F_t and E_{t+1} is no longer unambiguously defined. If a researcher estimates equation (1) and finds that F_t is a biased predictor of E_{t+1}, it does not necessarily follow that the forward market is inefficient. It can be argued that the *general* rather than the *simple* market efficiency hypothesis holds and that the researcher did not properly account for the risk premium. However, to avoid this rationalisation becoming a *tautology*, we need to have some measure of risk. If there is such a measure, say Z, the researcher can estimate an equation of the form:

(10) $\quad E_{t+1} = \alpha + \beta F_t + \chi Z_t + u_t$

Unfortunately, current research indicates that the risk premium can change signs over time and this makes it extremely difficult to measure.

Note:
This is a further complication in testing for market efficiency. Investors may not, in fact, be rational in formulating forecasts. In testing for market efficiency the researcher must therefore correctly measure *both* the manner in which expectations are formed and risk. If the market efficiency hypothesis is rejected it may be because expectations or risk or both were incorrectly modelled. This issue makes it extremely difficult to test the market efficiency hypothesis.

In international literature, Cornell (1977) and Levich (1979) find evidence to support the simple market efficiency hypothesis and Levich (1981) finds that the forward exchange rate out-performs forecasting agencies in predicting the future exchange rate. However, Hansen and Hodrick (1980) reject the simple market efficiency hypothesis and Frankel (1982) finds that a time varying risk premium is important in explaining why the simple market efficiency hypothesis is rejected. At the present time, the consensus in international literature seems to be that the unbiasedness hypothesis does *not* hold. The implication is that if a rule can be developed to out-perform the forward exchange rate in forecasting the future spot rate, profits can be made from forward market speculation. The results relating to market efficiency are less decisive and, because of the estimation difficulties involved, will probably never be satisfactorily resolved. More recently, Taylor (1988) presented results which indicated that investors were *irrational* in processing information about the future exchange rate. This result conforms with the earlier findings in Dooley and Shafer (1983) that rules found to be profitable in one period continued to be profitable in later periods even after the rule became publicly known. The implication is that profits can be made from forward market speculation.[5] In the Irish context, very little work has been published to date on these issues.[6]

16.5 Interest Rate Parity Theory

Interest rate parity theory (IRPT) states that the forward premium or discount on the foreign exchanges is determined by the differential between domestic and foreign interest rates. It is important to note that the investor is assumed to cover forward in order to avoid exchange rate risk. (The use of the forward exchange rate removes the uncertainty from the return on a foreign investment and for this reason the theory is referred to as "covered interest rate parity" theory.)[7]

In order to illustrate IRPT, we compare the return from an investment in Ireland with the return from an investment in the US. At the end of the period, the total amount of money received (principal plus interest) from IR£1 investment in Ireland equals:

(11) $(1 + r_{irl})$

Therefore IR£1,000 invested in Ireland at an interest rate of 10 per cent (or 0.1) would give a total return of £1,100 at the end of the period:

IR£1,000$(1 + 0.1) = $ IR£1,100

The return from a US investment is more complicated. First we must convert Irish pounds into dollars using today's spot exchange rate, E_t. Second, we must invest the dollars in the US and receive interest at the rate r_{us}. Third, we must contract forward so as to convert the total US return (principal plus interest) back into Irish pounds at the end of the investment period. If he uses the forward exchange rate, F_t, for this purpose, the investor is not exposed to any exchange rate risk. The total return from a US investment, denominated in Irish pounds, is given by:

(12) $(1 + r_{us})E_t/F_t$

Note:
The exchange rate E_t is first used to convert Irish pounds to dollars. The total dollar return is $(1 + r_{us})$. Today's forward rate, $1/F_t$, is used to convert the dollars back into Irish pounds.

As an example, suppose that an Irish investor wishes to invest £1,000 in the US and the following rates apply:

E_t = $1.599/IR£1   Today's spot exchange rate
F_t = $1.5734/IR£1   Today's one year forward
                                        exchange rate.

r_{us} = 8.25 per cent (or 0.0825) per annum   US interest rate.

First convert, say, IR£1,000 into dollars using E_t and obtain $1,599 ($1,599 = 1.599 × IR£1,000).

Second, invest $1,599 in the US at an interest rate of 8.25 per cent and receive $131.9 ($1,599 × 0.0825) at the end of the investment period. This gives a total return (principal plus interest) of $1,730.9.

Third, contract forward to convert $1,730.9 back into Irish pounds at F_t. This gives an Irish pounds return of IR£1,100. This is calculated; $1,730.9 × 1/1.5734 = IR£1,100.

The same result could have been obtained by inserting the relevant data into equation (12):

$$[IR£1,000(1 + 0.0825)1.599]/1.5734 = IR£1,100$$

While the interest rate in the US is only 8.25 per cent, the overall return from a US investment denominated in Irish pounds, is 10 per cent. The reason for this difference is that the Irish pound forward exchange rate is at a discount relative to the spot exchange rate so that the investor gains on the foreign exchange market.

Arbitrage should now ensure that the return from an Irish investment and a US investment should be the same. Equating equation (11) with equation (12) gives:

(13) $(1 + r_{irl}) = (1 + r_{us})E_t/F_t$

Rearranging

(14) $F_t/E_t = (1 + r_{us})/(1 + r_{irl})$

Subtracting 1 from both sides and rearranging:

(15) $(F_t - E_t)/E_t = (r_{us} - r_{irl})/(1 + r_{irl})$

Equation (15) is the most common way of expressing IRPT. It states that the forward premium or discount (left-hand side) equals the interest differential (right-hand side). If the Irish pound is at a premium ($F_t > E_t$), the foreign interest rate will exceed the domestic interest rate. Conversely, if the Irish pound is at a discount ($F_t < E_t$), the Irish interest rate will exceed the foreign interest rate. The reader can verify by inserting the relevant data into equation (15) that IRPT holds in our example. An investment in Ireland or the US gives the same return, 10 per cent.

We now turn to the case where IRPT does *not* hold and we explain how arbitrage would equate the forward premium or discount to the interest differential.

Note:
We have used the dollar in the above example to develop the basic IRPT equation, but the theory can be generalised to include any currency and foreign interest rate. Hence in equation (15), the US can be replaced by the more general term of "interest rate in the rest of the world".

Arbitrage

We mentioned that arbitrage would ensure covered interest rate parity. In order to illustrate how arbitrage brings about convergence, consider what would happen if equation (15) did not hold. In particular assume the following data apply:

E	=	STG£0.942/IR£1	Spot exchange rate
F	=	STG£0.951/IR£1	1 year forward exchange rate
r_{irl}	=	10 per cent per annum	Domestic interest rate
r_{uk}	=	14 per cent per annum	UK interest rate.

Inserting this information into equation (15) it is clear that covered interest rate parity does not hold. The interest differential on the right-hand side of the equation exceeds the Irish pound forward premium on the left-hand side. A speculator could benefit from this situation.

One option is to borrow, say, IR£5 million in Ireland for a period of one year. The steps involved are then as follows.

Today
1. Convert the IR£5 million into UK pounds using today's spot exchange rate, E_t, and receive STG£4,710,000.
2. Invest STG£4,710,000 in the UK for one year at an interest rate of 14 per cent and receive interest of STG£659,400 at the end of the period. Total UK receipts at the end of the year (principal plus interest) equals STG£5,369,400.
3. Contract to sell (deliver) STG£5,369,400 forward at $1/F_t$ and receive IR£5,646,057 one year from now.

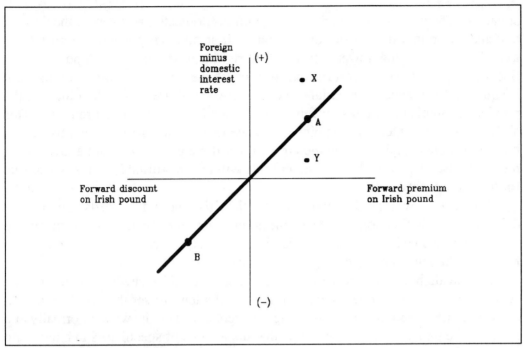

Figure 16.4 Interest rate parity theory

One year from now
4. Fulfil the forward contract by selling STG£5,369,400 and receive IR£5,646,057.
5. Repay the Irish pound loan of IR£5 million and the interest rate charges of 10 per cent or IR£500,000. Total repayments equal IR£5,500,000.

Overall
Proceeds	IR£5,645,057
Repayments	IR£5,500,000
Profit	IR£146,057

This example illustrates that if interest rate parity does not hold then it is possible for a speculator to profit from the situation with little or no risk. We have simplified the analysis by ignoring transaction costs, different taxation rates on deposit interest and restrictions on investments imposed by governments. In practice these factors are important. Furthermore we have assumed that interest rates remain constant in both countries for the duration of the transaction. This is unlikely to be the case, but investors could avoid this uncertainty by entering into fixed interest rate contracts.

In the above example it was profitable to borrow in Ireland and invest in the UK because the UK interest rate exceeded the Irish interest rate by more than the forward premium on the Irish pound. Figure 16.4 shows a graphical representation of the situation. The interest differential (foreign minus domestic) is given on the vertical axis and the premium (+) or discount (-) on the Irish pound is given on the horizontal axis. The line running upwards from left to right is the parity line. A point on this line indicates covered interest rate parity because the forward premium or discount is equal to the interest differential. The points A and B are two such points. In the previous example the interest differential exceeded the Irish pound premium. This situation is represented by the point X. As we saw, it was profitable in this case to borrow in Ireland and invest in the UK. In fact if we are at any point above and to the left of the parity line this investment rule will prove profitable. This is also true for the south-west quadrant.

Suppose now that the premium on the Irish pound exceeds the interest differential. This situation is given by the point Y in Figure 16.4. It is now profitable to borrow in the UK and invest in Ireland. In general, this rule will prove profitable for any point below and to the right of the parity line.

The available evidence for the Irish economy and elsewhere suggests that covered interest parity does hold.[8] In fact, banks tend to set the forward foreign exchange rate by looking at interest rate differentials. That is, we are normally at a point on the parity line. The reason is that the actions of speculators in attempting to profit from divergence bring about convergence. Recall that in the previous example it was profitable to borrow in Ireland and invest in the UK because the interest differential exceeded the Irish pound premium. Consider now how this investment rule might bring about interest parity.

First, borrowing in Ireland increases r_{irl} and investing in the UK lowers r_{uk}. The term on the right-hand side of the IRPT equation $(r_{uk} - r_{irl})/(1 + r_{irl})$, therefore decreases. Simultaneously, the conversion of Irish pounds into sterling means that the supply of Irish pounds on the foreign exchange market increases and E_t tends to depreciate (fall). The purchase of Irish pounds forward means that the forward exchange rate, F_t, will appreciate (rise). Hence the value of the left-hand side of the IRPT equation, $(F_t - E_t)/E_t$, tends to increase. With the value on the left-hand side increasing and the value on the right-hand side falling, convergence comes about. Allowing for transaction costs, profits will no longer be available and covered interest rate parity is restored. It is in this sense that arbitrage ensures that IRPT will hold.

Note:
It is possible that exchange controls might prevent arbitrage restoring the values on the left- and right-hand sides of the IRPT equation. However, the leading and lagging by exporters and importers respectively (see Chapter 10) cannot be prevented by exchange controls and this would have the effect of re-establishing any divergence from IRPT.

16.6 Exchange Rate Expectations

In this section we draw together some of the theories developed in this and previous chapters in order to explain how exchange rate expectations are formed. Recall from

Chapter 12 the theory of purchasing power parity (PPP). The PPP equation can be written as:

(16) $P_{irl} \times E = P_{world}$

where P_{irl} and P_{world} are prices in Ireland and the "rest of the world" respectively. According to PPP, exchange rates must, in the long run, tend to levels that equalise the purchasing power of currencies internationally. We saw that, at its simplest, this implied that price differentials would tend to be reflected in movements in exchange rates. For example, re-arranging equation (16) as, $E = P_{world}/P_{irl}$, an increase in Irish prices relative to "world" prices would lead to a devaluation of the Irish pound in the EMS.

The PPP equation can also be expressed in terms of rates of change as:

(17) $\Delta E = \Delta P_{world} - \Delta P_{irl}$

where ΔP_{world} and ΔP_{irl} denote the inflation rate in the "world" and Ireland respectively. This says that high inflation countries tend to have depreciating currencies, low inflation countries appreciating currencies. This generalisation provides us with a basis on which to build *expectations* about movements in exchange rates. High inflation in Ireland (relative to other countries) would lead markets to anticipate a fall in the value of the Irish pound. Logically, this should cause an outflow of funds from Ireland, in order to avoid the capital losses that will be incurred when the Irish pound falls.

Thus, we can see that according to PPP theory, differences in international price levels, or differential rates of inflation, will be the driving force behind exchange rate expectations.

We can go a stage further and ask why inflation rates differ from country to country? Monetarists would answer: "because countries expand their money supplies at different rates". Increases in the money supply, via the quantity theory of money, lead to increases in inflation. According to this view, everything is ultimately driven by the rate of monetary expansion in each country. Schematically, these interrelationships can be summarised as follows:

Differentials in rate of money expansion → (Quantity Theory) → differentials in rates of inflation → (PPP) → expected changes in exchange rate.

If the reader refers back to our discussion of our decision to participate in the ERM (Chapter 13), it can be seen that one of the expected benefits was a rapid decline in inflation and interest rates. In effect, it was hoped that instead of relying on the transmission mechanisms outlined above, expectations would have been abruptly changed by the change in the exchange rate commitment. By breaking the

465

expectation of continued depreciation with respect to the DM, it was hoped that price-wage formation process would be changed and consequently the rate of inflation would have quickly subsided. The hoped-for sequence of events can be depicted as follows:

Change in exchange rate regime → change in expected rate of inflation → change in wage-price formation → change in actual rate of inflation.

We can also link exchange rate expectations to interest rates by looking at the question from a slightly different perspective. The *Fisher equation*, which we have used implicitly in earlier chapters, states that the nominal rate of interest, r_n, equals the real rate of interest, r_r, plus the expected rate of inflation, ΔP^e. Assuming that inflation expectations are realised (next period's inflation is what was expected this period) and assuming constant real interest rates, then an increase in (expected) inflation leads to an increase in nominal interest rates.

Interest rate parity theory (IRPT) yields the same prediction: if (expected) inflation in Ireland is high by international standards, markets will anticipate a devaluation of the Irish pound and investors will move money out of Ireland in order to avoid incurring exchange rate losses. This outflow could, however, be staved off by a rise in Irish interest rates which would compensate investors for the eventual fall in the Irish pound and persuade them to leave their money in Ireland. Hence, an increase in (expected) inflation would lead to higher domestic nominal interest rates and a discount on the forward exchange rate. To complete the circle, bear in mind that the forward exchange rate is an unbiased predictor of the future spot exchange rate. That is, over time, the forward exchange rate is a reasonably good predictor of the future spot exchange rate. A fall in the forward exchange rate is therefore an indication that the future spot exchange rate of the Irish pound will fall.

The equations showing these relationships are:

(17) $\Delta E = \Delta P_{world} - \Delta P_{irl}$ PPP theory

(18) $r_n = \Delta P^e + r_r$ Fisher equation

(19) $(F - E)/E = (r_{world} - r_{irl})/(1 + r_{irl})$ IRPT

(20) $E_{t+1} = \alpha + \beta F_t$ Forward exchange rate as an unbiased predictor of the future spot exchange rate.

where

ΔP_{irl}	=	Domestic inflation rate	r_r	=	Real interest rates
ΔP_{world}	=	"World" inflation rate	ΔP^e	=	Expected inflation rate
E	=	Exchange rate, defined	F_t	=	Forward exchange rate

		as indirect quote	r_{irl}	=	Nominal interest rate
r_n	=	Nominal interest rate			in Ireland
r_{world}	=	Nominal "world"	E_{t+1}	=	Future spot
		interest rate			exchange rate.

Note:
We are using the term devaluation rather than depreciation as the analysis relates to the Irish pound which is semi-fixed in the ERM. If the Irish pound were in a freely floating exchange rate system, we would use the term depreciation.

In summary, inflation differentials between countries lead, via the Fisher equation, to differentials in nominal interest rates. Nominal interest rate differentials in turn, via IRPT, determine the premium or discount of the forward exchange rate. The two most common methods of predicting or forecasting the future spot exchange rate are deviations from PPP and the forward exchange rate. Both of these methods should give consistent forecasts of future exchange rates.

The impact of joining the ERM on interest rates can therefore be depicted as follows:

Fall in expected and actual rate of inflation $\rightarrow$ fall in nominal interest rate $\rightarrow$ reduction in forward foreign exchange rate discount $\rightarrow$ stability of exchange rate.

We saw in Chapter 13, however, that the simple commitment to participate in the ERM was not sufficient to break inflationary expectations and the expected fall in inflation and interest rates took some years to materialise.

16.7 Internal Hedging Techniques

In this section we outline some of the more common *internal* hedging techniques. These techniques enable firms to hedge against exchange rate risk and are less costly than external hedging techniques.

Use domestic suppliers One way of eliminating exchange rate risk is to switch from a foreign supplier to a domestic. This may not, however, be possible. A great deal of the raw materials imported into Ireland have no domestic substitutes. The alternative is to use a supplier from a country participating in the ERM. The stability of the Irish pound within the ERM in recent years offered protection against exchange rate movements. If such a supplier cannot be found, then a supplier operating out of a weak currency country is preferable to a strong currency country supplier. If the foreign currency depreciates, imports will cost less in Irish pounds.

Invoice in Irish pounds If a company can invoice in Irish pounds, then exchange rate risk is eliminated. In effect, the exchange rate exposure is transferred to the other party in the transaction. Whether or not this is possible will probably depend on the relative strength of the parties to the deal. For example, a large buyer may be able to pressurise a small supplier into accepting the exchange rate risk. On occasions, both parties may agree to trade on the basis of a mutually acceptable hard currency such as the DM.

Leading and lagging of payments or receipts　In Chapter 10 we discussed how importers and exporters can speculate on future exchange rate movements by leading and lagging. Importers and exporters can also minimise exchange rate losses through leading (paying before time) and lagging (delaying receipts for as long as possible). Under Irish circumstances, this technique is easy to resort to if one is convinced the Irish pound is going to rise or fall. As always, the problem is the difficulty of predicting exchange rate movements. Given the very high exports/GNP and imports/GNP ratios a concerted use of this strategy can have a very significant impact on the level of external reserves. For example, in January 1985, despite the existence of exchange controls, the official external reserves fell by approximately IR£1,000 million in just over a week on the expectation that the Irish pound would be devalued in an EMS realignment. In fact the Irish pound was not devalued on that occasion.

Match assets (liabilities) against liabilities (assets) in the same currency　Consider the case of an Irish firm with foreign assets, for example, a subsidiary company in France. All of the assets and liabilities of the company in France will have to be translated from francs to Irish pounds in order to prepare the balance sheet of the parent company in Ireland. If the Irish pound appreciates on the foreign exchange market, then the value of the French subsidiary will, in Irish pound terms, have fallen and this will lower the value of the parent company. This type of exchange risk is referred to as *translation exposure*. One way to avoid or minimise this risk is to match overseas assets with liabilities in the same currency by, for example, borrowing in French francs. Hence if the Irish pound exchange rate appreciates, this will reduce the value of both assets and liabilities.

Match foreign currency payments (receipts) against receipts (payments) in the same currency　Consider the case of an exporter whose receipts, denominated in Irish pounds, could be reduced by an appreciation of the Irish pound exchange rate. This type of exchange rate risk is called *transaction exposure* or economic exposure. One way of avoiding this type of exposure is to match foreign currency receipts (from the sale of output) against foreign currency payments to suppliers. That way a loss on receipts will be matched by a reduction in payments. This technique will not however be possible unless the firm has a reasonable two-way flow in the same foreign currency.

Transfer pricing   Transfer pricing is concerned with setting intra-firm prices so as to minimise tax burdens. It is also possible to use transfer pricing (allowing, of course, for customs duties and tax laws) to reduce exchange rate exposure. For example, suppose a company has two subsidiaries, one in a strong currency country and the other in a weak currency country. If the subsidiary in the weak currency country sells at cost to the other subsidiary, profits are maximised in the hard currency country and minimised in the weak currency country. The company will then gain if currencies move in the expected direction.

16.8   Futures Contracts

The function of a financial futures contract is to enable companies and individuals with positions in money, securities and foreign exchange markets to reduce their exposure to risk. Financial futures trading is conducted on the floor of an organised exchange. The main futures exchanges include (the year indicates the starting date):

International Money Market (IMM) of Chicago: 1972
Singapore International Monetary Exchange (SIMEX): 1979
New York Futures Exchange: 1979
London International Financial Futures Exchange (LIFFE): 1982.

There are also other exchanges in Sweden, New Zealand, France and Canada. In terms of trading volume, the IMM is by far the largest and most important exchange. In May 1989, the Irish Futures/Options Exchange (IFOX) commenced trading. IFOX trades in three different types of contracts:

Future on long-term Irish gilt
Future on short-term Irish gilt
Future on three month DIBOR (Dublin inter-bank offer rate)
Future on an Irish stock exchange index.

Each of these contracts has its own specifications. The contracts are for a standardised amount and are delivered on a standardised date in the future. The contracts can be used to hedge against *interest* rate risk. When IFOX was first established it was possible to hedge against *exchange* rate risk by using a future on an Irish pound/dollar exchange rate. However, that type of contract has since been terminated. In what follows we give an example of how the 3 month DIBOR contract might be used in practice. The operation of the other contracts is very similar.

Interest rate risk   As an example of interest rate risk consider the case of a treasury manager who, in July 1992, anticipates a cash surplus of IR£1 million between mid-September and mid-December 1992. The treasury manager proposes to place this money in a bank deposit. The current interest rate is 10 per cent but the treasury manager expects interest rates to fall to 8 per cent sometime in September. If interest rates do fall, then the interest received on the deposit will be reduced. For example, if the interest rate equals 10 per cent the return on the deposit is:

Deposit interest = IR£1 m × 10/100 × 90/360 = IR£25,000

that is, the deposit interest equals the sum deposited multiplied by the interest rate multiplied by the duration (90 days). If the interest rate falls to 8 per cent:

Deposit interest = IR£1 m × 8/100 × 90/360 = IR£20,000

Hence a reduction in interest rates from 10 per cent to 8 per cent leads to a loss of IR£5,000 on deposit interest. (If the treasury manager was borrowing money instead of depositing money the opposite would be the case.) It is possible to hedge against this type of risk by using the three month DIBOR contract.

Interest rate futures contract The specifications of the DIBOR contract are:

Contract size:	IR£100,000
Settlement date:	Third Wednesday of March, June, September, December
Quotation price:	100 minus the rate of interest
Tick size	0.01 per cent
Tick value	IR£2.50
Contract	cash settlement.

The DIBOR contract is a standardised size of IR£100,000. The standardised settlement dates are the third Wednesday of March, June, September and December. The quotation price is calculated as 100 minus the interest rate (the Dublin inter-bank offer rate). Hence, if the interest rate is 10 per cent, the quotation price is 100 - 10 = 90. If the interest rate is 8 per cent, the quotation price is 100 - 8 = 92. This means that if interest rates decrease, the quotation price increases and (as explained below) the buyer of the futures contract gains. If, on the other hand, interest rates increase, the quotation price falls and the buyer incurs a loss.

The *tick size* is the minimum price movement and is set at 0.01 per cent. The tick value is calculated as the value of the contract multiplied by the tick size multiplied by the duration of the contract (3 months or 90 days).

Tick value = IR£100,000 × 0.0001 × 90/360 = IR£2.50

This means that the price has to move by IR£2.50 before the price movement will be recorded.

Hedging   To hedge against falling interest rates the treasury manager enters into a futures contract. The basic idea is to set up in the futures market an equal but opposite position to that in the deposit or cash market. If interest rates fall, the value of the futures contract will increase and the profits on the futures contracts will compensate for the loss of interest on the IR£1 m deposit.

In order to "lock-in" an interest rate of 10 per cent on a *deposit* of IR£1 m, the treasury manager must *purchase* 10 contracts of IR£100,000. (A *borrower* in the cash market would *sell* futures contracts.)   Ten contracts at a price of 90.00 would cost IR£225,000.

$$10 \text{ contracts} \times 9000 \text{ ticks} \times IR£2.50 = IR£225,000$$

Suppose that in September the treasury manager's expectations are realised and interest rates fall from 10 per cent to 8 per cent and the contract price rises from 90 to 92. Having bought the 10 contracts for IR£225,000, the treasury manager now sells the 10 futures contracts for IR£230,000.

$$10 \text{ contracts} \times 9200 \text{ ticks} \times IR£2.50 = IR£230,000$$

The profit on the futures contract of IR£5,000 exactly offsets the loss on the deposit interest. In effect, the treasury manager has achieved a "perfect hedge".

The profit (or loss) on the futures contract can also be calculated using the tick values. The difference between the sell price (92) and the purchase price (90) is equivalent to 200 ticks. The profit is equal to the number of ticks multiplied by the tick value multiplied by the number of contracts.

$$\text{Profit on futures contract} = 200 \times IR£2.50 \times 10 = IR£5,000$$

The treasury manager by "fixing" the interest on a floating rate deposit also trades-away any potential gains. If interest rates increased over the period, the gain made on deposit interest is offset by a loss on the futures contract. It should be borne in mind that it takes two parties to complete a transaction. If someone is purchasing a futures contract, someone else must be selling. This means that the two parties are taking opposing views on how interest rates will move in the future. If the buyer of the futures contract gains, the seller of the contract loses and vice versa.

Note:
Because of arbitrage between the cash and futures markets, the interest rates on futures contracts are very closely related to the interest rates embodied in the yield curve (see Chapter 12). Hence, if the yield curve is upward sloping indicating that interest rates will increase in the future, the interest rate

on futures contracts will be greater than current interest rates. This means that futures contracts only offer insurance against *unexpected* changes in interest rates, that is changes in interest rates over and above changes reflected in the yield curve.

Variation margin   The purchaser of a futures contract is required to deposit, as collateral, with IFOX a sum of money known as the *initial margin*. This money is returned on completion of the contract. Each day the clearing exchange mark all accounts to the current market value and the purchaser is refunded or required to pay a maintenance margin, known as the *variation margin*, in cash each day. The variation margin is equivalent to the difference between yesterday's and today's closing price. This feature of futures contracts is known as *mark-to-market*. As an example of how the variation margin works consider the data in Table 16.2.

Table 16.2
Variation margin

Day	Price	Initial margin IR£	Variation margin IR£
Monday	90	3,000	
Tuesday	89		(2,500)
Wednesday	87		(5,000)
Thursday	92		+ 12,500
Close			+ 5,000

Note: A + sign indicates a payment from IFOX whereas an ( ) sign indicates a payment from the depositor to IFOX.

On Monday the treasury manager buys 10 contracts at a price of 90. Each contract requires an initial margin of IR£300. Hence the manager must deposit IR£3,000 with IFOX. Suppose now that on Tuesday the contract price *falls* to 89 (a decrease equivalent to 100 ticks) reflecting an increase in interest rates. Because the price has fallen the manager must now *pay* IFOX IR£2,500 as a variation margin. This is calculated as:

10 contracts × IR£2.50 × 100 ticks = IR£2,500

Suppose that on Wednesday the contract price again falls this time to 87. The treasurer must pay a further variation margin of IR£5,000.

10 contracts × IR£2.50 × 200 ticks = IR£5,000

Finally, suppose that on Thursday interest rates decrease and the contract price rises to 92. The treasury manager now *receives* IR£12,500 from IFOX.

10 contracts × IR£2.50 × 500 ticks = IR£12,500

Having incurred a loss of IR£7,500 on the first two days and a profit of IR£12,500 on the third day the treasury manager has made an overall profit of IR£5,000. The treasury manager now closes out her position by selling the 10 contracts. As mentioned, the gain on the futures contract offsets losses in the cash market. The main point about the variation margin is that gains and losses are paid for on a daily basis. If the purchaser cannot pay the variation margin, the clearing exchange will close out his position and make good any losses from the initial margin. In this regard, the clearing exchange guarantees the performance of the futures contract.

Forward and futures contracts Foreign currency futures contracts are very similar to forward contracts. (The current futures contracts offered by IFOX cannot be used to hedge against foreign currency risk.) The two types of contracts differ however in a number of respects.

1. Forward contracts are negotiated with a bank at any location. Futures trading is conducted by brokers on the floor of an organised exchange. The IFOX system is a computerised trading system where dealers are linked via screens to a central computer.

2. Banks will enter into a forward contract for any amount. Futures contracts are for a standard size contract for delivery at a standard maturity date in the future.

3. Forward contract prices are expressed by a bank in the form of bid and offer rates. Some futures prices are determined on the floor of the exchange by an "open outcry" system. The IFOX system is based on an electronic automated system rather than "open outcry" and there is no actual trading floor.

4. Futures contracts require the purchaser to put up an initial margin as a good-faith gesture. A variation margin is then required each day as the price of the contract is mark-to-market. Forward contracts require no margin prior to the settlement date. This is one of the most important differences between futures and forward contracts.

16.9   Conclusion

The main points discussed in this chapter include:

- A forward exchange transaction is an agreement to buy or sell a specified amount of currency at an agreed date in the future

- The premium or discount on forward exchange rates is related to the difference between domestic and foreign interest rates. The theory underlying this relationship is known as "covered interest parity theory"

- Covered interest rate arbitrage is the process that ensures that "covered interest parity" holds

- The hypothesis that the forward exchange rate is an unbiased predictor of the future spot exchange rate states that on average the forward exchange rate is a good predictor of the future spot rate and that the prediction error will be random

- The concept of forward market efficiency

- The role of risk premia

- PPP and the forward exchange rate are related through the Fisher equation and interest rate parity theory

- How a change in the exchange rate system could alter expectations about inflation and reduce interest rates

- A number of internal hedging techniques that can be used to reduce exposure to exchange rate risk

- Financial futures contracts can be used to reduce interest rate and exchange rate risk

- A foreign currency futures contract is similar to a forward contract. One of the main differences is that in a futures contract the purchaser is required to put up an initial margin as collateral.

1. Surveys of forward market efficiency are given in R. A. Hodrick, *The Empirical Evidence on the Efficiency of Forward and Futures Foreign Exchange Markets*, Harwood Academic Publishers, 1987. R. M. Levich, "Empirical Studies of Exchange Rates, Price Behaviour, Rate Determination and Market Efficiency", in R. H. Jones and P. B. Kenen (eds), *Handbook of International Economics*, Vol. II, North Holland, 1985. R. Baille and P. McMahon, *The Foreign Exchange Market: Theory and Evidence*, Cambridge University Press, 1990.

2. E. F. Fama, "Efficient Capital markets: A Review of Theory and Empirical Work", *Journal of Finance*, 25, 1970, p. 383-417, distinguishes between three forms of market efficiency. Weak form efficiency is where current prices reflect only the information contained in historical prices. Semi-strong efficiency is where current prices reflect all public information. Strong efficiency is where current prices reflect all information, including insider information.

3. As an example of how expected values are calculated consider a lottery where half the tickets sold carry no prize money and the other half carry a prize of IR£10. This means that if someone were to purchase a ticket there is a 50 per cent chance of winning IR£10 and a 50 per cent chance of winning nothing. The following table shows the two possible outcomes and their associated probabilities (note that the sum of the probabilities add to one). The third column shows the product of column 1 and column 2. The sum of the two products is the expected value. In this case the expected value is IR£5. What this means is if someone were to buy, say, 100 tickets they would expect to win on average IR£5. The first few tickets may or may not carry any winnings but, on average, over a hundred or so tickets the purchasor could expect average winnings of IR£5. The expected value is, in effect, the most likely average outcome from purchasing tickets. (Note that no one ticket actually carries a prize of £5.) In formulating a forecast of the exchange rate, the task of deciding on the probabilities associated with each possible outcome will, of course, be considerably more complex than in the above example.

Outcome	*Probability*	*Outcome* × *Probability*
IR£0	0.5	0
IR£10	0.5	IR£5
Expected value		IR£5

4. Associated with the unbiasedness and market efficiency hypothesis is the concept of a *random walk*. A variable is said to follow a random walk if changes from one period to the next are unpredictable or random, which will ensure that it tends to return to its original value. For example a drunk wandering along the street might follow a random walk. His next step could be to the left, to the right, straight ahead or even backwards. He should end up going round in circles. There is some evidence that the Irish pound exchange rate follows a random walk: see A. Leddin, "Interest and Price Parity and Foreign Exchange Market Efficiency: The Irish Experience in the European Monetary System", *The Economic and Social Review*, Vol. 19, No. 3, April 1988. The implication is that historical exchange rate data cannot be used to forecast the future exchange rate.

5. B. Cornell "Spot Rates, Forward Rates and Exchange Market Efficiency", *Journal of Financial Economics*, 5, pp. 55-65, 1977. M. P. Dooley and J. R. Shafer, "Analysis of Short-run Exchange Rate Behaviour: March 1973 to November 1981", in *Exchange Rate and Trade Instability*, D. Bigman and T. Taya (eds), Cambridge Ma., Ballinger, 1983. J. A. Frankel, "In Search of the Exchange Risk Premium: A Six-Currency test Assuming Mean-Variance Optimization", *Journal of International*

Money and Finance, 1, pp. 255-74, 1982. L. P. Hansen and R. J. Hodrick, "Forward Exchange Rates as Optimal predictors of Future Spot Rates: An Econometric Analysis", *Journal of Political Economy*, 88, pp. 829-53, 1980. R. J. Levich "On the Efficiency of Markets for Foreign Exchange", in R. Dornbusch and J. Frenkel (eds), *International Economic Policy: An Assessment of Theory and Evidence*, Johns Hopkins University Press, Baltimore, 1979. R. M. Levich, "How to Compare Chance with Forecasting Expertise", *Euromoney*, August 1981. M. P. Taylor, "What do Investment Managers Know? An Empirical Study of Practitioners' Predictions", *Economica*, 54, pp. 185-202, 1988.

6. A. Leddin, 1988, *op. cit.* using quarterly data, found that the forward exchange rate for the Irish pound was an unbiased predictor of the future spot rate in the case of sterling and the DM but not the dollar. B. Lucy, "Efficiency in the Forward Exchange market: An Application of Co-Integration", *The Economic and Social Review*, Vol. 20, No. 1, October 1988, using the cointegration technique presents evidence to the contrary. Lucy's findings are however disputed in A. Leddin, "Efficiency in the Forward Exchange market: An Application of Co-Integration: A Comment", *The Economic and Social Review*, Vol. 20, No. 3, April 1989.

7. For a review of the literature on interest rate parity, see R. M. Levich, *op. cit.*

8. See F. X. Browne, "Departures from Interest Rate Parity", *Journal of Banking and Finance*, Vol. 7, 1983, and A. Leddin, 1988, *op. cit.*

9. A very good treatment of IFOX forward contracts is given in M. O'Dea, "A Financial Futures Market", Central Bank of Ireland, *Quarterly Bulletin*, Winter, 1990. For an introductory textbook on futures markets, see J. Hull, *Introduction to Futures and Options Markets*, Prentice Hall, 1991. For a more advance treatment, see D. Duffie, *Futures Markets*, Prentice Hall, 1989. The reader should also consult, R. Breen, "Hedging and Speculating in Financial Futures Markets, *Irish Bank Review*, Summer, 1988. D. Bradley, "Irish Futures and Options Exchange", *Irish Bank Review*, Summer, 1991.

Chapter 17

Economic Growth and Longer-Term Policy Issues

Little else is requisite to carry a state to the highest degree of opulence from the lowest barbarism, but peace, easy taxes, and tolerable administration of justice.
Adam Smith.[1]

17.1   Introduction

Throughout this book we have been mainly concerned with the short-term performance of the economy. In Chapter 1 we looked at inflation and unemployment since the Second World War. In Chapter 3 we examined in some detail the evolution of the components of national income since 1980. In other chapters we explored the impact of fiscal, monetary and exchange rate policies on cyclical fluctuations in the level of activity. In this chapter we look first at the longer-term performance of the Irish economy and then examine some broad issues of development policy.

17.2   Irish Economic Performance
Since Independence

This section contains a brief summary of the development of the Irish economy since Independence under a few key headings.

Population and migration
In 1916 Padraic Pearse expressed the hope that in a

... free Ireland gracious and useful industries will supplement an improved agriculture, the population will expand in a century to 20 million and it may even in time go up to 30 million.[2]

In reality, large-scale emigration continued after Independence until it was interrupted by the Great Depression and started up again during and after the Second World War. The population continued to decline. A Commission on *Emigration and Other Population Problems* was established in 1948. The reports, published in 1954, explored at length the reasons for emigration, and recommended policies which it was believed would help to reduce it. The analysis focused on the fact that emigration was heaviest outside the main urban areas and consisted to a large extent of a movement from rural Ireland to urban Britain and America. While some limited proposals were put forward to encourage industrial development, the main emphasis was placed on agricultural development with a view to retaining a larger population in the rural areas.

Ironically, in the years immediately following the publication of the Reports of this Commission the annual rate of emigration soared to almost 3 per cent of the population, the highest recorded since the 1880s (see Figure 9.1 in Chapter 9), and the pace of rural depopulation accelerated. The population of the Republic of Ireland fell to 2,818,000 in 1961, compared with over 6 million in the corresponding area in 1841. This long-run decline of population is the most remarkable feature of Irish economic history. It is usually viewed as a symptom of failure and under-achievement. Obviously it is dispiriting if almost half of the school-leaving cohort leaves the country, at least temporarily, as was the case during the 1950s.[3] However, given the apparent inability of the Irish economy to absorb the potential growth of its labour force into worthwhile employment, emigration at least afforded young Irish people the opportunity of raising their living standards and relieved pressure on wage levels and welfare services in Ireland. We saw in Chapters 3 and 9 how, during the early 1980s, when high unemployment throughout the western world virtually closed off the safety valve of emigration, there was a sharp increase in unemployment and an unprecedented decline in living standards in Ireland.

A high birth rate, and hence a high rate of natural increase, persisted in Ireland long after fertility in other European countries had fallen below the replacement level. However, the fall in the birth rate since 1980 has been dramatic. The fertility rates recorded in 1991 were only just high enough to ensure the long-run replacement of the Irish population.[4] As a result of the drop in the number of births, the median age of the population is now rising markedly. (It was almost 30 in 1991, compared with 26 years in 1981.)

Projections prepared in the early 1980s, based on the assumption of a low rate of emigration, indicated that the population might pass 4 million by the end of the century. However, the resumption of large-scale emigration in the mid-1980s and the drop in the birth rate have made it likely that the population will stabilise in the region of 3.5 million, compared with just under 3 million at the time of Independence. The result will be that independent Ireland, despite having had one of the highest rates of natural increase of any European country in the twentieth century, will have achieved a cumulative growth of population of less than 20 per cent, proportionately less than that of any other European country over the same period.

Growth in output

We noted in Chapter 1 that in 1990 Irish GDP per person was the third lowest of the 24 countries in the OECD. There has been much discussion of the long-run performance of the Irish economy and whether any evidence of a catching-up with the richer countries can be discerned.[5] Many commentators have expressed disappointment at the failure to close the gap in living standards between Ireland and rich industrialised countries of the world, as well at the fact that several countries (Italy and Spain, for example) have overtaken Ireland in the course of the twentieth century. The similarity of Irish and British growth rates, inflation and other economic indicators throughout most of the twentieth century is striking and hardly surprising in view of the close integration of the two economies until very recently. The poor performance of the Irish economy should be viewed in the light of the performance of the British economy and its dominant influence on Ireland.

In Chapter 11 we saw that there has been no dramatic catching-up between Ireland and the average of the EC countries since 1975. Table 17.1 compares the performance of Ireland and the OECD as a whole since 1960. It may be seen that the Irish growth rates in total and *per capita* GDP was slightly *higher* than those of the OECD over this entire period and also over the 1970s and 1980s. During the 1960s the Irish record was worse than the OECD, and this would presumably also be true of the 1950s (reliable data are unavailable before 1960).

Table 17.1
Annual average growth rates in volume of GDP, 1960-90, %

	GDP		GDP/person	
	Ireland	OECD	Ireland	OECD
1960-70	4.1	4.9	3.6	3.8
1970-80	4.3	3.2	2.8	2.3
1980-90	3.2	2.9	2.9	2.1
1960-90	3.8	3.6	3.1	2.7

Source: OECD, *Principal Economic Indicators*, November 1991 and earlier editions; Ireland *National Income and Expenditure*, 1990, Table A.

This comparison uses *GDP*. As we noted in Chapter 3 the gap between GNP and GDP has widened during the 1980s due to the outflow of national debt interest and repatriated profits. The growth of GNP during the 1980s was lower in Ireland than in the OECD, but for the whole period 1960-90 we estimate that the growth of GNP *per capita* was almost exactly the same in the two areas.

To summarise, since the 1960s Ireland's economic growth has been broadly in line with that achieved in the OECD as a whole. While it is disappointing not to be able to record any marked catching-up with the richer countries, very pessimistic judgments about the country's relative performance are not warranted.

17.3 Industrial Policy

Background Reports such as that of the Commission on Emigration (1954) looked to the agricultural sector to absorb Ireland's growing population and labour force, but in reality this sector has steadily declined in relative importance. The decline of the rural population and the slow but steady growth of urban Ireland has resulted in a marked increase in the proportion of the population living in cities and towns. In 1926 only 32 per cent of the population was classified as urban; by 1986 this had risen to 56 per cent.[6] The growth in urbanisation has been accompanied by an even faster decline in the importance of agriculture, which accounted for only 14 per cent of the labour force in 1991. Over the years the emphasis in Irish development policy shifted from agriculture to industry as the sector which would provide employment and income for the population. It is informative to review the development of thinking on this issue.

Early years In the brief period between the end of the Civil War in Ireland and the onset of the Great Depression in 1930, a strategy of limited state intervention in economic affairs was pursued in the hope that by concentrating on agriculture, where it was believed our comparative advantage lay, the foundations for economic development would be built. Even during these years, however, the state was prepared to supplement private enterprise by creating a state monopoly, Electricity Supply Board, and to grant a limited number of tariffs to help selected industries that made the case that they were facing unfair competition from abroad. Due to a lack of data it is not possible to draw any firm conclusions about the results of this early economic strategy.

Economic and political circumstances, both in Ireland and abroad, changed dramatically during the 1930s. The collapse of world trade in the Great Depression and the return flow of emigrants to Ireland probably resulted in a sharp fall in living standards. (There are no annual estimates of GNP for these years.) In response to the changed situation, the newly elected Fianna Fáil government embarked on a programme of generalised protectionism in 1932. Foreign investment was virtually excluded from Ireland and if anyone was willing to manufacture a product in Ireland a very high tariff was imposed on competing imports. As a result of these policies, the level of effective protection of Irish industry was extremely high throughout the next four decades. Even as late as 1966, the average rate of effective protection of Irish manufacturing industry was almost 80 per cent, one of the highest in the western

480

world.[7] The firms that set up behind these high tariffs were Irish owned, although in many cases British firms went into joint ventures with Irish residents and set up subsidiaries to cater for the Irish market. British car manufacturers, for example, put together special kits in England that were shipped to Ireland and assembled here by their subsidiaries. The limited number of semi-skilled jobs created in the Irish car assembly industry in this manner were paid for by the very high cost of cars in Ireland. Less than twenty years after protectionism gave way to free trade, none of these jobs survived.

In judging Ireland's long-term growth record, account should be taken of the fact that between 1932 and 1966 the Irish economy was one of the most heavily protected in the world. Prolonged reliance on generalised protectionism has not proved to be an effective way of promoting economic development anywhere in the world. Whatever the merits of imposing tariffs on selected "infant industries" at the early stages of industrialisation, no example can be found of a country that has successfully used indiscriminate protectionism extending for over a generation to create a viable industrial sector.[8]

The 1930s also witnessed a marked expansion in the direct activities of the state in the commercial life of the economy. A strategy of creating state sponsored bodies to fill the gaps believed to have been left by private enterprise was adopted. State companies were established in areas such as radio broadcasting, the development of the peat bogs, the provision of agricultural and industrial credit, life insurance, air, sea, road and rail transport, running hotels, producing food, steel and chemical fertilisers - the list is long. Most of these bodies enjoyed significant monopoly rights of one sort or another. In addition, a plethora of state boards was created to foster the development of almost every sector in the economy. By the 1970s the role of the state in the commercial life of the country was probably more extensive in Ireland than in any other country that had not formally adopted a socialist political economy.

Transition to outward-looking policies Although the Industrial Development Authority was established as early as 1949 to attract foreign industry to Ireland and in 1952 An Foras Tionscal was established to provide grants to these industries, policy remained highly protectionist until the 1960s. Tariffs did not begin to be dismantled until after the coming into force of the Anglo-Irish Free Trade Area Agreement in 1966, first for Britain and then for the rest of Europe after our entry into the EEC in 1973. The remaining restrictions on direct foreign investment were replaced by generous grants and tax incentives to attract export-orientated manufacturing firms to Ireland. The new outward-looking approach was designed to replace our reliance on firms catering for the small and stagnant domestic market with firms that would grow through exporting. There was also a shift from giving priority to Irish-owned firms to welcoming inward investment from the rest of the world.

By the 1980s the level of public sector support to Irish industry had reached a very high level. The value of all the state aids to industry (exclusive of foregone tax revenue) varied between £370 and £400 million over the period 1983-86.[9] This implies that about three per cent of GNP was being spent each year to promote industrial development, equal to over one eighth of the total value added in the industrial sector. To this should be added the value of indirect aids to industry, channelled through the training budgets of the Departments of Labour and Education, for example, and tax reliefs that do not appear as expenditure in the budget. During the second half of the 1980s the total budget for industrial aid declined, but an estimate prepared for the Review Group in 1991 put the total bill for the total "package" of state support for industry in the region of £600 million.[10]

Table 17.2 displays data collected by the Commission of the European Community on the level of state aids to industry in member states. It shows that in the mid-1980s Ireland was third after Greece and Italy in the level of its aids relative to value added in industry.

Table 17.2
Aids to manufacturing industry as percentage of gross value added (excluding shipbuilding and steel)

	Average 1981-86
Greece	13.9
Italy	8.2
Ireland	7.3
France	3.6
Netherlands	4.1
Denmark	1.7
Germany	2.9
UK	2.9
Belgium	4.5
Luxembourg	3.5

Note: "Aids" excludes tax reliefs, etc.
Source: Commission of the European Community, Directorate General for Competition (DG IV), *Second Report on State Aids*.

The high level of state aid to industry shows that the contrast between the protectionist and outward-looking phases of Irish industrial policy is not as clear cut as is often made out. The array of grants and tax concessions offered to industries setting up in Ireland after the removal of the tariffs in effect replaced "commodity-based protection" with "factor-based protection". Just as a tariff on the price of a product allows a firm to incur higher costs than its competitors in the rest of the world, subsidies on its inputs drive a wedge between domestic and world costs.

It has been estimated that the industrial incentive package offered by the Irish government in the 1970s was equivalent to an effective protection rate of 24 per cent.[11]

The new firms that came to Ireland to avail of the generous incentives provided by the government, and to locate in a relatively low-cost environment inside the enlarged EEC, accounted for most of the growth of industrial employment, output and exports during the 1970s and 1980s. The old, formerly protected firms contracted or went out of business in the new competitive environment. By 1990 it is estimated that 93,000 out of a total of 212,000 jobs in manufacturing were in foreign-owned firms.[12] As we saw in Chapter 9, over the longer run the industrial sector as a whole has not expanded rapidly enough to absorb much of the growth of the labour force, and despite a very active industrial policy the problems of unemployment and migration remain as severe as ever.

The nature of the aid offered has had a significant effect on the type of industry that has been attracted to Ireland. Irish industrial growth in the 1980s has been dominated by a small group of sectors: pharmaceuticals and fine chemicals, electronic engineering and data processing equipment, and "other foods". Firms in these sectors are able to take maximum advantage of the opportunities offered by the Irish corporate tax code to use transfer pricing to increase their world-wide after-tax profits. Net output per head in these "modern" sectors averaged £57,700 in 1984, compared with only £19,300 in the rest of Irish industry, but earnings per employee were actually slightly *lower* in the former (£8,148 compared with £8,731), indicating the vastly greater profitability of the "modern" sector.[13] Repatriated profits from the foreign-owned sector account for about half of the gap between GDP and GNP, which now amounts to about 11 per cent of GNP.

There is a growing awareness of the need for international action to curb the level of state aids to industry. The Commission of the EC has had some success in reducing existing aids, but the magnitude of expenditure at national level still dwarfs the spending from the structural and cohesion funds of the EC and could offset the attempts to equalise the level of economic achievement between the regions of the EC.

An undesirable effect of the subsidisation of industry has been to change the factor price ratio in favour of capital and against labour.[14] Most Irish state aids to industry, capital grants, accelerated depreciation allowances, etc. have the effect of lowering the cost of capital. On the other hand, as pointed out in Chapter 9, the rise in the rate of income taxation and social insurances charges has raised the cost of employing labour. It is inappropriate to subsidise capital and tax labour in a relatively poor, labour-exporting economy.

Much of this criticism was accepted in the 1992 Report of the Review Group on Industrial Policy. It recommended a fundamental reorientation of industrial policy, with less emphasis on state grants and more on creating a favourable environment for industry. The main elements of such an environment are:

- A tax system that provides incentives for enterprise and risk taking, with few distortions

- An efficient infrastructure that does not penalise industry relative to its international competitors

- An educational system that equips job seekers with the technical, vocational and managerial skills required by modern industry

- An industrial promotion process that places less emphasis on grants and subsidies and is willing to invest in joint projects with the private sector.

In the 1990s changes were also apparent in the philosophy, dominant since the 1930s, of direct state intervention in the commercial life of the country. A gradual programme of deregulation and privatisation has been implemented. Nitrigin Éireann, Irish Life Assurance Company and the Irish Sugar Company have been privatised and the Industrial and Agricultural Credit Corporations are ready for privatisation. The monopoly rights of the state-owned companies in areas such as inter-city bus transport, broadcasting and air transport have also been removed.

17.4   Economic Planning

Many people were infatuated with French planning [in 1962]. The combination of intellectual rigour, as suggested by the word "planning", and romance, as suggested by the word "French" was extremely tempting. So a group of us went to Paris. We met with officials of the Commissariat du Plan, with French businessmen, and with economists. By the time we returned I had concluded, in a line that I could not get out of my mind: "Le Plan français, il n'existe pas." The French government had forecasts about the economy, it made certain interventions in the economy - but it had no plan.
Herbert Stein, former Chairman of the US Council of Economic Advisers, in *Fortune*, 14 November 1983.

In Ireland in the 1950s there was also a fascination with the idea that an economy could be "planned" or "programmed" in some gentle, indicative way that bore no relation to the horrors of soviet regimentation. From 1958 into the 1980s a stream of government publications attempted to chart a medium-term course for the Irish economy. In this section we review these documents and assess their contribution to the development of the Irish economy.

Origins The *Public Capital Programme* was introduced after the Second World War in an attempt to systematise the public sector's annual budget for capital or development expenditure. This was the first tentative step on the road to economic planning. Another factor that contributed to thinking in terms of more than just the annual budget was our participation in the European Recovery Programme (Marshall Aid) in 1949. Ireland, although neutral during the war, was offered some of this aid.

484

The US authorities were anxious to see integrated proposals for spending the large amounts of aid that were made available. The Department of Finance opposed borrowing, even on very favourable terms, for ambitious new projects. In fact there were those who deplored the indignity of accepting US aid at all.[15] However, the Department of Foreign Affairs, where Sean MacBride was Minister, prepared a long-term recovery programme consisting mainly of schemes for the development of forestry and agriculture, and for spending on local authority housing and hospitals. The loans received under Marshall Aid were spent on these projects.

These tentative steps towards "planning" were overtaken by the stagnation of the early 1950s and the crisis of 1955 and 1956. Emigration soared to a record level as employment fell and unemployment rose. Living standards, which had not kept pace with expectations since the war, fell during the recession and an even sharper fall was only averted by the mass exodus from the country. T. K. Whitaker, who was Secretary of the Department of Finance at the time, has described the situation as follows:

The mood of despondency was palpable. Something had to be done or the achievement of national independence would prove to have been a futility. Various attempts were made to shine a beam forward in this dark night of the soul; they at least agreed on the need to devote more resources on an orderly basis to productive investment. Finally, over the winter and spring of 1957/58, a comprehensive survey of the economy, extending to its potentialities as well as to its deficiencies, was prepared in the Department of Finance. This was presented to the Government in May 1958 and was published under the title Economic Development in November of that year, simultaneously with the *First Programme for Economic Expansion*, which was acknowledged to be based largely upon it.
T. K. Whitaker, "Ireland's Development Experience", paper read to the Annual Conference of the Development Studies Association, Dublin, 1982.

The principal guidelines for economic policy set out in the *First Programme* were:

- To escape from stagnation, "public and private development of a productive character must be stimulated and organised so as to overshadow the non-productive development which now bulks so largely in public investment and in national capital formation as a whole"

- To achieve this, capital spending on local authority housing and hospitals was to be reduced and additional resources invested in agriculture and industry

- Fiscal policy should give priority to a significant reduction in taxation, particularly income taxation, because "high taxation is one of the greatest impediments to economic progress because of its adverse effects on saving and on enterprise"

- The increase in wages and salaries should for a time lag behind that in Britain.

485

There followed pages of detailed recommendations designed to foster increased efficiency in agriculture, industry and services such as banking.

A number of features of this Programme strike the reader today. In the first place, the hope was still that agriculture would provide the engine of growth for the development of the economy.[16] The conflict between trying to pursue our comparative advantage in agriculture while at the same time maintaining exceptionally high protective tariffs on industrial products was not discussed.[17] In fact the question of the failure of protectionism and the need to move to an export-oriented strategy was not explicitly addressed. In the brief section that touched on this issue, the achievements of the protected industries were listed (100,000 new jobs and a trebling of the volume of industrial production), but it was acknowledged that tariffs "might impair the incentive to reduce costs and increase efficiency". Despite the fact that, as we have seen, extraordinarily high levels of effective protection had been in force in Ireland for over a generation, and was acknowledged to offer no prospect for further development, there was no clarion call to face up to the rapid dismantling of these tariffs. Instead it was rather blandly stated that

it is obviously essential not only that existing industries should become progressively more efficient, but also that new industries should be competitive in export markets and capable of withstanding the challenge presented by the Free Trade Area.

The *First Programme* attached little weight to Keynesian demand management. Instead, the emphasis was placed on the need to raise productivity in the individual sectors of the economy, what we should today call "supply-side" measures. It has been criticised for this,[18] but in view of the painful lessons that we learned from an inappropriate use of Keynesian policies in the 1970s, the balance it struck between supply- and demand-side measures was probably the right one as Ireland moved into the 1960s.

It has become the accepted wisdom to attribute the contrast between the economic stagnation of the 1950s and the expansion of the 1960s to the impact of the *First Programme*. The contribution it made to economic policy and the performance of the economy is difficult to establish, however. Few of its recommendations were implemented. The burden of taxation was not eased. Instead, as we noted in Chapters 2 and 4, income tax in particular rose inexorably. Moreover, as Kennedy and Dowling point out,

There is no evidence of a rise in the level of manufacturing investment, or its share in GNP, prior to the increase in the growth rate of GNP. Neither does it emerge that cutting back housing investment in any way helped to raise the level of manufacturing investment.[19]

Nor did agriculture prove to be the engine of growth as envisaged in the First Programme: even after entry into the EEC and a massive injection of subsidies from

486

the EC, the share of GNP originating in this sector declined steadily and the number employed on family farms continued to fall. The role of economic locomotive was assumed by industry, as the scale of the inflow of foreign capital far exceeded that in the First Programme's projections. The improved performance of industry was not, however, attributable to any of the policies introduced in the Programme: growth resumed in 1958/59, before any new policies contained in the Programme could have taken effect. In reality, the Irish economy recovered more or less spontaneously from the protracted recession of 1954-58 and then participated in the rapid expansion of the world economy during the 1960s. In fact, the target of 11 per cent growth in the volume of GNP over the period 1959-63 contained in the Programme was less than half the 23 per cent growth actually recorded.

However, there is no doubt that the *First Programme* captured the imagination of a much wider population than would normally be aware of a detailed discussion of economic policy. It served to gain acceptance of the importance of economic development as a policy objective, and the need to look outward rather than inward in order to generate this development, which could not be taken for granted in the conservative, agrarian-orientated Ireland of the 1950s.

The most puzzling aspect of Irish economic policy in the post-war period is that we waited 20 years after the end of the Second World War before finally abandoning the policy of protectionism that had been adopted as an expedient in the 1930s. The accelerated growth recorded after 1957 was largely due to the buoyancy of the world economy and the gradual opening up of the Irish economy to export-orientated investment, which allowed us to benefit more fully from favourable external developments. (Note from Table 17.1 that even though it was a period of almost unprecedented expansion and optimism in Ireland, we lagged behind the OECD during this decade of very rapid global growth.)

It was inevitable that the dramatic improvement in the performance of the Irish economy in the years following the publication of the *First Programme* would be attributed to the Programme itself, and, in view of the vogue of "indicative planning" at this time (see the quotation at the beginning of this section), it is understandable that the planning exercise was repeated in a much more ambitious form in subsequent years. A *Second Programme 1964-70* was published in 1964 and a *Third Programme, Economic and Social Development, 1969-72* in 1969. These contained much more detailed statistical analyses of the Irish economy than had been attempted in 1958. The national accounts framework used in the First Programme was supplemented by detailed sectoral projections based on an input-output model. As has been pointed out:

... the objective of both later programmes was to obtain a profile of the Irish economy at a specified later date (1970 for the Second, 1973 for the Third), which reflected the highest possible growth rates which could be achieved in the light of "policy possibilities, the probable development of the external environment and resource availability".
Bradley J., "Economic Planning: Lessons of the Past and Future Prospects", *Administration*, Vol. 36, No. 1, 1988.

Both of these programmes projected a growth rate of 4 per cent a year in real GNP, which was the actual outcome during the recovery from the deep recession of the 1950s. However, projections of the growth of the economy, in aggregate and by sector, proved as wide of the mark during the Second and Third Programmes as they had been in the First, with the added embarrassment that the greater detail contained in the later documents drew attention to their increasing lack of relevance as the planning periods progressed. The Second Programme was based on the assumption that Ireland would be a member of the EEC by 1970. As this was prevented by France's veto of Britain's entry shortly after its publication, a rationale was provided for abandoning the Programme in 1966. It also became clear very early on that the targets contained in the Third Programme, especially those relating to employment, would not be achieved.

The degree of disillusionment with the whole process of planning in the turbulent economic circumstances of the 1970s is reflected in the words of the Minister for Finance, Richie Ryan, in his 1975 budget speech:

... of all the tasks that could engage my attention, the least realistic would be the publication of a medium or long term economic plan based on irrelevances in the past, hunches as to the present and clairvoyance as to the future ...
quoted in Bradley, *op. cit.*

Recent developments Irish economic planning would thus seem to have died amid the unrealised targets of the 1960s and the global economic uncertainty of the oil-price crisis of 1973. But in fact it enjoyed renewed popularity after the formation of a new government in 1977. A Department of Economic Planning and Development was created.[20] A plan called *National Development 1977-80* was published, containing specific targets for the growth of output and employment, and above all the reduction in unemployment. It was envisaged that the public sector would provide an initial boost to the economy, after which the private sector would take up the running. This would require increased government spending and recruitment in the public sector as a job-creation measure. The adverse effects of implementing these policies on the public finances and the structure of the economy were outlined in Chapter 5. As we noted, the projections contained in this plan proved to be far too optimistic and were rendered irrelevant by the second oil-price crisis in 1979. This exercise in planning hindered, rather than helped, the implementation of an appropriate policy response as the country faced into the most protracted recession in its post-war history.

Subsequent statements on national development increasingly focused on the constraints facing the economy rather than on specific targets for sectoral output. In the light of our membership of the ERM, it was recognised that pay moderation was essential if competitiveness was to be improved. In 1981 the Coalition government established a *Committee on Costs and Competitiveness*, which reported in October. The report set out calculations of a wage norm, taking into account the forecast increases in our competitors' wage costs and likely changes in exchange rates. The idea was that if this norm were adhered to there would be no deterioration in the country's competitiveness. Unfortunately, the norm proposed in October 1981 was rendered inappropriate almost as soon as it was published by a weakening of sterling. (The fall in sterling meant that greater wage moderation was required if Ireland was to maintain its competitiveness with the UK.) This episode provided a clear illustration of how difficult it is to frame policy in a small open economy where even short-run forecasts of key variables can be very wide of the mark.

A planning document, *The Way Forward*, was prepared by the Fianna Fáil government during 1982 and became the manifesto on which the party fought (and lost) the second general election of 1982. This document contained optimistic forecasts of economic growth based on a dramatic improvement in our international competitiveness, to be achieved by "moderate pay increases combined with increases in productivity".

In March 1983 the new Coalition government established an independent National Planning Board to prepare a study that would form the basis for a new plan.[21] *Proposals for Plan 1984-87* was published in April 1984. This document differed fundamentally from its immediate predecessors, and in some ways returned to the spirit of the *First Programme*, by presenting very detailed sectoral policy recommendations. It contained no fewer than 241 recommendations, ranging over many aspects of economic and social policy. Central to its recommendations was the need to reduce the level of public sector borrowing by expenditure cuts rather than increased taxation and to increase the efficiency of the public sector, particularly of the monopolistic state companies whose high costs were acting as a drag on the ability of the private sector to compete internationally. The Keynesian emphasis on demand management that had been influential in the late 1970s was emphatically rejected. The analysis of the unemployment problem focused attention on the growing proportion of long-term unemployed in the total and called for special, targeted measures, rather than across-the-board demand stimulus, to alleviate this problem. It applied the ideas of privatisation, deregulation and supply-side economics to the Irish case. In many respects the package proposed resembled a *structural adjustment programme* of the type supported by soft loans from the International Monetary Fund and World Bank in numerous developing countries in the 1980s.

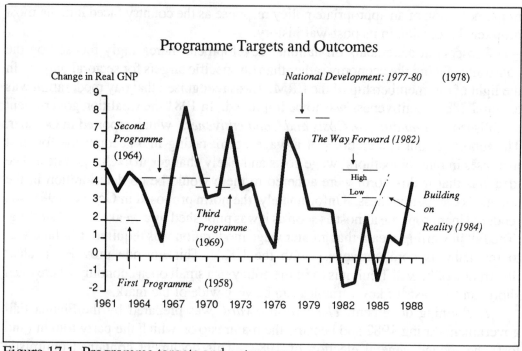

Figure 17.1 Programme targets and outcomes

The government's plan *Building on Reality* was published in autumn 1984. This generally endorsed the policy recommendations contained in *Proposals for Plan*. It emphasised the goal of stabilising the debt/GNP ratio and reducing the level of taxation. It forecast that total employment would increase over the next three years as employment in private sector services grew rapidly and industrial employment would begin to recover from the recession. These projections proved too optimistic. As we have seen in Chapter 5, the public finances continued to deteriorate until 1987 and employment did not begin to recover until 1988.

The minority Fianna Fáil government that was formed in 1987 published a *Programme for National Recovery 1987-90* in October 1987. This did not aspire to be a Plan in the way earlier documents had. At its core was an agreement between employers, trade unions and the government to adhere to a ceiling of 2.5 per cent annual increases in wages and salaries over a three-year period. A reduction in the rate of income taxation was promised and the prospect of increases in employment in selected state-sponsored enterprises was held out. A period of exceptionally low inflation facilitated adherence to the incomes policy agreed to in this document. A similar formula was accepted in the *Programme for Economic and Social Progress* (PESP) covering the period 1991-94, which provided for pay increases of 4 per cent in 1991, 3 per cent in 1992 and 3.75 per cent in 1993. Slight concessions in these terms were agreed before the 1992 budget in recognition of the financial problems created for the public sector by the recession.

Conclusions It is instructive to compare the projections/forecasts of economic growth they contained with the actual out-turn. This is done in Figure 17.1.[22] It is evident that the projections contained in all six Programmes or plans that were published bore virtually no relationship to the outcomes. The *First Programme*, as we saw, hoped for less than half the growth that occurred. At the other extreme, *National Development 1977-80* wildly overestimated the growth of the economy. *Building on Reality*, which was a sober document compared with *The Way Forward* published only two years earlier, was nevertheless very wide of the mark in its anticipation of a strong recovery in 1984/5. It is clear that medium-term economic forecasting in a small open economy is an extremely hazardous exercise, whose value is questionable. In fact, since the mid-1980s, government economic policy statements have remained relatively silent about the medium-term prospects for the economy.

One of the difficulties in evaluating the projections for the economy contained in these planning documents is that they did not make clear what these numbers represented. Were they forecasts of how the economy was expected to perform or estimates of what might have been achieved if the policies proposed in the document had been implemented? This is not made clear in any of the relevant documents.

A fundamental critique of the whole process of planning as it was attempted in Ireland is that it was based on a misunderstanding of the theory of economic planning as developed by economists such as Jan Tinbergen, Bent Hansen and Henri Thiel over the post-war period.[23] According to this theory, planning consists in setting values for the target variables (such as the growth in GNP) and trying to find values for the instrument or policy variables (e.g. government expenditure, taxes, the exchange rate) that will lead to the attainment of the targets, taking account of the structure of the economy and how it responds to changes in the values of the instrument variables. The central feature of the Plan is finding the (unknown) values of the instrument variables that will do the job. However, as has been pointed out, we in Ireland "have tended to view economic policy with its head upside down: we have tended to focus on targets and projections as the ultimate unknowns, as though in many cases the instruments could be taken for granted".[24] The plans published over the past thirty years did not tend to specify the policy instruments to be used to achieve the results that were sought. In some cases, for example, the very high growth rates in *National Development 1977-80*, it is unlikely that any values of the instrument variables (taxes, government spending, the exchange rate) would have been capable of attaining the targets, given the structure of the Irish economy.

17.5   The Future Role for Irish Economic Policy

The quotation from Adam Smith at the beginning of this chapter summarises one view of economic development. It is based on a belief that market forces and the self-interest of economic agents will lead to rapid economic growth unless obstructed by war, high taxation or insecurity of property rights. This view was not generally accepted in Ireland after Independence. Political nationalism tends to be linked with economic nationalism, which would see a much larger role for the state than is proposed under this laissez-faire philosophy. Economic nationalism intensified in the 1930s, when it was implicitly accepted that market failures and barriers to competition made it unlikely that private enterprise in an underdeveloped, late-industrialising country would be able to build up an industrial sector to provide employment for its population or close the gap in living standards with richer countries. This philosophy was modified by the adoption of more outward-looking policies in the 1960s and 1970s. However, in response to the perceived growth of the laissez-faire philosophy, the older interventionist argument was vigorously restated in the 1980s:

It is necessary to challenge the simplistic view that all that needs to be done is to unshackle the private sector from state interference and that this sector will then deliver the jobs [required to attain full employment]. This belief is now highly influential but it is not supported by the evidence of . . . Irish history or by the experience of most OECD economies since the end of the war. On the other hand, there is plenty of evidence of a weak response by private indigenous enterprise to the same environment in which foreign enterprise was able to generate large profits.
Employment and Unemployment Policy for Ireland by staff members of ESRI, edited by Denis Conniffe and Kieran A. Kennedy, Dublin: The Economic and Social Research Institute, 1984, p. 326.

In the same vein, it has been asserted that

Despite a level of public expenditure equivalent to more than 60 per cent of GNP, the capacity of the Irish State is in reality quite limited. Economic planning as practised in Ireland and the semi-peripheral status of the economy have meant that the State's ability to manage the economy has not increased commensurate with the share of total expenditure that is channelled through the State.
R. Breen, D. Hannan, D. Rottman and C. Whelan, *Understanding Irish Society*, Dublin: Gill and Macmillan, 1991, p. 47.

The first group of authors concluded that there should be a "substantially increased commitment of public funds" to help Irish firms overcome the structural barriers to competing successfully on world markets, the second favoured a more effective role for the state and more centralised control of the economy. The case for more state spending on industry has also been supported by the argument that only in this manner have late-industrialising countries from Sweden to Japan and Taiwan been able to compete with well-established rivals.[25]

However, there is now a general acceptance that the public sector does not enjoy a comparative advantage in the commercial areas of economic activity, and that its role should be confined to providing efficient infrastructure, essential public goods and the correction of clear market failures.

A recurrent theme of this book has been the increasing extent to which policy-makers in Ireland are constrained by international commitments as we approach the creation of an EMU in Europe. It is worth summarising these constraints in the context of the debate on the role of the state in the economy:

Exchange rate We are firmly committed to staying in the narrow band of the ERM and *de facto* the Irish pound is pegged to the DM at IR£1 = DM2.67. We are preparing to adopt the single European currency by the end of the decade.

Monetary policy Credit controls were allowed to lapse in 1984. Interest rate policy is confined to smoothing out short-run fluctuations in liquidity in the Dublin money market. The adoption of the European currency will entail the surrender of any residual scope for a national monetary policy. Ireland will, however, be represented at European level in the formulation of monetary policy by the proposed European Central Bank.

Fiscal policy The use of fiscal policy as an instrument of *demand management* is severely constrained by the binding rules laid down for participation in the EMU, namely, keeping the deficit under 3 per cent of GDP and reducing the debt/GDP ratio to 60 per cent by 1996. The pattern of *capital expenditure* is increasingly determined jointly with the EC Commission in order to secure funding from the European Regional Development Fund. Significant proportions of *current spending* on education and training are similarly geared to obtaining funding from the EC Social Fund. *Taxation* generally is constrained by the Laffer curve considerations we discussed in Chapter 4, which are very important in a small open economy. Moreover, *indirect taxation* is constrained by the objective of harmonisation at Community level.

Industrial policy Grants and other aids to industry require Commission approval. The recommendations of the Review Group on Industrial Policy, summarised above, if implemented, would markedly curtail the role of the public sector in the promotion of industry, which has been a central feature of Irish economic policy since the 1950s.

The macroeconomic instruments that remain under national control are few. Perhaps the most important is *incomes policy,* which in recent years has taken the form of the national agreements such as the PESP. Opinions differ as to how effective this approach to wage determination is but, as we argued in Chapter 9 and again in Chapter 12 in our discussion of the Irish experience in the EMS, in a small open economy the level of wage inflation is a major influence on the level of employment and unemployment.

The shrinking scope for an independent macroeconomic policy highlights all the more the need for effective and appropriate policies in other areas. Because of the size of the public sector in Ireland, the *structure* of taxation and spending have a major influence on the efficiency of the economy. As attention is shifted away from issues of macroeconomic policy, it should focus more clearly on the question of whether public spending and taxation are effectively promoting the goals of economic growth and employment creation.

"The romantic phase is over", Keynes wrote when England left the gold standard in 1932, "and we can now set about doing what is right for the economy". This advice is very appropriate to Ireland as we look forward to participating in a European economic and monetary union.

Notes

1. This is quoted in Paul Kennedy, *The Rise and Fall of Great Powers*, New York, Random House, 1987, p. 20. The exact source in Adam Smith's work is not given, but it captures the spirit of his discussion of the development of the New World in Book IV, Chapter VII of *The Wealth of Nations*, ("Causes of Prosperity of New Colonies").

2. Cited in J. F. Meenan, *The Irish Economy Since 1922*, Liverpool University Press, 1970.

3. In fact, it is surprisingly difficult to find evidence that high rates of emigration have an adverse effect on the rate of economic growth: see B. M. Walsh, "Testing for Macroeconomic Feedback from Large-Scale Migration based on the Irish Experience, 1948-87: A Note", *The Economic and Social Review*, Vol. 20, No. 3, April 1989, pp. 257-66, and J. J. Sexton, B. M. Walsh, D. F. Hannan and D. McMahon, *The Economic and Social Implications of Emigration*, Dublin: The National Economic and Social Council, March 1991.

4. The Irish net reproduction rate fell from 1.8 in 1970 to 1.0 in 1991. The net reproduction rate has to be greater than one to ensure a population is replacing itself in the long run.

5. For example: ". . . over the 70 years from 1913 to 1985, Ireland's growth rate of total real product . . . was below that of every other European country, apart from the UK," Kieran A. Kennedy, Thomas Giblin and Deirdre McHugh, *The Economic Development of Ireland in the Twentieth Century*, London: Routledge, 1988, p. 121, and "It is difficult to avoid the impression that Irish economic performance has been the least impressive in western Europe, perhaps in all Europe, in the twentieth century", J. J. Lee, *Ireland 1912-1985: Politics and Society,* Cambridge, Cambridge University Press, 1989, p. 521.

6. These are Census data relating to the population living in cities and towns with 1,500 or more inhabitants.

7. Dermot McAleese, *Effective Tariffs and the Structure of Industrial Protection in Ireland*, Dublin: The Economic and Social Research Institute, Paper No. 62, 1971. "Effective protection" is a measure of the extent to which a tariff allows an industry to be inefficient relative to international competitive standards and still survive.

8. The literature on protectionism is vast. For a review of the issues, see World Bank, *World Development Report 1991: The Challenge of Development*, Oxford University Press, 1991.

9. These figures are taken from *A Time for Change: Industrial Policy for the 1990s* , Report of the Industrial Policy Review Group, Dublin: The Stationery Office, 1992, p. 31.

10. *Review of Industrial Performance 1986*, Dublin: The Stationery Office, 1987.

11. Stephen E. Guisinger, "Do Performance Requirements and Investment Incentives Work?", *The World Economy*, Vol. 9, No. 1, March 1986, pp. 79-96.

12. See *A Time for Change: Industrial Policy for the 1990s, op. cit.* p. 31.

13. See T. J. Baker, "Industrial Output and Wage Costs 1980-87", *Quarterly Economic Commentary*, Economic and Social Research Institute, October 1988.

14. See Frances P. Ruane and Andrew A. John, "Government Intervention and the Cost of Capital to Irish Industry", *The Economic and Social Review*, Vol. 16, No. 1, October 1984.

15. See Ronan Fanning, *The Irish Department of Finance*, Dublin: The Institute of Public Administration, 1978.

16. Out of a total of 212 pages of text, 100 were devoted to a detailed discussion of agriculture, forestry and fisheries. The headline in the *Irish Independent* proclaimed: "Easier credit schemes for farmers proposed"!

17. A rationale for tariffs is to try to change a country's comparative advantage over time. The authors of the Emigration Commission Reports and of the First Programme did not seem to believe that this hope was being realised, yet they did not recommend that tariffs be dismantled.

18. "It is our contention that the desire to lay a basis for long-term growth, in particular by changing the composition of the Public Capital Programme, involved an excessive emphasis on supply aspects at the expense of demand considerations "(Kieran A. Kennedy and Brendan R. Dowling, *Economic Growth in Ireland: The Experience since 1947*, Dublin: Gill and Macmillan, 1975, p. 226). The perception remains, however, that the *First Programme* "installed Keynesian economic principles as the main item on the national agenda", Richard Breen, Damian F. Hannan, David F. Rottman and Christopher T. Whelan, *Understanding Contemporary Ireland: State, Class and Development in the Republic of Ireland*, Dublin: Gill and Macmillan, 1990, p. 5.

19 Kennedy and Dowling, *loc. cit.*, p. 176.

20. It is of interest to note that T. K. Whitaker, then a senator, spoke against this step.

21. One of the authors of the present book, Brendan Walsh, was a member of both the Committee on Costs and Competitiveness and the National Planning Board.

22. The idea of compiling this Figure, and the data for the earlier years, were provided by J. P. Neary.

23. See Desmond Norton, *Problems in Economic Planning and Policy Formation in Ireland, 1958-74*, Dublin: The Economic and Social Research Institute, 1975. See also O. Katsiaouni, "Planning in a Small Economy: The Republic of Ireland", *Journal of the Statistical and Social Inquiry Society of Ireland*, 23 (5), 1977/78, pp. 217-75.

24. Norton, *op. cit.*, p. 30.

25. For an example of this type of reasoning applied to the Irish case see Eoin O'Malley, *Industry and Economic Development, The Challenge for the Latecomer*, Dublin: Gill and Macmillan, 1989. It is beyond the scope of this chapter to explore this issue in detail, but so frequently is Japan cited as an example of the success of state aid to industry that it is worth looking at this instance. The Ministry of International Trade and Industry (MITI) played an active role in fostering Japan's outstanding economic performance after the Second World War. But MITI's role was primarily one of creating a favourable environment for Japanese industry at home and for its exports abroad. There was very little in the way of direct subsidies and grants to manufacturing industries. For example, it is estimated that in only one out of thirteen major industrial sectors did subsidies exceed 0.1 per cent of gross value added (compared with over 7 per cent in Irish industry). In the late 1970s the Japanese government funded no more than 1.9 per cent of all industrial research and development, far less than was the case in Europe and the US. Moreover, where MITI intervened and tried to control industrial development, it did harm, as well as good. It tried to "rationalise" the automobile industry by concentrating production in a few giant companies and discouraged Honda from entering. It wasted billions of dollars in trying to establish a Japanese aircraft industry, which went out of business after producing one prototype.

Index